ORDNANCE SURVEY
NATURE ATLAS
OF GREAT BRITAIN
Ireland and the Channel Isles

CLB 4640
This edition published 1995
exclusively by Colour Library Books Ltd
Godalming Business Centre, Woolsack Way,
Godalming, Surrey

Conceived, edited and designed by
Duncan Petersen Publishing Ltd,
5, Botts Mews, Chepstow Road, London, W2 5AG.

Text © 1989 Duncan Petersen Publishing Ltd
(individual contractors as listed)
Maps of Great Britain © Crown Copyright 1989
Maps of Northern Ireland © Crown Copyright 1989
Maps of Ireland © Irish State 1989

ISBN 1-85833-405-5

Printed and bound in Singapore

Whilst every care has been taken in the preparation of
this book, all the routes described are undertaken at the
individual's own risk. The publishers and copyright
owners accept no responsibility for any consequences
arising out of the use of this book, including
misinterpretations of the maps and directions.

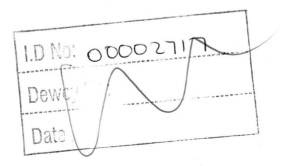

ORDNANCE SURVEY

NATURE ATLAS
OF GREAT BRITAIN
Ireland and the Channel Isles

CLB
Colour Library Books

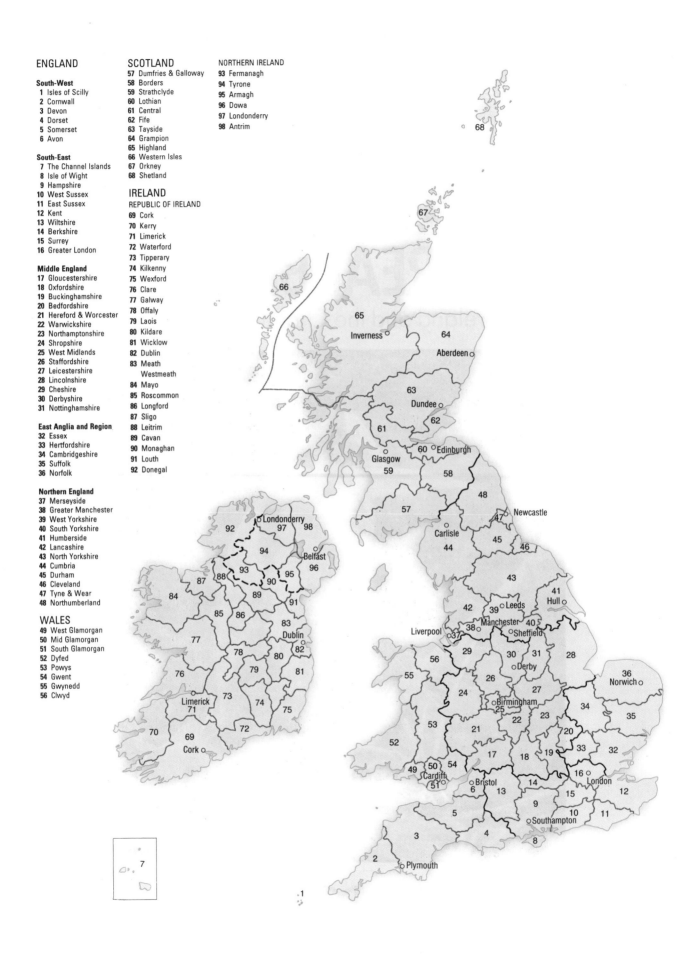

ENGLAND

South-West
1 Isles of Scilly
2 Cornwall
3 Devon
4 Dorset
5 Somerset
6 Avon

South-East
7 The Channel Islands
8 Isle of Wight
9 Hampshire
10 West Sussex
11 East Sussex
12 Kent
13 Wiltshire
14 Berkshire
15 Surrey
16 Greater London

Middle England
17 Gloucestershire
18 Oxfordshire
19 Buckinghamshire
20 Bedfordshire
21 Hereford & Worcester
22 Warwickshire
23 Northamptonshire
24 Shropshire
25 West Midlands
26 Staffordshire
27 Leicestershire
28 Lincolnshire
29 Cheshire
30 Derbyshire
31 Nottinghamshire

East Anglia and Region
32 Essex
33 Hertfordshire
34 Cambridgeshire
35 Suffolk
36 Norfolk

Northern England
37 Merseyside
38 Greater Manchester
39 West Yorkshire
40 South Yorkshire
41 Humberside
42 Lancashire
43 North Yorkshire
44 Cumbria
45 Durham
46 Cleveland
47 Tyne & Wear
48 Northumberland

WALES
49 West Glamorgan
50 Mid Glamorgan
51 South Glamorgan
52 Dyfed
53 Powys
54 Gwent
55 Gwynedd
56 Clwyd

SCOTLAND
57 Dumfries & Galloway
58 Borders
59 Strathclyde
60 Lothian
61 Central
62 Fife
63 Tayside
64 Grampion
65 Highland
66 Western Isles
67 Orkney
68 Shetland

IRELAND
REPUBLIC OF IRELAND
69 Cork
70 Kerry
71 Limerick
72 Waterford
73 Tipperary
74 Kilkenny
75 Wexford
76 Clare
77 Galway
78 Offaly
79 Laois
80 Kildare
81 Wicklow
82 Dublin
83 Meath
   Westmeath
84 Mayo
85 Roscommon
86 Longford
87 Sligo
88 Leitrim
89 Cavan
90 Monaghan
91 Louth
92 Donegal

NORTHERN IRELAND
93 Fermanagh
94 Tyrone
95 Armagh
96 Dowa
97 Londonderry
98 Antrim

CONTENTS

USING THIS BOOK   6

INTRODUCTION   8

THE MAJOR HABITATS:
  BACKGROUND   10

HABITAT DESCRIPTIONS   12

A NATURALIST'S YEAR   14

ACCESS AND OTHER
  PRACTICAL
  INFORMATION   15

ENGLAND   16

South–West   18

South–East   46

Middle England   74

East Anglia and Region   109

Northern England   126

WALES   168

SCOTLAND   200

IRELAND   248

REPUBLIC OF IRELAND   250

NORTHERN IRELAND   266

INDEX   282

ACKNOWLEDGEMENTS   288

USING THIS ATLAS

THE MAP EXTRACTS
The map extracts in the *Atlas* have been taken from sheet mapping produced by the Ordnance Surveys of Great Britain, Northern Ireland and Ireland.

Season
Different sites are at their best at different times of year. Where detailed guidance is appropriate, it is given. Otherwise, readers are left to follow the commonsense rules:

■ Sites where plants and breeding birds are the main interests will be best in spring and summer, 'dead' in autumn and winter.

■ Sites where migrating birds are the main interest will be best in spring and autumn.

County covered *mainly, but not exclusively* on this spread. (The map extracts may include sites in parts of adjoining counties.) The sequence in which the counties are featured in the book corresponds to the Ordnance Survey grid system which works from west to east and from south to north. Cornwall, furthest west and furthest south comes first; on the British mainland, Highland, furthest east and furthest north comes last, followed by the Western Isles, Orkney, Shetland and Ireland.

Site locations: the numerals key to the gazetteer entries, usually on the same page or spread, occasionally on a following page. In this case, 1 refers to A:1, the Axe Estuary; 4 refers to A:4, Golden Cap.

Map extract (scale 1:250 000 – 4 miles to one inch) and reference letter. All the gazetteer entries with the prefix 'A:' fall on this extract.

THE SOUTH-WEST
DORSET

MAP A

A:1 AXE ESTUARY
Near Seaton; roadside parking at approx SY 255905. Keep to public roads.
■ Estuary, mudflats, salt-marsh, flood meadows.
■ Used in winter by waders, wildfowl and gulls, often close to road: use car as hide.

A:2(a–b) AXMOUTH TO LYME REGIS UNDERCLIFFS*
Near Seaton/Lyme Regis; roadside parking at approx SY 265903, or in Lyme Regis. Keep to footpaths.
■ Wooded cliffs, gulleys.
■ This 800-acre reserve protects one of the most striking sections of coastline in S England. Over the years there have been many landslips; the largest, in 1839, formed the so-called Goat Island, leaving a huge chasm still visible despite colonization by woodland and scrub. In more sheltered places a mixed ash woodland has grown up with a rich and colourful ground flora of ferns and lime-loving herbs, many insects and a large population of birds.
NATURE CONSERVANCY COUNCIL

A:3 BLACK VEN & THE SPITTLES
Near Lyme Regis; park in Lyme Regis or Charmouth. Reserve entered along coastal public footpaths and marked routes. No access to landslip area.
■ Scrub-covered undercliff, grassland.

■ Constantly slipping undercliff provides variety of habitats from stable scrub and open grassland to wet flushes and mud. Rich insect and bird population.
DORSET TRUST FOR NATURE CONSERVATION/NATIONAL TRUST

A:4 GOLDEN CAP
Near Lyme Regis; car park at SY 421917. Site can be entered along coastal footpath from Seatown or Charmouth.
■ Scrub-covered undercliff, grassland.
■ Undercliff a rich habitat for butterflies and songbirds.
NATIONAL TRUST

A:5 WEST BEXINGTON
Near Bridport; park in West Bexington at SY 531865. Site entered along coastal footpath. No entry to reed-bed.
■ Shingle beach, reed-bed.
■ Shingle continuation of vast Chesil Beach supports good flora; reed-bed safe nesting for warblers and waterbirds with many spring and autumn migrants.
DORSET TRUST FOR NATURE CONSERVATION

A:6 POWERSTOCK COMMON
Near Bridport; entry to reserve from road at SY 547973 or bridle-path at 532963. Keep to footpaths or get DTNC permit.
■ Oak and mixed woodland, scrub, open

grassland, cutting.
■ Forestry plantations alternate with blocks of native woodland and open grassland where heavy clay soils encourage good ground flora, including many ferns. Drainage ditches colourful; railway cutting a habitat for lime-loving species. Important for butterflies.
DORSET TRUST FOR NATURE CONSERVATION

B:1 THE FLEET & CHESIL BEACH*
Near Weymouth; car parks and information centres at Ferry Bridge, SY 668755, and Abbotsbury Swannery. Sanctuary area closed at all times; part of beach closed in nesting season.
■ Tidal lagoon, shingle ridge.
■ The huge ridge, 17+ miles (25km) long, is one of the largest storm beaches in Europe and protects an important tidal lagoon. The landward side, where some humus has collected, has been colonized by many interesting plant species and by terns, protected by wardens in the nesting season. The aquatic vegetation is vital to the wildfowl wintering here, notably the 1,000 or so mute swans and large flocks of wigeon. Waders, including rarities, feed on the muddy margins of the Fleet, and communities of marine molluscs live in the stabilized shingle between the tide lines of the lagoon. **Plants** Eel grass, shrubby sea-blite. **Insects** Scaly cricket (only British site).

MAP B

34

Indicates a length of coastline or a group of related sites covered in one gazetteer entry.

The gazetteer entries relating to this extract all carry the prefix 'B:'.

Letter reversed out of box shows location of large-scale (1:50 000) map.

List of interesting species, given where space allows, generally in order of interest. Sometimes it is a supplement to the species mentioned in the general commentary. This is a selective, not an exhaustive list.

One star means don't miss if in the area.

Two stars means the site is worth a day's journey, but check opening times before departing.

THE SOUTH-WEST

DORSET

B:2 RADIPOLE LAKE**
Weymouth; car park at swannery at SY 677796. Access along public footpaths. Good information centre.
■ Reed-beds, lakes, lagoons, scrub.
■ Entirely surrounded by the town of Weymouth, the reserve which has three hides, offers the very best of urban bird-watching. Extensive reed-beds, home for many species of warbler, are used during migration by large numbers of roosting yellow wagtails, sedge warblers and swallows whose pre-roost display flights are a feature of evening bird watches in autumn. During winter, the numbers of gulls build up, often including rarities among them; Mediterranean and ring-billed gulls are regular. Many wildfowl use the lake, and up to 100 mute swans gather to moult; cormorants sit on the islands to dry their wings. **Birds** Cetti's, reed, sedge and grasshopper warblers, bearded tit, water rail.
ROYAL SOCIETY FOR THE PROTECTION OF BIRDS

B:3 LODMOOR COUNTRY PARK*
Near Weymouth; car park on A353 at SY 687807. Use public footpaths.
■ Freshwater marsh, pools, reed-beds, scrub, salt-marsh.
■ The marsh and shallow pools are used by large numbers of waders and wildfowl, especially during migration and in winter. Redshank, mallard, shelduck and yellow wagtail breed on the marsh, and the reed-beds shelter many warblers, including Cetti's. Almost any wader can be seen on the pools, including N American species such as

the pectoral sandpiper and lesser yellowlegs. In winter there are jack snipe and water pipits, and when flooded, the marsh holds many ducks. Linnets, stonechat and whitethroat breed in scrub patches, as do butterflies. Hides and a good perimeter path make viewing easy.
ROYAL SOCIETY FOR THE PROTECTION OF BIRDS

B:4 WHITE NOTHE UNDERCLIFF
Near Weymouth; access from Ringstead Bay at SY 760814.
■ Cliffs with landslips, scrub.
■ Great range of landslip-created micro-habitats with both wet and dry grassland, damp flushes, sheltered and exposed areas and steep crags. Plant and animal life equally varied; fine views of the Isle of Portland.
NATIONAL TRUST/DORSET TRUST FOR NATURE CONSERVATION

B:5 LULWORTH COVE*
Near Wool; car park at Lulworth Cove, SY 823801. Use footpaths. Danger of landslips near cliffs.
■ Rocky cove, seashore, coastal downland.
■ One of the most striking places on the Dorset coastline, the cove provides an ideal sheltered habitat for intertidal marine life. Many species reach almost their western limit in the England Channel here; cushion stars, brittle stars, wartlet anemones, star ascidians and many colourful seaweeds live among the tumbled boulders on the shore. Dense beds of kelp are exposed at low tide, although the tidal range is never very great. Squat lobsters and edibly, hairy and velvet

swimming crabs are all common, and fossil-bearing rocks are visible.

B:6 LULWORTH RANGE*
Near Wool; car parks at Lulworth Cove, SY 823801, and Tyneham, SY 882804. Footpaths open at certain times only as ranges still used; check local press, roadside notice boards, or tel. Bindon Abbey 462721.
■ Cliff tops, coastal downland.
■ Has escaped modern farming, due to use as range, and so has a rich chalk downland wildlife. Spectacular setting for seeing chalk downland as well as sea-birds.
MINISTRY OF DEFENCE

B:7 PURBECK MARINE WILDLIFE RESERVE*
Near Swanage; car parks at Kimmeridge Bay, SY 909791 (also display centre). Use coastal footpaths.
■ Cliff tops, rocky seashore.
■ Britain's first mainland marine reserve, the gently shelving Kimmeridge Ledges are exposed over a great area at low tide, making this an excellent site for studying marine life. Carpets of coralline seaweeds shelter large colonies of snakelocks anemones, top shells and periwinkles. Limpets and barnacles cover the rocks in exposed areas, but in many places there is a dense growth of colourful algae. The kelp beds at the low-water mark are home for blue-rayed limpets, hairy crabs, worm pipe fish and sea slugs; many species found only in the western Channel reach their eastern limit here.
PRIVATE OWNERSHIP/DORSET TRUST FOR NATURE CONSERVATION

Name of site, or its location.

Access information, including where possible, parking, is given in italics and includes, where relevant, notes on gaining permits/permission to visit. See also 'Contours'.

List of principal habitats found at the site.

General commentary on the site's key features.

Ownership or management details are included where they are of general interest or significant to obtaining further information or access permits. Where this information is omitted, however, it does not confer right of access to those sites beyond that afforded by designated public rights of way; see 'Access' on page 14.

B:A ISLE OF PORTLAND**
Near Weymouth; car parks well signposted. Access along many public footpaths.
■ Limestone peninsula, fields, scrub, quarries, rocky seashore.
① Check gulls feeding here for rarities; little gull often present. At low tide good marine life uncovered among large boulders and kelp beds. Black redstart on steps and sea-wall.
② Grey bush-cricket in scrub on under-cliff, plus migrant birds. Good marine life at low tide. Shags feed offshore.
③ Excellent views of Chesil Beach.
④ Check scrub patches and old quarries for migrants. Do not climb walls or stone piles which may be dangerous.
⑤ Continue to fence of Admiralty radio station, checking fields for migrants. Ortolan seen here at times. Auks may be seen from cliff near fence flying in and out of breeding ledges beneath.
⑥ Obelisk at tip is best place for watching migrating seabirds. Purple sandpiper on rocks below.
⑦ Check scrub between huts, old quarries and gardens for migrants. Bird observatory in old lighthouse can be checked for latest news. Great green bush cricket in scrub, and excellent limestone flora in open areas. Little owls hunt in quarries.
⑧ Sea lavender and golden samphire grow on cliff edge. Marine life shows effect of exposure. Shags, cormorants and gulls feed close inshore.
⑨ Another good area for migrant birds; check overgrown quarries for warblers, shrikes. Danewort grows here; stony areas have many land snails.
⑩ Excellent views of Dorset coast. Distant views of feeding gulls and terns below. Divers and grebes sometimes visible. Limestone flora.

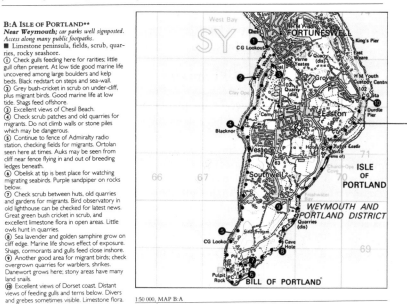

1:50 000, MAP B:A

35

Suggested walking route around the site and observation points. This may not be the only route around the site: but it has been chosen to allow it to be worked to advantage. Follow local directions, however, as authorized routes may change.

16th October, 1987
The night of the hurricane-force winds which swept the south and east of England. Many of the sites in the *Nature Atlas* are those which were worst-affected by the storm.
The millions of trees blown over seemed at first to be a great wildlife catastrophe, but it is now clear that the impact is really quite variable. Worst affected are collections, like Kew Gardens, and parks, where fine specimen trees will take hundreds of years to replace. Country hedgerows and small woodlands are a worry, too, – the first are difficult to re-establish, and the second may in many cases disappear under the plough.
But in large woods, especially nature reserves, regeneration is already beginning and the long-term preservation of the habitat is assured. Some of the sites may look odd – sheered-off and uprooted trees will litter the ground for years – but as woods they will remain.

Caution
'Keep to footpath(s)' is used throughout the text to indicate that access to a site is on public rights of way, and that visitors should not stray from them.

Map extract (scale 1:50 000 – one mile to 1¼ inches) showing a particularly interesting site in detail. Sites chosen for this treatment are always important, but they are not necessarily the most important sites in the book. They are shown on large-scale mapping because their topography justifies, or requires it.

The most useful tool available to the naturalist – besides notebook, pencil and binoculars – is a map. If you can read one, it will give up a huge amount of the countryside's secrets; better still, if you can pore over a map with an expert, you can get straight to the heart of where and how the most interesting natural history can be found.

Using *The Pan/Ordnance Survey Nature Atlas* is rather like poring over a good map with a natural history expert at your elbow. The map extracts are marked with the location of most of the interesting, visitable natural history sites in Britain and Ireland. This emphasis on visitability is, of course, appropriate: for this is a book not only to assist learning and planning, but above all to encourage people to get out and enjoy the countryside. The sites included are those which the contributors and owner/managers believe are representative of the most interesting of their kind; and which can tolerate visitor pressure.

You won't find all the great natural history sites in the *Atlas*; you may even find some surprising omissions. This will almost certainly be because we have been persuaded by those responsible that inclusion would damage the propects of wildlife in the area. But there is more than enough left for a lifetime of absorbtion and interest.

As well as the location of sites – all on mapping at the scale of 1:250 000 or 4 miles to one inch, and some on mapping at the larger scale of 1:50 000 – there is much practical information in the gazeteer entries. Access, habitat summaries, general descriptions and, on the Landranger extracts, observation points along a marked route to help you make the most of a visit.

Everyone has a different idea of what makes a worthwhile day out in the field. For the birder it might be a visit to an estuary to watch waders, ending with the incomparable sight of a flock being harried by a peregrine. For the botanist it could be the unexpected sight of thousands of orchids in flower on the bed of an old quarry. Having a red-letter day needs more than luck; you have to be in the right place at the right time; *The Pan/Ordnance Survey Nature Atlas* is the ideal means for achieving this goal.

The authors for each region are all noted for their breadth of natural history interest. Birders and botanists will, of course, find the *Atlas* especially valuable; but so will anyone prepared to widen their horizons.

The best of Britain and Ireland

Many of the sites in the *Atlas* are Sites of Special Scientific Interest (SSSIs), well known and managed as nature reserves; but many are unmanaged, waiting to be explored. Some, like the amazing natural bridge across the Tees at God's Bridge, can be seen if you have an hour to spare; others, such the Channel Islands and the Speyside sites, deserve a whole holiday.

There is, in short, an amazing amount of natural history packed into our islands. In Scotland you can visit birch woods and blanket bogs similar to those found in Norway. In the west of Wales and in Ireland you can find plants which otherwise only grow in Portugal. Sites in South Wales, Cornwall and Kent have French connections; the Channel Islands are positively Mediterranean. The mountain flowers of Upper Teesdale and Ben Lawers can be found in the Alps and Pyrenees, and the nearest thing to some Breckland grasslands are the steppes of Russia. Globally, the British Isles' most significant natural history feature is the sea-bird colonies. St. Kilda, for instance, is a World Heritage Site, on a par with the Serengeti and the Great Barrier Reef. Britain provides a home for enormous numbers of wildfowl and waders each winter; Ireland and the Flow Country of northern Scotland contain the best examples of blanket bog in Europe. The Burren, in the Republic of Ireland, with its upland and lowland plants on limestone pavement, can claim to be one of the botanical wonders of Europe. And Wexford Slobs is internationally important for wintering geese.

Origins of native species

Ten thousand years ago most of the British Isles were covered with ice. Trees, plants and animals followed the retreating glaciers across the land bridges that linked what are now the British Isles to Europe. The sea level rose as the ice melted, and the islands stood apart from the continent, covered, for the most part, by forest. Soon, in terms of pre-historical time scales, man became the major influence on the environment: cutting and burning, tilling and grazing, he created the countryside mosaic we know today. Indeed, few truly natural habitats remain once you move away from the coast: rivers and ponds are managed to supply water and drain the land; ancient meadows and pastures are the product of centuries of agriculture and the remaining woods have provided timber, fuel and forage for millennia. Even the wildest heather moors and finest chalk down were created by man and maintained by hungry sheep. Luckily animals and plants are adaptable and our flora and fauna are now composed of species which can thrive in the semi-natural landscape we have created.

Above left, bloody crane's-bill.

Opposite, typical Welsh wooded hillside: Dinas Valley, Dyfed.

Woods and coppices: The British Isles should have a cold climate. Edinburgh is further north than Moscow and the Shetland Islands are at the same latitude as Helsinki. Even the Channel Islands are on a level with Newfoundland. But the Atlantic keeps our climate relatively warm and damp, ideal conditions for the growth of trees. Our two species of oak are the most important woodland trees, but depending on the region and soil, ash, birch, beech, elm, hornbeam, juniper, Scots pine, small-leaved lime, yew and the aggressive sycamore can all form single species or **mixed woodland**. The shrubs which form the **understorey** can be an important part of the wood for wildlife. Some woods are managed as **coppices** where stumps are allowed to produce shoots which can be harvested as useful poles within a few years. The best woods are the natural ones, with trees of different ages and species; however some **plantations** of single species of uniform age can be interesting, particularly as shelters for mammals and birds.

Scrub and carr: When an area of ground is left to go wild, it is usually invaded by shrubs to form **scrub**. Eventually, trees become established, but the

Above, Upland habitats: Beinn Eighe NNR, Highlands.

Below right, classic downs: the Chilterns.

return to woodland can take a long time. The dominant scrub species are frequently birch, blackthorn and hawthorn. Areas of thorn scrub are sometimes called **spinneys**. In damp areas, alder and willows may form **carrs**.

Grassland: This is probably our most important habitat type after woodland. Unfortunately, there is little natural grassland left and the improved **pastures** and **leys** favoured by modern farmers are of little interest to wildlife or naturalists. **Hay meadows**, managed by cutting each summer, are undoubtedly the most attractive form of grassland, but good examples are few and far between. **Pasture grassland** can be attractive too, particularly if the soil is **calcareous** or **neutral. Acid grassland** is generally less interesting, with notable exceptions such as the **brecks** of East Anglia. The beautiful butterflies and flowers of the **chalk downs** are well known, but exciting species-rich grassland can be found on all the British limestones. In some places there is no soil and plants grow in the giant cracks in

limestone pavement. The traditional **parkland** or **deer park** landscape – grazing with venerable old trees – which surrounds many of our stately homes is important for wildlife, though it is the trees rather than the grass which provide the greatest interest.

Heath and moor: lowland heath is a fascinating habitat dominated by species of heather and found mainly in the lowland south. It is particularly important for reptiles, amphibians, dragonflies and Dartford warblers. In the colder and wetter north, heather tends to form **heather moor**; this is the most important vegetation over much of upland Britain. Grasslands do occur in upland Britain but most are dominated by mat grass or purple moor-grass, neither of which makes a very exciting habitat. These are collectively referred to as **grass moor**.

Wetlands: The uplands are the source of all of our rivers. The upland **becks** and burns are generally cold, clear, fast flowing and full of oxygen. The becks join together as they flow downstream to form **streams** and these may converge to make **lowland rivers**. By this time the water will be slow-moving, full of silt and the oxygen level will be much lower. All of these factors affect the animals and plants which live along the length of the river. Eventually, the river meets the sea at an **estuary**, where the silt it carries is deposited as **mudflats** which may support a **salt-marsh**. **Lakes** and **ponds** (and **lochs** and **lochans** in Scotland) are another important though diverse habitat, ranging from the enormous glacial lakes of upland Britain, with their unique species of fish, to bomb-craters from World War II which are now dragonfly refuges. Many important ponds have recently been created by flooding sand and gravel pits. **Canals**, **ditches**, **dykes** and **rynes** are all artificial, and form an interesting intermediate habitat between rivers and ponds.

Mires and wetlands: Just as grassland is invaded by scrub, open water is invaded by reeds, reed mace (*Typha*) and similar species, to form a mire. An acid mire is called a **bog** and the richer, more alkaline mires are called **fens**. Reed-beds are essential for birds such as bittern, bearded reedling and marsh harrier. In the north, where reeds do not grow well, reed mace provides a home for rails and crakes as well as a number of specialist moths. *Sphagnum* moss grows anywhere that is sufficiently damp and it forms enormous **blanket bogs** in parts of upland Britain and Ireland. These are important for breeding waders and several of our rarer birds of prey.

The seaside: On the coast, the harder rocks form **stacks** and **cliffs** which are important for breeding sea-birds and specialist plants such as wild cabbage. Where a hard rock lies on top of a softer rock, the cliffs can be undermined. This produces an **undercliff**, a wild jumble of broken rock covered with vegetation. The most famous undercliff is at Lyme Regis in Dorset, although there are also significant undercliffs on the Isle of Wight, at Folkestone and in North Yorkshire. The seashore can be rocky, sandy or muddy and though each of these has a unique flora and fauna, rocky shores with **rock pools** offer most to the naturalist. **Strands** of shingle can support an interesting flora, but the grinding action of the stones makes them inhospitable to most animals. Sand **dunes** are another complex habitat ranging from the **mobile dunes** near the sea to the vegetated **fixed dunes** further inland. There may also be shallow areas of water called **dune slacks** which are important for orchids and natterjack toads. In the Hebrides and Western Ireland, where the sand contains plenty of sea shells, **machair** grassland occurs. This is important for wild flowers and breeding corncrakes and waders.

Wood
Any natural or semi-natural group of trees and all the associated wildlife.

Caledonian pine forest
Scots pine woods found in the highlands of Scotland: part of our native flora, they are home to a wide variety of rare and exciting animals and plants.

Understorey
The shrub layer in a wood. Absent from woods that are grazed and from beech woods, but important for mammals, birds and insects.

Coppice
A wood managed by regular cutting. The cycle of light and shade makes coppices particularly rich in woodland flowers.

Plantation
Any group of planted trees, generally of uniform age and of a single species. Frequently conifers, but poplar plantations are grown in East Anglia for matchwood.

Scrub
Low, bushy vegetation that is both the first step in a return to woodland and an important habitat in its own right. Particularly important for some warblers.

Spinney
A small wood dominated by blackthorn or hawthorn.

Carr
A swamp woodland dominated by alder or willow. As it dries out, it will be invaded by birch and eventually oak.

Grassland
Any habitat dominated by grass, though flowers and other plants may also be present.

Pasture
Grassland managed by grazing.

Meadow
Grassland managed by cutting.

Water meadow
Grassland fertilized by allowing floodwater to cover it in winter. A rare but particularly rich habitat.

Ley
A grassland deliberately planted as pasture or meadow, agriculturally productive but generally uninteresting to naturalists.

Calcareous
Means a habitat on limestone or chalk.

Neutral
Means a habitat which is neither acid nor alkaline, often on clay.

Acid
In ecological terms, the opposite of calcareous. Acid habitats are often found on sandstones.

Limestone pavement
Striking habitat found in various locations in northern England and on Skye. The bare rock is split into blocks called clints by deep cracks called grikes. The grikes hold a specialized and interesting flora.

Parkland
Traditional landscape of pasture dotted with mature trees usually found associated with old estates and stately homes.

Deer park
Parkland which contains deer and possibly other stock as well. The trees have a characteristic shape caused by the animals browsing for fodder.

Heathland
Dry habitats dominated by heathers. Home for a wide variety of some of our rarest animals.

Moorland
The upland version of lowland heath. Generally cold and wet, moorland does not have to be dominated by heather.

Heather moor
Moorland dominated by heather. Often managed for grouse shooting and sometimes referred to as grouse moor.

Grass moor
Moorland dominated by mat-grass or purple moor grass.

Beck
An upland stream.

Burn
Same as a beck, though this word is more frequently used in Scotland.

Stream
A waterway intermediate in size between a beck and a lowland river.

Lowland river
A broad, slow-moving stream found in the lowlands.

Estuary
The tidal portion of a river where it starts depositing silt. Estuaries are particularly important as bird habitats in winter.

Corn poppies, corn marigold and scentless mayweed: Sheringham, Norfolk.

Mudflat Large expanse of mud or silt. Often provides an enormous amount of food for waders and some species of duck.

Salt-marsh Mudflat which has been colonized by salt-tolerant plants such as salt-marsh grass, sea arrow-grass or sea lavender. Salt-marsh is regularly covered by the highest tides.

Pond Any small body of water.

Lake A larger body of water. Rule of thumb: if it is too big to walk round easily, it is a lake.

Loch A Scottish lake.

Lochan A small loch, particularly in the highlands of Scotland. Important for breeding divers.

Gravel pit A steep-sided pond formed by flooding old gravel workings.

Canal An artificial river or artificially straightened section of an existing river. Canals are maintained for navigation and for land drainage.

Ditch Any small cut designed to carry water, though it may be dry for much of the year.

Dyke A drainage ditch that contains water all the year round.

Rynes As for dyke, particularly on the Somerset Levels.

Mire Any marshy or boggy habitat.

Bog A mire which is acid and generally short of nutrients.

Fen A mire which is alkaline and generally rich in nutrients.

Reed-bed A mire which is dominated by the common reed. An important habitat essential for a number of highly specialized birds and insects.

Typha bed A mire dominated by greater or lesser reedmace. Other species which can dominate mires include iris, saw sedge and the bur-reeds.

Blanket bog A type of *Sphagnum* bog found in flat or gently sloping upland areas with a high rainfall. Blanket bogs can extend for miles.

Stack Isolated pillar of rock, often important for nesting sea-birds.

Cliff Formed wherever hard rocks reach the coast. Important for breeding sea-birds.

Undercliff Habitat formed when a cliff is undermined by softer strata. The result is a highly broken habitat which is quickly colonized by shrubs.

Rock pool Pool of sea water trapped by a depression in the rock as tide falls.

Dune Large, naturally-formed pile of sand usually found by the sea, though they can occur inland on dry sandy sites such as in Breckland.

Mobile dune A dune which is not covered with vegetation so that the sand can be blown from one place to another.

Fixed dune A dune which is covered with vegetation and so unlikely to be blown about.

Dune slack Shallow, wet depression between dunes, important for orchids and natterjack toads.

Machair Pronounced mak-a this unique grassland habitat is only found on shell-rich sands in the Hebrides and in western Ireland.

Tombolo What was once a small island, now connected to the shore by a double curve of beach, one on either side.

Turlough A shallow, ground water-fed lake with a fluctuating water level.

Esker Mound of glacial gravel and sand.

A NATURALISTS' YEAR

JANUARY

The coast is seething with divers, ducks, waders and exciting buntings, so a day at **Seal Sands** and **Teesmouth** is a must. If the weather holds, we could even go up to **Holy Island** for the geese and whooper swans. A spare afternoon could be spent at **Tynemouth** looking for glaucous and Iceland gulls. The woodlands are quiet, but the bare trees make it easier to see squirrels and identification of trees by their winter twigs provides a challenge.

FEBRUARY

Snow gives a chance to look for mammal tracks and see how the local badgers and foxes have fared through the winter. The ducks at **Shibdon Pond** would be worth watching. With the half-term break, we might get across to **Caerlaverock** for the barnacle geese or down to the **Ouse Washes** for the Bewick's swans.

MARCH

Early in the month we must visit **Hawthorn Dene** to see the carpets of snowdrops and later we might look for kingfishers and the yellow star-of-Bethlehem at **Gainford Spa Wood**. March is a tricky month to plan: will spring be early or late? Our best bet is to visit some varied sites like **Shipley** and **Great Woods** or **Witton-le-Wear** which give an exciting day out, even if we fail to see any summer migrants.

APRIL

Spring at last. We plan to spend some time at **Washington Wildfowl Park** where the wild area attracts migrant warblers and waders. We also plan a visit to the **Rosa Shafto Nature Reserve** towards the end of the month because it is carpeted with spring flowers. There is less time to travel afield this month as the common bird census on our local patch will have started and we will have to check on our local reptile and amphibian breeding sites. The Easter holiday is a chance to get away for some sunshine. Anywhere on the coast in southern England would be good and of course, this is the best time to visit the Mediterranean for birds and flowers.

MAY

Everywhere is good at this time of year, so we decide to concentrate on the big woodland of **Brignall Banks** for maximum variety. The coast is still turning up waders and it is light enough to put in some field work first thing in the morning or after work. Bats will start to occupy their breeding roosts and insects, molluscs and other invertebrates start to be active. We start to run the moth trap every night from now on. We probably use the two bank holidays to visit some of the sites in Northumberland like **Cocklawburn Dunes** or **Gunnerton Nick**.

JUNE

We decide to do some exploration this month and have a look at some of the under-recorded carboniferous limestone quarries of **Weardale**. We get a permit for **Harehope Quarry** and decide to include **Slit Woods**. Everyone knows Harehope, but it is a superb site and the marsh orchids at the top end will be in full flower. We could check the big badger sett whilst we are there.

JULY

At the beginning of the month the magnesian limestone and **Teesdale Hay Meadows** are at their best. We should organize a couple of sleepless nights to look for glow-worms at **Thrislington** and a flying visit to **Muckle Moss** for the insects and bog flora. As soon as the school holidays start we will be off to Scotland or Wales to look at the big sea-bird colonies and chase the mammals, butterflies, dragonflies and birds of prey which we don't get at home.

AUGUST

We might treat ourselves to a trip to the **Farne Islands** to look at the seals and sea-birds: the best time to go is as soon as the terns finish breeding. **Upper Teesdale** would be worth a visit, though the sea watching off **Hartlepool Headland** will be starting to get exciting. Harvestmen and spiders should be adults now, so much easier to identify than they were earlier in the year. People with holiday to spare may pop down to Norfolk for birds or up to the Western Isles in search of whales.

SEPTEMBER

Autumn already. Most of the spare time will be spent chasing up the bat queries and dragonfly records left over from the summer. The nest boxes will need cleaning and repairing. It is a good month for looking at molluscs. The moth-trap will catch little: we will only run it on warm, muggy nights.

OCTOBER

I expect that we will be given some baby hedgehogs that need feeding up for the winter but, in general, October is a birder's month. A hint of an east wind would push Scandinavian migrants such as bluethroat and red-breasted flycatcher on to our coast. A weekend visit to **Holy Island** would be ideal, though a westerly could make it a waste of time. Those who stay on their home patch will be recording the departure of the house martins and the arrival of fieldfare, redwing and brambling.

NOVEMBER

A quiet month after October and the days are so short that we can only get out at weekends. There will still be some flowers along the disused railway lines such as the one at **Malton**. Wildfowl numbers should start building up, so a visit to **Hurworth Burn** would make sense. **Hamsterley Forest** is another place to visit. It will be relatively peaceful in winter and we are fairly sure to see red squirrels and roe deer if we start early. We might even be able to track down one of the elusive hawfinches.

DECEMBER

Christmas makes a big hole in December, though visits to friends and relatives who live near interesting reservoirs or on the coast could provide some days out. If we are at home, then **Whittle Dene Reservoir** and **Hadston Lake** are worth the effort. As for the New Year, perhaps we could get a cottage up on the Dornoch Firth: it has dolphins and ducks in mid-winter.'

ACCESS AND OTHER PRACTICAL INFORMATION

Many of the sites in the *Atlas* are privately owned and inclusion DOES NOT CONFER RIGHT OF ACCESS or freedom to wander off public rights of way.

Public rights of way in England and Wales are a network of footpaths, bridleways and by-ways over which the public has a right of passage. These are normally signposted or waymarked in yellow or blue. Ordnance Survey Landranger maps (1:50 000 scale) of England and Wales also show the routes of all definitive public rights of way. In addition, many areas of open country such as moorland and fell may be traversed by local or established custom, but seek local advice if you are unsure.

In Scotland, while there are designated rights of way, there is not the definitive national network that exists in England and Wales. Neither is there any law of trespass. You may traverse moorland and mountain paths taking due care to avoid damage to property and the environment; but landowners can and do impose restrictions on access. This is particularly so during the grouse shooting season (August 12th into September) and the deer stalking season (generally from the beginning of August well into October). Landowners also have a legal remedy against any person causing damage on or to the land and may use reasonable force to remove such a person. The basic rules are therefore: always avoid damaging property, and if you are not clear about access, seek permission of the landowner first.

In Northern Ireland, public rights of way do exist, but it is important to note that few are signposted. However, the process of waymarking public footpaths and bridleways is under way, prompted by access to the countryside legislation introduced in 1983. There is also public access to much of the open countryside of the uplands, for example the Mourne Mountains and the Antrim Plateau, seek local advice.

In the Republic of Ireland, there is no definitive network of public rights of way. Local rights of way do exist, but they are not signposted, so always seek local advice before proceeding.

Sites requiring access permits

Where a permit is necessary to gain access to a site, approach the owner/manager. Guidance is given on this in some of the gazeteer entries, but when specific instructions and/or addresses are not given, the local telephone directory is the simple solution. A large proportion of the sites in the *Atlas* come ultimately under the wing of four national parent bodies:

The Nature Conservancy Council, Northminster House, Peterborough, PE1 1UA. Tel: (0733) 40345.

The National Trust, 36 Queen Anne's Gate, London SW1H 9AS. Tel: (01) 222 9251.

The Royal Society for the Protection of Birds, The Lodge, Sandy, Bedfordshire SG19 2DL. Tel: (0767) 80551.

The Royal Society for Nature Conservation, The Green, Nettleham, Lincoln LN2 2NR. Tel: (0522) 752326.

If in difficulty obtaining permits locally, enquire at these head offices.

Please write in good time and remember to include a stamped addressed envelope. Please do not turn up and plead ignorance, it could spoil things for others. It is particularly important to contact the owner or manager if you intend to visit a site with a party.

Clothing

Naturalists sported waxed jackets and gum boots long before they became fashionable. Adequate outdoor clothing enables you to concentrate on natural history rather than on the weather, and this is especially important if you venture into the uplands.

Conservation

The *Atlas*'s contributors all round the U.K. have tried to include new areas of interest to the public. At the same time, they have had to recognize that some sites which, say, two or three years ago could have had a place are now too sensitive to be included. This is particularly true in Lincolnshire where, away from the coast, only a few small remnants of semi-natural habitats remain.

On an individual level, people can be the making or breaking of an interesting site from the conservation point of view. Some people who ought to know better have blind spots: birdwatchers are notorious for treading on rare plants; and botanists can be blissfully unaware of the chacking warbler that is trying to draw attention away from its nest.

Making the most of your interest

The first objective of anyone wanting to develop a real interest in natural history is to come to grips with the wildlife in their own area.

Wardens at the famous osprey hide at Loch Garten, Scotland, are often amazed to find out how popular the chaffinches are with visitors. It is quite obvious that many have never seen them before, yet they are one of the commonest birds. The lesson is obvious. Don't, if you live in a built-up area, take the line that your neighbourhood has no natural history worth knowing about. Even in the depths of the biggest cities, there are parks, churchyards, tow-paths and disused railway lines teeming with wildlife. The library will have information about your local natural history society, bird club, R.S.P.B. members' group or branch of the county's trust for nature conservation.

As you start getting to know your own locality's natural history, you will become more aware of what it lacks; going further afield will follow naturally. You will soon realize that the two main obstacles for naturalists are time and money, and surprisingly, it is the former which presents the greatest problems. There simply are not enough days in May and June to look at everything on one's home patch, let alone elsewhere in the country. So you have to plan ahead.

On the opposite page is a personal year plan developed by Durham schoolmaster, Noel Jackson, *Atlas* contributor and author of this introduction, for keen naturalists, some of them beginners, in Darlington. The approach could be adapted for anywhere in the U.K.

ENGLAND

Hedgerows and farmland are two habitats typical of the English countryside. Since 75 per cent of the British Isles is agricultural land, mature hedgerows have become important shelter for wildlife.

Siskins (above) were originally confined to Scottish pine-forests, where pine-seeds formed their spring and summer diet. Since conifers have spread throughout Britain during the last hundred years, the siskin has benefited and its high-pitched, musical song is heard in southern England, Wales and Ireland. Male siskins resemble a small male greenfinch, with distinctive black crown.

THE ISLES OF SCILLY

THE ISLES OF SCILLY★★

Regular sea crossings and helicopter flights from Penzance to Hugh Town, on St Mary's. Other islands reached by boat from St Mary's. Further details from Council of the Isles of Scilly and NCC.

■ Granite islands with cliffs, dunes, coastal heath, scrub, marshes, cultivated fields, sub-tropical gardens.

■ The Isles of Scilly, the most southerly land in the British Isles, enjoy a mild climate – frost and snow are rare – but there are many days of gales and plants have to cope with high levels of salt spray. The islands have a rich native flora, including many species found nowhere else in Britain, and many plants have been introduced from much warmer climates. The islands also attract a great number of rare birds during autumn migration.

DUCHY OF CORNWALL/PRIVATE OWNERSHIP

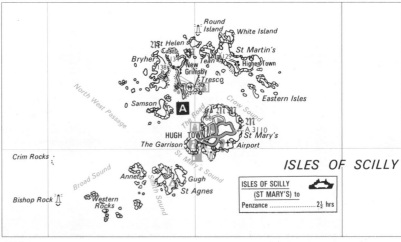

MAP A

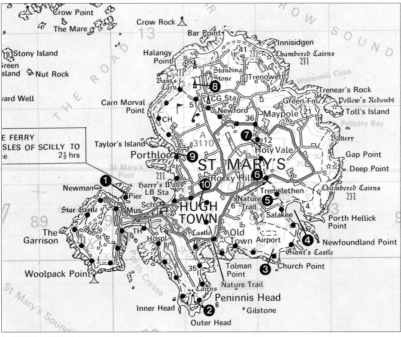

1: 50 000, MAP A:A

ST MARY'S

① From Hugh Town pier, walk W around Garrison, checking trees and bushes for migrants. Scan St Mary's Sound for sea-birds and divers. Porpoises sometimes pass through and grey seals are usually in the area. Cross Porth Cressa and follow footpath around Buzza Hill.

② Peninnis Head. Check open areas for larks, pipits and buntings, and continue to watch for sea-birds offshore. Many lichens on the granite outcrops; green tiger beetles common in summer. Coastal flowers here show effects of extreme exposure to wind and salt spray.

③ Continue along coastal path to airfield (do not cross fence) and in autumn check for dotterel, buff-breasted sandpiper and pipits. Spring migrants include wheateater and ring ouzel.

④ Sheltered bay of Porth Hellick where waders feed at low tide. Rich marine fauna and flora and, on shingle above high tide line, an interesting maritime flora. Check strand line debris for feeding pipits, wagtails and black redstart.

⑤ Nature trail leading up small valley from Porth Hellick passes a pool, overlooked by two hides, which attracts many migrant birds, including several rarities. A variety of aquatic plants grows around it. Eels and mullet sometimes reach the pool from the sea.

⑥ On leaving the pool the trail passes a series of large tussock sedge plants, each supporting several other plants and animals within the tangled root mass. Look for rails, crakes, herons and other marsh birds.

⑦ Holy Vale trail, following stream up the valley, is very sheltered: one of the best areas to look for warblers, flycatchers and other passerines. Note the luxuriant growth of ferns, mosses and lichens.

⑧ Follow lane to Telegraph Tower, checking tiny fields for migrants on the way, then cross golf course by footpath to coastal path. Dotterel and other waders may be present, and buntings feed in the rough grass.

⑨ Walk S to Porthloo where sanderling usually feed on the shore; check all waders carefully for unusual species. Pipits and wagtails often feed on strand line; debris may include many species of shells not normally found on shore.

⑩ Nature trail starts near Low Pool and follows a hedge and then a drainage channel to Old Town Bay. Sallows, planted to provide materials for lobster pots, now provide shelter for migrant birds. Water rail, snipe, mallard and teal may be found in marshy areas; a fine display of marsh flora in summer.

THE OTHER ISLANDS

Of the other main Scilly Isles, **Tresco** is best known for its sub-tropical gardens with a great range of exotic plants from around the world. The freshwater pools and dunes are important habitats for migrant and breeding birds.

Many rare birds have been recorded on **St Agnes**, but the island also has an interesting flora, including three species of adder's tongue fern. A small freshwater pool adds further interest.

The sand dunes on **Bryher** support many species scarce or absent elsewhere in Britain, and some of the headlands have a rich maritime flora. Pool, a brackish pond, attracts many migrant birds.

Maritime heath is well developed on **St Martin's**. Evidence of early settlers of the islands persists in the form of old field boundaries. Great Bay is a magnificent stretch of shell sand.

The Scillies' main sea-bird colonies are found on **Annet**, an uninhabited island; for permit to visit, apply to NCC. Annet has a striking display of thrift in spring.

Birds Auks, petrels, shearwaters, some song-birds. **Mammals** Lesser white-toothed (Scilly) shrew, grey seal, porpoise. **Plants** Dwarf and least adder's tongue ferns, royal fern, spring squill, orange bird's-foot, dwarf pansy, balm-leaved figwort, chaffweed. **Insects** Meadow brown and common blue butterflies (local forms), great green and grey bush crickets. **Amphibians** Common frog.

DUCHY OF CORNWALL/PRIVATE OWNERSHIP

Above, porpoise; opposite, Porth Hellick.

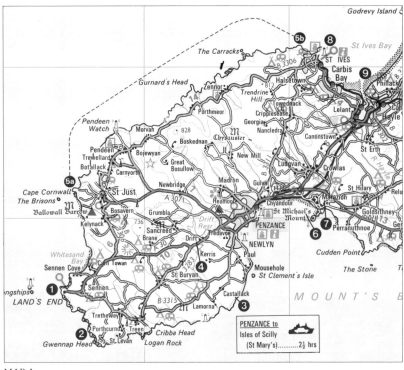

MAP A

A:1 LAND'S END

Near Penzance; car park and display centre at Land's End; access from A30 or along coastal footpath.

■ Granite cliffs, coastal heath.

■ Spectacular sea cliffs with views to the Isles of Scilly. Autumn gales best for bird-watching; spring best for coastal flowers.

A:2 PORTHGWARRA★

Near Penzance; car park at SW 370218. Keep to coastal footpath.

■ Granite cliffs, coastal heath.

■ The tiny valley, winding down to the sea between exposed coastal heathlands, acts as a trap for migrants, often extreme rarities. Willows with royal fern growing beneath offer the only luxuriant vegetation, and a pond at the head of the valley stream is the only other source of fresh water. Migrating sea-birds seen offshore in late summer include Cory's, sooty and great shearwaters, also auks, petrels and skuas. Spring brings returning divers and the first passerine migrants which make use of the scrub areas. Mediterranean visitors may include the woodchat shrike and migrant butterflies such as clouded yellows.

A:3 KEMYEL CREASE

Near Penzance; access from B3315, then minor road to footpath at SW 467257, or along coastal footpath from Lamorna Cove. Permit from CTNC needed for parts of reserve off footpaths.

■ Conifer plantation on cliff.

■ Trees planted as shelter on steeply sloping cliff have merged to form dense woodland with little ground cover. Feeding area for migrant birds.
CORNWALL TRUST FOR NATURE
CONSERVATION

A:4 DRIFT RESERVOIR

Near Penzance; from A30 take minor road to car park at SW 437288. Keep to footpaths.

■ Reservoir with grassy and part wooded margins.

■ Mainland Britain's most SW body of fresh water. Small number of waterbirds breed and many overwinter or pass through on migration. Noted for N American vagrants.
CORNWALL BIRDWATCHING AND
PRESERVATION SOCIETY

A:5 CAPE CORNWALL TO CLODGY POINT★

Near St Just/St Ives; access from Cape Cornwall car park at SW 353317, and many access points from B3306. Keep to footpaths.

■ Coastal cliffs, headlands.

■ This dramatic stretch of coastline gives good (if sometimes distant) views of sea-birds and marine mammals. Strong gales drive sea-birds close inshore, while calmer weather may reveal seals basking, or porpoises passing offshore. In summer, the cliffs are coloured by thrift, gorse and heather. Exposed patches of rock show a variety of lichens. Butterflies and moths, especially migrants, abound. **Birds** (Offshore) gannet, shearwater, petrel, gulls, auks; (cliffs) raven, wheatear, pipit. **Plants** Spring and autumn squill, maidenhair fern, sea and lanceolate spleenwort, lousewort, rock sea-spurrey.
NATIONAL TRUST/PRIVATE OWNERSHIP

A:6 BATTERY ROCKS, MOUNTS BAY

Near Penzance; car park at SW 506313. Access subject to tides: check times to avoid being stranded.

■ Rocky seashore.

■ Intertidal rocks of varied exposure, some supporting mainly barnacles, the more sheltered covered by dense seaweed with rich invertebrate fauna beneath. Divers and waders, some rare, in winter.

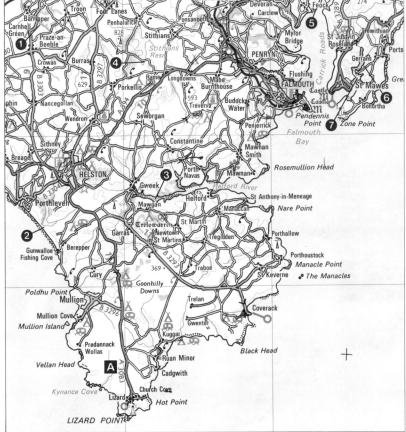

MAP B

A:7 MARAZION MARSH★

Near Penzance; car park at SW 506313. Good views from adjoining road; do not walk on to marsh.
■ Freshwater marsh, reed-beds.
■ Cornwall's largest reed-bed, excellent in spring for returning swallows, martins and other species en route. Many rarities seen in autumn. **Birds** Spoonbills, hoopoe, bittern, garganey, water rail.

A:8 ST IVES HEAD★★

St Ives; car park at SW 520410. Access on public rights of way. Excellent viewing from coastguard lookout.
■ Rocky headland.
■ Most species of sea-bird may be seen at some time; spectacular movements during autumn gales, with many birds rarely seen from shore elsewhere in Britain. **Birds** Phalaropes, black redstart, snow bunting, gannet, divers.

A:9 HAYLE ESTUARY★

Hayle; car parks at SW 544367 or in Hayle. Bird-watching hide in pub grounds at SW 545364. Keep to footpaths.
■ Estuary, brackish pools, sand dunes.
■ The only mudflats in the far south-west offering sheltered feeding and roosting for many waders, wildfowl and gulls (regularly including one or more ring-billed gulls from N America) and attracting numerous rarities when freezing temperatures further east drive them from their usual feeding grounds. Flocks of wigeon and teal, with some mallard and gadwall, feed at the edge of the salt-marsh in winter; careful searching usually reveals American wigeon or green-winged teal. In spring more waders return and terns begin to pass through. Mid-summer is quieter, but in autumn wader numbers increase and rarities may appear.

B:1 PENDARVES WOOD

Near Camborne; access from B3303 at SW 641376. Further details from CTNC.
■ Mixed woodland, lake.
■ Woods originally planted with ornamental species, but many native species present. Man-made lake attracts wildfowl in winter and supports many aquatic insects.
CORNWALL TRUST FOR NATURE CONSERVATION

B:2 THE LOE POOL & LOE BAR

Near Helston; parking at SW 652238, SW 637249 and SW 654252. Keep to footpaths.
■ Shingle beach, freshwater lake, mixed woodlands, scrub.
■ Beach supports interesting flora. Lake beyond important for overwintering wildfowl; waders feed along its shore, warblers breed in reed-beds. Good variety of woodland birds, and insects in scrub. **Plants** Sea-holly, yellow horned-poppy, sea sandwort.
NATIONAL TRUST

B:3 HELFORD RIVER

Near Helston; access at SW 705265, SW 717252 and SW 759260. Keep to footpaths.
■ Estuary, wooded shores, steep valley.
■ Large areas of mudflats rich in invertebrates – food for many waders and wildfowl in winter. Interesting flora and fauna in surrounding woodlands. **Birds** Godwit, curlew. **Plants** Thrift, wild madder.

B:4 STITHIANS RESERVOIR★

Near Redruth; good views from road at SW

708373, SW 715352. Hides available, keys from SWW.*
■ Reservoir, grassy shores, scrub.
■ Reservoir shores a great attraction to migrant waders in spring and autumn. Many wildfowl, including rarities, feed in shallows.
SOUTH WEST WATER

B:5 TRELISSICK

Near Truro; access from B3289 King Harry Ferry road, SW 837396. Closed in winter. Check times with NT.
■ Parkland, ancient woodland, estuary.
■ Notable ornamental tree collection.

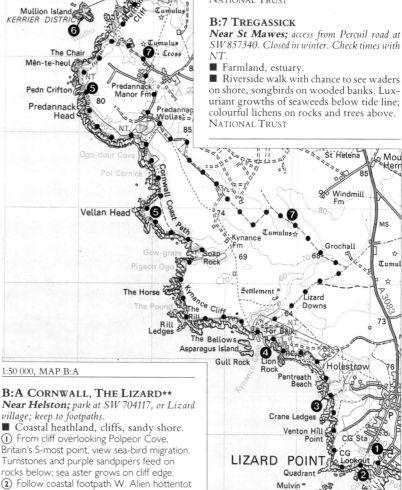

1:50 000, MAP B:A

B:A CORNWALL, THE LIZARD★★

Near Helston; park at SW 704117, or Lizard village; keep to footpaths.
■ Coastal heathland, cliffs, sandy shore.
① From cliff overlooking Polpeor Cove, Britain's S-most point, view sea-bird migration. Turnstones and purple sandpipers feed on rocks below; sea aster grows on cliff edge.
② Follow coastal footpath W. Alien hottentot fig grows down the cliffs and this is only British site for Lizard clover.
③ In spring and autumn check carefully for migrants. Wheatears are common, and many rarities. Continue to scan sea for sea-birds; some on isolated stacks. Green tiger beetles common in summer.
④ Rocks near Kynance Cove are of serpentine, which weathers to form soil suitable for lime-loving plants. Look for dropwort and bloody cranesbill, plus the rare Cornish heath, common here. In wetter areas are many orchids, especially heath spotted, with lousewort frequent. Royal fern grows in sheltered hollows.
⑤ Coastal path continues N over dramatic cliffs and valleys, and, where serpentine forms outcrops, there is a rich and varied flora, including many clover species rare elsewhere in

■ Old parkland trees provide valuable habitats for lichens, fungi, beetles and woodland birds. Cormorants and herons from adjoining estuary roost in woodland. Fine ground flora; many ferns.
NATIONAL TRUST

B:6 ST ANTHONY-IN-ROSELAND

Near St Mawes; access from minor road at SW 868329. Closed in winter. Check times with NT.
■ Farmland, ancient woodland, estuary, cliffs, coast.
■ Colourful hedgerows and lanes with many flowers; woodland and farmland birds. Cormorants, herons and waders seen on estuary, gulls and sea-birds from cliffs.
NATIONAL TRUST

B:7 TREGASSICK

Near St Mawes; access from Percuil road at SW 857340. Closed in winter. Check times with NT.
■ Farmland, estuary.
■ Riverside walk with chance to see waders on shore, songbirds on wooded banks. Luxuriant growths of seaweeds below tide line; colourful lichens on rocks and trees above.
NATIONAL TRUST

Britain. Look for hairy greenweed on rocky outcrops and patches of dwarf gorse, often infested with dodder. Burnet rose flowers in summer, but soon loses its petals. Flatter areas and shallow pools often attract migrant waders.
⑥ Mullion Island has breeding sea-birds. Cliffs support rich maritime flora, including lichens.
⑦ Alternative route back, over heath. Check open areas and pools for waders. Dragonflies in summer; butterflies include marsh fritillary. Look in cart ruts and wet hollows for pygmy rush, dwarf rush and pillwort. Fragrant orchid occurs, and Cornish heath is abundant in places.
PRIVATE OWNERSHIP/NATIONAL TRUST/ NATURE CONSERVANCY COUNCIL

MAP C

C:1 CAMEL'S COVE & THE STRAYTHE

Near Truro; *access from Portloe along coastal footpath to SW 931388. Check times of high tide before venturing on to rocks.*
■ Sheltered cove, cliffs.
■ Low tide reveals flourishing communities of algae and invertebrates. Cliffs have a rich coastal vegetation. **Birds** (Winter) black-throated diver, purple sandpiper. **Plants** Stinking iris, thrift, rock sea spurrey.
NATIONAL TRUST/PRIVATE OWNERSHIP

C:2 DODMAN POINT

Near St Austell; *access from minor road at SX 000404, or along coastal footpath from Gorran Haven.*
■ Exposed headland, scrub.
■ Dense scrub patches on headland attract migrant birds and are much used by resident songbirds for nesting. Hill fort and fine display of coastal flowers.
NATIONAL TRUST

D:1 CARNKIEF POND

Near Newquay; *access from minor road at SW 784524. Keep to footpaths.*
■ Pond, bog, damp woodland.
■ Good bog vegetation surrounding small pool; late summer good for dragonflies and damselflies. Many woodland mosses, lichens, ferns and birds.

D:2 PENHALE CAMP & PERRAN SANDS

Near Newquay; *car park at SW 766586. Use public rights of way. Check MOD notice boards carefully.*
■ Coast, calcareous dunes.
■ Some of the highest sand hills in Britain. Although much disturbed, characteristic lime-loving dune flora and fauna have developed. **Plants** Portland spurge, sea spurge, hound's-tongue, marsh- and spotted-orchids.
MINISTRY OF DEFENCE

D:3 KELSEY HEAD & HOLYWELL BAY

Near Newquay; *park at SW 767591 or SW 776598. Keep to footpaths.*
■ Exposed headland, grassland, scrub, dunes, offshore stacks.
■ From ancient settlement on headland breeding auks and other sea-birds may be watched offshore. Fine seasonal display of coastal flowers. **Plants** Sea spleenwort, Portland and sea spurge, sea campion.
NATIONAL TRUST/PRIVATE OWNERSHIP

D:4 GANNEL ESTUARY & CANTOCK BEACH

Near Newquay; *park at SW 788608 or SW 787614. Use public footpaths. Check times of*
tides before crossing estuary.
■ Sandy estuary, salt-marsh, dunes.
■ Variety of habitats within relatively small estuary, attracting migrant and overwintering birds; good populations of butterflies and ground beetles. **Birds** Whimbrel, curlew. **Mammals** Grey seal. **Plants** Sea spleenwort, sea campion.
NATIONAL TRUST/PRIVATE OWNERSHIP

D:5 BEDRUTHAN STEPS

Near Newquay; *car park at SW 849695. Keep to footpaths.*
■ Cliffs, coast.
■ Dramatic cliff scenery on stretch of coast exposed to full force of Atlantic gales. Much stunted vegetation, but very colourful display of spring flowers. Sea-birds offshore year-round.
NATIONAL TRUST/PRIVATE OWNERSHIP

D:6 DINAS HEAD & CONSTANTINE BAY

Near Padstow; *car park at SW 851763. Use public foorpaths; beware of strong currents if exploring seashore.*
■ Headland, cliffs, dunes.
■ Attractive cliff scenery on very exposed coastal headland and stable dune system. Colourful spring flowers, breeding gulls on cliffs, abundant marine life in intertidal pools.

E:1 CAMEL ESTUARY & WALMSLEY SANCTUARY*

Near Wadebridge-Padstow; *access from either town along shore of estuary. Amble Marshes can be viewed from road at SW 887743. Use public rights of way and disused railway line. CBWPS hide (permit needed) at SW 983743.*

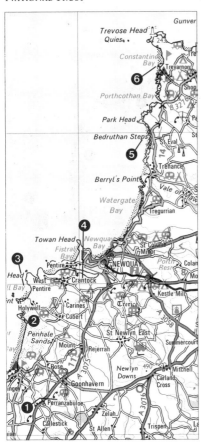

MAP D

MAP E

■ Mudflats, sandbanks, salt-marsh.

■ The largest estuary on Cornwall's N coast has a great range of habitats and a diverse wildlife. On the N shore near the mouth of the estuary a dune system supports species rare in the county. In the marshes at the head of the estuary are overwintering wildfowl and waders, notably white-fronted goose, golden plover, lapwings and dunlin. Birds feed close to the shore; a hide at the head of the estuary by the Amble River gives good views of wintering birds. In spring whimbrel and terns pass through near the mouth, while resident kingfishers and herons can be seen in the upper reaches where freshwater streams enter. **Birds** Buzzard, peregrine, white-fronted goose, wigeon, pintail, goldeneye, smew, green sandpiper, golden plover, greenshank. **Mammals** Fox.

PRIVATE OWNERSHIP/CORNWALL BIRDWATCHING AND PRESERVATION SOCIETY

E:2 HAWKE'S WOOD

Near Wadebridge; access from minor road at SW 987710. Keep to footpaths.

■ Mixed woodland, stream, quarry.

■ Formerly coppiced, sloping, woodland site supports good variety of native trees, birds and insects. Luxuriant ground flora of ferns and flowering plants best in spring and early summer.

CORNWALL TRUST FOR NATURE CONSERVATION

E:3 RED MOOR

Near Lostwithiel; access from minor road at SX 075623. Further details from CTNC; keep to footpaths.

■ Wet heath, scrub, woodland, ponds.

■ Mounds and hollows left by abandoned tin workings now colonized with woodland, heath and wetland plants and animals. Over 100 bird species and 11 dragonflies recorded. **Birds** Stonechat. **Mammals** Fox.

CORNWALL TRUST FOR NATURE CONSERVATION

E:4 LANHYDROCK

Near Bodmin; access from minor road at SX 099635. Closed during winter. Check times and further details with NT.

■ Mixed ancient woodland, parkland, river.

■ Ideal habitat for woodland birds and flowers; damp conditions aid luxuriant growth of ferns, mosses, liverworts and lichens. Many invertebrates and brown trout in river Fowey. **Birds** Buzzard, sparrowhawk, dipper. **Mammals** Fox, badger, wood mice, bats. **Plants** Royal fern, golden-saxifrage, Cornish money-wort, lichens, mosses. **Insects** Caddisflies, stoneflies, damselflies.

NATIONAL TRUST

E:5 CARDINHAM WOODS

Near Bodmin; access from minor road at SX 117688. Check current visiting arrangements with FC.

■ Conifer plantations, mixed woodland.

■ Nature trails through forestry plantations supporting dense growth of mosses, liverworts, ferns and lichens; used by many woodland birds and mammals. **Birds** Buzzard, woodpeckers, goldcrest, redpoll. **Plants** Golden-saxifrage, Cornish money-wort.

FORESTRY COMMISSION

Painted lady, typical in Cornwall.

E:6 PELYN WOODS

Near Lostwithiel; access from A390 at SX 087587. Further details from CTNC. Keep to footpaths; reserve closed at certain periods.

■ Mixed broad-leaved woodland, river.

■ Mixed woodland with good range of plants – especially ground flora.

CORNWALL TRUST FOR NATURE CONSERVATION

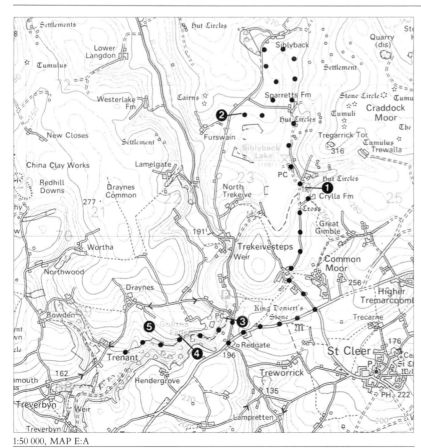

1:50 000, MAP E:A

E:A SIBLYBACK LAKE & DRAYNE'S WOOD★

Near Liskeard; car parks at reservoir and Drayne's Bridge. Keep to footpaths.

■ River, reservoir, muddy margins.

① Car park well signposted. Scan reservoir for grebes and diving ducks. Possible to walk along shore to dam: divers sometimes visit deeper water.

② Follow path N along shore to bird hide, checking patches of exposed mud for waders. Best in autumn, when low water levels offer chance of rare migrants.

③ From bridge follow path through woods alongside river. Clear waters support brown trout; many caddis flies, stone fly, and several dragonflies. Dippers are likely – look for droppings on stones. Grey wagtails (yellow underparts) breed.

④ The waterfalls and mossy boulders support a variety of damp woodland species, including filmy fern, mosses and liverworts. The rocks can be slippery: keep to paths to avoid damaging plants. Examine tree trunks and low branches for lichens which are luxuriant here: tree lungwort one of many species.

⑤ Woodland flora typical of acid soils is dominated by bilberry, great woodrush and hard fern, although sanicle grows in some spots on richer soils. Many mosses and liverworts. Treecreeper, nuthatch, woodpeckers and mixed flocks of tits inhabit canopy; buzzards usually present. Leaf litter supports many invertebrates, preyed on by shrews.

Birds Smew, goosander, goldeneye, teal, wigeon, black tern.

SOUTH WEST WATER/NATURE CONSERVANCY COUNCIL

CORNWALL

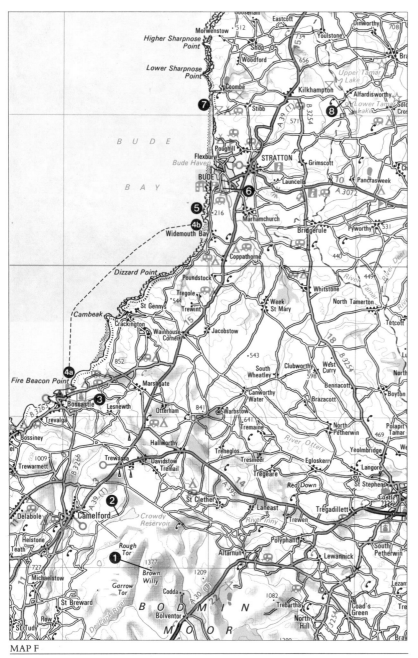

MAP F

F:1 BODMIN MOOR*

Near Bodmin; *minor road from A30 at SX 184768, Bolventor to Liskeard, gives good access to moorland. Many other minor roads enter moor from A30.*

■ Granite moorland, bogs, rivers, mixed woodlands, rough pasture.

■ Granite tors, slopes of tumbled boulders and heather moorland characterize the higher slopes. There is a typical wet moorland flora of acid-loving species, including both filmy ferns. Several streams and rivers flow off the moor and there is standing freshwater at the naturally formed Dozmary pool and artificially created reservoirs. Many shallow peaty pools make walking hazardous, but these mini-habitats are rich in aquatic plants and insects. Drier grassy areas can be botanically very rich with many orchids and other herbs of damp meadows. The bird life is typical of upland regions, with breeding waders and birds of prey in the more open areas. Large flocks of starlings and redwings overwinter near the plantations. **Birds** Buzzard, golden plover, curlew, dipper, raven. **Mammals** Fox, badger, otter, mink. **Plants** Cornish moneywort, pale butterwort, long-leaved sundew, lesser bladderwort. **Butterflies** Marsh fritillary. **Reptiles** Grass snake, adder. **Amphibians** Frog, toad, smooth and palmate newts.
PRIVATE OWNERSHIP/NATIONAL TRUST/ FORESTRY COMMISSION/CORNWALL TRUST FOR NATURE CONSERVATION

F:2 CROWDY RESERVOIR & MARSH

Near Camelford; *car park at SX 138834. Permits for hide and key from SWW.*

■ Reservoir, conifer plantation.

■ Extensive marshy margins of reservoir support interesting flora and invertebrates and are much used by waders and wildfowl. Old airfield good site for overwintering waders and birds of prey; large roosts of starlings found in conifer plantations. **Birds** Buzzard, curlew, woodcock, willow tit, raven. **Mammals** Fox, badger. **Plants** Ivy-leaved bellflower, pale butterwort, oblong-leaved sundew, bog orchid. **Insects** Marsh fritillary butterfly, dragonflies. **Reptiles** Grass snake, adder. **Amphibians** Frog, toad, smooth and palmate newts.
SOUTH WEST WATER/FORESTRY COMMISSION

F:3 PETER'S WOOD

Near Boscastle; *church car park at SX 111904. Keep to footpaths.*

■ Ancient oak woodland, valley.

■ Deep valley providing shelter along very exposed coastline. Vegetation luxuriant in damp conditions; large population of molluscs thrives in base-rich rocks of valley floor. **Birds** Buzzard, nuthatch, raven. **Mammals** Fox.
CORNISH TRUST FOR NATURE CONSERVATION/NATIONAL TRUST

F:4 BOSCASTLE TO WIDEMOUTH BAY*

Near Boscastle; *parking at many points along coastal road from Boscastle to Bude. Keep to footpaths. Do not climb cliffs; beware freak waves.*

■ Coastline, cliffs, coves, coastal scrub, woodland.

■ This geologically complex coastline is highly exposed, affecting plant and animal life. Stunted oakwoods cling to the spectacular cliffs, and a dense scrub of blackthorn and gorse fills many small valleys. Below are packed colonies of barnacles and mussels. Grey seals breed in sheltered sea caves, and Cornwall's largest puffin colony can be seen on the stacks just off Boscastle. Natural rock gardens have formed on slopes, making a colourful display in early summer; naturalized fuschias and montbretia give autumn colour. **Birds** Buzzard, peregrine, auks, stonechat, wheatear, raven. **Mammals** Grey seal, fox, badger. **Plants** Royal and shield ferns; sea and lanceolate spleenworts. **Butterflies** Pearl-bordered fritillary. **Moths** Thrift clearwing. **Reptiles** Slow-worm, common lizard, grass snake, adder.
NATIONAL TRUST/PRIVATE OWNERSHIP

F:5 PHILLIP'S POINT CLIFFS

Near Bude; *parking at SS 200044 on coastal road from Boscastle to Bude. Keep to footpaths (Cornwall Coast Path). Do not climb cliffs.*

■ Cliff-top grassland, coastal heath.

■ Exposed coastline supports many maritime plants on sunny rock faces. Ravens and fulmars breed on cliffs; seals and porpoises sighted offshore. **Birds** Buzzard, rock pipit, raven. **Mammals** Grey seal. **Plants** Sea and lanceolate spleenworts, sea campion, stonecrop. **Reptiles** Slow-worm, common lizard, adder.
CORNISH TRUST FOR NATURE CONSERVATION

F:6 BUDE CANAL & MARSHES

Bude; *park in Bude. Footpath alongside canal at SS 207062. Information centre with enclosed observation point on top, open Apr-Oct.*

■ Canal, freshwater marsh.

■ The disused canal and adjacent River Neet provide valuable stretches of freshwater. The marshland between them is used by many water-birds, and good views can be obtained from the hide; the elusive water rail is sometimes seen in winter. Hard

weather inland always increases the numbers and variety of species present. Spring brings returning migrants and the reed and sedge warblers sing from the reed-beds. Yellow iris colours the marsh and the first damselflies and dragonflies hatch; these increase as the summer progresses and the returning autumn migrants pass through. **Birds** Kestrel, water rail, reed warbler, kingfisher. **Insects** Dragonflies, damselflies. **Reptiles** Grass snake, common lizard, slow-worm. **Amphibians** Frog, toad.
NORTH CORNWALL DISTRICT COUNCIL

F:7 DUCKPOOL
Near Bude; parking at SS 202117. Keep to footpaths. Do not climb cliffs. Check tide times before venturing on to shore.
■ Tidal seashore.
■ Exposed stretch of rocky seashore with dense population of mussels and barnacles; noted for colonies of sand mason worms. **Birds** Fulmar, gulls, auks; wheatear, rock

pipit, raven. **Mammals** Grey seal. **Plants** Sea and lanceolate spleenworts; sea campion.

F:8 TAMAR LAKES
Near Bude; car park at SS 291117. Keep to footpaths. Permits and keys for hides from SWW. Information centre on site.
■ Reservoirs, scrub.
■ Set amid high, rolling farmland, both lakes have banks with natural vegetation; the larger, upper one is used as a reservoir. They attract a good variety of water-birds, including many rarities. Small numbers of swans, including occasional Bewick's, and some geese overwinter, and dabbling ducks appreciate the shallow grassy margins. Diving ducks, including goldeneye and goosander, feed in the deeper stretches, and waders probe on the muddy shores where hides have been placed. Dragonflies and damselflies breed in shallower, weedy backwaters and the feeder streams are used by king-

Above, Bedruthan Steps; below, water rail (F:8).

fishers. In winter birds of prey not normally resident, like the merlin and hen harrier, hunt over the margins and flocks of gulls leave the coast to bathe in fresh water. **Birds** Hen harrier, merlin, jack snipe, water rail; green and wood sandpipers, snipe, barn owl, kingfisher, sparrowhawk, buzzard. **Mammals** Otter. **Plants** Wavy St John's-wort. **Insects** Dragonflies, damselflies. **Reptiles** Grass snake, common lizard, slow-worm. **Amphibians** Frog, toad.
SOUTH WEST WATER

DEVON

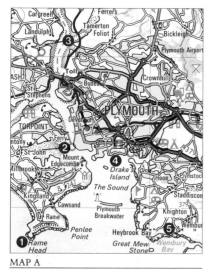

MAP A

A:1 RAME HEAD*

Near Plymouth; car park at SX 422487. Access largely unrestricted along coastal footpath. Summer weekends can be crowded.

■ Headland, cliffs, scrub, grassland.

■ Along this steeply sloping stretch of coastline bracken-covered banks are interspersed with dense thickets of blackthorn, stone hedge-banks and small rough fields. Open areas have an attractive display of coastal flowers in spring and summer. Scrub patches host birds like the Dartford warbler and cirl bunting, joined in spring and autumn by many migrants, including some rarities. Southerly winds bring migrating sea-birds close inshore in spring and autumn; divers, shearwaters, skuas, petrels, auks and terns of many species have been recorded. **Birds** Buzzard, raven; (offshore) sea-birds; (scrub) migrant warblers, Dartford warbler; cirl bunting, thrushes, finches, flycatchers. **Mammals** Fallow deer. **Plants** Sea campion, thrift, hare's-foot clover.

A:2 ST JOHN'S LAKE, TAMAR ESTUARY

Near Torpoint; access along public roads only. View from tidal road at SX 410540. Wildfowling in some areas. Check tide times carefully.

■ Tidal mudflats.

■ The 'lakes' are large expanses of mudflats uncovered at low tide in the Tamar estuary. Being deep in a valley, the site is very sheltered. The lakes are important feeding areas for many waders and wildfowl, and the mild SW climate encourages birds like the avocet and greenshank to overwinter. The deep-water channels are used by divers and grebes. Birdwatching often requires a telescope. **Birds** Great northern diver, black-tailed godwit, spotted redshank, great crested grebe, greenshank. **Plants** Sea-purslane, sea-lavender, stinking iris.

A:3 KINGSMILL LAKE, TAMAR ESTUARY

Near Saltash; park at Landulph Church, SX 432615 or at Cargreen, SX 437627 and follow footpaths to shore. Wildfowling in some areas. Check tide times carefully.

■ Tidal mudflats.

■ Favoured feeding place for waders and wildfowl; a large flock of avocets. The rocky shore is partly wooded, and rich salt-marsh flora in sheltered areas attract migrant butterflies and moths. **Birds** Avocet, black-tailed godwit, spotted redshank, green sandpiper.

A:4 PLYMOUTH SOUND*

Near Plymouth; park on sea-front (crowded during holidays), signposted from city centre. Access along footpaths and roads, and to most of shore. Some restrictions in MOD areas.

■ Harbour, rocky shoreline, sewage outfalls, fish quays.

■ A long breakwater protects this natural harbour which offers sheltered conditions to overwintering birds. The sewage outfalls and fish quays are further attractions to huge flocks of gulls, including rarities. Divers and grebes overwinter far out into the Sound. Oystercatchers, turnstones and purple sandpipers may be seen on the shoreline, and the rich and colourful marine fauna beneath the high-tide line includes many species unable to survive on exposed parts of the coast. The flora of limestone outcrops includes several rare British species. **Birds** Slavonian grebe, buzzard, goosander, red-breasted merganser, gulls; (migrant) terns. **Plants** Plymouth pear, field eryngo, Plymouth thistle, maidenhair fern.

PRIVATE OWNERSHIP/PLYMOUTH CITY COUNCIL

A:5 WEMBURY

Near Plymouth; park in Wembury (crowded at weekends). Access along footpaths, and to most of shore. Some restrictions in MOD areas. Check

range notice boards for firing times.

■ Rocky shoreline, scrub, grassland.

■ Reserve protecting the rich inter-tidal zone along a 4-mile (6-km) stretch of coastline. **Birds** Cirl bunting, Slavonian grebe, whimbrel, black redstart. **Butterflies** Green hairstreak.

PRIVATE OWNERSHIP/NATIONAL TRUST

B:1 COTEHELE

Near Tavistock; access off minor road at SX 423681. Closed in winter. Opening times from NT at Cotehele.

■ Woodland, estuary.

■ Nature trail leads through old estate woodlands and alongside upper reaches of estuary where marshland supports interesting salt-marsh flora.

NATIONAL TRUST

B:2 BURRATOR RESERVOIR

Near Yelverton; park on roads circling reservoir. Good views from road. Keep to footpaths. Permit from SWW office near dam required for access to banks.

■ Reservoir, conifer woods.

■ Dramatically set in a steep-sided valley amid high granite tors and dense conifer woodland. The acid water restricts the flora and the bird and animal life is less rich than in lowland waters. Brown trout and eels are present. The most abundant invertebrates are caddis flies. Several species of wildfowl overwinter. Small colonies of crossbills and

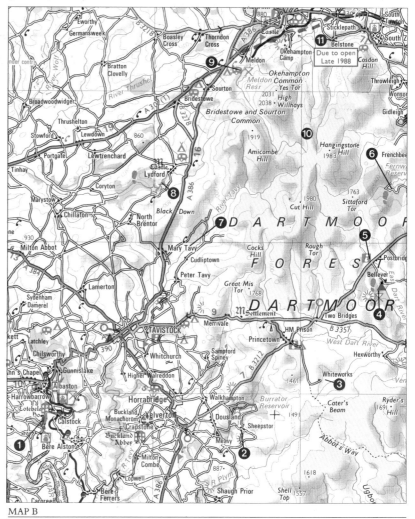

MAP B

the tiny lesser-spotted woodpecker may be seen in the surrounding woods. **Birds** Goosander, dipper, crossbill, kingfisher, buzzard. **Mammals** Otter.
SOUTH WEST WATER

B:3 FOXTOR MIRES
Near Yelverton; limited parking on minor road at SX 613710. Some footpaths. Take great care in boggy areas and do not walk on bright green mosses.
■ Moorland, valley bog.
■ This mire is an excellent example of a valley bog. The small pools and runnels at the edge of the mire are ideal for dragonflies and damselflies in late summer. There are white carpets of cotton grass in the wetter areas and yellow splashes of tormentil and hawkbit on drier tussocks. Herons stalk the mire and grass snakes may sometimes be glimpsed in the shallow pools. **Birds** Ring ouzel, dipper, wheatear, stonechat, whinchat, golden plover. **Mammals** Fox, badger, otter. **Plants** St John's-wort, bog pimpernel, sundews, ivy-leaved bellflower, bog asphodel. **Reptiles** Slow-worm, grass snake, adder.
DUCHY OF CORNWALL

B:4 BELLEVER PLANTATION
Near Ashburton; park at Bellever; follow signs from B3212 to approx SX 656773. Forest rides and paths; further details from FC.
■ Conifer plantation, moorland, river.
■ Mature plantation; one of the most productive winter bird-watching areas on the moor. River below wood rich in aquatic life. **Birds** Hen harrier, crossbill, ring ouzel, dipper, raven, buzzard, siskin. **Plants** Marsh St John's-wort, bog pimpernel, sundews, ivy-leaved bellflower, bog asphodel.
FORESTRY COMMISSION

B:5 EAST DART RIVER
Near Ashburton; park at Postbridge on B3212, SX 647788. Keep to footpaths. Further details from Dartmoor National Park Authority. Guided walks sometimes available.
■ Upland river, granite moorland.
■ The East Dart rises high on the moors in an area of blanket bog and flows off the plateau through a small rocky valley. Trout, salmon and eels feed on abundant insect life, and a rich moorland flora grows along its banks. **Birds** Ring ouzel, dipper, raven, buzzard, stonechat. **Mammals** Otter, weasel. **Plants** Marsh St John's-wort, bog pimpernel, sundews, ivy-leaved bellflower. **Insects** Caddis flies, stoneflies.
DUCHY OF CORNWALL

B:6 FERNWORTHY RESERVOIR
Near Chagford; car park at SX 659838. Follow signs to Fernworthy from B3212. Keep to footpaths. Details from SWW office on site.
■ Upland reservoir, conifer plantations, deciduous woodland, scrub.
■ Shallow, well-vegetated margins attract a variety of waterbirds, especially in winter. Nature reserve at the inlet, and forest trails. **Birds** Goosander, dipper, redstart, crossbill, raven, buzzard. **Insects** Caddis flies, stoneflies.
SOUTH WEST WATER/FORESTRY COMMISSION

B:7 RIVER TAVY
Near Tavistock; limited parking on minor road at approx SX 525795, or at edge of moor at SX 637824. Some footpaths. Check MOD firing times in local press, or look for red flags.
■ Moorland river.
■ The River Tavy rises on high moorland to the E, rushes through a dramatic rocky gorge at Tavy Cleave, continuing off moor through gentler farmland to join Tamar estuary. Clear, peaty waters ideal for trout and salmon; many aquatic insects. **Birds** Heron, buzzard, kestrel, dipper, grey wagtail, meadow pipit, skylark, wheatear, stonechat, ring ouzel, raven. **Mammals** Otter. **Plants** Marsh St John's-wort, bog pimpernel. **Insects** Caddis flies, stoneflies. Dragonflies Golden-ringed.

B:8 LYDFORD GORGE
Near Lydford; park at SX 509846 or in Lydford. Follow NT signs to Lydford Gorge. Keep to footpaths (may be slippery after heavy rain). Closed in winter.
■ Wooded gorge, waterfalls.
■ The River Lyd plunges through a dramatic ravine over a series of waterfalls, emerging into a gorge with typical western oakwood flora with luxuriant growth of ferns and mosses in wood. **Birds** Redstart, dipper, grey wagtail. **Mammals** Roe deer, mink. **Plants** Soft and hard shield-ferns. **Insects** Purple hairstreak, caddis flies.
NATIONAL TRUST

B:9 MELDON RESERVOIR
Near Okehampton; park near dam at SX 563916. Access unrestricted, apart from nature reserve area at inlet.
■ High moorland reservoir, willows.
■ Typical upland birds can be seen at the inlet, and migrants and some breeding birds in the scrub. Many dragonflies in feeder streams. **Birds** Goosander, dipper, stonechat, ring ouzel. **Mammals** Otter, mink. **Plants** Bog and heath spotted-orchids, sundews, lousewort, milkwort.
SOUTH WEST WATER/DEVON TRUST FOR NATURE CONSERVATION

B:10 YES TOR & CRANMERE POOL★
Near Okehampton; park on unclassified road from Okehampton; follow signs to Dartmoor National Park from town centre to SX 591932, then through gate on to moor. MOD firing ranges close large areas at times. Check in local press and on notice boards. Weather can deteriorate rapidly.
■ High granite moorland, rocky tors, heather moors, blanket bogs, pools, streams.
■ The highest and wildest part of Dartmoor rises to 2,038 feet (621 m) and is capped by the granite masses of High Willhays and Yes Tor. Red grouse breed in the heather, and a few pairs of dunlin and golden plover nest on the open moor. Foxes are often seen. A vast area of blanket bog lies S of the summit; Cranmere pool is a shallow, peaty depression near the source of the West Okement river. The heather, bell heather, cross-leaved heath and dwarf gorse make a colourful late summer display. Dragonflies and damselflies abound. **Birds** Red grouse, dipper, ring ouzel, dunlin, golden plover, wheatear. **Mammals** Fox.
DUCHY OF CORNWALL/MINISTRY OF DEFENCE

B:11 BELSTONE CLEAVE & TAW MARSH
Near Okehampton; park in Belstone at SX 620935 (limited on summer weekends). Footpaths and bridle-paths to most areas. MOD range on edge of area; check firing times in local press.
■ Granite moorland, rocky tors, grassland, heath, rivers, marsh, oakwoods.
■ The River Taw flows from the blanket bogs of northern Dartmoor across a flat boggy plain and plunges off the moor at Belstone. There is a good marsh flora and fauna, with many waterbirds. Snipe and lapwing breed and golden plover, and sometimes dotterel, pass through. Further downstream redstarts breed and buzzards nest in the oaks of the wooded banks. Heavy rain can turn the river into a raging torrent in a matter of hours. **Mammals** Otter, mink. **Plants** Sundews, heath spotted-orchid, lousewort, bog asphodel, sheep's-bit scabious. **Reptiles** Grass snake.
DUCHY OF CORNWALL/DARTMOOR NATIONAL PARK AUTHORITY

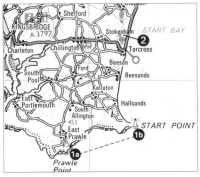

MAP C

C:1 PRAWLE POINT/START POINT★
Near Kingsbridge; car parks Prawle Point, SX 775355 and Start Point, SX 825373. Access along footpaths, and to most of shore.
■ Rocky coastline, scrub, grassland.
■ Some of the most attractive cliff scenery on the S coast, providing ideal conditions for migrant and resident birds. This is probably the best area in Britain to see cirl buntings and many migrants, including rarities, throughout spring and autumn. Scrub patches are often alive with small songbirds. Shearwaters pass by offshore and should be checked for unusual species, and many birds of prey pass overhead. Offshore, grey seals and basking sharks may be seen.
PRIVATE OWNERSHIP/NATIONAL TRUST

C:2 SLAPTON LEY★
Near Kingsbridge; car parks on A379 at SX 824424 and SX 828442. Access along footpaths and roads. Permits for woodland and reed-bed walk from Slapton Field Study Centre.
■ Freshwater lagoon, reed-beds, beach.
■ Cut off from the sea by a long shingle strand (which has its own interesting flora) Slapton Ley is Devon's largest natural lake. Only a few feet deep, it supports abundant fish populations, especially perch and eels, and has some of the region's most extensive reed-beds. Wildfowl come in winter and water rails and bitterns skulk in the reeds. In spring the reed-beds become home to migrant and breeding warblers and there are always rare migrants like hoopoes or purple herons. A marsh harrier may linger for a few days, and terns and whimbrel will pass through. Dragonflies and damselflies become active in the summer. **Birds** Bittern, Cetti's warbler, bearded tit, firecrest, garganey, ruddy duck, Slavonian grebe. **Mammals** Otter, mink.
FIELD STUDIES COUNCIL

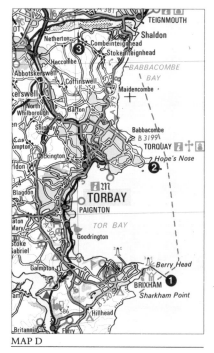

MAP D

D:1 BERRY HEAD*

Near Torbay; car park at SX 943564. Follow signs to Berry Head Country Park. Access along footpaths and roads. Permits for quarries from TBC.

■ Limestone headland, cliffs, quarries, grassland, scrub.

■ The headland offers a fine collection of plants found on few other sites in Britain. The white rock-rose grows on the exposed section of cliffs, alongside stonecrops and commoner plants like thrift and sea campion. The tiny honewort and even tinier small hare's-ear grow in the close-cropped turf which is coloured by autumn squill in late summer when the bugloss and ploughman's spikenard are past their best. Near to typical lime-loving plants may be small patches of bell heather, showing how a limestone 'heath' has been formed. On the cliffs is an important sea-bird colony and autumn

gales bring many migrants close inshore.
TORBAY BOROUGH COUNCIL

D:2 HOPE'S NOSE

Near Torbay; park on road at SX 944636. Keep to footpaths.

■ Limestone headland, cliffs, quarries, grassland, scrub.

■ Large flocks of gulls, some divers and sea-duck in winter. Good viewing from prominent headland.
TORBAY BOROUGH COUNCIL

D:3 TEIGN ESTUARY

Between Teignmouth and Newton Abbot; limited roadside parking. Some spaces on B3195. keep to footpaths, mostly on S shore. Avoid walking on mudflats.

■ Estuary, mudflats, salt-marsh.

■ Footpath along S of estuary gives good views of intertidal mud and sand with waders and wildfowl. Upper reaches support more wildfowl in winter and have good salt-marsh flora. **Birds** Red-breasted merganser, green sandpiper, kingfisher, gulls.

E:1 BOVEY VALLEY WOODLANDS

Near Newton Abbot; car park near SX 757804 off B3344 signposted Becky Falls. Keep to woodland paths and tracks. NCC permit needed for other areas.

■ Oak/birch woodland, streams.

■ Some of the richest remaining mixed woodlands on Dartmoor with luxuriant ferns, mosses, liverworts and lichens; rich in fungi in autumn. **Birds** Pied and spotted flycatchers, redstart, wood warbler, woodpeckers. **Butterflies** Fritillaries, white admiral, purple and green hairstreaks.
NATURE CONSERVANCY COUNCIL

E:2 YARNER WOOD*

Near Newton Abbot; car park at SX 786788 off B3344. Keep to woodland paths or obtain NCC permit.

■ Oak/birch woodland, conifers, open moorland, streams.

■ The wood, which includes many deciduous tree species, is extremely rich in woodland birds – flycatchers, redstarts and warblers – during the breeding season. This is partly due to the abundance of insects in-

cluding moths, butterflies and beetles. A nest-box scheme has encouraged many formerly scarce species, most notably the pied flycatcher. Large wood ant nests can be seen throughout the drier parts of the wood, and in autumn there is an impressive display of fungi. **Birds** Pied flycatcher, nightjar, redstart, wood warbler, dipper. **Butterflies** Purple and green hairstreaks, holly blue, white admiral. **Mammals** Dormouse.
NATURE CONSERVANCY COUNCIL

E:3 CHUDLEIGH KNIGHTON HEATH

Near Newton Abbott; parking possible at SX 838776 off B3344.

■ Lowland heath, ponds, scrub, woodland.

■ A reserve with a mosaic of heathland habitats and a good selection of typical plants and animals (including dragonflies and damselflies). **Plants** Sundews, bladderwort, pale dog-violet. **Amphibians** Palmate newt.
DEVON TRUST FOR NATURE
CONSERVATION

E:4 TEIGN VALLEY WOODS

Near Exeter; car park at SX 805884 off B3212. Keep to woodland paths.

■ Mixed woodland, river valley.

■ Visit in spring to see impressive displays of wild daffodils and at any time to see many other woodland plants and animals. **Birds** Buzzard, sparrowhawk, kestrel, pied flycatcher. **Butterflies** Brimstone, purple hairstreak, pearl-bordered and silver-washed fritillaries.
DEVON TRUST FOR NATURE
CONSERVATION

E:5 HALDON WOODS

Near Exeter; car parks at SX 877856, SX 882847, SX 885842. Forest walks signposted off A38. Keep to woodland paths and rights of way. Further information from FC office at Buller's Hill.

■ Coniferous woodland, open heath, grassland.

■ The woods support a typical range of conifer wood species and their high position makes watching migrants very rewarding; several forest trails reveal characteristic flora

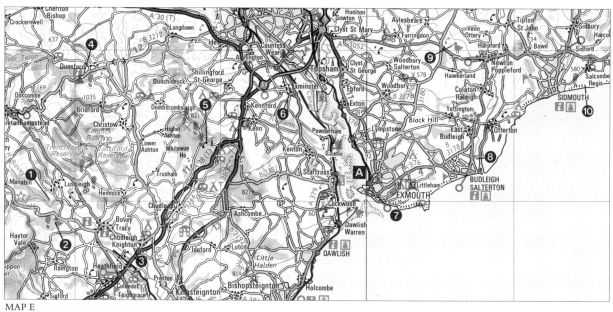

MAP E

in the damp rides and open clearings.
FORESTRY COMMISSION

E:6 EXE REED-BEDS
Near Exeter; park at SX 959875 on narrow track and take footpath across meadows to canal towpath, or use canal footpath from Exeter.
■ Tidal reed-bed, freshwater canal, scrub.
■ Extensive reed-beds used by nesting warblers and roosting starlings and swallows, which attract predators such as hobby and sparrowhawk. Many waders, especially in winter; dragonflies in summer.
DEVON TRUST FOR NATURE
CONSERVATION

E:7 MAER ROCKS & ORCOMBE POINT
Near Exmouth; park along sea-front or in town. Access along coastal footpath and sea-front.
■ Red sandstone cliffs, intertidal rocks.
■ Marine algae, molluscs and other invertebrates cover rocks, riddled with holes made by piddocks. Good feeding ground for waders, useful watchpoint for sea-birds in stormy weather. Migrant and breeding butterflies on cliffs.
NATIONAL TRUST

E:8 OTTER ESTUARY★
Near Budleigh Salterton; park at SY 073819. Many footpaths.
■ Estuary, pebble beach, salt-marsh, reed-bed, meadows, scrub.
■ The pebble ridge and intertidal rocks are used by waders and sea-ducks and the mud-flats and salt-marsh attract feeding and roosting waterbirds. Grebes fish in the deep-water channel; dippers, kingfishers and water rails may be found in the fresh water upstream. In autumn, herons stalk hundreds of tiny flatfish in the shallows. Flooded meadows adjacent to the estuary are used by snipe and wildfowl in winter. Birds in the surrounding patches of woodland and scrub may include serins. The estuary also tends to act as a trap for migrant birds in spring.

E:9 AYLESBEARE COMMON
Near Sidmouth; car park at SY 057898. Keep to public footpaths. Trail shows main features of reserve.
■ Wet/dry lowland heath, woodland.
■ Fine stretch of heathland with many typical plants and animals. **Birds** Dartford warbler, nightjar, stonechat. **Plants** Bog

Dragonfly – see E:6

pimpernel, sundews, pale butterwort, dwarf gorse, dodder.
ROYAL SOCIETY FOR THE PROTECTION OF BIRDS

E:10 SALCOMBE HILL
Near Sidmouth; car parks in Sidmouth and on minor road at SY 138881. Keep to footpaths. Nature trail shows best features; leaflet from DTNC.
■ Cliff-top grassland, scrub, undercliff.
■ The scrub supports good population of insects and is used by many birds for breeding and shelter on migration. Well-vegetated undercliff.
DEVON TRUST FOR NATURE
CONSERVATION

E:A DAWLISH WARREN & EXE ESTUARY★★
Near Dawlish; park at Dawlish Warren or on roadside and keep to footpaths.
■ Estuary, mudflats, sand dunes, sandstone cliffs, parkland.
① From top of rock or sea-wall scan for divers, grebes and sea-duck in winter. Terns in late summer; purple sandpipers feed on the rocks below. Check scrub behind railway line for migrants and cirl bunting (use binoculars).
② At entrance to reserve check scrub for migrants, and ponds for dragonflies and bush crickets in summer.
③ Follow path through dunes. Flora in large stony slack: yellow bartsia, centaury, evening primrose, eyebright.
④ Back along shore to hide overlooking estuary. Excellent at high tide as flocks of gulls and waders roost in front of it. Brent goose in winter.
⑤ Follow shore to far point; Slavonian grebes and mergansers in deepwater channel in winter, terns in summer. Typical dune flora.
⑥ Return along shore, taking care in winter not to disturb roosting waders. Look for interesting shells such as pelican's foot. Divers and grebes offshore, terns in summer.
⑦ Park beside road at SY 976804, cross railway line with care, and scan mudflats for waders, especially godwits. Cormorants roost on old wreck. Oystercatchers and turnstones feed on mussel beds.
⑧ Waders and gulls in Cockwood harbour, marsh for snipe and green sandpiper.
⑨ Park beside road at SY 974832. Deer park on W of road has large herd of fallow deer. Waders roost here at high tide and huge numbers may be present; telescope needed for good views, but 'fly-over' as birds return to feed is impressive. When flooded, park holds many pintail, teal and wigeon and there is a heronry. Rail-line can be crossed here. Greenshank in freshwater outfall and curlew, godwits and dunlin picking around for food in the mud.
⑩ Park at SY 873844 and follow path along river to lock gates at Turf. Waders at low tide, flooded fields may hold wildfowl.
PRIVATE OWNERSHIP/DEVON TRUST FOR NATURE CONSERVATION

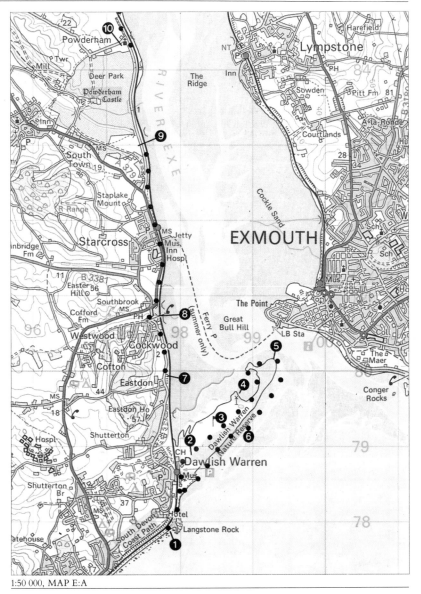

1:50 000, MAP E:A

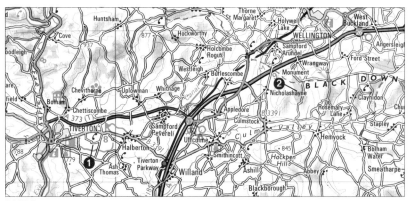

MAP F

MAP H

F:1 GRAND WESTERN CANAL
Near Tiverton; car park in town at *SS964124; limited parking on roadsides elsewhere. Use canal towpath. Exhibition in Tiverton (may be very busy on summer weekends). Horse-drawn boat operates in summer.*
■ Canal; country park.
■ Recently restored canal is one of few stretches of slow-moving water in Devon with good population of coarse fish. Banks colonized by marginal plants and many dragonflies and damselflies breed.
DEVON COUNTY COUNCIL

F:2 WELLINGTON HILL
Near Wellington; entry from minor road to monument at ST 143167. Keep to footpath.
■ Ancient woodland, meadow.
■ The woodland has many indicator species of ancient woodland, and the meadow a variety of flowers and butterflies.
SOMERSET TRUST FOR NATURE CONSERVATION

G:1 HARTLAND POINT*
Near Bude; car park at SS 235275. Use

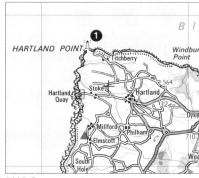

MAP G

coastal footpath and other rights of way. Toll road for cars. Do not climb cliffs.
■ Cliffs, grassland, scrub, hedgerows.
■ Lighthouse is good spot for watching breeding, migrating and wintering seabirds. Seals, dolphins, porpoises and basking sharks offshore; cliffs in spring and summer support colourful flora and many butterflies. **Birds** Shearwater, red-throated

diver, black redstart, lesser whitethroat, auks.

H LUNDY★★
In Bristol Channel; regular sailings from Bideford, sometimes from Ilfracombe. Information from office on Bideford Quay, or from Landmark Trust. Accommodation. Landing fee.
■ Granite island, cliffs, moorland, rough pasture, stony beach, caves.
■ Derived from Norse, Lundy means 'puffin island'. Only a few pairs remain now, but guillemots, razorbills, kittiwakes, shearwaters and gulls make Lundy the most important sea-bird colony in the SW. Its isolated position attracts many migrant birds; spring and autumn are the best times to see rarities. Lundy's unique plant, the cabbage, which grows on the cliffs by the landing bay, is one of the many interesting features of the island's vegetation; several plants found here in profusion are now scarce elsewhere. Grey seals breed in deep sea caves, and the surrounding waters are a marine nature reserve.
Mammals Soay sheep, Sika deer.
LANDMARK TRUST

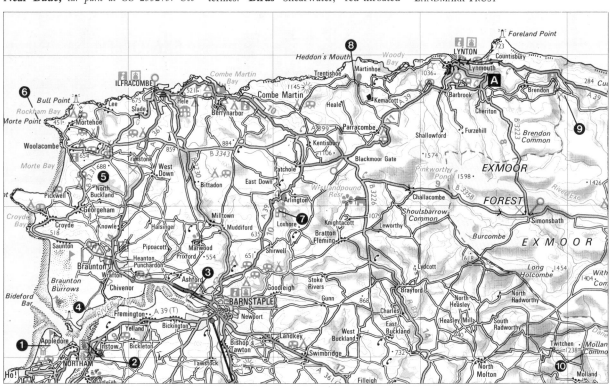

MAP I

I:1 NORTHAM BURROWS*

Near Bideford; car park (fee) at SS 440307. Guided walks, Apr-Oct. Access to dunes restricted in order to combat erosion.
■ Sand dunes, pebble ridge, sandy beach, salt-marsh.
■ Massive pebbles form ridge protecting dunes, grazing marsh and salt-marsh; interesting flora and many insects. Flocks of waders and wildfowl feed in estuary and on marsh; seashore with varied marine life.
DEVON COUNTY COUNCIL

I:2 TORRIDGE ESTUARY

Near Bideford; car park at SS 474310 or park along Instow sea-front. Keep off mudflats when tide is rising.
■ Sand dunes, sandy beach, rock pools, salt-marsh, deep-water channel.
■ Bass, salmon and sea trout use the deep-water channel. Intertidal rocks at estuary mouth have rich marine life, including the edible seaweed, laver. Birds roost and feed on the rocks. Many butterflies, grasshoppers and bush-crickets.

I:3 TAW ESTUARY

Near Barnstaple; park in Barnstaple, or on A361 between SS 510349 and SS 550334. Keep to footpaths; keep off mudflats when tide is rising. No access in front of Chivenor airfield.
■ Estuary, mud/sand flats.
■ Expanses of sand and mud are exposed at low tide; grazing marshes at the sides. Estuary mouth is guarded by the vast dune system of Braunton. High tide brings the birds closer to shore, and more unusual species may be seen when hard winter weather increases their numbers using the area. The marshes are important for both birds and aquatic plants; the numerous drainage ditches are very colourful in summer, and support many dragonflies. Salmon and sea trout swim up the estuary to reach their spawning sites high on Dartmoor; otters occasionally seen.

I:4 BRAUNTON BURROWS**

Near Barnstaple; park at SS 463351 and SS 467327 (toll road). Military zone closed when red flags are flying; check notice boards. Some dune areas restricted.
■ Dunes, sandy beach, salt-marsh.
■ A vast beach provides the wind-blown sand to form the sweeping line of dunes (the largest in N Europe) running from Taw mouth to the low cliffs at Saunton Down. Tellins, razor shells and heart urchins are strewn in thousands after gales, and the salt-wort and sea-rocket above the tide line may be almost buried by new deposits of sand. Under strand-line refuse, the large gregarious yellow-and-black ground beetle *Eurynebria*, may be abundant. Marram grass has stabilized the dunes allowing plant colonies; the wet dune slacks are particularly rich, with some British rarities. Orchids abound and yellow rattle, dune pansy, storksbill and bugloss colour the area in summer. Large

Nightjar – see E:9, previous page.

Grey seal – see Lundy, opposite page.

numbers of land snails live here, due to the abundant calcium, and there is a rich insect fauna, especially butterflies and moths, as well as grasshoppers, crickets and a great variety of beetles, flies and bugs, including many rarities. Snow buntings and golden plover appear in hard winter weather.
NATURE CONSERVANCY COUNCIL

I:5 CHAPEL WOOD

Near Braunton; park on roadside at SS 483413. Access by permit only from RSPB warden, Mr C. Manning, 8 Chichester Park, Woolacombe, Devon (send s.a.e.).
■ Mixed woodland, stream.
■ Variety of native and alien species in attractive valley setting with ruined 13thC chapel and Iron Age hill fort. Ground flora.
ROYAL SOCIETY FOR THE PROTECTION OF BIRDS

I:6 MORTE POINT & DEVON NORTH COAST PATH

Near Woolacombe/Ilfracombe; park in Woolacombe, Mortehoe, Lee Bay or Ilfracombe. Steep, grassy slopes may be very slippery. Avoid climbing cliffs.
■ Rocky cliff tops, coastal heath, scrub.
■ A well-placed headland for watching sea-birds, although north-westerlies are needed to bring them close to the shore. Ravens and buzzards are always present, and in winter a merlin or peregrine may also be seen pursuing prey along the cliffs. The small areas of woodland may have flycatchers and redstarts. Coastal flowers flourish along the cliff edge and many butterflies breed.
NATIONAL TRUST/PRIVATE OWNERSHIP

I:7 ARLINGTON COURT

Near Barnstaple; park at SS 611405. Follow signs from A39. Open Apr-Oct.

■ Lake, river, woodland, parkland.
■ Nature trail leads through attractive park and wood with substantial heronry and many breeding songbirds. Waterbirds and damselflies on river and lake.
NATIONAL TRUST

I:8 HEDDON VALLEY WOODS*

Near Lynton; park at SS 655482. Use public and coastal footpaths. Busy at Aug weekends.
■ Wooded valley, stream, sea.
■ The river Heddon rushes off Exmoor through a deep, densely-wooded valley holding many typical West-country woodlands birds and flowers, best seen May to June. Where the river later flows across a stony beach sea-birds and waders may be seen.
NATIONAL TRUST

I:9 GLENTHORNE ESTATE WALKS

Near Lynton; approach from A39 at SS 794484; nature trails.
■ Coastal woodlands.
■ A surprising variety of habitats in a small area, including steep, densely wooded slopes, a pinetum and a stony beach. Varied ground flora. **Birds** Cormorant, oystercatcher, gulls, buzzard, sparrowhawk, raven, redstart, nuthatch, woodpeckers. **Mammals** Red deer, badger.
EXMOOR NATIONAL PARK

I:10 MOLLAND COMMON

Near South Molton; park at SS 808305 or SS 835297.
■ Moorland, bog, woodland, scrub.
■ Moorland is home to many birds of prey in winter, and a good point for watching migration. Interesting moorland flora; many red deer. Exmoor ponies, dragonflies and damselflies.
PRIVATE OWNERSHIP/EXMOOR NATIONAL PARK

Opposite: grey wagtail; right, common lizards.

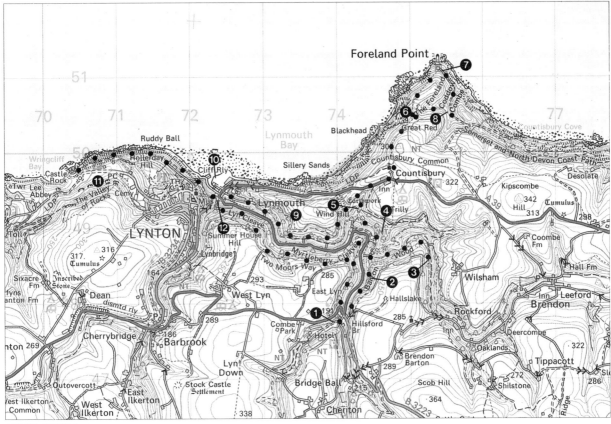

1:50 000, MAP I:A

I:A LYN VALLEY WOODLANDS**
Near Lynton; car park at Hillsford Bridge.
Keep to footpaths.
■ Woodland, rivers, streams, moorland.
① From parking at Hillsford Bridge, cross B3223 and enter woods through gate on E bank of river; follow path downstream. Rich, acid-loving flora here, including many ferns, wood sorrel and Irish spurge.
② Welsh poppy grows on stony outcrops; golden saxifrage covers damp rocks.
③ Continue downstream to bridge and take path to the right up the East Lyn. Dippers and grey wagtails common here, and crystal-clear water allows close views of brown trout and salmon.

④ Return downstream to bridge, cross East Lyn and follow river downstream on N bank. Typical oak-woodland birds here, including redstart and pied flycatcher, while glimpses of open sky through trees often reveal buzzards.
⑤ Cross road and follow footpath N.
⑥ Typical heather moorland plants, with coastal species on cliff edge. Take care. Near lighthouse is best area to watch sea-birds.
⑦ Follow path S through Coddow Combe. Check scrub patches for migrant birds. Lizards and adders bask on sunny banks.
⑧ Return across common to coast path and back to Lyn valley at ⑤. Ravens common on open moor; meadow pipits and skylarks breed in open grassy areas. Fox and emperor moths

present but difficult to find. Listen for willow tits nasal, grating calls while descending through woods and scrub.
⑨ The valley suffered a disastrous flood in 1952, but plants have recolonized this section.
⑩ From the harbour wall gulls and waders may be seen feeding at low tide.
⑪ The Valley of the Rocks is reached by a footpath running W from the B3234 over the cliffs. Ravens and feral goats inhabit this rocky valley, best avoided on summer weekends. Sea-birds, including auks, viewed from cliffs.
⑫ Footpath to Lyn Cleave. Scan skies for birds of prey, especially buzzard, sparrowhawk and kestrel.
PRIVATE OWNERSHIP/NATIONAL TRUST

DORSET

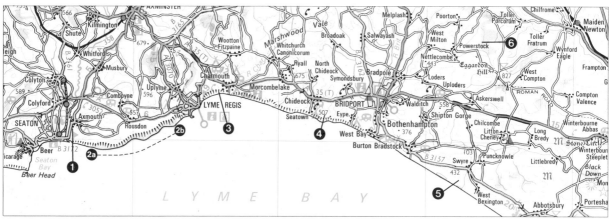

A:1 AXE ESTUARY
Near Seaton; roadside parking at approx SY 255905. Keep to public roads.
■ Estuary, mudflats, salt-marsh, flood meadows.
■ Used in winter by waders, wildfowl and gulls, often close to road: use car as hide.

A:2(a-b) AXMOUTH TO LYME REGIS UNDERCLIFFS★
Near Seaton/Lyme Regis; roadside parking at approx SY 265903, or in Lyme Regis. Keep to footpaths.
■ Wooded cliffs, gulleys.
■ This 800-acre reserve protects one of the most striking sections of coastline in S England. Over the years there have been many landslips; the largest, in 1839, formed the so-called Goat Island, leaving a huge chasm still visible despite colonization by woodland and scrub. In more sheltered places a mixed ash woodland has grown up with a rich and colourful ground flora of ferns and lime-loving herbs, many insects and a large population of birds.
NATURE CONSERVANCY COUNCIL

A:3 BLACK VEN & THE SPITTLES
Near Lyme Regis; park in Lyme Regis or Charmouth. Reserve entered along coastal public footpaths and marked routes. No access to landslip area.
■ Scrub-covered undercliff, grassland.

■ Constantly slipping undercliff provides variety of habitats from stable scrub and open grassland to wet flushes and mud. Rich insect and bird population.
DORSET TRUST FOR NATURE CONSERVATION/NATIONAL TRUST

A:4 GOLDEN CAP
Near Lyme Regis; car park at SY 421917. Site can be entered along coastal footpath from Seatown or Charmouth.
■ Scrub-covered undercliff, grassland.
■ Undercliff a rich habitat for butterflies and songbirds.
NATIONAL TRUST

A:5 WEST BEXINGTON
Near Bridport; park in West Bexington at SY 531865. Site entered along coastal footpath. No entry to reed-bed.
■ Shingle beach, reed-bed.
■ Shingle continuation of vast Chesil Beach supports good flora; reed-bed safe nesting for warblers and waterbirds with many spring and autumn migrants.
DORSET TRUST FOR NATURE CONSERVATION

A:6 POWERSTOCK COMMON
Near Bridport; entry to reserve from road at SY 547973 or bridle-path at 532963. Keep to footpaths or get DTNC permit.
■ Oak and mixed woodland, scrub, open

grassland, cutting.
■ Forestry plantations alternate with blocks of native woodland and open grassland where heavy clay soils encourage good ground flora, including many ferns. Drainage ditches colourful; railway cutting a habitat for lime-loving species. Important for butterflies.
DORSET TRUST FOR NATURE CONSERVATION

B:1 THE FLEET & CHESIL BEACH★
Near Weymouth; car parks and information centres at Ferry Bridge, SY 668755, and Abbotsbury Swannery. Sanctuary area closed at all times; part of beach closed in nesting season.
■ Tidal lagoon, shingle ridge.
■ The huge ridge, 17+ miles (25km) long, is one of the largest storm beaches in Europe and protects an important tidal lagoon. The landward side, where some humus has collected, has been colonized by many interesting plant species and by terns, protected by wardens in the nesting season. The aquatic vegetation is vital to the wildfowl wintering here, notably the 1,000 or so mute swans and large flocks of wigeon. Waders, including rarities, feed on the muddy margins of the Fleet, and communities of marine molluscs live in the stabilized shingle between the tide lines of the lagoon. **Plants** Eel grass, shrubby sea-blite. **Insects** Scaly cricket (only British site).

B:2 RADIPOLE LAKE★★

Weymouth; car park at swannery at SY 677796. Access along public footpaths. Good information centre.

■ Reed-beds, lakes, lagoons, scrub.

■ Entirely surrounded by the town of Weymouth, the reserve which has three hides, offers the very best of urban bird-watching. Extensive reed-beds, home for many species of warbler, are used during migration by large numbers of roosting yellow wagtails, sedge warblers and swallows whose pre-roost display flights are a feature of evening bird watches in autumn. During winter, the numbers of gulls build up, often including rarities among them; Mediterranean and ring-billed gulls are regular. Many wildfowl use the lake, and up to 100 mute swans gather to moult; cormorants sit on the islands to dry their wings. **Birds** Cetti's, reed, sedge and grasshopper warblers, bearded tit, water rail.
ROYAL SOCIETY FOR THE PROTECTION OF BIRDS

B:3 LODMOOR COUNTRY PARK★

Near Weymouth; car park on A353 at SY 687807. Use public footpaths.

■ Freshwater marsh, pools, reed-beds, scrub, salt-marsh.

■ The marsh and shallow pools are used by large numbers of waders and wildfowl, especially during migration and in winter. Redshank, mallard, shelduck and yellow wagtail breed on the marsh, and the reed-beds shelter many warblers, including Cetti's. Almost any wader can be seen on the pools, including N American species such as the pectoral sandpiper and lesser yellowlegs. In winter there are jack snipe and water pipits, and when flooded, the marsh holds many ducks. Linnets, stonechat and whitethroat breed in scrub patches, as do butterflies. Hides and a good perimeter path make viewing easy.
ROYAL SOCIETY FOR THE PROTECTION OF BIRDS

B:4 WHITE NOTHE UNDERCLIFF

Near Weymouth; access from Ringstead Bay at SY 760814.

■ Cliffs with landslips, scrub.

■ Great range of landslip-created microhabitats with both wet and dry grassland, damp flushes, sheltered and exposed areas and steep crags. Plant and animal life equally varied; fine views of the Isle of Portland.
NATIONAL TRUST/DORSET TRUST FOR NATURE CONSERVATION

B:5 LULWORTH COVE★

Near Wool; car park at Lulworth Cove, SY 823801. Use footpaths. Danger of landslips near cliffs.

■ Rocky cove, seashore, coastal downland.

■ One of the most striking places on the Dorset coastline, the cove provides an ideal sheltered habitat for intertidal marine life. Many species reach almost their western limit in the England Channel here; cushion stars, brittle stars, wartlet anemones, star ascidians and many colourful seaweeds live among the tumbled boulders on the shore. Dense beds of kelp are exposed at low tide, although the tidal range is never very great. Squat lobsters and edibly, hairy and velvet swimming crabs are all common, and fossil-bearing rocks are visible.

B:6 LULWORTH RANGE★

Near Wool; car parks at Lulworth Cove, SY 823801, and Tyneham, SY 882804. Footpaths open at certain times only as ranges still used; check local press, roadside notice boards, or tel. Bindon Abbey 462721.

■ Cliff tops, coastal downland.

■ Has escaped modern farming, due to use as range, and so has a rich chalk downland wildlife. Spectacular setting for seeing chalk downland as well as sea-birds.
MINISTRY OF DEFENCE

B:7 PURBECK MARINE WILDLIFE RESERVE★

Near Swanage; car parks at Kimmeridge Bay, SY 909791 (also display centre). Use coastal footpaths.

■ Cliff tops, rocky seashore.

■ Britain's first mainland marine reserve, the gently shelving Kimmeridge Ledges are exposed over a great area at low tide, making this an excellent site for studying marine life. Carpets of coralline seaweeds shelter large colonies of snakelocks anemones, top shells and periwinkles. Limpets and barnacles cover the rocks in exposed areas, but in many places there is a dense growth of colourful algae. The kelp beds at the low-water mark are home for blue-rayed limpets, hairy crabs, worm pipe fish and sea slugs; many species found only in the western Channel reach their eastern limit here.
PRIVATE OWNERSHIP/DORSET TRUST FOR NATURE CONSERVATION

B:A ISLE OF PORTLAND★★★

Near Weymouth; car parks well signposted. Access along many public footpaths.

■ Limestone peninsula, fields, scrub, quarries, rocky seashore.

① Check gulls feeding here for rarities; little gull often present. At low tide good marine life uncovered among large boulders and kelp beds. Black redstart on steps and sea-wall.

② Grey bush-cricket in scrub on under-cliff, plus migrant birds. Good marine life at low tide. Shags feed offshore.

③ Excellent views of Chesil Beach.

④ Check scrub patches and old quarries for migrants. Do not climb walls or stone piles which may be dangerous.

⑤ Continue to fence of Admiralty radio station, checking fields for migrants. Ortolan seen here at times. Auks may be seen from cliff near fence flying in and out of breeding ledges beneath.

⑥ Obelisk at tip is best place for watching migrating seabirds. Purple sandpiper on rocks below.

⑦ Check scrub between huts, old quarries and gardens for migrants. Bird observatory in old lighthouse can be checked for latest news. Great green bush cricket in scrub, and excellent limestone flora in open areas. Little owls hunt in quarries.

⑧ Sea lavender and golden samphire grow on cliff edge. Marine life shows effect of exposure. Shags, cormorants and gulls feed close inshore.

⑨ Another good area for migrant birds; check overgrown quarries for warblers, shrikes. Danewort grows here; stony areas have many land snails.

⑩ Excellent views of Dorset coast. Distant views of feeding gulls and terns below. Divers and grebes sometimes visible. Limestone flora.

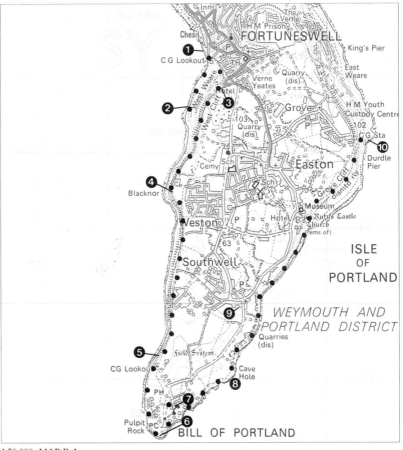

1:50 000, MAP B:A

DORSET

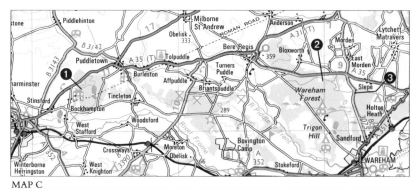

MAP C

C:1 THORNCOMBE WOOD & BLACK HEATH

Near Dorchester; *access from Higher Bock-hampton, off A35, at SY 727925. Use nature trails. Leaflet from DCC.*

■ Heath, mixed woodland, scrub, ponds.
■ Range of habitats provides homes for a wide variety of woodland and heathland plants and animals, including many butterflies. Hardy's birthplace and Roman road add interest.
DORSET COUNTY COUNCIL

C:2 WOOLSBARROW

Near Wareham; *park by FC tracks off Bere Regis-Wareham road at SY 889916. Keep to footpaths. Leaflets from DTNC.*

■ Dry heathland. Iron Age hill fort.
■ Valuable small heathland area for many plants and animals unable to compete with surrounding conifer plantations.
DORSET TRUST FOR NATURE CONSERVATION/FORESTRY COMMISSION

C:3 MORDEN BOG

Near Wareham; *park by B3075 at Sherford Bridge, SY 919926. Entry by permit only off bridle-path.*

■ Dry heath, wet heath, bog, birch scrub, ponds.
■ Mosaic of habitats in small area; important remnants of once-extensive Dorset heathlands, with boggy flushes holding many rare species. Conservation work vital here. **Birds** Nightjar, stonechat. **Mammals** Roe deer, fox. **Plants** Dorset heath, marsh gentian, brown beak sedge. **Insects** Silver-studded blue butterfly, heath and large marsh grasshoppers. **Reptiles** Sand lizard, smooth snake.
NATURE CONSERVANCY COUNCIL

D:1 STUBHAMPTON BOTTOM & CRANBOURNE CHASE

Near Shaftesbury; *access from minor road at ST 897168. Keep to footpaths and bridle-paths.*

■ Mixed woodland, scrub, grassland.
■ Wide variety of woodland birds and mammals, and rich and varied ground flora. Fine display of fungi in autumn.

MAP D

E:1 ST ALBAN'S HEAD*

Near Swanage; *car park at Worth Matravers, SY 974776. Access along coastal footpath.*

■ Limestone cliffs.
■ Its prominent position on the Dorset coast makes St Alban's Head a natural landfall for migrants and a good vantage point for watching sea-birds. Fulmars, kittiwakes and guillemots nest on the cliffs, and offshore passing gannets, terns and skuas may be seen. The tangled scrub of the undercliff provides excellent cover for migrants and breeding songbirds, making a spring visit very rewarding. Little owls and kestrels hunt overhead, while nightingales sing from dense thickets. In late summer bush crickets, grasshoppers and butterflies abound. The cliff-top flowers can be spectacular; careful searching will reveal many orchid species.

E:2 WINSPIT*

Near Swanage; *car park at Worth Matravers, SY 974776. Access along coastal footpath.*

■ Limestone valley, grassland, scrub, stream.
■ Tiny valley with many lime-loving plants and migrant birds in scrub areas.

Cove has wave-washed platform of rock colonized by seaweeds and molluscs; auks.

E:3 DURLSTON COUNTRY PARK**

Near Swanage; *park at information centre, SZ 031774. Use coastal footpath.*

■ Limestone cliffs, grassland, scrub, quarries, caves.
■ From the security of the stone walls it is possible to lean over the cliffs at Durlston Head and watch the nesting guillemots, razorbills and kittiwakes, or view fulmars and gulls using updraughts. A little further West, a few puffins breed and migrant birds are a feature of the cliff tops in spring. The abandoned quarries and caves are important to many bat species, including greater horseshoe, Bechstein's and grey long-eared. Rock- and golden-samphire grow on the exposed limestone and the grassland above is rich in lime-loving herbs, including orchids. Adonis, small, common and chalk-hill blue butterflies are seen here in summer, with several species of land snails and crickets.
NATIONAL TRUST/DORSET COUNTY COUNCIL

E:4 TOWNSEND

Near Swanage; *reserve reached along footpath at SZ 022784.*

■ Limestone grassland, scrub, quarries.
■ Sheltered, scrub-filled hollows provide good cover for nesting birds; exposed stony banks excellent for lime-loving herbs and butterflies. **Birds** Nightingale. **Plants** Horseshoe vetch, sainfoin. **Butterflies** Lulworth skipper, small blue.
DORSET TRUST FOR NATURE CONSERVATION

E:5 HARTLAND MOOR

Near Wareham; *park on road at SY 964854. Access along footpath only; NCC permit needed for most of reserve. Reserve office at Slepe Farm.*

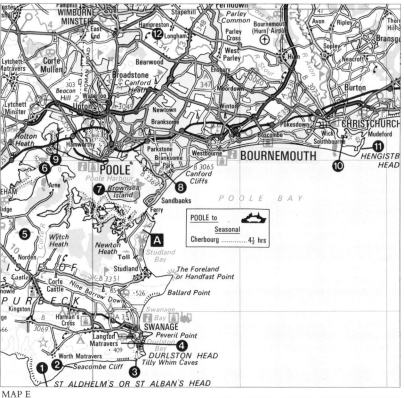

MAP E

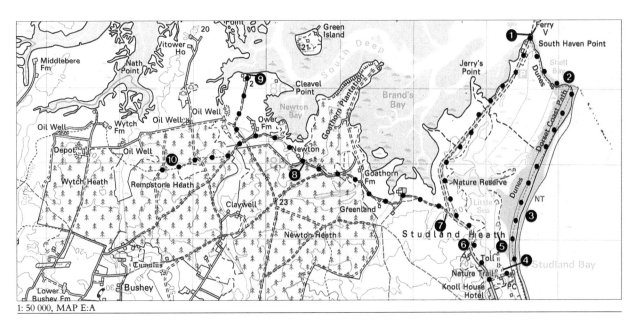

1: 50 000, MAP E:A

E:A STUDLAND HEATH★★

Near Studland; car parks at South Haven Point, near Knoll House Hotel and some roadside parking. Enter at toll road or toll ferry. Access along many footpaths. Details from NCC.

■ Estuary, sand/mudflats, acid sand dune system, heathland, woodland, freshwater lake, reed-beds.

① From car park at SZ 036865 walk down road to ferry slipway and scan deep water channel for grebes in winter, terns in summer.

② Walk along shore of Shell Bay looking for strand line debris. Pandora shell and grooved razor shell should be among many species found. Waders feed on exposed rocks; sea-ducks may be present in winter. Pipits and wagtails feed on strand line.

③ Continue along dunes edge looking for typical flora such as marram and sea bindweed. NCC dune trail enters dunes here. Note change to acid-loving flora, unusual in sand dunes. Bush-crickets common here.

④ NCC woodland trail starts here. Migrants and resident birds.

⑤ Hide overlooking Little Sea. Note royal fern growing in wetter areas. Many wildfowl present in winter, but few stay to breed.

⑥ Walk or drive along road; after leaving the woods, good view of heath to W. Hobbies may be seen over heath in summer; hen harriers in winter.

⑦ Turn W along track over heath. Smooth snakes, adders and sand lizards living here but very difficult to spot. Keep to path, but inspect

sunny banks and bare sand patches. Dartford warblers in patches of mature gorse.

⑧ Roe deer may be spotted in this wood, which has a good population of breeding birds and butterflies.

⑨ Many waders feed here, especially in winter; sea-duck, cormorants and grebes usually present in deep water channels.

⑩ Follow track over Rempstone Heath for woodland birds and butterflies; clearings, rides and woodland edges most productive.

⑪ Return to ⑦; then follow bridle-path back towards South Haven Point and ferry. From shore, more views of waders on mudflats, and excellent heathland flora along track.

PRIVATE OWNERSHIP/NATURE CONSERVANCY COUNCIL

■ Wet heathland, bog.

■ One of the best examples of wet heath habitat remaining and home to many rare plants and animals, including 14 species of ants and many damselflies.

NATURE CONSERVANCY COUNCIL

E:6 ARNE HEATH★

Near Wareham; park on minor road in Arne village at SY 973882. Keep to public footpath; permit from RSPB needed for most of reserve. Nature trail to Shipstal Point open at all times.

■ Dry heathland, bog, salt-marsh.

■ Primarily a bird reserve, set up to protect heathland species like the Dartford warbler, the heath can boast all our native reptiles and many rare heathland insects and plants. Twenty-two species of dragonfly have been recorded here and many other aquatic insects live in the pools. Woodpeckers and sparrowhawks breed in the surrounding woods where royal fern grows and many fungi are found in autumn. Roe and sika deer stray out of the woods to browse on the nearby marshes, and at low tide the creeks and mudflats are good places to watch waders such as black-tailed godwits and spotted redshank. Goldeneye, wigeon and mergansers overwinter in the harbour.

ROYAL SOCIETY FOR THE PROTECTION OF BIRDS

E:7 BROWNSEA ISLAND★

Near Poole; boats for Brownsea Island leave

from Poole Quay or Sandbanks Ferry. Access by permit only. Guided walks available. Leaflet from DTNC.

■ Wooded island, freshwater lagoon, salt-marsh.

■ Shallow, reed-fringed lagoon a nesting area for terns and waders; herons, red squirrels, sika deer and exotic plants in adjoining pines. In winter many waders use shores for feeding and roosting.

NATIONAL TRUST/DORSET TRUST FOR NATURE CONSERVATION

E:8 LUSCOMBE VALLEY

Near Poole; park along B3369 at SZ 045891. May be crowded at weekends.

■ Scrub, grassland, heathland, stream.

■ Valley with good range of wildlife; mixture of heathland and meadow plants among pine and birch trees and a good bird-watching site for warblers, woodland species and migrants.

POOLE BOROUGH COUNCIL

E:9 UPTON COUNTRY PARK

Near Poole; access from A35 at SY 992933. Open all year (crowded at weekends).

■ Salt-marsh, mudflats, woodland, fields, formal gardens.

■ Hide overlooking mudflats of Poole Harbour gives good views of waders, wildfowl and salt-marsh flora.

POOLE BOROUGH COUNCIL

E:10 STANPIT MARSH

Near Christchurch; park on minor road at SZ 173925. No access off rights of way. Check times of high water.

■ Salt-marsh, mudflats, grazing marsh.

■ Marsh an excellent area for wading birds and wildfowl; many rare species recorded. Interesting salt-marsh flora, and many aquatic plants grow in ditches.

CHRISTCHURCH BOROUGH COUNCIL

E:11 HENGISTBURY HEAD★

Near Bournemouth; park at SZ 163911. Use nature trail. Leaflet from Bournemouth BC.

■ Sandstone headland, woodland, scrub, salt-marsh, seashore.

■ A nature trail laid out around this prominent headland shows the main habitats. The low cliffs and breakwater are good vantage points for watching sea-birds and the woods and scrub attract many migrant birds, including rarities, in spring and autumn.

BOURNEMOUTH BOROUGH COUNCIL

E:12 RIVER STOUR

Near Wimborne Minster; access from B341 at SZ 031988 or from A31 at SU 000042. Use public footpath.

■ Riverside.

■ Footpath follows river for a short way giving opportunity to see water-birds such as heron and kingfisher, and attractive aquatic vegetation. Many dragonflies and damselflies in mid-summer.

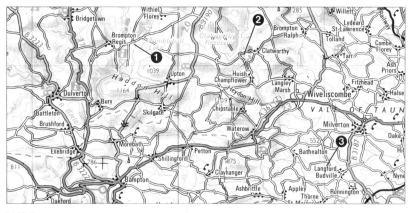

MAP A

A:1 HURSCOMBE (WIMBLEBALL LAKE)

Near Dulverton; *entry from minor road at SS 874317; keep to footpaths. Leaflet dispenser.*

■ Farmland, hedgerows, scrub, marshy fields, larch plantation.

■ The reservoir attracts wildfowl and Many butterflies breed.

SOUTH WEST WATER/SOMERSET TRUST FOR NATURE CONSERVATION

A:2 CLATWORTHY RESERVOIR

Near Wiveliscombe; *entry from minor road at ST 042308; keep to footpaths and nature trail. Leaflet dispenser on site.*

■ Woodland, reservoir.

■ The reservoir attracts wildfowl and gulls. The woodland has a rich ground flora and many ferns and lichens. Dam building has exposed interesting rock formations. **Birds** Great spotted woodpecker, long-tailed tit. **Plants** Opposite-leaved golden saxifrage, wood anemone.

WESSEX WATER

A:3 LANGFORD HEATHFIELD

Near Wellington; *entry from minor road at ST 102237; permit required to wander off foot-paths. Apply STNC.*

■ Ancient woodland, lowland heath.

■ A variety of habitats in a relatively small area, including birch and willow scrub, and both dry and damp acid heathlands. Warblers breed in the scrub and butterflies are numerous. **Plants** Cow wheat, betony.

SOMERSET TRUST FOR NATURE CONSERVATION

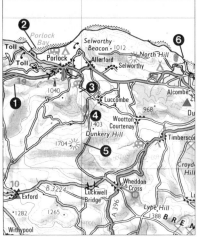

MAP B

B:1 PORLOCK COMMON

Near Porlock; *access from A39 at SS 855463.*

■ Heather moorland, mixed woodland.

Birds Buzzard, stonechat, raven, sparrow-hawk, tree pipit. **Mammals** Badger, red deer. **Plants** Sheep's-bit scabious, ivy-leaved bellflower.

EXMOOR NATIONAL PARK COMMITTEE

B:2 PORLOCK BAY★

Near Porlock; *parking at Porlock Weir, SS 865479.*

■ Shore, submarine forest, salt-marsh, brackish pools.

■ At low tide evidence that trees once grew here is uncovered in the form of well pre-served stumps and trunks. The muddy shore provides feeding grounds for many birds, especially in winter and during migration. Sea-bird watching during gales; shingle flora.

B:3 HORNER WOOD★

Near Porlock; *parking at Horner, SS 897454; permit required off footpaths.*

■ Mixed deciduous woodland.

■ Ancient woodland with a rich ground flora, plus many lichens. **Birds** Pied fly-catcher, redstart, woodwarbler, buzzard, dipper, grey wagtail, sparrowhawk. **Plants** Cornish money-wort, slender St John's-wort.

NATIONAL TRUST

B:4 CLOUTSHAM NATURE TRAIL★

Near Porlock; *access from minor road at SS 903438. Booklet from ENP Information Centre, Minehead.*

■ Mixed deciduous woodland, moorland edge, stream.

■ Red deer often seen. **Birds** Pied fly-catcher, redstart, wood warbler, buzzard, dipper, grey wagtail, sparrowhawk.

NATIONAL TRUST/EXMOOR NATIONAL PARK

B:5 DUNKERY BEACON★

Near Porlock; *access from minor road at SS 903419. Booklets from ENP Information Centre, Minehead.*

■ Upland moorland.

■ The highest point of Exmoor, at 1,705 feet (519m), Dunkery commands sweeping views. Flowering bell heather colours huge areas in late summer, but many other moor-land plants grow on the high tops including bilberry, bristle bent, western gorse, cotton-grass and heath-spotted orchids. Heavily grazed by Exmoor ponies, domesticated

sheep and cattle and the native red deer, the moorlands are bleak in winter, but in early summer many birds nest and the flowers are at their best. Many northern plant species approach their southern limit here and grow alongside southern species like pale butter-wort. Both northern and oak eggar moths breed here and emperor moth cocoons are often seen on the heather. **Mammals** Badger, red deer, fox. **Birds** Ring ouzel, wheatear, stonechat, raven, buzzard, dip-per, grey wagtail.

NATIONAL TRUST/EXMOOR NATIONAL PARK

B:6 NORTH HILL NATURE TRAIL

Near Minehead; *access from minor road, SS 970473. Booklet from ENP Information Centre, Minehead.*

■ Foreshore, woodland, moorland.

■ Contrast the gorse, western gorse, bell heather, ling and bilberry which grow on the tops with the honeysuckle and madder scrambling through the hawthorn scrub on the way up the cliff. Warblers and woodland birds; waders and gulls.

EXMOOR NATIONAL PARK

C:1 SUTTON BINGHAM RESERVOIR

Near Yeovil; *good views from causeway at ST 547114, or from road at ST 545100. S end can be viewed from bridle-path at ST 545094. Do not enter fields.*

■ Reservoir, grassy margins, scrub.

■ Good habitat for breeding warblers, migrant waders (including rarities) and overwintering wildfowl. Plenty of bird life at all seasons but migration times are best. **Birds** Warblers, migrant waders, mallard, wigeon, teal, great crested grebe. **Reptiles** Slow-worm, grass snake. **Amphibians** Frog, toad.

WESSEX WATER

C:2 HAM HILL COUNTRY PARK

Near Yeovil; *approach from minor road out of Stoke Sub Hamdon.*

■ Disused limestone quarries.

■ Quarrying has left a variety of micro-habitats encouraging an abundance of lime-loving plants and associated insects.

Plants Autumn lady's tresses, plough-man's-spikenard, rock-rose, marjoram. **Butterflies** Marbled white.

YEOVIL DISTRICT COUNCIL

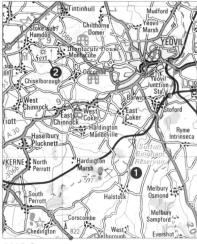

MAP C

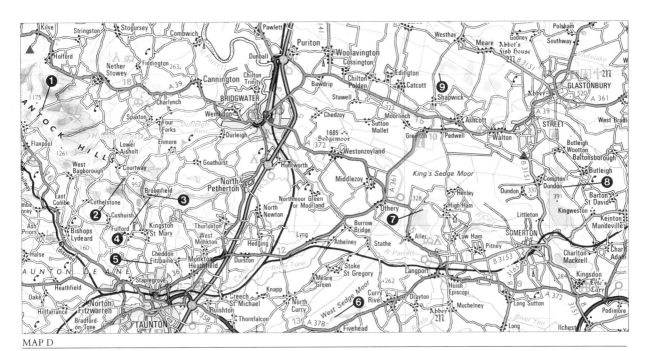

MAP D

D:1 QUANTOCK HILLS
Near Watchet; *access via numerous public footpaths.*
- Ancient oak woodland, conifer plantation, birch scrub, parkland, moorland.
- Interesting ground flora under the oaks, with many butterflies in clearings. Between the woodlands are pastures and patches of moorland covered with bracken. There are red deer, and an abundance of woodland birds and mammals.
PRIVATE OWNERSHIP/NATIONAL TRUST

D:2 BROOMFIELD HILL & BUNCOMBE WOOD
Near Bridgwater; *enter from crossroads at ST 208329; keep to footpaths.*
- Mixed woodland, stream, moorland.
- An interesting variety of habitats. Dawn chorus good in early spring.
Mammals Roe and red deer, fox, badger.
NATIONAL TRUST/PRIVATE OWNERSHIP

D:3 BROOMFIELD WALK
Near Bridgwater; *enter from minor road at ST 222322; keep to footpaths.*
- Woodland, conifer plantation, farmland.
- The mixed woodland has a good spring flora and there are many fungi in the autumn.
SOMERSET TRUST FOR NATURE CONSERVATION

D:4 FYNE COURT
Near Bridgwater; *enter from minor road at ST 222322.*
- Woodland, parkland, *arboretum.*
- The headquarters of the STNC, situated among mixed habitats which support an interesting range of plants and animals.
SOMERSET TRUST FOR NATURE CONSERVATION

D:5 FIVE POND WOOD TRAIL
Near Taunton; *enter from minor road at ST 224275; keep to nature trail. Further details from STNC.*
- Woodland, stream.
- Varied spring flora with many species typical of wet meadows.

SOMERSET TRUST FOR NATURE CONSERVATION

D:6 SOMERSET LEVELS & WEST SEDGEMOOR★
Near Taunton; *car park at ST 361238; keep to footpaths; permit required for restricted areas.*
- Marsh, peat diggings, woodland.
- This expanse of low-lying wet meadows, criss-crossed by drainage ditches provides the South-West with its most important site for breeding waders, which include an important population of black-tailed godwits. Nightingales, yellow wagtails and whinchats also breed. Short-eared owls hunt in winter when many wildfowl, including Bewick's swans, are present. The shallow pools are important staging posts for migrant waders; whimbrel and golden plover are often abundant. There is a colourful display of water plants in the ditches with water violet and southern marsh-orchids present in large quantities. Rich in aquatic and marsh insects. Visit in spring and autumn for migrant waders; wildfowl in winter.

D:7 BEER WOOD
Near Bridgwater; *enter along footpath from minor road at ST 414316.*
- Ancient woodland.
- A fine mixture of broad-leaved trees provides food for insects and many woodland birds; the rich understorey and ground flora is of further interest.
SOMERSET TRUST FOR NATURE CONSERVATION

D:8 GREAT BREACH & NEW HILL WOODS
Near Street; *enter along footpath from minor road at ST 505326.*
- Woodland, limestone grassland.
- A mixture of mainly oak and ash trees on a heavy clay soil, with slopes of grassland on limestone nearby. There is a rich ground flora, plus, in autumn, an impressive display of fungi. **Birds** Nightingale, woodcock.
SOMERSET TRUST FOR NATURE CONSERVATION

Sundew – see D:9. Shapwick Heath.

D:9 SHAPWICK HEATH
Near Glastonbury; *enter on footpath from minor road at ST 421406; permits required for restricted areas.*
- Marsh, fen, peat workings.
- The reserve is one of the few places where the formerly extensive 'raised mires' can be seen. Much of the peat which built up on the ancient estuarine clays has been cut and the surrounding areas drained, but here a small area is maintained by pumping water into it, not out, as happens elsewhere. A mosaic of wet habitats remains, with acid bog, marsh, fen and drainage ditches providing ideal conditions for aquatic vegetation. Birch and alder carrs have developed in some areas, with royal and marsh fern growing in abundance. The scrub areas are rich in bird life and many rare aquatic invertebrates are common here in the ditches and pools. **Birds** Nightjar, nightingale, willow tit, warblers. **Plants** Milk-parsley, lesser butterfly-orchid, sundew, bog pimpernel, white and brown beak-sedges. **Insects** Butterflies, moths, dragonflies, water beetles. **Reptiles** Adder.
NATURE CONSERVANCY COUNCIL

SOMERSET

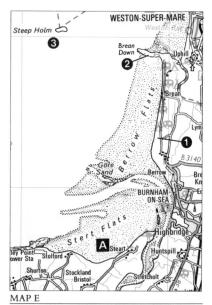

MAP E

E:1 BERROW DUNES*

Near Burnham-on-Sea; access at many points on footpaths between Burnham and Berrow; mostly unrestricted, apart from golf links.
■ Sand dunes, foreshore.
■ This extensive dune system sweeps up the coast from Burnham-on-Sea to Brean and shows an interesting transition from strand line through shifting dunes to stable grassland with wet dune slacks and pools. The strand line is strewn with seaweeds, driftwood and shells and is especially rich in

marine debris after storms. In winter it provides interesting pickings for turnstones, rock pipits and starlings. The foredunes are colonized by sea rocket and marram, while further inland, where the sand is more stable, an interesting flora has built up and many insects are present, plus a high population of land snails. The marshy areas support many wet meadow species, including orchids. **Plants** Marsh helleborine, marsh-orchids, heath spotted-orchid, lesser bulrush. **Insects** Butterflies, moths.
SEDGEMOOR DISTRICT COUNCIL

E:2 BREAN DOWN*

Near Weston-super-Mare; car park at ST 296587; mostly unrestricted.
■ Limestone headland, intertidal rocks.
■ This dramatic limestone ridge jutting out into the Severn Estuary is of great interest to botanists for the number of
unusual species, especially white rock-rose, found here and in few other sites. The extreme exposure limits plant growth to stunted hawthorns and brambles, but the close-cropped turf is rich in lime-loving species such as thyme, salad burnet and horse-shoe vetch. Maritime species such as rock samphire, thrift and white campion grow at lower levels. The prominent headland is a landfall for migrant birds and insects. Excellent views of the surrounding sand and mudflats reveal large concentrations of waders and wildfowl in winter.

E:3 STEEP HOLM ISLAND**

Off Weston-super-Mare; park in Weston near Knightstone causeway or Cave Caf slipway, from where boats leave; details, phone 0963

32307 – bad weather can interrupt service. Access by permit only; details from KAMT, Knock-na-Cre, Milborne Port, Sherborne, Dorset.
■ Limestone island, cliffs.
■ The 48-acre limestone island lies in the Bristol Channel 5 miles (8.5 km) off Weston-super-Mare. It has a long history of human occupation. Mediaeval monks introduced many plants – some (including the wild peony which flowers in May) still surviving – for medicinal and culinary use. Large areas of alexanders now cover the debris of old fortifications. Thriving gull colonies on the cliffs and a large number of cormorants make this an important sea-bird site. Peregrine and raven returned to breed in the mid-1970s. The cliff-top scrub provides cover for migrants in spring and autumn and for the rarely seen muntjac deer and hedgehogs. Unusual blue-coloured slow-worms can be 12+ in (50 cm) long. The loose limestone scree on the cliff-edge supports many species of woodlice which are preyed on by purse-web spiders. Mid-May best for wild peony and birds. **Plants** (Naturalized) Peony, wild leek, caper spurge. **Birds** Lesser black-backed gull, great black-backed gull, cormorant. **Arachnids** Purse-web spider.
KENNETH ALLSOP MEMORIAL TRUST

F:1 CHEDDAR GORGE*

Cheddar; limited parking in gorge, or park in Cheddar and walk up road; keep to footpaths, permits required for restricted areas.
■ Limestone gorge.
■ The deep limestone gorge's cliffs face in many directions, thus providing varying degrees of light and shade, shelter and

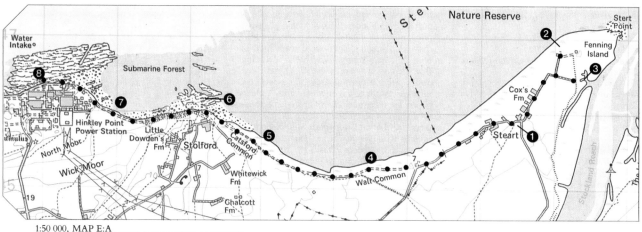

1:50 000, MAP E:A

E:A BRIDGWATER BAY*

Near Bridgwater; reserve may be entered from Stolford ST 234548 or Steart ST 273458. Some areas closed in winter, NCC permits needed for rest of year. Beware rapidly rising tides.
■ Tidal bay, mudflats, saltmarsh.
① Park at car park near warden's house in village. Follow footpath sign to Fenning Island. Keep to path and do not enter gardens or fields. Check scrub for migrants.
② Scan with binoculars or telescope for waders and wildfowl, especially shelduck, on mudflats. Geese and pintail may be present on grassy areas. Mud can be dangerous here, and tides rise rapidly.
③ Look for waders in creek, best as tide rises and pushes them nearer. Saltmarsh flora good

here. Do not stray on to mudflats, especially Nov-Mar when this is important roosting and feeding area.
④ Return through village and join sea-wall. Scan flats for waders and gulls on shore. There may be thousands of curlew and dunlin here in winter. Best on rising tide when they are pushed nearer shore.
⑤ Check small pools for waders and ducks. In summer look for clovers and shingle flora.
⑥ Intertidal rocks used as a roost. Check for waders before going on to rocks at low tide to look for unusual gulls and terns in spring and autumn.
⑦ At low tide remains of 'submarine forest' may be seen. Shore very muddy here, so do not stray too far. Check fields behind sea-wall for ducks and short-eared owl in winter.

Dunlin.

⑧ Hot water outfall from power station should be checked for feeding gulls and terns; rarities may be present. Good marine life on rocks. Beware rapidly rising tides. Fossils may be seen in exposed rocks.
Plants Knotted and sea clover, yellow horned-poppy.
NATURE CONSERVANCY COUNCIL/WESSEX WATER AUTHORITY

humidity. A rich flora has developed, including many rare species such as the Cheddar pink, found nowhere else in Britain. Typical limestone-loving plants grow in open areas; butterfly populations are present. Scrub has developed on scree slopes and in sites where soil can build up, and a number of species of whitebeam grow on the cliffs with ash, guelder-rose, dogwood, spindle and wayfaring-tree. Jackdaws nest in holes in the cliffs. The cliffs are dangerous. **Plants** Green-winged orchid, stonecrop, lesser meadow-rue, rock-rose.
NATIONAL TRUST

F:2 BUBWITH ACRES
Near Cheddar; footpath from Cheddar at ST 470537; keep to footpaths; permits required for restricted areas.
■ Limestone heath, downland, scrub.
■ Outcrops of limestone support rich fern and lichen populations, while acid-loving plants grow in pockets of deeper soil alongside typical limestone species. The scrub patches are used by many breeding birds and butterflies. **Plants** Rusty-back, maidenhair spleenwort, stemless thistle, salad burnet.
SOMERSET TRUST FOR NATURE CONSERVATION

F:3 BLACK ROCK DROVE
Near Cheddar; enter on footpath from B3135 at ST 484545; keep to footpaths; permit required for restricted areas.
■ Limestone grassland, woodland.
■ The Black Rock Reserve is a steeply sloping area of close-cropped limestone grassland. Areas of conifers and native broad-leaved woodland increase the variety of habitats and over 200 species of flowering plants have been found. The limestone flora is rich and the area is much used by butterflies and other insects.
SOMERSET TRUST FOR NATURE CONSERVATION

F:4 VELVET BOTTOM★
Near Cheddar; enter on footpath from minor road at ST 503556; keep to footpaths; permit required for restricted areas.
■ Limestone valley.
■ Although lead mining has long-since ceased, the soil in the valley bottom is still contaminated and grazing is restricted. Grassland and woodland plants thrive, with many orchids and butterflies.
SOMERSET TRUST FOR NATURE CONSERVATION

F:5 DRAYCOTT SLEIGHTS
Near Cheddar; enter on footpath from Draycott or from minor road at ST 483513. Keep to footpaths.
■ Limestone grassland.
■ A mixture of limestone grassland plants and an important colony of chalk-hill blue butterflies.
SOMERSET TRUST FOR NATURE CONSERVATION

F:6 EBBOR GORGE★
Near Wells; car park at ST 524483; keep to footpaths; permit required for restricted areas.
■ Limestone gorge, ancient woodland.
■ The deep dry valley was carved out of the Mendip carboniferous limestone by an ancient river. The exposed limestone is rich in fossils. Many water-formed caves contain the remains of animals long extinct in Britain. Damp woodland on north-facing

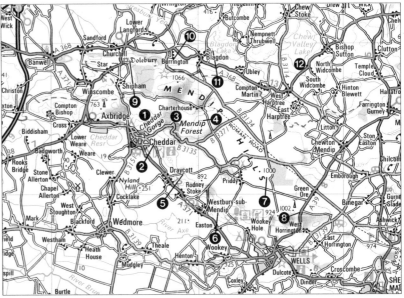

MAP F

slopes is rich in ferns, while the hornbeam reaches its western limit here. Mixed ash woodland dominates some areas with small-leaved lime and whitebeams also present. Coppicing has been practiced here for centuries in order to maintain the richness of the habitat with its outstanding ground flora. Small areas of open limestone grassland remain with typical species, and in deeper pockets of soil, acid-loving plants grow.
NATIONAL CONSERVANCY COUNCIL

F:7 PRIDDY MINERIES
Near Wells; enter on footpath from minor road at ST 548513; keep to footpaths; permit required for restricted areas.
■ Limestone grassland, meadow, pools.
■ The area was once mined and the spoil tips and hollows left behind have been colonized by a range of limestone and wetland species. One of the richest sites in the region for dragonflies. **Insects** Water beetles. **Amphibians** Great crested newts.
SOMERSET TRUST FOR NATURE CONSERVATION

F:8 BIDDLE COMBE NATURE TRAIL
Near Wells; enter on bridle-path from A39 at ST 569488.
■ Wooded valley.
■ Limestone grassland provides a range of typical species while the stream and woodland add further diversity.
WELLS NATURAL HISTORY AND ARCHAEOLOGY SOCIETY

F:9 DOLEBURY WARREN
Near Bristol; park on B3134 at ST 476587 (limited on summer weekends); site can be entered from road at ST 475589.
■ Limestone grassland, acid soils.
■ Limestone hilltop with characteristic rock-rose, orchids and milkwort. Adjoining hill fort with views to N; slopes below hill have acid soils with western gorse, heather, bell heather, bilberry. **Birds** Nuthatch.
AVON WILDLIFE TRUST

F:10 BURRINGTON COMBE
Near Blagdon; park at ST 489582 and ST 476589. Keep to footpaths. Leaflet from Avon Wildlife Trust. Keep away from cave entrances.

■ Limestone gorge, woodland, scrub, grassland, small ponds.
■ Fossils reveal the formation of the combe by upheavals of the earth's crust and subsequent glacial erosion. Creatures living today on tropical coral reefs can be recognized in the remains of animals which lived 340 million years ago. Bats roost in the many caves and potholes in winter, and in some have been found bones of creatures long extinct such as the mammoth and woolly rhinoceros. Woodland in steeper areas supports a rich plant and animal life. The open grassland supports a typical limestone flora and fauna. The area, with dark, peaty soil known as Blackdown, has a quite different acid-loving fauna.
THE BURRINGTON CONSERVATORS

F:11 BLAGDON RESERVOIR★
Near Bristol; view from road over dam at ST 504600. Access to hides by permit only, from BWWC Recreations Department.
■ Reservoir.
■ Large, deep resevoir, attractive to aquatic life, supporting, in turn, an abundant bird-life. Banks are well grown and there is plenty of submerged aquatic vegetation. Winter brings wildfowl and waders such as goosander, gadwall, ruddy and tufted duck, kingfisher, curlew. Little owl and woodpeckers are resident.
BRISTOL WATERWORKS COMPANY

F:12 CHEW VALLEY LAKE★
Near Bristol; view from Herriot's Bridge, ST 572583, or Heron's Green, ST 555595, or the two public car park and picnic areas. Otherwise, access to shores by BWWC Recreations Department permit only. Do not enter sanctuary area, even with permit.
■ Reservoir, vegetated on banks, shallows.
■ The large size and shallow water of the reservoir make it attractive to winter wildfowl, but many species (including passerines, prey for sparrowhawks) breed on the richly vegetated banks. **Birds** (Winter) Bewick's swan, goosander, goldeneye, wigeon; (breeding) ruddy and tufted duck; (migration) osprey, marsh harrier, spotted redshank, grey plover, sandpiper, terns.
BRISTOL WATERWORKS COMPANY

AVON

A:1 WESTON WOODS

Near Weston-super-Mare; enter from road at ST 328633.
■ Mixed woodland.
■ Mainly sycamore, also oak, ash, poplar, sweet chestnut. Parasitic toothwort and several fern species. Migrant birds in spring and autumn. **Birds** Chiffchaff, blackcap; (breeding) nuthatch. **Butterflies** Brimstone, comma, speckled wood. **Plants** Toothwort, ferns.
WOODSPRING DISTRICT COUNCIL

A:2(a-b) BLACKSTONE ROCK TO WOODSPRING BAY

Near Weston-super-Mare; access to shore from footpath at ST 394700, or view from St Thomas's Head at ST 348669.
■ Muddy seashore, salt-marsh.
■ Vast areas of mud and rocks exposed at low tide, providing excellent feeding areas for waders and wildfowl. Good salt-marsh vegetation including, in sheltered spots, English scurvy-grass and sea-lavender. **Birds** Scoter, eider, shelduck; (shore) oystercatcher, curlew, redshank, turnstone; (freshwater ditches) green sandpiper.

A:3 GOBLIN COMBE

Near Bristol; enter reserve on footpath starting at ST 459654.
■ *Limestone grassland, steep wooded valley.*
■ This typical limestone woodland of ash, beech, yew and hazel has a rich understorey of dog's mercury and enchanter's-nightshade. Badger and deer tracks run through

the vegetation and many woodland birds can be heard overhead. The more open areas have a downland type of vegetation, with a colourful turf, rich in herbs, clothing the flatter areas; many species of butterflies live here, including blues, small copper, marbled white and skippers. Best May to September. **Plants** Stinking hellebore, madder, hart's-tongue; (open areas) yellow-wort, rockrose.
AVON WILDLIFE TRUST

A:4 BROCKLEY COMBE

Near Bristol; access at ST 483663 along bridle-path.
■ Wooded limestone valley.
■ Nature trail through typical Mendips valley, with extensive plantations nearby. Abundant woodland birds and small mammals, and a rich ground flora including hart's-tongue and wood melick.
FOUNTAIN FORESTRY

A:5 WESTON MOOR

Near Clevedon; reached at ST 436739 on B3124. Entry by AWT permit only, Sep–Feb; at other times, keep to trail; hide
■ Reed-bed, fen, alder carr, damp grassland.
■ A breeding area for wetland birds, with typical wet-meadow vegetation; receives lime-rich water from the surrounding limestone ridges. Best May to August. **Birds** (Reed-beds) Grasshopper and reed warblers; **Plants** Marsh fern, greater bird's-foot trefoil, devil's-bit scabious.

AVON WILDLIFE TRUST

A:6 CADBURY CAMP & TICKENHAM HILL

Near Clevedon; park in Tickenham; footpath at ST 454718.
■ Limestone grassland, mixed woodland.
■ Hill-top with ancient earthworks overlooking surrounding woodlands and birds such as kestrel and sparrowhawk; good selection of woodland mammals and flora on slopes, with hill-top flora and butterflies.
NATIONAL TRUST

A:7 LIME BREACH WOOD

Near Nailsea; bridle-path at ST 480730. Keep to footpaths.
■ Ancient woodland, small-leaved lime coppice.
■ A good selection of woodland birds, mammals and flora; spring best for woodland flora and bird song.
AVON WILDLIFE TRUST

A:8(a-b) BATTERY POINT TO LADYE POINT

Near Portishead; keep to footpath, access at various points between ST 464776 and ST 409730.
■ Muddy/shingle shore, salt-marsh, exposed rocks, coastal scrub.
■ Bird numbers highest in winter, with waders – redshank, oystercatcher, turnstone, dunlin – feeding on shore; also shelduck and other wildfowl. Interesting plants along low cliff edge, including English scurvy-grass, sea-lavender, sea-spurrey.

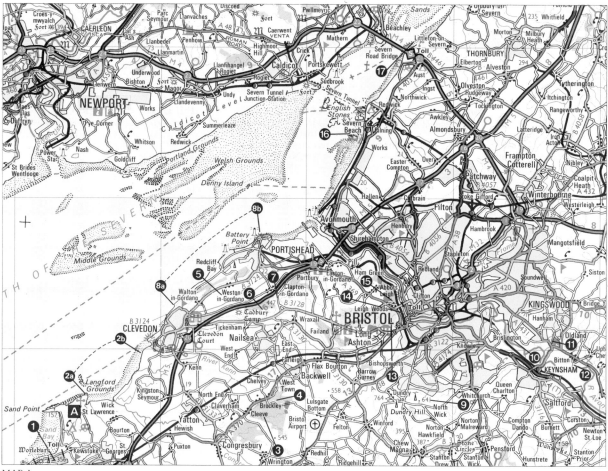

MAP A

A:9 DUNDRY SLOPES
Near Bristol; access from footpath at ST 582669.
■ Scrub, woodland, wetter areas.
■ Look for warblers (breeding) in scrub, woodland birds in more dense areas. Good butterfly numbers in sunnier patches with wet-meadow plants in damp places.
AVON WILDLIFE TRUST

A:10 AVON WALKWAY (1)
Near Bristol; keep to public footpath; access at ST 632720.
■ Riverside woodland.
■ Footpath runs SE through a steep-sided wooded valley allowing good views of woodland birds and freshwater species. Interesting marginal vegetation on banks.

A:11 WILLSBRIDGE MILL
Near Bristol; park at ST 665707. Restricted opening times – contact AWT.
■ Valley, stream, quarry, woodland, scrub, meadow, pond.
■ Quarry and disused railway cutting of interest to geologists. Woodland birds and warblers in scrub areas, butterflies plentiful.
AVON WILDLIFE TRUST

A:12 AVON WALKWAY (2)
Near Bristol; park at Swineford at ST 690690. Keep to public footpath.
■ Riverbank, watermeadows.
■ Flat floodmeadows provide winter feeding areas for wildfowl, including green sandpiper, teal, mute swan, mallard. Interesting meadow flora survives alongside in drainage ditches.

A:13 ASHTON COURT ESTATE
Near Bristol; park at ST 554726 to join nature trail.
■ Limestone/acid grassland, woodland.
■ Trail meanders through a surprising variety of habitats with many species, both typical and exotic. **Plants** Green hellebore, rock-rose. **Birds** (Breeding) wood warbler, goldcrest. **Butterflies** Silver-washed fritillary, holly blue. **Mammals** Fallow deer.
BRISTOL CITY COUNCIL/BRISTOL NATURALIST'S SOCIETY

A:14 AVON GORGE★
Near Bristol; enter at ST 554732 near warden's hut.
■ Wooded limestone gorge.
■ A Mecca for botanists wishing to study the rare flora, including some species found nowhere else in Britain. The woodland is mainly oak – unusual on Carboniferous limestone – with ash, elm, birch, small-leaved lime and several species of white-beam, including the endemic Bristol. More open areas show typical woodland-floor species and an abundance of hart's-tongue. Traveller's joy and madder scramble for light. Woodland birds, butterflies and small mammals are plentiful. An Iron Age hill fort adds further interest. Spring and early summer best for flora. **Plants** Spiked speedwell, Bristol whitebeam, Bristol rock-cress, fingered sedge.
NATIONAL TRUST/NATURE CONSERVANCY COUNCIL

A:15 AVON WALKWAY (3)
Near Bristol; join riverside path at ST 564761.
■ Wooded limestone gorge, tidal river.
■ A place to observe the River Avon's huge

Oystercatchers – see A:A.

tidal range. Exposed mud with occasional feeding wader or gull. Plants include ivy broomrape, little-robin, green hellebore.
BRISTOL CITY COUNCIL

A:16 SEVERN BEACH★
Near Avonmouth; access on footpath from ST 549837.
■ Tidal coast, rocky outcrops.
■ Falling tides expose vast areas of mud, sand and rock, providing a valuable feeding ground for wildfowl, waders and gulls.

A:17 AUST ROCK
Near Avonmouth; park at motorway service station at ST 568898. Access to shore along footpaths.
■ Tidal coast, rocky outcrops.
■ Strong Severn tides uncover large areas of rock and sand, providing vital winter feeding grounds for waders, wildfowl and gulls. Interesting fossil-bearing rocks.

A:A SAND POINT & MIDDLE HOPE★
Near Weston-super-Mare; park at Sand Point at ST 330659. Access over NT and AWT property.
■ Limestone headland, scrub, grassland, rocky shore, salt-marsh.
① Park at ST 330659. From car park, track leads W over ridge towards Sand Point, giving good views over tidal flats and salt-marsh below. English scurvy-grass covers large areas, and some waders use exposed mud. Usual maritime plants on hillside, plus rue-leaved saxifrage.
② An interesting limestone flora, including honewort, on slopes; migrant birds use scrub areas in spring and autumn. Good area for butterflies in sunny weather.
③ Flatholm and Steepholm islands may be seen from W point. Sea-bird movements in Bristol Channel easily watched; oystercatchers

and gulls feed on rocks below. Beware rapidly rising tides.
④ Walk E on N slopes, continuing to watch for sea-birds, and migrants in scrub areas. Many cowslips here, with orchids and other meadow species present in sheltered areas. Continue E to metalled road and a fence.
⑤ Enter AWT reserve by gate at S end of fence. Many birds winter in Woodspring Bay, with unusual migrants. Salt-marsh supports varied flora, with adjacent meadows rich in flowers, including orchids. (NB – there is no access at Woodspring Priory.)
Birds Stonechat, turnstone. **Plants** Honewort, rue-leaved saxifrage, orchids, dropwort, henbane, sea wormwood, English scurvy-grass. **Butterflies** Marbled white, blues, browns. **Reptiles** Slow-worm.
PRIVATE OWNERSHIP/NATIONAL TRUST/AVON WILDLIFE TRUST

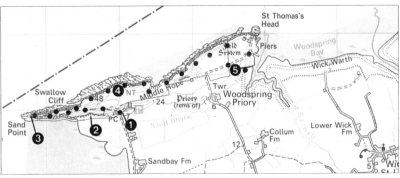

1:50 000, MAP A:A

THE CHANNEL ISLANDS

THE CHANNEL ISLANDS

Although highly populated and cultivated, the Channel Islands still have much to offer the naturalist. Cars can be hired, but it is quite possible to explore the islands by public transport, or on foot. Many books are available on the islands to help the holiday-maker and naturalist.

The Jersey North Coast Path, extending from Grosnez Point to Tour de Rozel, is ideal for observing cliff flora and sea-birds, as is the **Guernsey Coastal Path**, round the S and E coasts from Pleinmont Point to St Peter's Point.

A:1 JERSEY, NOIR MONT HEADLAND*
Open access to headland; keep to paths around fields.
■ Cliffs, coastal grassland.
■ Explore the grassy scrub for migrants and plants. Scan the sea for sea-birds.
Birds Dartford warbler. **Plants** Autumn squill, spotted rock-rose, Jersey forget-me-not.
STATES OF JERSEY

A:2 JERSEY, LES QUENNEVAIS**
■ Sand dunes.
■ Explore sand dunes for plants. Together with the rest of the St Ouen's Bay area, it forms part of Les Mielles, Jersey's mini-national park. Further information from Interpretative Centre at Kempt martello tower.
Plants Dwarf pansy, sand crocus, Jersey thrift **Reptiles** Green lizard.
STATES OF JERSEY

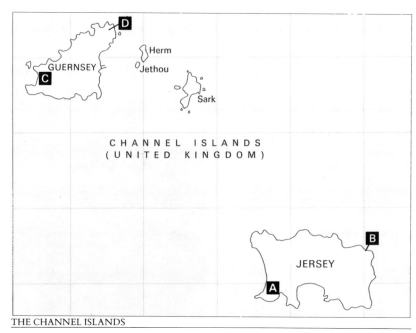

THE CHANNEL ISLANDS

A:3 JERSEY, LES MIELLES*
■ Sand dunes, heath, pond, reedbed, shore.
■ Scan the beach and sea for sea-birds and explore the dunes and meadows inland. RSPB birdwatching hide at La Mielle de Morville.
Birds Waders, reed warbler, Cetti's warbler, seasonal migrants. **Plants** Dune flora, Jersey orchid.

A:4 JERSEY, ST PETER'S VALLEY
Access from A11.
■ Woodland.
■ Explore on foot.
Birds Short-toed treecreeper. **Plants** Spring woodland flora, bryophytes.
JERSEY
NATIONAL TRUST

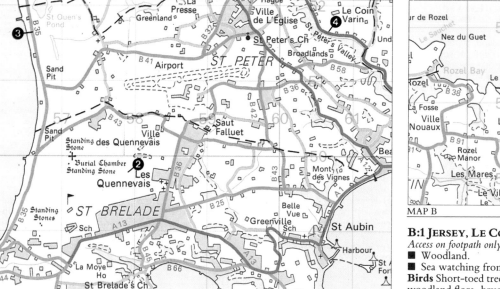

MAP B

B:1 JERSEY, LE COUPERON
Access on footpath only from B38.
■ Woodland.
■ Sea watching from the coast.
Birds Short-toed treecreeper **Plants** Spring woodland flora, bryophytes.
JERSEY NATIONAL TRUST

MAP A

Above: puffin; opposite, coppiced woodland.

THE CHANNEL ISLANDS

C:1 GUERNSEY, PLEINMONT POINT
Car park at Les Pezeries.
■ Cliffs, scrub, sea.
■ Sea watching in spring and autumn. Migrants and Dartford warblers in the scrub.
STATES OF GUERNSEY

C:2 GUERNSEY, SILBE NATURE RESERVE
Access from Rue de Quanteraine; limited parking near Htel du Moulin; keep to the paths.
■ Mixed woodland, stream.
■ Short valley walk past reservoir.
Birds Short-toed treecreeper.
LA SOCIETE GUERNESIAISE

C:3 GUERNSEY, LA CLARE MARE
No public access, view from surrounding road and lanes.
■ Marsh, freshwater.
Birds Waders, migrant passerines.
LA SOCIETE GUERNESIAISE

C:4 GUERNSEY, VAZON BAY
■ Shore.
■ Explore from coast road: waders, sea-birds and migrants.

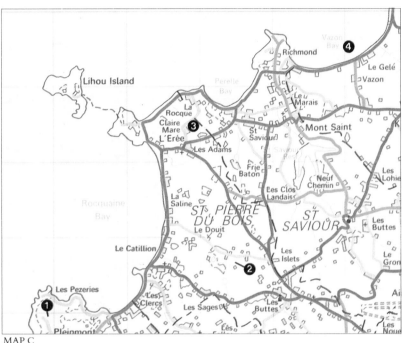

MAP C

D:1 GUERNSEY, VALE POND*
No access to the pond, but public hide overlooks it.
■ Brackish pond, reedbed, saltmarsh.
■ Waders, wildfowl and migrants. Interesting emergent plants.
PRIVATE OWNERSHIP/LA SOCIETE GUERNESIAISE.

D:2 GUERNSEY, L'ANCRESSE COMMON*
■ Sand dunes.
Migrant waders and passerines, sea-birds.
Plants Autumn squill.

THE SMALLER ISLANDS
Alderney is served by hydrofoil from Guernsey. Numerous footpaths aid exploration of rugged granite cliffs in the SW and sand dunes in NE.

Sark is reached by boat from St Peter Port, Guernsey. Bikes can be hired to explore lanes and tracks. Plants include sand crocus; butterflies.

Herm, famous for its shell beach, is reached by boat from St Peter Port, Guernsey. Plants include sand crocus; birds: puffin.

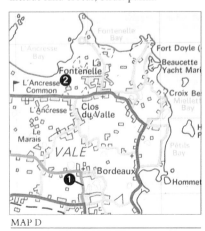

MAP D

ISLE OF WIGHT

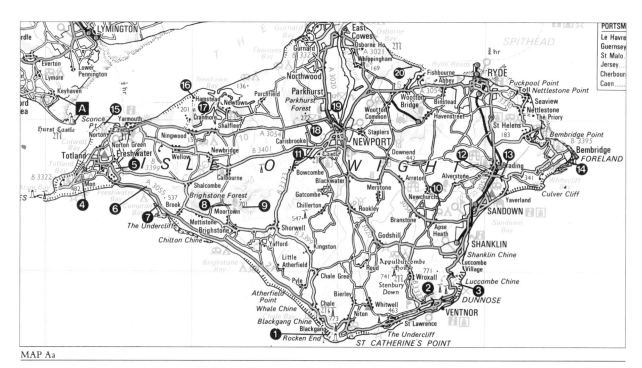

MAP Aa

Aa:1 ST CATHERINE'S POINT★★

Near Ventnor; park at SZ 488767 and explore on paths and tracks.

■ Undercliff, scrub

■ An extremely productive area of cliff and undercliff forming the most southerly part of the Isle of Wight. Much of it is covered by scrub but annual landslides help maintain open and grassy patches.

Its position in the English Channel makes St Catherine's Point an important landfall for migrant birds and butterflies. Clouded yellows are recorded every year and fly with the area's most interesting resident species, the glanville fritillary. Its larvae feed on sea plantain and large swarms occur in the summer.

The area has many other interesting insects, notably cepero's groundhopper which likes the puddled areas of clay landslide. This elusive species dives under water to escape danger. **Birds** Migrants, fulmar. **Insects** Glanville fritillary, cepero's groundhopper, great green bush-cricket.

NATIONAL TRUST

Aa:2 VENTNOR DOWNS

Near Ventnor; covers SZ 5678–SZ 5778. Park off main road or in Ventnor. Open access except where cultivated.

■ Chalk downland, scrub.

■ **Plants** Cowslip, hairy violet, dumpy centaury. **Butterflies** Marbled white, blues, skippers.

NATIONAL TRUST

Aa:3 LUCCOMBE CHINE★

Near Ventnor; access from SZ 583793.

■ Undercliff, scrub.

■ **Insects** Glanville fritillary, cepero's groundhopper, grey bush-cricket. **Birds** Migrants.

NATIONAL TRUST

Aa:4 TENNYSON DOWN & THE NEEDLES★★

Near Freshwater; *park in Freshwater or on minor roads leading to Alum Bay. Open access between SZ 3084–SZ 3385; take care near cliff*

edge. This is a superb walking area, with well-signposted paths.

■ Chalk down, cliffs.

■ The chalk cliffs and the eroded Needles provide a stunning backdrop for the excellent chalk flora of Tennyson Down.

Near the cliff edge, grazing rabbits and the constant wind have produced a herb-rich community of stunted plants; away from the edge and among the scrub, growth is more luxuriant. Unusually, both chalk-loving and heath plants can be found side-by-side in places. Interesting species include early gentian, bastard-toadflax, early purple orchid, white horehound and sea stock. The last of these grows on the sheer cliff faces and should be viewed with caution.

NATIONAL TRUST

Aa:5 FRESHWATER MARSH★

Freshwater; access from SZ 348858. Keep to nature trail.

■ Marsh, river.

■ Nature trail beside river. **Plants** Flowering rush, yellow loosestrife. **Birds** Reed warbler, sedge warbler, nightingale, cuckoo.

SOUTH WIGHT BOROUGH COUNCIL

Aa:6 COMPTON DOWN★★

Near Freshwater; park at SZ 368854.

■ Chalk down, scrub.

■ Most of this exceptional chalk down faces south, looking out over the English Channel. During late spring and summer the area is a riot of colour with knapweeds, bee and pyramidal orchids, yellow-wort and horseshoe vetch. The last of these is food for the larvae of adonis and chalkhill blue butterflies; careful inspection of the leaves may reveal the symbiotic relationship between the grub-like larvae and red ants which 'milk' them for their honeydew. Common and small blues are also present together with marbled whites and dark-green fritillaries, and there are interesting communities of spiders, snails and other invertebrates to be found.

NATIONAL TRUST

Aa:7 COMPTON BAY

Compton; park at SZ 372848, accessible to wheelchairs. Muddy landslides can be treacherous: take due care.

■ Cliffs, undercliff.

Butterflies Glanville fritillary.

NATIONAL TRUST

Aa:8 BRIGHSTONE DOWN

Near Brighstone; park carefully off the road at SZ 420848 or walk from Brighstone village. Access from network of footpaths.

■ Mixed woodland, chalk downland.

■ Plants and butterflies associated with this habitat. **Birds** Nightjar, woodcock, grasshopper warbler.

Aa:9 WORSLEY TRAIL

Near Brighstone; trail starts at SZ 432842 and runs E to Shanklin. Keep to the route. Detailed leaflet from County Council.

■ Chalk downland, mixed woodland.

■ Long-distance walk along chalk ridge. Route intercepts various roads so catch bus back to starting point. **Mammals** Red squirrel. **Butterflies** Dingy skipper.

Aa:10 BORTHWOOD COPSE

Near Sandown; access from SZ 570844; keep to footpaths.

■ Oak woodland.

■ A relic of ancient woodland, once covering much of the Isle of Wight. Fine display of bluebells in spring. **Birds** Lesser spotted woodpecker, buzzard. **Mammals** Red squirrel.

NATIONAL TRUST

Aa:11 SHEPHERDS TRAIL

Carisbrooke; trail starts at SZ 487874 and runs to Shepherd's Chine, Atherfield SZ 448798. Keep to the route. Detailed leaflet from County Council.

■ Chalk downland, cliffs.

■ Long-distance walk which intercepts various roads. Catch bus back to starting point. **Birds** Stonechat, corn bunting. **Mammals** Red squirrel. **Reptiles** Slowworm, common lizard, adder.

ISLE OF WIGHT

Aa:12 BRADING DOWN

Brading; park in Brading (SZ 610870) or off one of the minor roads running W.
■ Chalk downland, scrub.
■ Ungrazed, old quarries. **Birds** Lesser whitethroat. **Insects** Dingy skipper.
SOUTH WIGHT BOROUGH COUNCIL

Aa:13 BRADING MARSH

Brading; park in Brading and walk E to SZ 615872. Keep to footpaths.
■ Grazing marsh, reed-bed, ponds.
■ Reclaimed inter-tidal basin dotted with ponds and reed-beds. Footpaths along old sea wall give view over marsh. **Birds** Coot, reed bunting, reed warbler, waders. **Insects** Short-winged conehead.

Aa:14 BEMBRIDGE LEDGES

Near Bembridge; park in Bembridge, walk to SZ 662875.
■ Foreshore.
■ The best rocky ledges on the Isle of Wight, rich in inter-tidal life. Check tide table. **Invertebrates** Crabs, marine molluscs, anemones. **Plants** Seaweeds. **Birds** Waders.

Aa:15 FORT VICTORIA COUNTRY PARK

Near Yarmouth; nature trail starts at SZ 338898.
■ Cliff, undercliff, scrub.
■ The undercliff is much overgrown in parts, providing cover for a variety of plants and migrant birds.
ISLE OF WIGHT COUNTY COUNCIL

Aa:16 HAMSTEAD TRAIL

Near Yarmouth; trail starts at Brook Bay (SZ 385836) and runs to Hamstead Ledge (SZ 405920). Keep to the route. Detailed leaflet from County Council.
■ Chalk downland, cliffs.
■ Long-distance walk along chalk ridge. Route intercepts various roads so catch bus back to starting point. **Birds** Buzzard, corn bunting. **Mammals** Red squirrel. **Reptiles** Slow-worm, common lizard, adder.

Aa:17 NEWTOWN HARBOUR*

Newtown; park in Newtown and follow route through village around the old harbour. Permit required for access off footpath.
■ Salt-marsh, mudflat.
■ Interesting salt-marsh plants in summer; wide variety of birds during winter.
NATIONAL TRUST

Aa:18 PARKHURST FOREST*

Near Newport; park at SZ 480900. Other car parks nearby.
■ Mixed woodland.
■ Although largely planted with conifers, Parkhurst Forest still contains remnants of ancient hunting forest. Stands of mature beech and oak are in the N, while elsewhere plantations of varying ages are found.
  Its wildlife value has dwindled but the woodland rides are especially rewarding for butterflies such as white admiral, silver-washed fritillary and purple hairstreak. You may glimpse the red squirrel, most at home in the broad leaved woodland but sometimes entering the plantations. The grey squirrel never crossed the Solent, so any squirrel you see on the Isle of Wight is sure to be red.
FORESTRY COMMISSION

Aa:19 MEDINA ESTUARY

Newport; park in Newport and walk from Newport Quay (SZ 500898) along banks of River Medina, keeping to Nature Trail.
■ River, salt-marsh.
■ Good for salt-marsh plants (summer) and birds (autumn, winter). Trail guide essential, obtain from IOWNH & AS.
ISLE OF WIGHT NATURAL HISTORY & ARCHAEOLOGY SOCIETY

Aa:A PENNINGTON & KEYHAVEN MARSHES/HURST SPIT**

Near Lymington.
■ Coastal marsh, foreshore, shingle beach.
① Pull in on corner and scan fields. Waders at high tide; thrushes, raptors and short-eared owl in winter.
② Limited parking. Look for waders and wildfowl in fields.
③ Sewage outfall attracts large numbers of gulls. Terns feed offshore and in landward pools. Grass contains lesser marsh grasshopper and short-winged conehead.
④ Walk around sea wall and scan grazing marsh and pools on landward side. Wildfowl and waders including grey phalarope in autumn. At low tide, brent geese and waders on mudflats.
⑤ Traditional sea watching point. Unusual species have included long-billed dowitcher and buff-breasted sandpiper. Good at high tide when waders fly over the sea-wall to the pool on the other side.
⑥ Walk along sea wall to pools and marsh which attract waders such as ruff and little stint; occasional rarities.
⑦ Track from Pennington to Keyhaven leads through gorse which holds migrants in spring and autumn.
⑧ Car park overlooks harbour and mudflats.
⑨ From bridge, scan the pool and reed-bed for grebes and migrants.
⑩ Pull off the road. Excellent on a rising tide as the birds on the salt-marsh are pushed towards the car.
⑪ Limited parking beside the road. Scan fields for waders at high tide. Sea watching from shingle ridge is best in spring when there are strong onshore winds. Skuas and divers often seen.
⑫ Walk along sea wall to brackish pool which, in spring and autumn, attracts migrants and gulls including little and Mediterranean.
⑬ Either walk along the shingle beach from (11) or catch the ferry from Keyhaven at (8). Good maritime flora around Hurst Castle, including sea-lavender, little-robin, golden-samphire and, surprisingly, autumn lady's-tresses. Terns nest and feed offshore in summer. Good for migrants in autumn and the occasional black redstart or snow bunting in winter.
HAMPSHIRE COUNTY COUNCIL/HAMPSHIRE AND ISLE OF WIGHT NATURALISTS' TRUST

Aa:20 COASTAL TRAIL

Brighstone; this section starts at St Catherine's Point (SZ 498753) and runs along coast to Totland. Keep to the route. Detailed leaflet from County Council.
■ Cliffs, chalk downland.
■ Fifteen-mile (24-km) walk which intercepts various roads. Catch bus back to starting point. **Birds** Shag, fulmar, corn bunting. **Reptiles** Adder, common lizard. **Butterflies** Glanville fritillary.

Adder – see Aa:16 and Aa:20.

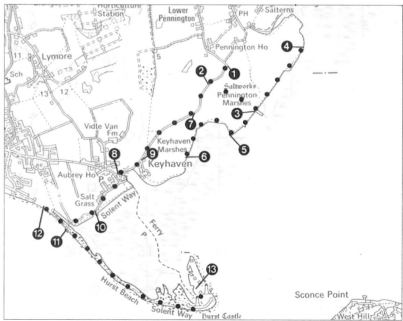

1:50 000, MAP Aa:A

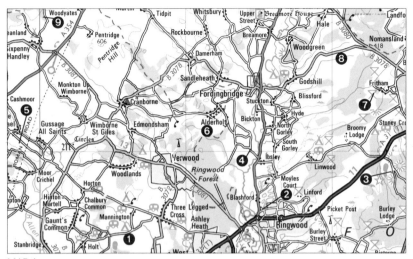

MAP A

A:1 HOLT HEATH

Near Wimborne Minster; car park at SZ 047037 or access from minor road at SZ 057046. Use public footpaths. Further details from NCC.

■ Wet/dry heath, oak wood.

■ Mixture of dry and damp heathland together with valley bogs make this a rich site; oak wood supports high population of insects and lichen. **Birds** Nightjar, stonechat.

Mammals Fox, badger, roe deer. **Plants** Sundews, bog asphodel, heath spotted-orchid. **Reptiles** Slow-worm.
NATURE CONSERVANCY COUNCIL

A:2 BLASHFORD & RINGWOOD GRAVEL PITS

Near Ringwood; park in Blashford or at SU 161077 and use public footpaths.

■ Freshwater lakes.

■ A series of flooded gravel pits, some stocked by anglers; good for wildfowl, winter and spring. **Birds** Wigeon, great crested grebe. Occasional rarities, e.g. ring-necked duck.

A:3 BOLDERWOOD★

Near Lyndhurst; park in FC car park at SU 243087 and follow trails (leaflets available from FC's Lyndhurst office).

■ Mature native woodland, arboretum.

■ Highlights include a fallow deer sanctuary with a hide affording good views. The impressive arboretum has some majestic redwoods and cedars. A longer walk passes through it into Mark Ash Wood; interesting variety of trees and typical New Forest birds. **Birds** Redstart, buzzard, sparrowhawk, woodpeckers. **Mammals** Fallow deer, roe deer, badger. **Insects** Wood ant.
FORESTRY COMMISSION

A:4 AVON FLOODMEADOWS AT IBSLEY

Near Ringwood; park on roadside at SU 147099 and use car as hide.

■ Floodmeadows.

■ Best visited in winter to see numerous wildfowl; in summer, supports a variety of breeding birds. **Birds** (Winter) Bewick's swan, white-fronted goose, teal; (summer) redshank, yellow wagtail, snipe.

B:A NEW FOREST★
Near Lyndhurst.

■ Heath, woodland, pond.

■ There are numerous Forestry Commission car parks in this central part of the Forest from the great beech and oak woods, and the New Forest's diverse other habitats can be explored. The following are a typical selection.

(1) FC car park under mature conifers. Inspect trees for crossbill and siskin.
(2) Walk SW across heath looking out for heathland birds. Dragonflies and damselflies breed in wetter areas. Cotton-grass, sundew and bog asphodel indicate boggy areas.
(3) Denny Wood, criss-crossed by tracks, is good for woodland birds. Listen for the faint song of the wood cricket. The immense ash-black slug is sometimes seen in wet weather.
(4) Follow path along S edge of Bishop's Dyke. Look for fallow and roe deer feeding on the woodland edge. Buzzards sometimes soar overhead.
(5) From the railway bridge, hobbies are sometimes seen in summer feeding on dragonflies. In winter, look for hen harrier and great grey shrike.
(6) Search trees for redstart and hawfinch. Numerous tracks allow exploration.
(7) Pond with boggy margin. Gulls and wildfowl feed around the edges. Aquatic life is rich. Interesting flora includes Hampshire-purslane.

Birds (Summer) Dartford warbler; hobby, nightjar, crossbill, stonechat; (winter) hen harrier, merlin, great grey shrike; (Matley Wood) redstart, buzzard, hawfinch; (Hatchet Pond) ducks, common tern. **Plants** Sundews, bog myrtle, bog asphodel; (Hatchet Pond) bladderwort, Hampshire purslane, chaffweed, slender centaury, bog orchid. **Insects** Bog bush-cricket, dragonflies. **Molluscs** (Matley Wood) ash-black slug. **Spiders** Swamp spider.
FORESTRY COMMISSION

1:50 000, MAP B:A

A:5 SOVELL DOWN

Near Wimborne Minster; *access from minor road at ST 993109. Keep to footpaths.*
- Chalk grassland, scrub.
- Unimproved grassland has abundance of chalkland plants, including orchids, with correspondingly high number of butterflies. Scrub areas used by nesting song birds.
DORSET TRUST FOR NATURE CONSERVATION

A:6 AVON FOREST

Near Ringwood; *car park at SU 128023. Keep to footpaths.*
- Coniferous woodland, grassland, heath.
- This tiny fragment of the formerly vast Dorset heathlands is home for some of the rare species of this habitat. Many butterflies, moths, grasshoppers and bush crickets. **Birds** Nightjar, stonechat, Dartford warbler. **Mammals** Fox, badger, roe and sika deer. **Plants** Sundews, bog asphodel, heath spotted-orchid. **Reptiles** Slow-worm, common and sand lizards, adder, smooth and grass snakes.
DORSET COUNTY COUNCIL

A:7 EYEWORTH POND*

Near Cadnam; *FC car park at SU 229148.*
- Woodland, heath.
- An excellent area of New Forest woodland with all the associated bird species. Numerous paths from car park; further information from FC. Close by is a former gunpowder works. **Birds** Hawfinch, redstart, wood warbler, buzzard.
FORESTRY COMMISSION

A:8 ASHLEY WALK**

Near Fordingbridge; *FC car park at SU 186157.*
- Heathland, bog.
- A typical area of heathland and valley bog. **Birds** (Summer) Dartford warbler, stonechat; (winter) great grey shrike, hen harrier, merlin. **Plants** Bog myrtle, pale dog-violet. **Insects** Dragonflies, bog bush-cricket.
FORESTRY COMMISSION

A:9 GARSTON WOOD

Near Sixpenny Handley; *access from minor road at SU 004194. Use footpaths.*
- Mixed woodland.
- Good variety of woodland birds and mammals, interesting ground flora.
ROYAL SOCIETY FOR THE PROTECTION OF BIRDS

B:1 RHINEFIELD*

Near Lyndhurst; *car park at SU 268048, others nearby. Often muddy. Beware the bite of 'clegs' (horseflies).*
- Woodland, heath.
- The magnificent Rhinefield Ornamental Drive leads to a car park at Pound Hill from which numerous tracks and trails lead through the forest and eventually on to open heath and bog. The route N passes through the Tall Trees walk towards Brock Hill, whereas a walk in the opposite direction leads to Puttles Bridge and the Ober-Water. Sharp eyes may spot the camouflaged pine hawk moth resting on the bark of Scots pine. In the more open areas of heath you will see dragonflies, such as the four-spotted chaser hunting over the heather and possibly that most elegant of falcons, the hobby.
FORESTRY COMMISSION

C:1 BUCKLERS HARD*

Near Beaulieu; *car park at Bucklers Hard. Follow riverside path upstream.*
- River, salt-marsh.
- The charming wooded valley of the Beaulieu River. Details of trail from Bucklers Hard Maritime Museum. **Birds** Little tern, common tern, brent goose, dunlin, godwits. **Plants** Sea-lavender, glasswort, cord grass.

C:2 LEPE COUNTRY PARK

Near Southampton; *car park at SZ 456986 (small fee in summer).*
- Foreshore, stabilized shingle.
- Good views of waders and brent geese at low tide in winter. Spring sea-bird migration occasionally good during onshore gales. **Birds** Brent goose, oystercatcher,

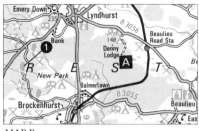

MAP B

dunlin, gulls.
HAMPSHIRE COUNTY COUNCIL

C:3 HAYLING ISLAND

Near Portsmouth; *car parks (fee) at SZ 695996 and SZ 688998. Crowded in summer. Keep to public footpaths.*
- Stabilized shingle, coastal.
- Highly trampled shingle supporting variety of coastal plants; views of the Solent and Langstone Harbour. **Birds** Slavonian grebe, Mediterranean gull, terns, brent goose. **Plants** Yellow horned-poppy, sea-milkwort, rough clover, hare's-foot clover.

C:4 EAST HEAD, WEST WITTERING*

Near Chichester; *approach from West Wittering and park at SZ 765990; keep to public footpaths.*
- Dunes, foreshore.
- Stabilized dunes with views N into Chichester harbour and S into Solent. **Birds** Godwit, brent goose, terns, gulls. **Plants** Yellow horned-poppy, sea-holly.
NATIONAL TRUST

C:5 CHICHESTER HARBOUR*

Near Chichester; *use footpaths round perimeter.*
- Mudflats, salt-marsh.
- This immense natural harbour is of national importance as a wintering ground for thousands of ducks, geese and waders. Vast areas of mud are uncovered at low tide and birds feed on the exposed marine animals. As the tide rises, the birds are

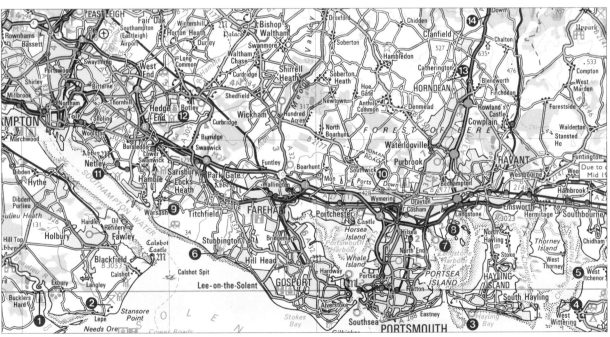

MAP C

HAMPSHIRE

pushed closer to the shore and can be viewed from numerous points such as Hayling Island and East Head (see above). At high tide the birds fly into the surrounding fields and pastures: consult a tide timetable.

Terns and gulls breed here and in the late summer the drier areas of salt-marsh provide a colourful display of plants such as golden-samphire and sea-lavender. **Birds** Godwits, brent goose. **Plants** Yellow horned-poppy, sea-holly.
CHICHESTER HARBOUR CONSERVANCY

C:6 TITCHFIELD HAVEN★★

Near Fareham; parking on foreshore and at reserve centre at SU 535024. Permit required from Naturalist Ranger, Titchfield Haven, but part of reserve can be overlooked from road (SU 533024) or from footpath along reserve edge.
■ Freshwater lagoons, marsh.
■ Titchfield is of interest to the birdwatcher, with several hides overlooking shallow lagoons and reed-beds. During the winter hundreds of dabbling ducks such as wigeon and teal congregate here, and in most years there is a bittern. On calm winter days small flocks of bearded tit are sometimes seen or heard.

In spring and autumn the reserve attracts migrant terns and waders such as wood sandpiper and spotted redshank, and there is always the chance of a rarity. Both spotted sandpiper and sociable plover were present on the same pool in autumn 1986.
HAMPSHIRE COUNTY COUNCIL

C:7 FARLINGTON MARSHES★★

Near Portsmouth; access from roundabout at SU 675043; parking limited. View from sea wall footpath (wet underfoot); no access to grazing marsh.
■ Grazing marsh, salt-marsh, mudflats.
■ These 300 acres of coastal marsh, freshwater pools and scrub, jutting into Langstone harbour, provide a roosting and feeding area for thousands of wildfowl and waders during the winter. brent geese may arrive as early as September, followed by wigeon, teal, godwits and curlew. Access along the sea wall allows excellent views of the mudflats and marshes. Parts of the wall support interesting maritime plants.

The hordes of wintering birds also attract visiting raptors and owls. Peregrine, merlin and hen harrier are regularly seen, together with the day-flying short-eared owl. Rarities have included Franklin's gull and marsh sandpiper. Information boards give details of recent sightings.
HAMPSHIRE & ISLE OF WIGHT NATURALISTS' TRUST

C:8 LANGSTONE HARBOUR★★

Near Portsmouth; park near roundabout on A27 at SU 697058. Coastal footpath along N shore allows good views.
■ Salt-marsh, coastal marsh.
■ This vast area of mudflats and salt-marsh is an important wintering place for species such as brent goose and godwits. At low tide the exposed surface attracts thousands of feeding birds which, as the tide comes in, are pushed closer to the edge of the mudflats. At high tide they fly to adjacent areas.

The area can also be viewed from Hayling Island and from paths around Langstone village. **Birds** Black-tailed and bar-tailed godwit, shelduck. **Plants** Cord-grass.
ROYAL SOCIETY FOR THE PROTECTION OF BIRDS

C:9 HOOK AND WARSASH NATURE RESERVE

Near Fareham; park in Warsash or at SU 490061 and walk S along the Hamble. Reserve starts at SU 490053. Access along footpaths and foreshore.
■ Foreshore, salt-marsh, freshwater, woodland.
■ A variety of habitats. **Birds** Brent goose, waders, terns. **Plants** Slender hare's-ear, sea-holly, yellow horned-poppy, sea milkwort. **Insects** Long-winged conehead, lesser marsh grasshopper.
HAMPSHIRE COUNTY COUNCIL

C:10 PORTSDOWN HILL★

Near Portsmouth; stretches from SU 618065 to SU 660064.
■ Chalk downland.
A chalk anticline with commanding views; chalk flora. **Plants** Bee orchid, bastard toadflax, early gentian. **Insects** Great green bush-cricket.
PORTSMOUTH CITY COUNCIL

C:11 ROYAL VICTORIA COUNTRY PARK

Near Southampton; car park at SZ 457080. Entry fee in summer. Crowded at weekends.
■ Woodland, foreshore, parkland.
■ An interesting mixture of varied woodland and foreshore.
HAMPSHIRE COUNTY COUNCIL

C:12 UPPER HAMBLE COUNTRY PARK

Near Southampton; park at SU 490114. Entry fee in summer.
■ Woodland, tidal river.
■ Pleasant walks through ancient woodland and along the Hamble. **Butterflies** Purple hairstreak, white admiral.
HAMPSHIRE COUNTY COUNCIL

C:13 CATHERINGTON DOWN★

Near Horndean; access at SU 690143 along minor road from Lovedean to Clanfield.
■ Chalk down.
■ This fine area of chalk downland is now managed as a local nature reserve. On the slopes, the presence of strip lynchets (a medieval system of farming) indicates that much of the land has not been ploughed for centuries. This has allowed an extremely rich plant community to develop.

The striking clustered bellflower is present in large numbers, as is round-headed rampion, normally rare in Hampshire. The chalk-loving stemless thistle and squinancywort are common, and later in the season autumn lady's-tresses and felwort can be found.
HAMPSHIRE & ISLE OF WIGHT NATURALISTS' TRUST/HAMPSHIRE COUNTY COUNCIL

C:14 QUEEN ELIZABETH COUNTRY PARK

Near Petersfield; park at SU 717186 (small fee). Well signposted N of Horndean.
■ Chalk down, scrub, woodland.
■ Trails and paths lead through 1,400 acres of downland and woods, dominated by Butser Hill. Information centre and Iron Age farmstead. Birds include kestrel, yellowhammer and whitethroat; one of the few areas where golden pheasant is regularly seen; marbled white and common blue butterflies.
HAMPSHIRE COUNTY COUNCIL/FORESTRY COMMISSION

D:1 FARLEY MOUNT★

Near Winchester; car park at SU 409293.
■ Chalk downland.
■ Fine downland scenery and associated flora. **Plants** Orchids, bastard-toadflax. **Molluscs** Round-mouthed snail.
HAMPSHIRE COUNTY COUNCIL

D:2 CRAB WOOD★

Near Winchester; park at SU 436298. Open access, but keep to footpaths.
■ Woodland.

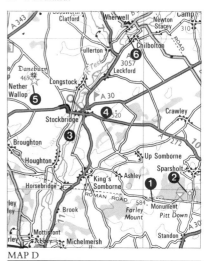

MAP D

■ This superb piece of woodland is an LNR actively managed area maintaining a wide diversity of tree species and age structure. Many mature oaks and beeches remain, the latter with an understorey of bluebells in the spring. Other areas have been opened up, and the increased light has encouraged plants such as primrose and violets. These more open glades are also favoured by sun-loving woodland butterflies such as silver-washed fritillary, white admiral and speckled wood.

The woodland supports a wide variety of birds. Nightingales and blackcaps are found in thickets while woodpeckers and nuthatches prefer the more mature areas. **Birds** Woodpeckers, nightingale. **Butterflies** White admiral. **Plants** Bluebell, earlypurple orchid, Solomon's seal.
HAMPSHIRE COUNTY COUNCIL/HAMPSHIRE & ISLE OF WIGHT NATURALISTS' TRUST

D:3 COMMON MARSH, STOCKBRIDGE

Near Stockbridge; access at SU 351340. Open access, follow paths.
■ Water meadow.
■ Rich wet meadows next to River Test. **Plants** Hemp agrimony, marsh orchids, yellow flag, ragged robin. **Birds** Sedge warbler, reed bunting.
NATIONAL TRUST

D:4 STOCKBRIDGE DOWN★

Near Stockbridge; park at SU 377347.
■ Chalk down, scrub.
■ This remnant of the downland which once stretched across Salisbury Plain supports all the typical members of a chalk community such as thyme, kidney vetch and lady's bedstraw. In addition, more unusual plants such as squinancywort and dropwort can be found, and the whole area provides a colourful spectacle at the height of summer.

Birds such as yellowhammer and whi-

tethroat haunt the scrub, while linnets and skylarks prefer the more open areas of herb-rich grassland. Various butterflies are present, as well as the day-flying six-spot burnet moth and common forester. The site also holds several unusual bugs, such as the conspicuous, lurid green flower-beetle and the bishop's-mitre bug. On damp days or towards the evening, you may find several species of snail.
NATIONAL TRUST

D:5 DANEBURY RING
Near Andover; car park at SU 324376.
■ Chalk downland.
■ Iron Age hill fort with commanding views and chalk flora.
HAMSHIRE COUNTY COUNCIL

D:6 CHILBOLTON COMMON
Near Andover; park in Chilbolton or Wherwell. Common is at SU 387402.
■ Meadow.
■ Grazed wet meadows in the Test valley, with plants more often associated with fens. **Plants** Water avens, southern marsh-orchid, marsh arrow-grass, tawny sedge.
CHILBOLTON PARISH COUNCIL

E:1 ST CATHERINE'S HILL
Near Winchester; park at SU 490275.
■ Chalk downland, scrub.
■ An interesting relict of downland near A33 with better-than-average selection of chalk-loving plants and animals. **Plants** Carline thistle, bastard-toadflax. **Butterflies** Chalkhill blue, marbled white.
HAMPSHIRE AND ISLE OF WIGHT NATURALIST'S TRUST

E:2 WEALDEN EDGE HANGERS*
Near Petersfield; reserve from SU 728256 to SU 749271. Keep to footpaths.
■ Beech/yew/ash woodland.
■ This dramatic woodland lies on eroded chalk scarps overlooking the Weald of Sussex. The dense beech canopy allows little light to penetrate, and so only early spring flowers like bluebell and early-purple orchid can thrive, as well as saprophytic bird's-nest

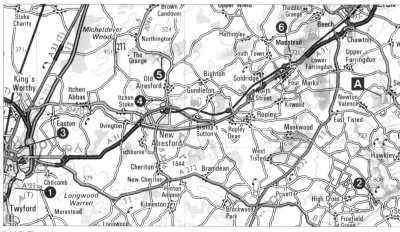

MAP E

orchid which lacks chlorophyll and is found in the deepest shade. In more open areas plants such as ramsons and dog's mercury grow, and there are butterflies such as the speckled wood and other insects. Where these clearings are on chalk rather than clay, there is a surprising display reminiscent of chalk downland, with thyme and rock-rose. **Plants** Bird's-nest orchid, white hellebore-rine, wood spurge, nettle-leaved bellflower.
HAMPSHIRE COUNTY COUNCIL

E:3 WINNALL MOORS
(SOUTHERN AREA)
Near Winchester; access at SU 486300. Park in North Walls Recreation Ground car park. Keep to paths.
■ Water meadow, fen.
■ Ungrazed, wet meadows which have developed a rich variety of fen plants and associated animals. **Plants** Marsh-orchids, ragged robin. **Birds** Grasshopper, reed and sedge warblers.
HAMPSHIRE AND ISLE OF WIGHT NATURALIST'S TRUST

E:4 ALRESFORD POND
In Alresford; park in Broad Street and walk N

Nettle-leaved bellflower – see E:A.

along Basingstoke road to pond. Numerous public footpaths by cress beds.
■ Lake, carr.
■ Good wintering spot for dabbling and diving ducks; unusual birds during migration, eg osprey. **Birds** Kingfisher, grey heron, pochard, tufted duck.

E:5 ABBOTSTONE DOWN
Near Alresford; car park at SU 585362. Keep to footpaths beyond parking area.
■ Chalk down, woodland, scrub.
■ Footpaths lead through wood and scrub containing nightingales and garden warblers to rolling downland, most of which is under the plough. **Butterflies** Grizzled skipper.
HAMPSHIRE COUNTY COUNCIL

E:6 CHAWTON PARK WOOD
Near Alton; park in FC car park at SU 672361. Keep to paths and woodland rides. Adders; wellington boots necessary.
■ Mature forestry plantation; mainly conifers but many broad-leaved trees as well.
■ After a wet summer can be exceptional for fungi. **Fungi** Dog stinkhorn, stinkhorn, fly agaric, *Boletus* spp. **Plants** Violet hellebore-rine, broad-leaved helleborine. **Birds** Siskin, goldcrest, redpoll, sparrowhawk.
FORESTRY COMMISSION

E:A SELBORNE HILL
Near Alton; public car park in Selborne village behind Selborne Arms.
■ Beech wood.
① From NT car park, take the Zigzag Path up through the beeches on Selborne Hanger. Look for woodland flowers such as nettle-

leaved bellflower and sanicle.
② At the top, turn left for a fine view. Retrace steps and walk along the Hanger. Various tracks also lead through Selborne Common, an area of mixed woodland on clay with flints. Listen for wood warbler and chiffchaff in spring.
③ At the viewpoint seat, the path bears right and descends to Selborne. Views of the village.
④ Cross road to churchyard containing ancient yew and Gilbert White's simple grave. Good range of lichens on gravestones.
⑤ Cross church meadow, enter woodland and follow path to left of cottage along the Short and Long Lythe. Mature beech woodland rich in fungi.
⑥ Footpath continues to Priory Farm. Then follow the bridle-path sign to return towards Selborne via Dorton Wood.
⑦ Footpath passes through fine old beechwood containing green hellebore. The autumn colours can be stunning and the good range of fungi includes death cap, oyster mushroom and scarlet elf cup.
⑧ At the stream look for opposite-leaved golden-saxifrage; return to village up Huckers Lane.
NATIONAL TRUST/PRIVATE OWNERSHIP

1:50 000, MAP E:A

WEST SUSSEX

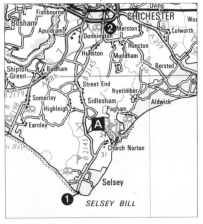

MAP A

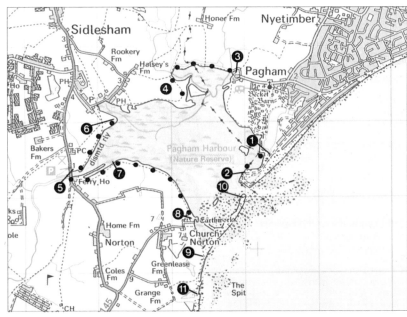

1:50 000, MAP A:A

A:1 SELSEY BILL

Near Chichester; park at Selsey Bill (SZ 850923) or in village. Access to coastal path and foreshore only; crowded in summer holidays.

■ Shingle shore, open sea.

■ Excellent for migrating sea-birds, spring and autumn: best during onshore winds. Tideline debris interesting after gales. **Birds** Skuas, terns, divers, grebes, gulls, scoters, black redstart.

A:2 CHICHESTER GRAVEL PITS

Near Chichester; limited parking at SU 869034, but many other access points (see Landranger 197). View from roads and public footpaths only.

■ Lakes, exposed gravel workings.

■ Many pits of varying size, depth and use; new lakes appear after gravel extraction. Best in winter. **Birds** Terns, waders, grebes, grey heron.

B:1 KINGLEY VALE

Near Chichester; best approached from unclassified road at West Stoke.

■ Yew forest, chalk down.

■ Undoubtedly the finest yew forest in Britain, Kingley Vale NNR sits high on the slopes of the South Downs with outstanding views S to Chichester and the Isle of Wight.

Although the yews are dramatically gnarled and aesthetically appealing, very little grows under them. However, there are many clearings and open areas where a chalk heath community has developed: look for plants normally associated with chalk, such as bee and fragrant orchids and clustered bellflower. Insects also prefer these more open areas and several species of grasshopper, including the stripe-winged, can be found, together with a wide variety of butterflies. Best in spring and summer. **Plants** Round-headed rampion, common gromwell, orchids. **Butterflies** Purple emperor, adonis blue, purple emperor, silver-washed fritillary, chalkhill blue.

NATURE CONSERVANCY COUNCIL

B:2 ARUNDEL WILDFOWL REFUGE

Near Arundel; car park at TQ 020082. Admission fee; open all year.

■ Ponds, reed-beds.

■ An impressive collection of wildfowl mingles with a variety of wild birds attracted by the food and lack of human interference. In winter moorhens and the occasional

A:A PAGHAM HARBOUR**

Near Chichester; keep to footpaths.

■ Mudflats, salt-marsh, ponds, grazing marsh.

① Pagham lagoon attracts wildfowl such as smew in winter. Grebes and divers often seen offshore.

② Shingle spit affords good views of the harbour and supports excellent flora, including yellow horned-poppy, sea kale and small numbers of childling pink.

③ Limited parking near Pagham church. Walk W along sea-wall to view harbour. Good for Brent geese in winter.

④ Continue along wall for further views. 5 Park in reserve car park and view Ferry Pond from hide or road. Excellent for waders, wildfowl and the occasional rarity.

⑥ Walk NE along sea wall to view mudflats.

⑦ Walk E along sea wall to Church Norton.

⑧ At Church Norton, inspect bushes and scrub for migrants. Firecrest usually present during autumn and winter and short-eared owls often seen over the fields. Tidal creeks good for salt-marsh plants, waders and wildfowl.

⑨ Shingle ridge affords good views of sea; look for sea-duck and divers. Waders and passerines feed in the grazing fields.

⑩ The shingle spit is open outside the breeding season (consult notice-board for times). Interesting maritime flora; snow bunting sometimes seen in winter.

⑪ Small pools and reed-beds called the 'Severals'. Good for migrants and vagrants which have included purple heron. **Birds** Ruff, grey plover, godwits, turnstone, oystercatchers, short-eared owl. **Insects** Short-winged conehead.

WEST SUSSEX COUNTY COUNCIL

water rail feed among the pinioned ducks.

Two viewing hides overlook meadows, man-made scrapes and reed-beds. From November to March hundreds of wildfowl, including pochard and teal, and waders including lapwing and redshank, can be seen at close quarters. In good years, bearded tits and bittern may be present.

A late spring visit is perhaps most rewarding: in addition to the wild birds, the captive ducks are seen displaying. Listen for the song of Cetti's warbler which lurks in the reed-beds. In summer, duck are in heavy moult. **Birds** Bewick's swan, water rail, shoveller.

WILDFOWL TRUST

B:3 AMBERLEY MOUNT

Near Arundel; park in Amberley or catch train to Amberley and walk to TQ 034125 from where there is a network of public footpaths, including the South Downs Way.

■ Chalk down, scrub.

■ A small stretch of the South Downs Way with superb views over the flood plain of the River Arun. **Plants** Cowslip, orchids, squinancywort. **Butterflies** Chalkhill blue, marbled white.

B:4 GREATHAM BRIDGE

Near Pulborough; take unclassified road E from Coldwaltham to approx. TQ 028163 and look for flooded fields: the exact site varies each year. View from road, using car as hide.

■ Floodmeadow, grazing marsh.

■ Important wintering area for wildfowl and waders. **Birds** Bewick's swan, short-eared owl, pintail, wigeon, redshank, snipe, teal, lapwing.

B:5 BURTON MILL POND

Near Petworth; reserve starts at SU 979180 – open access around walkway.

■ Lake, reed-bed, carr.

■ Reed-fringed lake margins and alder carr showing an interesting diversity of habitat. **Plants** Cowbane, yellow water lily. **Birds** Water rail, siskin, redpoll.

WEST SUSSEX COUNTY COUNCIL/SUSSEX TRUST FOR NATURE CONSERVATION

C:1 WIDEWATER & SHOREHAM BEACH

Near Hove; car park at TQ 205043.

■ Lake, shingle shore, open sea.

■ The area can be good for migrant and wintering birds. Widewater Lake often har-

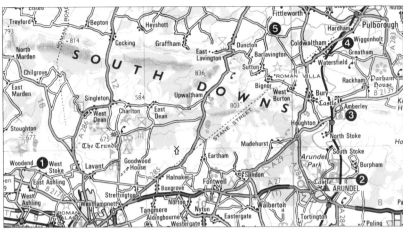

MAP B

Chalkhill blue – see B:1, B:3, C:5.

bours a few interesting waders and, occasionally, even Baird's sandpiper in recent years. Sea watching can also be productive in spring and autumn with pomarine skuas occasionally seen during onshore gales in early May. On calm winter days, scan the water for divers and grebes.

Winter gulls often include Mediterranean; black redstarts sometimes shelter between the beach huts. If there is nothing about, walk to the River Adur, now an RSPB re-

serve, and scan the mud from the banks (crowded in summer). **Birds** Grebes, divers.

C:2 CASTLE HILL
Near Brighton; *park at TQ 377074 and follow track heading E; permit required to stray from footpaths – apply local NCC.*
■ Chalk down.
■ Exceptional flora and fauna at this NNR, which is managed to maintain grazing pressure from cattle and sheep, which has encouraged species diversity. Best in spring

and summer. **Plants** Field fleawort, round-headed rampion, carline thistle, orchids, squinancywort. **Butterflies** Chalkhill blue, adonis blue. **Birds** Stonechat.
NATURE CONSERVANCY COUNCIL

C:3 CISSBURY RING
Near Worthing; *car parks at TQ 130077 and TQ 138087; walk to TQ 140080.*
■ Chalk down.
■ Although a popular spot, with its large Iron-Age hill fort and fine views, Cissbury Ring retains an interesting selection of chalk-loving plants and animals. Knapweeds, clustered bellflower and the occasional orchid provide colour and a wide variety of insects occur in the grasses. Burnet moths are conspicuous.

Cissbury also the site of a Neolithic flint-mining industry – remains on the W end of the hill.
NATIONAL TRUST

C:4 DEVIL'S DYKE
Near Brighton; *car park at TQ 258111.*
■ Chalk down, scrub, hill-fort remains.
■ A dramatic N-facing scarp of the South Downs which can be busy in summer. **Plants** Clustered bellflower, common spotted-orchid.
BRIGHTON BOROUGH COUNCIL

C:5 DITCHLING BEACON★
Near Brighton; *car park at TQ 329133.*
■ Chalk down.
■ The remains of an ancient hill fort mark the summit, from which there are magnificent views towards the North Downs and Ashdown Forest. The NT car park is a useful starting point from which to explore the area or to walk the South Downs Way.

Despite its proximity to Brighton, the whole area still supports chalk-loving plants such as fragrant orchid and lady's bedstraw and a rich variety of butterflies. In the evening stroll snails and sometimes glow-worms start to appear, and you might see the unusual caterpillars of the chalkhill blue being 'milked' by ants. **Plants** Fragrant orchid, round-headed rampion, orchids, squinancywort, sainfoin. **Invertebrates** Chalkhill blue, brown argus and marbled white butterflies, round-mouthed and pointed snails.
NATIONAL TRUST/SUSSEX TRUST FOR NATURE CONSERVATION

C:6 WOODS MILL★
Near Brighton; *car park and information centre at TQ 218135; access details from centre.*
■ Lake, woodland (once coppice), marsh, hay meadow.
■ Woods Mill is not only the centre for the STNC but also its showpiece reserve. Much of the woodland was formerly coppiced and bluebells and wood anemones still carpet the ground in these areas.

The wetland is perhaps of more interest with a mixture of marsh, carr and open water giving variety. The small area of reed-bed harbours sedge and reed warblers and the surrounding bushes provide perches for reed buntings. Emergent plants thrive with colourful displays of bogbean, marsh marigold and yellow iris. **Birds** Sedge and reed warblers, reed bunting, kingfisher, grey heron. **Dragonflies** Broad-bodied chaser, emperor, large red damselfly.
SUSSEX TRUST FOR NATURE CONSERVATION

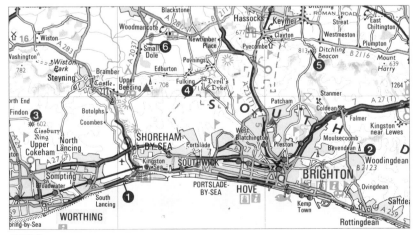

MAP C

53

EAST SUSSEX

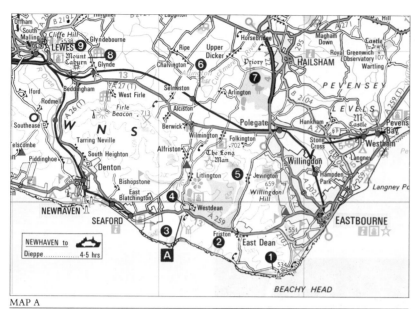

MAP A

A:1 BEACHY HEAD★★

Near Eastbourne; car parks at Birling Gap (TV 554961), Belle Tout (TV 565955), Hodcombe Farm (TV 571954) and Beachy Head itself (TV 583954).

■ Chalk down, cliffs, scrub.

■ As well as superb scenery – close-cropped downland turf, wind-pruned scrub and dramatic chalk cliffs – Beachy Head's chalk flora includes rarities such as the diminutive small hare's-ear and a wealth of interesting butterflies and other insects.

The area is an ornithologist's Mecca, particularly during spring and autumn migrations. Wryneck, hoopoe, golden oriole and tawny pipit are recorded annually and recent rarities have included bee-eater, rustic bunting and black-eared wheatear. The small wood at Belle Tout is always good for firecrest in the autumn and in a recent spring boasted a singing greenish warbler. Sea-bird passage past Birling Gap can be interesting, particularly during onshore spring gales. **Plants** Clustered bellflower, autumn gentian, bastard-toadflax, orchids. **Butterflies** Chalkhill blue, marbled white, grizzled skipper.

EASTBOURNE BOROUGH COUNCIL

A:2 CROWLINK

Near Eastbourne; car park at TV 549978 and footpath to the Seven Sisters.

■ Chalk down, cliffs.

■ Dramatic cliffs topped with rich chalk flora and fauna. Some interesting cornfield 'weeds' around field margins. Best in spring and summer. **Plants** Clustered bellflower, autumn gentian, bastard-toadflax. **Butterflies** Chalkhill blue, marbled white, grizzled skipper.

NATIONAL TRUST

A:3 SEAFORD HEAD★★

Near Seaford; car park at TV 505980 or walk down E side of River Cuckmere from Exceat Bridge, TV 512992.

■ Chalk down, cliffs.

■ Dramatic chalk cliffs and a view towards the Seven Sisters form a background to the plants and animals of the short chalk turf. The area contains Britain's best population of the umbellifer moon carrot as well as im-

pressive numbers of orchids and autumn gentian.

On the way to the cliff edge, you pass through large patches of scrub which harbour breeding birds such as stonechats as well as migrants, for example wryneck and warblers. During onshore winds in spring and autumn, sea-birds on passage may include the elegant Mediterranean gull.

A:4 FRISTON FOREST

Near Seaford; car parks at TQ 518003 and TV 556998.

■ Mixed woodland, conifer plantation, scrub, chalk down.

■ Extensive forest walks and trails pass through beech and pine plantations of varying ages and open areas with natural scrub. A range of chalk-downland butterflies and plants can be found, often in sheltered surroundings. The plantations support birds such as goldcrest and coal tit and a variety of fungi in the autumn. More rewarding perhaps are the forest rides where many interesting plants grow in the better light.

Friston Pond on the opposite side of the A259 is worth a look for plants such as greater spearwort and the alien *Crassula helmsii*. Best in spring and summer. **Plants** Wood-sorrel, sanicle, Italian lords-and-ladies, fungi. **Butterflies** Green hairstreak, brown argus.

FORESTRY COMMISSION

A:5 LULLINGTON HEATH

Near Eastbourne; access along footpaths from Jevington and Littlington; permit required to wander off footpaths.

■ Chalk heath.

■ This NNR is the best example in East or West Sussex of chalk heath, an unusual habitat that develops where a superficial layer of acid soil overlies chalk. The resulting flora and fauna contain elements from both types of habitat, heathers growing alongside dropwort and other chalk plants.

A rich community of insects and spiders has developed, particularly bush-crickets and grasshoppers. Scrub has begun to invade many parts of the reserve and this supports a variety of breeding birds.

NATURE CONSERVANCY COUNCIL

A:6 ARLINGTON RESERVOIR★

Near Hailsham; free car park at TQ 529077 with facilities for the disabled; footpath round perimeter.

■ Lake.

■ Attracts many species of wintering wildfowl and includes a designated bird sanctuary. A circuit takes about 40 minutes. **Birds** Canada geese, grey geese, wigeon, tufted duck, osprey.

EASTBOURNE WATERWORKS COMPANY

A:7 ABBOT'S WOOD

Near Hailsham; car park at TQ 556073; numerous forest walks.

■ Conifer plantation, mixed woodland, pond.

■ Conifers have diminished the area's wil-

A:A SEVEN SISTERS COUNTRY PARK★★

Near Seaford.

■ *River*, *grazing marsh, chalk grassland, ponds, salt-marsh.*

① From the car park, follow path heading S towards sea. River banks attract gulls and waders. Dragonflies breed in the ditches. Look out for occasional patches of red star-thistle.

② Scan the marshes and pools for waders and migrants; jack snipe in winter. The banks to the E support good chalk flora.

③ Follow track up hillside. Good chalk flora and insects including chalkhill blue butterfly and stripe-winged grasshopper. Either continue E along South Downs Way or W to return to car park.

④ An excellent wader pool which has attracted grey phalarope and little stint in the past. Black terns sometimes stop to feed in spring and autumn.

⑤ Walk back along river-bank. Gulls, waders and wildfowl feed while the tide is out. Sea-lavender and sea-purslane grow along the edge.

⑥ Good view from Exceat Bridge down river (look out for kingfishers) and across grazing marsh. Grey geese and swans sometimes occur in cold winters.

Birds Heron, gulls, hen harrier, short-eared owl. **Plants** Orchids, centaury.

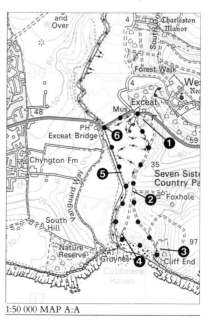

1:50 000 MAP A:A

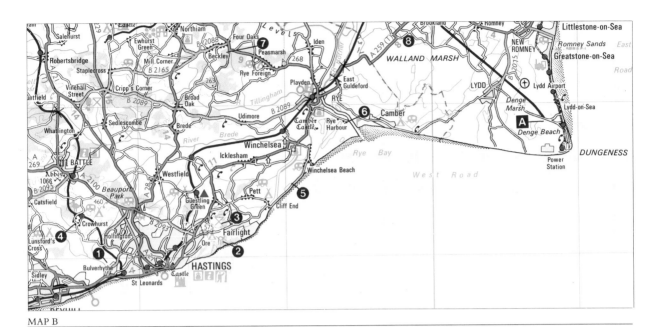

MAP B

dlife appeal, but the forest rides and pond are still interesting. **Birds** Woodpeckers, woodcock, goldcrest. **Plants** Common spotted-orchid, lousewort, cow-wheat. **Insects** Dragonflies, bush-crickets; grizzled skipper and speckled wood butterflies.
FORESTRY COMMISSION

A:8 MOUNT CABURN
Near Lewes; access along footpaths from Lewes or Glynde to TQ 456090.
■ Chalk down, scrub.
■ Excellent chalk flora and fauna; stunning views. **Plants** Deadly nightshade, burnt orchid, squinancywort. **Butterflies** Marbled white.

A:9 MALLING DOWN*
Near Lewes; park in Lewes and walk to TQ 430108.
■ Chalk down, scrub.

■ This excellent area of downland has views across Lewes and the Ouse River and levels. Patches of scrub support breeding whitethroats and yellowhammers. In the open areas of downland, typical plants such as bird's-foot-trefoil and horseshoe vetch thrive. These in turn feed the caterpillars of the blue butterflies which grace the area: the azure-winged adonis blue is on the wing in late spring and again in the autumn, and the single-brooded chalkhill blue, in August.

Chalk-loving plants are well represented with several species of orchid, including the charming pyramidal. The many species of snail are most evident after wet weather. **Plants** Autumn gentian, field fleawort.
SUSSEX TRUST FOR NATURE CONSERVATION

B:1 FILSHAM REEDBEDS
Near Hastings; may be overlooked from foot-

path at TQ 775098; strictly no access to reserve itself.
■ Reed-beds, grazing marsh.
■ The wet meadows, drainage ditches and reed-beds attract breeding birds as well as migrants and winter visitors. **Birds** (summer) Reed and sedge warblers, yellow wagtail; (winter) jack snipe, snipe.
HASTINGS BOROUGH COUNCIL/SUSSEX TRUST FOR NATURE CONSERVATION

B:2 HASTINGS COUNTRY PARK
Near Hastings; car park at TQ 860116.
■ Cliff, heath, woodland.
■ Three nature trails illustrate most habitats of this area of outstanding natural beauty. Leaflets from Visitor Centre. **Birds** Fulmar, stonechat. **Plants** Mosses and liverworts. **Insects** Grey bush-cricket.
HASTINGS BOROUGH COUNCIL

B:A DUNGENESS**
Near New Romney; small entrance fee to RSPB reserve for non-members. Other areas are open or can be viewed from roads.
■ Stabilized shingle, ponds, open sea.
① RSPB reserve reached via a rough track signposted at Boulderwall Farm. Several hides give views over flooded gravel pits and scrapes. Breeding waders and wildfowl are supplemented by migrants. Mediterranean and little gulls and black tern are regular.
② Limited space to pull off road and view extensive flooded gravel workings. Excellent for wildfowl such as tufted duck and pochard. Smew and long-tailed duck are regular in winter and rarities sometimes occur.
③ The bird observatory is surrounded by bushes and scrub which provide cover for migrants. Do not hinder ringing activities. Barred warbler, wryneck and bluethroat are recorded almost annually. Grey bush-crickets in grassy areas.
④ Walk to beach and scan sea for gulls which congregate over the warm-water outflow from the nuclear power station. Excellent sea watching in spring during onshore winds. Pomarine skuas are invariably seen during May when SE winds prevail.
⑤ Walk along shore to view deep water, with

divers, grebes and skuas. Shingle flora may include Nottingham catchfly.
⑥ Park near pub to watch sea. Mud and sand

attract feeding waders at low tide.
ROYAL SOCIETY FOR THE PROTECTION OF BIRDS/PRIVATE OWNERSHIP

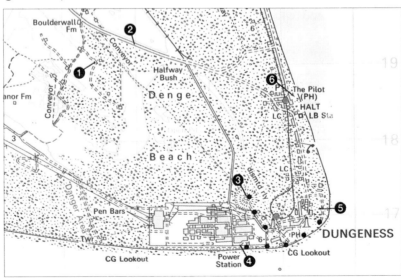

1:50 000 MAP B:A

EAST SUSSEX

B:3 MALLYDAMS WOOD

Near Hastings; field centre at TQ 857122; open access to paths.

■ Mixed woodland, heath.

■ Educational woodland reserve with wide rides rich in flowers; also more open areas of heath and bog. **Plants** Milkwort, common spotted-orchid, bluebell, broom. **Birds** Long-tailed tit, nuthatch.

ROYAL SOCIETY FOR THE PREVENTION OF CRUELTY TO ANIMALS

B:4 FORE WOOD★

Near Battle; park by village hall – TQ 756128.

■ Mixed woodland.

■ Hazel and hornbeam coppice with oak standards, actively managed to allow plenty of light through the canopy. **Birds** Hawfinch, woodpeckers, tawny owl, sparrowhawk. **Plants** Early-purple orchid, common twayblade.

ROYAL SOCIETY FOR THE PROTECTION OF BIRDS

B:5 PETT POOLS★

Near Rye; no access, so view from road at TQ 902146, using car as hide.

■ Pools.

■ The pools can attract an amazing variety of waders in spring and autumn, sometimes rarities. **Birds** Curlew, ruff, little stint, dunlin, redshank.

B:6 RYE HARBOUR★★

Rye; park at TQ 942187; access to LNR restricted to designated paths.

■ Stabilized shingle, ponds, salt-marsh, grazing marsh.

■ A variety of birds breed on this vast area adjoining the mouth of the River Rother, upon which a variety of birds breed, including oystercatcher and ringed plover. Well-placed hides (one with access for the disabled) overlook pools which attract large numbers of migrant waders and wintering wildfowl, including many rarities, and support breeding colonies of terns and black-headed gulls. Wintering Mediterranean gulls often linger well into the spring.

The shingle supports a superb range of maritime plants such as yellow horned-poppy. Of more interest to botanists are colonies of slender hare's-ear and small-red goosefoot as well as nationally important populations of least lettuce.

NATURE RESERVE MANAGEMENT COMMITTEE

B:7 FLATROPERS WOOD

Near Rye; footpaths from A268 and unclassified roads lead to reserve at TQ 862229.

■ Mixed woodland.

■ Coppiced sweet chestnut and oak and birch woodland with an interesting understorey and good butterfly populations. **Butterflies** Pearl-bordered and small pearl-bordered fritillaries. **Birds** Nuthatch, treecreeper, woodpeckers.

SUSSEX TRUST FOR NATURE CONSERVATION

B:8 WALLAND MARSH

Near Rye; use footpaths and roads which dissect the marsh, eg at TQ 978244.

■ Grazing marsh, agricultural land.

■ A bleak and inhospitable place, best visited in winter when it is the haunt of geese and swans. Also attracts raptors and owls. **Birds** Bewick's and whooper swans, white-

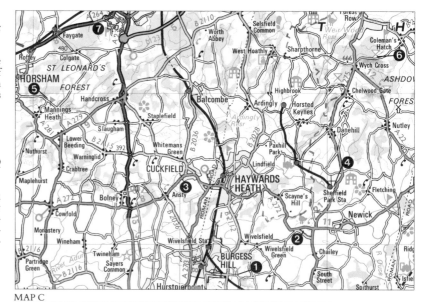

MAP C

fronted and pink-footed geese, hen harrier, short-eared owl.

C:1 DITCHLING COMMON COUNTRY PARK

Near Brighton; car park at TQ 336181.

■ Acidic heath grassland, oak wood, lake.

■ All the elements of a typical Wealden common, with woodland grading into gorse scrub and acid grassland. **Butterflies** Small pearl-bordered fritillary, green hairstreak. **Birds** Nightingale, stonechat.

C:2 CHAILEY COMMON

Near Haywards Heath; park at TQ 391218 and walk to TQ 386210.

■ Heath, scrub.

■ The reserve lies on common land and has all the features of lowland heath. **Birds** Siskin, redpoll, tree pipit, stonechat. **Plants** Petty whin, lousewort, bell heather, cross-leaved heath. **Insects** Grayling, green tiger beetle.

NATURE RESERVE MANAGEMENT COMMITTEE

C:3 NEWBURY POND

Near Haywards Heath; park at TQ 306243; access easy at S end only; keep to footpaths.

■ Pond, marsh.

■ Interesting variety of plants, insects and birds. **Insects** Dragonflies, damselflies, water beetles, water boatmen. **Plants** Yellow iris, hornwort. **Birds** Reed bunting.

SUSSEX TRUST FOR NATURE CONSERVATION

C:4 SHEFFIELD PARK

Near Crowborough; park at TQ 415240. Open Apr-Nov, Tue-Sun afternoons; entrance fee. Facilities for the disabled.

■ Parkland, formal garden, lakes, woods.

■ A hundred acres, landscaped by Capability Brown; best spring to autumn. **Birds** Hawfinch, siskin, redpoll. **Plants** Specimen trees.

NATIONAL TRUST

C:5 ST LEONARD'S FOREST

Near Horsham; three small reserves at TQ 208299, TQ 216303 and TQ 212308 within larger area of FC plantations; keep to footpaths.

■ Beech wood, birch coppice, pine plantation.

■ Relics of the types of woodland formerly found in Wealden forests, destroyed by planting conifers. Best in spring and summer. **Birds** Nightingale, siskin, woodpecker, redpoll. **Plants** Lily-of-the-valley.

SUSSEX TRUST FOR NATURE CONSERVATION/FORESTRY COMMISSION

C:6 ASHDOWN FOREST★★

Near East Grinstead; numerous car parks: see Landranger 187.

■ Heath, mixed woodland, bog.

■ The wild heather-clad landscape is dotted with patches of birch scrub, clumps of pine and valley bogs.

Gorse, heather and bell heather grow in the dry areas and this was one of the few sites outside Cornwall for hairy greenweed. Nightjars are relatively common.

In the boggy areas, bog-moss grows in carpets together with insectivorous sundews. The whole area is rich in invertebrate life and butterflies recorded include four species of fritillary. **Birds** Hobby, nightjar, stonechat, tree pipit. **Plants** Round-leaved sundew, bog asphodel, petty whin. **Insects** Bog bush-cricket, dragonflies; silver-studded blue butterfly, silver-washed fritillary. **Mammals** Fallow deer, badger. **Reptiles** Adder, common lizard.

CONSERVATORS OF ASHDOWN FOREST

C:7 BUCHAN PARK★

Near Crawley; car park and information centre just off A264 at TQ 246348.

■ Conifer wood, hazel coppice, parkland, lakes.

■ Buchan Park contains a remnant of Wealden forest, and the woodland includes some ancient oaks and beeches.

Insect life is rich and varied with purple emperor, white admiral and purple hairstreak butterflies in summer. More than 20 species of dragonfly and damselfly have been recorded on the lakes including numbers of the local downy emerald.

The usual woodland birds are found, including the occasional crossbill. Woodcock can be heard in the rides at dusk and roe deer sometimes venture into the open.

WEST SUSSEX COUNTY COUNCIL

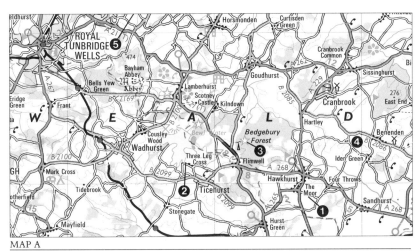

MAP A

A:1 COLLINGWOOD
Near Hawkhurst; *park at TQ 761292.*
- Mixed woodland, lake.
- A long strip of woodland containing native and introduced species. Best in spring and summer. **Birds** Kingfisher, marsh tit, nuthatch, blackcap.
KENT TRUST FOR NATURE CONSERVATION

A:2 BEWL BRIDGE*
Near Hawkhurst; *Visitors' Centre, picnic area and viewing point at TQ 677317. Reserve overlooked from TQ 678318 and from footpaths; access restricted to footpaths and road.*
- Lake.
- Water levels on this massive reservoir fluctuate, but when low in autumn, margins harbour waders. A variety of ducks is always present in winter. **Birds** Goosander, great crested grebe, shoveler – telescope essential.
SOUTHERN WATER

A:3 BEDGEBURY PINETUM*
Near Tenterden; *park at TQ 715338.*
- Mixed woodland, parkland.
- This important arboretum was established by the Forestry Commission and the Royal Botanic Gardens, Kew. The rolling parkland, criss-crossed by paths and tracks, has over 200 species of tree. The area is of interest throughout the year, with a fine display of flowering trees in spring and stunning autumn colours.

During the winter Bedgebury provides good birdwatching with roving flocks of redpoll, siskin and sometimes crossbill. It is also a regular haunt of the elusive hawfinch, most often to be seen perched on the tops of conifers. Because of their dry diet of seeds, they frequently come down to drink from areas of standing water. **Trees** Conifers. **Birds** Hawfinch, crossbill, woodpeckers.
FORESTRY COMMISSION

A:4 PARSONAGE WOOD
Near Tenterden; *footpaths from B2086 to reserve at TQ 794329.*
- Oak and beech woodland.
- Wealden woodland with rich understorey on clay overlying sandstone. Good bryophyte communities. **Plants** Wood spurge, violet helleborine, mosses, liverworts. **Birds** Blackcap, garden warbler.
KENT TRUST FOR NATURE CONSERVATION

A:5 BRENCHLEY WELLS
Near Tunbridge Wells; *access TQ 648418.*

- Weald woodland.
- Woodland on sandstone, mainly oak and beech with interesting mosses and liverworts. Best for birds in spring and summer. **Plants** Sanicle, mosses, liverworts. **Birds** Wood warbler, nightingale, garden warbler, woodcock.
KENT TRUST FOR NATURE CONSERVATION

B:1 HAM STREET WOODS*
Near Ashford; *car park and information centre at TR 009347. Keep to footpaths.*
- Coppiced woodland with oak standards.
- This area of coppiced hornbeam, hazel and sweet chestnut with oak standards is managed to preserve a diversity of plant life. In the autumn and winter, the hornbeam seeds are a favourite food for the hawfinch and Ham Street supports a small breeding population. Nightingales and blackcaps also breed and are easier to detect, especially when singing. The many and varied insects include orange tip, brimstone and speckled wood butterflies which favour the woodland rides. Where the tree canopy lets through sufficient light, the woodland floor is particularly colourful in spring with wood sorrel, wood anemones and cowslips.
NATURE CONSERVANCY COUNCIL

C:1 STAFFHURST WOOD
Near Limpsfield; *park near St Silvan's Church at TQ 410487 and walk east.*
- Old coppiced woodland.
- Here is one of the last remaining areas of Wealden forest left in Surrey – now designated a Local Nature Reserve. Until recently it was managed as a coppice system with hornbeam, ash and beech growing under standards of oak, leaving many parts of the woodland open and airy, with a good growth of bluebells in spring.

Shrubs and trees of the understorey include yew, holly and the occasional wild ser-

vice-tree. All the usual woodland birds are found in the area and the dawn chorus repays the effort of arriving early. **Birds** Nuthatch, woodpeckers.
SURREY COUNTY COUNCIL

C:2 BOUGH BEECH RESERVOIR*
Near Tonbridge; *Information Centre and footpath at TQ 495494. Permit required for access to nature reserve, but both reserve and reservoir can be seen from the B2042 at TQ 497492.*
- Reservoir, wader pits.
- Of interest all year, mainly to the birdwatcher. Many breeding species and variety of migrant waders, depending on water level. **Birds** Garganey, little ringed plover, great crested grebe, waders, winter wildfowl.
KENT TRUST FOR NATURE CONSERVATION

C:3 TOYS HILL
Near Westerham; *car park at TQ 469517.*
- Beech and mixed woodland, heath.
- Extensive woodland with superb views across the Weald. **Birds** Stonechat, willow tit, green woodpecker, long-tailed tit. **Plants** Fungi.
NATIONAL TRUST

C:4 IDE HILL
Near Westerham; *car park at TQ 487517.*
- Mixed woodland, heath.
- Wooded ridge close to Toys Hill, with superb views of the Weald on a clear day. Plants Fungi.
NATIONAL TRUST

C:5 HANGING BANK & BROCKHOULT MOUNT
Near Sevenoaks; *park at Ide Hill (TQ 487517) and walk E to TQ 497518.*
- Mixed woodland.
A wooded ridge with magnificent views towards the Weald and Bough Beech reservoir. **Birds** Sparrowhawk, blackcap. **Plants** Fungi.
NATIONAL TRUST

Little ringed plover – see C:2.

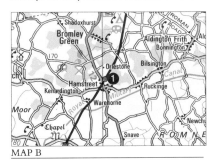

MAP B

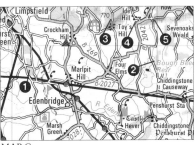

MAP C

KENT

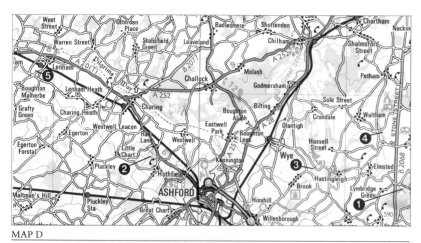

MAP D

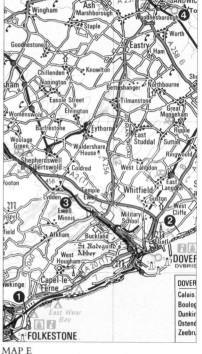

MAP E

D:1 LYMINGE WEST WOOD

Near Canterbury; car park and picnic area at TR 138443.

■ Mature conifer plantation.

■ A 2¼-mile (3.5-km) forest walk, best in spring and summer. **Birds** Crossbill, goldcrest, woodpeckers, coal tit, sparrowhawk.

FORESTRY COMMISSION

D:2 HOTHFIELD COMMON

Near Ashford; parking and numerous footpaths at TQ 972458.

■ Mixed woodland, heath, valley bog.

■ This LNR, consisting of acid heath and valley bog lying on sand and clay, is almost the only wet peat in Kent. It is managed to prevent invasion by bracken. **Birds** Tree pipit, green woodpecker. **Plants** Heath spotted-orchid, sundews, bog asphodel. **Insects** Dragonflies, bugs, beetles, sand wasps.

KENT TRUST FOR NATURE CONSERVATION

D:3 WYE DOWNS★

Near Wye; car park and information centre at TR 077455. Keep to footpaths, unless permit obtained.

■ Chalk downland, scrub.

■ In an impressive area of steep chalk slopes, much of this reserve is still open downland, despite invasion by scrub. There is plenty to see from the public paths in both spring and summer: typical chalk-loving plants, such as salad burnet, dropwort and horseshoe vetch and an impressive number of orchids, including fragrant, pyramidal and bee as well as several Kent specialities.

Insects abound in the herb-rich grassland and include stripe-winged and several other species of grasshopper. **Plants** Orchids, stemless thistle, sainfoin, milkwort. **Butterflies** Blues, skippers, marbled white.

NATURE CONSERVANCY COUNCIL

D:4 YOCKLETTS BANK★★

Near Canterbury; park at T-junction near Yockletts Farm (not near reserve entrance) and walk to reserve at TR 125477. Keep to footpaths and tracks.

■ Mixed woodland.

■ Nearly 59 acres of mixed, coppiced woodland are maintained to encourage the plants in the understorey and in woodland glades. Tree species include hornbeam, ash, field maple, beech, oak, hazel, spindle and purging buckthorn. But the reserve is famous for its orchids. Impressive lady orchids grow alongside early-purple and greater butterfly-orchids; other flowers include wood anemone, wood spurge and primrose.

Coppicing has encouraged a variety of warblers to nest and in late spring nightingales compete with blackcaps and garden warblers for the richest song. **Plants** Lady, fly, early-purple and greater butterfly-orchids.

KENT TRUST FOR NATURE CONSERVATION

D:5 KILN WOOD

Near Ashford; reserve lies at TQ 888513. Open access but keep to footpaths.

■ Coppiced woodland.

■ Coppices of varying age provide a mixture of woodland habitats and a good ground flora; there is also a small pond. Best in spring and summer. **Plants** Herb Paris, early-purple orchid, common twayblade. **Birds** Woodcock.

KENT TRUST FOR NATURE CONSERVATION

E:1 FOLKESTONE WARREN★

Near Folkestone; park near coast and walk to TR 242373.

■ Cliff, undercliff, grassland, foreshore.

■ This excellent area of chalk cliffs, landslips and scrub supports both chalk-loving and maritime plants. Orchids, spiny restharrow, rock sea-lavender and sea-heath are among the more unusual plants which grow in the open areas. This has been a classic site for entomologists for more than a century; the rich and varied insect community includes many rare species of bugs and beetles. It is boosted in spring and summer by migrant *Lepidoptera* from the Continent such as the painted lady and clouded yellow butterflies and the humming-bird hawk-moth. Birds include resident fulmars and, in spring, a variety of common migrants. In winter, black redstarts feed along the cliff edge, and the sewage outfall at nearby Copt Point regularly attracts Mediterranean gulls. **Insects** grey and great green bush-crickets; chinch-bug.

SHEPWAY DISTRICT COUNCIL

E:2 SOUTH FORELAND CLIFFS

Near Dover; park on nearby minor roads and head for TR 340427. Open access from numerous paths.

■ Chalk downland, scrub, cliffs.

■ Magnificent chalk cliffs and downland. **Plants** Knapweed broomrape, Nottingham catchfly. Insects Great green bush-cricket; chalkhill blue and clouded yellow butterflies.

E:3 LYDDEN DOWN★

Near Dover; reserve lies at TR 278453. Open access.

■ Chalk downland.

■ One of Kent's finest areas of chalk downland, on steep, rabbit-grazed slopes, Lydden Down is a riot of colour in early summer with the yellow of common rock-rose, yellow-wort and horseshoe vetch contrast-

Badger – see C:6, Ashdown Forest.

ing with the pink of centaury and several species of orchid. These downland plants provide food for the larvae of many species of butterfly; chalkhill blue and marbled white are among the more interesting. Grasshoppers and bush-crickets thrive in the short turf; at least eight species have been recorded.

Gorse and hawthorn provide cover for birds such as whitethroat and yellowhammer.

KENT TRUST FOR NATURE CONSERVATION

E:4 SANDWICH BAY*

Near Sandwich; take toll-road from Sandwich and park on sea-front. Keep to footpaths.
■ Sand dune, foreshore, grazing marsh.
■ Fine area of sand dune, coastal marsh and foreshore. Sandwich is well known for its plants, notably a variety of orchids and both clove-scented and carrot broomrapes. Above the high-tide line are sea-holly and yellow horned-poppy; in more stabilized areas, look carefully to find sand catchfly and spring vetch. The whole area is excellent for migrant birds and winter visitors and a bird observatory keeps records of sightings. During the breeding season, terns and waders are protected. In winter the beach regularly has a sizable flock of snow buntings.

KENT TRUST FOR NATURE
CONSERVATION/ROYAL SOCIETY FOR THE
PROTECTION OF BIRDS/NATIONAL TRUST

F:1 KEMSING DOWNS

Near Sevenoaks; reserve starts at TQ 550594; keep to footpaths.
■ Chalk downland, scrub, broad-leaved woodland.
■ Good chalk downland with invasive scrub and an old chalk pit. **Plants** Common spotted-orchid, spurge-laurel. **Butterflies** Chalkhill blue, grizzled and Essex skippers, brown argus.

KENT TRUST FOR NATURE CONSERVATION

F:2 TROSLEY
COUNTRY PARK

Near Maidstone; parking and numerous footpaths at TQ 644613. Open 9 am – dusk.
■ Mixed woodland, scrub, chalk downland.
■ Offers a variety of interesting chalk habitats. **Birds** Lesser whitethroat. **Plants** Yellow-wort, orchids. **Insects** Stripe-winged grasshopper.

KENT COUNTY COUNCIL

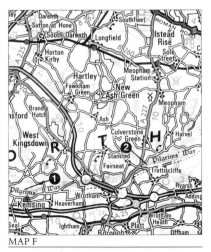
MAP F

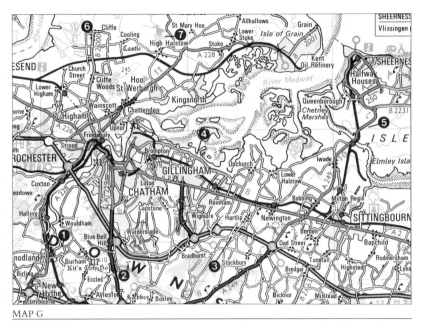
MAP G

G:1 BURHAM MARSH

Near Chatham; keep to footpath from TQ 716619.
■ Marsh, reed-bed, river.
■ A pleasant walk along the banks of the river Medway overlooking marshes and other wetland habitats; best in spring and summer for the migrant birds and rare plants such as marsh sow-thistle.

KENT TRUST FOR NATURE CONSERVATION

G:2 WESTFIELD WOOD

Near Maidstone; various footpaths lead to reserve at TQ 757610 and 754603.
■ Yew forest, mixed woodland.
■ On the steep slopes of the North Downs close to the Medway Gap. Best in spring and summer. **Trees** Yew, spindle. **Plants** Common twayblade, green hellebore.

KENT TRUST FOR NATURE CONSERVATION

G:3 QUEEN DOWN WARREN*

Near Sittingbourne; park at junction of Yaugher Lane and Hartlip Road at TQ 827629; open access.
■ Chalk downland.
■ Managed to maintain high species diversity, this reserve merits both the SSSI and LNR status. Lying on the south-facing slope of a valley in the North Downs, it was originally managed as a rabbit warren. Centuries of nibbling have produced rich downland turf with many species of orchid along with thyme, yellow-wort and cowslips.

The site is good for butterflies, with chalkhill and Adonis blues and brown argus among the more interesting. The wide variety of invertebrates includes many snails and grasshoppers such as the stripe-winged. **Plants** Early spider, fragrant and bee orchids.

KENT TRUST FOR NATURE CONSERVATION

G:4 RIVERSIDE
COUNTRY PARK*

Near Rainham; signposted car park off B2004.
■ River, salt-marsh, mudflat, ponds, meadows, chalk pit.
■ A variety of habitats along the S shore of the river Medway (leaflets available from GBC). **Birds** Kingfisher, waders, wildfowl.

Plants Round-leaved wintergreen, longleaf, sea-lavender. **Insects** Roesel's bush-cricket, dragonflies, damselflies, lesser marsh grasshopper.

GILLINGHAM BOROUGH COUNCIL

G:5 ELMLEY MARSHES**

Near Sittingbourne; take track heading E off A249 one mile (1.5 km) N of the Kingsferry Bridge on to Isle of Sheppey at TQ 926708. One-mile walk from information centre to hides; disabled persons may drive. Open 9am – 9pm (or dusk) exc Tue; small fee unless RSPB member.
■ Grazing marsh, freshwater scrapes.
■ Elmley includes fine areas of undisturbed and undeveloped coastal marsh, mudflat and salt-marsh. During the summer, yellow wagtail, snipe and redshank breed and ruff often stay late enough to show off their summer plumage. Autumn brings thousands of waders, among them curlew and dunlin, as well as wildfowl such as wigeon and teal. Raptors, including hen harrier, merlin and short-eared owl are also frequently recorded.

Strategically placed hides afford excellent viewing; rarities recorded in recent years include lesser golden plover and black-winged stilt.

ROYAL SOCIETY FOR THE PROTECTION OF BIRDS

G:6 CLIFFE
MARSHES*

Near Rochester; parking in Cliffe village. Keep to tracks and footpaths across marsh.
■ Grazing marsh, pools, mudflats.
■ A remnant of the once extensive North Kent marshes, Cliffe provides some excellent birdwatching, particularly in spring and summer. Part of the area is reclaimed salt-marsh, now grazed. In these fields both yellow wagtails and snipe breed, and summer-plumage ruff often linger late enough in the spring to provide courtship displays.

Several pools attract waders, especially at high tide. Unusual birds are often recorded and have included broad-billed sandpiper as well as regular sightings of curlew sandpiper and Temminck's stint. **Plants** Small-red goosefoot (Chenopodium botryodes), glasswort.

KENT

G:7 NORTHWARD HILL*

Near Rochester; entry from Northwood Road in High Halstow at TQ 784759. Open access to public area; sanctuary requires escort.

■ Oak woodland, scrub.

■ Part of the Kent marshes, this is one of the richest and most impressive woodlands in southern England. The RSPB's woodland reserve contains a thriving heronry, the largest in Britain, and can be viewed from an elevated hide. Hawfinch and long-eared owl are also occasionally seen and nightingales can be heard during spring.

The water meadows, grazing marsh and pools around the area attract huge numbers of migrant and wintering waders and wildfowl; there are excellent views from the road and many tracks. **Butterflies** White-letter hairstreak, Essex skipper.
ROYAL SOCIETY FOR THE PROTECTION OF BIRDS

H:1 CHURCH WOOD**

Near Canterbury; car park at TR 123593.

■ Coppiced woodland.

■ From the RSPB car park several nature trails lead through splendid mixed woodland. The habitats include mature oak stands, coppiced areas and wide woodland rides which insects favour. Woodland birds are well represented, with woodpeckers, nuthatch and redstart much in evidence. The rich plant life inclues an abundance of cowwheat, providing food for the larvae of Church Wood's most interesting butterfly, the heath fritillary; the many other species include speckled wood and purple hairstreak. **Birds** Woodpeckers, redstart, nuthatch. **Plants** Wood anemone. **Insects** Dark bush-cricket.
ROYAL SOCIETY FOR THE PROTECTION OF BIRDS

H:2 BLEAN WOODS*

Near Canterbury; footpaths to reserve at TR 118611. Permit required to stray off footpaths.

■ Coppiced woodland.

■ Coppiced hornbeam, ash and sweet chestnut with oak standards. Leaflet available from NCC. **Plants** Wood anemone, bluebell, wood sorrel. **Birds** Woodpeckers, nuthatch. **Insects** Purple hairstreak and heath fritillary butterflies; oak bush-cricket.
NATURE CONSERVANCY COUNCIL

H:3 OARE MEADOW

Near Faversham; reserve starts at TR 007627. Keep to footpaths.

■ Pasture.

■ A small, grazed meadow with wet hollows and a tidal stream.
KENT TRUST FOR NATURE CONSERVATION

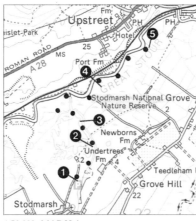

1:50 000, MAP H:A

H:A STODMARSH**

Near Canterbury.

■ Reed-bed, lakes, grazing marsh.

① Park in NCC car park, reached along a rough track from Stodmarsh village. Inspect alders for flocks of siskin and redpoll.

② Walk along raised bank, called the Lampen Wall, through carr and reed-bed. Reed and sedge warblers are heard in summer, water rails in winter. Cetti's warbler and bearded tit occur throughout the year.

③ Continue along Lampen Wall until you reach open water to the W and reed-bed to the E. Excellent for grebes, wildfowl, hirundines and swifts in summer. Savi's warblers may sing close to the path. Marsh harriers pass through in spring and hen harriers feed and roost in the reed-bed in winter. The ditches contain greater spearwort, water dock, frogbit and bogbean.

④ The walk continues along the bank of the River Stour with reed-beds on the right. Almost every bush will contain a Cetti's warbler. The path leads to grazing fields which occasionally flood: good for yellow wagtail and garganey in spring; snipe and redshank breed here.

⑤ Continue to Grove Ferry. Hen harrier and merlin are regular in winter. Great grey shrike and rough-legged buzzard are sometimes seen in the area.
NATURE CONSERVANCY COUNCIL

Long-eared owl – see G:7, Northward Hill.

H:4 SOUTH SWALE

Near Faversham; use coastal footpath; keep to footpaths.

■ Foreshore, salt-marsh.

■ Migrant and wintering wildfowl and waders; maritime plants around the high-tide line. **Birds** Brent goose, wigeon, dunlin, knot, redshank, oystercatcher. **Plants** Sea-lavender, yellow horned-poppy.
KENT TRUST FOR NATURE CONSERVATION

H:5 EAST BLEAN WOOD

Near Canterbury; reserve lies at TR 182647. Keep to footpaths.

■ Coppiced woodland.

■ Typical of the woods round Canterbury: oak standards with mixed coppice below and a wealth of spring flowers.
KENT TRUST FOR NATURE CONSERVATION

H:6 RECULVER MARSHES

Near Whitstable; view from roads, public footpaths and sea wall.

■ Grazing marsh, foreshore.

■ In winter, a haunt of wildfowl and raptors on the grazing marsh and waders and wildfowl on the foreshore; in summer, a holiday spot. **Birds** (winter) Hen harrier, rough-legged buzzard, merlin, greylag goose, ruff, waders, Lapland bunting. **Plants** Sea-lavender, yellow horned-poppy.

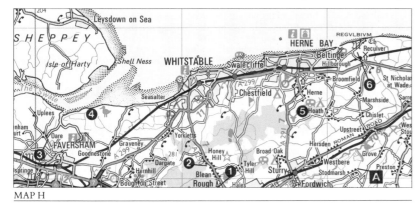

MAP H

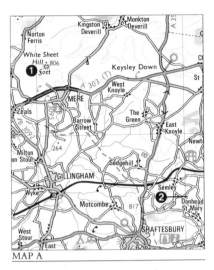

MAP A

A:1 WHITE SHEET HILL★
Near Mere; park at ST 798350 (limited space); keep to footpaths.
■ High quality chalk grassland.
■ An abandoned chalk pit has been colonized by typical chalk grassland species; impressive butterfly population.
Plants Orchids (especially common spotted), rock-rose, cowslips. **Butterflies** Dark green fritillary and marbled white breed. **Birds** Corn bunting.
WILTSHIRE TRUST FOR NATURE CONSERVATION

A:2 OYSTERS COPPICE
Near Shaftesbury; park on green at ST 894259; enter wood on public footpath by bungalow on N of green.
■ Derelict hazel coppice.
■ Coppicing and re-planting are restoring diversity of plant/animal life. **Birds** Winter flock of siskins and tits, breeding wood warblers. **Mammals** Badger, fox.
WILTSHIRE TRUST FOR NATURE CONSERVATION

B:1 STOCKTON WOOD & EARTHWORKS
Near Wylye; park in lay-by on A303 at ST 965356; enter by bridle-paths at ST 961354 or ST 975356. Access restricted to bridle-paths.
■ Mixed woodland, steep chalk down.
■ Celtic field system and other archaeological remains add interest.

B:2 WYLYE DOWN★
Near Wylye; enter reserve by public footpath

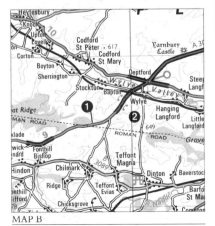

MAP B

which leaves Wylye village at SU 004377. Permit required to leave right of way – apply NCC.
■ Outstanding chalk downland and Celtic field systems.
■ The 84-acre reserve was acquired in 1978 to protect the exceptionally rich chalk downland flora which survives here, maintained by a traditional grazing pattern. No ploughing, re-seeding or fertilizer application has taken place, so the rich flora has survived intact. Over 40 species of flowering plants can occur within a square yard. Dwarf sedge and quaking-grass are common and rock-rose blooms on steep slopes in summer. Among the grasses is an abundance of herbs and an impressive population of butterflies and grasshoppers. The numerous ant-hills also support a rich flora. **Plants** Frog, bee and burnt orchids, round-headed rampion, field fleawort. **Butterflies** 32 species recorded; chalk-hill, small blue and others breed.
NATURE CONSERVANCY COUNCIL

C:1 PEPPERBOX HILL
Near Salisbury; park in lay-by on A36 at SU 212248; access on bridle-path only.
■ Juniper scrub invading chalk grassland.
■ Several stages visible in the progression from open downland to beech woodland; rich variety of shrub species and chalk flora. **Plants** Juniper, pyramidal orchid, small scabious, guelder-rose. **Trees** Whitebeam, wayfaring-tree.
NATIONAL TRUST

C:2 BLACKMOOR COPSE
Near Salisbury; limited parking on verge at SU 231289. Use footpaths.
■ Ancient woodland, 19thC woodland, coppice.
■ Ground flora typical of woodland on clay, includes some meadow species. The site is specially noted for butterflies. **But-**

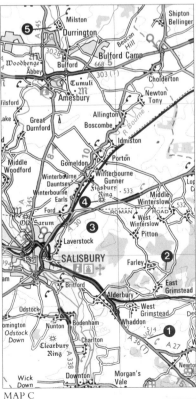

MAP C

terflies Purple emperor. **Birds** Woodcock, nightingale. **Plants** Adder's-tongue, devil's-bit scabious.
WILTSHIRE TRUST FOR NATURE CONSERVATION

C:3 COCKEY DOWN
Near Salisbury; park near school in Laverstock at SU 160310, follow track east on to the downs. Keep to footpaths.
■ Chalk grassland.
■ Rich chalk flora and associated insects.
WILTSHIRE TRUST FOR NATURE CONSERVATION

C:4 FIGSBURY RING
Near Salisbury; park near church in Winterbourne Dauntsey and follow lane SE on to down. Open all year, keep to footpath.
■ Chalk grassland, scrub.
■ Chalk flora.
NATIONAL TRUST

C:5 RIVER AVON
Near Durrington; park near church in Durrington and follow footpath signs. Keep to footpaths.
■ Chalk stream, watermeadows.
■ Managed as a trout fishery. Very clear water allows close views of aquatic life.
Insects Damselflies, mayflies. **Birds** Kingfisher, grey wagtail.

Kingfisher – see C:5.

MAP D

The golden blooms of **marsh marigold** *(above) brighten damp woodland marshes, fens and ditches, from Mar until late summer, flowering best in partial shade. In southern England, the flowers reach 2 in (5 cm) across on tall, upright stems and the bright green leaves are heart-shaped with glossy surfaces.*

Only the male **purple emperor** *(left) has the beautiful iridescent, purple-blue sheen on the wings; the upper wing surfaces of the larger female are dark brown. Southern oak-woods are its stronghold, where males perform gliding, soaring flights across the glades and tree tops from Jul to Aug. It is an elusive butterfly because it prefers the canopy of oak, ash and beech trees, where it feeds on a sweet aphid secretion called honey dew.*

WILTSHIRE

D:1 BROWN'S FOLLY★
Near Bath; public footpaths from Bathford at ST 789665 or ST 797664. Do not enter old mine shafts.
■ Rocky outcrops (Bath stone), old quarry workings, scrub, limestone grassland.
■ Abandoned quarry terraces provide superb range of sheltered habitats for limestone flora, insects and the greater horseshoe bat. Rich downland-type turf in some places; scrub of dogwood, privet, spindle, wayfaring tree and whitebeam in others, and some dense woodland.
AVON WILDLIFE TRUST

D:2 KENNET AND AVON CANAL
Near Trowbridge; access along towpaths and bridle-path.
■ Canal, meadows.

D:3 RACK HILL
Castle Combe; park in Castle Combe at ST 845777. Approach on foot, cross bridge next to Bybrook House. Keep to footpaths.
■ Valley on limestone, grassland, scrub.
■ The turf supports limestone plant species. Scrub clearance takes place occasionally and no fertilizers are used.
WILTSHIRE TRUST FOR NATURE CONSERVATION

E:1 JONES'S MILL
Near Pewsey; park after crossing railway bridge; enter reserve by green lane.
■ Wet meadow, chalk stream.
■ Contains many species scarce in the area that grow in waterlogged peat. **Plants** Bog pimpernel, flea sedge, bogbean, marsh arrow-grass. **Birds** (Winter) five species of tits, water rail, kingfisher. **Butterflies** Marsh fritillary.
WILTSHIRE TRUST FOR NATURE CONSERVATION

E:2 KENNET AND AVON CANAL
Near Pewsey; join towpath near Pewsey at SU 174617 and follow E to Newbury and beyond.
■ Canal.
■ The canal was built to link the Avon and Kennet waterways, thus joining London with Bristol via the Thames. It meanders through lowland England, fed largely from chalk streams. This has encouraged the growth of a rich and varied plant life which in turn supports an abundance of invertebrates such as dragonflies, damselflies, water beetles and molluscs. Many species of water birds live along the canal, including kingfisher, water rail, reed and sedge warblers, reed bunting and sand martin. At intervals along the canal 'flashes' were built to provide water storage for the locks and turning areas for long barges. These quiet backwaters provide excellent habitats for stillwater species of fish, especially the pike, which can sometimes be seen resting quietly in the weeds. **Plants** Fringed water lily.

E:3 ROUNDWAY HILL COVERT
Near Devizes; SU 005647. Leaflet available from FC for countryside trail.
■ Mixed woodland with box understorey.
■ Small clearings with chalk flora add diversity. Woodland birds, butterflies, grasshoppers in clearings.
FORESTRY COMMISSION

E:4 SAVERNAKE FOREST★
Near Marlborough; entry at various points where roads and paths cross the forest. Keep to footpaths.
■ Ancient woodland.
■ Until the 16thC Savernake was a royal hunting forest. Much of the ancient woodland has been felled and replanted with conifers but many very old trees remain and large areas of broadleaved woodland can still be found. The clay-with-flints soil encourages plants which thrive in damper conditions. Rides and clearings provide enough light for agrimony, willowherbs, lady's bedstraw and meadowsweet to grow. The abundance of old trees and leaf litter provides ideal conditions for fungi in autumn. Deer are present, though seen closely only by the quiet observer. Good populations of woodland birds. **Mammals** Roe and muntjac deer. **Birds** (Breeding) woodcock, tawny owl; (winter) brambling, tits.
FORESTRY COMMISSION

E:5 CHERHILL DOWN
Near Calne; rights of way lead on to down from A4. Keep to footpaths/bridle-paths.
■ Chalk grassland.
■ Good range of chalk grassland plants (including orchids), insects and butterflies. Extensive views.

E:6 FYFIELD DOWN★
Near Marlborough; park in Avebury and enter reserve from footpath which leaves Avebury at SU 103700. Off right of way, NCC permit required.
■ Chalk grassland.
■ The reserve is of interest for the vast number of sarsen stones which litter the surface of the 613-acre site. The sarsens support an important lichen population which owes its richness to the lack of pollution and the great age of the stones. The many voles and field mice in turn encourage birds of prey to live here. Skylarks, corn buntings and wheatears breed in summer; short-eared owls patrol in winter. Small ponds and scrub patches add diversity to the reserve. **Plants** Meadow saxifrage, frog orchid, chalk milk-

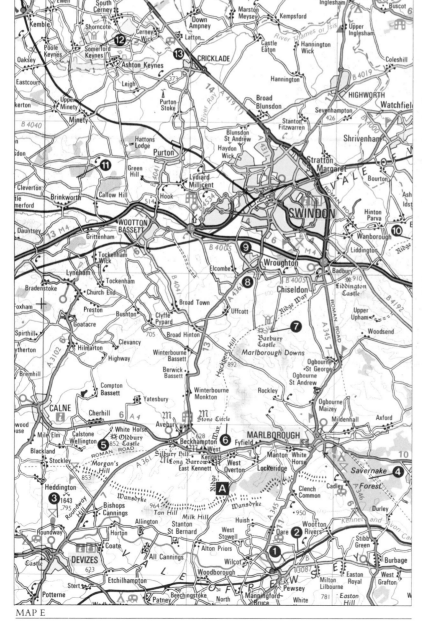

MAP E

wort, salad burnet, early gentian; acid-tolerant species such as thyme-leaved sandwort near Sarsen stones.
NATURE CONSERVANCY COUNCIL

E:7 BARBURY CASTLE COUNTRY PARK
Near Swindon; entrance on Marlborough Downs at SU 157761.
■ Chalk grassland.
■ Good range of chalk grassland plants (including orchids) and insects; extensive views N. Short turf maintained by grazing.
WILTSHIRE COUNTY COUNCIL

E:8 CLOUTS WOOD NATURE TRAIL
Near Wroughton; park in lay-by on A361; follow sign to 'Clouts Wood'; keep to footpaths.
■ Mixed oak/ash woodland.
■ Steep chalk hillside with old coppiced areas, regenerating wych elms and rich ground flora. **Mammals** Bats roost in older trees, badger, fox. **Plants** Bath asparagus, wood vetch.
WILTSHIRE TRUST FOR NATURE CONSERVATION

E:9 COATE WATER COUNTRY PARK
Near Swindon; access from roundabout on A345 at junction with B4006. Car park at SU 177827. Permit required for bird reserve, available from warden's office.
■ Lake, wetland.
■ An impressive variety of birds has been recorded, especially during migration; many species breed.
THAMESDOWN BOROUGH COUNCIL

E:10 THE RIDGE WAY PATH*
Near Avebury; the long distance waymarked route starts near Avebury at SU 118681, and ends at Ivinghoe Beacon in Buckinghamshire. Guide book from HMSO.
■ Ancient track on chalk downs.
■ Dating from at least 2500 BC the Ridge Way runs from Avebury, once the cultural centre of Britain, to the Thames near Streatley. It is strewn with ancient monuments, as it was once a vital trade and military route. Lapwings and partridges breed in the fields and interesting chalk flora survives on ancient grassy banks. Foxes and badgers are present and many small mammals breed in the grassier areas. Birds of prey may be seen in winter, including short-eared owls, buzzard and, rarely, rough-legged buzzards. The path provides a vital link between the isolated outcrops of unimproved chalk downland. **Plants** Bee, frog and butterfly orchids. **Mammals** Roe deer, several badger setts.

E:11 SOMERFORD COMMON
Near Swindon; enter reserve at SU 024863.
■ Mixed woodland on clay, rides and clearings.
■ Originally part of the mediaeval Braydon Forest, felled by the FC in the late 1950s. Regeneration has taken place. **Plants** Early-purple orchid, false oxlip. **Birds** Nightingales breed.
WILTSHIRE TRUST FOR NATURE CONSERVATION

E:12 COTSWOLD WATER PARK
Near Cirencester; access at SU 027955, from A419 and minor road to South Cerney. Permits needed for some areas: apply warden's office. Leaflets from GCC or WCC.
■ Abandoned, flooded gravel workings.
■ A vast network of lime-rich lakes with abundant invertebrate life, supporting many species of fish, birds and aquatic plants. **Birds** Marsh warbler, regular garganey, water rail, little ringed plover, great crested grebe, grasshopper warbler.
WILTSHIRE COUNTY COUNCIL/ GLOUCESTERSHIRE COUNTY COUNCIL

E:13 NORTH MEADOW**
Near Cricklade; park in large lay-by on B4041 at SU 099944. Keep to footpath. Permit required to leave right of way: apply NCC.

Butterfly orchid – see E:10.

■ Meadow, river.
■ North Meadow is one of the finest examples of an ancient meadow in Britain. Particularly noteworthy is the huge population of snake's head fritillaries, making up 80 per cent of the British total. There is an abundance of other meadow plants which make the site one of great beauty in early summer. The cycle of hay-making, grazing and winter flooding is thought to have continued for over 800 years and is responsible for the richness of the wildlife. By the time the hay is cut in July the meadow flowers have set seed and the subsequent grazing helps maintain the diversity of flora. The infant river Thames alongside has a healthy fish and invertebrate population; many water birds feed and breed here. **Plants** Meadow rue, adder's tongue, southern marsh orchid. **Birds** Kingfisher, grey wagtail. **Insects** Dragonflies, damselflies.
NATURE CONSERVANCY COUNCIL

E:A KNAP HILL & PEWSEY DOWNS**
Near Pewsey; park just off road at SU 116638. Enter reserve along bridle-paths. Leaflets and permit for Milk Hill from NCC. Access unrestricted except on Milk Hill where visitors must keep to paths.
■ Chalk escarpment.
① Follow bridle-path SE on to down; look and listen for corn buntings along fences.
② Follow track down steep gulley; banks excellent for chalk flora including round-headed rampion. Warblers breed in scrub patches and in sunny weather, bank is good for butterflies.
③ Retrace steps to bridle-path, then cross stile to reach top of Knap Hill. Slopes have many orchids, including bee and frog, and other chalk herbs such as field fleawort. Tuberous thistle may be found on S slopes. Remains of Neolithic causeway camp may be identified on hill top.
④ Return to road and walk down to cutting at SU 109628, part of ancient 'Ridge Way'. Kestrels usually hunt over edge of downs, and there are fine views of Vale of Pewsey.
⑤ Follow footpath back up hill to summit and along top to White Horse. Many ant-hills here, indicating ancient grassland, each with its own collection of chalk grassland plants, worth close examination. Look for thyme, bastard toadflax

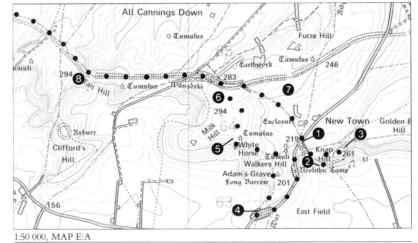

1:50 000, MAP E:A

and horseshoe vetch.
⑥ Grassland here very rich with excellent mixture of herbs, grasses and sedges. Glaucous sedge and sheep's fescue dominate with stemless thistle and salad burnet. Good on sunny days for butterflies. Look for brown argus, chalk-hill and little blues; marsh fritillary present in this dry site because of abundance of devil's-bit scabious.

⑦ Return to starting point along bridle-path. Note marked contrast between ancient pasture of reserve and intensively farmed land N of track.
⑧ It is possible to continue along the Wansdyke path for many miles where more chalk flora and fauna abounds. Best June for orchids and other flora.
NATURE CONSERVANCY COUNCIL

BERKSHIRE

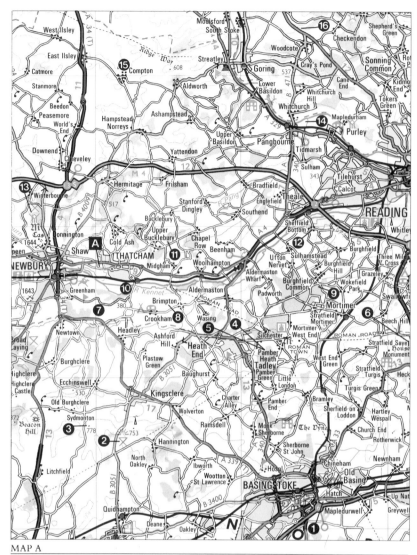

MAP A

A:1 BLACK DAM

Near Basingstoke; *park by Black Dam Lake (SU 651518) and take subway under motorway to nature reserve. Keep to footpaths. Permit required off footpaths.*
■ Wet woodland, scrub.
■ Surprisingly good for woodland birds. Kingfisher or grey wagtail occasionally at lakes by car park.
HAMPSHIRE AND ISLE OF WIGHT NATURALISTS' TRUST

A:2 WHITE HILL

Near Kingsclere; *park in lay-by at SU 516565 or in Kingsclere and walk S. Keep to footpaths.*
■ Chalk downland.
■ A remnant of chalk downland in a 'sea' of arable. **Invertebrates** Marbled white, common blue, grasshoppers, round-mouthed snail.

A:3 LADLE HILL

Near Kingsclere; *park in lay-by at SU 492566 or in Burghclere village and walk. Keep to footpaths.*
■ Chalk downland.
■ Good chalk flora on an ancient hill fort; excellent views. In some years grazing pressure reduces species. **Plants** Cowslip, frog orchid, clustered bellflower, squinancy-

wort. **Birds** Skylark, kestrel. **Insects** Grasshoppers, marbled white butterfly, six-spot burnet moth.

A:4 SILCHESTER COMMON

Near Tadley; *park on Impstone Road (SU 617623) and follow tracks.*
■ Heath, birch scrub, bog.
■ A relict area of N Hampshire heath, subject to considerable public disturbance. The burnt areas can be good for reptiles and butterflies, while the dead trees provide perches for heathland birds. **Birds** Stonechat, nightjar. **Reptiles** Common lizard, adder. **Butterflies** Silver-studded blue, grayling. **Orthoptera** Woodland grasshopper, bog bush-cricket. **Plants** Bog asphodel, sundew, bell heather.

A:5 PAMBER FOREST★★

Near Tadley; *park on Impstone Road (SU 617623) and keep to footpaths criss-crossing the forest.*
■ Mature, broad-leaved woodland.
■ The best example in N Hampshire of mature woodland, Pamber Forest contains many ancient stands of oak. The area is actively managed with conservation and species diversity in mind. In early spring, the forest is alive with bird song and the drumming of woodpeckers, which nest in the

older trees. Selective coppicing has produced patches of open woodland which are good for spring flowers. Later in the season, many insects including at least 15 species of butterfly are attracted to the bramble patches and hogweed umbels. Mammals are well represented, with dormouse and yellow-necked mouse among the more unusual. Foxes and roe deer are present, but are retiring and seldom seen. **Plants** Wood anemone, early purple orchid, twayblade, wood sorrel. **Butterflies** Silver-washed fritillary, purple emperor, white admiral.
ENGLEFIELD ESTATE

A:6 WELLINGTON COUNTRY PARK

Near Basingstoke; *access from A33 between Basingstoke and Reading at SU 724627. Small entrance fee.*
■ Lake, mixed woodland.
■ Five nature trails pass through woodland and around the lake. Wildfowl, interesting marginal plants. **Birds** Goosander, great crested grebe, nuthatch, woodpecker. **Mammals** Roe deer, fallow deer. **Butterflies** Comma, white admiral, speckled wood.
WELLINGTON ENTERPRISES

A:7 BOWDOWN WOODS

Near Newbury; *access via rights of way from Greenham or Thatcham to reserve at SU 504647. Keep to footpaths.*
■ Mixed woodland.
■ The woodland is ancient. **Birds** Green woodpecker, nuthatch. **Plants** Opposite-leaved golden saxifrage. **Butterflies** White admiral, speckled wood.
BERKS, BUCKS & OXON. NATURALISTS' TRUST

A:8 BRIMPTON GRAVEL PITS★

Near Newbury; *limited parking at SU 568650. Keep to footpaths.*
■ Lake.
■ A series of flooded gravel pits – colonized by aquatic life and attractive to birds, including migrants and winter wildfowl.

A:9 WOKEFIELD COMMON

Near Reading; *limited parking at SU 653662.*
■ Heathland, woodland, ponds.
■ Rather spoilt by public pressure, but still retains much of its wildlife interest. **Birds** Siskin, goldcrest, green woodpecker. **Insects** Silver-studded blue butterfly, pine hawk moth. **Reptiles & amphibians** Palmate newt, common lizard.

A:10 KENNET & AVON CANAL TOWPATH

Thatcham; *park in Thatcham and join towpath at SU 528663. Walk E or W.*
■ Canal.
■ Pleasant walks along towpath; aquatic life. **Birds** Water rail, grey wagtail, moorhen, little grebe, reed bunting. **Insects** Dragonflies, damselflies, aquatic insects. **Plants** Flowering rush.

A:11 BUCKLEBURY COMMON★

Near Newbury; *park off road at SU 555692.*
■ Heathland, woodland, ponds.
■ This area of heathland is now much overgrown with birch and conifer woodland. The few heathland pools support several species of dragonfly and damselfly.
Many characteristic heathland birds have disappeared, but green woodpeckers, tree

BERKSHIRE

pipit and the occasional nightingale can be found. Flocks of siskin and redpoll are most evident in winter.

Bucklebury Common boasts an impressive array of fungi, particularly after a wet summer. The colourful fly agaric is common around the base of birch trees. There are several species of *Boletus* present as well as earth-star fungi and the strangely convoluted *Helvella*. **Birds** Siskin, redpoll, tree pipit, long-tailed tit. **Plants** Fungi.

A:12 THEALE GRAVEL PITS★
Near Reading; Gravel pits centred around SU 649699; view from roads and keep to footpaths.
■ Lakes.
■ The vast gravel deposits of the Thames basin have been extensively exploited by man for decades. In the Theale area this has left a complex network of gravel pits.

The flooded ones attract vast numbers of wildfowl, great crested grebe and gulls together with a splendid variety of migrants and vagrants. In the drier areas, little ringed plover and lapwing may try to nest, and numerous waders pass through on passage. Canada geese and yellow wagtails prefer the grassy slopes around the banks of these pits. **Insects** Dragonflies.

A:13 SNELSMORE COMMON COUNTRY PARK★
Near Newbury; park at SU 463711.
■ Heathland, woodland.
■ One of Berkshire's best areas of heathland, woodland and valley bog is here. The heath and birch scrub contain characteristic birds such as stonechat, tree pipit and willow warbler in addition to more unusual species like nightjar, woodcock and grasshopper warbler. On a warm evening in early summer you might hear their calls, and perhaps even get a fleeting glimpse of them. **Birds** Stonechat, green woodpecker. **Plants** Round-leaved sundew, bog asphodel, bogbean. **Insects** Dragonflies, damselflies.
NEWBURY DISTRICT COUNCIL

A:14 RIVER THAMES
Pangbourne; View from footpath which starts at SU 635768.
■ River, water meadow.
■ Flower-rich water meadows along the banks of the Thames – one of the river's most popular spots. **Insects** Club-tailed dragonfly, damselflies.
NATIONAL TRUST

A:15 COMPTON & BLEWBURY DOWNS
Near Newbury; walk N from Compton or SW from Blewbury to area around SU 513827. Keep to footpaths.
■ Chalk downland, scrub.
■ The downland has been much altered by modern agriculture but small pockets and strips still remain; interesting for wintering birds. **Birds** Hen harrier, short-eared owl, merlin, thrushes. **Plants** Chalk flora.

A:16 NORTH GROVE WOOD
Near Wallingford; entrance along footpath where the woodland adjoins A4074.
■ Woodland.
■ Mature beechwood with areas of ash/hazel coppice (rare in the Chilterns) supporting a typical chalk flora.
WOODLAND TRUST

Nightjar – see A:4, opposite page.

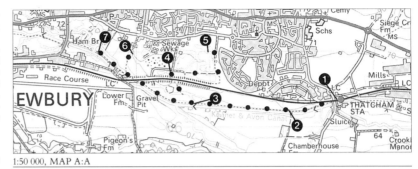

1:50 000, MAP A:A

A:A THATCHAM REED-BEDS★★
Near Newbury; limited parking at Thatcham Station. Keep to footpaths.
■ Reed-beds, lakes, carr.
① Follow towpath along N side of canal towards Newbury. Little grebe, moorhen and grey wagtail on canal and emergent vegetation along the margins.
② Towpath passes through alder carr and reed-beds. Listen for calls of siskin and redpoll in trees. Water rails much in evidence in winter and bearded tit occasionally heard.
③ Just before the canal and river meet, path leads off to right through reed-beds and ponds towards railway. Reed warblers in reed-beds and grebes and wildfowl on water. Hirundines hunt insects in summer. Take great care when crossing the railway.
④ Thatcham Moors nature reserve car park reached by rough track from Thatcham village

or from canal towpath. Lake margins excellent for emergent plants such as greater water plantain and yellow flag. Many interesting species of insect.
⑤ Alternative access point from anglers' car park. Footpaths have changed due to presence of new flooded pits so follow signs. Excellent water-meadow vegetation and interesting water-birds including kingfisher.
⑥ Canal towpath crosses railway and track to right leads through areas of water-meadow plants and reed-beds. Also reached from rough track called Prince Hold Road.
⑦ Path continues towards Newbury.
Birds Great crested grebe, grey heron, sedge warbler. **Plants** Butterbur, common meadow rue. **Dragonflies** Banded agrion, broad bodied libellula, common blue damselfly.
NEWBURY DISTRICT COUNCIL

BERKSHIRE

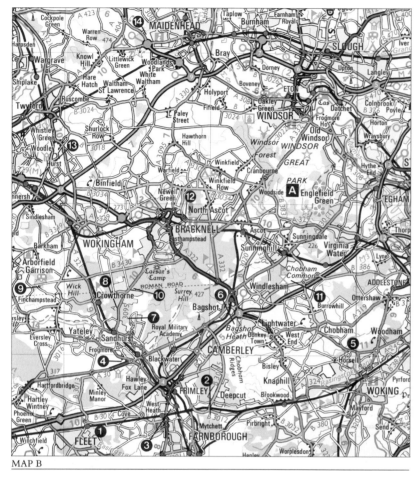

MAP B

B:1 FLEET POND*
Near Aldershot; park at SU 816553 or use small roads leading to water's edge. Footpath runs around margin of lake; wet underfoot.
■ Lake, reed-bed, carr.
■ This is a sizable lake, with extensive reed-beds and carr around its margins and adjoining areas of woodland and heath. It is noted for attracting unusual birds: marsh harrier, bittern and bearded tit are seen annually and rarities have included ring-necked duck, great reed warbler and collared pratincole.

During spring and summer, the lake acts like a magnet to swallows and martins, and hobbies visit regularly. Great crested grebes breed in some numbers together with a healthy population of reed warblers.

There are also good populations of plants such as yellow flag and bladderwort, and a thriving community of aquatic invertebrates such as dragonflies and the raft spider.
HART DISTRICT COUNCIL

B:2 BASINGSTOKE CANAL TOWPATH
Near Woking; A useful starting point is SU 901567.
■ Fresh water.
Not as good as it used to be, but still plenty to see. **Birds** Water rail, grey wagtail, little grebe. **Plants** Lesser water plantain, hornwort. **Insects** Dragonflies, damselflies, water insects.

B:3 FARNBOROUGH & FRIMLEY GRAVEL PITS*
Near Farnborough; approach from Farnborough North railway station at SU 878567.

Keep to footpaths.
■ Lakes.
■ A series of flooded gravel pits attracting a variety of breeding birds but of particular interest for winter wildfowl. **Birds** Smew, great crested grebe, kingfisher.

B:4 YATELEY COMMON
Near Yateley; park at SU 802592.
■ Heath, pond.
■ This extensive area of heath shows all the stages of succession, from recent burning to invasive birch scrub, as well as Sphagnum bog. There is open access but it is worth following the 1-mile (2-km) nature trail. This starts by Wyndham's Pool, which contains a wide variety of aquatic life despite its popularity with anglers and picnickers.

During summer, dragonflies such as the ruddy darter and the emperor hunt over the open areas of heath. In wet autumns, fungi are abundant, especially under the birch scrub. Most of the typical heathland birds breed in the area. During winter, there are roving flocks of siskin, redpoll and long-tailed tit, and you may see great grey shrike. **Plants** Bell heather, cross-leaved heath, marsh St John's wort. **Birds** Stonechat, jay, redpoll. **Fungi** Fly agaric. **Butterflies** Silver-studded blue.
HAMPSHIRE COUNTY COUNCIL

B:5 HORSELL COMMON
Near Woking; car park at TQ 015611.
■ Heathland, scrub.
■ Directions for 4 walks will help you explore the heath; leaflets from Horsell Common Preservation Society. Birds Stonechat.

Plants Dodder. **Insects** Silver-studded blue, grayling, emperor moth.
HORSELL COMMON PRESERVATION SOCIETY/SURREY TRUST FOR NATURE CONSERVATION

B:6 LIGHTWATER COUNTRY PARK
Camberley; park near the sports complex at SU 921622.
■ Heath, woodland, pond.
■ A well-marked nature trail takes in the interesting habitats; leaflet from SHBC. **Birds** Stonechat. **Plants** Heath spotted-orchid, ragged robin. **Reptiles** Common lizard. **Insects** Wood ant, dragonflies.
SURREY HEATH BOROUGH COUNCIL

B:7 OWLSMOOR BOG AND HEATH*
Near Bracknell; access from A3095 or nearby Crowthorne Woods to SU 842622. Open access via obvious tracks.
■ Bog, heathland, woodland.
■ Seventy acres of bog and wet heath adjacent to Edgbarrow Wood and Crowthorne Wood. **Birds** Siskin, goldcrest, green woodpecker. **Insects** Fox moth, dragonflies, damselflies. **Plants** Round-leaved sundew, cottongrass, dwarf gorse.
BERKS, BUCKS & OXON. NATURALISTS' TRUST

B:8 EDGBARROW WOODS*
Near Bracknell; park off the Crowthorne Road (A3095) at SU 837632.
■ Woodland, heath, bog.
■ There are 78 acres of heathland, bog and mixed woodland here, much of it an SSSI. The woodland supports birds such as great spotted woodpecker, siskin and redpoll with a ground cover containing bilberry.

Elsewhere, dry heath grades into bog, providing a rich variety of species in a relatively small area. Silver-studded blues and graylings are common butterflies of the dry parts; common lizards and adders bask in open, sandy patches. The bog is the haunt of several species of dragonfly. Plants such as cottongrass and bog asphodel are characteristic. **Insects** Emperor moth, damselflies.
BRACKNELL DISTRICT COUNCIL

B:9 CALIFORNIA COUNTRY PARK*
Near Wokingham; car park at SU 785651.
■ Woodland, heath, ponds.
■ A variety of rich habitats. Leaflets available for nature walks from Wokingham DC. **Birds** Woodcock, goldcrest, woodpeckers, coal tit. **Reptiles** Grass snake, common lizard. **Amphibians** Palmate newt.
WOKINGHAM DISTRICT COUNCIL

B:10 CROWTHORNE WOOD
Near Bracknell; park at SU 844644 and explore the woodland rides.
■ Mature pine plantation.
■ Extensive woodland with heathland flora in open area; wide rides. **Birds** Crossbill, siskin, green woodpecker. **Mammals** Fallow and roe deer. **Insects** Pine hawk-moth, wood ant.
FORESTRY COMMISSION

B:11 CHOBHAM COMMON
Near Chertsey; numerous car parks in the area, eg off the Chobham Road (B383).
■ Heathland, bog.
■ Renowned amongst Victorian entomologists and spider-hunters as an exceptional area, Chobham Common still retains much of its former interest. This is despite the

occasional fire, increased public pressure and the encroaching birch scrub.

In the wettest areas round-leaved sundew, cottongrass and bog asphodel grow. On higher ground the vegetation is dominated by bell heather and gorse. Many of the invertebrates are of national importance; specialist knowledge is often required to identify them. But the conspicuous bog bush-cricket and the mottled grasshopper should be easily recognized. **Birds** Woodlark, nightjar, stonechat, tree pipit. **Insects** Silver-studded blue, grayling.

SURREY COUNTY COUNCIL

B:12 LILY HILL PARK

Near Bracknell; turn into Lily Hill Road off A329 at Running Horse public house. Car park after ½ mile (0.8 km) at SU 887694.
■ Mixed woodland, parkland.
■ Park and woodland (67 acres) with a marked tree trail and 55 tree species labelled. Information leaflet from Bracknell DC. Woodland birds. **Plants** Rhododendrons.

BRACKNELL DISTRICT COUNCIL

B:13 DINTON PASTURES COUNTRY PARK

Near Wokingham; access from B3030 at SU 785718.
■ Lakes, scrub.
■ A series of flooded gravel pits; rich wetland insect fauna. **Plants** Summer snowflake. **Insects** Ground beetles, soldier-flies.

WOKINGHAM DISTRICT COUNCIL

B:14 MAIDENHEAD THICKET

Maidenhead; park at SU 854815 or SU 855810.

MAP C

■ Scrub, mixed woodland.
■ Features Robin Hood's Arbour, site of a prehistoric farm.

NATIONAL TRUST

C:1 HAM HILL

Near Shalbourne; park at entrance to quarry at SU 333617, just S of Ham village. Permit required: apply WTNC, 19 High Street, Devizes Wiltshire SN10 1AT.
■ Unimproved chalk grassland, scrub.
■ A selection of chalk flora present with associated insects, birds and butterflies.

WILTSHIRE TRUST FOR NATURE CONSERVATION

C:2 INKPEN & WALBURY HILLS★

Near Newbury; park near SU 369621 and follow the ridge. Keep to footpaths.
■ Chalk downland.
■ Migrant birds pass through in spring and autumn, raptors occur in winter. Stunning views N. **Birds** Buzzard, short-eared owl, sparrowhawk, corn bunting.

C:3 INKPEN COMMON★

Near Newbury; reserve lies at SU 382641. Open access, but keep to tracks.
■ Heathland, bog.
■ In the drier parts of this heathland, grassland with gorse and heather predominates. Invading birch controlled occasionally. This habitat supports breeding populations of typical heathland birds – linnet, stonechat and tree pipit. Nightjars attempt to nest in open patches and their strange churring song can be heard from dusk onwards.

The bogs and wet flushes support a rich and varied plant community with bog asphodel and bogbean adding splashes of colour to the lush green *Sphagnum* moss. In the shade of overgrown and wooded areas, marsh marigolds produce their bright yellow flowers in spring. **Birds** Nightingale. **Plants** Heath milkwort, cross-leaved heath, ragged robin.

BERKS, BUCKS & OXON. NATURALISTS' TRUST

C:4 SEVEN BARROWS

Near Wantage; access from minor road at SU 329828.
■ Chalk downland.
■ Chalk flora on a site of some archaeological interest. **Plants** Sainfoin, common rock-rose. **Insects** Common blue, skippers grasshoppers.

BERKS, BUCKS & OXON. NATURALISTS' TRUST

C:5 WHITEHORSE HILL★

Near Wantage; park at SU 297864 and explore the area.
■ Chalk downland.
■ From the hill fort near the highest point, magnificent views can be had over the Vale of the White Horse. Both hill and valley gain their names from the figure of a horse, 374 ft (114 metres) long, carved into the chalk hillside, probably in Saxon times. It is thought to represent a pagan god.

From near the car park you can join a long-distance path, the Ridge Way, and walk either east or west. Modern arable agriculture has altered the area once covered by sheep-grazed downland. However, many of the typical chalk-loving flowers are still present in good numbers. **Birds** Corn bunting. **Plants** Common-spotted orchid, hairy violet, horseshoe vetch, milkwort.

B:A VIRGINIA WATER & WINDSOR GREAT PARK★

Near Windsor.
■ Lake; oak/beech woodland, parkland.
① Park in the large car park and walk NW towards Virginia Water. Search the trees for woodland birds including nuthatch and woodpeckers. In winter, hawfinches, feeding on hornbeam seeds, are more obvious than at other times of year. Beechmast on the ground attracts chaffinch flocks which generally contain a few brambling.
② Walk to the bridge, which gives pleasant views of the lakes. Look for grebes and wildfowl, and in particular mandarin duck which has its British stronghold in the area. The male has splendid wing fans and side whiskers. The female is plain. Splendid mistletoe in the surrounding trees.
③ Numerous tracks and paths lead N through the parkland. Ancient oaks are important for insects. White admirals frequent the bramble flowers in summer. Birds include sparrowhawk and woodpeckers.
④ More views of Virginia Water. Scan the lake for water birds. Carp and tench can sometimes be seen in spring spawning near the edge.
⑤ There are several car parks in the north of Windsor Great Park from which the woodland can be explored. Avoid the plantations and concentrate on the ancient woodland and park. Look for fallow deer, woodland birds and insects; butterflies include white admiral, purple hairstreak, holly blue and large skipper.

Birds (Water) tufted duck, pochard, mallard, great crested grebe, grey heron, coot; (woods and park) redstart, hobby, siskin, redpoll.

CROWN ESTATES COMMISSIONERS

1:50 000, MAP B:A

SURREY

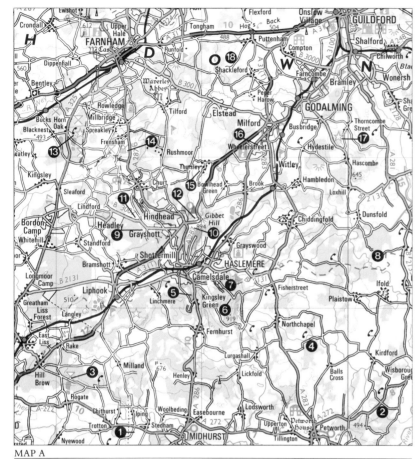

MAP A

A:1 IPING & STEDHAM COMMONS
Near Midhurst; park at SU 845224. The two commons lie S of the A272 to the W and E of the unclassified road S.
■ Heath, scrub.
■ Remnants of heath with communities of representative plants and animals. Best in spring and summer. **Plants** Ling, bell heather, cotton grass, bog asphodel. **Insects** Grayling, mottled grasshopper.
WEST SUSSEX COUNTY COUNCIL/SUSSEX TRUST FOR NATURE CONSERVATION

A:2 THE MENS★★
Near Petworth; parking at TQ 024236.
■ Mixed woodland.
■ An outstanding area of mature woodland, mainly beech, which has remained largely untouched for nearly a century. Many of the trees have reached an immense size. In spring there is a carpet of woodland flowers, particularly in clearings. Bluebells, wood anemone, wood sorrel and wood spurge contrast with the rich brown of the fallen beech leaves. In the canopy, wood warblers sing their trilling song.

Because most of the fallen timber decays where it falls, The Mens is exceptionally rich in slugs, snails and woodlice.
SUSSEX TRUST FOR NATURE CONSERVATION

A:3 TULLECOMBE FOREST
Near Petersfield; car park and picnic area at SU 805255.
■ Mature pine plantation.
■ Signposted forest walk from picnic area along South Downs escarpment.
FORESTRY COMMISSION

A:4 EBERNOE COMMON★
Near Petworth; parking at TQ 976278.
■ Beech and oak woodland.
■ Mature beech woodland with younger areas of oak. Best in spring and summer.
SUSSEX TRUST FOR NATURE CONSERVATION

A:5 MARLEY COMMON
Near Haslemere; park at TQ 890309.
■ Heath, scrub.
■ Heath on sandstone, best in spring and summer. **Birds** Stonechat, tree pipit, linnet, yellowhammer. **Butterflies** Grayling, small copper. **Reptiles** Common lizard, slow-worm.
NATIONAL TRUST

A:6 BLACK DOWN NATURE TRAIL
Near Haslemere; trail starts at SU 921309.
■ *Mixed woodland, grassland.*
■ Wooded slopes surround this the highest point in West Sussex, with commanding views S to the coast. **Birds** Yellowhammer, blackcap. **Butterflies** Speckled wood, silver-washed fritillary.
NATIONAL TRUST

A:7 BARFOLD COPSE
Near Haslemere; access off B2131 ½ mile (0.8 km) E of Haslemere. Park by second turning to Black Down and take footpath to reserve at SU 914324.
■ Mixed woodland, hazel coppice. **Plants** Wild daffodil, pendulous sedge. **Insects** Golden-ringed dragonfly, white admiral butterfly.
ROYAL SOCIETY FOR THE PROTECTION OF BIRDS

A:8 SIDNEY WOOD
Near Dunsfold; car park and access at TQ 023336. Keep to footpaths.
■ Mixed woodland.
FORESTRY COMMISSION

A:9 WAGGONERS WELLS
Near Haslemere; park at SU 863354.
■ Mixed woodland, ponds.
■ Footpaths and nature trails through woodland and beside man-made ponds.
NATIONAL TRUST/LUDSHOTT COMMON COMMITTEE

A:10 HINDHEAD COMMON
Near Hindhead; car park at SU 890357.
■ Heathland, woodland.
■ Extensive common land, much of it with heathland characteristics. **Birds** Sparrowhawk, yellowhammer, whitethroat, green woodpecker.
NATIONAL TRUST

A:11 LUDSHOTT COMMON
Near Haslemere; nature walks start at SU 850360.
■ Heath.
■ Walks of varying length over the heathland which adjoins Waggoner's Wells. **Birds** Nightjar, stonechat.
NATIONAL TRUST/LUDSHOTT COMMON COMMITTEE

A:12 DEVIL'S PUNCHBOWL & GIBBET HILL
Near Hindhead; car park and nature trails at SU 890357.
■ Mixed woodland, heathland.
■ Two walks through pleasant woodland and heathland; views from Gibbet Hill.
NATIONAL TRUST

A:13 ALICE HOLT FOREST
Near Guildford; main car park and information centre at SU 810417; several other car parks nearby.
■ Mixed woodland, pond.
■ Numerous footpaths through pine, beech and oak woods. Signposted walk (suitable for wheelchairs) starts from the information centre.
FORESTRY COMMISSION.

A:14 FRENSHAM COUNTRY PARK
Near Farnham; car park and interpretive centre at SU 849406. Open access.
■ Heathland, scrub, lake.
■ This remnant of Surrey heath has all the characteristic plants of this habitat. Part of the area has been designated a nature reserve but the rest can be explored freely.

Although a popular tourist spot, the Great Pond still attracts a variety of birds, including great crested grebe and interesting wildfowl in winter. The Little Pond's substantial reed-bed supports numerous reed warblers in summer and the occasional bittern in winter.

The heath, covered in heather, gorse and bracken, provides cover for spiders and insects. These, in turn, fall victim to common lizards and adders.
WAVERLEY BOROUGH COUNCIL

A:15 THURSLEY COMMON★
Near Farnham; car park off minor road on W side of Thursley Common. Keep to footpaths.
■ Heathland, bog.
■ Once covered in broad-leaved woodland and then cleared by man, Thursley is one of

the most important heathland areas left in southern England. Bog grades into dry heath and finally to birch and pine woodland.

The wetter areas are home to plants such as bladderwort, bog asphodel and round-leaved and oblong-leaved sundew. Invertebrates include the raft spider and up to 26 species of dragonfly, most notably the nationally scarce white-faced dragonfly.

The drier areas, characterized by heather, bell heather and gorse, provide a suitable habitat for silver-studded blues and bog bush-crickets.

A variety of raptors are recorded in most winters and these often include merlin and hen harrier. Thursley is also a regular haunt of that elusive predator, the great grey shrike.
NATURE CONSERVANCY COUNCIL

A:16 WITLEY COMMON*
Near Godalming; *the common lies at SU 936409.*
■ Heathland, woodland.
■ **Birds** Stonechat, whinchat, tree pipit.
NATIONAL TRUST

A:17 WINKWORTH ARBORETUM
Godalming; *access on E side of B2130, 2 miles (3 km) SE of Godalming at SU 990412. Entrance fee. Open all year during daylight hours.*
■ Parkland, woodland.
■ Fine display of unusual foreign trees.
NATIONAL TRUST

A:18 PUTTENHAM COMMON
Near Guildford; *common lies at SU 919461. There are three car parks; access from Suffield Lane leading from Puttenham village.*
■ Heathland, woodland, ponds.
■ Sandy heathland sloping away from the Hog's Back. **Birds** Stonechat, tree pipit, green woodpecker. **Insects** Dragonflies, damselflies, water insects.
SURREY COUNTY COUNCIL

B:1 HACKHURST & WHITE DOWNS
Near Dorking; *reserve lies at TQ 096486.*

■ Chalk downland.
■ This extensive area of fine chalk downland, scrub and woodland runs along the spine of the North Downs Way. Parts are owned by the National Trust and SCC; the many footpaths allow further exploration.

A variety of orchids are present as well as most of the common chalk indicator plants. Many of these provide food for the larvae of butterflies, hence chalkhill blue caterpillars are found feeding on horseshoe vetch. Round-headed rampion adds to the area's botanical interest.

Grasshoppers and bush-crickets are well represented, with the extremely local rufous grasshopper a highlight.
NATIONAL TRUST/SURREY COUNTY COUNCIL

B:2 ABINGER ROUGHS
Near Dorking; *NT car park at TQ 111480. Other car parks in the vicinity allow exploration of Abinger Common and Abinger Forest.*
■ Woodland.
NATIONAL TRUST

B:3 RANMORE COMMON*
Near Dorking; *car park and footpaths from TQ 141503.*
■ Woodland, chalk downland.
■ Broken areas of woodland and scrub surround patches of chalk downland, and the shelter encourages many butterflies. In late spring and summer numerous blue butterflies, including adonis and chalkhill, add colour while later in the year silver-spotted skipper and dark-green fritillary can be found. As well as a good range of chalk-loving plants, Ranmore supports many downland and scrub birds such as lesser whitethroat and blackcap.

B:4 BOX HILL COUNTRY PARK
Near-Dorking; *NT car park at TQ 179513.*
■ Chalk downland, woodland.
■ Despite visitor pressure there is still much of interest. The area earns its name from the box trees which, together with yew, form the climax woodland vegetation

Stonechat – see A:18.

over part of the steep slopes. Much of Box Hill is open chalk grassland but, here and there, scrub has started to invade. An impressive range of orchids are found along with unusual chalk-loving plants such as deadly nightshade.

Invertebrates include the Roman snail – Britain's largest species. In the spring they can be seen performing their extraordinary mating rituals among the scrub. Butterflies are abundant and include several species of blue and the local silver-spotted skipper.
NATIONAL TRUST

B:5 HEADLEY HEATH*
Near Leatherhead; *NT car park at TQ 204538.*
■ Heathland, scrub, pond, chalk grassland.
■ This extensive heathland grades into chalk downland and scrub, an unusual combination producing an impressive diversity of species. Areas of birch and pine scrub have developed on the heathland and several small pools hold water all year.

The heathland is a riot of colour in spring and holds typical birds such as stonechat, tree pipit and the occasional nightjar. As the acid soil is lost, chalk-loving plants appear and a greater variety of butterflies take to the wing, including chalkhill blue and dark green fritillary. In wet autumns the heath can be good for fungi. Particularly impressive are the colourful fly agarics which grow under birch.
NATIONAL TRUST

B:6 GREAT BOOKHAM COMMON
Near Leatherhead; *park near TQ 121567. Numerous public footpaths and tracks.*
■ Woodland, scrub, grassland.
■ **Birds** Nuthatch, nightingale, woodpeckers.
NATIONAL TRUST

B:7 EPSOM COMMON
Epsom; *park in Epsom. Nature trail starts at TQ 196609.*
■ Woodland, scrub, heath, grassland.
EPSOM & EWELL BOROUGH COUNCIL

B:8 HORTON COUNTRY PARK
Near Epsom; *car park at TQ 191618.*
■ Woodland, meadow.
EPSOM & EWELL BOROUGH COUNCIL

B:9 HOGSMILL OPEN SPACE
Near Kingtson; *area lies around TQ 214641. Open access.*
■ River, parkland.
EPSOM & EWELL BOROUGH COUNCIL

B:10 BRAMLEY BANK
Croydon; *access from Riesco Drive or Broadcombe to TQ 352635. Open access.*
■ Mixed woodland.
■ Oak and sycamore woodland with a relict patch of heath.
LONDON WILDLIFE TRUST

MAP B

GREATER LONDON

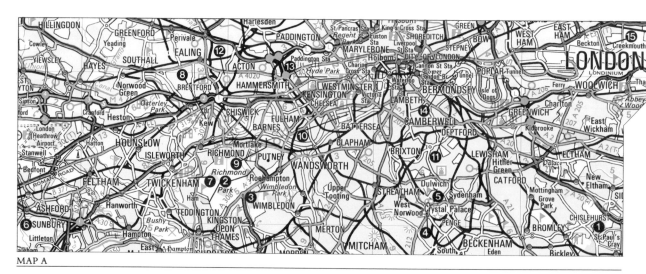

MAP A

A:1 SCADBURY PARK
Sidcup; *access from Perry Street.*
■ Woodland, grassland, stream.
■ Formerly an old hunting forest and farm, now managed to maintain a diversity of plants and animals.
LONDON BOROUGH OF BROMLEY

A:2 RICHMOND PARK*
Richmond; *several gates allow access to cars, e.g. at TQ 211721.*
■ Parkland, woodland.
■ Despite its proximity to London, Richmond Park is a haven for many sorts of wildlife. Particularly noticeable are the red and fallow deer. Use the car for a hide. A visit any time of year can be profitable; in autumn the rutting male deer compete for females.
A small pool and areas of scrub and woodland add to the park's wildlife interest. Both speckled and oak bush crickets are found among the rhododendrons. A variety of birds occur; with many of them almost indifferent to the presence of man, interesting views can be had.
ROYAL PARK

A:3 WIMBLEDON COMMON
Wimbledon; *many points of access eg at TQ 235724.*
■ Woodland, scrub, heath, bog.
■ **Birds** Redstart, stonechat, tree pipit. **Plants** Bogbean, round-leaved sundew.

A:4 UPPER WOOD
Crystal Palace; *access from Farquhar Road to TQ 337712.*
■ Mixed woodland.
■ Formerly neglected woodland, now managed to increase the diversity of plant and animal life.
ECOLOGICAL PARKS TRUST

A:5 SYDENHAM HILL WOOD
Southwark; *access from Crescent Wood Road to TQ 344724.*
■ Mixed woodland.
■ A rich area of ancient forest with mature oaks and beeches; an understorey of holly, coppiced hornbeam/hazel. **Birds** Woodland birds including nuthatch, treecreeper, great spotted woodpecker. **Plants** Solomon's seal.
LONDON WILDLIFE TRUST

A:6 STAINES RESERVOIR*
Staines; *no official parking place but many resi-*

dential roads in vicinity. Access restricted to causeway, entered at TQ 057733.
■ Lakes.
■ Staines reservoir is effectively split into two by a causeway which offers excellent views. Despite close proximity to Heathrow airport the reservoir attracts vast numbers of water birds and the area is nationally important for several species of duck. In November 1979 there were over 5,000 pochard and 4,000 tufted duck present.
Occasionally the Thames Water Authority drains one side of the reservoir and this draws in surprising numbers of waders including a few rarities. In recent years Wilson's phalarope and Baird's sandpiper have been recorded, and marsh terns occur in spring and autumn. Other terns, and grebes, are likewise notable features.
THAMES WATER AUTHORITY

A:7 HAM LANDS
Near Twickenham; *access from Riverside Drive, Ham at TQ 171727. Open access.*
■ Grassland, scrub.
■ An area of old workings on the banks of the Thames.
LONDON BOROUGH OF RICHMOND

A:8 ROYAL BOTANIC GARDENS, KEW*
Kew; *entrance at TQ 189771; entrance fee.*
■ Plant collection; formal gardens.
■ Extensive collection of native and exotic species, many in natural-looking settings, but tragically damaged by the storm of 16th October, 1987.
ROYAL BOTANIC GARDENS

A:9 BARNES COMMON
Barnes; *the common lies at TQ 227758.*
■ Scrub, grassland.
■ A typical London common with grassland plants, including burnet rose.

A:10 BATTERSEA PARK
Battersea; *the park lies at TQ 286777.*
■ Grassland, scrub.
■ A nature reserve was established here in 1985 – a haven for wildlife of open habitats.
LONDON WILDLIFE TRUST

A:11 NUNHEAD CEMETERY
Peckham; *access to reserve from Linden Grove, Peckham at TQ 352756.*
■ Woodland, grassland.
■ Mainly sycamore woodland with under-

storey plants. Several species of butterfly in open areas; woodland birds and flowers.
LONDON BOROUGH OF SOUTHWARK

A:12 GUNNERSBURY TRIANGLE
Hounslow; *approach from Bollo Bridge Road; restricted access: contact LWT.*
■ Scrub, woodland.
■ A valuable wildlife site enclosed by railway lines; much used as an educational area. Some scarce invertebrates.
LONDON WILDLIFE TRUST

A:13 HYDE PARK & THE SERPENTINE
Kensington; numerous entrances, locked at night.
■ Parkland, lakes.
■ Typical London parkland with patches of dense cover. The Serpentine holds ornamental wildfowl, but also attracts wild species. Deciding which is which can sometimes be difficult.
ROYAL PARK

A:14 LAVENDER POND
Bermondsey; *access from Rotherhithe Street to TQ 348797.*
■ Pond, reed-bed.
■ An entirely man-made nature reserve representing many freshwater habitats. Aquatic animals, marsh plants.
ECOLOGICAL PARKS TRUST

A:15 THAMESIDE ECOLOGICAL PARK
Barking; *access from River Road, Creekmouth to TQ 457820.*
■ Grassland, ponds, salt-marsh.
■ Interesting reserve on waste land left after power station was demolished. **Birds** (Winter) short-eared owl. **Plants** Marsh- and common spotted-orchids.
THAMESIDE ASSOCIATION

B:1 CAMLEY STREET NATURE PARK
St Pancras; *access, (also for disabled), from Camley St NW1 to TQ 299834. Open daily, 10 am-5 pm or daylight hours.*
■ Meadow, pond, willow coppice.
■ An ecological park established on site of old depot beside Regent's Canal; educational centre.
LONDON WILDLIFE TRUST

B:2 GILLESPIE ROAD OPEN SPACE
Islington; *the area lies at TQ 315862.*

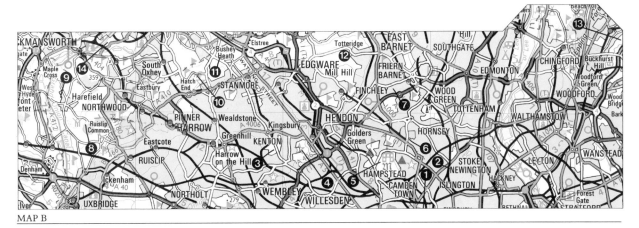

MAP B

■ Scrub, grassland, pond.
■ Old railway sidings, imaginatively landscaped to encourage wildlife.
LONDON BOROUGH OF ISLINGTON

B:3 FRYENT COUNTRY PARK
Hendon; entrance at TQ 192875.
■ Woodland, farmland.
■ Managed to maintain wildlife and rural interest. Nature trail, leaflet available.
LONDON BOROUGH OF BRENT

B:4 BRENT RESERVOIR
Hendon; reservoir situated at TQ 216876.
■ Lake, carr, marsh, reed-bed.
■ Part of the reservoir's margins are silted; the succession of emergent plants encourages breeding birds. **Birds** Gadwall, reed warbler.
BRITISH WATERWAYS BOARD

B:5 HAMPSTEAD HEATH
Hampstead; the area lies at TQ 264867; guide book available from the London Ecology Unit.
■ North London's best-known open area which still holds many interesting meadow and woodland flowers.

B:6 PARKLAND WALK
Highgate; two walks, one from Highgate tube station to Finsbury Park, the other from Highgate Woods to Alexandra Park. Open access.
■ Woodland, scrub.
■ A disused railway line colonized by wildlife; now managed to maintain diversity. Woodland birds and flowers.
LONDON BOROUGH OF HARINGEY

B:7 COPPETTS WOOD
Barnet; access from Colney Hatch Avenue to TQ 276916. Restricted access.
■ Mixed woodland.
■ Oak woodland with an understorey of hazel, hornbeam and sweet chestnut. Woodland birds and flowers.
LONDON WILDLIFE TRUST

B:8 BAYHURST WOOD COUNTRY PARK
Near Ruislip; situated at TQ 073891. Open access.
■ Woodland, lake.
■ Mixed woodland with oak and beech standards and hornbeam coppice. Leaflet available for nature trail.
LONDON BOROUGH OF HILLINGDON

B:9 OLD PARK WOOD★
Rickmansworth; public footpath at TQ 051914. Open access.
■ Mixed woodland.
■ Splendid ancient oak woodland with hazel understorey and a fine showing of spring flowers.
HERTS & MIDDLESEX TRUST FOR NATURE CONSERVATION

B:10 HARROW WEALD COMMON
Near Stanmore; the common is at TQ 143927.
■ Grassland, scrub.
■ Heathy grassland, invading birch scrub.

B:11 STANMORE COMMON
Stanmore; the common lies at TQ 161937. Permit required for HMTNC reserve at nearby Bentley Priory.
■ Grassland, woodland.

B:12 DARLANDS LAKE
Barnet; lake lies at TQ 244934. Public footpath to W. Restricted access to the lake itself.
■ Lake, marsh.
■ The lake, surrounded by marsh and alder

Southern marsh orchid – see B:13.

carr, is a haven for water birds.
HERTS AND MIDDLESEX TRUST FOR NATURE CONSERVATION

B:13 RODING VALLEY MEADOWS★
Near Loughton; park in Oakwood Hill Road N of reserve. Use trails. Parts wet underfoot.
■ Hay meadows, green lane.
■ One of the largest and finest flower-rich meadows remaining in Essex. Best from May to July. **Plants** Southern marsh-orchid, pepper-saxifrage, ragged-robin, sneezewort.
ESSEX NATURALISTS' TRUST

B:14 CROXLEY COMMON MOOR
Croxley Green; park in village. Common lies 440 yards (400 m) SE of station; across bridge over Grand Union Canal and River Gade.
■ Grass heath, marsh.
■ Extensive area with rich community of plants. Best in spring and summer. **Plants** Fen bedstraw, marsh pennywort, large thyme, betony, common cat's-ear.

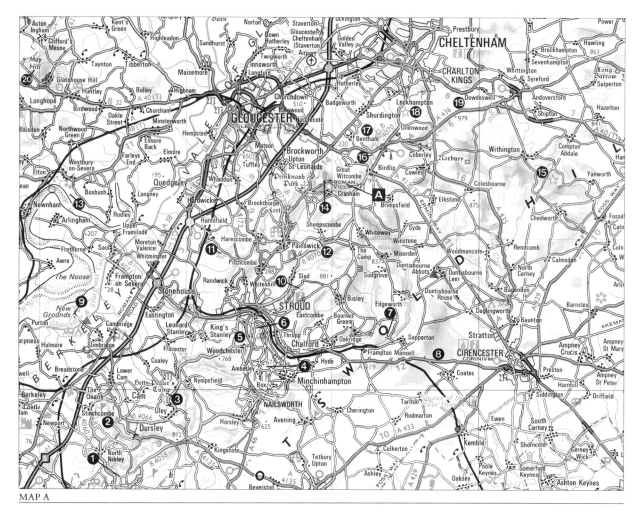

MAP A

A:1 WOTTON HILL
Near Wotton-under-Edge; *leave Wotton-under-Edge on minor road N up Wotton Hill. Grassland on W side of road, woodland on E.*
■ Grassland, woodland.
■ Some good examples of Cotswold beechwoods and areas of herb-rich limestone grassland. Whole area worth exploring.
PRIVATE OWNERSHIP/NATIONAL TRUST

A:2 STINCHCOMBE HILL*
Near Dursley; *park at top of hill; explore area to NW on foot; part of site is golf course.*
■ Limestone grassland.
■ A large area of herb-rich limestone grassland supporting a typical range of limestone plants and butterflies. **Plants** Bee, wasp, fly, fragrant and pyramidal orchids, sainfoin, clustered bellflower.

A:3 COALEY WOOD
Near Dursley; *entrance to wood from B4066 at Westhill.*
■ Woodland, quarries.
■ Ancient woodland on steep scarp slope containing oolite quarries of geological interest. The wood is dominated by beech and ash and supports a fairly rich ground flora.
WOODLAND TRUST

A:4 MINCHINHAMPTON COMMON*
Near Nailsworth; *leave Minchinhampton on any minor road heading W. Common in about ½ mile (0.8 km).*
■ Limestone grassland.

■ Extensive area of common land holding rich and diverse limestone flora.
NATIONAL TRUST

A:5 SELSEY COMMON
Near Stroud; *access off B4066 one mile (1.5 km) S of A46 crossroads.*
■ Limestone grassland, quarries.
■ A large area of limestone grassland rich in flora with several old quarries of geological interest. **Plants** Musk, frog, bee, wasp and fly orchids, stemless thistle, woolly, carline thistle, small scabious, autumn gentian.

A:6 RODBOROUGH COMMON**
Near Stroud; *easiest access from minor road at SO 852035.*
■ Limestone grassland, scrub, woodland.
■ A large area of commonland on a plateau and extending down Cotswold scarp slopes. Mostly rich limestone grassland, but there is scrub invasion, and woodland on some of the lower slopes. The soil depth is variable from shallow scree-like areas to deep soils, a variation which gives rise to diverse floral communities. It is one of the finest examples of Cotswold limestone grassland and there are some rarities. Ten species of orchid are found, including bee, frog and greenwinged. The national rarities pasque-flower and purple milk vetch occur along with more widespread calcicoles such as horseshoe and kidney vetch, sainfoin, carline thistle, salad burnet, autumn gentian, yellowwort, clustered bellflower.
NATIONAL TRUST

A:7 SICCARIDGE WOOD & DANEWAY BANKS*
Near Cirencester; *approach Sapperton to Daneway; Siccaridge Wood is on W of minor road above Frome; Daneway Banks to E of road. Access to Daneway Banks on footpath only.*
■ Woodland, grassland, scrub.
■ Siccaridge is a rather open ancient woodland supporting a rich ground flora. Daneway is a steep limestone bank bearing scrub grassland and scree with a wide range of limestone plants.
GLOUCESTERSHIRE TRUST FOR NATURE CONSERVATION

A:8 CIRENCESTER PARK
Near Cirencester; *woods either side of A419 at Tumbledown 3½ miles (5.5 km) W of Cirencester.*
■ Woodland, grassland.
■ Extensive ancient woodland, mostly oak but with some softwood plantations; system of grassy rides and glades, and a rich flora. **Plants** Lesser butterfly-orchid, herb Paris, meadow saffron, downy-fruited sedge.

A:9 SLIMBRIDGE**
Near Dursley; *signposted from Slimbridge village; entrance fee.*
■ Marsh, grassland, pools.
■ A series of ornamental pools holding a superb wildfowl collection. Hides overlook river estuary and grazing marsh which support exceptional numbers of winter wildfowl.
WILDFOWL TRUST

A:10 SWIFT'S HILL*
Near Stroud; *access directly off minor road at Swift's Hill, approached from B4070 ½ mile (0.8 km) S of Stroud.*
■ Limestone grassland.
■ Common land supporting a rich limestone flora, also noted for invertebrates.
Plants Autumn lady's-tresses, musk, frog, bee and fly orchids, carline thistle, autumn gentian.
GLOUCESTERSHIRE TRUST FOR NATURE CONSERVATION

A:11 HARESFIELD BEACON
Near Stroud; *footpaths from S side of Haresfield-Harescombe minor road at SO 824090 and SO 832086.*
■ Limestone grassland.
■ Cotswold limestone grassland on steep N-facing scarp. Fairly rich flora. **Plants** Musk and bee orchid.
NATIONAL TRUST

A:12 BULL'S CROSS & JUNIPER HILL*
Near Painswick; *alongside B4070 at Bull's Cross and extending SW one mile (1.5 km).*
■ Limestone grassland, woodland, scrub.
■ A mixed area of ecological interest on the Cotswold limestones. Woodland (The Frith) occupies a large proportion of the site. This is a typical Cotswold beechwood, with oak, whitebeam, cherry, small-leaved lime and a rich calcareous ground flora, including yellow bird's-nest, wood barley, bird's-nest orchid and green hellebore.
Parts of the site are occupied by rich calcareous scrub communities with species such

as juniper, wayfaring-tree, spurge-laurel, deadly nightshade, Solomon's-seal and gromwell.
Areas of herb-rich limestone grassland complete the picture. Most of the typical species are present and several rare ones.
The site is noted for its entomological interest and there is a breeding bird community including wood warbler and nightingale.
Plants Lesser, butterfly-, musk and bee orchids, columbine, hound's-tongue, clustered bellflower.

A:13 GARDEN CLIFF
Near Cinderford; *from A4151 at Westbury-on-Severn head S for ½ mile (0.8 km). Turn right down lane to river and park; footpath S along river; cliff starts in 100 yards (90 m).*
■ River cliff.
■ A fine exposure of fossil-bearing jurassic limestone.

A:14 COOPER'S HILL
Near Gloucester; *leave A46 at Green Street and follow lane down to wood.*
■ Woodland, grassland, scrub.
■ A fairly large area of Cotswold beech woodland with a characteristic flora. Open areas of scrub, limestone grassland and quarries add to the diversity and interest.
GLOUCESTERSHIRE COUNTY COUNCIL

A:15 CHEDWORTH RAILWAY CUTTING
Near Cirencester; *entrance from minor road from Cirencester to Compton Abdale where road crosses over old railway.*
■ Disused railway line.

■ Cuttings exhibit exposures of oolitic limestone and support a fairly rich limestone flora. Surrounded by woodland they create glades, good for invertebrates.
GLOUCESTERSHIRE TRUST FOR NATURE CONSERVATION

A:16 BARROW WAKE
Near Gloucester; *car park on A417 ¼ mile (0.5 km) S of Air Balloon pub. Site on steep slopes below.*
■ Limestone grassland.
■ An example of Cotswold limestone grassland with a rich and diverse flora.

A:17 CRICKLEY HILL COUNTRY PARK
Near Gloucester; *entrance from N side of roundabout at junction of A436 and A417.*
■ Grassland, woodland, scrub, rock exposures.
■ A diverse site on the Cotswold limestones: ash/beech woodland, species-rich calcareous scrub communities and herb-rich grassland.
GLOUCESTERSHIRE COUNTY COUNCIL

A:18 LECKHAMPTON HILL
Near Cheltenham; *several tracks lead up hill from B4070 2 miles (3 km) S of Cheltenham.*
■ Limestone grassland, scrub, quarries.
■ Predominantly herb-rich limestone grassland invaded by scrub. The quarries exhibit fine exposures of oolitic limestone, with fossils.

A:19 LINEOVER WOOD
Near Cheltenham; *park in lay-by on A436*

A:A COTSWOLD COMMONS & BEECHWOODS**
Near Gloucester.
① Parking as marked
② Painswick Hill (partly golf course) is a superb area of limestone grassland and calcareous scrub with a rich flora including many orchids – autumn lady's-tresses, fly, bee, wasp, musk, frog and greater butterfly-orchid; also stemless and woolly thistles, sainfoin, small scabious, juniper, squinancywort. Good for butterflies, including chalk-hill and small blue.

③ Buckhold Wood, one of Britain's finest examples of a mature beech woodland, has trees up to 300 years old and a rich ground flora which includes red and white helleborine, greater butterfly-orchid, bird's-nest orchid, herb Paris, columbine, lily-of-the-valley, green hellebore and yellow bird's-nest.
④ Scattered parking along road.
⑤ Cranham Common is an excellent area of limestone grassland with invading scrub and woodland. The rich flora includes juniper, whitebeam; musk, frog, fly, bee, greater and

lesser butterfly-orchids, moonwort, sainfoin and narrow-lipped helleborine.
⑥ Scattered parking along road.
⑦ Witcombe Wood is beech partially replanted with conifers but still supporting a rich ground flora including mezereon, red and white helleborine, greater butterfly and bird's-nest orchids, narrow-lipped helleborine, angular Solomon's-seal, herb Paris, columbine.
NATURE CONSERVANCY COUNCIL/ GLOUCESTER TRUST FOR NATURE CONSERVATION

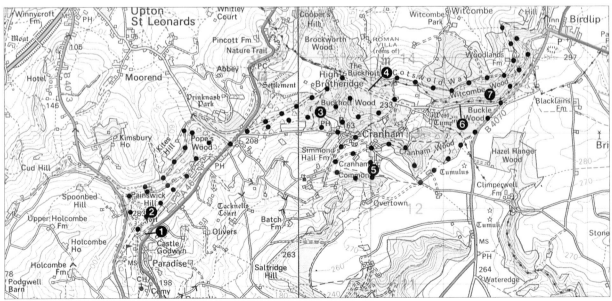

1:50 000, MAP A:A

GLOUCESTERSHIRE

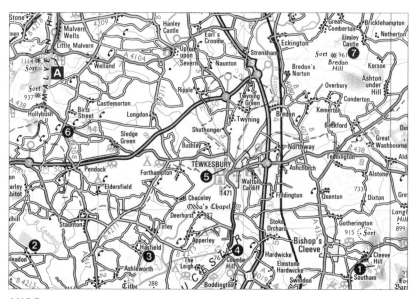

MAP B

B:A MALVERN HILLS

Near Malvern; parking at Herefordshire Beacon, Castlemorton Common, bottom of Swinyard Hill; car park.

① Herefordshire Beacon has a fine Iron Age fort. Tops and slopes mainly acid grassland.
② Ancient wood with both large- and small-leaved limes, good for wood warbler and dormouse.
③ Swinyard Hill is acid grassland/bracken, with some calcides. Spring cinquefoil, carline thistle.
④ Gullet Quarry and surrounding grassland/ scrub are very good for butterflies: high brown, dark green, pearl-bordered and small pearl-bordered fritillaries, grayling, green hairstreak, marbled white.
⑤ Gullet/News Wood are ancient woodland.

Rich flora – wild daffodil, purple and broad-leaved helleborines, columbine, greater butterfly-orchid, herb Paris. Butterflies.
⑥ Midsummer Hill has acid grassland and oak/ ash wood on E slope; noted for ancient holly trees. Woodland birds.
⑦ Eastnor Park has herd of red deer. Fine old parkland trees and lichens.
⑧ Castlemorton Common is unimproved grassland and grass heath with scrub, marsh, stream, pools. Rich flora with over 270 species. Wet areas best.
⑨ Hollybed Common has pool with interesting flora including fringed water-lily.
⑩ Combegreen Common is unimproved grassland with rich flora.
MALVERN HILLS CONSERVATORS

1:50 000, MAP B:A

just E of wood at Pegglesworth. Entrance across road.
■ Woodland.
■ Ancient broad-leaved woodland of ash/ lime/beech/field maple over hazel coppice supporting a rich ground flora.
WOODLAND TRUST

A:20 MAY HILL

Near Ross-on-Wye; path leads up hill from Yartleton Lane (SO 691211).
■ Grassland, woodland, scrub.
■ One of the best examples of acidic grass-land in Gloucestershire. Areas of scrub and bracken invasion; typical range of flora and fauna.
NATIONAL TRUST

B:1 CLEEVE COMMON★★

Near Cheltenham; from Cleeve Hill on A46 take one of many footpaths up scarp.
■ Limestone grassland and heath, scrub, quarries, scree, woodland.
■ A large area situated among plateaux, scarp slopes and dry valleys of the Cotswolds: diverse, with a variety of habitats including extensive limestone grasslands on deep and shallow soils, limestone scree quarry faces, old spoil heaps, leached soils holding limestone heath with heather and bracken, extensive gorse scrub, a golf course and peripheral woodlands. The rich flora includes at least 13 species of orchid. The invertebrates are equally diverse and there is a variety of breeding birds.

B:2 COLLINPARK WOOD

Near Newent; entrance to wood off minor road 400 yards (365 m) N of Upleadon crossroads. Only NW part is nature reserve. Access to rest of wood on footpath only.
■ Woodland.
■ A fine example of an oak/small-leaved lime wood with extensive coppiced lime and damp areas. The ground flora is predominantly acidic, spring flora particularly notable, with fine stands of bluebell.
GLOUCESTERSHIRE TRUST FOR NATURE CONSERVATION/PRIVATE OWNERSHIP

B:3 ASHLEWORTH HAM

Near Tewkesbury; leave B4213 at Tirley crossroads; in about 1½ miles (2.5 km) hides alongside road; do not enter on foot.
■ River meadows.
■ Extensive area of low-lying alluvial meadow adjoining the Severn, with a characteristic flora. Prone to winter flooding. Winter wildfowl, including Bewick's swan.
GLOUCESTERSHIRE TRUST FOR NATURE CONSERVATION

Feeding geese, typical postures.

B:4 COOMBE HILL CANAL

Near Tewkesbury; access off A38 down track opposite A4019. Towpath along canal; access to meadows on footpaths only.
■ Disused canal, grassland.
■ A disused canal adjoining the Severn supporting a rich aquatic flora. The alluvial meadows on either side have a characteristic flora and are attractive to wildfowl in winter when flooded.

Flocking fieldfares – see A:3, Port Meadows, this page.

B:5 SEVERN HAM

Tewkesbury; *access from Mill St., opposite abbey. Access to Upper Lode (oxbow) is down lane, first on left on A438 after crossing Severn from Tewkesbury. Take care of hay crop in early summer.*

■ River meadow, oxbow lake.

■ A large riverside hay meadow supporting a typical grassland flora, also fairly good for breeding birds and winter wildfowl. The old Severn at Upper Lode holds an interesting flora.

TEWKESBURY BOROUGH COUNCIL

B:6 DUKE OF YORK MEADOW★

Near Rye Street; *park in pull-in picnic area next to Duke of York pub. Entrance to meadow through gate. No access into meadow when up for hay.*

■ Hay meadow.

■ An excellent example of a herb-rich grassland with abundant wild daffodils.

WORCESTERSHIRE NATURE CONSERVATION TRUST

B:7 BREDON HILL★

Near Pershore; *approaching from N, take road on right in front of Elmley Castle church; follow road to end then take footpaths up hill. Explore NW scarps. Keep to footpaths.*

■ Limestone grassland, scrub, woodland, old quarries, arable.

■ This large hill, an outlier of the Cotswolds, has interesting limestone grassland and scrub communities. The old quarries are of note and the arable weed flora is good.

A:1 SHOTOVER COUNTRY PARK★

Oxford; *entrance from minor road, Shotover Hill (SP 051063).*

■ Woodland, heath, scrub, grassland.

■ A diverse site once part of a royal hunting forest. The woods are ancient, rich in species and there are areas of heath (rare in the county) and bird-rich scrubland. **Mammals** Fallow and muntjac deer. **Butterflies** Purple, emperor, white admiral.

OXFORD CITY COUNCIL

A:2 FARMOOR RESERVOIR

Near Oxford; *W side of B4017 ¼ mile (0.5 km) S of Farmoor; footpath crosses between reservoirs.*

■ Lake.

■ A large water supply reservoir attractive to winter wildfowl and passage waders, terns, etc.

OXFORD CITY COUNCIL

A:3 PORT MEADOW★

Oxford; *along track over Oxford Canal and railway at SO 4073.*

■ Meadow.

■ A large alluvial meadow bordering the Thames and Oxford Canal on the NW fringe of Oxford. Its long-documented history of management has made it important in the study of grassland floristics. It is annually grazed and exhibits a range of grassland communities varying in relation to height above the river. The richest areas are the wettest, low-lying parts near the river which support species such as spike rush, great burnet, tubular water dropwort, sedges and round-fruited rush. The meadow is also a valuable habitat for birds providing

extensive feeding areas for grassland species, particularly in autumn/winter. Large flocks of thrushes (fieldfare, redwing), waders (lapwing, curlew, golden plover), finches; during periods of inundation wildfowl can be seen.

A:4 OT MOOR

Near Oxford; *park in Beckley village; proceed N on bridleway across moor.*

■ Marsh.

■ Extensive area of low-lying grazing marsh prone to winter flooding. Attractive to a wide range of wetland birds, including breeding species. Important for wetland insects. In winter: wildfowl, raptors; in summer: garganey, shoveller, redshank, grasshopper warbler, snipe.

A:5 BLENHEIM PARK

Woodstock; *entrance to park from lane past church in Woodstock (SP 442168).*

■ Parkland, woodland, lake.

■ A good example of traditional parkland with some fine old trees and a good range of woodland and lake birds.

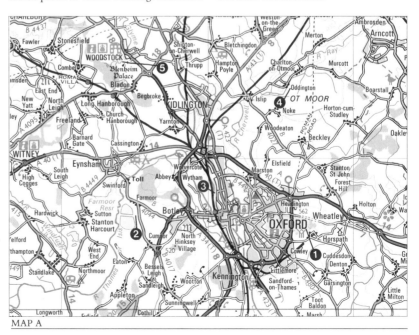

MAP A

BUCKINGHAMSHIRE

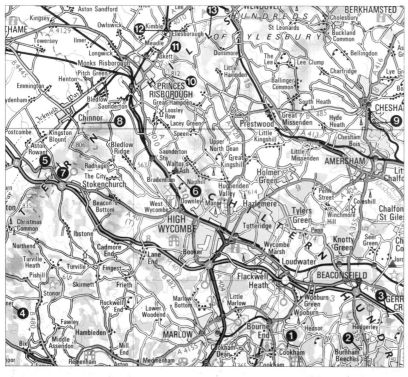

MAP A

A:1 CLIVEDEN
Near Maidenhead; access is along towpath S from Hedsor Wharf.
- Woodland, river.
- A fine broad-leaved woodland on a steep river cliff adjacent to the River Thames. Plants include summer snowflake.
NATIONAL TRUST/PRIVATE OWNERSHIP

A:2 BURNHAM BEECHES★★
Near Slough; car park in woods , mile (0.5 km) W of A355 in Farnham.
- Woodland, scrub, grassland.
- Burnham Beeches, an extensive ancient semi-natural woodland, is on a low plateau intersected by shallow valleys; it overlies acidic gravelly soils. The wood is structurally diverse with ancient pollards, stands of mature trees, old coppice, scrub and open grassy glades. Beech is the dominant tree with pedunculate oak, holly, birch, rowan, hornbeam and wild cherry. Although sparse in parts, the ground flora, characterized by acid-loving species, is rich; damp/wet areas are particularly interesting. Plants include heath cudweed, marsh St John's-wort, small skullcap, orpine, juniper, bladderseed, sundew, saw-wort, bog asphodel, wood horsetail, alder buckthorn, hoary cinquefoil. The diverse woodland structure encourages a varied bird life which includes lesser spotted, greater spotted and green woodpeckers, nuthatch, redstart, woodcock, hawfinch, tree pipit, wood warbler, sparrowhawk.
CITY OF LONDON

A:3 CHURCH WOOD
Near Gerrards Cross; access along track S of church in Hedgerley village (SU 973873).
- Woodland, scrub, pond.
- Woodland is mixed birch, oak and ash. Good range of breeding birds and fairly diverse plants. **Butterflies** White admiral, purple and white-letter hairstreak. **Mam-**mals Muntjac. **Plants** Solomon's seal, green hellebore, butcher's-broom, box.
ROYAL SOCIETY FOR THE PROTECTION OF BIRDS

A:4 WARBURG★
Near Henley-on-Thames; take Bix Bottom road off A423 at Bix. Reserve car park 2 miles (3 km) down lane. Keep to marked paths.
- Beechwood, chalk grassland, scrub.
- A rich Chiltern beechwood with open grassy areas and meadows which support a typical chalk grassland flora. Good range of typical birds, mammals and reptiles. Amongst 17 species of orchid: greater and lesser butterfly, frog, fly, bee; also meadow clary, herb Paris, Solomon's seal, green hellebore, columbine.
BERKS, BUCKS & OXON NATURALISTS' TRUST

A:5 ASTON ROWANT★★
Near Thame; from Stokenchurch take A40 W. After 1½ miles (2.5 km) turn left at crossroads, take first right; reserve car park after about ½ mile (0.8 km) on right. Keep to nature trail and footpaths.
- Chalk grassland, scrub beechwood.
- A NNR on the steep Chiltern Scarp adjoining the M40 with superb views over the Vale of Aylesbury. Small area of chalk heath with heather but most of the soils are lime-rich. Extensive area of chalk downland with a very rich flora: candytuft, Chiltern and autumn gentian, yellow-wort, bee and frog orchids. Where grazing is less intense species-rich scrub communities have developed: juniper, buckthorn, spindle, whitebeam, wayfaring-tree. The hilltop has fine beechwoods with a sparse but varied ground flora: purple helleborine, bird's-nest orchid, herb Paris, wood barley. Birds and mammals (harvest mouse, deer) are varied. Butterflies include silver-spotted, grizzled and dingy skippers, chalkhill and small blue,

Duke of Burgundy, dark green fritillary, green hairstreak.
NATURE CONSERVANCY COUNCIL

A:6 BRADENHAM WOODS★
Near High Wycombe; woods adjoin the W side of Walter's Ash and Naphill. Keep to extensive woodland footpath network.
- Oak and beech woodland.
- Site comprises the almost contiguous Naphill, Bradenham and Park Woods, considered the best example of ancient semi-natural woodland in the Chilterns. They vary in composition. Naphill is a moderately acid oak (both species) and beech wood with holly, rowan, birch, yew and an acidic ground flora including heather. Bradenham is a well-grown beech wood with an acid ground flora; a dew pond adds diversity. Park Wood, a pedunculate oak/beech wood is richer in trees and shrubs; clematis, wild cherry, wayfaring-tree with a correspondingly large ground flora. Some trees are considered amongst the oldest in the Chilterns. Overall there are rich invertebrate and plant communities. Most of the woodland breeding birds are present.

A:7 ASTON WOODS★
Near Stokenchurch; park in lanes around Crowell Hill or Chinnor Hill or park at Aston Rowant NNR and keep to footpaths.
- Woodland.
- Extensive areas of mature beechwood as well as more mixed woodland with small-leaved lime, hornbeam, whitebeam, etc. Chalk/woodland plant species thrive: purple helleborine, fly and bird's-nest orchids, herb Paris, box orchid.

A:8 CHINNOR HILL
Near Princes Risborough; access from car park at end of Hilltop Lane (SP 766005) off Chinnor-Bledlow Ridge road.
- Chalk, scrub, wood, grassland.
- Downland reverted to scrub. Woodland includes some mature beechwood and species-rich grassland with typical plants such as autumn gentian. Good range of chalk trees and shrubs such as yew, juniper, wayfaring-tree, whitebeam. Scrub birds include seven species of warbler.
BERKS, BUCKS & OXON NATURALISTS' TRUST

A:9 CHESHAM BOIS WOOD
Near Amersham; access from A416 between Amersham and Chesham.
- Woodland.
- A mature beechwood noted for its bluebells in spring.
Plants Coralroot, bird's-nest orchid.
WOODLAND TRUST

A:10 WINDSOR HILL
Princes Risborough; entrance to wood along a footpath on N side of lane at Parslow's Hillock (SP 827020).
- Woodland.
- A fine example of a mature beechwood on a steep scarp slope. Plants include a number of rare species.

A:11 GRANGELANDS AND PULPIT HILL★
Near Princes Risborough; park in lay-by at top of Longdown Hill; take bridle-path through wood on N side of road (SP 834045) down towards Upper Icknield Way.
- Chalk grassland, woodland, scrub.

■ A varied site rich in chalk-loving species. 50 species of birds breed locally. **Butterflies** Chalkhill and small blue, marbled white.
BERKS, BUCKS & OXON NATURALISTS' TRUST

A:12 ELLESBOROUGH WARREN*
Near Wendover; park in Ellesborough (B4010) and take footpath up on to Beacon Hill; keep to footpaths.
■ Chalk, scrub, grassland.
■ Site supports the largest stands of box scrub in Britain. A range of other scrubs occur as well as areas of herb-rich grassland.
Plants Deadly nightshade, spurge laurel.

A:13 COOMBE HILL
Near Wendover; access off lane between Dunsmore and Coombe on sharp bend.

■ Chalk scrub and heath, grassland.
■ Situated on the steep Chiltern scarp with commanding views over the Vale of Aylesbury. Diverse chalk shrub community contrasting with acidic scrub and heath.
NATIONAL TRUST

B:1 FOXCOTE RESERVOIR
Near Buckingham; leave A413 at Maids Moreton; take minor road towards Leckhampstead; reservoir adjacent to road one mile (1.5 km) N of Maids Moreton. View lake from road.
■ Lake.
■ Reservoir noted for its variety of birdlife: winter wildfowl, great crested grebe, passage waders and terns.

Grizzled skipper – see A:5, Ashton Rowant, opposite page.

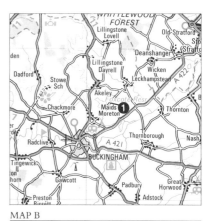

MAP B

BEDFORDSHIRE

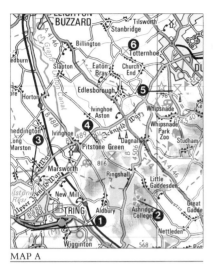

MAP A

A:1 TRING WOODLANDS

Near Tring; park on top of Hastoe Hill. Access to woods running along scarp from many footpaths.

■ Beech woodland.

■ Ancient semi-natural Chiltern beech woodland with range of typical birds, on steep NW-facing escarpment; rich ground flora including several orchid species. Best in spring and summer. **Plants** Narrow-lipped and white helleborines, yellow bird's-nest, fly orchid, common wintergreen.

A:2 ASHRIDGE*

Near Berkhamsted; park at Ashridge. Toll gates sometimes operated on estate road. Footpaths from Berkhamsted, Potten End or Little Gaddesden.

■ Mixed woodland, plantation, bracken, grassland.

■ Woodland with national rarities among the ground flora, and a large herd of fallow deer. Best in late spring and early summer. **Birds** Firecrest, redstart, hawfinch, lesser spotted woodpecker, nightingale, wood warbler, nuthatch. **Mammals** Fallow deer, muntjac. **Plants** Narrow-lipped and green-flowered helleborines, fly orchid, yellow bird's-nest, stinking hellebore.

NATIONAL TRUST

A:3 TRING RESERVOIRS

Near Tring; park in Wilstone Green or Tringford. Footpath access to Wilstone, Startop's End, Marsworth and Tringford reservoirs; nature trail and hides.

■ Reservoir, tall fen, marshy grassland.

■ Waterfowl in winter; breeding birds include one of Britain's few reed-bed heronries. **Birds** (Passage) little gull, black tern, waders.

NATURE CONSERVANCY COUNCIL/HERTS & MIDDLESEX WILDLIFE TRUST

A:4 IVINGHOE BEACON*

Near Tring; park off minor road between B489 and B4506 at SP 963159. Explore on foot.

■ Chalk grassland, scrub.

■ An extensive site occupying the Chiltern scarp and plateau. Large areas hold herb-rich chalk grassland, with areas of scrub invasion and secondary woodland. **Butterflies** Duke of Burgundy fritillary, Chalkhill and small blue, brown argus. **Plants** Pasque-flower, adder's-tongue.

NATIONAL TRUST

A:5 DUNSTABLE & WHIPSNADE DOWNS*

Near Dunstable; signposted from town, about 2 miles (3 km) SW, adjoining B4541. Car park, lavatories, refreshments and information centre. Busy in summer.

■ Chalk down, scrub.

■ Steep, W-facing escarpment on the Middle Chalk extends for 2 miles (3 km) between Dunstable and Whipsnade, providing fine views over Vale of Aylesbury. Late spring and summer best for flowering plants and butterflies. **Plants** Frog orchid, great pignut, field fleawort, dwarf thistle, autumn gentian, small and devil's-bit scabious. **Butterflies** Chalkhill blue, small blue, dark green fritillary.

BEDFORDSHIRE COUNTY COUNCIL/ NATIONAL TRUST

A:6 TOTTERNHOE KNOLLS*

Near Totternhoe; park at picnic site on NE side of Totternhoe-Stanbridge road, N of village. Sticky mud after rain.

■ Chalk grassland, quarry, beech woodland, scrub.

■ Chalk hill topped by Norman earthworks and old stone quarry workings, with rich flora and 20 butterfly species. Managed to control further colonization by scrub; small area of beech plantation with ash. Best in late spring and summer.

BEDFORDSHIRE COUNTY COUNCIL/BEDS & HUNTS WILDLIFE TRUST

B:1 GALLEY & WARDEN HILLS

Near Luton; reached by track leading E to golf club, off A6 on N outskirts of town.

■ Chalk downland.

■ W-facing chalk escarpment comprising much unimproved grassland with a fine flora and a national rarity, great pignut. **Plants** Pignut, broomrape, purple milk-vetch, field fleawort, yellow rattle, common rockrose, salad burnet.

LUTON BOROUGH COUNCIL

B:2 DROPSHORT MARSH

Near Toddington; on W side of A5120 on S outskirts of town. B&HWT Permit required.

■ Spring-fed marsh, wet meadow.

■ A wetland habitat type now scarce in this part of England, with a varied flora. **Plants** Marsh valerian, ragged robin, lady's mantle, marsh arrowgrass, fen bedstraw, pennywort, betony.

BEDS & HUNTS WILDLIFE TRUST

B:3 SUNDON HILLS

Near Luton; on road between Upper Sundon and Harlington. Car park, waymarked walks.

■ Chalk downland.

■ Country park on chalk escarpment downlands offers fine views over mid-Bedfordshire countryside.

BEDFORDSHIRE COUNTY COUNCIL

B:4 BARTON HILLS*

Near Barton-Le-Clay; footpath from B655 just SE of town.

■ Grazed chalk down, hawthorn scrub, beech woodland, stream.

■ An important research site and National Nature Reserve, with a rich and varied plant and insect life including many rare beetles. Best in spring and summer. **Plants** Pasque flower, white helleborine, bee, fragrant and spotted orchids, herb Paris, field fleawort,

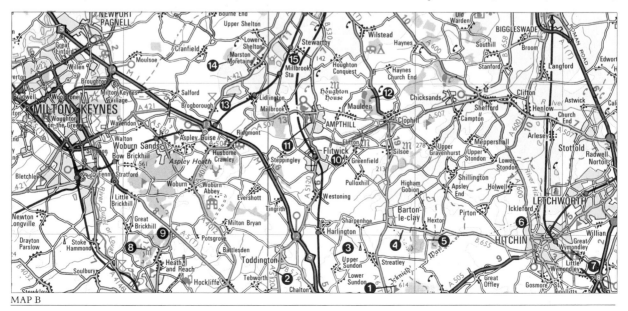

MAP B

clustered bellflower, woolly thistle and carline thistle.
NATURE CONSERVANCY COUNCIL

B:5 HEXTON CHALK PIT
Near Hexton; park near pit along minor road just S of crossroads at Hexton village.
■ Chalk pit, downland.
■ Tiny reserve containing rich flora.
HERTS & MIDDLESEX WILDLIFE TRUST

B:6 OUGHTON HEAD COMMON
Near Hitchin; park at Westmill. Public footpath on S bank of Oughton Head. H&MWT permit needed for entry to N bank woodland.
■ Marsh, river, alder/willow woodland.
■ Variety of wetland habitats on either side of clear chalk stream holding brown trout and other fish. Best in spring and summer, with good stonefly and dragonfly communities. **Birds** Kingfisher, reed warbler; (winter) water rail, siskin, redpoll. **Fish** Brown and rainbow trout, ten-spined stickleback.
HERTFORDSHIRE COUNTY COUNCIL/HERTS & MIDDLESEX WILDLIFE TRUST

B:7 PURWELL NINESPRINGS
Near Hitchin; park beside River Purwell on E side of Hitchin, N of minor road to Great Wymondley.
■ Alder woodland, wet meadows, reeds.
■ A small wetland reserve of year-round interest, with breeding reed and sedge warblers and reed buntings; alders attract siskins and redpolls in winter.
HERTS & MIDDLESEX WILDLIFE TRUST

B:8 STOCKGROVE
Near Leighton Buzzard; adjoining road to Great Brickhill, signposted from A418. Situated on W side of much larger woodland including B&HWT reserve in Kings Wood (permit needed).
■ Mixed woodland, meadow, lake.
■ Country park with mostly ancient oak wood, with a wide structural variety and composition; stand-types include birch-oak, small-leaved lime coppice, oak-ash-maple; hornbeam, hazel and aspen also present. Fragments of remnant lowland heath. **Plants** Lily-of-the-valley, wood vetch, saw-wort, climbing corydalis, wood spurge, yellow archangel, heath speedwell, bilberry, great wood-rush.
BEDFORDSHIRE COUNTY COUNCIL

B:9 KING'S WOOD & GLEBE MEADOWS
Near Houghton Conquest; reached by track from Rectory Lane. B&HWT permit needed.
■ Ash/maple woodland, hay meadows.
■ Ancient semi-natural woodland on heavy clays, with diverse shrub and ground flora communities. Best spring/summer. **Plants** (Woodland) Violet helleborine, pendulous sedge, wood millet, thin-spiked wood-sedge; (meadow) dropwort, saw-wort, pepper-saxifrage, yellow rattle, cowslip.
BEDFORDSHIRE COUNTY COUNCIL/BEDS & HUNTS WILDLIFE TRUST

B:10 FLITWICK MOOR*
Near Flitwick; take track at Folly Farm on Flitwick to Maulden road. Park at end on right. Access off public rights of way open to any member of a county naturalists' trust, otherwise by B&HWT permit. Wet underfoot.
■ Bog, wet meadow, damp birch/alder/oak woodland.

Yellow rattle: see B:9.

■ Strange remnant of once extensive marshland; variety of wetland and damp woodland habitats with almost 200 species of flowering plants and many scarce insects. **Plants** Common cottongrass, butterbur, water figwort, mosses, fungi. **Birds** Water rail; (summer) grasshopper warbler; (winter) siskin, redpoll.
BEDS & HUNTS WILDLIFE TRUST

B:11 COOPER'S HILL
In Ampthill; situated in W part of town. Keep to footpaths. Part also known as the Firs. Often crowded on fine days.
■ Greensand heathland, mixed woodland, mire.
■ The best remaining area of heathland on Bedfordshire greensand. Best in spring and summer. **Plants** Marsh violet. **Birds** Lesser and great spotted woodpecker.
BEDS & HUNTS WILDLIFE TRUST

B:12 MAULDEN WOOD
Near Ampthill; park at Maulden Wood picnic site, about 1½ miles (2 km) N of Clophill, on W side of A6 at summit of Deadman's Hill. Forest walks start here.
■ Mixed deciduous/coniferous plantation woodland.
■ Mainly plantation woodland but a few relict fragments of semi-natural woodland and heath. Rich invertebrate fauna, particularly Hymenoptera, Heteroptera and Lepidoptera; range of woodland birds. Nuthatches, coal tits and finches are especially confiding at the picnic site. **Plants** Wild service-tree, green-flowered helleborine.
FORESTRY COMMISSION

B:13 BROGBOROUGH LAKE
Near Brogborough; park at Brogborough Hill picnic site, adjoining A5140 Bedford-M1 link road, close to M1 junction 13.
■ Flooded brick pit.
■ One of the largest of the deep Bedfordshire claypits, attracting waterfowl, especially in winter.
BEDFORDSHIRE COUNTY COUNCIL

B:14 MARSTON THRIFT
Near Bedford; turn W off A421 just S of Marston Moretaine. Enter from track or footpaths at Wood End. Entry to reserve area by B&HWT permit only.
■ Ash/oak/maple woodland.
■ An ancient, semi-natural wood, within which a traditional coppice with standards management regime is being re-established. Characteristic ground flora and good butterfly population. Best in spring and summer. **Plants** Forster's woodrush, wood spurge. **Butterflies** Purple hairstreak.
BEDS & HUNTS WILDLIFE TRUST

B:15 STEWARTBY LAKE
Near Bedford; about 7 miles (10 km) SW of town, adjacent to A5140 Bedford-M1 link road, on Stewartby turn; ample parking.
■ Flooded clay pit.
■ Large flooded lake in the Bedfordshire brickfields, with extensive bankside walks and good bird-watching. Least disturbance from boating in winter. **Birds** (All year) Great crested grebe; (summer) little ringed plover, common tern, lesser whitethroat, reed warbler; (passage) black tern, little gull; (winter) red-throated diver, ruddy duck.
BEDFORDSHIRE COUNTY COUNCIL

BEDFORDSHIRE

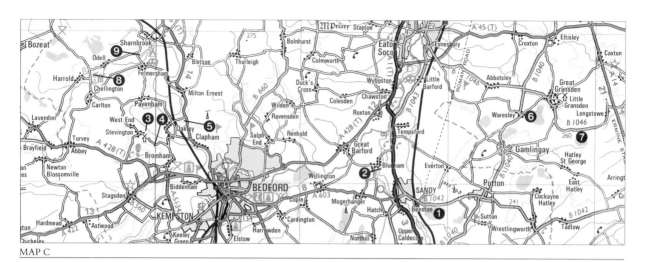

MAP C

C:1 THE LODGE, SANDY

Near Sandy; park at site on S side of B1042, Sandy to Potton road, one mile (1.5 km) E of Sandy station. Closed Sun exc to RSPB and B&HWT members; fee for non-members.

■ Heath, mixed woodland, parkland, pool.

■ Reserve surrounds RSPB headquarters. Natterjack toads have been successfully reintroduced. Good bird-watching all year. **Birds** Nightjar, crossbill, lesser spotted woodpecker; (winter) siskin. **Plants** Meadow saxifrage. **Mammals** Muntjac.

ROYAL SOCIETY FOR THE PROTECTION OF BIRDS

C:2 BLUNHAM GRAVEL PITS

Near Sandy; 2 miles (3 km) N of Sandy turn W into Blunham village, park near church. Lane S from church to footbridge over River Ivel and footpaths on S and W sides of pits.

■ Flooded gravel pits, river.

■ Established gravel pits offering a good range of wildfowl, especially in winter. **Birds** Gadwall, goosander.

C:3 HOLYWELL MARSH

Near Bedford; park at site in village of Stevington.

■ Wet grassland.

■ Tiny wetland reserve with rich variety of wetland plants, including much butterbur along a limestone spring line. At its best in summer.

BEDS & HUNTS WILDLIFE TRUST/ STEVINGTON PARISH COUNCIL

C:4 STEVINGTON

Near Bedford; entrance and car park beside Bromham-Stevington road, roughly mid-way between the two villages.

■ Disused railway, scrub.

■ A 2-mile (3-km) country walk following part of the former Bedford to Northampton railway line providing fine views across the Ouse Valley. A variety of common flowering plants, butterflies and birds.

BEDFORDSHIRE COUNTY COUNCIL

C:5 JUDGE'S SPINNEY

Near Bedford; from A6 3½ miles (5 km) N of town take second left turn to Oakley; site is on left.

■ Beech woodland.

■ A small beech hanger containing spurge laurel. Best in spring and summer.

BEDFORDSHIRE COUNTY COUNCIL/BEDS & HUNTS WILDLIFE TRUST

C:6 WARESLEY WOOD & GRANSDEN WOOD★

Near St Neots; limited parking on road verge; access along concrete road to sewage works. Free access to members of B&HWT and CWT, otherwise permit required. Parts of wood used for shooting; N part of Gransden wood private; no dogs please.

■ Hazel coppice/oak standard woodland, hawthorn, blackthorn.

■ Excellent example (in April and May) of the bluebell and oxlip woods found on boulder clay in this area; stream and wide rides add to mainly botanical interest. **Plants** Early purple, bird's nest, greater butterfly and fly orchids, adder's tongue, fungi.

BEDS & HUNTS WILDLIFE TRUST

C:7 HAYLEY WOOD★

Near Great Gransden; park 2 miles (3 km) S on B1046 where trail starts. Open to members of CWT and B&HWT or by permit from CWT. Bridle-path skirts perimeter. Often wet.

■ Coppiced ash/field maple/hazel/hawthorn/oak standards, rides, pond.

■ At least a million springtime oxlips in this classic boulder clay coppice wood with a recorded history of over 700 years. A superb mosaic of habitats restored after vigorous CWT management. Outstanding autumn fungi (250 species). **Mammals** Fallow deer. **Plants** Crested cow-wheat, dyers' greenwood, adder's tongue fern, orchids, fungi, mosses, liverworts.

CAMBRIDGESHIRE WILDLIFE TRUST

C:8 HARROLD-ODELL

Near Bedford; park at site just E of Harrold village on NW bank of River Ouse, entrance N of Harrold Bridge. Open all year, but visitor centre weekends only.

■ Landscaped flooded gravel pit, river bank, meadows, developing willow woodland.

■ A new country park, still being developed; already known as a good site for waterbirds and dragonflies. **Birds** (Winter) smew, red-necked grebe, goldeneye.

BEDFORDSHIRE COUNTY COUNCIL

C:9 FELMERSHAM GRAVEL PITS★

Near Bedford; park at entrance on minor road between Felmersham and Sharnbrook. Reserve on both sides. Open to any member of a county naturalists' trust. Otherwise by B&HWT permit. May be wet underfoot.

■ Shallow flooded pits, neutral grassland, developing willow/alder woodland.

■ An attractive area of old, small flooded gravel pits, sheltered by trees and scrub, and having an especially rich dragonfly fauna, best seen in summer. The varied habitats also support a diverse bird community.

BEDS & HUNTS WILDLIFE TRUST

Opposite, a fallow deer buck – see C:7, Hayley Wood. Below, pasque-flower – see A:4, Ivinghoe Beacon, page 80.

HEREFORD & WORCESTER

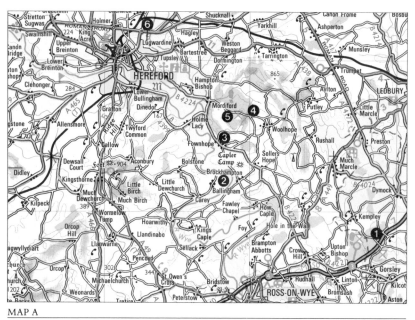

MAP A

A:1 DYMOCK WOODS

Near Ledbury; *turn W from B4215 at Gospel Oak; after 1½ miles (2.5 km) small wood S of road is reserve. From here cross M50 into main block of FC woodland.*

■ Woodland.

■ Extensive oak woodland with characteristic flora and fauna, particularly noted for show of spring wild daffodils.

Butterflies White admiral, purple hairstreak. **Plants** Wild service-tree.

GLOUCESTERSHIRE TRUST FOR NATURE CONSERVATION/FORESTRY COMMISSION

A:2 RIVER WYE & CAPLER WOOD

Near Hereford; *park in Fownhope. Take*

footpath down to river. Footpath follows river as far as Brockhampton.

■ River, woodland.

■ One of the finest natural rivers in Britain, the Wye supports a very rich invertebrate community especially in the water crowfoot beds. Capler Wood, situated on a steep river cliff, is a rich broad-leaved woodland. **Plants** Toothwort, herb Paris, wild service tree. **Insects** Club-tailed dragonfly, white-legged damselfly, beautiful demoiselle. **Birds** Dipper, pied flycatcher, kingfisher, grey wagtail, sand martin. **Fish** Salmon.

A:3 COMMON HILL

Near Hereford; *areas of interest sited along*

Wye Valley long distance path on Common Hill above Fownhope. Access from minor roads either at SO 595345 or SO 582352. Keep to footpaths.

■ Limestone, grassland, scrub, woodland.

■ A series of wildlife habitats consisting of herb-rich limestone grassland with invading scrub reverting to woodland, rich in invertebrates. **Plants** Green-winged orchid, adder's tongue, pale St John's wort, spring cinquefoil, yellow-wort. **Insects** Glow-worm, pearl-bordered fritillary, wood white, green hairstreak, brown argus, marbled white.

HEREFORD & RADNOR NATURALISTS' TRUST

A:4 BROADMOOR COMMON

Near Hereford; *site is crossed by minor road from Mordiford to Woolhope, ½ mile (0.8 km) W of Woolhope.*

■ Mixed heath, scrub, grass heath community.

■ An unusual habitat for the area with a fairly diverse plant and animal life. **Plants** White-horehound.

HEREFORD & WORCESTER COUNTY COUNCIL

A:5 HAUGH WOOD

Near Hereford; *leave Mordiford on minor road to Woolhope. After the steep hills road passes through the wood. Car park in ½ mile (0.8 km). Nature trail to N of road but worth exploring beyond this.*

■ Woodland.

■ A large wood, partly replanted with conifers. Rich flora and fauna particularly along stream valleys. **Plants** Marsh helleborine, herb Paris, lily-of-the-valley, stinking hellebore, wild service-tree, meadow saffron, columbine, marsh valerian, early-purple orchid. **Insects** Silver-washed fritillary, wood white, white admiral, white-letter hairstreak. **Birds** Hawfinch, crossbill,

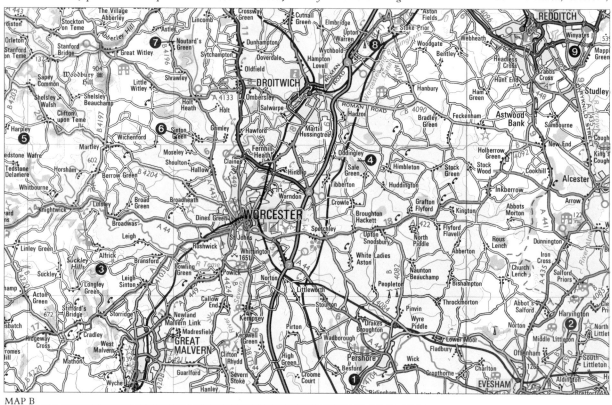

MAP B

HEREFORD & WORCESTER

wood warbler, woodcock, tree pipit. **Mammals** Polecat, fallow deer.
FORESTRY COMMISSION/NATIONAL TRUST

A:6 LUGG VALLEY MEADOWS

Near Hereford; *take footpath S from bridge over Lugg on A4103. Meadows adjoin river in about 400 yards (365 m). Keep to footpaths.*
■ Grassland.
■ Riverside alluvial hay meadow with a rich unimproved grassland flora. Winter flooding attracts wildfowl. River supports club-tailed dragonfly.

B:1 TIDDESLEY WOOD

Near Pershore; *wood adjoins A4104, 1½ miles (3 km) W of Pershore. Turn W off A44, down road to Besford ½ mile (0.8 km) W of Pershore. After ¾ mile (one km) turn S down track to wood and car park (SO 929460).*
■ Woodland.
■ Ancient woodland with a varied structure. Large rides particularly noted for flora and butterflies. **Plants** Bird's-nest orchid, herb Paris, narrow-leaved everlasting-pea, meadow saffron, adder's-tongue, thin-spiked wood-sedge. **Insects** White admiral, purple hairstreak. **Birds** Nightingale.
WORCESTERSHIRE NATURE CONSERVATION TRUST

B:2 WINDMILL HILL

Near Evesham; *entrance to Windmill HIll on S side of B5410 on sharp bend at top of Cleeve Hill (SP 0724477). Park on verge. Access along bridle-path, which also runs N to the Cleeve Hill NR.*
■ Limestone, grassland, woodland, scrub.
■ Scarp slope with fine views over the Vale of Evesham. **Plants** Deadly nightshade, bee and pyramidal orchids, wild liquorice, carline thistle, crested hair-grass. **Invertebrates** Snails.
WORCESTERSHIRE NATURE CONSERVATION TRUST

B:3 KNAPP & PAPERMILL NATURE RESERVE*

Near Malvern; *leave A4103 on sharp bend at Bransford down minor road to Leigh and Alfrick. Take first left and after 3 miles (5 km) reserve is on left by bridge over stream (SO 750521).*
■ Woodland, grassland, stream, orchard, ponds.
■ Site is within the secluded wooded valley of Leigh Brook. The varied geology gives a range of soil conditions from fairly acid to calcareous. Fast-flowing trout stream has good invertebrate fauna and supports dipper, grey wagtail and kingfisher, with plants such as monk's-hood, nettle-leaved bellflower and small teasel on the banks. Meadows and orchards of the lower valley support a rich flora including green-winged orchid, adder's-tongue, yellow rattle, and greater broomrape. The adjoining ancient semi-natural woodlands have abundant wild service-tree and small and large-leaved limes. The varied ground flora includes purple helleborine, toothwort, early-purple orchid. Rich invertebrate, bird and mammal communities.
WORCESTERSHIRE NATURE CONSERVATION TRUST

B:4 TRENCH WOOD*

Near Droitwich; *park in Trench Lane alongside wood; W part private – keep to footpath.*
■ Broad-leaved woodland.
■ Ancient woodland site with important

Nightingale – see B:1.

glade ride system supporting, amongst others, woodland butterflies, nightingales, six orchids, herb Paris, hornbeam, wild service-tree.
WORCESTERSHIRE NATURE CONSERVATION TRUST

B:5 SAPEY BROOK VALLEY

Near Bromyard; *take minor road linking B4203 and B4204 at Clifton-upon-Teme. In ½ mile (0.8 km) W of Clifton on S side of road, follow small lane over bridge and park in space on left after 100 yards (91 m). Take footpaths S through wood. Difficult terrain.*
■ Mixed broad-leaved woodland, stream.
■ A fine example of the steeply incised wooded dingles in the area, with extensive tufa deposits. First recorded site of the ghost orchid in Britain which, although not seen for over 100 years, may still linger in some undisturbed corner. **Plants** Herb Paris, wood vetch, stinking hellebore, wild service-tree. **Birds** Dipper, raven, buzzard. **Mammals** Dormouse, polecat.

B:6 MONKWOOD & MONKWOOD GREEN

Near Worcester; *small car park off lane through wood (SO 805606); green open on to roads.*
■ Woodland, grassland, ponds.
■ An ancient semi-natural woodland with an important insect site. Plants **Orchids,** lily-of-the-valley, meadow saffron, petty whin, grass vetchling, greater spearwort, black poplar. **Insects** Terrestrial caddis, glow-worm, wood white. **Birds** Woodcock, grasshopper warbler, tree pipit.
WORCESTERSHIRE NATURE CONSERVATION TRUST

B:7 SHRAWLEY WOOD*

Near Stourport-on-Severn; *entrance along track opposite New Inn pub in Shrawley village. Keep to footpaths in S part of wood.*
■ Woodland, lake.
■ Large ancient semi-natural woodland on a plateau and cliffs above the Severn and its tributary the Dick Brook. Some replanting with conifers has occurred but the wood mainly consists of almost pure small-leaved lime coppice, considered the best example of a lime wood in the W Midlands. A large,

dammed pool supports red-eyed and emerald damselflies, and scarce hawker. Flora includes lily-of-the-valley, spreading bellflower, heath cudweed, thin-spiked wood sedge, narrow-leaved bittercress and a fine display of spring bluebells; also rich in fungi. Typical range of breeding birds.
FORESTRY COMMISSION

B:8 UPTON WARREN*

Near Bromsgrove; *turn E off A38 by AA box 200 yards (182 m) N of Swan Inn, Upton Warren down small track 150 yards (137 m) to small car park on left. Entry by WNCT permit only.*
■ Lakes, marsh, salt-marsh, grassland, woodland.
■ A diverse wetland site with interesting series of saline subsidence pools, saltier than seawater, surrounded by one of the best inland salt-marshes in Britain, areas of bare mud and grazed marsh. There is a large freshwater subsidence pool, an old gravel pit and several smaller pools. The range of wetland habitats also includes fen communities, reed-bed, alder wood, wet grassland, river and stream. Flora includes golden dock, black poplar, giant bellflower, lesser sea-spurrey, round-leaved mint, round-fruited and blunt-flowered rush. Over 200 bird species recorded, including many rarities. Good for winter wildfowl and spring and autumn wader passage. Breeding birds include great crested and little grebes, up to ten species of warbler, ruddy duck, redshank, little ringed plover, water rail, sparrowhawk and little owl; hobby is a regular summer visitor.
WORCESTERSHIRE NATURE CONSERVATION TRUST/HEREFORD & WORCESTER COUNTY COUNCIL

B:9 IPSLEY ALDERS MARSH

Near Redditch; *enter reserve off Alders Drive mid-way between A4023 and A4189.*
■ Marsh, wet meadow, pools, woodland.
■ One of the largest fen-peat marshlands in the county. Grazed floristically-rich meadow, pools and woodland add diversity. **Plants** Adder's-tongue, blunt-flowered rush, horned pondweed. **Insects** Red-eyed damselfly.
WORCESTERSHIRE NATURE CONSERVATION TRUST

HEREFORD & WORCESTER

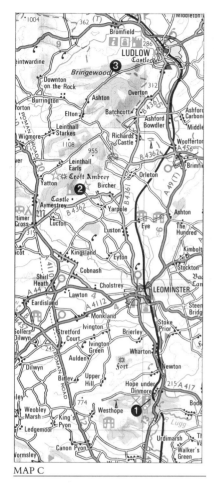

MAP C

C:1 QUEENS WOOD

Near Leominster; *A49 runs through wood-land at Hope-under-Dinmore. Car park off main road one mile (1.5 km) S of village.*
■ Woodland.
■ A large woodland including an Arbore-tum with an important collection of rare trees. The native woodland is a rich mixed broad-leaved type. **Plants** Herb Paris, wild service-tree, early-purple orchid. **Birds** Hawfinch, redstart, wood warbler. **Mammals** Polecat, fallow deer.
HEREFORD & WORCESTER COUNTY COUNCIL

C:2 CROFT CASTLE

Near Leominster; *entrance to castle off B4362 3 miles (5 km) E of A4110 crossroads.*
■ Woodland, parkland, stream, grassland.
■ A fine parkland backed by extensive woodlands and rough common land. The Fishpool Valley series of woodland ponds is particularly interesting. **Plants** Toothwort, alternate- and opposite-leaved golden saxifrage, thin-spiked wood-sedge. **Birds** Pied flycatcher, redstart, wood warbler, buzzard. **Mammals** Dormouse, polecat, fallow deer, badger.
NATIONAL TRUST

C:3 MORTIMER FOREST

Near Ludlow; *minor road from Ludlow to Wigmore passes through wood one mile (1.5 km) W of Ludlow.*
■ Woodland, quarries.
■ This large area of woodland, which extends into Shropshire, has been much planted with conifers but the remaining

broad-leaved wood is rich, particularly the Whitcliffe Wood towards Ludlow. Geological nature trail exhibits good exposures of the Silurian system. Fossils. **Birds** Hawfinch, pied flycatcher, redstart, wood warbler.
FORESTRY COMMISSION

D:1 HARTLEBURY COMMON★★

Near Stourport-on-Severn; *A4025 E of Stourport crosses the common; several parking areas.*
■ Heathland, bog, lake, woodland, scrub.
■ Local Nature Reserve and one of the finest heathlands in the Midlands, situated on light sandy soils and river terraces with an unusual inland blown dune system. Large areas are dominated by ling and bell heather with stands of gorse broom scrub. Mixed oak/birchwood has encroached on to the E part of the site. Small valley on the E has extensive reed swamp, alder carr and old woodland with large beeches and hornbeams. The range of habitats is further diversified by a small bog and pool. The very rich flora includes sundew, cranberry, bog-bean, striated catchfly, hoary cinquefoil, spring vetch, flixweed, tower mustard, shepherd's cress and knawel.
   The rich invertebrate fauna includes uncommon spiders and beetles, over 100 species of moths and a varied dragonfly fauna. There is a diverse bird community.
HEREFORD & WORCESTER COUNTY COUNCIL

D:2 DEVIL'S SPITTLEFUL

Near Kidderminster; *from Sutton Park Road (B4549) turn W down Rifle Range Road. Heath adjoins car park at end and extends W.*
■ Heathland, woodland, acid grassland, scrub.
■ Site dominated by calluna-heath with open sandy areas – one of the largest and richest heaths in the county. Also fairly large areas of birch woodland and grass heath. **Plants** Moonwort, grey hair-grass, pale toadflax.
WORCESTERSHIRE NATURE CONSERVATION TRUST/WYRE FOREST DISTRICT COUNCIL

D:3 TITTERSTONE CLEE HILL★

Cleobury Mortimer; *turn off A4117 one mile (1.5 km) W of Cleehill; follow unclassified road to top of hill; several footpaths cross hill.*

Stonechat – found on Hartlebury Common.

■ Upland grassland, moorland, bog, scree.
■ Isolated upland supporting series of habitats including Calluna heath, grassland, boggy areas and open rock.

D:4 CATHERTON COMMON★

Cleobury Mortimer; *unclassified road crosses common ¾ mile (one km) from A4117.*
■ Heath, grass heath, wet heath, scrub.
■ A large area of open common land noted for wet heathland communities which are particularly well developed along stream.

D:5 KINVER EDGE

Kinver; *leave A449 W along unclassified road into Kinver and turn left half way through village; woodland in ½ mile (0.8 km) (SO 834835).*
■ Woodland, heath.
■ An extensive area of oak/birch woodland on a ridge of sandy soils. Areas of scrub, heath and bracken add diversity.
STAFFORDSHIRE COUNTY COUNCIL
NATIONAL TRUST

MAP D

D:A WYRE FOREST
Bewdley; *park at Forestry Commission centre.*
(1) New Parks – mainly conifers with young and mature plantations. Birds – crossbill, siskin, goldcrest, occasional firecrest.
(2) Shelf-held Coppice – typical acid Wyre Forest sessile oakwood over bilberry, heather, bell heather, cow-wheat. Occasional sword-leaved helleborine, lily-of-the-valley. Fallow deer. Hawfinch, all three woodpeckers, nuthatch, wood-warbler. Terrestrial caddis-fly.
(3) Park Brook Valley – rich oak/ash/elm wood with wild service-tree, small-leaved lime, alder. Flush sites rich. Flora includes fragrant orchid, alder buckthorn, wood crane's-bill, wood horsetail, broad-leaved and common cottongrasses, soft-leaved sedge.
(4) Old Railway Line – rich flora. Adder and tree pipit common. Good site for butterflies seeking nectar: high-brown, silver-washed, pearl-bordered and small pearl-bordered fritillaries, dark green, wood white, purple hairstreak.
(5) Meadows are scattered through the forest. Many are unimproved with rich flora: green-winged orchid, meadow saffron, adder's-tongue, betony, lady's-mantle.
(6) Dowles Brook Valley – The Dowles is a fast-flowing unpolluted stream with a rich invertebrate fauna: crayfish, beautiful demoiselle damselfly. Fish: salmon, stone loach, bullhead, trout. Birds: dipper, kingfisher, grey wagtail. The woods are mixed broad-leaved good for pied flycatcher, redstart. Plants: bloody and wood crane's-bill, oak fern.
(7) Limited parking.
(8) Parking.
(9) Hawkbatch Valleys – mainly conifer plantation with some typical acid oak wood.
(10) Seckley Wood – rich mixed broad-leaved

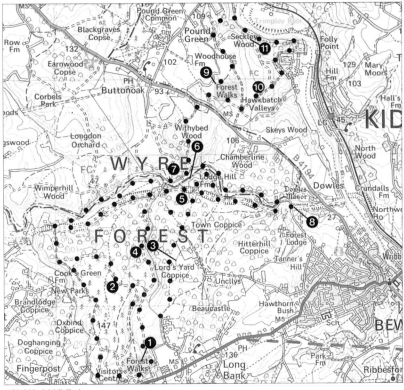

1:50 000, MAP D:A

wood with small-leaved lime, wild service tree on very steep river cliff. Good for bryophytes. River Severn holds extensive beds of river crowfoot, noted for club-tailed dragonfly, white-legged damselfly, dipper, kingfisher, otter.
NATURE CONSERVANCY COUNCIL/
FORESTRY COMMISSION/WORCESTERSHIRE
NATURE CONSERVATION TRUST

E:1 CHADDESLEY WOODS⋆
Near Bromsgrove; *leave A448 N on lane to Woodcote (SO 916720). Take left fork after ½ mile (0.8 km); park on roadside about 300 yards (274 m) into wood. Keep to footpaths.*
■ Woodland, grassland.
■ A remnant of the old Forest of Feckenham. Some areas have been planted with conifers but the majority is ancient semi-natural woodland with a series of old meadows supporting plants such as green-winged and spotted orchids, saw-wort, betony, adder's-tongue, lady's-mantle.

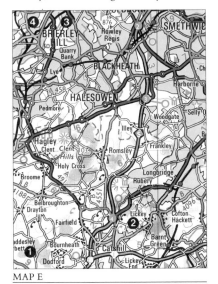

MAP E

Scattered ponds add diversity and hold good invertebrate communities. The woodlands are predominantly oak but hold a wide range of trees and shrubs including small- and large-leaved lime, wild service-tree, hornbeam, spurge-laurel. The woods are unusual in having both northern and southern community types towards the limit of their ranges and represent a transition between 'lowland' and upland' Britain. Ground flora includes toothwort, purple and broad-leaved helleborine, rough horsetail tutsan, ivy broomrape, lily-of-the-valley, heath cudweed. Good range of mammals including muntjac.
NATURE CONSERVANCY COUNCIL/
WORCESTERSHIRE NATURE CONSERVATION
TRUST/PRIVATE OWNERSHIP

E:2 LICKEY HILLS COUNTRY PARK
Near Birmingham; *car park off B4096 at SO 996759.*
■ Heathland, broad-leaved woodland, grassland, conifer plantation.
■ An extensive area on a small hill system overlying ancient acidic rocks. Fine areas of bilberry heath and a range of woodlands – birch, alder, mature beech, mature conifer plantations, ancient coppice add diversity. **Mammals** Muntjac. **Reptiles** Adder, common lizard. **Birds** Redstart, crossbill, wood warbler, woodpeckers. **Plants** Bell heather, heath rush.
BIRMINGHAM CITY COUNCIL

E:3 SALTWELLS WOOD & DOULTON'S CLAY PIT
Near Brierley Hill; *entry points from most*

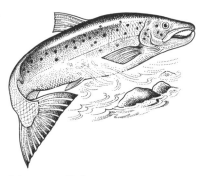

Salmon – see D:A.

adjoining roads (eg Heath Lane or Saltwell Lane).
■ Pool, marsh, stream, broad-leaved woodland, scrub, grassland, heath, cliff.
■ Clay pit with fine exposures of coal measures and diversity of habitats. **Plants** Southern marsh-orchid, lesser reedmace, ploughman's-spikenard. **Butterflies** Dingy skipper.
DUDLEY BOROUGH COUNCIL

E:4 PENSNETT POOLS
Near Brierley Hill; *access from Blewitts Road or Wallows Road adjoining.*
■ Lakes, marsh.
■ Three large pools with adjoining marsh, particularly noted for wetland birds – wildfowl year round, waders on passage – also plants. **Plants** Adder's-tongue fern, southern marsh-orchid, mare's-tail, shining pondweed.

WARWICKSHIRE

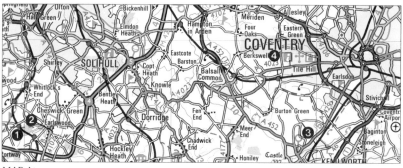

MAP A

A:1 CLOWES WOOD*

Near Solihull; *approach along path from minor road 200 yards (180 m) E of Earlswood Lakes Station (SP 098742). Permit required from WNCT.*

■ Woodland.

■ An ancient semi-natural woodland of oak, beech, birch, alder and aspen. Rich herbaceous flora and notable mosses and fungi. Varied birdlife; moths. **Plants** Lily-of-the-valley, wood horsetail, elongated and smooth-stalked sedges. **Birds** Wood warbler. **Mammals** Muntjac.

WARWICKSHIRE NATURE CONSERVATION TRUST

A:2 EARLSWOOD LAKES*

Near Solihull; *car park off Malthouse Lane.*

■ Lakes, woodland, willow carr.

■ The three large canal-feeder reservoirs are good for wildfowl and water plants. The surrounding broad-leaved woodland supports a range of plants and birds. **Plants** Lesser water-plantain, mudwort, elongated sedge, shining and flat-stalked pondweeds. **Birds** Great crested and little grebes, kingfisher, terns, winter wildfowl.

BRITISH WATERWAYS BOARD

A:3 CRACKLEY WOODS

Near Kenilworth; *site is ½ mile (0.8 km) N of A429. Park in lay-by beside wood (SP 287737).*

■ Woodland.

■ An ancient semi-natural woodland dominated by oak/birch with a hazel and rowan understorey. Noted for its birds and an excellent spring flora.

WARWICK DISTRICT COUNCIL

A:4 TILEHILL WOOD

Coventry; *entrance off Banner Lane (SP 279790). Permit needed from Coventry CC or Coventry Natural History Society.*

■ Woodland, bog.

■ A relic of the Forest of Arden, mainly ancient semi-natural oak with some areas of conifers. *Sphagnum* mosses are present. A prime invertebrate site, with many ancient woodland species.

COVENTRY CITY COUNCIL

B:1 HARTSHILL HAYES COUNTRY PARK

Near Nuneaton; *entrance off minor road at SP 315945.*

■ Woodland.

■ An ancient semi-natural woodland – mainly oak standards over hazel and small-leaved lime coppice. Good spring flora. **Plants** Wild service-tree, guelder-rose, large-leaved lime.

WARWICKSHIRE COUNTY COUNCIL

B:2 SUTTON PARK**

Sutton Coldfield; *access for cars at Stonehouse Road, SP 103963. Many pedestrian entry points.*

■ Heath/grass heath, bog/marsh, woodland, pools, stream, scrub.

■ The park extends over 2,000 acres. It contains a relict landscape of woodland heath interspersed with a fine series of wetlands – streams, lakes, bogs, marshes, alder carr. The woods are varied – broad-leaved and conifer plantations with native woods mostly oak/birch with much holly (good for holly blues) and woodland birds over bilberry. There are extensive areas of calluna and grass heath and gorse scrub. The bogs have many rare plants – cranberry, crowberry, cowberry, sundew, butterwort, grass-of-Parnassus, bog pimpernel, meadow thistle, sedges. The whole site is excellent for birds and invertebrates.

CITY OF BIRMINGHAM DISTRICT COUNCIL

B:3 KINGSBURY WATER PARK*

Near Coleshill; *access to car parks via Bodymoor Lane off A4097. Way-marked nature trails.*

■ Old gravel workings, pools, willow carr, rough grassland, scrub.

■ The Water Park consists of over 600 acres of old gravel workings making it one of the finest wildlife refuges in the county.

Cliff Pool Nature Reserve is a specially developed lake with islands and foreshore where in winter large congregations of pochard, shoveler, teal and goldeneye are recorded, whilst in summer common tern, shelduck, great crested grebe and little grebe breed along with nine species of warbler.

Fifteen species of dragonflies and damselflies have been noted including the ruddy darter and the red-eyed damselfly.

WARWICKSHIRE COUNTY COUNCIL

B:4 ALVECOTE POOLS*

Near Tamworth; *car park at Alvecote Priory for Pooley Fields nature trail. Pools can be viewed from road at SK 254047; otherwise permit needed from WNCT.*

■ Lakes, river, canal, marsh, wet grassland, scrub woodland.

■ A series of reed-fringed pools caused by mining subsidence enclosed between Coventry Canal and River Anker. Areas of scrub and marsh add diversity. **Plants** Bladderwort, bog mosses (six species). **Birds** Wildfowl, swans, migrating waders and terns, kingfisher, reed warbler.

WARWICKSHIRE NATURE CONSERVATION TRUST

C:1 EDGE HILL

Near Banbury; *park in Edge Hill village 1½ miles (2.5 km) N of A422. Footpaths lead N and S through woods.*

■ Woodland, grassland.

■ Ancient semi-natural woodland on steep scarp slope supporting a rich calcareous flora and a typical range of woodland birds and invertebrates.

WARWICKSHIRE NATURE CONSERVATION TRUST

C:2 BURTON DASSETT COUNTRY PARK

Near Banbury; *entrance one mile (1.5 km) E of A41 at Temple Herdewyke.*

■ Grassland.

■ A range of unimproved grassland from neutral acid to an unusual calcareous flora on old ironstone quarries. **Plants** Stemless thistle, salad burnet, crested hair-grass.

WARWICKSHIRE COUNTY COUNCIL

C:3 BADBY WOOD

Near Daventry; *park in Badby (just off the A361) near church. Keep to footpaths leading S from church to wood.*

■ Oak/hazel woodland, bracken glades, stream, marsh.

■ Ancient woodland with occasional ash and birch; varied ground flora with local rarities and good range of breeding birds. Best in spring and early summer. **Plants** Wood horsetail, blinks, hairy wood-rush, marsh valerian, wood vetch. **Birds** (Breeding) nuthatch, redstart, wood warbler, tree pipit. **Mammals** Badger.

C:4 UFTON FIELDS**

Near Leamington Spa; *entry by permit only, from WNCT.*

■ Old limestone workings, pools, willow

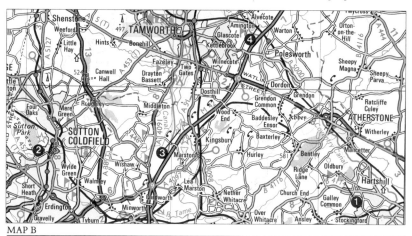

MAP B

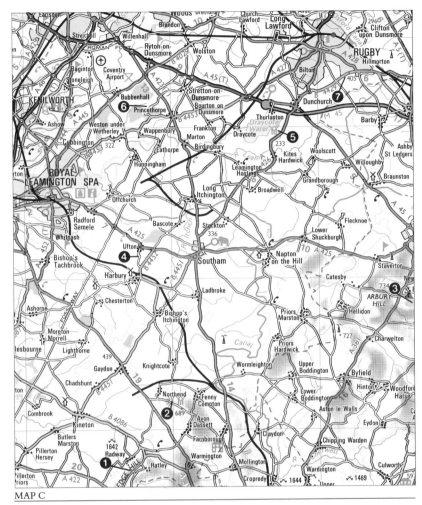

MAP C

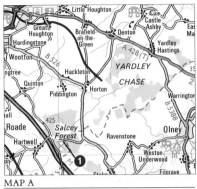

MAP A

NORTHAMPTONSHIRE

A:1 SALCEY FOREST*

Near Northampton; *car park in forest 2 miles (3 km) S of Quinton. For Trusts' reserve continue to crossroads, turn left, and site is in 1½ miles (2 km) on left. Open access to FC walks and conservation trail; two compartments (Great and Little Straits) on E edge of forest area are a reserve, open to members of county naturalists' trusts, otherwise by permit from either NTNC or BBONT.*

■ Oak/hazel/ash woodland.

■ The largest remaining ancient wood in Northamptonshire, much of Salcey has been commercially reafforested. FC walks on the W side of the forest offer sights and sounds of a wide range of woodland birds, including tame nuthatches at the picnic site, nightingales, lesser spotted woodpeckers, and occasional hobbies. The W part of the forest is structurally and botanically the most natural, and holds most of the scarcer plants of woodland and ride grasslands.

FORESTRY COMMISSION/
NORTHAMPTONSHIRE TRUST FOR NATURE
CONSERVATION/BERKS, BUCKS AND
OXON. NATURALISTS' TRUST

B:1 RAMSDEN CORNER PLANTATION

Near Daventry; *from Daventry, E on A45 then S for 1½ miles (2 km) on A5, turn right along minor road through Church Stowe; site is in 1½ miles (2 km), to N of road. Access by permit from NTNC.*

■ Acidic grassland, oak/ash/hazel woodland, scrub, stream valley.

■ Plants of local interest, including tormentil, cat's-ear, broad-leaved helleborine, bitter-vetch, wood horsetail and opposite-leaved golden saxifrage.

NORTHAMPTONSHIRE TRUST FOR NATURE
CONSERVATION

B:2 DAVENTRY COUNTRY PARK

Near Daventry; *car park off B4036 on N edge of Daventry.*

■ Reservoir.

■ Mainly of interest to birdwatchers, the park includes a nature trail, hide and reserve. Look for great crested grebes, wildfowl and a gull roost in winter, and waders, terns and occasional rarities (for example osprey) on passage.

B:3 RAVENSTHORPE RESERVOIR

Near Northampton; *from A428 going NW, turn right (N) on minor road to Coton; ½ mile (0.8 km) after Ravensthorpe, road crosses reservoir causeway. View from there, or obtain birdwatching permit at Holcot information centre, Pitsford Reservoir (see site D:A).*

---

and alder carr, scrub/woodland, calcareous grassland.

■ Quarrying and restoration in the 1950s have left their mark on this LNR in the form of deep pools and a series of limestone spoil ridges, much of which have been colonized by typical calcareous flora. Fifteen species of dragonfly and damselfly have been recorded around the pools including red-eyed damselfly and ruddy darter damselfly. The deep fresh waters hold other unusual insects, like the water stick-insect. Around the pool fringes willow and alder grow vigorously.

Under the deep shade of the conifers are many fungi and the saprophyte yellow bird's-nest. Where the soils consist of limestone spoil, the typical species-rich calcareous sward has developed, with abundant butterfly, bee and spotted orchids, and stemless thistle.

On a sunny day over 20 species of butterfly can be seen including small blue, marbled white, dusky and dingy skippers and green hairstreaks. A hard winter will bring in predatory birds such as short- and long-eared owls, sparrowhawk and kestrel, while the pools may hold bittern.
WARWICKSHIRE NATURE CONSERVATION
TRUST

C:5 DRAYCOTE WATER COUNTRY PARK*

Near Rugby; *car park off access road to Draycote Reservoir. Access to part of foreshore from park.*

■ Reservoir, grassland.

■ A large water supply reservoir noted as one of the best bird-watching sites in the region with 208 species recorded, including passage osprey, waders, terns, winter wildfowl, divers, grebes. Best visited in winter and during passage periods.
WARWICKSHIRE COUNTY COUNCIL

C:6 RYTON/WAPPENBURY WOODS

Kenilworth; *access along public bridleway off minor road (SP 383709) 1½ miles W of Princethorpe. Keep to footpaths, otherwise permit required: apply WNCT.*

■ Woodland.

■ Extensive broad-leaved (mainly oak) woodlands supporting a rich flora and fauna including the county's largest nightingale 'colony'. **Birds** Warblers, tree pipit, woodcock, woodpeckers. **Plants** Greater butterfly- and early-purple orchids, broad-leaved helleborine.
WARWICKSHIRE NATURE CONSERVATION
TRUST

C:7 ASHLAWN RAILWAY CUTTING

Near Rugby; *parking in small car park next to Ashlawn Bridge (SP 516732).*

■ Calcareous grassland, scrub, woodland.

■ Excellent example of species-rich grassland. **Plants** Green-winged orchid, twayblade, adder's tongue fern, broom-rape, quaking grass. **Butterflies** Small blue, green hairstreak, marbled white, brown argus.
WARWICKSHIRE NATURE CONSERVATION
TRUST

Emperor moths *are seen throughout the British Isles in Apr and May, when the males fly rapidly across heathland during the day. Females are mainly nocturnal, but sometimes perch on heather to bask in the daytime sun, revealing large false eyes on each wing which ward off predators. Emperor moths are the only British member of the silkmoth family, but their cocoons are unsuitable for producing silk.*

*Once common on heathlands, the **natterjack
toad** is almost restricted to a few sandy heaths
and coastal dunes in north-west England, East
Anglia and Hampshire. Winter is spent buried
in the sand but in Apr the natterjack emerges to
seek pools for breeding. Males sit around pool
margins croaking to attract nocturnal females.
The trilling croak is heard up to ½ mile (one
km) away, making the toad Britain's noisiest
amphibian.*

NORTHAMPTONSHIRE

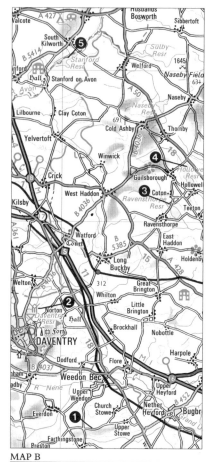

MAP B

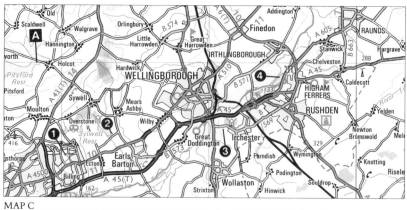

MAP C

■ Reed-beds, scrub, woodland.

■ Small reservoir in relatively steep valley; W end maintained as nature reserve. Of ornithological interest all year, with many wildfowl in winter. **Birds** (Winter) smew, grebes.

ANGLIA WATER AUTHORITY

B:4 HOLLOWELL RESERVOIR

Near Northampton; *from A50 going NNW, turn left (W) to Guilsborough after 10½ miles (15 km); access track and car park on left, , mile (0.5 km) from turn. Entry by permit from Holcot information centre, Pitsford Reservoir (see site D:A).*

■ Reservoir, grassland, woods.

■ A small reservoir, less sheltered than that at Ravensthorpe. A birdwatching site, best in winter for waterfowl; attracts waders, terns and occasional rarities on passage. **Birds** Little and black-necked grebes, goosander.

ANGLIA WATER AUTHORITY

B:5 STANFORD RESERVOIR

Near Rugby; *leave Rugby NE on B5414, taking second turn (right) after 7½ miles (11 km) to Stanford-on-Avon; reservoir on left just after turn. Entry by permit from S-TW; nature reserve area open to any member of a county naturalists' trust or by permit from NTNC.*

■ Reservoir.

■ Small reservoir attracting a variety of birds at all seasons, but best in autumn and winter when waders and terns (some rarities) on passage may be seen.

SEVERN-TRENT WATER/
NORTHAMPTONSHIRE TRUST FOR NATURE
CONSERVATION

C:A PITSFORD RESERVOIR✶✶

Near Northampton; *footpath/cycle track (free access) around S part of reservoir; permit needed for N (and best) part, from AW visitor centre.*

■ Reservoir, scrub, developing woodland.

■ An outstanding bird site, this 640-acre reservoir is shallow at its N (more interesting) end, where much muddy foreshore is exposed when water levels are low. Scrub and planted woodland, found mainly on the N and NW sides, add to the diversity of scenery and natural history.

① Park at AW centre, where birdwatching permits (daily or annual) to visit the NW section may be bought.

② Walk down to causeway. Goosanders and goldeneye often close by in winter.

③ Car park with views over, and access to, the deepest part near the dam, which attracts cormorants and, in hard weather, concentrations of duck as well as occasional stray divers and sea-duck.

④ On winter evenings a useful point to watch gull roost. Occasional 'white-winged' gulls – Mediterranean, glaucous, Iceland – recorded most years.

⑤ Start of public footpath running N; AW permit holders get closer access and views.

⑥ Birdwatching hide of Northampton Bird Club; sometimes open.

⑦ Area of woodland and scrub surrounding NE (Scaldwell) arm, the margins of which are much liked by snipe.

⑧ Car park.

⑨ Hide and walk (NTNC members or permit holders only) through young woodland around shallow NE (Walgrave) arm, often the best for waders and dabbling duck.

ANGLIA WATER AUTHORITY/
NORTHAMPTONSHIRE TRUST FOR NATURE
CONSERVATION

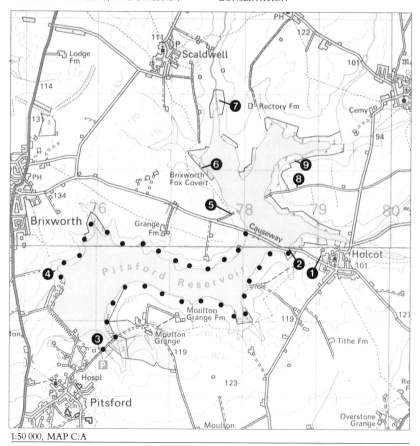

1:50 000, MAP C:A

C:1 LINGS WOOD

Near Northampton; car park on Lings Way, a turning off A45 on E outskirts of Northampton.
■ Mixed secondary woodland.
■ NTNC headquarters with visitor centre and nature trail. Formerly heathland, but now woodland with many alien species.
NORTHAMPTONSHIRE TRUST FOR NATURE CONSERVATION

C:2 SYWELL COUNTRY PARK

Near Earls Barton; car park and information centre 1½ miles (2 km) NW of Earls Barton (between Northampton and Wellingborough).
■ Reservoir, parkland.
■ Well-stocked bird-feeders attract large numbers of tits and finches in winter when reservoir holds small numbers (but good variety) of waterfowl; butterfly garden.
Birds Gadwall, lesser spotted woodpecker.
NORTHAMPTONSHIRE COUNTY COUNCIL

C:3 IRCHESTER COUNTRY PARK

Near Wellingborough; car parks SE of Wellingborough, off A509, on B570 Irchester to Little Irchester road. Nature trail; leaflet available on site.
■ Plantation woodland, scrub, grassland.
■ Developed on site of former ironstone quarry, planted with larch and Scots pine, plus some broadleaves supporting rookery and usual woodland birds; best in spring and summer. **Mammals** Muntjac.
NORTHAMPTONSHIRE COUNTY COUNCIL

C:4 HIGHAM FERRERS GRAVEL PITS

Near Higham Ferrers; park in Higham Ferrers at bottom of Wharf Road. Cross by-pass by footbridge and view gravel pit lakes from public footpaths. Alternative access by footpaths from Irthlingborough. Clay soils sticky after rain.
■ Flooded gravel pits.
■ Extensive, shallow flooded gravel pits, chiefly of interest for wildfowl and other water birds (including rarities), breeding, wintering or on passage.

D:1 WICKSTEED PARK

Near Kettering; park between A604 and A509 on SE outskirts of Kettering.
■ Lake, pools.
■ Urban bird-watching site, with green sandpipers and other waders on passage; redpolls and siskins in alders in winter.
WICKSTEED VILLAGE TRUST

D:2 THRAPSTON & TITCHMARSH GRAVEL PITS*

Near Thrapston; three main access points to public footpaths W from A605 in and N of Thrapston: 270 yards (250 metres) N of junction with A604; one mile (1.5 km) N; and down track 1¾ miles (2.5 km) N, opposite turn to Titchmarsh. Heronry closed during breeding season.
■ Flooded gravel pits, meadows, scrub.
■ Series of large flooded pits along River Nene, together with adjacent grassland and woodland, holds an interesting variety of breeding, migrant and passage birds. **Birds** (Breeding) herons, common tern, little ringed plover; (winter) goosander, goldeneye, wigeon; (passage) osprey, garganey, little gull, black tern, waders. **Plants** Cotton thistle.
NORTHAMPTONSHIRE WILDLIFE TRUST

D:3 BRIGSTOCK COUNTRY PARK

Near Corby; on S side of Brigstock just off A6116 along Barnard's Way.
■ Chalk grassland, scrub, marshy ponds,

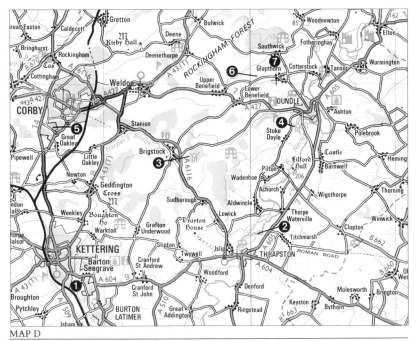

MAP D

oak woodland.
■ Wide variety of plants and butterflies associated with chalk grassland. Range of breeding woodland birds.
NORTHAMPTONSHIRE COUNTY COUNCIL/ FORESTRY COMMISSION

D:4 BARNWELL COUNTRY PARK

Near Oundle; car park just S of Oundle on A605. Information centre.
■ Flooded gravel pits, grassland, scrub.
■ Small, popular country park by tributary of river Nene of ornithological interest all year. **Birds** (Breeding) common tern; (winter) water rail; (passage) black tern, common sandpiper. **Dragonflies** Banded demoiselle.
NORTHAMPTONSHIRE COUNTY COUNCIL

D:5 KING'S WOOD

Near Corby; park on SE outskirts of Corby; 2 miles (3 km) from centre turn right at roundabout on A6014; wood is in ¼mile (0.5 km) on right.
■ Oak/ash woodland.
■ Urban remnant of ancient Rockingham Forest, with outstanding lichen community, fine ground flora and good variety of woodland birds. Best in spring and summer.
Plants Early-purple orchid, bluebell, common spotted orchid, common twayblade,

wood-sorrel.
NORTHAMPTONSHIRE TRUST FOR NATURE CONSERVATION

D:6 GLAPTHORN COW PASTURE

Near Oundle; park opposite site in green lane one mile (1.5 km) from Benefield. Keep to footpath. Entry open to any member of a county naturalists' trust. Otherwise NTNC permission required.
■ Scrub, ash/maple woodland.
■ Old pasture which has reverted to dense blackthorn scrub and damp woodland; a site for black hairstreak butterfly. **Plants** Great dodder. **Birds** (Breeding) nightingale.
NORTHAMPTONSHIRE TRUST FOR NATURE CONSERVATION

D:7 SHORT WOOD

Near Oundle; lies W of minor road from Oundle to Southwick; approach from bridle-path leading W from point ¾ mile (one km) S of Southwick, just S of water tower. Footpath along S side. Open to members of county naturalists' trusts, otherwise by permit from NTNC.
■ Oak/ash/maple woodland.
■ A relic of the ancient Rockingham Forest (includes Midland hawthorn, field maple and spindle) with rich ground flora including several locally rare species. **Plants**

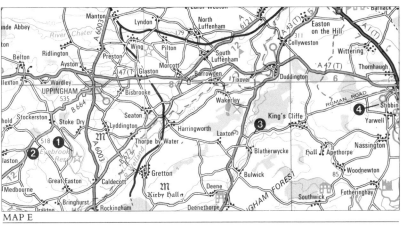

MAP E

NORTHAMPTONSHIRE/SHROPSHIRE

Greater butterfly and bird's-nest orchids.
NORTHAMPTONSHIRE TRUST FOR NATURE
CONSERVATION

E:1 EYEBROOK RESERVOIR★★

Near Corby; *lies just W of A6003 Corby to
Uppingham road; 1¾ miles (2.5 km) S of latter,
minor road leads through Stoke Dry to N and W
sides of reservoir. No public access but good views
from roads, especially along the W shore.*
■ Reservoir.
■ A 395-acre reservoir holding a range of
wintering wildfowl and attracting scarcer
species on passage and in hard weather. Set
in an attractive valley, the N shallow end is
especially good for passage waders, gulls
and dabbling duck. Good all year, but
autumn to spring best. **Birds** Garganey,
Bewick's swan, ruddy duck, goosander,
pintail; (passage) osprey, hobby, little gull,
black tern, black-necked grebe, little stint;
(cold weather) great northern diver, Slavonian and red-necked grebes.
CORBY & DISTRICT WATER COMPANY

E:2 GREAT MERRIBLE WOOD

Near Corby; *lies 5½ miles (8 km) NNW of
town. Entrance ¾ mile (one km) S of crossroads
of B664 and Great Easton to Horninghold road.
Park on roadside; then by foot across two fields to
wood. Open to members of a county naturalists'
trust; otherwise by permit from L&RTNC.*
■ Ash/maple woodland.
■ A fragment of the ancient Leighfield
forest which once covered large areas in this
part of the county; retains a varied flora and
breeding bird population. Best in spring and
summer. **Plants** Violet and broad-leaved
helleborine, herb Paris, giant bellflower,
early-purple orchid.
LEICESTERSHIRE & RUTLAND TRUST FOR
NATURE CONSERVATION

E:3 BLATHERWYCKE LAKE

Near King's Cliffe; *no access to private estate
but lake and parkland may be viewed from minor
road from King's Cliffe to Blatherwycke. Telescope recommended.*
■ Lake, parkland.
■ Private park lake, formed by impound-
ing Willow brook, and of considerable wildfowl interest. Best in winter.

E:4 OLD SULEHAY FOREST

Near Peterborough; *at Wansford on A1 7
miles (10 km) W of Peterborough, turn S on
minor road to Yarwell; wood is to W between the
two villages. Keep to footpaths.*
■ Oak/ash woodland.
■ Remnant of the ancient Rockingham
Forest on acid soils; contains several unusual
coppice types with good understory.
Ground flora includes a number of locally
uncommon species.

E:5 COLLYWESTON QUARRY

Near Easton on the Hill; *park in Easton.
Turn W down Westfield and Ketton Drift, taking
footpath to S just beyond recreation ground. Off
footpath, permit required from NTNC.*
■ Jurassic limestone grassland.
■ Former limestone quarry with species-
rich grassland dominated by upright brome
and tor grass with downy oak and quaking
grass. Good butterfly populations. **Plants**
Broomrape, pyramidal orchid, Dyer's
greenweed, clustered bellflower, dropwort.
NORTHAMPTONSHIRE TRUST FOR NATURE
CONSERVATION

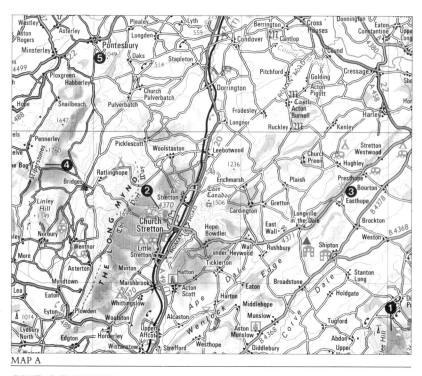

MAP A

SHROPSHIRE

A:1 BROWN CLEE HILL

Cleobury Mortimer; *parking and access to
nature trail from unclassified road one mile (1.5
km) W of Cleobury North at SO 607782.*
■ Upland grassland, heath, woodland.
■ The trail leads through plantation woodland, but the best areas of this large isolated
hill are the tops and valleys to the W, occupied by hill grassland, heath and scrub.

A:2 THE LONG MYND

Church Stretton; *park at head of Cardingmill
Valley, then explore on foot.*
■ Moorland, streams, bog, rock outcrops.
■ A huge, whale-backed plateau whose
slopes are cut by deep winding valleys cut by
springs.
Most of the site is dominated by heather
moorland with sweeps of bilberry and
bracken. Some of the sheltered slopes support acid grassland scattered with hawthorn
and rowan scrub. Plants of the moorland include shepherd's cress, navelwort, Wilson's
filmy fern and greater broomrape. The flush
sites hold bog-loving species such as marsh
lousewort, round-leaved sundew, bog pimpernel and butterwort.
The unpolluted water of the streams supports rich invertebrate fauna; also brown
trout, dipper and grey wagtail. **Birds** Red
grouse, ring ouzel, pied flycatcher, redstart,
wood warbler, raven, wheatear, whinchat,
buzzard.
NATIONAL TRUST

A:3 WENLOCK EDGE★

Much Wenlock; *many access points from the
B4371; keep to the network of footpaths.*
■ Woodland, grassland.
■ One of the major landscape features of
Shropshire. Much of the Edge is composed
of limestones and calcareous shales and
clays. The ridge presents a near-continuous
line of woodland; although much has been
replanted with conifers, there are still considerable areas of ancient woodland worthy

of exploration. In addition to the woodland,
small banks of limestone grassland, disused
quarries and flush sites add to the interest.
The flora is exceptionally rich, especially
in calcicoles even though much exploration
is needed to uncover the treasures. Notable
species include herb Paris, yellow bird's-
nest, gromwell, autumn gentian, wood
vetch, rock stonecrop, wood barley, sainfoin and at least 12 orchids.
NATIONAL TRUST/SHROPSHIRE TRUST FOR
NATURE CONSERVATION

A:4 STIPERSTONES★★

Bishop's Castle; *parking at S end of reserve on
N side of unclassified road from bridges to the bog.
Foot access unrestricted.*
■ Moorland.
■ The rocks on this 2-mile (3-km) range of
hills are predominantly acid and there are a
series of striking quartzite tors on the summit, which is also renowned for its stone
stripes and polygons. A number of steep
dingles run W from the ridge. Most of the
area is dominated by heathland with sub-
montane characteristics. Heather is the
dominant plant with a large proportion of
bilberry. Other heathland plants include
cowberry, crowberry, western gorse and
bell heather.
Other areas support acidic grassland
which, although generally species-poor,
holds populations of the mountain pansy.
There are several wet flushes and boggy
areas with cottongrass, butterwort, bog
asphodel and marsh violet.
NATURE CONSERVANCY COUNCIL

A:5 EARL'S HILL

Pontesbury; *park in Pontesford village; follow
narrow lane S – path to reserve and visitor centre
are signposted.*
■ Grassland, woodland, scree, scrub,
stream.
■ A striking steep-sided bluff rising above
the N Shropshire plain, Earl's Hill is an outcrop of ancient pre-Cambrian rocks surrounded by younger sedimentary rocks.

MAP B

The tops and slopes to the SW hold acid grassland with some scrub invasion: plants include smooth cat's-ear, harebell, greater broomrape. The sunny SW slopes are good for butterflies

The steep cliffs on the side give way to scree which supports bloody crane's-bill and rock stonecrop. Lower slopes are clothed in species-rich ancient woodland with uncommon trees – large-leaved lime, wild service-tree and herbs such as meadow saffron. SHROPSHIRE TRUST FOR NATURE CONSERVATION

B:1 BENTHALL EDGE WOOD

Ironbridge; park in Ironbridge and cross River Severn. Enter wood from disused railway line to W of Ladywood.
■ Oak/lime woodland, river.
■ A large, ancient semi-natural woodland on the steep slopes of the Severn gorge with a rich flora and fauna. **Plants** Herb Paris, wild service-tree, butterfly and early-purple orchids, large-leaved and small-leaved lime, thin-spiked wood-sedge.

C:1 LLYNCLYS COMMON★

Near Oswestry; from the Llynclys crossroads, take A495 and turn first left up lane on to common.
■ Limestone grassland, woodland, scrub.
■ A fine area of limestone grassland with a rich flora being invaded by scrub and birch woodland. Ten species of orchid, including bee, frog, lesser and greater butterfly, pyramidal and fragrant.
SHROPSHIRE TRUST FOR NATURE CONSERVATION

C:2 CRAIG SYCHTYN

Near Oswestry; leave B4396 just before Welsh border going N along minor road. Take first right and follow road for about 2 miles (3 km); wood on left (SJ 234252).
■ Woodland, cliffs.
■ A mixed broad-leaved woodland of oak, ash and elm, with a rich calcareous flora set beneath a cliff of carboniferous limestone.
SHROPSHIRE TRUST FOR NATURE CONSERVATION

MAP C

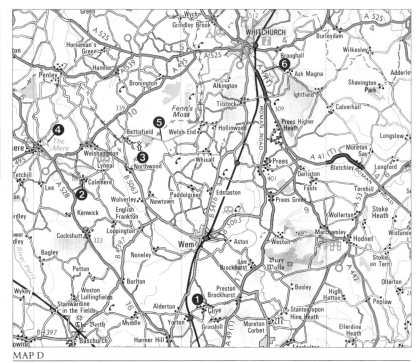

MAP D

D:1 CORBET WOOD

Wem; turn W off A49 at Preston Brockhurst, then first left up to car park on edge of wood.
■ Woodland, quarries.
■ A mixed broad-leaved woodland of wild cherry, oak, beech, birch and rowan with some conifers and an acidic ground flora. Old quarries, of geological interest, add diversity. **Plants** Alkanet, common spotted orchid, bilberry.
SHROPSHIRE TRUST FOR NATURE CONSERVATION

D:2 COLEMERE COUNTRY PARK

Ellesmere; park at E end of mere.
■ Lake, woodland, grassland.
■ A large natural lake set within fringing woodlands. Beds of emergent vegetation and open grassland to the SE add diversity. **Birds** (Winter) goosander, goldeneye, shoveler, wigeon; (passage) waders and terns.
SHROPSHIRE COUNTY COUNCIL

D:3 WEM MOSS★

Ellesmere; turn off B5063 at Northwood down unclassified road to Dobson's Bridge. In ¼ mile (0.5 km) a track heads N: follow this for about ½ mile (0.8 km). Moss is on right within wood. A footpath gives access, but a permit must be obtained, apply STNC.
■ Raised bog, woodland.
■ A fine example of a lowland raised mire developed on a glacial mere exhibiting a good pool and ridge network and surrounded by woodland. The variation in surface wetness has given rise to a remarkably rich flora and fauna. **Plants** Bog rosemary, bog asphodel, meadow thistle, cranberry, early marsh- and lesser butterfly-orchids.
SHROPSHIRE TRUST FOR NATURE CONSERVATION

D:4 THE MERE, ELLESMERE

Ellesmere; car park off the main road through Ellesmere where it adjoins the Mere.
■ Lake.
■ The largest of the Shropshire meres: heavy recreational use has led to some degradation, but this is still an important site, particularly for winter wildfowl and the gull roost. **Birds** Smew, goosander, goldeneye, shoveler, wigeon. **Plants** Marsh cinquefoil, marsh violet, cottongrass, needle spike-rush, horned pondweed.
SHROPSHIRE COUNTY COUNCIL

D:5 SHROPSHIRE UNION CANAL – PREES BRANCH★

Wem; at Waterloo Park take towpath N along canal.
■ Disused canal.
■ Here is a fine succession of aquatic plants from closed reed swamp with invading alder to open water communities.

Reed swamp with water dock dominates the S end; towards the N this gives way to communities dominated by frogbit and hornwort which in turn are succeeded by open communities with yellow water-lily, water-milfoil and pondweeds. The canal is one of the richest sites in Britain for pondweeds with ten species recorded including red, long-stalked, flat-stalked and grass-wrack.

The invertebrate fauna includes several species of dragonfly, including red-eyed damselfly and it is particularly good for water snails including uncommon species. There is a varied fish community which includes the introduced and scarce bitterling.
SHROPSHIRE TRUST FOR NATURE CONSERVATION

D:6 BROWN MOSS★

Whitchurch; parking in wood adjoining site.
■ Pools, bog, heath, woodland.
■ A former peat bog now with a series of pools; peripheral heath and woodland. The wetland flora is rich and the site is locally important for birds. **Plants** Floating water-plantain, marsh St John's-wort, sundew, cranberry, water-violet, marsh violet, lesser water-plantain, lesser marshwort, least bur-reed, purple small reed, floating clubrush.
SHROPSHIRE COUNTY COUNCIL

WEST MIDLANDS/STAFFORDSHIRE

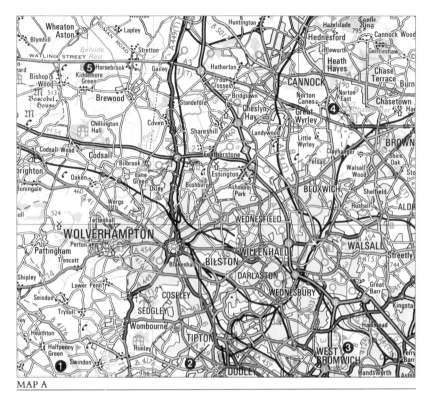

MAP A

A:1 HIGHGATE COMMON
Stourbridge; *common is one mile (1.5 km) W of Swindon.*
■ Heathland, woodland.
■ A fairly extensive tract of heather heathland with areas of birch woodland. **Birds** Tree pipit, sparrowhawk, woodpeckers, redpoll. **Plants** Shepherd's cress, sea stork's-bill, viper's-bugloss.
STAFFORDSHIRE COUNTY COUNCIL

A:2 WREN'S NEST★
Near Dudley; *entrance to nature trail off Wren's Nest Road. Fossil collecting not allowed.*
■ Disused quarry, rock faces, wood, grassland.
■ Fine exposures of Silurian limestone with abundant fossils. Calcareous plants such as autumn gentian and invertebrates well represented. Mons Hill to N worth a visit.
NATURE CONSERVANCY COUNCIL

A:3 SANDWELL VALLEY
Near West Bromwich; *entrance to nature trails from Salter's Lane, SP 017914. Entrance to RSPB reserve from Tanhouse Lane (car park) off Hamstead road, SP 036931.*
■ Lakes, woodland, parkland, grassland, marsh.
■ Extensive area of open country with a wide variety of habitats. Wetlands and lakes of particular interest for wildfowl (best in winter, spring and autumn) and other wetland birds.
SANDWELL BOROUGH COUNCIL/ROYAL SOCIETY FOR PROTECTION OF BIRDS

A:4 CHASEWATER
Near Brownhills; *car park at S end of site, GR 035072. Footpath along W shore of lake. Intensive recreational use.*
■ Lake, lowland heath.
■ A large pool of regional importance for birds. Winter wildfowl and gull roost; passage waders, terns, rarities. Small but interesting areas of heath at S end.

Lesser spotted woodpecker – see A:2.

A:5 BELVIDE RESERVOIR
Cannock *on S side of A5 4 miles (6.5 km) W of M5. Keep to bridle-path along W boundary, otherwise permit required – apply WMBC.*
■ Lake, marshy meadows.
■ A large canal feeder reservoir with a marshy fringe and surrounded by grassland. One of the best lakes for wildfowl/water birds in the region; winter gull roost often includes Iceland and glaucous gulls. **Birds** (Breeding) Garganey, gadwall, ruddy duck, shoveler, teal, great crested grebe; (winter) goosander, goldeneye, ruddy duck, wigeon, sea duck; (passage) black, common and Arctic terns, waders, hirundines.
BRITISH WATERWAYS BOARD/WEST MIDLAND BIRD CLUB

STAFFORDSHIRE

A:1 TILLINGTON-DOXEY MARSHES★
Stafford; *off A5013 at SJ 909248. The site lies alongside the A5013 in Stafford; take path on to marsh.*
■ Marsh, pools, river.
■ At first sight, Tillington appears to be an unlikely place for a bird site of regional importance, being hemmed in on three sides by houses, on the fourth by the M6 and dissected by a railway. However, Tillington is an extensive area of marshland centred around the confluence of the Darling and Doxey Brook and the River Sow. It consists of a mosaic of small pools, grazed wet pasture, marsh, reed-beds and ditches. The complex provides ideal conditions for a wide range of wetland birds. The diverse breeding community includes redshank, snipe, ruddy duck, teal, whinchat, kingfisher and reed and grasshopper warblers. There are a good passage of waders, hobby in summer and occasional rarities. Winter brings snipe (up to 600), jack snipe, water rail, wildfowl, stonechat, short-eared owl and occasional great grey shrike.
STAFFORDSHIRE NATURE CONSERVATION TRUST

A:2 LOYNTON MOSS★
Near Newport; *park to W of canal bridge, one mile (1.5 km) SW of Woodseaves on A519. Access along lane 300 yards (270 m) towards Woodseaves; follow lane over canal into site. Keep to footpaths, otherwise permit required – apply SNCT.*
■ Reed-bed, raised bog, woodland, fen.
■ An important wetland complex lying in a glacial basin and showing a fine transition from reed-bed through alder carr to raised bog. A calcareous embankment adds floristic diversity. **Birds** Lesser and greater spotted woodpeckers, reed and sedge warblers. **Plants** Greater spearwort, bog myrtle, elongated and bladder sedges.
STAFFORDSHIRE NATURE CONSERVATION TRUST

A:3 COP MERE
Eccleshall; *from Eccleshall take B5026 W. In 1½ miles (2.5 km) turn W; after ½ mile (0.8 km) pool on left. Keep to footpath which runs along E side of lake.*
■ Lake, woodland.
■ A natural mere of glacial origin fringed with reeds and broad-leaved woodland on three sides. **Birds** (Breeding) Redstart, wood warbler, woodpeckers, ruddy duck, water rail, great crested grebe, grasshopper and reed warblers, sparrowhawk; (winter) ruddy duck, goosander, water rail, goldeneye, wigeon. **Plants** Shoreweed.

B:1 BLITHEFIELD RESERVOIR★
Rugeley; *leave Rugeley N on B5013; in 4 miles (6.5 km) a causeway crosses reservoir; view from causeway or unclassified road on E side; permit required to visit hides available from West Midland Bird Club.*
■ Reservoir.
■ A large water-supply reservoir ranked third in Britain for wildfowl numbers. Passage periods bring waders, terns, rarities and in winter there is a large gull roost. **Birds** (Winter) Iceland and glaucous gulls, divers, grebes, ruddy duck, goosander; (passage) black and common terns, more than 20 wader species.
SOUTH STAFFS WATERWORKS COMPANY

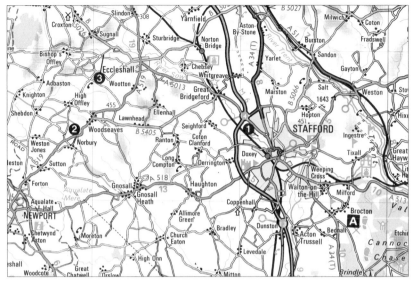

MAP A

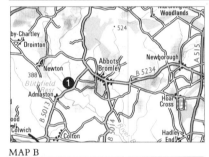

MAP B

C:1 DIMMINGS DALE
Cheadle; *from Alton take unclassified road NW along Churnet Valley. In one mile (1.5 km) bridle-path on left leads up Dimmingsdale; keep to footpaths.*

■ Woodland, grassland, stream.

■ An attractive wooded valley running along a fast-flowing stream. A range of woodland plants and animals are represented. **Birds** Redstart, wood warbler, dipper, woodcock, sparrowhawk, woodpeckers. **Plants** Upland enchanter's-nightshade.

C:2 HAWKSMOOR WOOD★
Cheadle; *on the N side of the B5417 2 miles (3 km) E of Cheadle.*

■ Heath, woodland.

■ Hawksmoor occupies a prominent posi-

tion on the steep valley slopes of the attractive Churnet Valley. The site overlies sandstone giving rise to acid soils. Large areas are birch- and bracken-clad hillside. Other parts hold more mature woodland of oak, both pedunculate and sessile, and birch with holly, rowan and alder buckthorn. The ground flora is typical of acid oak woodland with species such as cow-wheat, wood horsetail and wood-sorrel. Fallow deer are present. The birdlife is rich, with grey wagtail and dipper along the river, while the heath and wood support tree pipit, woodcock, redpoll, woodpeckers, nuthatch, sparrowhawk, redstart, pied flycatcher, willow and marsh tits.
NATIONAL TRUST

C:3 PARK HALL COUNTRY PARK
Stoke-on-Trent; *from A520 turn W on to B5040; after ¾ mile (one km) turn right on unclassified road to car park.*

■ Heath, pools, woodland, grassland, canyons.

■ A diverse site with a range of habitats on the site of former sand and coal extraction. The heath and pool areas are best for wildlife. **Birds** (Breeding) whinchat, stonechat, grasshopper warbler, sand martin, redshank; (winter/passage) short-eared owl, golden plover, wildfowl.
STAFFORDSHIRE COUNTY COUNCIL

A:A CANNOCK CHASE
Stafford.

① Heathland – this is outstanding, representing a transition between southern lowland heath and northern moor, supporting many species common to both. The flora is dominated by ericaceous shrubs with scattered trees and scrub – bell heather, crowberry, cowberry, bilberry, sheep's-bit and the best population of the hybrid bilberry (cowberry × bilberry) in Britain. Birds include meadow pipit, whinchat, grasshopper warbler and stonechat. Winter brings great grey shrike, hen harrier, short-eared owl, merlin and buzzard.

The extensive conifer plantations should not be ignored. Young plantations hold nightjar, grasshopper warbler and the pipit, while mature areas have long-eared owl, siskin, crossbill, and redpoll. Many paths cross the area.

② Good site for nightjar.

③ The Sherbrook Valley, lined with alders, is good for moths, small pearl-bordered fritillary, lesser spotted woodpecker, siskin and redpoll.

④ Oldacre Valley has extensive stands of willow scrub.

⑤ Brocton Coppice: This sessile oak/birch wood is the best area of native woodland on the Chase with old oaks up to 300 years old. It has plants such as cow-wheat and climbing corydalis and a rich fungus flora. It is also rich in beetles and moths associated with old woodland and has a diverse bird community – hawfinch, redstart, wood warbler, woodcock, woodpeckers, tree pipit.

⑥ Brocton Pool, the largest pool on the Chase, good for breeding and wintering wildfowl.

The Chase is noted for its deer: muntjac, red, roe, sika and fallow.
STAFFORDSHIRE COUNTY COUNCIL

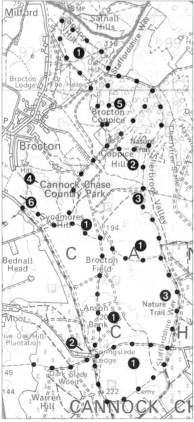

1:50 000, MAP A:A

MAP C

STAFFORDSHIRE

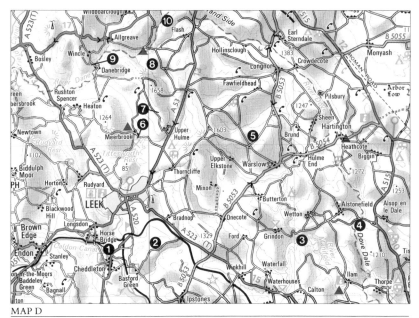

MAP D

D:1 DEEP HAYES COUNTRY PARK

Leek; *from Leek take A53 and W after 3 miles (5 km) turn left to horse bridge. Entrance to park is over Caldon Canal.*

■ Lake, marsh, meadow, woodland.

■ A small but diverse country park centred around a large pool with fringing marsh. Grassland and small areas of woodland increase the range of habitats. **Birds** Kingfisher, grey wagtail, sedge warbler. **Plants** Greater butterfly-orchid, dwarf elder, dyer's greenweed, adder's-tongue fern.

STAFFORDSHIRE COUNTY COUNCIL

D:2 COOMBES VALLEY*

Leek; *reserve on the Cheddleton to Bradnop road, 4 miles (6.5 km) S of Leek. Report to RSPB information centre on arrival (visiting arrangements may be variable – contact RSPB).*

■ Woodland, grassland, scrub, stream, heath.

■ A wooded valley with species-rich stream-side meadows and areas of heath. The oak wood is species rich and the whole area is good for invertebrates. **Birds** (Breeding) long-eared and tawny owl, redstart, pied flycatcher, dipper, kingfisher, woodpeckers, grey wagtail, sparrowhawk. **Butterflies** High brown fritillary. **Plants** Greater butterfly- and early-purple orchids.

ROYAL SOCIETY FOR THE PROTECTION OF BIRDS

D:3 MANIFOLD VALLEY**

Leek; *park at Weags bridge 1½ miles (2.5 km) E of Grindon (SK 100543); trails are marked from car park.*

■ Woodland, grassland, cliffs, river.

■ A rich and varied limestone valley with a wealth of high-quality calcareous habitats. Riverside meadows, limestone grassland, wooded slopes, towering cliffs, caves and old quarries set within a beautiful valley make this a naturalist's paradise. **Birds** Redstart, wood warbler, dipper, common sandpiper, kingfisher, grey wagtail, whinchat. **Plants** Mezereon, Nottingham catchfly, orpine, greater butterfly- and green-winged orchids, Jacob's-ladder, mountain currant, narrow-leaved bittercress, sweet cicely.

NATIONAL TRUST

D:4 DOVEDALE**

Ashbourne; *from Ashbourne head N on A515; in one mile (1.5 km) turn left (signpost) for Dovedale. From car park in Dovedale head N on footpaths up valley.*

■ Limestone grassland, woodland, cliff/scree.

■ The River Dove flows through carboniferous limestone country and is set within a spectacular, deep valley. It supports a diverse range of semi-natural habitats. The whole area, from Dovedale in the S through Milldale, Beresford Dale to Wolfscote Dale and the side valley Biggin Dale, are worthy of exploration – a total length of 6 to 7 miles (9.5 to 11 km). Dovedale itself supports a fine limestone ash woodland with oak, beech, rowan, whitebeam, rock whitebeam and mountain currant. A series of rich calcareous grasslands, exhibiting a range of variation dependent on aspect and soil condition, occupy many of the valley sides. Cliffs and screes, some wooded, hold many rare plants and the river itself has a diverse fauna.

Most of the widespread limestone plants are present, plus others such as green spleenwort, limestone fern, wall whitlow-grass, mountain St John's-wort, Nottingham catchfly, large-leaved lime, orpine, mossy saxifrage, wood fescue, hutchinsia, dark-red helleborine, narrow-leaved hempnettle and spring sandwort. Butterflies include brown argus, green and white-letter hairstreak, dingy and grizzled skipper. The varied birdlife includes dipper, kingfisher, grey wagtail, redstart, buzzard, wood warbler, tree pipit.

NATIONAL TRUST

D:5 SWALLOW MOSS

Leek; *leave B5053 along unclassified road leading W at Warslow; Swallow Moss is by road after 2 miles (3 km).*

■ Moorland, blanket bog.

■ An extensive area of upland blanket bog dominated by *Sphagnum* and cottongrass with areas of moorland. **Birds** Twite, whinchat. **Plants** Bog asphodel, violet.

D:6 RUDYARD RESERVOIR

Leek; *lane to reservoir from Harper's Gate; nature trail runs along old railway on E side, or*
take footpath through woods on W side.

■ Lake, woodland, old railway, marsh.

■ A long, narrow canal feeder reservoir with mixed woodland on the W and a disused railway on the E side. Marsh/wetland occurs at the N end and along the E shore. **Birds** (Breeding) redstart, wood warbler, sparrowhawk, great crested grebe; (winter) Bewick's and whooper swans, goosander.

STAFFORDSHIRE NATURE CONSERVATION TRUST

D:7 THE ROACHES

Leek; *footpaths lead up on to The Roaches from unclassified road at Roach End (SJ 995645).*

■ Moorland, cliff, woodland.

■ A prominent hill clothed in heather moorland. The ridge line is dominated by a line of cliffs. **Birds** Red grouse, ring ouzel, twite, whinchat. **Plants** Mountain pansy, cowberry, crowberry. **Mammals** Red-necked wallaby, mountain hare.

PEAK PARK JOINT PLANNING BOARD

D:8 BLACKBROOK VALLEY & GOLDSITCH MOSS*

Buxton; *turn W off A53 at Morridge Top on to unclassified road past Gibtor; Goldsitch is in 1½ miles (2.5 km). Explore the Moss and follow footpath down Black Brook.*

■ Moorland, blanket bog, rock, stream.

■ Goldsitch is a blanket bog of floristic and ornithological interest, drained by the Black Brook, which runs through an interesting valley with moorland, rock outcrops and scrubby woodland. **Birds** Black and red grouse, ring ouzel, short- and long-eared owls, twite, golden plover, whinchat. **Plants** Bog rosemary, bog asphodel.

D:9 DANE VALLEY*

Near Congleton; *Danebridge (limited car parking), 1¼ miles (2 km) SE of A54, via unclassified road which leaves A54 at SJ 953619; keep to footpaths.*

■ River, broad-leaved woodland, upland heather moor, blanket bog.

■ A fast-flowing upland river passing from open moorland to a heavily wooded valley. The high-quality water supports a substantial fish population and attracts typical birds.

D:10 GOYT VALLEY

Near Macclesfield; *approach on A5002 or A54 and A537. Car parks at Derbyshire Bridge (SK 017718) and elsewhere. Traffic control schemes operate during peak periods. Contact Peak District National Park for details.*

■ Moorland, flushed grassland, open water, coniferous plantation, blanket bog.

■ The Goyt Valley is surrounded by high gritstone moorland which overlies Carboniferous Coal Measures. The land is used for sheep farming, forestry and water catchment, and in the past had a thriving farming community, a gunpowder factory, a paint works and a railway. Most of this has now gone, though you can still trace part of the railway track. Errwood Hall, is now a ruin, but the surrounding grounds have been developed as a woodland walk.

Flooding the valley floor created Fernilee and Errwood Reservoirs. The surrounding moors are important for nesting waders and other moorland birds. There are several botanically interesting flush areas. **Birds** Red grouse, dipper, ground-nesting waders. **Plants** Shoreweed, deergrass.

FORESTRY COMMISSION/PEAK DISTRICT NATIONAL PARK

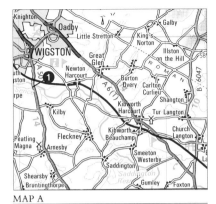

MAP A

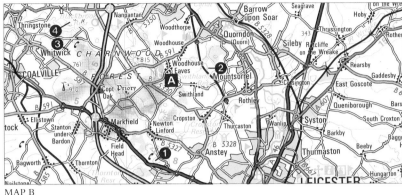

MAP B

A:1 GRAND UNION CANAL

Near Leicester; section from Kilby Bridge (on A50 just S of Leicester) to Foxton Locks (near Market Harborough). No general right of way but access from many points where roads and footpaths cross the canal.

■ Canal.

■ The 12½-mile (18-km) stretch of navigable canal is an SSSI, with a varied aquatic and marginal plant community, as well as dragonflies. Tunnels between Fleckney and Saddington hold colonies of Daubenton's

and Natterer's bats. Best in spring and summer. **Plants** Flowering-rush, frogbit, arrowhead, sweet-flag.
BRITISH WATERWAYS/LEICESTERSHIRE & RUTLAND TRUST FOR NATURE CONSERVATION

B:1 GROBY POOL

Near Leicester; near A50 NW of town on Groby to Newton Linford road. Free car park just S of Groby pool. Pool itself is private, but footpath on E side leading from car park gives views.

■ Open water, reed swamp.

■ The largest (32 acres) sheet of natural open water in the county, fringed with reeds and trees, and attracting numbers of ruddy duck and other wildfowl, esp. in winter.

B:2 SWITHLAND RESERVOIR

Near Loughborough; lies 1½ miles (2 km) W of Mountsorrel, reached by minor roads, one of which, between Rothley Plain and Swithland crosses S part of reservoir. No access but may be viewed from public road.

B:A BRADGATE PARK – CROPSTON RESERVOIR – SWITHLAND WOOD – THE BRAND – BEACON HILL – THE OUTWOODS – CHARNWOOD FOREST**

Near Leicester; car park and information centre (Marion's Cottage) at the S entrance to Bradgate Park.

■ Grassland, heath, deciduous/mixed woodland, reservoir, muddy shoreline.

■ A series of sites open to the public centered 7 miles (10 km) NW of Leicester, offering a wide range of habitats and natural history interest. Each may be visited in turn by car or, better, as a 7-mile (10-km) one-way walk. (Arrange lift from far end.)

① **Bradgate Park**, a large area of grassland and heath, dotted with small woods, plantations and rocky outcrops, where common lizards bask in the sun. Tormentil and harebells provide summer colour, when there is a varied bird community, including whinchat. Fallow deer 'sanctuary' at S end.

② E side of park overlooks **Cropston Reservoir**, which often has ruddy duck and holds large numbers of mallard, wigeon, and teal in winter. Shallow, S end attracts yellow wagtails and common sandpipers, greenshank and scarcer waders such as spotted redshank on passage.

③ **Swithland Wood**, remnant of the ancient **Charnwood Forest** (car parks to N and S). Rich ground flora – wood sage, enchanter's-nightshade, wood-sorrel, wood melick, bluebell, yellow pimpernel and hairy wood-rush. Excellent range of woodland birds includes wood warbler and hawfinch.

④ A small, old pasture holds common spotted-orchid, saw-wort and adder's-tongue. Just N is small but deep and dangerous old slate quarry, water-filled, with harebells and other flowers in the short turf around its perimeter. More plants species present in Swithland than in any equivalent area in Leicestershire.

⑤ Further water-filled quarries found at **the Brand**.

⑥ On a clear day, **Beacon Hill** provides

superb all-round views over the surrounding countryside. Its crags are among the oldest rocks in Britain. Top of hill dominated by tufted hair-grass and fescues; slopes covered by bracken, with scattered birch and rowan.

⑦ **The Outwoods** are oak woodland, the centre of which has been planted with conifers. Waymarked nature trails.
BRADGATE PARK TRUST/CHARNWOOD BOROUGH COUNCIL

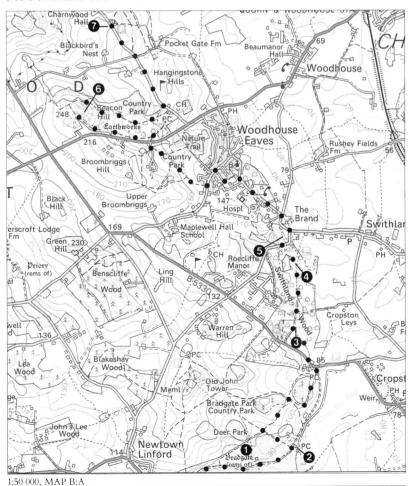

1:50 000, MAP B:A

■ Reservoir.
■ Bird-watching site, with good numbers of wintering waterfowl, including up to 100 ruddy duck, and a variety of migrants on passage. Reservoir is fringed with mixed woodland and has small area of fen at its S end. Good all year but best for wildfowl in winter. **Birds** Ruddy duck, gadwall, shoveler, goldeneye; (passage) hobby, Arctic tern, waders.
SEVERN-TRENT WATER AUTHORITY

B:3 CHARNWOOD LODGE

Near Loughborough; from town, go W on A512, turning S on minor road 1½ miles (2 km) after crossing M1 (junction 23); entrance on left (E) in 2 miles (3 km). Entry by permit from the L&RTNC.
■ Moorland.

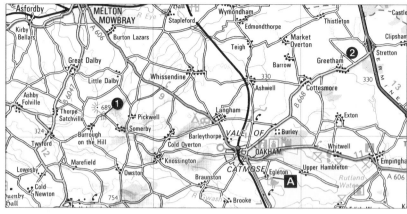

MAP C

C:A RUTLAND WATER**

Near Oakham; car parks at site. Footpaths, cycle tracks, and one nature trail around reservoir. Permits required for non-members of L&RTNC to reserve areas.
■ Reservoir, lagoons, reed-bed, old meadow grassland, reseeded grassland, scrub, secondary woodland.
■ Large, new (1977) reservoir has created major wetland, combining vast 3,065-acre water surface with variety of wetland and lakeside habitats, some semi-natural (old meadows, reedswamp, scrub) some artificial (lagoons, islands, muddy margins and flats, reseeded grassland, secondary woodland). Recreational use is zoned, and the W end actively managed as nature reserve. One of the best reservoir sites for wintering and moulting wildfowl in the country and holds outstanding concentrations of mallard, shoveler, wigeon, gadwall, teal, pochard, tufted duck and goldeneye. Great variety of waders (up to 19 species in a day) and other migrants recorded on passage. One of the best inland bird-watching sites in the country.
① Egleton reserve (closed weekdays exc Wed); fee for entry by day permit (9 am–5 pm) from information centre in car park gives access to trail and ten hides overlooking lagoons and reservoir. Control of water levels in lagoons provides for different habitat requirements of waders and wildfowl.
② From road at Manton Bridge look for waders on muddy water's edge.
③ Lyndon reserve (closed weekdays in winter, Mon and Fri, May–Oct), fee for entry by day permit (10 am–4 pm) from interpretive centre. Nature trail and three hides provide views of wildfowl in SW corner of reservoir.
④ Sykes Lane car park is close to dam, hence deepest part of reservoir, and last area to freeze in exceptionally severe winters. Numbers of diving ducks often concentrate here, and rarer sea ducks or divers may be seen.
⑤ Whitwell car park, from which nature trail runs along reservoir boundary to
⑥ Barnwell car park, and footpath to NW corner of reservoir, nearest to Oakham.
⑦ Shallow bays and foreshore in this section hold many wildfowl and waders.
⑧ Total shoreline is nearly 28 miles (40 km); 4-mile (6-km) circular walk around 'island' of Hambleton gives good impression of scale of this, one of Britain's largest man-made lakes; an increasingly important refuge for waterfowl.
Birds Ruddy duck, shelduck; (breeding) long-eared owl, little ringed plover, oyster-catcher, common tern, reed warbler; (hard weather) rarer grebes, smew, scaup; (winter) short-eared owls, ruff, green sandpiper; (passage) osprey, hobby, terns.
ANGLIA WATER/LEICESTERSHIRE & RUTLAND TRUST FOR NATURE CONSERVATION

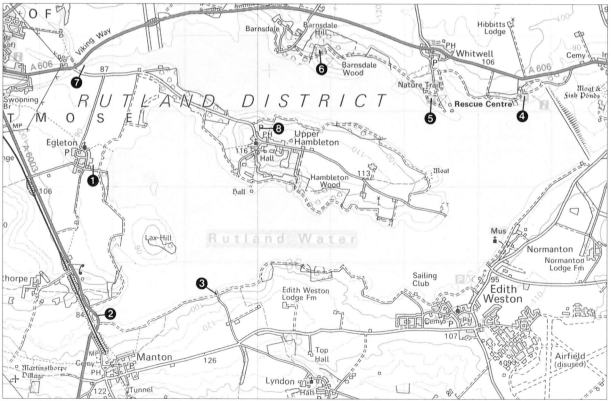

1:50 000, MAP C:A

LEICESTERSHIRE/LINCOLNSHIRE

■ The largest and best remaining area of moorland in the E Midlands, with many rocky outcrops. Good range of bryophytes, lichens and heathland invertebrates. **Birds** Wheatear, whinchat, curlew. **Plants** Moonwort, petty whin, bog pimpernel, lemon-scented fern, lesser skullcap.
LEICESTERSHIRE & RUTLAND TRUST FOR NATURE CONSERVATION

B:4 BLACKBROOK RESERVOIR

Near Loughborough; just S of the A512 W of Loughborough and 2 miles (3 km) W of junction 23 on M1.
■ Reservoir.
■ The marginal plant community is unusual being more akin to some sites much farther N. The thread rush *Juncus filiformis* is common here, its most S locality in Britain. **Plants** Small water-pepper, lesser marshwort, floating club-rush, shoreweed, trifid bur-marigold. **Birds** Great crested and little grebe, teal. **Invertebrates** Native crayfish.
SEVERN-TRENT WATER AUTHORITY

C:1 BURROUGH HILL

Near Melton Mowbray; about 5½ miles (8 km) S of town on N side of minor road midway between Burrough-on-the-Hill and Somerby. Waymarked paths lead from clearly signposted car park (lavatories closed in winter).
■ Limestone grassland, scrub, secondary woodland.
■ One of the highest hills in E of county, topped by Iron Age fort and providing extensive views. Site supports a good range of plants, butterflies and birds, best seen, as might be expected, in spring and summer. **Plants** Meadow saxifrage.
LEICESTERSHIRE COUNTY COUNCIL/ ERNEST COOK TRUST

C:2 GREETHAM MEADOWS

Near Stretton; lies just W of Ram Jam Inn at Stretton on A1 about 8½ miles (12 km) N of Stamford, Lincolnshire. By permit (fee payable) from L&RTNC.
■ Hay meadow.
■ One of the best 'ridge and furrow' hay meadows remaining in this part of England and the only known county site for frog orchid. Best in late spring and summer. **Plants** Green-winged and heath spotted-orchid, pepper-saxifrage, adder's-tongue, salad burnet.
LEICESTERSHIRE & RUTLAND TRUST FOR NATURE CONSERVATION

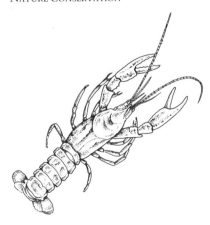

Native crayfish – see Blackbrook Reservoir.

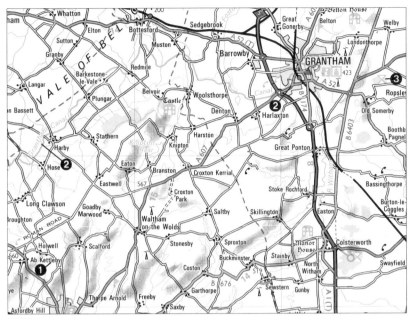

MAP A

LINCOLNSHIRE

A:1 HOLWELL QUARRIES & MINERAL LINE

Near Melton Mowbray; about 3½ miles (5 km) N of town, Holwell lies E of Ab Kettleby and the A605. Owing to risk of subsidence cars should be parked along road or opposite Brown's Hill Quarry. Open to any member of a county naturalists' trust; otherwise by permit from L&RTNC.
■ Disused railway line, quarries, limestone grassland.
■ A rich area botanically, with meadow crane's-bill, cowslip, common spotted-orchid and bee orchid along the railway line or in the quarries. Wetter parts of the reserve hold sedges, giant horsetail and willows.
LEICESTERSHIRE & RUTLAND TRUST FOR NATURE CONSERVATION

A:2 GRANTHAM CANAL

Near Lincolnshire; reserve runs W from Grantham (Lincolnshire) to Harby (Leicestershire). Access from many minor roads crossing canal. Keep to footpaths, or get permit from L&RTNC.
■ Disused canal.
■ A 17-mile (24-km) reserve, this canal – unused for 50 years – holds a variety of aquatic plants and animals. Its reed-beds are a local stronghold of reed warblers.
BRITISH WATERWAYS/LEICS & RUTLAND TRUST FOR NATURE CONSERVATION

MAP B

LINCOLNSHIRE

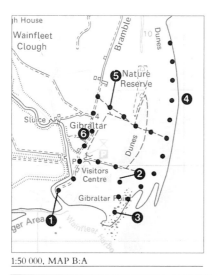

1:50 000, MAP B:A

B:A GIBRALTAR POINT★★

Near Skegness; park at reserve. Nature trails open all year; visitor centre closed on weekdays in winter months.

■ Dunes, salt-marsh, tidal sand flats.

① From car park, walk as shown on map to point SW of visitor centre to view curlew and wildfowl flocks on extensive, developing salt-marsh.

② After crossing the old salt-marsh, lilac-hued with sea-lavender in summer, reach the bird-ringing station in the East Dunes. Sea buckthorn is the dominant shrub, its berries forming an important food source for immigrant winter thrushes and occasionally waxwings. Thousands of migrant passerines are ringed here each year. Avoid the area of the traps when catching is in progress.

③ The Point itself, constantly changing through tidal action, is the nesting place of ringed plovers and little terns, and the site on high autumn tides of large roosts of oystercatchers, bar-tailed godwits, knot and other waders.

④ A winter walk on the East Dunes may produce snow buntings and twite along the shore; eiders, shelduck, scoter and red-throated divers on the sea, and the occasional hen harrier or short-eared owl hunting over the marsh. Look for common seals on sandbanks, and passing skuas in autumn.

⑤ A hide overlooks a mere where herons, kingfishers, waders (including occasional rarities) and waterfowl occur. The freshwater marsh in this area attracts many dragonflies.

⑥ Return along the older West Dunes, where elder, hawthorn and sycamore, as well as dense sea buckthorn grow. Pyramidal orchids are among the flowers found here, while the scrub attracts many migrant birds during E winds in spring and especially autumn.
Plants Sea-holly. **Mammals** Common seal.
LINCOLNSHIRE & SOUTH HUMBERSIDE TRUST FOR NATURE CONSERVATION

A:3 ROPSLEY RISE WOOD

Near Ropsley; park at picnic site 1½ miles (2 km) off B1176 on Old Somerby to Ropsley road. Keep to forest trail.

■ Mixed coniferous/deciduous woodland.

■ Excellent variety of woodland birds from woodpeckers to warblers, throughout year, but late spring and early summer, early morning, best for song birds. **Birds** Long-eared owl, all three woodpeckers, nuthatch, redpoll; (summer) nightjar, warblers; (winter) siskin.
FORESTRY COMMISSION

B:1 FRAMPTON MARSHES★

Near Boston; 3½ miles (5 km) S of Boston turn E off A16 at Kirton on minor road through Frampton to sea wall. Keep to sea walls.

■ Salt-marsh, tidal mudflats.

Two adjoining reserves containing some of the highest, oldest salt-marsh on the Wash, with excellent salt-marsh plant communities. Of major ornithological (and botanical) importance; large numbers of breeding common tern, shelduck and redshank, but even better in winter. **Birds** (Winter) brent goose, twite, Lapland bunting. **Mammals** Common seal.
LINCOLNSHIRE & SOUTH HUMBERSIDE TRUST/ROYAL SOCIETY FOR THE PROTECTION OF BIRDS

B:2 FREISTON SHORE

Near Boston; park near public house at Freiston Shore, and walk along new sea wall to mouth of River Witham. Keep to footpaths.

■ Salt-marsh, tidal mudflats.

■ Salt-marsh here is narrower than at Frampton opposite, giving better opportunities at high tide (check times) of seeing sea-birds; best during autumn migration when waders, terns and skuas abound. **Birds** Brent and pink-footed geese, snow bunting, twite, skuas, terns, waders, divers, grebes.

C:1 SNIPE DALES NATURE RESERVE & COUNTRY PARK

Near Winceby; car parks at Winceby for nature reserve and one mile (1.5 km) E towards Spilsby for country park.

■ Valley grassland, stream, conifer woods, ponds.

■ One of few wet habitats to survive the onslaught of modern agriculture in this part of England, the nature reserve comprises two main valleys fretted by streams, with dry grassland and some scrub on the upper slopes, and wet areas in the bottoms. Oak, ash, alders and willows have recently been planted in suitable areas. Immediately E lies the country park, consisting mainly of Corsican pine but with some native deciduous trees. Siskins were recently found breeding. Newly dug ponds are being colonized by frogs, toads and dragonflies, and 18 species of butterflies have been recorded. Six waymarked paths cover the reserve and country park: keep to them. **Plants** Alternate- and opposite-leaved golden saxifrage, meadow saxifrage, water avens. **Birds** Grasshopper warbler, sand martin, coal and willow tits, goldcrest, barn owl. **Mammals** Badger.
NATURE CONSERVANCY COUNCIL/ LINCOLNSHIRE COUNTY COUNCIL

C:2 CHAMBERS WOOD

Near Bardney; car park at site, one mile (1.5 km) off B1202. Permit required off marked walks.

■ Mixed woodland, clay soils.

■ Several marked walks of varied length in this predominantly oak woodland. Good populations of insects and birds. **Plants** Lily-of-the-valley, giant bellflower.
FORESTRY COMMISSION

C:3 RED HILL

Near Goulceby; parking at top end of reserve, 1½ miles (2 km) NE of Goulceby on minor road to Raithby.

■ Chalk down, quarry.

■ One of the few remnants of Lincolnshire Wold downland, together with a disused quarry with red chalk cliffs, and fine views towards Lincoln. **Plants** Bee orchid, pyramidal orchid, basil thyme, yellow-wort. **Mammals** Badger. **Reptiles** Common lizard.
LINCOLNSHIRE & SOUTH HUMBERSIDE TRUST FOR NATURE CONSERVATION

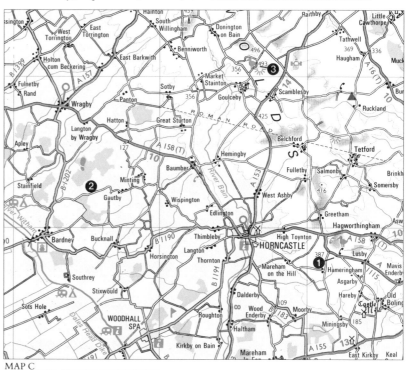

MAP C

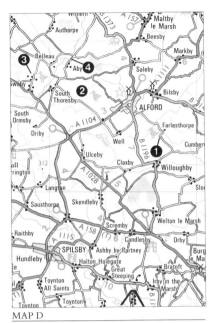

MAP D

tebrates along its 21-mile (30km) length from source (near Brinkhill) to mouth (at Saltfleet). Above Aby it is less than 6 feet (2m) wide and 8 inches (20 cm) deep and even supports stoneflies; below it widens out to about 30 feet (10 m), while lower still it becomes a sluggish drain through arable fenland. The water is clear throughout. **Plants** Horned, curly, fennel, flat-stalked and opposite-leaved pondweeds, water crowfoot, river water-dropwort.

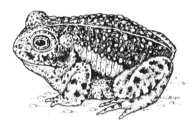

Natterjack toad – see Saltfleetby Dunes.

D:1 WILLOUGHBY-FARLESTHORPE RAILWAY LINE
Willoughby; entrance from B1196 at E end of Willoughby village.
■ Grassland, scrub.
■ A 1½-mile (2-km) stretch of disused railway, converted to pleasant walk and small nature reserve, with grassy banks and hawthorn scrub. **Plants** Adder's-tongue.
LINCOLNSHIRE & SOUTH HUMBERSIDE TRUST FOR NATURE CONSERVATION

D:2 RIGSBY WOOD
Near Alford; park by wood ¾ mile (one km) on right beyond Rigsby. Closed on a few days each winter for shooting.
■ Ash/oak woodland, ash/hazel coppice.
■ Ancient woodland with rich ground flora, and various species of woodland bird who breed here. **Plants** Early-purple orchid, wood anemone, woodruff. **Birds** (Winter) woodcock.
LINCOLNSHIRE & SOUTH HUMBERSIDE TRUST FOR NATURE CONSERVATION

D:3 SWABY VALLEY
South Thoresby; park near South Thoresby Church and follow path waymarked by LCC NW across Calceby beck to Swaby beck and valley. Keep to footpaths.
■ Lime-rich valley grassland, calcareous marsh.
■ Calceby and Swaby becks join just downstream to form the river Great Eau. Plants characteristic of dry chalk grassland present on valley sides, and of marsh in valley bottom. Best in summer with 16 species of butterflies recorded. **Plants** (Valley sides) bee and pyramidal orchid, small scabious, salad burnet; (marsh) early and southern marsh-orchids, marsh arrowgrass. **Birds** Snipe, lapwing.
LINCOLNSHIRE & SOUTH HUMBERSIDE TRUST FOR NATURE CONSERVATION

D:4 GREAT EAU
Near Aby; access from several public footpaths at South Thoresby, Aby, Tothill and Gayton.
■ Chalk stream.
■ The largest of the streams draining from the chalk of the Lincolnshire Wold, this has a great diversity of aquatic plants and inver-

E:1 SALTFLEETBY – THEDDLETHORPE DUNES**
Near Mablethorpe; car parks in dunes off A1031 at reserve site. Tides dangerous, keep off MoD ranges when in use.
■ Tidal sand, mudflats, salt-marsh, dunes, freshwater marshes, scrub.
■ This large reserve provides superb examples of the ecology of a low, sandy coastline. Extensive sandflats, rich in invertebrates, support thousands of waders and waterfowl. The low salt-marsh supports hundreds of skylarks and other birds in winter, but because of tidal inundation is unsuitable for breeding birds. The stable dune system has a variety of orchids, carline thistle and other lime-loving plants, while the sea buckthorn scrub holds many grounded migrant birds in spring and autumn. Freshwater marshes behind the dunes are the home of natterjack toads, snipe and redshank, and a great variety of plants including the rare marsh pea. **Birds** (Nesting) shelduck, ringed plover, oystercatcher; (migrants) skuas, terns, waders; (winter) hen harrier, snow bunting, shore lark. **Plants** Marsh pea, bee and pyramidal orchids, bog pimpernel, autumn gentian, carline thistle. **Insects** (Butterflies) green hairstreak, dark green fritillary; good dragonflies. **Amphibians** Natterjack toad.
LINCOLNSHIRE & SOUTH HUMBERSIDE TRUST FOR NATURE CONSERVATION

E:2 COVENHAM RESERVOIR
Near Utterby; car park at NW corner of reservoir.
■ Reservoir.
■ Only large area of open fresh water in this part of the county, attracting a variety of waterfowl (notably divers and rarer grebes) in hard weather and on migration. Bird-

watching best in autumn and winter. **Birds** (Winter) divers, rarer grebes, long-tailed duck, scaup, goosander; (passage) little gull, black tern, waders.
LINCOLNSHIRE & SOUTH HUMBERSIDE TRUST FOR NATURE CONSERVATION

E:3 DONNA NOOK*
Near Louth; approach from North Somercotes, parking by dunes at end of Marsh Lane. Part of area is bombing range; must not be entered when red flags are flying.
■ Dunes, salt-marsh, tidal sand flats.
■ Important landfall for migrant birds in spring and autumn, when many passerine rarities have been recorded, especially after E winds. Good all year. **Birds** (Breeding) little tern, ringed plover; (winter) hen harrier, short-eared owl, shore lark, Lapland bunting, shore waders. **Plants** Bee and pyramidal orchids, yellow-wort. **Mammals** Grey and common seals.
LINCOLNSHIRE & SOUTH HUMBERSIDE TRUST FOR NATURE CONSERVATION

E:4 TETNEY MARSHES*
Near Cleethorpes; park near Tetney Lock. Reserve may be entered on foot via river bank or through the (normally locked) entrance gate. Access at all times on sea wall. Tides dangerous; don't stray on to salt-marsh.
■ Tidal sandflats, salt-marsh, low dunes.
■ Notable as site of one of Britain's largest colonies of little terns, of interest all year. **Birds** (Breeding) ringed plover, oystercatcher, shelduck, redshank; (migration) whimbrel and other waders; (winter) brent goose, bar-tailed godwit, grey plover, knot.
ROYAL SOCIETY FOR THE PROTECTION OF BIRDS

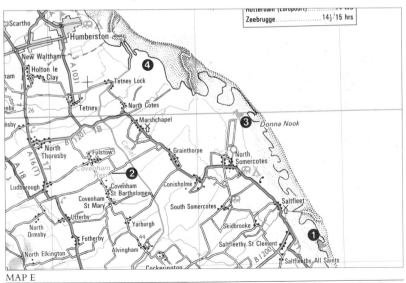

MAP E

CHESHIRE

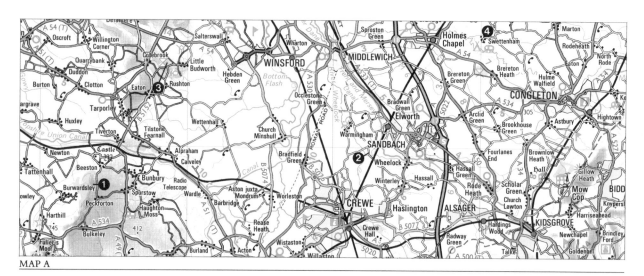

MAP A

A:1 PECKFORTON HILLS
Near Tarporley; access from car park at SJ 540590 – keep strictly to the signposted Sandstone Trail.

■ Sessile oak woodland, heathland, acid grassland, conifer plantation.

■ An area of heavily wooded sandstone hills with excellent views of the Cheshire Plain. **Birds** Pied flycatcher, redstart, wood warbler.

TOLLEMACHE ESTATE

A:2 SANDBACH FLASHES
Near Sandbach; S of the A533; Elton Hall Flash is either side of Clay Lane which is reached via Elton Road and Hall Lane from Ettiley Heath or via Haslington on the A534. Good views are available from surrounding roads. No access to the flashes, which lie within private farmland.

■ Inland salt-marsh, open water, reed-beds.

■ A series of pools formed as a result of subsidence due to the solution of the underlying salt deposits. This is still occurring, though at a much reduced rate. The water quality varies from fresh water to highly saline. Inland saline sites are rare in Britain and the pools contain species characteristic of marine salt-marsh, including sea aster, sea spurry and tiger shrimp. Elton Hall Flash in particular is an important birdwatching area and attracts passage migrants as well as to resident species. These include wigeon, teal, snipe, curlew and other waders.

A:3 LITTLE BUDWORTH COMMON
Near Kelsall; from A54 or A49 follow Little Budworth or Oulton Park signs; parking and lavatories.

■ Dry and wet heathland, deciduous woodland.

■ **Plants** Sundew, cranberry, white sedge, hare's-tail cottongrass.

DEPARTMENT OF COUNTRYSIDE AND RECREATION, CHESHIRE COUNTY COUNCIL

A:4 PICKERING'S PASTURE
Near Widnes; off unclassified road from Ditton to Hale, car park at SJ 488837.

■ Grassland, estuarine foreshore, salt-marsh.

■ Former industrial waste tip on Mersey Estuary now covered by species-rich grassland and providing excellent birdwatching facilities on both the river and adjacent salt-

marsh. Waterfowl and waders; grassland plants.

HALTON BOROUGH COUNCIL

B:1 DELAMERE FOREST
Near Northwich; car parks at Flaxmere, Linmere, Barnesbridge Gates and at points off the B5152. Pedestrian access via network of forest roads and footpaths.

■ Peat mossland, open water, wet and dry heathland, broad-leaved woodland, coniferous plantation.

■ One of the largest blocks of woodland in Cheshire with many varied walks showing a rich variety of wildlife habitats within a small area. Best Jun-Jul. **Plants** Bog-rosemary, sundew, cottongrass. **Birds** Various waterfowl, goldcrest. **Insects** White-faced dragonfly.

FORESTRY COMMISSION

B:2 MARBURY COUNTRY PARK
Near Northwich; signposted from A559 at junction at SJ 649785. Car park open 8 am-dusk.

■ Open water, reed-bed, broad-leaved woodland.

■ Area of landscaped parkland laid out in the 18thC and recently restored by Cheshire County Council. The adjacent Budworth Mere is an important ornithological site (part Cheshire Conservation reserve).

CHESHIRE COUNTY COUNCIL

B:3 WEAVER BEND★★
Frodsham; use private road running NW from Marsh Lane, Frodsham; parking area at SJ 508788. Keep to footpaths.

■ Lagoons, rough grassland, river.

■ One of Cheshire's foremost ornithological sites. Important for passage migrants, especially waders, of which 45 species are recorded, including several American vagrants. Best in autumn. Winter brings waterfowl.

BRITISH WATERWAYS BOARD/MANCHESTER SHIP CANAL COMPANY

B:4 RISLEY MOSS★★
Near Warrington; follow signs from M62,

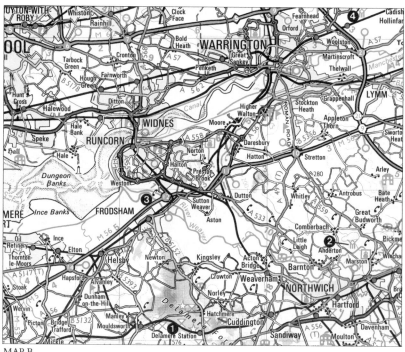

MAP B

Junction 11, or A574 from Warrington; ample parking; closed Fridays, permit needed for access to wet mossland.

■ Peat mossland, heathland, oak/birch woodland, open water, grassland.

■ A remnant of the once-extensive mosslands which covered the Mersey Valley. Following extensive habitat management, the peatland has been restored to a fascinating area of wilderness. Visitor centre and observation tower. **Birds** Long-eared owl (winter), woodcock, curlew, snipe, teal, warblers. **Plants** Cottongrass, bog-mosses. **Insects** Dragonflies.
CHESHIRE COUNTY COUNCIL

C:1 DANES MOSS
Near Macclesfield; limited parking (2-3 cars) at SJ 903701; keep to footpath, or obtain permit from CCT, Marbury Country Park, Northwich, Tel 0606 781868.

■ Peat mossland, heathland, oak/birch woodland, open water.

■ An area of raised bog which has been badly affected by peat-cutting, but is now being restored to its former interest by management of the water table. Many species of dragonfly; cottongrass, bog-moss, Labrador-tea and various waterfowl. Best Jun-Jul.
CHESHIRE CONSERVATION TRUST/
CHESHIRE COUNTY COUNCIL

C:2 TRENTABANK RESERVOIR*
Near Macclesfield; approach on unclassified road from Langley to Forest Chapel; car park at Visitor Centre (SJ 961711); access at all times to lay-by viewing point and disabled access trail. Access to reservoir catchment by permit available from CCT, Marbury Country Park, Northwich, Cheshire CW9 6AT.

■ Open water, broad-leaved and coniferous plantation, grassland, heathland.

■ Water catchment reservoir attracting large numbers of waterfowl. Active heronry clearly visible from public lay-by, also birdwatching area. Best Mar-May.
NORTH WEST WATER AUTHORITY/
CHESHIRE CONSERVATION TRUST

C:3 ALDERLEY EDGE
Near Wilmslow; access from B5087: the edge is one mile (1.5 km) SE of Alderley Edge town.

■ Broad-leaved and coniferous woodland, dry heathland, bare rock.

■ Prominent sandstone ridge, covered with broad-leaved and coniferous wood-

land, providing excellent views of the Cheshire Plain and Pennines. Copper ore has been mined here since Roman times. **Birds** (Winter) siskin, redpoll; (breeding) redstart, wood warbler, tree pipit, woodpeckers, treecreeper.
NATIONAL TRUST

C:4 TATTON PARK
Near Knutsford; signposted from A50 and A556; off M6 Junction 19 and M56 Junction 17; tel 0565 54822 for opening times, admission charge to park.

■ Open water, reed-beds, grassland, broad-leaved and coniferous plantation.

■ A large area of landscaped parkland which includes two major areas of open water, Tatton Mere and Melchett Mere.

Ramsons or wild garlic – see C:5, Styal.

Birds Waterfowl, passage migrants.
NATIONAL TRUST/CHESHIRE COUNTY COUNCIL

C:5 STYAL
Near Wilmslow; signposted from A538, A34 and from M56 Junction 6. Car park off Holt's Lane and Bank Road (SJ 835830) – fee. Keep to footpaths.

■ Broad-leaved woodland, grassland.

■ Attractive valley, heavily wooded. The Styal Cotton Mill is an attractive working museum. **Plants** Moschatel, ramsons.
NATIONAL TRUST

C:6 ROSTHERNE MERE**
Near Knutsford; in Rostherne village, ¾ mile (one km) SE of the A556. The warden's house and Bird Observatory are adjacent to the church yard, N of Manor Lane. Access to Mere restricted to permit holders: also to A.W. Boyd Memorial Observatory. Contact Reserve Warden, The Rowans, Rostherne, Knutsford. Birdwatching from Rostherne churchyard is unrestricted.

■ Lake, reed-bed, broad-leaved woodland.

■ Rostherne Mere is a lowland lake, one of the series of meres' in Cheshire and adjacent counties. It was probably formed by glacial action, though its depth may have been increased by natural salt subsidence. The Mere attracts many breeding and visiting waterfowl (including wigeon, pintail, shoveler; also waders, raptors and various passerines. Due to the lack of food in the Mere, waterfowl tend to use the site as a day-time roost, moving at dusk to other feeding areas. Best spring and summer for breeding waterfowl and autumn for passage migrants.
NATURE CONSERVANCY COUNCIL

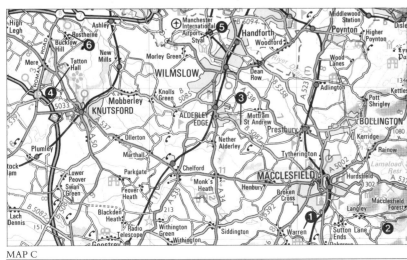

MAP C

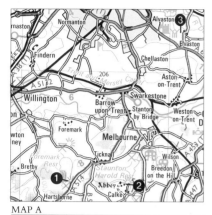

MAP A

A:1 FOREMARK RESERVOIR
Near Burton upon Trent; off the Ticknall-Milton road; car parks on E bank and S tip. Open all year exc Christmas and Boxing Day, 9 am to 4 pm.
■ Open water, woodland, marsh.
■ Birds (Water) divers, grebes, goldeneye, wigeon, terns; (woodland) woodpeckers, nuthatch, woodcock.
SEVERN-TRENT WATER

A:2 STAUNTON HAROLD RESERVOIR★
Near Derby; car parks adjacent to Calke Park, also Windmill car park on the Melbourne to Ashby road. Open all year: permit required for Spring Wood and hide.
■ Open water, woodland.
■ Reservoir of considerable importance for wintering wildfowl; some ancient woodland. **Birds** Red-throated diver, grebes, long-tailed duck, smew, goldeneye, terns.
SEVERN-TRENT WATER

A:3 ELVASTON CASTLE COUNTRY PARK
Near Derby; car park (free Mon-Fri); disabled access. Grounds open daily 9 am to dusk.
■ Mature woodland, parkland.
■ Busy site with formal gardens and pockets of interesting habitats, easily accessible. Up-to-date species lists available from rangers or information centre.
DERBYSHIRE COUNTY COUNCIL

B:1 SHIPLEY COUNTRY PARK
Near Heanor; signposted at M1 Junction 26; car park and visitor centre off Thorpes Road.
■ Mature deciduous woodland, reservoirs, ponds, plantations, rough grassland, pasture, hedgerows.
■ Remains of former private country estate, with large areas of land reinstated following coal mining operations. A wide range of wildlife habitats with extensive network of footpaths and bridle paths. **Plants** Yellow-fringed water lily, common spotted orchid. **Mammals** Bats.
DERBYSHIRE COUNTY COUNCIL

MAP B

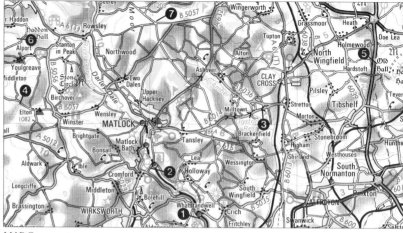

MAP C

C:1 SHINING CLIFF WOOD
Near Matlock; turn W off A6 on unclassified road about 200 yards (183 m) S of A6/A610 junction. Road crosses River Derwent. Small parking place immediately over bridge. Walk N on footpath to Shining Cliff Wood, about one mile (1.5 km). Observe FC byelaws.
■ Springs, wet flushes, grassy heath.
■ A varied wood overlooking the River Derwent with some pleasant paths for the walker. Good for birds: pied flycatcher and wood warbler breed; large winter flocks of brambling.
FORESTRY COMMISSION

C:2 CROMFORD CANAL★
Near Matlock; car parks at SK 306520 and SK 312560; access along towpath.
■ Open water, reed swamp, neutral grassland.
■ A 4-mile (6.5-km) length of disused canal partly restored to navigation. S section is an LNR. **Birds** Kingfisher, siskin, redpoll. **Invertebrates** Hoverflies, dragonflies. **Plants** Water plantain, arrowhead, sweet flag.
DERBYSHIRE COUNTY COUNCIL/
DERBYSHIRE WILDLIFE TRUST

C:3 OGSTON RESERVOIR★
Near Matlock; two car parks; permit required for access to reservoir banks. Three hides, Ogston Bird Club members only, 2.50 a year.
■ Open water, scrub, woodland, rough grassland.
■ Best to visit at migration times and in winter, but narrow country lanes and bad weather frequently make it hazardous. More than 200 bird species recorded, including regular Iceland and glaucous gulls in winter.
SEVERN-TRENT WATER

C:4 GRATTON & LONG DALE
Near Matlock; use Fridon car park; footpaths run length of dales. Permit required from NCC to stray from footpaths.
■ Limestone grassland, woodland, scrub.
■ A gentle, rolling dale, lacking the grandeur of the deep' Dales to the N. However, its open grassland has the full range of acid- and lime-loving plants. The calcareous areas bear great similarity to the chalk grassland of the S, with an abundance of chalk species such as stemless thistle and dropwort. The acid plants include heather, bilberry, dwarf gorse and mountain pansy.

Lead mining took place in the dale and the spoil heaps have their own floristic interest, with spring sandwort and alpine penny-cress.

The woodland and scrub areas in Gratton Dale attract a range of typical woodland birds, but are of particular note for their high density of nesting pairs compared with the surrounding areas. These include hole-nesting redstarts. The cliffs in the woodland attract kestrels and jackdaws. Dippers and grey wagtails can be seen around the stream.
NATURE CONSERVANCY COUNCIL

C:5 HARDWICK PARK
Near Mansfield; signposted from M1 Junction 29 and from A617.
■ Parkland, woodland, grass paddocks, lakes, ponds.
■ Wide variety of flora and fauna, with managed rare breeds – longhorn cattle and white-faced woodland sheep. Specimen carp in the ponds. **Birds** (Water) kingfisher, great crested grebe, little grebe, water rail; (parkland) sparrowhawk, kestrel, tawny and little owls.
NATIONAL TRUST

C:6 LATHKILL DALE★
Near Bakewell; park in Over Haddon, where an information centre is planned. Further information (including details of a concessionary path) from the Warden, NCC, Riversdale House, Dale Road North, Darley Dale, Matlock, who can advise on facilities for educational groups – permit required from NCC to wander off footpaths.
■ Woodland, limestone grassland, river.
■ The ash woodland S of the Lathkill River is thought to be one of the finest examples of its type. The understorey is dominated by hazel, with guelder rose, dogwood and hawthorn, and the ground flora by dog's mercury and tufted hair-grass, with flowers such as red campion and yellow archangel.

The wide range of grassland towards the W end of the dale is of particular interest. On the warmer and drier S-facing slopes, the most species-rich areas occur, characterized by meadow oat-grass and glaucous sedge with common rock-rose, salad burnet and wild thyme. The tall, moist herb grassland on the N-facing slopes have an abundance of meadowsweet, crosswort, dog's mercury, common valerian and burnet saxifrage. In the upper W end of the dale this grassland supports a large population of the nationally rare Jacob's-ladder.

The river itself supports an abundance of wildlife, and the purity of the water is of par-

ticular note. Brown trout and bullheads are clearly visible.
NATURE CONSERVANCY COUNCIL

C:7 EASTERN MOORS
Near Sheffield; the numeral on the map marks an area which, at going to press, had changed its status during the compilation of the Atlas and had become unsuitable for visitors. Broadly similar country is, however, managed for public access about 10 miles (16 km) SW of Sheffield off A621; please respect the National Park's access system, which includes access areas, wildlife sanctuary zones, public footpaths and concessionary paths. Use specific access points and car parks, for example at SU 263747.
■ Moorland.
■ Large expanse of mixed moorland vegetation including areas of pure heather, purple moor-grass, exposed gritstone edges and botanically diverse wet flushes. Typical moorland flora and fauna.
PEAK PARK JOINT PLANNING BOARD

D:1 BUXTON COUNTRY PARK★
& POOLE'S CAVERN★★
Near Buxton; car park; woodland open all year, Easter-Oct.
■ Beech/oak/sycamore woodland.
■ The woodland was planted on a lime waste tip around 1820. **Plants** Green hellebore, northern marsh and frog orchids, mountain everlasting, creeping willow, grass-of-Parnassus.
BUXTON AND DISTRICT CIVIC ASSOCIATION

D:2 CRESSBROOK DALE
Near Bakewell; car park for 10 cars at Ravensdale; access by footpath from Wardlow, Litton or Ravensdale; footpaths run length of dale excepting woodland in S. Permit required for access away from footpaths – contact NCC warden.
■ Limestone grassland, woodland, hazel scrub.
■ A rich botanical site, part of the Derbyshire Dales NNR, containing the full range of limestone plants, which can be clearly seen from the footpaths. The Ravensdale limestone cliffs are spectacular. **Plants** Bird cherry, field maple, guelder rose, ramsons, lily-of-the-valley, spurge laurel, bloody crane's-bill, Nottingham catchfly, stemless thistle, spring sandwort. **Butterflies** Brown argus.
NATURE CONSERVANCY COUNCIL

D:3 CHEE & MILLER'S DALE★
Near Buxton; car parks at SK 138734 and SK 108725. Access from footpaths via Monsal Trail. Permit required for parties of more than 12 off footpaths. Some precipitous terrain – keep to foot-

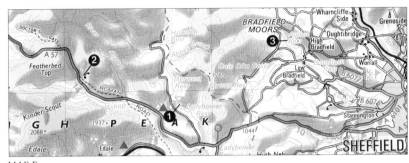

MAP E

paths.
■ Woodland, limestone grassland, river.
■ Typical mature and colonising limestone dale woodland: species-rich grassland with developing communities on old quarry workings including lead spoil heaps. **Birds** Redstart, house martin (cliff-nesting), dipper. **Plants** Yew, whitebeam; Alpine currant, bee orchid, fragrant orchid, globeflower, mountain pansy.
DERBYSHIRE WILDLIFE TRUST

D:4 MONKS DALE/DERBYSHIRE DALES NATIONAL NATURE RESERVE
Near Buxton; parking for 70 cars at Miller's Dale; access via footpath from Miller's Dale and Wormhill. Footpath runs length of dale – permit required to wander away from footpaths – contact NCC warden. Please keep dogs under strict control, stay on footpaths and take litter home.
■ Ash woodland, limestone grassland, stream.
■ A peaceful dale, but the path is difficult and rock-strewn: not recommended for children or the elderly.
The woodlands are abundant with local tree and shrub species with areas of bird cherry at the S limit of its range.
The grasslands range from open, scrub-free areas to patches of dense hazel and hawthorn. This mixture provides habitats for an enormous range of plant, bird and insect species. With early-purple orchids growing in profusion on the open grasslands, bloody crane's-bill and Nottinghams catchfly growing in the scrub areas. The top of the dale edges have a range of acid-loving plants.
The rock screes are of interest for plants which can tolerate extremely dry conditions: stonecrop, shining crane's-bill and limestone polypody.
Another feature of Monks Dale is the number of springs and flushed sites with tufa forming moss communities. These are best seen by the footbridge at S end of dale.
NATURE CONSERVANCY COUNCIL

D:5 LONGSHAW ESTATE★
Near Sheffield; car parks; dogs on leads.
■ Gorge, woodland (including ancient sessile oak woods), unimproved grassland, dwarf-shrub and grass heath.
■ The wide range of habitat types, and its location on the S or SE limit of the breeding range for many species, make the Longshaw Estate an area of great interest. The woodlands of Padley Gorge and Sheffield Plantation are of major importance for birds, including pied flycatcher, wood warbler, redstart, hawfinch and overwintering crossbill. There are more than 300 species of fungi, many rare and uncommon; also the lichen *Umbilicaria torrefacta.*
NATIONAL TRUST

E:1 LADYBOWER RESERVOIR★
Near Sheffield; on A57, extensive parking. Way-marked public and concessionary paths. Information centre at Fairholmes.
■ Upland reservoirs, mixed woodland, ancient woodland, moorland.
■ The reservoirs are in a most attractive setting with woodland walks giving access to open country. The surrounding land is being managed with sensitivity.
SEVERN-TRENT WATER

E:2 BLEAKLOW/KINDER
Near Manchester; car parks in Edale, Hayfield, Glossop and at Snake Pass, with paths to the moorland indicated by signs. See O.S. Dark Peak map. Keep dogs on leads at all times.
■ Blanket bog, upland heath, upland dwarf shrub vegetation, cloughs, streams.
■ Considering its closeness to major conurbations, the survival of this vast upland heath as semi-wilderness is remarkable. Extensive sheep grazing and some grouse shooting are the main economic land uses, but recreational use by walkers is now a major feature. The famous mass trespass of 1932 took place on part of Kinder Scout. Unfortunately, owing to atmospheric pollution, overgrazing by sheep, accidental fires and increasing recreational activity, many parts are severely degraded and eroded. The National Trust is trying to reverse the damage. **Birds** Golden plover, ring ouzel, dunlin, red grouse, snipe, lapwing, curlew, occasional merlin, peregrine, goshawk. **Mammals** Mountain hare, fox.
NATIONAL TRUST

E:3 AGDEN BOG
Near Low Bradfield; park on road skirting Agden reservoir. Footpath from road to reserve.
■ Bog, acid grassland and millstone grit.
■ Many acid-loving plants in the bog, also some richer wetland communities. Insectivorous plants of particular interest, and invertebrates. Forty bird species.
YORKSHIRE WILDLIFE TRUST

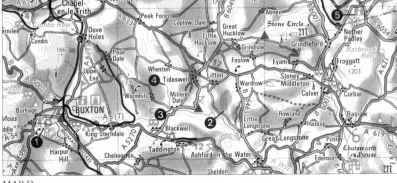

MAP D

NOTTINGHAMSHIRE

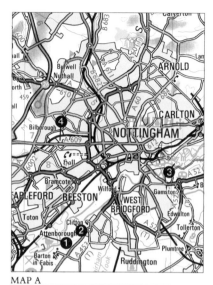

MAP A

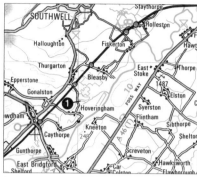

MAP B

A:1 ATTENBOROUGH GRAVEL PITS★

Near Nottingham; 5½ *miles (9 km) SW of Nottingham on A6005 to Long Eaton. Take road through Attenborough to Strand car park near River Trent. Permit from NTNC required off paths, or Trust's caravan at car park on Sunday afternoons.*

■ Flooded gravel pits, fen, wet meadows.
■ Disused gravel pits show varying development of natural vegetation over some 50 years and provide habitats for a wide range of breeding birds, a large, diverse population of wintering wildfowl, and many rarities on spring and autumn migration. **Birds** (Breeding) common tern, kingfisher, great crested grebe, sand martin, grasshopper and reed warblers; (winter) ducks. **Plants** Meadow saxifrage, flowering-rush, arrowhead, ragged-Robin, yellow rattle.

NOTTINGHAM TRUST FOR NATURE CONSERVATION

A:2 HOLME PIT

Near Nottingham; off A453 to Clifton 1½ *miles (2.5 km) from junction turn right (N) in Clifton to church beside bend on river Trent; site is 650 yards (600 m) S along footpath.*

■ Open water, marsh.
■ One of the best remaining areas of marsh, reedswamp and open water in the county, with a rich plant community and attracting many birds. Good to visit any time of year. **Plants** Tubular water-dropwort, meadow rue.

A:3 COLWICK

Near Nottingham; signposted off B686, 2 *miles (3 km) E of city centre.*

■ Lakes, parkland.
■ Country park with heavy recreational use in summer, but best in winter when a wildfowl refuge, with Canada goose, mallard, wigeon, tufted duck and pochard all occasionally topping 100. The unexpected (scaup, kittiwake) sometimes turn up, too.

NOTTINGHAM CITY COUNCIL

A:4 MARTIN'S POND

Near Nottingham; 1½ *miles (2 km) W of city ring road, turn right (N) off A609 to entrance in Russell Avenue, Wollaton. Popular with fishermen, so least disturbed during mid-Mar-mid-Jun close season.*

■ Pool, marsh, scrub.

■ A shallow pond, fringed with reed swamp and willows, which has survived the threat of urban development and is maintained as a nature reserve and for anglers. It has varied plant and bird communities, including some migrant waders. **Plants** Golden dock, marsh arrow-grass. **Birds** Great crested and little grebe, reed warbler; (winter) water rail.

NOTTINGHAM CITY COUNCIL/ NOTTINGHAMSHIRE TRUST FOR NATURE CONSERVATION

B:1 HOVERINGHAM GRAVEL PITS

Near Nottingham; NE *of city, turn right off A612 to Hoveringham or Bleasby; footpaths between these two villages and along River Trent provide views of site. Keep to footpaths which cross the area.*

■ Flooded gravel pits.
■ One of several gravel pit complexes in the Trent valley, of importance for wintering wildfowl and attracting many migrants on passage. As well as numbers of Canada geese and commoner duck, smew, goosander and up to 100 goldeneye may be present in hard weather.

C:1 RUFFORD

Near Ollerton; signposted off A614 2 miles (3 km) S of town.

■ Parkland, lake, stream.
■ The varied parkland habitats of this country park provide opportunities for seeing a range of common birds at close quarters – Canada goose, ruddy duck and other wildfowl on the lake (beware, some wildfowl are pinioned, not wild!) and such breeding passerines as tree sparrows, pied wagtails, spotted flycatchers and long-tailed tits.

NOTTINGHAMSHIRE COUNTY COUNCIL

C:2 SHERWOOD FOREST

Near Ollerton; signposted off B6005, A6075 and A616. Car park, picnic site, visitor centre. The paths and nature trails are heavily used on fine summer days.

■ Ancient oak forest.
■ Heavily used country park containing some of the oldest and largest oaks in Britain. Birch and bracken glades also present but acidic soils support a poor ground flora. Rich beetle fauna with a number of rare species. Typical woodland birds. Early morning in spring and early summer best for bird song.

NOTTINGHAMSHIRE COUNTY COUNCIL

C:3 WELBECK PARK

Near Worksop; turn W off B6005 along minor road to Norton; after 1½ miles (2 km) park on N side of road overlooking central part of Great

lake. Estate strictly private with no rights of way. View from road. Expect other bird watchers to be there too.

■ Parkland, deciduous woodland, lake.
■ One of few places in Britain where honey buzzards can be seen regularly. Look for them soaring over wood and lake, late morning or early afternoon on fine days between May and early Aug. **Birds** Honey buzzard, sparrowhawk, kingfisher, great crested and little grebes.

C:4 CLUMBER PARK★

Near Worksop; signposted off minor road between Carburton and A1-A614 junction. Entrance fee.

■ Mature deciduous/mixed woodland, heathland, scrub, young plantation, marsh, stream, lake.
■ Once forming the northern, rather open (heathland, scattered oaks) part of the Royal Forest of Sherwood, this large estate was landscaped and developed by successive dukes. The park overlies Bunter sandstones. Much of it is sympathetically managed for nature conservation. Mature broad-leaved woodland supports a rich breeding bird community. The ornamental lake has a large flock of Canada geese, and attracts other wildfowl, particularly in winter. Occasional flash flooding brings passage waders in spring and autumn. **Birds** (Breeding) nightjar, long-eared owl, redstart, nightingale, nuthatch, woodpeckers, tree pipit, gadwall, ruddy duck.

NATIONAL TRUST

C:5 CRESWELL CRAGS★

Near Creswell; on B6042 just E of Creswell (Derbyshire). Signposted car park and picnic site. Visitor centre closed Mon (except Bank Holidays) Feb-Oct, and all days exc Sun Nov-Jan.

■ Limestone gorge, lake.
■ A narrow limestone gorge containing a series of caves, one of the richest British localities for fossil mammals, birds and fish. Although primarily a palaeontological site, a range of common birds can be seen in the woodland and around Crags Pond.

NOTTINGHAMSHIRE COUNTY COUNCIL/ DERBYSHIRE COUNTY COUNCIL

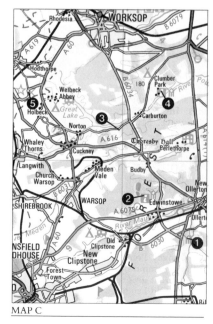

MAP C

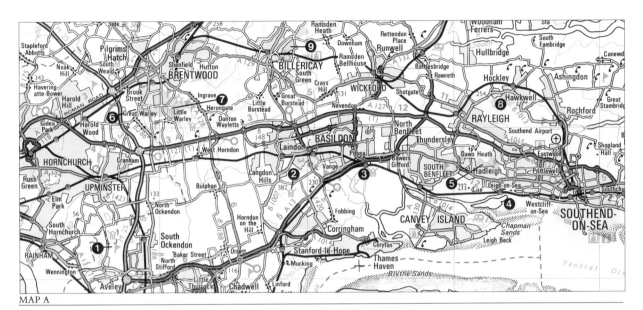

MAP A

A:1 BELHUS WOODS
Near South Ockenden; car park, visitor centre at Country Park site, across from Romford Road, Aveley (close to M25 junction 30).
■ Woodland, gravel pits, parkland, lake.
■ A variety of wildlife easily accessible in this otherwise built-up area of Essex/ Greater London.
ESSEX COUNTY COUNCIL

A:2 LANGDON HILLS
Near Basildon; country park SW of town, including One Tree Hill (E) and Westley Heights (W). Access to both from Dry Street and B1007 (W). Information room at One Tree Hill.
■ Former farmland, mixed woodland, meadows.
■ Attractive woodland but most valuable are three herb-rich meadows, part of One Tree Hill. This rare area of old pasture in Essex has substantial numbers of green-winged orchid and yellow rattle. **Plants** (Trees) wild service-tree, hornbeam; (meadows) pepper-saxifrage.
ESSEX COUNTY COUNCIL

A:3 WAT TYLER COUNTRY PARK*
Near Pitsea; car parks S of Pitsea Station.
■ Scrub, salt-marsh, reed-bed, salt/fresh open water, grassland.
■ Thick scrub supports large numbers of redwing and fieldfare plus a winter long-eared owl roost. In summer, listen for Roesel's bush-cricket in long grass and for reed and sedge warblers in the adjoining reed-beds. **Insects** (Scarce) emerald damselfly; rosy wave, Matthew's wainscot and star-wort moths.
BASILDON COUNCIL

A:4 SOUTHEND FLATS**
Southend; parking on Southend sea front, Old Leigh, Two Tree Island. Small fee for Southend Pier.
■ Intertidal flats, salt-marsh, grassland, scrub.
■ The sheer numbers of waders coming to their high tide roosts on Two Tree Island and Canvey Point compete as a spectacle with the autumn sight of up to 10,000 dark-bellied brent geese seen beyond the cockle sheds at Old Leigh. From Shoeburyness to Leigh the mud- and sand-flats are among the most important wintering areas for waders

in the UK. Benfleet Downs have several scarce flowers and butterflies.
NATURE CONSERVANCY COUNCIL/ESSEX NATURALISTS' TRUST

A:5 BELFAIRS
Near Southend; enter from Poors Lane (N) or Warren Road (S).
■ Hornbeam/sweet chestnut coppice, oak standards.
■ The newly-opened areas of the reserve are the most interesting. Best in spring for flowers, summer for butterflies, autumn for fungi. **Plants** Wild service-tree, common cow-wheat, broad-leaved helleborine. **Mammals** Dormouse. **Butterflies** White admiral.
SOUTHEND-ON-SEA BOROUGH COUNCIL

A:6 WARLEY PLACE
Near Brentwood; cross privately-owned field.
■ Garden, arboretum.
■ Nature trail through abandoned ornamental garden and arboretum reached across field containing the rare spring crocus, a red data book species.
ESSEX NATURALISTS' TRUST

A:7 THORNDON PARK (NORTH & SOUTH)
Brentwood; enter N part from The Avenue, S part from the A128.
■ Birch/oak/hornbeam coppice woodland, old parkland, oak pollards.
■ These woodlands are particularly noted

for their beetles; flora generally poor, dominated by bramble and bracken, but lily-of-the-valley occurs and there is a small area of heath. **Plants** Moschatel, pendulous sedge.
ESSEX COUNTY COUNCIL/BRENTWOOD DISTRICT COUNCIL

A:8 HOCKLEY WOODS
Hockley; car park at B1013 at Hockley.
■ Sessile oak wood, hornbeam/sweet chestnut coppice.
■ Largest population of sessile oak in East Anglia, with added attraction of widespread wild service-tree and hornbeam. Interesting ground flora includes three orchids. **Plants** Greater butterfly and bird's-nest orchids, water-violet.
ROCHFORD DISTRICT COUNCIL

A:9 NORSEY WOOD*
Near Billericay; car park on E side off Outwood Common Road. Information centre, nature-trail.
■ Mixed chestnut/hornbeam coppice, pedunculate/sessile oak standards, birch.
■ This wood has a history dating back to the Bronze Age. External boundary banks are from its use as a medieval deer park. It has a rich flora under the coppice. **Plants** Herb Paris, water-violet, narrow and broad buckler-fern, butcher's broom. **Butterflies** Purple hairstreak.
BASILDON COUNCIL

White admiral – see Belfairs, A:5 on this page.

ESSEX

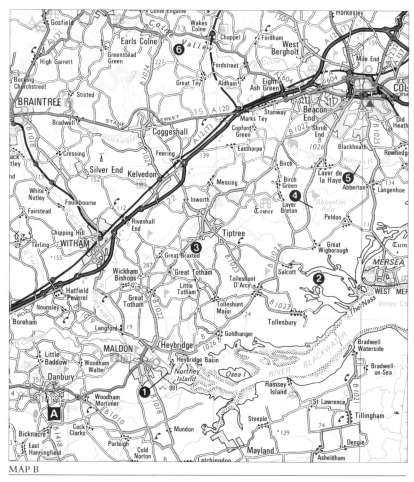

MAP B

B:1 BLACKWATER ESTUARY

Maldon; park in town. Footpaths follow both N and S shores.

■ Estuary, mudflats, salt-marsh, gravel pits.

■ Superb estuary for wintering waders and wildfowl. Heybridge gravel pits attract goldeneye, grebes and divers, especially in hard weather. **Birds** (Estuary) brent goose, bar-tailed godwit, grey plover, ringed plover.

B:2 OLD HALL MARSHES

Near Tollesbury; enter from minor road N of town. Limited car parking (do not use approach road). Keep to footpaths. Walk below the sea wall.

■ Grazing marsh, salt-marsh, reed-bed, fleets.

■ The 1,134 acres are the largest remaining block of the once-extensive Essex grazing marshes.

Continuing the grazing is a crucial aspect of the management, not least for the wintering flocks of brent geese, taking the pressure off surrounding farmland. Winter also brings hunting hen harriers and short-eared owls, with twite flocks on the salt-marsh.
ROYAL SOCIETY FOR THE PROTECTION OF BIRDS

B:3 TIPTREE HEATH*

Several car parks along road in Tiptree Heath.

■ Heath, scrub, birch/oak woodland.

■ A tiny fragment of the once extensive heaths between Colchester and Chelmsford, at 62 acres this is still the largest heath in Essex.

The complete succession through gorse and birch scrub to secondary oak woodland occurs, carefully maintained by management. A stream side supports lemon-scented, royal and hard ferns.

The tiny flower allseed occurs at its only Essex locality. Best in Jun and Jul.
TIPTREE PARISH COUNCIL

Birds-nest orchid – see A:8, previous page.

B:4 ABBERTON RESERVOIR

Near Colchester; parking along causeways across reservoir, which offer best views; no public access on perimeter; small fee to visit hide, open dawn to dusk.

■ Man-made reservoir.

■ Thousands of wintering wildfowl and a steady stream of scarce waders have established the causeway S of Layer-de-la-Haye as one of East Anglia's top bird-watching spots. A unique colony of tree-nesting cormorants, and common terns on a platform add to the year-round interest. Winter best for ducks.
ESSEX WATER COMPANY

B:5 ROMAN RIVER VALLEY*

Near Colchester; car park at W of site on Layer-de-la-Haye to Colchester road. At the E end occasionally no access to MoD area, watch for flying flags.

■ Mixed woodland, grassland, scrub, fen, heath.

■ The diversity of habitat in this area is shown by the variety of breeding birds and over 1,000 species of moths and butterflies.

Friday and Donyland woods have the remains of a coppice-with-standards structure but also contain some mixed and coniferous plantation.

Berechurch Common is mainly acic grassland, with plenty of sheep's sorrel and heath bedstraw, but with more neutral, damp and marsh grassland by the Roman River. The wetland habitat includes a reed-bed S of Donyland wood, and there is fen with willow pollards.

Thick gorse, broom and thorn scrub complete the mosaic.
MINISTRY OF DEFENCE

B:6 CHALKNEY WOOD

Near Halstead; enter from Tey Road.

■ Mixed woodland/small-leaved lime.

■ An ancient woodland, including some of the best small-leaved lime in Essex. Rarer plants include violet helleborine and narrow buckler-fern; mosses and liverworts are well-recorded including several scarce species.
ESSEX COUNTY COUNCIL

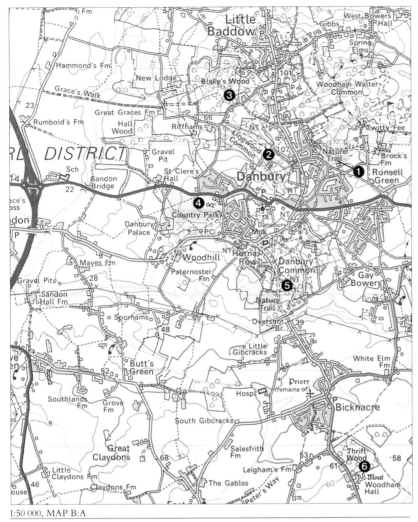

1:50 000, MAP B:A

B:A DANBURY RIDGE
Near Chelmsford.

■ Woodland, heath.

① Woodham Walter Common: An ancient oak-hornbeam woodland with some heath and wet flushes. Speckled wood butterflies dance in clearings; badgers and sparrowhawks also in area.

② Lingwood Common: Now almost entirely oak and birch woodland, although there are small heathy patches. Butcher's broom and dog's mercury grow in shaded areas. Nightingales can be heard in scrub.

③ Blakes Wood: Bluebells under the sweet chestnuts and, unusually, both hornbeam and alder coppice. Classic ancient woodland flowers include wood anemone, wood-sorrel and yellow archangel.

④ Danbury Country Park: Some fine old oaks and ornamental trees by the car park, but lakes and park have little wildlife interest.

⑤ Danbury Common: One of the largest remaining heaths in Essex. Meadow saxifrage and green-winged orchids can be found in unimproved meadows in NE corner while ponds have fringed water-lily and mare's-tail. This is the principal British stronghold of rosy marbled moth.

⑥ Thrift Wood: Mainly hornbeam coppice with oak standards, excellent for wood ants. Huge drifts of common cow-wheat in open areas. Heath fritillary has been re-introduced.

ESSEX NATURALISTS' TRUST/NATIONAL TRUST

Sparrowhawk.

C:1 HOLLAND HAVEN
Near Clacton; car park at site.

■ Coastal grazing marsh, sea wall, scrub.

■ Superb winter bird-watching with waders. brent geese and winter thrushes on the rich old pasture. The hawthorn scrub often has a long-eared owl roost, and purple sandpipers are regular on the shore beyond the new sea wall. Best Oct-Apr.

C:2 FINGRINGHOE WICK★
Near Colchester; turn off B1025 at Abberton on minor road signposted Fingringhoe. After 1½

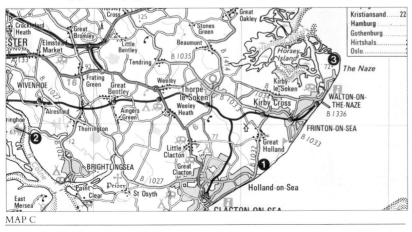

MAP C

miles (2.5 km), turn right following sign to South Green; reserve signposted. Information centre, car park.

■ Scrub, old gravel workings, salt-marsh, mudflats, scrape.

■ Old gravel workings the Wick may be, but it has developed into a superb and diverse nature reserve under the management of the ENT, headquartered here.

The thorn and willow scrub is mature enough for a range of warblers and there are more nightingales than anywhere else in Essex. Large flocks of redwings and fieldfares move in during the autumn.

Waders on the Colne estuary are joined by wintering brent geese. The salt-marsh alongside has sea asters and sea-lavender.

The new scrape attracts passage waders and the recently excavated sand martin cliff has attracted scores of this declining bird.

ESSEX NATURALISTS' TRUST

C:3 THE NAZE, WALTON★★
Walton-on-the-Naze; car park at site. *Access to ENT reserve restricted, but elsewhere access always open.*

■ Thorn/gorse scrub, tidal flats, salt-marsh, low cliff, grassland.

■ Fossils found in the cliff here have included a parrot and a falcon; today it is an excellent bird-watching spot.

The combination of the scrub and its exposed position brings in many migrants, including regular autumn wrynecks and firecrests. In Oct arrivals of Continental blackbirds and chaffinches can number thousands; long-eared owls hide in the scrub from Nov onwards.

The mudflats and salt-marshes of the otherwise almost inaccessible Hamford Water are a major wintering area for wildfowl, notably brent geese, shelduck, teal, wigeon and pintail, and waders including black-tailed godwit.

TENDRING DISTRICT COUNCIL. SMALL PART ESSEX NATURALISTS' TRUST.

HERTFORDSHIRE

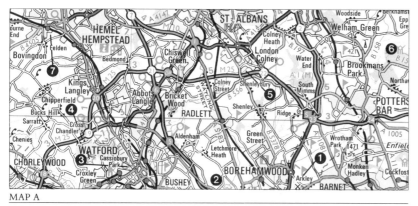

MAP A

A:1 ROWLEY GREEN COMMON
Barnet; entrance at Rowley Green Lane to TQ 217960.
■ Heath, scrub, bog.
Birds Long-tailed tit, reed bunting. **Plants** *Sphagnum* moss, heathland plants.
LONDON WILDLIFE TRUST

A:2 HILFIELD PARK RESERVOIR
Near Elstree; park just before entrance. Follow footpath to view reservoir from N.
■ Open water.
■ Good for wintering waterfowl which regularly include pochard, tufted duck, goldeneye, also goosander, wigeon and occasional rarities. Mornings and evenings best.

A:3 CASSIOBURY PARK
Near Watford; park on side of Watford beside river Gade. Free public access to most parts, but one area of watercress beds private; to enter reserve requires permit from HMWT.
■ River, watercress beds, mixed woodland.
■ The clear River Gade has excellent aquatic fauna (including 30 species of river molluscs) and many dragonflies. Wintering

birds found on cressbeds. **Birds** Woodpeckers, nuthatch, treecreeper, tits, kingfisher; (winter) grey wagtail, water rail, snipe, teal, siskin. **Aquatic fauna** Crayfish.
HERTS & MIDDLESEX WILDLIFE TRUST

A:4 WHIPPENDELL WOOD
Near Chandler's Cross; car parks on SW and NE sides of wood; open access.
■ Oak/hazel/ash, oak/hornbeam woodland.
■ Large, ancient woodland, containing mix of woodland habitats and rich bird community. Best in spring and summer.
Birds Hawfinch, wood warbler.

A:5 BROAD COLNEY LAKES
Near London Colney; car park on W side of reserve adjoining Shenley Lane (B5378).
■ Flooded gravel pits, river.
■ A variety of waterfowl including nesting great crested grebe, while developing ash, alder and willow around lakes provides habitat for passerines.
HERTS & MIDDLESEX WILDLIFE TRUST

Great crested grebe on nest – typical of many freshwater sites, including A:5, above.

A:6 NORTHAW GREAT WOOD
Near Cuffley; car park off the Ridgeway, road running W from Cuffley to Brookmans Park.
■ Mixed deciduous woodland.
■ Traditional coppicing and pollarding woodland management ensures retention of important wildlife. Large nightingale population in summer. **Birds** Hawfinch, nightingale, nuthatch, willow tit, tree pipit.
WELWYN HATFIELD DISTRICT COUNCIL/ HERTFORDSHIRE COUNTY COUNCIL

A:7 ROUGHDOWN COMMON
Near Hemel Hempstead; at roundabout junction of A41 and A417 W of Hemel Hempstead, follow minor road S for 300 yards (275 m) over railway; park near chalk quarry.
■ Chalk grassland, quarry.
■ Small area of grassland on N-facing chalk escarpment containing rich community of plants; only site in county for naturally regenerating juniper. **Plants** Fly orchid, large thyme, pyramidal orchid, dwarf and carline thistle, autumn gentian.
BOXMOOR TRUST

B:1 LEMSFORD SPRINGS
Near Welwyn Garden City; park beside river Lee, off roundabout (B197 leading to Lemsford, just W of A1 (M). Access by prior arrangement with warden, 7 Lemsford Village, Welwyn Garden City AL8 7TN.
■ Shallow lagoons, butterbur marsh, willow woodland.
■ Hide overlooks spring-fed lagoons providing one of Britain's best wintering sites for green sandpipers. A variety of molluscs; autumn and winter best for birds. **Birds** Green sandpiper, water rail, jack snipe. **Plants** Star-of-Bethlehem.
HERTS & MIDDLESEX WILDLIFE TRUST

B:2 SHERRARDSPARK WOOD
Near Welwyn Garden City; park in side roads W of railway station. Many footpaths enter wood.
■ Oak/hornbeam woodland.
■ Part of wood now mature sessile oak high forest with trees up to 250 years old. Site bisected by disused railway. Best in spring and summer. **Plants** Violet and broad-leaved helleborines, moschatel.

B:3 MARSHALLS HEATH
Near Wheathampstead; park on minor road to Marshalls Heath, just N of crossroads on A6129 1½ miles (2 km) W of roundabout at Wheathampstead.
■ Lowland heath.
■ Small remnant of acid heath, now rare in county, containing plants and insects characteristic of habitat.
HERTS & MIDDLESEX WILDLIFE TRUST

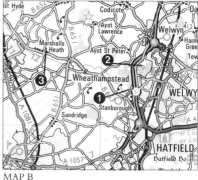

MAP B

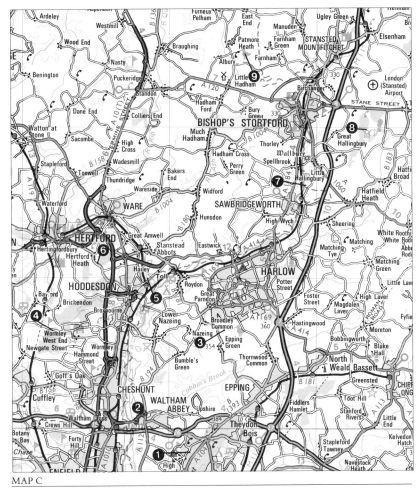

MAP C

C:1 EPPING FOREST

Near Loughton; many car parks throughout forest off A104. Parts of wood wet underfoot.
■ Ancient woodland, grass heath, ponds.
■ There are many outstanding individual trees – mainly beech, oak and hornbeam. Many have been pollarded, but now this practice, along with coppicing, has largely ceased so the ground flora is relatively poor except in the rides. Redstarts and nightingales have declined, but redpolls are commonly heard in the birch in many open heathy areas, and the elusive hawfinch is regularly seen.

Epping was threatened in the 19thC by enclosure, but saved by act of Parliament in 1878, since when it has been administered by the Corporation of London.
CORPORATION OF LONDON

C:2 CORNMILL STREAM & OLD RIVER LEA

Waltham Abbey; footbridges in NE and SE corners.
■ Slow-moving streams, rough grassland.
■ An outstanding site for dragonflies and damselflies with 18 species recorded. Added interest comes from aquatic plants, freshwater snails and other invertebrates. Best in spring and summer. **Insects** White-legged damselfly, variable damselfly, red-eyed damselfly, ruddy darter. **Plants** Flowering rush, shining pondweed.

C:3 HARLOW WOODS

Near Harlow; follow signs to Parndon Wood Cemetery and Crematorium.

■ Ash/maple and oak/hornbeam woodland, rides, clearings, ponds.
■ Bramble and bracken dominate the ground flora although bare leaf litter covers large areas under hornbeam coppice. Recent coppicing has encouraged flowers including early-purple orchid and violets.
HARLOW COUNCIL

C:4 WORMLEY WOOD

Near Hoddesdon; car park on minor road to Epping Green 1¾ miles (3 km) W of roundabout on A1170 in Broxbourne.
■ Mixed woodland, scrub.
■ Mixed wood, mainly sessile oak standards over hornbeam coppice, with some high forest, wild service-trees and scrub. **Birds** Nightjar, woodpeckers, nuthatch, woodcock, grasshopper warbler.
WOODLAND TRUST

C:5 RYE HOUSE MARSH★

Near Hoddesdon; car park opposite Rye House railway station, just E of Hoddesdon. Reserve and information/education centre open to public at weekends.
■ Mixed fen, wet meadow, scrub, stream, lagoons.
■ Small, varied, wetland reserve lying between the river Lee and lagoons of Rye Meads sewage works. Hides provide excellent views of wetland birds at all times of year, with many waders, hirundines and warblers on passage. **Birds** (Breeding) common tern, reed and sedge warblers; (winter) water pipit, green sandpiper, jack snipe, kingfisher; (passage) waders, hirundines and

warblers. **Mammals** Harvest mouse, bats. **Reptiles** Grass snake.
ROYAL SOCIETY FOR THE PROTECTION OF BIRDS

C:6 HERTFORD HEATH

Near Hertford; park in village of Hertford Heath, avoiding private roads. Site is in two parts on W and S sides of village.
■ Lowland heath, scrub, oak/hornbeam woodland, ponds.
■ Rare surviving remnant of southern heathland; patchwork of other habitats contributes to natural history interest. **Plants** Water-violet, creeping willow, heath grass.
HERTS & MIDDLESEX WILDLIFE TRUST

C:7 SAWBRIDGE MARSH

Near Sawbridgeworth; park beside Sawbridgeworth to Little Hallingbury road. Entry on W side. Open to members of county naturalists' trusts, otherwise by permit from HMWT.
■ Valley marshland.
■ Habitat and diverse flora maintained through grazing and rotational cutting. Snipe breed, and mollusc fauna includes national rarity, slender amber snail. Best in summer. **Plants** Marsh valerian, southern marsh-orchid, ragged-robin.
ESSEX NATURALISTS' TRUST/HERTS & MIDDLESEX WILDLIFE TRUST

C:8 HATFIELD FOREST

Near Bishop's Stortford; on S side of A120 E of town. Car park free to NT members.
■ Mixed/hornbeam woodland, lake, rides. **Plants** Black poplar, mistletoe, herb Paris, wild daffodil, adder's tongue, dwarf thistle. **Birds** Water rail, nightingale. **Mammals** Badger.
NATIONAL TRUST/ESSEX NATURALISTS' TRUST

C:9 PATMORE HEATH

Near Bishop's Stortford; park on roadside beyond 'Catherine Wheel' pub.
■ Grass heath, pools, scrub, developing oak woodland.
■ One of best remaining areas of acid grassland in county, also containing marshy areas and ponds with rich flora and dragonflies. **Plants** Southern marsh-orchid, marsh speedwell, common cottongrass.
HERTS & MIDDLESEX WILDLIFE TRUST

D:1 BLACKGROVE COMMON

Near Buntingford; park off Beckfield Lane, just W of village. Keep to footpaths crossing common, otherwise obtain permit from HMWT.
■ Wet grassland, stream.
■ Orchid-rich meadow bisected by a stream. Best in spring and early summer. **Plants** Early marsh-, southern marsh- and common spotted-orchids, ragged-robin.
HERTS & MIDDLESEX WILDLIFE TRUST

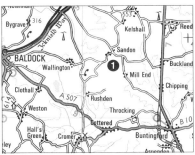

MAP D

CAMBRIDGESHIRE

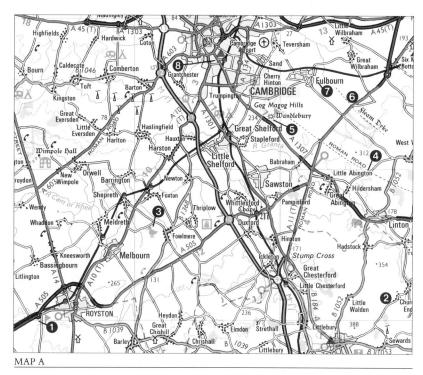

MAP A

A:1 THERFIELD HEATH*

Royston; park E side of town. Keep to foot-paths.

■ Chalk grassland, beech woodland, scrub.
■ Now rare example of East Anglian chalk grassland with various recreational uses, part local nature reserve, part mature, managed beechwood. **Plants** Spotted cat's-ear, pasque flower, white helleborine, bee and fragrant orchids, bastard toadflax, wild candytuft. **Butterflies** Chalkhill, blues, brown argus.
HERTS & MIDDLESEX WILDLIFE TRUST

A:2 SHADWELL WOOD

Near Saffron Walden; tracks lead from minor road to E of wood. Permit required from ENT.

■ Ash/maple woodland.
■ Oxlip, confined to woods on boulder clay in NW Essex and E Cambridgeshire, occurs here. Seven species of orchid have been recorded and a range of ancient woodland flowers. **Plants** (Shrubs) wayfaring-tree, guelder-rose; (flowers) greater butterfly-orchid, tutsan, herb Paris, bird's-nest orchid, narrow-leaved everlasting pea.
ESSEX NATURALISTS' TRUST

A:3 FOWLMERE

Near Fowlmere; S of village turn off A10 Cambridge-Royston road by Shepreth and follow sign. Limited parking on road verge. Nature trail, tower hide.

■ Reed-bed, open water, scrub.
■ Once part of the Cambridgeshire fens, this reserve is now surrounded by arable.

The reed-bed, spring-fed from the chalk, is alive with reed warblers (about 70 pairs) and sedge warblers. Little grebes, moorhens and water rail breed and bearded tits have done so, but are more regular in winter. Pied wagtails and corn buntings roost in the reeds in winter.

Chalky outcrops support bee orchids and cowslips; adder's-tongue and deadly night-shade can be found. Parts of former water-cress beds can be seen from the nature trail towards the S of the reserve. Spring is best,

but any time is good. **Birds** Kingfisher, siskin, green sandpiper, redpoll. **Plants** Guel-der-rose, small scabious. **Mammals** Water, pygmy and common shrews, weasel, stoat.
ROYAL SOCIETY FOR THE PROTECTION OF BIRDS

A:4 ROMAN ROAD

Between Cambridge and Haverhill; entire 5 miles (7 km) is road used as a public path.

■ Chalk grassland, hedges.
■ This pre-Roman trackway connected Cambridge and Haverhill. Chalk grassland is now scarce in Cambridgeshire and thick hedgerows enhance this green lane, at its best in Jun-Jul. **Plants** Purple milk-vetch, dropwort, salad burnet.

A:5 WANDLEBURY & BEECHWOOD

Near Cambridge; SE of town by A604. Car park at Wandlebury, road access to Beechwood.

■ Beech woodland, chalk grassland.
■ The old Wandlebury Ring was an Iron-Age fort on the chalk of the Gog Mahog hills. The planted woodland is good for birds, particularly warblers, and the remaining chalk turf – including the old lawn – has a range of chalk-loving wild flowers.

Just N of Wandlebury, Beechwood is an almost pure beech wood, where white helleborine is one of the few flowers not inhibited by the heavy shade. Best visited in Jun.
CAMBRIDGESHIRE WILDLIFE TRUST

A:6 FLEAM DYKE

Fulbourn; dyke runs SE from town. Access from footpath.

■ Chalk grassland, chalk scrub.
■ An ancient linear earthwork with chalk grassland; the only site for juniper in Cambridgeshire. Best Jun-Jul. **Plants** Purple milk-vetch, dropwort.
CAMBRIDGESHIRE WILDLIFE TRUST

A:7 FULBOURN

Fulbourn; entry by permit: apply CWT.

■ Chalk grassland, fen woodland, secondary woodland.

■ The variety of different habitats makes this reserve of particular educational value. Although rather modified by planting, the woodland areas add to the bird- and insect life here.
CAMBRIDGESHIRE WILDLIFE TRUST

A:8 UNIVERSITY BOTANIC GARDEN

Cambridge; in Bateman Street, off A10. Closed after 6 pm, Sun exc 2.30-6.30.

■ Gardens, glass houses.
■ Collection has plants from all over the world but especially Europe, including many rare British wild flowers. The birds have been well studied and include communal roosting robins.
UNIVERSITY BOTANIC GARDEN

B:1 LITTLE PAXTON GRAVEL PITS*

Near St Neots; car park at S end of pits (NE of Little Paxton village). Still a working gravel pit in parts; keep to footpaths; leaflet available from Huntingdonshire District Council.

■ Open water, reed, willows, willow carr.
■ These pits are the most interesting of dozens along the Ouse Valley. The wintering wildfowl include many gadwall, while sand spits support breeding and passage waders. One island has a small heronry; another a common tern colony in most years. Warblers and nightingales can be heard in the willow and osier scrub.

The pit margins support marsh plants like purple loosestrife and a range of dragonflies and damselflies. Evening-primroses and rosebay willowherb provide splashes of colour on poor sandy soil.

The nearby grassland and ponds of St Neots Common are also worth visiting. **Birds** Kingfisher, ringed plover. **Plants** Small balsam, bee orchid.

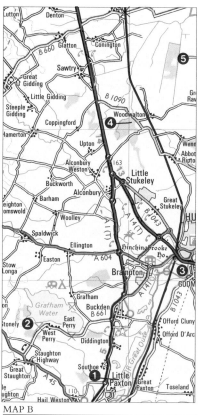

MAP B

B:2 GRAFHAM WATER

Near St Neots; at roundabout at Buckden on A1 take B661 signposted Grafham Water. Two large public car parks on S side of reservoir allow easy viewing. Cross to hide on foot from second (Mander) car park. B&HWT reserve at W of reservoir has no public access, except to hide open Oct-Mar for which non-members pay a small fee. Choppy water may cause wildfowl to retreat to sheltered W end of reservoir.
- Man-made reservoir, grassland, scrub marsh, shoreline.
- One of the largest inland waters in England, attracting large numbers of wintering wildfowl, smaller numbers of breeding wildfowl; outstanding in spring, late summer and autumn for passage migrants and rare birds. **Birds** (Winter) rarer grebes, sea duck, shearwater, goosander, cormorant, petrel; (breeding) gadwall, water rail, ringed plover.
BEDS & HUNTS WILDLIFE TRUST

B:3 PORT HOLME MEADOW*

Godmanchester; park in Godmanchester car park or near Chinese Bridge; walk through public park and over lock. Also footpath from Huntingdon or Brampton. Essential to visit before hay cut in early Jul. Wet underfoot.
- Dry/wet meadow.
- The River Ouse forks to run either side of this remarkable ancient meadow. It has been managed for hay in much the same way for centuries, allowing a wonderful range of wild flowers to prosper.

The footpaths, one of which runs along a route once used by the nuns at Hinchingbrooke, first cross dry meadow grassland characterized by lady's bedstraw, great burnet and pepper-saxifrage. In mid-summer the distinctive sound of yellow rattle seed heads will be heard as you brush past them. Wetter, low-lying parts in the middle have tubular water-dropwort, meadowsweet and marsh ragwort.

The river supports dragonflies including the scarce chaser. May and Jun are best. **Flowers** Fritillary, great yellow-cress, meadow crane's-bill. **Birds** Corn bunting.

B:4 MONKS WOOD

Near Huntingdon; Wood Walton is nearest village. By permit from NCC only.
- Ash/maple woodland, rides, neutral grassland, ponds, streams.
- One of Britain's most important lowland woodlands; a National Nature Reserve listed in *A Nature Conservation Review* and thoroughly described in the book *Monks Wood: A Nature Reserve Record.* Best visited in spring. **Plants** Crested cow-wheat, oxlip, wild service-tree, early-purple orchid, adder's-tongue, primrose. **Birds** Nightingale, woodcock. **Butterflies** Black hairstreak.
NATURE CONSERVANCY COUNCIL

B:5 WOODWALTON FEN

Near Ramsey; track from Ramsey Heights village. Access by permit from NCC only.
- Mixed fen, swamp, meres, birch/alder woodland.
- A remnant of the once vast fens, this area was dug for peat in the 19thC exposing the underlying fen peat. The range of fen, swamp and wet woodland habitats make this one of East Anglia's most important wetlands, best in spring and early summer. One of the last UK sites for the now extinct large copper butterfly, and still outstanding

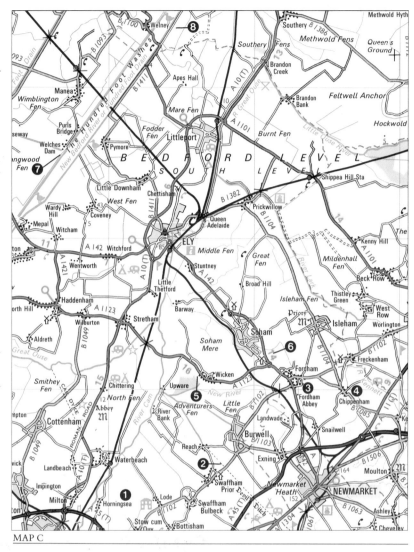

MAP C

for most insect orders. **Plants** Fen violet, fen wood-rush, bladderwort, water-violet, bog myrtle. **Birds** Woodcock; (winter) hen harrier.
NATURE CONSERVANCY COUNCIL

C:1 STOW CUM QUY FEN

Near Anglesey Abbey; leave A45 Cambridge by-pass at Stow cum Quy turn-off. Common land with many footpaths.
- Chalky pasture, pools.
- Although no true fen vegetation remains, the transition from dry chalk grassland to wetland habitats is interesting. Some semi-improved rough pasture being colonized by flowers from richer grassland nearby. **Plants** (Wetland) bladderwort, mare's-tail, unbranched bur-reed.

C:2 DEVIL'S DYKE**

Near Newmarket; park by road where B1102 crosses the embankment. Keep to footpath.
- Chalk grassland, chalk scrub.
- The dyke is an ancient linear earthwork and is the best and biggest area of chalk grassland in Cambridgeshire. Plants include several national rarities; best in Apr for pasqueflower, otherwise Jun-Jul. **Plants** Bloody crane's-bill, purple milk-vetch, wild asparagus, dropwort, rockrose, bastard toadflax, salad burnet. **Butterflies** Brown argus. **Invertebrates** Purse-web spider,

glow-worm.
CAMBRIDGESHIRE WILDLIFE TRUST

C:3 FORDHAM WOODS

Near Newmarket; entrance at N end of wood. CWT members and their guests only.
- Mature alder coppice/ash/crack willow/silver birch.
- Wetter areas of the wood have a fen vegetation including reed, meadowsweet and yellow flag. **Birds** Nightingale, kingfisher, woodcock.
CAMBRIDGESHIRE WILDLIFE TRUST

C:4 CHIPPENHAM FEN

Near Newmarket; park one mile (1.5 km) SW of Chippenham village where footpath crosses fen. Permit from NCC required.
- Fen, reed-bed, rough pasture, old planted woodland.
- Rich plant life includes bog-bean and fragrant orchid and a nationally rare umbellifer, Cambridge milk-parsley. **Plants** Grass-of-Parnassus, marsh helleborine, butterwort, southern marsh-orchid. **Birds** Water rail, nightingale, warblers.
NATURE CONSERVANCY COUNCIL

C:5 WICKEN FEN

Near Burwell; car park on site, NW of town. Walkway for wheelchairs. Admission fee. Wet underfoot.

CAMBRIDGESHIRE

■ Fen, reed-bed, scrub, open water.
■ This artificially maintained wetland is one of the most famous in East Anglia. Water pumped into the area has conserved a rich variety of habitats, while the surrounding countryside has sunk because of drainage. Wide grassy rides take you from the sedge fen to scrub of buckthorn, alder and guelder-rose.

The fen is rich with meadowsweet, yellow loosestrife and hemp agrimony. The scarce greater spearwort and lesser water-plantain can be found in the water courses while rough pasture, reed-bed and pools attract wintering wildfowl and breeding birds. The winter hen harrier roost can be watched from the tower hide at dusk. The site supports many rare insects. Take appropriate footwear – wet underfoot. **Birds** Wigeon, shoveler, woodcock, long-eared owl, great grey shrike, grasshopper warbler. **Plants** Milk-parsley, great fen-sedge, southern marsh-orchid, yellow rattle.
NATIONAL TRUST

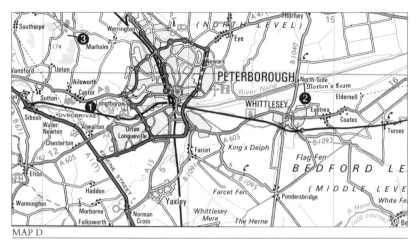

MAP D

C:6 SOHAM MEADOWS

Near Newmarket; entrance along track to W of reserve. Access to members of CWT only; keep to footpaths.
■ Neutral grassland, hedgerows.
■ Green-winged orchid and pepper-saxifrage demonstrate traditional grazing management on superb meadows, best from May to Jul. Wetter parts still have breeding snipe; hawthorn hedges attract winter thrush flocks. **Flowers** Meadow saxifrage, bee orchid, adder's-tongue. **Birds** Short-eared owl, snipe.
CAMBRIDGESHIRE WILDLIFE TRUST

C:7 OUSE WASHES★★

Near Chatteris; signposted from Manea village.
■ Grazing marsh, flooded in winter.
■ When the fens were drained in the 17thC, this flood reservoir was created between two parallel drainage channels. In winter the grasslands are dominated by thousands upon thousands of birds including 30,000 wigeon and the three species of swan (10 per cent of the world's Bewick's swans, some 3,000 or more).

In spring the wet meadows are outstanding for breeding waders, including 800 drumming snipe and a regular ruff lek. Black-tailed godwits first re-colonized Britain here, but have varied breeding success due to spring flooding. **Birds** (Winter) whooper swan, pintail shoveler, hen harrier roost; (summer) short-eared owl, spotted crake, redshank.
ROYAL SOCIETY FOR THE PROTECTION OF BIRDS/CAMBRIDGESHIRE WILDLIFE TRUST

C:8 WELNEY★

Near March; in winter, main access point is hides overlooking swans; in summer, there is also a walk across the washes. Permits from WT reception. Closed 24 and 25 Dec. Open daily 10 am-5 pm. Evening visits for 'swans under floodlight' 7 Nov-1 Mar, advance booking from WT.
■ Wet meadows.
■ Part of the Ouse Washes, described in C:7 above; thousands of wintering swans and wild duck attracted by regular feeding. The Welney summer walk crosses otherwise inaccessible washes. Winter best for birds, summer for flowers. See C:7 for selective species list.
WILDFOWL TRUST

D:1 FERRY MEADOWS

Near Peterborough; on A605 W of Peterborough, well signposted. Large car park.
■ Wader scrape, lakes, woodland.
■ The artificial wader scrape brings birds such as little ringed plover close to town. The lakes support easily observed birds such as Canada goose and tufted duck, and scarcer species such as wintering goldeneye. **Birds** Ringed plover, common tern, snipe, greylag goose.
PETERBOROUGH DEVELOPMENT CORPORATION

D:2 NENE WASHES★

Near Whittlesey; from the B1040, park by Dog in a Doublet sluice. By written application to RSPB only, otherwise keep to footpaths.
■ Flood plain.
■ Winter flooding of meadows between retaining banks attracts thousands of wildfowl, many of which move between here

Fieldfare in hawthorn – see Soham Meadows.

and the nearby Ouse Washes. Breeding birds include garganey and waders; rarities seen on passage. **Birds** Hen harrier, Bewick's swan, pintail, wigeon; (passage) black-tailed godwit, marsh harrier; (summer) garganey.
ROYAL SOCIETY FOR THE PROTECTION OF BIRDS

D:3 CASTOR HANGLANDS

Near Peterborough; park in Ailsworth. Bridle-path access from village through middle of site; no access to wood.
■ Ash/maple woodland, limestone grassland, neutral/acid grassland, ponds, ditches.
■ Ancient woodland with ramsons and yellow archangel. Grassland varies from wet to dry, chalky to acid, and contains many wild flowers, including orchids. **Plants** Purple milk-wort, pyramidal orchid, marsh valerian, marsh-orchids. **Amphibians** Crested newt. **Birds** Long-eared owl, nightingale, sparrowhawk, woodcock.
NATURE CONSERVANCY COUNCIL

SUFFOLK

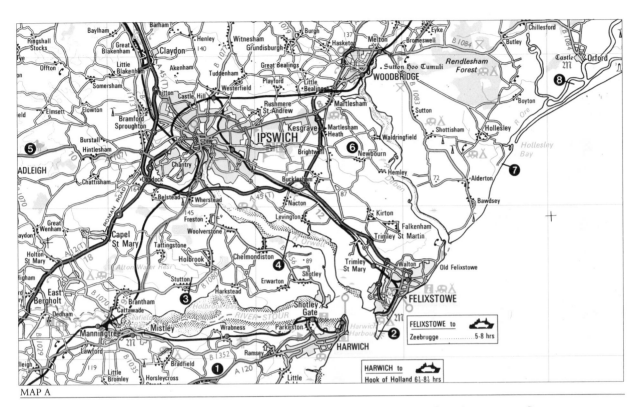

MAP A

A:1 STOUR & COPPERAS WOODS★★
Near Harwich; car park on B1352 Manningtree to Harwick Road, one mile (1.5 km) E of Wrabness.

■ Estuary, woodland, scrub, salt-marsh.

■ The unusual combination of woodland and coast side by side makes this one of the best wildlife sites in Essex. The sweet chestnut coppice of Stour Wood has little ground flora, but open areas offer bluebells and wood anemone.

The gently-shelving Stour Estuary regularly supports nine species of waders and wildfowl in nationally important numbers, and Copperas Bay is as good as anywhere to see them. The large black-tailed godwit flock is remarkable – a species otherwise scarce in East Anglia in winter.
ROYAL SOCIETY FOR THE PROTECTION OF BIRDS

A:2 LANDGUARD
Felixstowe; car park at S tip of town.

■ Sand/shingle spit, stablized inland, herb/grass mix, scrub.

■ Both sand and shingle areas have an exceptionally rich flora. Exposed position makes it an ideal landfall for migrant birds, including rarities. Also good for sea-birds, especially spring and autumn. **Plants** (Shingle) sea pea, sea-kale; (inland) viper's-bugloss, dittander, rare clovers.
SUFFOLK WILDLIFE TRUST/LANDGUARD BIRD OBSERVATORY

A:3 ALTON WATER★
Near Ipswich; site S of town E of the A137 Ipswich to Manningtree road. Four car parks at various points around reservoir. Footpath access to most areas.

■ Reservoir, woodland.

■ Although only completed in 1978, this reservoir already attracts large numbers of winter wildfowl, with waders and rarities on passage. Three areas are managed as nature reserves by the SWT.

ANGLIAN WATER/SUFFOLK WILDLIFE TRUST

A:4 ORWELL ESTUARY★
Near Ipswich; view S side from B1456 Holbrook road; for Pin Mill walk E then N alongside Shotley Marshes; view N side from Levington Creek (turning just E of Levington village); for Fagbury, footpaths from roundabout at TM 278343.

■ Intertidal mudflats, salt-marsh, grazing marsh.

■ This long estuary – with salt-marsh at Fagbury and Levington Creeks, and grazing marsh at Shotley – is good any time for birdwatching, but especially Aug to Apr.

A:5 WOLVES WOOD
Near Hadleigh; reserve entrance on N side of A1071 Ipswich-Hadleigh road 1½ miles (2.5 km) E of Hadleigh.

■ Broad-leaved woodland, coppice, rides, ponds, ditches.

■ One of the largest remaining coppice-with-standards woodland areas in Suffolk, its history can be traced back to the 12thC. A medieval boundary bank, ditches and some 43 ponds are archaeological features as well as being good for dragonflies and flowers. Thickets from many years of coppicing attract increasing numbers of nightingale. Hawfinch is regular in the hornbeam and cherry areas. The roadside verge has an exceptionally large colony of Essex skipper butterflies.

Sweet chestnut – see A:1, this page.

A:6 NEWBOURNE SPRINGS
Near Ipswich; E of town off A1093, car park beside The Fox in Newbourne village. Take sandy track to the left. Footpaths always open; otherwise SWT members and visitors are asked to call at Anglian Water's Bucklesham pumping station to make themselves known.

■ Valley, alder carr, fen, oak/ash/hazel woodland, heath, scrub.

■ Impressive variety of habitats in compact area. Spring-fed slopes, stream banks and recent coppice are particularly good for flowers.
SUFFOLK WILDLIFE TRUST

A:7 SHINGLE STREET
Near Woodbridge; follow road going E from Hollesley.

■ Shingle.

■ An excellent site for the specialized wild flowers of shingle, including sea pea, sea-kale, sea campion and yellow horned-poppy. The lagoons have a number of unusual brackish water invertebrates and the site has several rare spiders. Summer is best.

A:8 HAVERGATE ISLAND★★
By boat from town quay, Orford; permits needed from RSPB. Closed Sep-Mar and Tue, Wed, Thu. Winter visitng and permits by written application to warden. Entry fee.

■ Shallow lagoons, rough grassland, shingle.

■ The island is best known for its avocets, which became extinct in Britain in the 19thC and recolonized both Minsmere and Havergate in 1947. What began with four pairs has now built up to about 100 pairs in most years. Unusually, they winter here too, sharing the islands in the lagoon with common and Sandwich terns and in most years a pair or two of Arctic terns at their most southerly regular E coast site. The shingle in summer supports the rare yellow vetchling.
ROYAL SOCIETY FOR THE PROTECTION OF BIRDS

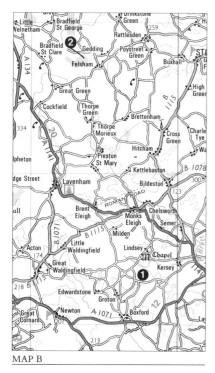

MAP B

B:1 GROTON WOOD★

Near Hadleigh; *gate at SW of wood which lies on minor road NE of Groton village.*
Small-leaved lime coppice, mixed secondary oak/ash woodland.

■ Suffolk's largest small-leaved lime wood, documented back to 1279. The S two thirds of the wood were probably planted in the 17thC; wild cherry is common. **Birds** Hawfinch, woodpeckers, woodcock, night-

ingale. **Plants** Violet helleborine, herb Paris, stinking iris, wood spurge, woodruff.
SUFFOLK WILDLIFE TRUST

B:2 BRADFIELD WOODS★★

Near Bury St Edmunds; *between A45 and A134 SE of town; car park off Bradfield St George to Gedding minor road.*

■ Diverse coppice-with-standards woodland, rides, meadow, pond.

■ Monkspark and Felshamhall Woods together make up the largest actively coppiced wood in Suffolk. Their size and variety account for some 370 recorded species of plants, surpassed only by two or three other woodlands in Britain. Coppicing has been carried out here since at least 1252 and continues today, with contrasts in the wildflower communities in different aged plots easy to see. The coppice suits dormice and a large number of nightingales.
SUFFOLK WILDLIFE TRUST

Hawfinch – see Groton Wood, this page.

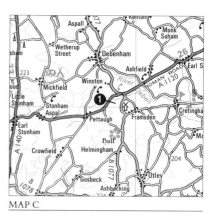

MAP C

C:1 FOX FRITILLARY MEADOW

Near Framlingham; *in the middle of Boundary Farm, Framsden, on S side of the A1120 just W of its intersection with the B1077. Park in farmyard with care not to obstruct; please identify yourself to the owners. Members of SWT only, exc on reserve open days.*

■ Wet meadow.

■ Biggest of the four fritillary meadows in Suffolk; fritillaries are now almost confined to Suffolk and the Thames-valley. Best from late Apr to mid May. **Plants** Ragged-robin, cowslip, lady's-smock.
SUFFOLK WILDLIFE TRUST

D:1 WEST STOW★

Near Bury St Edmunds; *from A1101 between Icklingham and Lackford take turning for West Stow. Park at site.*

■ Breck heath, alder woodland, gravel pits, birch/Scots pine woodland.

■ A range of Breckland habitats within a relatively small area, plus the added attraction of water-filled gravel pits. The scarce

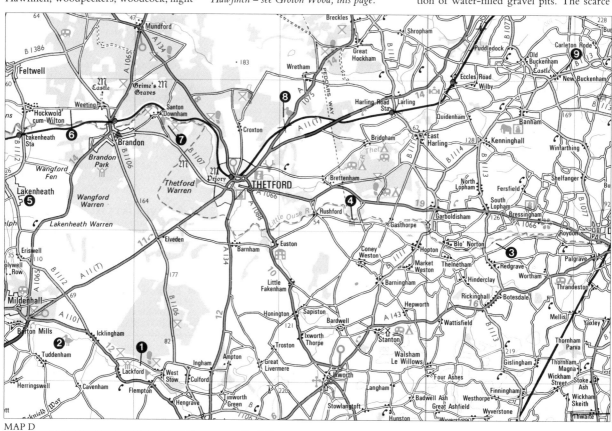

MAP D

maiden pink is widespread in short turf.
ST EDMUNDSBURY DISTRICT COUNCIL

D:2 CAVENHAM HEATH
Near Mildenhall; SE of town, access from Tuddenham village, signposted from A11 by Barton Mills roundabout. Permit needed from NCC, exc for public right of way and S section of reserve.
■ Breck heath, birch-oak/-alder woodland, wet meadow.
■ A large, mainly acidic breck with more woodland than most of the heaths in this area. The wet grassland in the floodplain of the River Lark adds to the variety.
NATURE CONSERVANCY COUNCIL

D:3 REDGRAVE & LOPHAM FENS★★
Near Diss; from B1113 take first turning E on Norfolk side; in 1/3 mile (0.5 km) fen entrance on right leads to car park.
■ Fen, reed-beds, sedge beds, sallow/alder carr, oak/birch woodland.
■ The largest remaining area of the once-extensive fens of the Little Ouse-Waveney Valley. Both rivers have their source here, fed, like the fen, by chalky springs, whose purity and low fertility are shown by plants like the insectivorous bladderwort.

Old peat diggings have left pools – the only place in Britain where the great raft spider is found. The reed- and sedge beds are still harvested and support reed and sedge warblers while the drier sandy ridges have a heathy vegetation.
SUFFOLK WILDLIFE TRUST

D:4 KNETTISHALL HEATH★
Near Thetford; car park and nature trails at site. Open daylight hours.
■ Breck heath, calcareous grassland, oak/pine/birch woodland, fen.
■ Characteristic Breckland with a range of heath and grassland types. **Birds** Nightjar, nightingale, green woodpecker, lesser whitethroat.
SUFFOLK COUNTY COUNCIL

D:5 MAIDSCROSS HILL★
Lakenheath; park at E end of town on edge of site.
■ Breck grassland, gorse scrub.
■ A sizeable area of dry Breck grassland with several rare plants, including Spanish and sand catchflies, Breckland thyme, sickle medick.

D:6 WEETING HEATH★
Near Brandon; car park by B1106 Weeting to Hockwold road. Hides. No access to most of reserve. Closed Sep-Mar. Permit needed from warden on site.
■ Breck heath, arable weed plot, pine plantation.
■ The short, rabbit-grazed turf supports several pairs of stone-curlew and is the best place in Britain to see them (usually visible but inactive during day). Several rare Breckland plants occur, notably spiked speedwell. **Plants** Lichens, Breckland and three-fingered speedwells, field wormwood (Breckland mugwort), Spanish catchfly.
NORFOLK NATURALIST'S TRUST/NATURE CONSERVANCY COUNCIL

D:7 SANTON DOWNHAM BIRD TRAIL★★
Near Brandon; car park at start of trail in St Helen's picnic site, Santon Downham. Bird trail leaflet from FC.

■ Forestry clearfell, pine forest, scrub, river.
■ Trail arranged to make it easy for birdwatchers to see many of the Breckland specialities, notably those found on forestry clearfells such as woodlarks and nightjars. **Birds** Red-backed shrike, goshawk, crossbill, hawfinch, siskin, woodcock, golden pheasant, nightingale.
FORESTRY COMMISSION

D:8 EAST WRETHAM HEATH★
Near Thetford; car park off A1075. Touch trail for the visually handicapped. The Drove Road is a public right of way. Otherwise, nature trail open every day exc Tue 10 am-5 pm. Permits from the warden's house; small fee.
■ Meres, grassland, pine/deciduous woodland, scrub.
■ Most of the dry heath and grassland of Breckland has disappeared under Thetford forest. Ringmere and Langmere are notable because their water level fluctuates with the ground water and is generally higher in summer. The acid, neutral and chalky grassland has a variety of grasses and flowers and many ant-hills. An arable weed plot has been created. The old Scots pine, planted in Napoleonic times, attracts red squirrels and crossbills. Hawfinches feed under the hornbeams.
NORFOLK NATURALISTS' TRUST

D:9 NEW BUCKENHAM COMMON★
Near Attleborough; N of B1113 immediately E of New Buckenham. Parking by road, easiest on N side of common. Take care not to disturb nesting lapwings when searching for orchids.
■ Neutral, acidic and calcareous grassland, scrub, ponds.
■ Norfolk's largest colony of green-winged orchids (best in May and Jun), reflecting the common's traditional management of light grazing. The scrub, dykes and ponds add interest.
NORFOLK NATURALISTS' TRUST

E:1 NORTH WARREN
Near Aldeburgh; entrance to car park off Aldeburgh to Leiston road.
■ Heath, fen, scrub.
■ Remnant of the once-extensive Sandlings heaths of coastal Suffolk, mainly grass with some heather and bell heather. Fen has sedge and reed warblers and marshland plants include bogbean. **Birds** Marsh harrier, nightingale.
ROYAL SOCIETY FOR THE PROTECTION OF BIRDS

E:2 WALBERSWICK★★
Near Southwold; car park part way along Walberswick village to Westwood Lodge road. Keep to footpaths.
■ Reed-bed, coastal lagoons, scrub, heath, woodland.
■ The vast reed-bed has breeding marsh harriers and bitterns, yet it is as a winter bird-watching site that it is best known. The view from Westwood Lodge is outstanding for birds of prey; hen harriers are reliable and rough-legged buzzards are often seen.

The walk from the car park takes you across heath; through reed beds with bearded tits; and by coastal lagoons with passage waders. Shorelarks and snow buntings are regular on the beach.

Next to Walberswick – a long way by road – are the town marshes and common of Southwold, also worth visiting. **Birds**

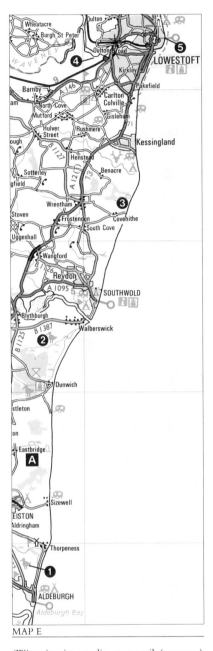
MAP E

(Winter) twite, merlin, water rail; (summer) Savi's warbler, avocet.
NATURE CONSERVANCY COUNCIL

E:3 COVEHITHE & BENACRE★
Near Kessingland; park with care by no-through-road to Covehithe cliffs, or park in Kessingland or Benacre and take footpaths.
■ Open water, reed-bed, woodland, beach, scrub.
■ The broad, pits and scrub right on the coast attract many wintering and passage birds. Benacre broad is still separated from the sea by a narrow spit of beach and attracts wintering wildfowl; smew are regular in hard weather.

Little tern nest on the shingle while the pits further N are often visited by sea-duck in winter. A Mediterranean gull regularly puts in an appearance in any season.

The dead oaks on the edge of the wood are striking – dying back as the sea eats into the land.
NATURE CONSERVANCY COUNCIL

SUFFOLK

E:4 CARLTON MARSHES*

Near Lowestoft; approach from Burnt Hill Lane off A146 Lowestoft-Beccles road ¾ mile (one km) W of Oulton Broad Station. Car park at site.

■ Grazing marsh, fen, open water, carr.

■ Many typical Broadland habitats within a relatively small area which escaped the pollution and agricultural 'improvement' of elsewhere in the Broads. **Birds** (Summer) marsh harrier, bearded tit, Cetti's warbler. **Plants** (Dykes) water-violet, water-soldier, flowering-rush; (grazing marsh) marsh pea, marsh-orchids; (fen) greater spearwort, marsh sow-thistle.

SUFFOLK WILDLIFE TRUST

E:5 LOWESTOFT NESS

Lowestoft; car park by coastguards.

■ Concrete sea defences, warehouses, harbour.

■ East Anglia's most regular purple sandpiper flock winters here, feeding among the breakwaters and on the sea wall. Gulls winter in large numbers with regular scarcer gulls (including glaucous), and the nearby harbour and lake Lothing may have sea-duck, grebes or divers in hard weather.

E:A MINSMERE, DUNWICH & WESTLETON HEATHS**

Near Saxmundham; car park at Sizewell. Minsmere open every day but Tue, fee to non-members of RSPB. Permit needed from RSPB for much of reserve. NT car park, fee for non-members. Entry to Westleton Heath by permit from NCC except area between Roman carriageway and Dunwich road.

■ Scrape, reed-bed, open water, heath, woodland, scrub, grazing marsh.

① Gull, terns and cormorants feed at warm water outflow; black redstarts nest on building. Flowers in turf include sheep's-bit.

② Tree lupins and scrub attract migrant birds in both spring and autumn.

③ Minsmere RSPB reserve justly famous for its reed-beds and artificial scrapes. Waders and wildfowl seen well from public hides on beach. There are tens of thousands of visitors to Minsmere each year and the RSPB is increasingly worried about disturbance to some of the species. Approaching from Sizewell or Dunwich Heath along the seaward boundary therefore does the birds a service.

④ Superb oak woodland, includes canopy hide; look for redstarts and woodpeckers.

⑤ W of road, meadow is good for southern marsh-orchids. Look towards sea for wintering swans on the Minsmere Levels.

⑥ When gorse stops flowering, dwarf gorse starts on Dunwich Heath, supporting linnets and stonechats. Look out for adders on footpaths from heath and fulmars from cliff top.

⑦ Access to most of Westleton heath by NCC permit, but heather heath between Roman carriageway and Dunwich road unrestricted.

⑧ Sand wasps burrow into sandy slopes on gorse-covered common. On bare areas, mossy stonecrop and parsley-piert are seen.

Birds (Breeding) avocet, marsh harrier, bittern, bearded tit, little tern, nightingale. **Plants** Water-violet, marsh-orchids, ragged-robin, marsh sow-thistle. **Mammals** Otter, harvest mouse, mink, water vole.

ROYAL SOCIETY FOR THE PROTECTION OF BIRDS/NATIONAL TRUST/NATURE CONSERVANCY COUNCIL

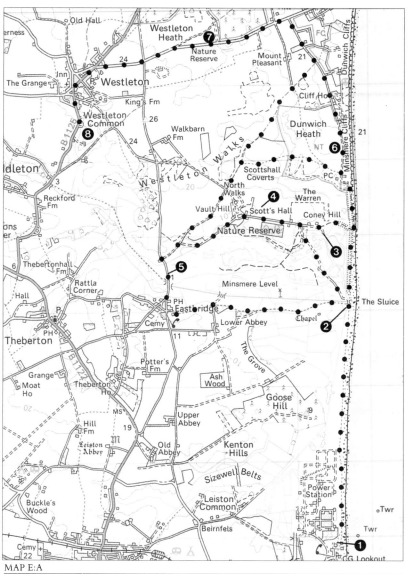

MAP E:A

Above, roe deer, seen at Thompson Common. Above left, water-violet – see E:4.

A:1 THOMPSON COMMON**
***Near Watton;** car park in Butters' Hall Lane, E of Thompson village. Public nature trail.*
■ Pingos, grassland, woodland, scrub.
■ High botanical interest maintained by grazing Shetland ponies, but huge variety of vegetation in the pingos (glacial features – see B:1) makes this one of the richest places for plants in the county, notably the scarce water-violet in May and large stands of southern marsh-orchid in Jun. Also outstanding for insects, and some rare snails. **Plants** Water-violet, green-winged orchid, bog-bean, greater spearwort. **Mammals** Roe deer. **Birds** Nightingale. **Insects** Red-eyed damselfly, ruddy darter. **Snails** Shining ram's-horn.
NORFOLK NATURALISTS' TRUST

A:2 WAYLAND WOOD*
***Near Watton;** by A1075 Thetford Road one mile (1.5 km) S of town.*

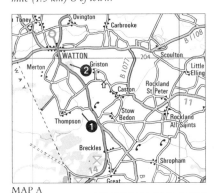

MAP A

■ Oak woodland, hazel/bird cherry coppice.
■ Wood's history traceable to the Domesday Book and reputedly the setting for *Babes in the Wood*. Many typical ancient woodland flowers, and the only Norfolk colony of the

MAP B

yellow star-of-Bethlehem. Best Apr-Jun.
NORFOLK NATURALISTS' TRUST

B:1 FOULDEN COMMON*
***Near Swaffham;** common is either side of Gooderstone to Foulden road.*
■ Fen, chalk grassland, scrub, heath, open water, neutral grassland.
■ A rich and diverse site with excellent flowers and a large population of nightingales. There are many pingos – small periglacial ground ice depressions – containing varying amounts of water, which support a wide range of spiders and dragon- and damselflies. Best May to Jul.

B:2 NARBOROUGH RAILWAY EMBANKMENT*
***Near Swaffham;** from W end of embankment, road S from A47 in Narborough.*
■ Chalk grassland, scrub.
■ The best chalk grassland in Norfolk – a country generally poor for chalk-loving flowers. Excellent butterfly site with 26 species recorded, including dingy skipper, green and purple hairstreaks, brown argus and grayling.
NORFOLK NATURALISTS' TRUST/BRITISH BUTTERFLY CONSERVATION SOCIETY

B:3 ROYDON COMMON*
***Near King's Lynn;** car park down public track at W of reserve, which lies S of Roydon to King's Lynn road. Members and holders of NNT handbook free to visit at any time.*
■ Heath, oak/birch woodland.
■ One of the best lowland heath and bog sites in Britain with a fine range of plant communities including a large heather heath. Roost of hen harriers in winter can be watched from car park at dusk.
NORFOLK NATURALISTS' TRUST

NORFOLK

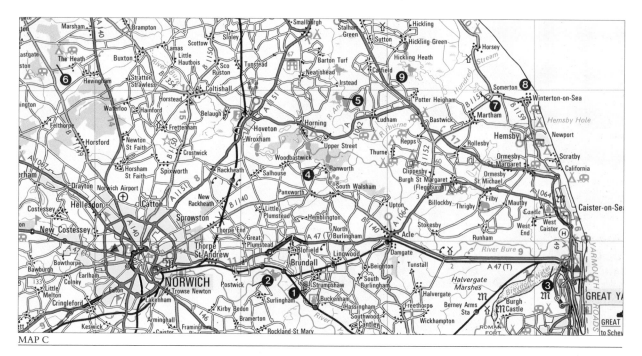

MAP C

C:1 STRUMPSHAW FEN★★

Near Norwich; car park reached by turning sharp right and right again into Low Road from Brundall; cross level crossing for fen. For Buckenham marshes park by Buckenham BR station. Trails, hides.

■ Fen, reed-bed, open water, grazing marsh, wet woodland.

■ All the Broadland habitats are here, and as they used to be. Dykes are full of the water plants that were once widespread, including the now scarce water-soldier, and they support Norfolk aeshna dragonfly. The fen, managed by mowing and grazing, is rich with flowers.

Marsh harriers are easy to see, while the explosive song of the Cetti's warbler is hard to miss; the Yare valley is its British stronghold.

The only bean goose flock in England feeds regularly on the grazing marshes by Buckenham Station.

ROYAL SOCIETY FOR THE PROTECTION OF BIRDS

C:2 SURLINGHAM & ROCKLAND MARSHES

Near Norwich; park by Surlingham church, about 3 miles (5 km) N of A146 Norwich to Beccles road. Follow trail. Wet underfoot in parts.

■ Open water, islands, marsh, reed-bed, scrub.

■ A charming walk taking in a range of Broadland habitats within a small area; Cetti's, grasshopper, reed and sedge warblers all breed and dusk is good for bats, especially noctule. Best in spring and early summer.

ROYAL SOCIETY FOR THE PROTECTION OF BIRDS

C:3 BREYDON WATER & BERNEY MARSHES★

Near Great Yarmouth; park at Great Yarmouth BR station, footpaths along N and S shores of Breydon. No road access to Berney Marshes, use Weavers Way long distance footpath or train to Berney Arms Halt.

■ Mudflats, grazing marsh, salt-marsh.

■ A key position to attract wintering and migrating birds, with many rarities recorded over the years. Being next to the huge Halvergate Marshes used to add to Breydon's wildfowl numbers but drainage and ploughing caused a decline. This trend is reversing with the development of the RSPB reserve at Berney Marshes.

Common terns nest on platforms near the hides. Wigeon, shelduck and pintail are the most notable wildfowl, with Bewick's swans on the grazing marshes. Sea-duck and sawbills appear in hard weather. Best visited in winter.

ROYAL SOCIETY FOR THE PROTECTION OF BIRDS/NORFOLK COUNTY COUNCIL/GREAT YARMOUTH BOROUGH COUNCIL

C:4 BURE MARSHES★★

Near Wrexham; park in village of Ranworth by staithe. Mooring for small boats at conservation centre. Centre open Apr-Oct (10.30 am-5.30 pm; Sat 2-5 pm only; closed Mon). Fee. Access from Cockshoot along boardwalk at all times from end of Ferry Road, Woodbastwick.

■ Fen, open water, carr.

■ Ranworth and Cockshoot Broads between them illustrate the problems and some of the solutions to broadland's decline.

At Ranworth a boardwalk takes you through the succession of habitats from oak woodland to open water in just 490 yards (450 m).

There are few water birds because of the poor water quality, although common terns nest on a platform.

Cockshoot Broad has been isolated from the polluted water and years of accumulated mud have been pumped out. The contrast is plain – a dyke full of water weeds and damselflies, wildfowl on the broad, plus Cetti's warbler and bearded tit.

NORFOLK NATURALISTS' TRUST/NATURE CONSERVANCY COUNCIL/BROADS AUTHORITY

C:5 HOW HILL★

Near Wroxham; signposted near Ludham on A1062 Wroxham to Potter Heigham road. Car park at site.

■ Reed-bed, grazing marsh, woodland, formal gardens, dykes, wader scrape.

■ Nature trail through broadland in miniature on this estate, with all the typical habitats which support marsh harrier, bearded tit and Cetti's warbler. Commands broadland's best view and formal gardens' flowers attract swallowtail butterflies.

HOW HILL TRUST

C:6 BUXTON HEATH★

Near Norwich; take turn signposted 'The Heath' off B1149 Norwich to Holt Road. Park by road.

■ Heath, fen, birch/oak scrub, reed-bed.

■ Large heath with excellent flora, especially in valley mire, with fine variety of orchids. The even larger Causton Marsham heaths to the N are dryer and have western gorse, more usually found on the Atlantic coast. Best in Jun and Jul. **Birds** Tree pipit, redpoll, whitethroat.

C:7 MARTHAM BROAD

Near Great Yarmouth; footpath runs to S of reserve, but no access to most of reserve. Park in West Somerton village.

■ Open water, reed-/sedge beds, alder carr woodland.

■ One of only four of the broads not damaged by poor water quality; the water plants therefore excellent, notably the nationally rare holly-leaved naiad. **Plants** Mare's-tail, marsh sow-thistle, milk parsley (supporting swallowtail butterflies), greater water-parsnip, parsley water-dropwort. **Birds** (Summer) bearded tit, marsh harrier.

NORFOLK NATURALISTS' TRUST

C:8 WINTERTON DUNES★

Near Great Yarmouth; park by road to Winterton Beach.

■ Acid sand dune system, damp hollows, scrub.

■ An extensive coastal dune system best known for the natterjack toads in the largely seasonal ponds. Wintering birds of prey are sometimes outstanding, and Winterton Great Valley S of the beach road has breeding stonechats, rare in Norfolk.

NATURE CONSERVANCY COUNCIL

C:9 HICKLING BROAD★★

Near Stalham; car park signposted in Hickling Broad. Footpath along S edge of broad at TG 412208. N from Potter Heigham, one mile (1.5 km) take right turn into through road. Park in about ½ mile (0.8 km) by gate and stile on right. Closed Nov-Mar and Tue. Advance permits from warden's office, Stubb Road, Norwich NR12 OBW; unsold permits may be available on the day. Advance booking also for water trail.

■ Reed-/sedge beds, open water, grazing marsh, woodland.

■ Largest of the Norfolk broads and probably the best for birds, this is the classic site to hear the reeling song of the rare Savi's warbler (but beware the similar grasshopper warbler).

Swallowtail butterflies here are best seen on a still summer day.

Pools by the trails are excellent for passage waders.

Grazing marsh is good for wintering swans, and the declining bittern still survives in the reed-beds, alongside the now increasing marsh harrier.

NORFOLK NATURALISTS' TRUST

D:1 SNETTISHAM★★

Near Hunstanton; park at Snettisham beach (small fee in summer).

■ Intertidal flats, flooded gravel pits, shingle ridge.

■ Thousands of waders moving ahead of the incoming tide on the wash can provide an unforgettable spectacle roosting undisturbed on islands in the gravel pits. The pits are excellent for winter wildfowl, especially goldeneye and red-breasted merganser.

ROYAL SOCIETY FOR THE PROTECTION OF BIRDS

D:2 SYDERSTONE COMMON

Near Fakenham; site is NE of B1454. Take care near pools not to tread on toads.

■ Heath, pools, hawthorn/birch scrub.

■ One of just three East Anglia sites for the rare natterjack toad, and the only inland one. The toads live in and around the alkaline pools on the otherwise acid heath.

NORFOLK NATURALISTS' TRUST

D:3 HUNSTANTON CLIFFS

Hunstanton; car park at top of cliffs open in summer (small fee).

■ Cliff, foreshore.

■ A classic winter sea-watching site, especially for eiders and common and velvet scoters. Cliff geologically interesting, part of it carstone rich in ammonite fossils, with largest breeding colony of fulmars on cliff face.

D:4 HOLME DUNES★

Near Hunstanton; at end of road to Holme Beach take unclassified road on right, car park at end. NNT/NOA permits sold on site. Caution – like many bird observatories, it is often almost completely without birds.

■ Sand dunes, sand flats, beach, pine shelter belt, salt-marsh, grazing marsh, dune slacks, sea buckthorn scrub.

■ Site on NW tip of Norfolk ideal for attracting migrant birds which is why NOA

Bittern, bird of Norfolk reed-beds.

bird observatory is here. Of year-round interest, with wintering and breeding birds, and botanically rich dune slacks.

NORFOLK NATURALISTS' TRUST/NORFOLK ORNITHOLOGISTS' ASSOCIATION

D:5 TITCHWELL MARSH★★

Near Hunstanton; car park to N of A149 coast road W of Titchwell village.

■ Fresh/brackish coastal lagoons, reedbed, salt-marsh, sand flats, dunes.

■ One of Britain's top bird-watching spots – the created coastal lagoons have attracted, among many others, breeding avocets.

The foreshore often has large numbers of estuary waders such as knot, bar-tailed godwit and oystercatchers. Sanderling and turnstone feed among the peaty remains of the ancient forest. Little and common terns nest on the shingle and sand and can be seen from a hide sunk into the dunes.

ROYAL SOCIETY FOR THE PROTECTION OF BIRDS

D:6 SCOLT HEAD ISLAND & BRANCASTER MANOR★★

Near Hunstanton; access by boat from Brancaster Staithe to Scolt Head; walking across at low tide not advisable without a local guide. Brancaster Manor car park at end of beach road (fee in summer); walk E for view towards Scott Head.

■ Salt-marsh, sand dunes, shingle, spit, beach, mudflats, grassland.

■ An offshore shingle spit where sand dunes have stabilized and extensive salt-marsh has grown on the sheltered S side, this island with its changing shape is of enormous interest to geographers.

The salt-marshes are remarkable in having three species of sea lavender along with sea aster and sea purslane. Bee orchids grow on some of the older dunes, and yellow horned-poppy flowers through to Oct on the shingle.

Brancaster Manor includes more salt-marsh and dunes, with sheets of flowering yellow rattle in spring.

NATIONAL TRUST/NATURE CONSERVANCY COUNCIL/NORFOLK NATURALISTS' TRUST

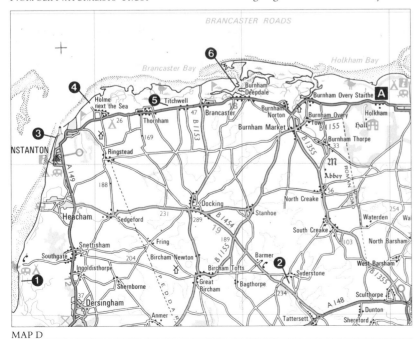

MAP D

NORFOLK

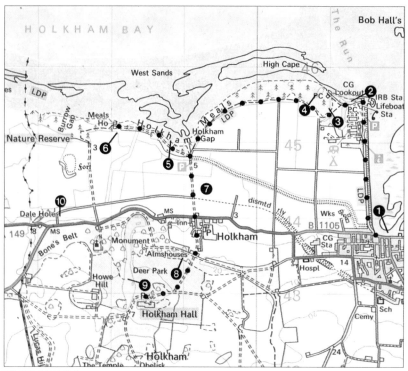

1:50 000, MAP D:A

D:A HOLKHAM MEALS★★

Wells-next-the-Sea; *park at Wells Quay, lifeboat station, Lady Anne's drive (Holkham Gap), Holkham village.*

■ *Pine woods, grazing marsh, intertidal flats, parkland, sand dunes, lake.*

① Views of waders; also of little grebes.
② Parrot crossbills bred by car park in 1984 and 1985; boating lake has goldeneye and scaup in winter. Waders on sand flats over ridge include sanderling.
③ Birch dell famous for autumn migrants; red-breasted flycatchers and yellow-browed warblers are annual.
④ Pool amid conifers attracts drinking birds including crossbill and siskin.

⑤ Corsican and Scots pine fringed by birch hold falls of migrant birds in autumn when they are often alive with goldcrests or blackcaps.
⑥ New scrape excellent for waders, especially in late summer.
⑦ Look out for wintering geese and resident Egyptian geese.
⑧ Huge holm oaks by car park, and regular spot for hawfinch and brambling under the beeches just inside Holkham Park.
⑨ Passing fallow deer in park; lake has greylag and Canada geese with cormorant roost on island.
⑩ Park with care by road for views of wintering geese.

NATURE CONSERVANCY COUNCIL

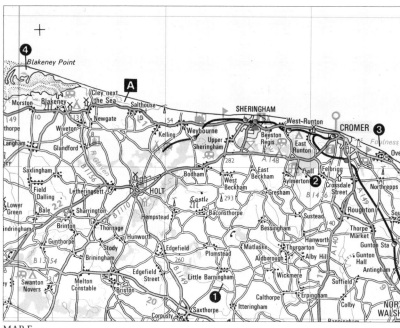

MAP E

E:1 MANNINGTON HALL★

Near Holt; *Park on roadsides. Signposted from Saxthorpe on B1149 Norwich-Holt road. Use marked trails.*

■ Farmland, mixed woodland, meadows, lakes.

■ One of the less well-known but nonetheless loveliest areas of N Norfolk – several unspoiled valley bottom meadows are colourful in spring. Birds include shelduck, breeding well inland here.

Up to 1,500 wildfowl have been counted on Wolterton Hall lake, and more wetland has been created at Mannington Hall as part of the Mannington Countryside Project.

Best from May to Jul.

E:2 FELBRIGG WOODS

Near Cromer; *SW of town, S of A148 Holt road; park by road at Lion's Mouth or at Hall when open. (Felbrigg Hall closed Tue & Fri and Nov-10 Apr).*

■ Beech woodland, old deer park.

■ Ancient beech woodland at far N of its range. The old trees there and in the deer park carry many species of lichen, including Graphis elegans and Parmelia perlata, more commonly found in SW Britain. Some trees are pollarded. **Birds** Wood warbler, redstart.

NATIONAL TRUST

E:3 NE NORFOLK CLIFFS & BEACHES★★

Near Cromer; *car parks at regular intervals along cliff-top, especially by bathing beaches.*

■ Cliff, sand/shingle beach, rock pools, grassland.

■ The cliffs from Weybourne to Happisburgh are all geologically important, especially those at the Runtons, which are rich in fossils.

There is chalk grassland on several of the clifftops; it is outstanding at Beeston where purple and knapweed broomrapes occur. Nearby chalky springs add variety.

The cliffs have many sand martin colonies and scattered nesting fulmars.

Sea-watching can reveal large bird movements, including divers, auks and gannets.

All the beaches attract wading birds on passage and in winter. Beware of crumbling cliff tops; beaches busy with tourists in summer.

E:4 BLAKENEY POINT★★

Near Holt; *access by boat from Morston quay or on foot from Cley coastguards – a long trudge on shingle. Car park by Blakeney Harbour (fee in summer except for NT members).*

■ Shingle spit, sand dunes, mudflats, saltmarsh, grazing marsh.

■ Blakeney Point draws many naturalists in summer. The tern colonies (best from May-Jul) are famous while other typical breeding birds here are ringed plovers on the shingle and shelducks in the rabbit burrows. The point's exposed position means migrant birds are excellent in both spring and autumn; regular rarities here include wrynecks and bluethroats.

Common seals bask on a sand spit off the point and grey seals occur regularly.

Blakeney Harbour is good – especially for brent geese and waders. Marshes along the sea wall have short-eared owls and golden plovers.

NATIONAL TRUST

Golden plover – see E:A, opposite.

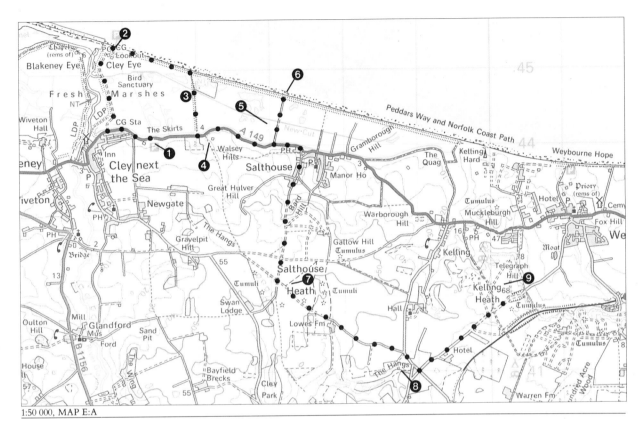

1:50 000, MAP E:A

E:A CLEY & SALTHOUSE MARSHES/ SALTHOUSE & KELLING HEATH**

Near Holt; car parks at information centre, *Cley beach, Cley East Bank, Salthouse beach, Kelling Heath. Permit required for NNT reserve from visitor centre.*

■ Coastal lagoons/scrapes, reed-bed, grazing marsh, heath, scrub, woodland.
① Roadside scrape has teal and wigeon in winter; avocet and yellow wagtail in summer. Access to reserve hides from here.
② Field has regular flocks of golden plovers, brent geese and ruffs. Skuas, auks and divers

pass at sea; on the shingle ridge snow buntings feed alongside winter finch flocks which include twite. In summer, yellow horned-poppies and sea campion grow.
③ The famous East Bank affords views over Arnold's Marsh where almost any wader species can appear. The reed-beds have bitterns and bearded tits; alexander grows, especially by the car park.
④ Walsey hills migration watch point good for warblers; look for little grebe on Snipe's Marsh alongside.
⑤ The regular gull flock here often includes a

glaucous gull.
⑥ Another good sea-watching point; shorelarks occur on the marshes.
⑦ Listen for nightjars and nightingales from road at dusk; in winter, hen harriers and great grey shrike.
⑧ Kelling Triangle good for wood warblers, scarce in East Anglia.
⑨ Superb coastal views; heath ablaze with dwarf gorse in late summer.
NORFOLK NATURALISTS TRUST/NORFOLK ORNITHOLOGISTS' ASSOCIATION/NATIONAL TRUST

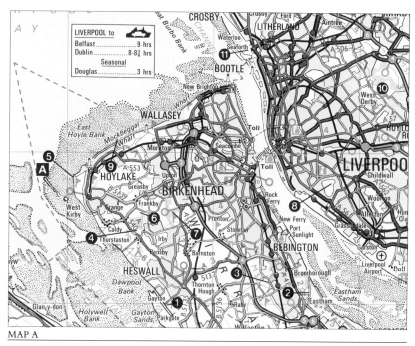

MAP A

A:1 GAYTON COTTAGE LANE

Near Heswall; *Gayton Cottage Lane (parking) runs from Gayton village (off A540) to River Dee. Gayton can also be reached on foot along Wirral Way from Parkgate.*
■ Salt-marsh, mudflats, estuary, hedgerows, meadows.
■ Easy access to a good site at high tide with views across the River Dee to Wales. Best visited one hour before and after high tide in winter. **Birds** Peregrine, water rail, hen harrier, short-eared owl, merlin, brambling, water pipit. **Mammals** Fox.
WIRRAL BOROUGH COUNCIL

A:2 EASTHAM COUNTRY PARK

Near Ellesmere Port; *park at Eastham Ferry one mile (1.5 km) N of Eastham village.*
■ Mixed woodland, meadows, river.
■ An excellent viewpoint for the River Mersey and a valuable wildlife site with fine stands of beech and oak close to motorways and oil terminals. **Plants** Solomon's seal, fungi. **Birds** Nuthatch, treecreeper, great spotted woodpecker.
WIRRAL BOROUGH COUNCIL

A:3 DIBBINSDALE

Near Bebbington; *S of Spital Station on B5137.*
■ Ancient mixed woodland, marsh, meadows, parkland, stream, pond.
■ An attractive local nature reserve with a diversity of habitats.
WIRRAL BOROUGH COUNCIL

A:4 THURSTASTON COMMON

Near Heswall; *park on A540.*
■ Acid heath, upper mottled sandstone.
■ The Wirral Country Park, West Kirby marine lake and shore are nearby. **Plants** Sundew.
NATIONAL TRUST

A:5 WEST KIRBY MARINE LAKE, FORESHORE AND RED ROCKS★

West Kirby; *from West Kirby Station take Dee Lane N to Marine Lake. Walk over foreshore to reach Red Rocks.*
■ Lake, sand flats, rocks, mudflats.

■ Red Rocks are situated at the mouth of the River Dee with a vast area of sand flats between Red Rocks, West Kirby Marine Lake and Hilbre Island at low tide. The main attraction of the foreshore is the large numbers of waders: sanderling, grey plover, bar-tailed godwit, turnstone, ringed plover, knot are all likely. In spring, look for Slavonian grebe, Sandwich tern, little tern, black-tailed godwit and little ringed plover. In the scrub you may find bluethroat, ring ouzel, wheatear, whinchat and stonechat. Winter visitors include long-tailed duck, snow bunting, scaup, common scoter, red-breasted merganser, purple sandpiper, hooded crow and rock pipit.
WIRRAL BOROUGH COUNCIL

A:6 ROYDEN PARK

Near West Kirby; *from the A540 take the B5140; entrance to park on right.*
■ Mixed woodland, meadows.
■ This site is close to Thurstaston Common and Thurstaston Hill and could be visited on the same day, ideally in spring or early summer. **Plants** Adder's-tongue fern.
WIRRAL BOROUGH COUNCIL

A:7 ARROWE PARK

Near Birkenhead; *park off A552.*
■ Park with mature trees.
■ All three species of British woodpecker occur, rare for this part of Britain. Wood warbler is an irregular species in spring. **Plants** include fungi and sundew.
WIRRAL BOROUGH COUNCIL

A:8 SEFTON PARK

Liverpool; *close to A561 between Toxteth and Aigburth, SE of city centre.*
■ Town park, lake.
■ A large town park completely surrounded by buildings. Brambling, siskin and little grebe sometimes visit in winter; treecreeper and nuthatch are more common.
LIVERPOOL CITY COUNCIL

A:9 DOVE POINT

Hoylake; *view Dove Point and East Hoyle Bank from promenade at N end of Hoylake.*

■ Sand, mudflats.
■ Dove Point is a convenient vantage point for wader watching, Best just before and during high tide. **Birds** Bar-tailed godwit, sanderling, grey plover, knot, ringed plover, curlew.
WIRRAL BOROUGH COUNCIL

A:10 CROXTETH COUNTRY PARK

Near West Derby, Liverpool; *enter from A5049 (Muirhead Avenue East) at junction with Oak Lane. Ample parking. Open daylight hours.*
■ Parkland, farmland, broad-leaved and coniferous woodland.
■ Expanse of varied habitat where more than a hundred bird species have been recorded. **Plants** Fungi.
LIVERPOOL CITY COUNCIL

A:11 SEAFORTH COASTAL NATURE RESERVE★

Seaforth, Crosby; *within Liverpool Freeport at N end of Docks complex. Freeport entrance at Crosby Road South on A5036(T). Don't enter enclosures, keep to footpaths.*
■ Freshwater pool, seawater pool, overgrown rubble mounds, derelict sand dunes.
■ A key position at the mouth of the River Mersey, overlooking Liverpool Bay. The reserve was formed during land reclamation and the habitats, including marshy areas, bulrush beds (*Typha*) and dry sandy areas, support over 150 plant species and a respectable insect fauna. Over 190 bird species have been recorded and it is probably the best site in Britain for gulls, with as many as 11 species present together, including many little gulls in Apr with a British record of 650 in 1987. Autumn gales, especially in Oct, bring large numbers of sea-birds. **Birds** Ring-billed, Mediterranean and glaucous gulls; (at sea) Leach's and storm petrels, long-tailed and pomarine skuas, sooty shearwater. **Plants** Southern marsh-orchid. **Lepidoptera** Clouded yellow, painted lady, silver Y.
MERSEY DOCKS AND HARBOUR CO/ LANCASHIRE TRUST FOR NATURE CONSERVATION

Solomon's seal – found at Eastham Country Park, A:2, this page.

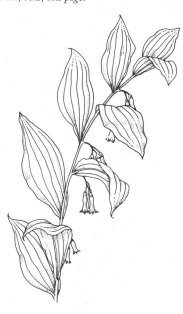

A:A HILBRE ISLAND★★

Near West Kirby; *use Marine Lake car park. WBC permit required: apply Wirral Country Park Estate, Station Road, Thurstaston, Wirral, L61 0HN.*

■ Rocky islands, inter-tidal sands.

① Access to ② Little Eye from slip. Consult signpost for directions on safe crossing and adequate time allowance for visiting Hilbre.

③ On Little Hilbre Island (The Middle Eye) western gorse and heath groundsel occur. N end suitable for hide photography: see booklet available locally.

④ Hilbre Island: cliffs with rock sea-lavender and sea spleenwort, thrift and other plants.

⑤ Bird observatory.

⑥ Lifeboat slip and sea watching hide, excellent in autumn and winter: great northern and red-throated divers, red-breasted mergansers, grebes, skuas, fulmar, shearwaters, Leach's and storm petrels, gannet, geese, auks, terns and gulls all possible. Scaup in substantial numbers off shore in winter; W winds best.

The whole island group is an important high-tide roost for waders, especially when the landward alternatives are covered by the tide, or disturbed. Thousands of knot, dunlin, oystercatcher, sanderling and ringed plover; also godwits, grey plover, redshank, turnstone and a regular winter flock of 40 or more purple sandpipers.

A spectacular sight from Hilbre are the grey seals on sand banks to the W.
WIRRAL BOROUGH COUNCIL

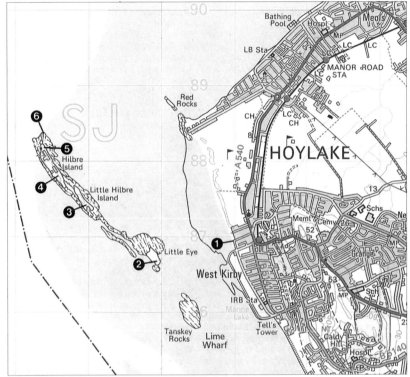

1:50 000, MAP A:A

B:1 SIDINGS LANE NATURE TRAIL

Near Rainford; *entrance just off A570 (T) N of junction with B5203.*

■ Woodland, colonized spoil tips.

■ An attractive area with intensive farming all round.
ST HELENS BOROUGH COUNCIL

B:2 HIGHTOWN
DUNES & ALT ESTUARY★

Near Formby; *from Hightown Station go S down Blundell Road with railway on left; park at end of road.*

■ River estuary, mudflats, sandy shore, sand dunes, fen, meadow.

■ Although small, the Alt is one of the best estuaries in the country for autumn and wintering waders, especially sanderling. The dunes are rich in both plants and birds. Breeding birds include stonechat and shelduck. Other regular species include redpoll and wheatear. Regular breeding birds of nearby private farmland include ringed plover, lapwing, oystercatcher and kestrel. Waders seen in the vicinity of the river include ringed plover, sanderling, grey plover, bar-tailed godwit, knot and turnstone. Late summer brings large numbers of common and Arctic terns, often with attendant skuas.
SEFTON BOROUGH COUNCIL

B:3 CABIN HILL★

Near Formby; *pass Formby oil station on right, continue (road turns to left) to St Lukes Church and park on minor road where there are trees on left. Don't enter fenced area: keep to footpaths.*

■ Sand dunes, man-made pool, cattle-grazed area, spinney of American balsam poplar, sea-buckthorn.

■ An NNR, excellent for amphibians and migrant birds in spring and autumn, especially from first light until 9 am. Many dune plants. **Amphibians** Natterjack toad, common toad, common frog. **Reptiles** Sand lizard. **Birds** Shelduck, snipe, wheatear, sparrowhawk, stonechat.
NATURE CONSERVANCY COUNCIL

B:4 RAVEN MEOLS HILLS

Near Formby; *leave the A565 (T) for Formby Station. Pass station and continue to St Luke's Church; turn right into Lifeboat Road. Car park; keep to footpaths where possible.*

■ Sandy shore, sand dunes, slacks, scrub.

■ This local nature reserve's S section contains the best example of early stages of dune formation to be found on the Sefton coast. The N is more mixed with wet slacks and light woodland. The formation is one of three parallel ridges. **Plants** Sea-holly, pyra-

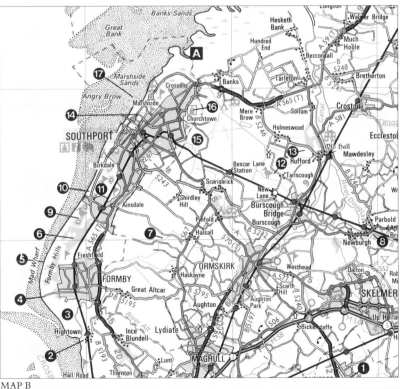

MAP B

MERSEYSIDE

midal orchid. **Amphibians** Natterjack toad. **Reptiles** Sand lizard.
SEFTON BOROUGH COUNCIL

B:5 FORMBY POINT★
Near Formby; park at Freshfield Station and walk to shore down Victoria Road or drive to NT hut and pay parking fee. Don't enter enclosures, and keep to footpaths.
■ Woodland, sand dunes, beach.
■ Includes a red squirrel reserve. The squirrels are descended from the darker continental form, not the British: very bold. **Birds** Waders, gulls, stonechat, treecreeper.
NATIONAL TRUST

B:6 AINSDALE SAND DUNES★★
Ainsdale; entrance on W side of A565(T) S of Southport. No parking at reserve entrance, but near Pontins.
■ Sand dunes.
■ An NNR, notable for its sand dune system showing the succession from fore dune to old dune with associated vegetation. Interesting animal and plant species include natterjack toad, sand lizard and dune and green-flowered helleborines. The natterjack toad requires wet slacks for breeding; management to counter the slow drying out of the slacks is also helping *odonata*; recently the emperor dragonfly has bred at perhaps its northern limit on the W coast. Resident birds include the lapwing, which does not commonly nest on the Sefton dunes. In winter, thrush flocks feed on the sea buckthorn berries which are found in the fixed dunes. **Birds** Woodcock. **Plants** Grass-of-Parnassus, round-leaved wintergreen, bog pimpernel, yellow-wort, balsam poplar, sea-buckthron. **Mammals** Red squirrel (continental form), fox, stoat, water vole. **Insects** Tiger beetle, sand wasps. *Lepidoptera* Dark green fritillary, oak eggar.
NATURE CONSERVANCY COUNCIL

B:7 PLEX MOSS★
Ainsdale; view from roads only.
■ Mosslands, birch woods, farmland.
■ This is one of the best places to see the pink-footed goose feeding in the early winter months. The mosslands are now used for intensive farming. **Birds** Short-eared owl, barn owl, wigeon, teal; (winter) hen harrier, grey wagtail; (spring) dotterel.

B:8 LEEDS &
LIVERPOOL CANAL TOWPATH,
PARBOLD TO APPLEY BRIDGE
Parbold, near Wigan; from the A5209 at Parbold or at Appley Bridge from B5375.
■ River valley, canal.
■ An attractive area, good for plants, birds and dragonflies. **Birds** Great grey shrike, kingfisher, siskin, goldcrest.

B:9 AINSDALE SAND DUNES★
Ainsdale; from Ainsdale Station, take Shore Road to beach; park at Sands Club Lake near Pontins Holiday Camp. Keep to footpaths.
■ Sand dunes, wet and dry slacks.
■ This local nature reserve is adjacent to the Ainsdale NNR, but there are no restrictions of access. Similar flora and fauna deserving the same respect. See B:6. **Birds** Snow bunting, hen harrier, short-eared owl, stonechat. **Plants** Marsh and dune helleborines, bee orchid, grass-of-Parnassus, round-leaved wintergreen. **Amphibians** Natterjack toad. **Reptiles** Sand lizard.
SEFTON BOROUGH COUNCIL

B:10 SANDS CLUB LAKE
Ainsdale. Car park by lake.
■ Lake, sand dunes, island, marsh.
■ Well worth a stop for birds at any time of year, and for plants in summer and autumn. Masses of grass-of-Parnassus in dune slacks on seaward side of lake, Jul-Oct.
SEFTON BOROUGH COUNCIL

B:11 BIRKDALE HILLS
Southport; turn W off A565 just N of Hillside Station, park in Hastings Road.
■ Sand dunes with wet and dry slacks.
■ Part of the same system of dunes represented in the Ainsdale NNR with similarly rich flora and fauna, and with easy access. Early spring is best for amphibians, Jul for plants. **Birds** Short-eared owl, stonechat, grasshopper warbler, redpoll. **Plants** Marsh helleborine, grass-of-Parnassus, round-leaved wintergreen, bee orchid. **Reptiles** Sand lizard, common lizard.
SEFTON BOROUGH COUNCIL

B:12 MARTIN MERE★★
Near Ormskirk; turn W off the A59(T) just N of rail bridge at Burscough Bridge; reserve is 2 miles (3 km) on left hand side. Fee (except Trust members).
■ Lake, marsh, cultivated mossland.
■ Beyond the pens of world wildfowl is a large area outstanding for its visiting waders and wildfowl, including a man-made lagoon where, in winter, herds of whooper and Bewick's swans return annually. Around the lagoon is a complex of wet fields, some grazed and some arable, with drainage gulleys overlooked by a series of hides.
Several thousand pink-footed geese winter in the area and are often accompanied by other species such as bean and barnacle geese and migrant swans. Gadwall and shelduck breed, and teal and mallard winter in large numbers, with pintail, tufted, wigeon, pochard and goldeneye. Ruff winter in respectable numbers and stay to leck in full breeding plumage. Black-tailed godwit is another speciality, present in most months.
Most British passage and breeding waders pass through or breed here, and from late summer to late spring there is the chance of rarities and vagrants. Gulls, terns and raptors also provide interest, with regular black, Arctic and common terns, frequent hen harriers, short-eared owls, peregrine and merlin. Marsh harrier, garganey, waders such as Temminck's stint, and occasional hobby and shrike underline the site's attraction to passing migrants.
WILDFOWL TRUST

B:13 MERE SANDS WOOD★
Near Rufford; about 2 miles (3 km) from A59 (T) opposite Rufford Hospital. Signposted: short track into free car park. Keep to paths. Car park closed after 5 pm, but limited parking outside gate after that.
■ Lake, mixed woodland, heath, wader scrape.
■ The reserve was created from land which had been a sand quarry for the glass industry. There is a large lake with a sand and cockleshell island created to encourage breeding waders. There are five hides and a nature trail.
Birds are the main attraction, but the reserve also has red squirrels, four bat species and some interesting plants and insects. Trees include scots pine, oak, beech, rowan, an old stand of alder, birch, ash and recent plantings of willows and poplars. Notable plants include a rare inland colony of yellow bartsia; yellow-wort; early and southern marsh-orchids.
Odonata include common, southern and brown hawkers, four-spotted chaser and golden-ringed dragonflies. There is a good fungus flora most evident in autumn.
Breeding birds include ruddy duck, great crested and little grebes, ringed and little ringed plovers, reed bunting, sedge and willow warblers, blackcap, whitethroat and spotted flycatcher. Visitors include the woodpeckers, long-eared owl, hawfinch, merlin, greenshank, spotted redshank, whimbrel, green sandpiper, woodcock and terns. In winter, pochard, tufted duck, teal and gadwall join the resident mallard. Whooper swans and various duck species may also arrive then, and pink-footed goose flies over frequently.
Best in spring for the birds.
LANCASTER TRUST FOR NATURE CONSERVATION

B:14 SOUTHPORT MARINE LAKE
Southport; public access all round the lake; parking alongside. No access to islands.
■ Marine lake with islands.
■ Always worth a look in winter for ducks, waders, mute swans and divers, including the occasional long-tailed duck. Redshank rest on the edge of the island, which is covered with sea-buckthorn. Redwing and fieldfare feed on its berries.
SEFTON BOROUGH COUNCIL

B:15 HESKETH PARK
Southport; N of town centre, reached from N end of Lord Street via Albert Road.
■ Town park on sand dune site.
■ Well-wooded park with formal gardens and a lake. **Birds** Black tern, scaup. **Mammals** Red squirrel.
SEFTON BOROUGH COUNCIL

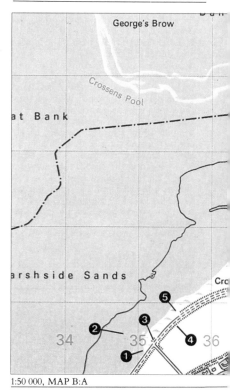

1:50 000, MAP B:A

B:16 BOTANIC GARDENS

Churchtown, Southport; *at N end of Southport. Open daylight hours.*

■ Well-wooded park with lake and small marsh.

■ The Botanic Gardens Museum has a natural history section including the Pennington collection of stuffed birds.

SEFTON BOROUGH COUNCIL

B:17 SOUTHPORT FORESHORE PIER TO SAND WASHING PLANT⋆

Southport; *off Southport Marine Drive. Park alongside marine lake or in car park near sand washing plants at Marshside, N Southport.*

■ Sand and mudflats, controlled Spartina grass.

■ In late summer and autumn, the numbers of waders using this area for feeding can be exceptional. **Birds** Peregrine, hen harrier, bar-tailed godwit, sanderling, turnstone.

SEFTON BOROUGH COUNCIL

B:A RIBBLE ESTUARY⋆⋆

Between Preston and Southport; *from Preston take the A59(T) then the unclassified road through Tarleton and Hesketh Bank to Banks, or the A565(T) to Crossens. There is no unauthorized entry to the NNR or the reclaimed salt-marshes (Marshside Marsh and Crossens Marsh), but all the birds can be seen from adjacent roads and embankments.*

■ Salt-marsh, fen, mudflats, wet pasture, farmland, sandy shore, rivers.

(1) Car park near sand washing plant.

(2) At low tide take rubble road towards the Ribble to look for bar-tailed godwit, ruff and sanderling.

(3) In winter, look for wigeon, black redstart and stonechat behind the sand washing plant.

(4) From the edge of the coastal road, look over the fields of Marshide and Crossens Marshes. Large numbers of pink-footed goose, golden plover, curlew and gulls here in winter.

(5) Look over the *Spartina* in winter for hen harrier, peregrine, merlin, short-eared owl, pink-footed goose, pintail, and, at high tide, water rail.

(6) From opposite the large pumping station follow embankment along one side of the Ribble Marshes NNR. Good chance of seeing large numbers of pink-footed goose, whooper and Bewick's swans.

(7) From Hundred End, another embankment can be walked as far as the River Douglas.

(8) Best area for large wintering herds of swans and often up to 12 short-eared owls. In summer, black-tailed godwit, marsh harrier and many pairs of yellow wagtail can be seen.

(9) The salt-marsh N of the river is not extensive but still good for birdwatching. Walk from Freckleton to the river to see wildfowl and waders.

NATURE CONSERVANCY COUNCIL/SEFTON BOROUGH COUNCIL/NORTH WEST WATER AUTHORITY/PRIVATE OWNERSHIP

GREATER MANCHESTER

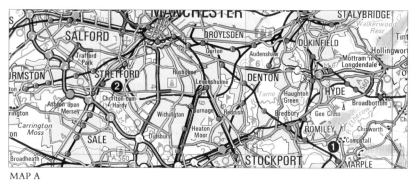

MAP A

A:1 ETHEROW COUNTRY PARK

Near Stockport; entrance at SJ 965909 on B6104 between Romiley and Marple Bridge.

■ River, pond, watercourse, woodland, fen.

■ The ponds or 'lodges' associated with the old mill are used by wildfowl and feral geese. A hide overlooks the river Etherow and a marshy area; interesting woodland. **Birds** Great crested and little grebes, kingfisher, lesser and great spotted woodpeckers, grey wagtail. **Plants** Early-purple orchid, common spotted-orchid.

STOCKPORT BOROUGH COUNCIL

A:2 SALE WATER PARK

Near Manchester; signposted from M63, Junction 8; car parks.

■ Man-made wetland, shingle islands, mudflats, meadow, planted trees.

■ Extensive man-made wildlife habitats in a heavily built-up area. **Birds** (Breeding) little ringed plover, little grebe; (passage) waders and terns; (winter) snipe, teal, cormorant, water pipit.

MANCHESTER BOROUGH COUNCIL

B:1 CARR MILL DAM

Near St Helens; entrance at junction of A580(T) and A571 at St Helens; ample parking.

■ Lake, farmland, woodland.

■ Easy and quick access for watching wildfowl including great crested grebe.

ST HELENS BOROUGH COUNCIL

B:2 SANKEY VALLEY PARK*

Near St Helens; entrance to car park and visitor centre behind Ship Inn at Blackbrook on A58.

■ Long valley with ponds, reed swamp, woodland, overgrown banks, surrounded by houses and industry.

■ A surprising diversity and number of species in a highly industrialized area. Birds include kingfisher. **Plants** Fungi. **Insects** Moths and butterflies.

ST HELENS BOROUGH COUNCIL

B:3 PENNINGTON FLASH COUNTRY PARK**

Near Leigh; on A572 look for large sign; ample parking.

■ Lake, ponds, bog, carr, alder carr, birch spinney, managed scrape, meadow, colliery spoil tip, canal and bank, mown grass on golf course.

■ The walk round the flash (lake) is well worthwhile and there are many other interesting shorter paths and five hides for birdwatching. Mute swan and shoveler are among breeders and after the breeding season large numbers of great crested grebes use the flash. Snipe and lapwing breed and

visit the new scrapes as do passage waders. The maturing of planted birch and alder should lead to increasing numbers of siskin. Winter is often good for wildfowl and birds such as smew occur with goldeneye and ruddy duck. Over 200 species of *Lepidoptera* have been recorded. **Birds** Bittern, water rail, curlew, garganey, black-tailed godwit, black tern, whimbrel, ruff, wood, green and common sandpipers, red-breasted merganser, greenshank, little ringed and ringed plovers, lesser whitethroat.

WIGAN BOROUGH COUNCIL

B:4 WIGAN FLASHES*

Near Wigan; limited parking at St James' Church, Poolstock. Best at Trencherfield Mill car park by Wigan Pier. Walk along canal bank to Scotsman's Flash.

■ Ponds, spoil heaps, birch and willow scrub, marshy areas, canal and banks.

■ Flash is a local word for pools formed by subsidence as a consequence of mining operations. Of the five here, Scotsman's Flash is used for sailing, while the others are less disturbed, though they are fished. The spoil heaps are well vegetated and the whole complex is a rich area for plants, birds and insects. Nine species of *Odonata* have been recorded including emerald damselfly and broad-bodied chaser. Birds include visiting passage migrants such as black tern, as well as wintering wildfowl and breeding warblers. **Birds** Great crested grebe. cormorant, goldeneye, little owl, common tern, stonechat, reed warbler. **Plants** Marsh helleborine, marsh orchids, teasel. **Insects** Large red damselfly, four-spotted chaser and brown hawker dragonflies.

WIGAN BOROUGH COUNCIL

B:5 HAIGH HALL COUNTRY PARK

Near Wigan; access for cars N of Haigh Hall at SD 596087. There are signs on the B5238 Wigan to Aspull road. Pedestrians only opposite Wigan Infirmary (A49).

■ Large plantation, open grassy areas, canal.

■ Developed from the parkland surrounding Haigh Hall, the site provides a green avenue into the heart of Wigan with red and grey squirrels, butterflies and fungi. Over 80 species of birds have been recorded and the canal adds aquatic interest. **Mammals** Water vole, water shrew. **Insects** Brown hawker dragonfly.

WIGAN BOROUGH COUNCIL

B:6 RIVINGTON RESERVOIRS

Near Horwich; on A673 turn right at Headless Cross then right again across reservoir; parking at Rivington village.

■ Lake, emergent edge vegetation, woodland.

■ The lower of three reservoirs are all worth visiting for wildfowl in winter. Footpaths around them allow access to the varied flora and insect fauna. **Birds** Great crested grebe, goldeneye, tufted duck, pochard, gadwall, raptor, waders.

NORTH WEST WATER AUTHORITY

B:7 CUERDEN VALLEY COUNTRY PARK

Bamber Bridge; four car parks, easiest of which is on B5256 between Clayton-le-Woods and Clayton Green. Country park with free access except for small area managed as nature reserve: apply to LTNC for permit.

■ River, grassland, mixed woodland, lake, marshy scrub.

■ Although much visited by the local city dwellers, this is a pleasant site with good insect fauna and the only known colony of *Calopteryx splendens* (banded demoiselle) in the county. The variety of trees yields an interesting fungus flora and the river and marshy areas attract insects and birds. There is a visitor centre. Best spring to late autumn. **Birds** Lesser spotted woodpecker, kingfisher, sedge warbler. **Fungi** *Melanoleuca cognata, Hebeloma strophosum, Leucocoprinus brebissonii.*

LANCASHIRE COUNTY COUNCIL/
LANCASHIRE TRUST FOR NATURE
CONSERVATION

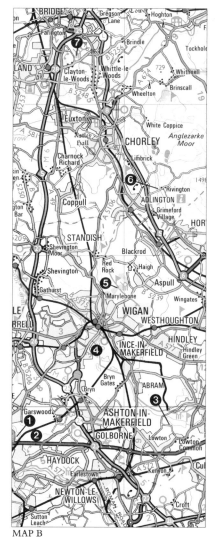

MAP B

GREATER MANCHESTER

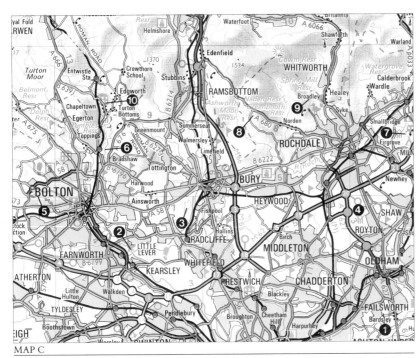

MAP C

C:1 DAISY NOOK COUNTRY PARK

Near Oldham; the country park is just off Newmarket Road (from A627); car park at Crime Lake, off Cutler Hill Road.

■ Canal and river valley in industrial area.

■ Undeveloped space within urban area: excellent for common plant and bird species.
MEDLOCK VALLEY WARDEN SERVICE

C:2 CROAL IRWELL VALLEY*

Near Bolton; from A6053 between Little Lever and Farnworth turn S to Rock Hall visitor centre at SD 742068; parking.

■ River, lakes, derelict industrial site.

■ The lakes are now used for public amenity but the derelict site includes poor soils, some with chemical contamination which support interesting plants. Reduced atmospheric pollution and import of seeds has helped. Walking on the transient soils can cause damage in places. **Plants** Orchids, Indian balsam, willowherbs.
BOLTON BOROUGH COUNCIL

C:3 ELTON RESERVOIR

Near Bury; access near sailing club; parking nearby. Footpath around most of the reservoir.

■ Lowland reservoir, bog.

■ A longstanding favourite birdwatching site. **Birds** Great crested grebe, wigeon, whooper swan, buzzard, grey plover, knot.
NORTH WEST WATER AUTHORITY

C:4 TANDLE HILL COUNTRY PARK

Near Oldham; on A627, turn W at sign at hill top between Oldham and Rochdale. Entrance at SD 907087. Open all daylight hours.

■ Beech wood, conifers, heath, grassy hillside.

■ Substantial numbers of jay and a feeding site for wintering birds especially in hard weather. In winter, birds come to roost at dusk.
OLDHAM BOROUGH COUNCIL

C:5 DOFFCOCKER RESERVOIR

Near Bolton; park in nearby streets; access by footpath.

■ Reservoir, fen, hawthorn, meadow.

■ Excellent site for snipe in autumn and winter when many are ringed. Great grey shrike has wintered here.
NORTH WEST WATER AUTHORITY

C:6 JUMBLES COUNTRY PARK*

Near Bolton; park is signposted W off A676 N of Bradshaw; parking.

■ Lake, mixed woodland, grassland, stream, marshy areas.

■ Although new in 1971 and described as a 'low-key recreation area', this site is becoming an interesting mixed habitat for birds, plants and insects. **Birds** Kingfisher, great crested grebe, snipe.
NORTH WEST WATER AUTHORITY

C:7 HOLLINGWORTH LAKE COUNTRY PARK

Near Rochdale; two miles (3 km) NW of Rochdale, signposted from B6225 between Milnrow and Littleborough. Car park.

■ Reservoir, bog, meadow.

■ A reservoir which is far less bleak than others in the area, with good moorland nearby. Excellent for watching breeding great crested grebes. Avoid bank holidays and Sundays for birdwatching. **Birds** Great

Bewick's swans and little owl – see C:10, Wayoh Reservoir, this page.

crested grebe, golden plover, snipe; (passage) bar-tailed godwit, sanderling, knot, ringed plover, common sandpiper, dunlin.
ROCHDALE BOROUGH COUNCIL

C:8 ASHWORTH MOOR RESERVOIR

Near Bury; parking in lay-by close to reservoir off A680 Rochdale to Edenfield road.

■ Reservoir, sheep-grazed grassland, acid moorland.

■ Less well known than some of the Greater Manchester ornithological sites, but very attractive to many species, especially on passage. Worth visiting for the chance of less common species such as black-tailed godwit, Temminck's stint, black tern, ruff, sandpiper, curlew.
NORTH WEST WATER AUTHORITY

C:9 HEALEY DELL

Near Rochdale; take A671 Rochdale to Bacup road to Healey. *Minor road runs into reserve. Easy public access and parking by roadsides.*

■ Upland river, oak and birch woodland, heath, disused railway line, marshy areas, acidic grassland and meadow.

■ This local nature reserve is a steep-sided narrow wooded valley, (locally known as a clough) cut by the River Spodden. The rock and soils are sandy with attendant acidic soil flora. However the limestone ballast of the old railway track provides a calcareous base for supporting other species. The river attracts dipper and grey wagtail, and snipe frequent the marshy areas. Ferns, mosses and liverworts are a feature of the site. **Birds** Twite, siskin, tawny owl, redpoll. **Plants** Northern marsh-orchid, common spotted-orchid, marsh violet, broad-leaved helleborine, water avens, ragged-robin, large bitter-cress.
ROCHDALE BOROUGH COUNCIL

C:10 WAYOH RESERVOIR

Near Bolton; from B6391 at Chapeltown, N of Bolton. Park on unmade road on SW corner of reservoir. Footpath around reservoir.

■ Lake, marsh, scrub, woodland, grassland.

■ A blend of waterside, open grass and woodland which holds a good variety of plants and insects. Great crested grebes breed and in winter it is good for wildfowl and gulls. **Birds** Whooper and Bewick's swans, merlin, short-eared owl, lesser spotted woodpecker, kingfisher, little owl, woodcock, pintail, passage waders, terns, gulls.
NORTH WEST WATER AUTHORITY/
LANCASHIRE TRUST FOR NATURE
CONSERVATION

WEST YORKSHIRE

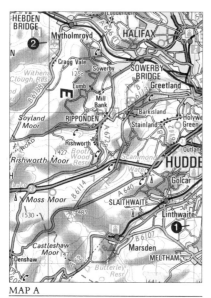

MAP A

A:1 BLACKMOORFOOT

Near Meltham; turn E from B6107 N of Meltham; road alongside reservoir gives good views across water. Bird-watching permits for entry on to reserve available from YW on request.

■ Reservoir.

■ Over 150 species of bird have been recorded breeding, overwintering or passing through, including ducks, waders and a gull roost.

YORKSHIRE WATER

A:2 BROADHEAD CLOUGH

Near Hebden Bridge; park just before Dauber Bridge, signposted to Frost Hole. Fork right and left on to concrete road to reserve. Access track must be kept clear of cars. Avoid wet areas.

■ Dry/wet deciduous woodlands, bog.

■ Clough is cut into Millstone Grit and carries varied flora and bird fauna. Best in spring and summer. **Plants** Heath spotted-orchid, lemon-scented fern, marsh valerian, cow-wheat, bilberry, *Sphagnum,* fungi. **Birds** Redstart, wood warbler, tree pipit, redpoll.

YORKSHIRE WILDLIFE TRUST

B:1 THORPE MARSH★

Near Doncaster; park at end of Marsh Lane. Footpath alongside Ean Beck Drain to reserve. Field Centre open to parties and school groups all year. Day permit available from warden on site.

■ Ancient pastures, embankment, pond, lake.

■ The ancient ridge-and-furrow grassland has a rich flora. The ridges have pepper-saxifrage, sneezewort, and great burnet.

Tubular water-dropwort grows in furrows. The limestone railway embankment is covered with dense scrub and open areas display common spotted-orchid, wild carrot and cowslip. The lake's reed-beds and woodland fringe are good for waders. Butterflies include uncommon speckled wood. Best in summer and autumn. **Birds** (Lake) mute and whooper swans, heron, common sandpiper; (hunting) short-eared owl.

YORKSHIRE WILDLIFE TRUST

B:2 BRETTON LAKES

Near West Bretton; park by Bretton Hall College kennel block. Keep to footpaths; do not cut across college grounds.

■ Freshwater lake, river bank, deciduous woodland, plantation, willow carr.

■ Lakes with over 100 Canada geese and many other birds, especially water fowl; other reserve habitats important for insects and birds. Best in spring and mid-winter, with good fungi in autumn. **Plants** Devil's-bit scabious. **Birds** Kingfisher, tits, warblers, great crested grebe; (winter) goldeneye, wigeon, teal, pintail. **Mammals** Water vole.

YORKSHIRE WILDLIFE TRUST/BRETTON HALL COLLEGE

B:3 WINTERSETT RESERVOIR

Near Wakefield; access from minor road which leaves B6132 Wakefield to Royston road.

■ Reservoir, plantation, parkland.

■ Valuable area all year for water birds and passing waders. Waterton Park was originally established as a bird sanctuary, but is now much disturbed. **Birds** (Reservoir) Black tern, Sabine's gull, red-necked grebe, divers; (plantation) long-eared owl.

YORKSHIRE WATER

B:4 STOCKSMOOR COMMON★

Near Wakefield; park on edge of reserve off B6117. Used extensively for research; keep to footpaths and do not touch equipment.

■ Sandy heath, grassland, scrub regeneration.

■ Heath and scrub woodland with dense ground litter important for many ground and rove beetles (some nationally rare), especially in winter. **Mammals** Red squirrel, fox.

YORKSHIRE WILDLIFE TRUST

B:5 STONEYCLIFFE WOOD★

Near Wakefield; park either in village of Netherton (on B6117 from Wakefield) or Stocksmoor Common Reserve car park. Footpaths opposite Star Inn or from Denby Grange NCB Colliery.

■ Mixed age deciduous woodland, stream.

Water vole – see Bretton Lakes, this page.

■ This is a good example of a mixed woodland on coal measures shales. The birch thickets, hazel and holly understories and mature woodlands provide an excellent range of habitats for birds, which can be seen from the paths (suitable for wheelchairs) and vantage points. There is an abundant ground flora, and dead wood provides a rich environment for birds and invertebrates. **Plants** Wood anemone, yellow archangel, ramsons. **Birds** tits, warblers.

YORKSHIRE WILDLIFE TRUST

B:6 BROCKADALE★

Near Wentbridge; Kirk Smeaton road from the A1, just S of Wentbridge viaduct. Pasture N of road containing electricity pylons marks entrance.

■ Mixed woodland, calcareous pastures, riverside grassland.

■ The reserve lies in the deep gorge of the River Went through Magnesian limestone and has a flat alluvial bottom which sometimes floods. The flora and fauna are rich with many breeding birds, including most of the warblers, slow-worm, grass snake, common lizard and a variety of mammals. Woodland supports good molluscs, and flora includes four species of violet, rock-rose, carline thistle, squinancywort. Calcareous pastures have cowslips, early-purple orchid, hoary plantain, twayblade, quaking-grass, milkwort. Riverside grassland has hound's-tongue and various crane's-bills species.

YORKSHIRE WILDLIFE TRUST

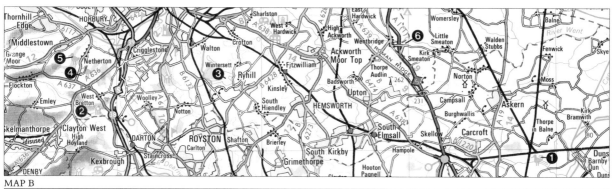

MAP B

A:1 MALTBY LOW COMMON

Maltby; park where road turns left into housing estate after Maltby Crags School sports ground. Follow footpath over bridge to reserve.

■ Dry acid basic grassland, scrub, marsh, oak wood.

■ Several uncommon invertebrates, close to their N limits, provide main interest in this highly varied reserve on magnesian limestone. Wide variety of flora. **Plants** (Acid soil) Meadow thistle, pepper-saxifrage, mat-grass; (drier heath) pill sedge, dog-violet; (banks) orchids, grass-of-Parnassus, small scabious.

YORKSHIRE WILDLIFE TRUST

A:2 DENABY INGS★

Near Mexborough; car park at reserve just through Denaby. Easy access for disabled visitors

Bee orchid may be found at Potteric Carr, A:4, this page. It likes recently disturbed ground.

to public hide on pastures lane.

■ Wet grassland, marsh, mixed deciduous woodland.

■ This is a good example of the marshland once much more extensive by the River Dearne. The *Glyceria* dominated area is grazed by cattle in summer. There is outstanding value in insect life, including a number of species with very restricted national distribution. Worth visiting at all times, but especially spring and autumn. **Trees** (River bank) ancient crack willows. **Birds** (Marsh) great crested grebe, shoveler; (winter) great grey shrike, merlin; (passage) common and black terns, waders.

YORKSHIRE WILDLIFE TRUST

A:3 SPROTBROUGH FLASH

Near Doncaster; park at rear of bridge toll house by River Don. Follow tow path upstream to reserve.

■ Fresh water flashes, emergent vegetation, willow stands.

■ High water level, originally created by subsidence, has been artificially maintained and makes for valuable bird life (more than 140 species recorded), particularly passage warblers. Best in autumn. Pot Riding Wood, close the the flash, has hawfinch, green hellebore, danewort, pale St John's-wort and interesting molluscs. **Birds** Little and great crested grebes; (passage) waders, terns, swallows, martins. **Mammals** Water shrew, stoat, fox, weasel.

YORKSHIRE WILDLIFE TRUST

A:4 POTTERIC CARR★

Near Doncaster; car park at reserve. Small part of reserve is accessible to public; remainder to YWT members with permit only.

■ Reed-beds, open water, meadows, streams, woodland, limestone embankments.

■ Old fenland, modified by drainage and mining subsidence. Known for nesting waterfowl, passage and rarer visiting birds. Interesting marsh flora and insect population. Some drier grassy areas also interesting. Best in breeding season. **Plants** Water-violet, bladderwort, bee orchid. **Birds** (Winter) bittern, water rail, great grey shrike, hen harrier, short-eared owl; (summer) garganey; (passage) marsh harrier, black tern, wood sandpiper. **Mammals** Harvest mouse, water shrew.

YORKSHIRE WILDLIFE TRUST

A:5 WATH INGS★

Near Wath upon Dearne; park off B6273 near village of Broomhill. Proceed on foot along concrete road, bear right at fork, follow signs across meadow to flood bank where hides overlook marsh. Footpaths open at all times, main hide locked unless warden on duty. Remaining two hides open at all times. Key and permit for hides can be purchased from management committee (Trust members only).

■ Cattle pasture, reed/rush areas.

■ The reserve, which is mainly flood grassland with *Glyceria* marsh and large *Juncus* areas, is very important for the study of migrant wading birds. All common European species have been recorded. The high numbers of overwintering duck have to be protected by wardens. Altogether some 160 species of bird are recorded each year, with best viewing in autumn and winter. **Birds** (Winter) whooper and Bewick's swans, pintail; (breeding) short-eared owl, little ringed plover, redshank, snipe, whinchat; (passage) osprey, marsh harrier, terns, waders.

YORKSHIRE WILDLIFE TRUST

A:6 BROOMHILL FLASH

Near Wombwell; park at reserve beyond The Railway public house. Footpath to hide (also wheelchair access).

■ Open water, muddy margins, arable/pasture land.

■ Reserve lying on coal measures, created by mining subsidence; water over 6 feet (2 m) deep. Main interest ornithological (over 100 species recorded); best in autumn and winter, when waders on migration. **Birds** (Winter) golden plover.

YORKSHIRE WILDLIFE TRUST/WOMBWELL GUN CLUB

MAP A

MAP A

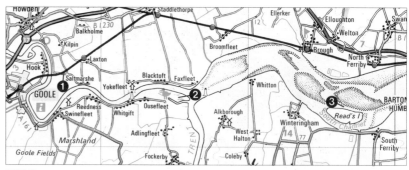

MAP B

A:1 SPURN HEAD★★

Near Kilnsea; car park at end of YWT penin-sular road. Full-time warden; certain parts of re-serve closed to public; entry fee. No dogs. Bird observatory must be booked.

■ Shingle/sand spit, salt-marsh, mudflats.

■ This unique peninsula, 3½ miles (5 km) long, funnels birds flying along the North Sea or Humber on to a narrow flight path. The reserve was established to protect a resting place for migrant birds and for ornithological, botanical, entomological (it is one of the richest places for insects in Yorkshire) and geomorphological study. Spectacular autumn migrations can be watched from the bird observatory. Both little tern (no longer breeds) and ringed plover (greatly reduced) have suffered from increased public pressure. **Plants** (Mobile sand dunes) sea-holly, sea rocket. **Birds** (Passage) Pallas's warbler, yellow-browed warbler, red-backed shrike, icterine warbler, bluethroat, wryneck, red-breasted flycatcher; (winter) shore lark, Lapland bunting, snow bunting, great grey shrike, twite, brent goose, waders; (passage at sea) skuas, terns. **Mammals** Rabbit, fox, seals. **Insects** Roesel's bush-cricket, short-winged conehead.
YORKSHIRE WILDLIFE TRUST

A:2 HUMBER ESTUARY (EAST)

Near Patrington; access to sea wall from Old Hall and Sunk Island from A1033. Tracks and side roads to coast from Kilnsea. Keep to shore areas.

■ Mudflats, salt-marsh.

■ Estuary of nearly 15,000 acres, important for overwintering geese, ducks and resident waders; also some passage migrants on N-S and E-W corridors. **Birds** Pink-footed goose, ruff, bar-tailed godwit, whimbrel, sanderling, knot, turnstone, divers, terns.

B:1 SALTMARSHE DELPH

Near Laxton; take road for Howden Dyke from A614. Follow to riverside jetties, follow river, take second left by railway; reserve is in ½ mile (0.8 km). Several parking places with view-points. Key to hide available to YWT members only. Do not use gate at W end of reserve.

■ Lake, reed-beds, pools.

■ Wet area created by excavation for rail-way embankment in 1872. Nutrient-rich water with a large and varied microfauna. Birdlife abundant, with 83 species. **Birds** Bearded tit, marsh harrier, great crested and little grebes. **Mammals** Harvest mouse.
YORKSHIRE WILDLIFE TRUST

B:2 BLACKTOFT SAND★

Near Ousefleet; car park ½ mile (0.8 km) E of Ousefleet off A161 from Goole. Footpath along

sea wall. Five hides; fee if non-member. Closed Tue.

■ Tidal reed-bed, salt-marsh, artificial brackish lagoons.

■ This is a valuable area for a wide variety of birds at all times of year. The habitats in-clude artificial lagoons, while the reed-beds contain bearded tits and warblers; occasion-ally marsh harriers have nested. Various rap-tors visit in winter and assorted passage migrants and many wildfowl are to be seen. **Birds** (Passage waders) avocet, stints, god-wits, greenshank, spotted redshank, sand-pipers; (nesting) bearded tit, shoveler, redshank, little ringed plover, shoveler, redshank; (winter) hen harrier, short-eared owl, merlin.
ROYAL SOCIETY FOR THE PROTECTION OF BIRDS

B:3 HUMBER WILDLIFE REFUGE★

Near Barton upon Humber; N side, view from shores at Faxfleet off A63, Broomfleet or Brough. S side, A1077 skirts Read's Island near South Ferriby, also Winteringham and Whitton. Access to refuge prohibited. Binoculars or tele-scope recommended.

■ Estuary, mudflats.

■ Bank-to-bank refuge originally estab-lished to preserve winter-roosting pink-footed geese which have declined in recent years. **Birds** Knot, sanderling, turnstone, curlew, shelduck, wigeon, oystercatcher, dunlin, redshank.

C:1 NORTH CLIFFE WOOD

Near Market Weighton; leave A63 2 miles (3 km) E of Holme-upon-Spalding moor, turn into sand lane leading to wood. Limited parking at entrance to reserve on NE side. Closed Mar-Jun.

■ Mixed oak woodland, high water table in winter.

■ Mature ancient woodland on acid, peaty soils. Much secondary tree growth, a rich ground flora and varied bird population. **Plants** Herb Paris, climbing corydalis, water avens, guelder rose. **Birds** Wood warbler, tree pipit, woodcock, sparrow-hawk, great spotted and green woodpeck-ers.
YORKSHIRE WILDLIFE TRUST

C:2 SKIPWITH COMMON★

Near Selby; car park on runway 2 of old air-field at beginning of reserve.

■ Wet/dry heath, open water, marsh, woodland.

■ Nationally important for insect fauna and with a rich ground flora. Nightjars, although scarce, are of special interest. Best in spring, summer and autumn. **Plants** Sun-dew, bog pimpernel, spotted-orchids, broad-leaved helleborine. **Mammals** Fal-low deer.
YORKSHIRE WILDLIFE TRUST

C:3 KIPLINGCOTES CHALK PIT

Near Market Weighton; car park on Kiplingcotes road, , mile (0.5 km) from site. Access on foot on Wolds Way which follows old railway track. Keep gates clear at all times. No dogs.

■ Chalk quarry.

■ Shows a succession of plants which colo-nize disturbed chalk; managed to keep down coarse grasses and maintain plant and insect diversity. **Plants** Autumn gentian, carline thistle, adder's-tongue, orchids, stonecrop. **Butterflies** Dingy skipper. **Birds** Whin-chat.
YORKSHIRE WILDLIFE TRUST

C:4 WHELDRAKE INGS★

Near York; take Thorganby road from Whel-

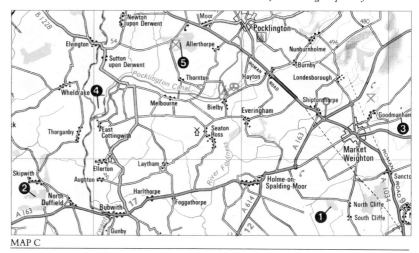

MAP C

drake, ½ mile (0.8 km) on, road forks left to Wheldrake Bridge. Parking limited. Ground often soft in flood conditions.

■ Flood meadows, drains, reed-beds, pool.

■ The grassland communities are almost unique due to traditional method of management by hay cropping with grazing and absence of agricultural chemicals. Land enriched by river silt from winter floods, which also make this an important refuge for Bewick's swan and geese and ducks. **Plants** Narrow-leaved dropwort, pepper-saxifrage, great burnet. **Birds** Barn and short-eared owls, snipe, curlew, redshank. Yorkshire Wildlife Trust

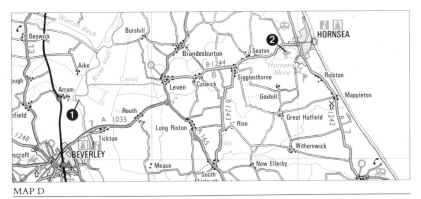

MAP D

C:5 ALLERTHORPE COMMON

Near Pocklington; E access by track from Allerthorpe, S of A1079 York to Hull road. W access 9 miles (13 km) E of York on A1079 from Thornton road.

■ Wet heath, plantation.

■ Wet heath, once much more extensive, frequently flooded in winter. Acid peaty soils with range of heath flora and fauna; scrub invasion in some parts. **Plants** Heathers, purple moor grass, cotton grass, marsh cinquefoil, petty whin, bog moss. **Birds** Nightjar, tree pipit, whinchat, woodcock, green and greater spotted woodpeckers. **Reptiles** Adder.
Yorkshire Wildlife Trust

D:1 PULFIN FEN

Near Beverley; parking at Hull Bridge on old A1033. Access to river bank from front of public house. Walk 1½ miles (2 km) N; reserve behind tree belt where river turns W. Keep to footpath; reed swamp is extremely dangerous, keep to higher grassland.

■ Fen/carr on boulder clay, drains, old clay pit.

■ Frequently flooded area in tidal bend of River Hull, dominated by common reed swamp in S, reed grass in N. Wide range of wetland plants and birds.
Yorkshire Wildlife Trust

D:2 HORNSEA MERE★★

Near Hornsea; car park at information centre on Kirkholme Point, on B1242 from Hornsea. Views from road. Remain on footpath unless on pre-arranged escorted visit.

■ Freshwater lake, reed-beds, fen, woodland.

■ This large east-coast freshwater lake results from glacial-related conditions. The reed-fringed water, mixed woodland and farmland with the sea close by make this a site of national importance for nesting, migrating and over-wintering birds. The reed-beds are of special interest because of the large numbers of nesting warblers. **Birds** (Summer migrants) black tern, little gull; (spring and passage migrants) whea-tear, whinchat; (winter) great grey shrike, gadwall, pintail, goldeneye.
Royal Society for the Protection of Birds

E:1 NORTH SANDS

Bridlington; walk along coastal road and track to Sewerby.

■ Sandy foreshore, mudflats.

■ Relatively sheltered beach complex used by large number of waders, over-wintering and passage birds, all of which can be easily observed. **Birds** Sanderling, dunlin; (winter) little gull.

E:2 FLAMBOROUGH HEAD★

Flamborough; car park at Flamborough Head lighthouse, reached from B1259. Keep to footpaths.

■ Chalk cliff.

■ Promontory of geological interest marking end of massive chalk system. Good place to observe breeding sea-birds and passage migrants, best in spring, early summer, and in autumn for terns, skuas and shearwaters out at sea.
Heritage Coast

E:3 BEMPTON CLIFFS★★

Near Bridlington; car park (with seasonally manned information point) reached from cliff road from Bempton village on B1229 Flamborough to Filey road. Keep to footpath and observation points as cliffs are dangerous.

■ Sea-bird cliff, scrub, grassland.

■ There are 3½ miles (5 km) of sheer chalk cliffs which form one of the most important sea-bird cliffs in England. This is the only mainland gannetry (650 pairs in 1986). Thousands of other courting and nesting birds may be watched from the cliff-top path at close quarters. Many migrants pass through and the turf, cliff cracks and gulleys give rise to an attractive and varied coastal flora, best seen from May to mid-Jul. **Birds** (Nesting) gannet, puffin, razorbill, guillemot, fulmar, kittiwake, shag, rock dove; (offshore migrants) shearwaters, skuas, terns; (cliff-top) bluethroat, ring ouzel, merlin. **Plants** Thrift, scurvy-grass.
Royal Society for the Protection of Birds

E:4 FORDEN CHALK BANK

Near Hunmanby; reserve by roadside 3½ miles (5 km) E of Forden, off A1039. Part of a working farm: enter from either end, not across country. No dogs.

■ Chalk grassland.

■ S-facing dry wold in steep-sided valley. Regionally rare habitat, formerly grazed by rabbits, now by sheep. Best in spring and summer, but good all year. **Plants** Purple milk-vetch, rock-rose, clustered bellflower. **Butterflies** Brown argus, dingy skipper.
Yorkshire Wildlife Trust

E:5 FILEY DAMS

Near Filey; inland from town. Hide available.

■ Pond, marsh, woodland fringe.

■ Valuable area for a range of wetland plants, a variety of bird life and both smooth and great crested newts. High densities of water shrew have been recorded. **Plants** Adder's-tongue, nodding bur-marigold. **Birds** Ruff, lesser yellowlegs, rustic bunting, great grey and red-backed shrikes, ring ouzel, firecrest, flycatchers.
Yorkshire Wildlife Trust

E:6 FILEY BRIGG★

Near Filey; just N of town, park on cliff-top. Take care on the cliff and rocks.

■ Rock promontory, rock pools, cliff.

■ Varied rockpool life and excellent bird-watching, especially for passage and wintering species: sandpipers, red-breasted merganser, eider, long-tailed duck, shorelark, snow and Lapland buntings.

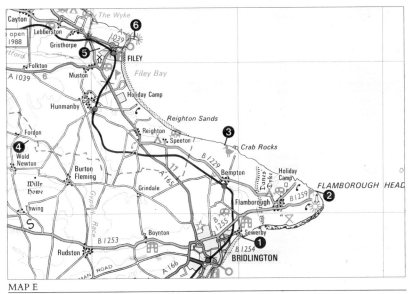

MAP E

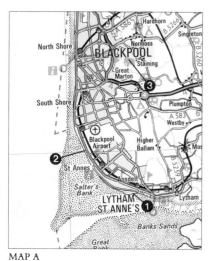

MAP A

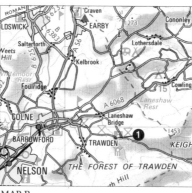

MAP B

A:1 FAIRHAVEN LAKE & SHORE*

Lytham St. Anne's; view from sea front.

■ Lake with islands, sandy shore.

■ The lake attracts wildfowl and passage waders and the shore is good for waders; in spring many grey plover occur in summer plumage. Knot, godwits and turnstone; rarities such as phalaropes may visit on passage. **Birds** Pochard, tufted duck, pintail, common scoter, dunlin, redshank.

A:2 ST ANNE'S DUNES & SHORE*

Lytham St Anne's; just S of holiday camp W of Blackpool Airport on A584. Parking on the road on Blackpool side. (S of here there are double yellow lines.) Reach shore by crossing main road and walking through the dunes opposite reserve. Reserve guide available from LTNC.

■ Sand dunes, wet slacks, sandy shore.

■ A small reserve, tucked away next to a fenced-in holiday camp, and safe from most interference.

This is a compact example of dune flora. One of the two wet slacks remains moist even when the water table is low. It overlies peat and, in spite of the surrounding calcareous sand, supports some cotton grass and marsh pennywort. Elsewhere, kidney vetch, trefoils, common restharrow and wild pansy attract the many insects. Early marsh orchid, bee orchid and yellow-wort stand out as features whereas marsh helleborine forms dense clumps in places. Round-leaved wintergreen and grass of Parnassus are also present.

The shore beyond the dunes across the road is excellent for birds; flocks of sanderling on passage often exceed a thousand birds; grey plover and godwits from the Ribble Estuary may also visit. This shore also provides sea watching with skuas,

shearwaters, common scoter, divers and kittiwakes.

LANCASHIRE TRUST FOR NATURE CONSERVATION

A:3 MARTON MERE*

Blackpool; going N along South Park Drive, fork right at Stanley Park and turn right into Lawson Road. Park and walk across playing field to path to Mere.

■ Lake with good edge vegetation.

■ A lake of this type close to the sea attracts many passage migrants and winter vagrants. It also has breeding grebes, diving and surface feeding ducks, shoveler, sedge and reed warblers, whitethroat and finches. **Birds** Little and great crested grebes, black tern, little gull, osprey, marsh harrier, snipe and jack snipe, wood and green sandpipers.

BLACKPOOL BOROUGH COUNCIL

Snipe – seen at Marton Mere.

B:1 WYCOLLER COUNTRY PARK

Near Colne; from Colne take the minor road to Trawden then follow signs for Wycoller; parking at site.

■ River, grassland, woodland, moorland edge.

■ A country park and conservation area with a clean upland stream where dipper and grey wagtail are frequent. Woodland, banks

and hillsides with flora and fauna characteristic of millstone grit soils. **Birds** Little owl, meadow pipit, curlew. **Plants** Wavy hair-grass, dog violets, heather.

LANCASHIRE COUNTY COUNCIL

C:1 ROSSALL PROMENADE & POINT

Fleetwood; public car parks, and some street parking, in Fleetwood.

■ Sea shore, playing fields, ponds.

■ Walk N along promenade for sea watching. Playing fields, golf links and amenity ponds provide resting places for migrants and wind-blown sea-birds. Dock and power station pools are also worth a look. Best Aug-Apr, especially after strong westerly winds. **Birds** Purple sandpiper, turnstone, common scoter, shearwaters, gannet, Leach's petrel, skuas, uncommon gulls, migrant terns, great crested, Slavonian and red-necked grebes, red-breasted merganser, red-throated diver, oystercatcher, sanderling, grey plover, black-tailed godwit, passage passerines.

C:2 BROCK VALLEY

Near Garstang; from A6 N of Bilsborrow take unclassified road E via Claughton to Higher Brock Mill at SD 572447; parking.

■ Upland river, grassland, woodland, marshy areas.

■ Nature trail beside the clean, fast flowing River Brock. Fine hardwood and open areas with meadowsweet and willowherb. Alive with insects in summer. **Birds** Dipper, grey wagtail, sand martin, great spotted woodpecker. **Plants** Sweet Ciceley, Indian balsam, yellow iris. **Dragonflies** Common hawker, golden-ringed.

LANCASHIRE TRUST FOR NATURE CONSERVATION

C:3 COCKERHAM AND WINMARLEIGH MOSSES

Near Garstang; from Cockerham several unclassified roads cross the Mosses and a footpath crosses Winmarleigh Moss from Crawley's Cross Farm (SD 436470). Parking difficult on these narrow roads; use lay-by just E of Cogie Hill Farm for the footpath walk. Keep to roads and footpaths.

■ Dry heath over deep peat, birch scrub, cultivated peat.

■ The last remnant of lowland raised bog in Lancashire, extensively modified, but still holding species characteristic of such habitats. The cultivated fields provide wintering sites for large flocks of geese, lapwing and golden plover. **Birds** Pink-footed goose, waders. **Insects** Large heath, hairstreak, purple-bordered gold, Manchester treble-bar, bog bush-cricket, black darter dragonfly. **Plants** Bog-rosemary, round-leaved sundew, white beak-sedge, cotton-grasses.

MAP C

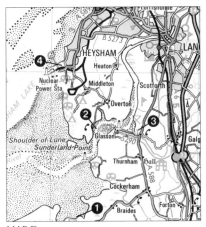

MAP D

D:1 PILLING MARSH & SHORES*

Pilling; on A588 between Cockerham and Pilling, opposite Lane Ends Farm, enter water board's public car park. Keep to roads and access area on sea wall provided by NWWA.

■ Salt-marsh, sea shore.

■ Excellent wader and duck watching from sea wall, with pink-footed goose flying from sea roost to fields. Migrants and winter visitors such as green sandpiper and snow bunting on and behind the sea wall, where there are pools. Raptors are seen regularly at the wader roost. Best Aug-May. **Birds** Wigeon, mallard, teal, shelduck, grey and golden plovers, lapwing, sanderling, knot, bar-tailed godwit, dunlin, ringed plover, merlin, peregrine, whimbrel, spotted redshank, greenshank.

NORTH WEST WATER AUTHORITY

D:2 SUNDERLAND POINT*

Near Morecambe; the unclassified road leading S from the B5273 is passable except at high spring tides. Car park at Sunderland village (SD 427560). Walk towards the point, then across to Middleton Sands using the footpath. Keep to roads and footpaths.

■ Shore, pasture.

■ An important high tide roost at the mouth of the Lune. Visit one to two hours before high tide, choosing tides of more than 27 feet (8.5 m). Particularly good for passage waders, with up to several thousand sanderling and knot. Hundreds of godwits and grey plover winter. Migrant passerines may also be seen in the fields and hedges. Best visited Aug-May. **Birds** Bar-tailed godwit, dunlin, grey plover, ringed plover, turnstone, curlew, redshank, oystercatcher, shelduck.

D:3 CONDER GREEN

Near Lancaster; from the A588 going S from Lancaster turn right at the Stork Inn just before crossing the River Conder; parking. Keep to footpaths.

■ Estuarine mud banks, salt-marsh, river.

■ Close views of waders and wildfowl feeding on exposed mud and as tides rise and fall at this point where the Conder enters the Lune. The salt-marsh and Lune beyond are also good for birdwatching. Interesting salt-marsh plants by the sea walls. Visit spring and autumn. Guide available from the LTNC. **Birds** Wigeon, teal, shelduck, dunlin, curlew, redshank, curlew sandpiper, little stint, spotted redshank, ruff, grey and golden plovers, snipe, gulls, terns.

D:4 HEYSHAM HARBOUR & POWER STATION*

Near Morecambe; approach Heysham along Morecambe promenade, A5105. Follow signs for the ferry; just before harbour take road along sea wall to sea-watching site. Just before this, Moneyclose Lane leads left to a public observation tower and reserve. Keep to roads and areas indicated on notices and leaflets.

■ Harbour, sea, intertidal sands and scars, dry scrub, grassland, pond, reed-bed.

■ Worthwhile sea watching from end of sea wall; but the highlight is the excellent daytime viewing of migrant passerines from the observation tower. Rarities include yellow-browed warbler. CEGB hide at Red Nab overlooking wader roost. Sea watching best at high tide with W winds and also in dead calm conditions; choose calm days for passerine migration. **Birds** Purple sandpiper, divers, grebes, auks, sea ducks, petrels, terns and gulls, especially little gull, migrant passerines, bar-tailed godwit, oystercatcher, knot, dunlin, turnstone, redshank, ringed, grey and golden plovers, curlew, sanderling.

CENTRAL ELECTRICITY GENERATING BOARD

E:1 RIVER WYRE GRAVEL PITS

Near Lancaster; limited roadside parking at Street; keep to footpaths.

■ Flooded gravel pits, spoil dumps, river.

■ SE of the River Wyre flooded pits attract great crested and little grebe, tufted duck, and peripheral plants such as bulrush. On the other side a rich spoil tip area is good for *Odonata* and passage waders. **Birds** Dipper, grey wagtail, grebes, green and common sandpiper, oystercatcher, ringed and little-ringed plover. **Dragonflies** Brown hawker, four-spotted chaser, dragonflies and emerald damselfly.

E:2 TROUGH OF BOWLAND*

Near Lancaster; signposted from Lancaster – the 'Through' is a pass through the Bowland fells leading to Dunsop Bridge and Clitheroe. Access to some of the fells open at certain times, contact local tourist office. Keep to footpaths.

■ River, woodland, heather moorland, grassland.

■ Roadside amenity areas make useful observation points: short-eared owl, hen harrier and merlin are possible. The fell tops are featureless and prone to low cloud. **Birds** Raptors, dipper, grey wagtail, golden plover, snipe, redshank, curlew, redstart, ring ouzel, red grouse.

E:3 STOCKS RESERVOIR & GISBURN FOREST

Near Clitheroe; view reservoir from road; pedestrians only on forest tracks.

■ Lake, grassland, marshy areas, river, conifer woodland with hardwood bands.

■ The artificial lake formed by the River Hodder has breeding wildfowl including red-breasted merganser; winter wildfowl in respectable numbers. The forest, mainly spruce, is being harvested so that an interesting succession of growth stages provides a variety of habitats. A hardwood section beside Bottom Beck is particularly good for plants and insects. **Birds** Pochard, tufted duck, migrant swans and waders, short-eared owl, black grouse, crossbill, twite, hen harrier, merlin, curlew, common sandpiper, dipper. **Plants** Water avens, marsh violet, early-purple orchid, spotted orchid, fungi.

NORTH WEST WATER AUTHORITY/
FORESTRY COMMISSION

E:4 CLOUGHA PIKE & BIRKBANK BOG*

Near Lancaster; take Quernmore fork by Knots Wood towards Bay Horse. Take first left past church; car park and picnic site in about ½ mile (0.8 km) at SD 527603. Read displayed regulations governing Bowland Forest access; dates are also posted giving notice of days during the grouse shooting season when access is barred.

■ Heather moorland, valley mire, oak woodland on millstone grit, upland stream.

■ This is probably the best site for a close look at the natural history of Bowland Forest. Beyond the car park a track leads to a small plateau with a valley mire: here are bog asphodel, sundew, and cottongrasses as well as rushes and sedges of acidic bogs.

A small hanging oak wood behind the bog continues along a stream and many interesting ferns including lemon-scented, male fern and scaly male fern grow here. In the rocky gullies, such as Windy Clough, on the drystone walls and the stoney tops, are wheatear, stonechat, ring ouzel, and common lizard. On the heather moorland there are golden plover and curlew with the chance of a passing hen harrier or merlin.

A large colony of lesser black-backed gulls breeds beside the access strip at Tarnbrook Fell. In Apr emperor moths can be seen over the heather and other *Lepidoptera* include green hairstreak and fox moth. The wet areas are excellent in May for displaying snipe; hares are common and roe deer frequent. Best Apr-Oct.

BOWLAND FOREST ACCESS AREA

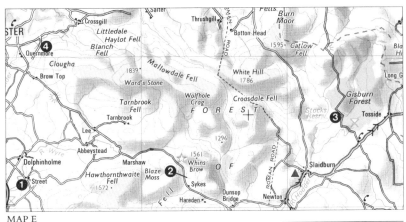

MAP E

LANCASHIRE

F:1 HEST BANK & MORECAMBE PROMENADE★★

Morecambe; easy access from A5105. Keep to footpaths.

■ Sandy shore, shingle banks, scars, salt-marsh, pasture.

■ Here is one of the best wader watching sites in the country, comprising several locations. The high-tide roost at Hest Bank is reached over the level crossing at SD 468665. It is an area of salt-marsh and flats holding thousands of oystercatcher, knot, dunlin, curlew; and hundreds of redshank, bar-tailed godwit, ringed plover, turnstone, lapwing, wigeon and shelduck. Ten to twenty thousand birds in all may be present at peak periods. Best viewing is when tides are as high as 27 to 33 feet (8.5 to 9.7 m): the birds are pushed beyond Red Bank Farm and in this area a flock of over one hundred golden plover winter, mainly on the pasture. At SD 461659, where the promenade starts, a' freshwater outfall attracts waders and wildfowl: a likely place to see pintail, wigeon and hundreds of shelduck.

By the golf course towards Morecambe is a shingle bank favoured by ringed plover, and just where The Broadway meets the promenade, turnstone can usually be seen close inshore. There are waders all along here, even at low tide. In Morecambe itself, a stone jetty projects from the promenade behind the Midland Hotel. This abuts deeper water and is good for sea watching at high tides, especially after westerly gales: Leach's petrel, kittiwake and little gull are regular, as well as sea ducks and red-breasted merganser.

ROYAL SOCIETY FOR THE PROTECTION OF BIRDS

F:2 THE RIVER LUNE★

Lancaster to Kirkby Lonsdale; approach from Caton via the Halton road, or from Hornby – Loyn Bridge. Keep to footpaths, which give access to most of the banks.

■ Upland river, pasture, woodland.

■ A clean salmon river, excellent for riverside birds, and a prime site in the British Trust for Ornithology's waterways survey. Any stretch is worth a visit; woodland sections contain interesting plants. **Birds** Goosander, common sandpiper, oystercatcher, ringed plover, redshank, curlew, yellow wagtail, dipper, kingfisher, sand martin. **Plants** Sweet Cicely, winter cress, Indian balsam, wood stitchwort.

F:3 LUNDSFIELD QUARRY

Near Carnforth; at bridge over M6 just W of Nether Kellet, take unclassified road N beside M6 on W side; park and follow footpath. Keep to footpaths, which criss-cross the site.

■ Pond, spoil tips, grassland, scrub, alder carr.

■ Disused quarry with a rich flora and consequent insect fauna; the pond is good for *Odonata*. In Jun there are drifts of spotted orchid and its hybrids, also northern marsh orchid. **Plants** Bee orchid, marsh helleborine, early marsh orchid, kidney vetch, trefoils. **Insects** Emerald, azure, large red and common blue damselflies, four-spotted chaser, common and black darter dragonflies, five- and six-spot burnet moths.

LANCASTER CITY COUNCIL

F:4 LORD'S LOT WOOD

Near Carnforth; park at picnic site, SD 547710. Pedestrians only on forest tracks.

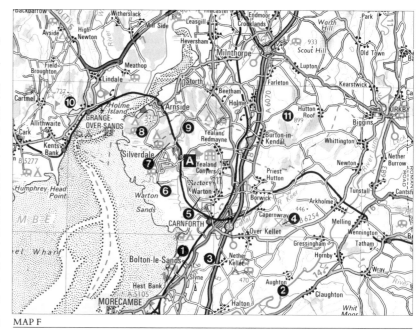

MAP F

■ Mixed and conifer woodland, *Sphagnum* bog.

■ A mixture of hemlock, pines, spruce, oak, birch, beech, sycamore and rowan makes this an interesting site for fungi. The wet area is good for insects, especially *Odonata*. Don't walk on the bog. **Birds** Crossbill, sparrowhawk, woodcock. **Dragonflies** Black darter, common hawker. **Plants** Lemon-scented fern, bog asphodel, round-leaved sundew; *Leccinum holopus, Lactarius flexuosus, Pluteus boudieri*.

FORESTRY COMMISSION

F:5 WARTON CRAG★

Near Carnforth; in Warton High Street turn W by Black Bull; parking in disused quarry on right just above hotel. LTNC guide available.

■ Limestone scars and pavement, scrub, limestone grassland.

■ A compact Local Nature Reserve providing abundant, effort-free opportunities for plant and insect photography, although paths are steep.

Deep soils formed by sediments blown in from Morecambe Bay occur in pockets on the terraces, providing a contrasting plant community. In late spring, the scars are yellow with vetches, trefoils and composites such as lesser dandelion; with thyme on the terraces, the rich insect fauna becomes obvious.

Day-flying species of *Lepidoptera* include the very local least minor and cistus forester, green hairstreak, common and holly blues, pearl-bordered, small pearl-bordered and high brown fritillaries. Hover-flies such as *Volucella pellucens* and *Eristalis* species are obvious on the flowers of the many shrubs. There are plenty of interesting grasses and sedges; ferns include moonwort. The pavement is among ash scrub with yew and juniper. Plants here include pale St. John's-wort and long-stalked crane's-bill. Primroses and violets are widespread. Take care on the pavement.

LANCASTER CITY COUNCIL

F:6 HEALD BROW & JENNY BROWN'S POINT

Near Carnforth; leave Silverdale on unclassi-

fied road going E in direction of station. About ¼ mile (0.5 km) after last buildings, turn right on to unclassified road; park in about 100 yards (90 m). Footpath leads S through wood at SD 470746.

■ Woodland, limestone bank, salt-marsh.

■ The path leads through a mixed wood with interesting plants and birds on to an open limestone bank, also rich in plants and insects, with a view over areas of salt-marsh. At the point, an old sea embankment provides a resting place for waders at high tide. Hundreds of wigeon favour this area and some sea watching is possible. **Plants** Herb Paris, wood anemone, vetches, crane's-bills, thyme. **Butterflies** Pearl-bordered fritillary, dingy skipper, grayling.

F:7 EAVES WOOD

Near Carnforth; head NE out of Silverdale on the unclassified road in direction of Waterslack and Beetham. Car park at SD 471760 shown on Landranger Sheet 97.

■ Mixed wood on limestone, (some pavement).

■ A rich and diverse wood with fungi, wood ants, red squirrels and shade-tolerant plants. Open areas have common rock-rose, dropwort and blue moor-grass with some calcifuge plants on the leached topsoil and associated with mounds made by the ant *Lasius flavus*. Best Apr-Nov. **Plants** Small-leaved lime, wild service-tree, spindle, juniper, yew, oak, beech, ash, broad-leaved helleborine, herb Paris, lily-of-the-valley, *Geastrum, Lepiota,* and 'fairy club' fungi species. **Mammals** Roe deer. **Birds** Redstart, woodcock.

NATIONAL TRUST

F:8 ARNSIDE KNOTT & SHORE★

Near Arnside; park opposite Knott at SD 460774 – obvious pull-off. Footpath on to Knott is opposite.

■ Limestone grassland scree, fragmented pavement outcrops, shore, salt-marsh, cliffs, oak-yew woodland.

■ For an interesting circular walk taking in Knott and shore, turn right opposite car park through yew trees. Follow path to New Barns, then head SW to shore, follow-

Kingfisher – see F:2, opposite page.

ing round to Far Arnside and back to start.

On the Knott there is a fine calcicole flora. The dominant grass, blue moor-grass, is restricted to the type of rock found here, and worth seeing in spring. Dark red helleborine is also characteristic. Keep off scree; path at bottom gives view of plants. Tiger beetle burrows are frequent on top path. **Plants** Rue-leaved saxifrage, spring sandwort, small scabious, autumn gentian, broad-leaved helleborine, bloody crane's-bill. **Insects** High brown fritillary, holly blue, green hairstreak.
NATIONAL TRUST

F:9 GAIT BARROWS★★
Near Carnforth; *from Silverdale take road through Waterslack; entrance on right in nearly one mile (1.5 km) after rail bridge. Car park for permit holders; entrance by permit only, apply NCC, NW Regional Office, Blackwell, Bowness-on-Windermere, Cumbria, LA23 3JR.*

■ Limestone pavement, woodland, grassland, alder carr, lake.

■ This National Nature Reserve is the finest example of limestone pavement in the country, notable for large areas of continuous smooth pavement with grikes (fissures). The whole outcrop slopes S and is surrounded by a zone of shattered pavement, then birch and hazel scrub which merges into woodland with mature trees.

The pavement is dotted with yew, holly, juniper, rowan, guelder-rose and ash growing from the grikes with exciting herbaceous flora. Ferns are in most grikes: tutsan, saw wort, angular Solomon's-seal and bloody crane's-bill are special to this area with an occasional dark-red helleborine.

The shattered area is interesting, too, with drifts of ploughman's spikenard and pale St. John's-wort and plenty of thyme and biting stonecrop. Here, and in the rides dividing the woodland, are interesting *Lepidoptèra* such as high brown and Duke of Burgundy fritillaries.

The mixed woodland contains small-leaved lime, oak and yew. The dominant grasses are mountain and wood melicks, with false brome and blue moor-grass. The wood ant *Formica rufa* is common (large nests). The uncommon hover fly *Microdon mutabilis*, which is associated with ants, is also present. The fungus flora is also rich with many rarities recorded. Beyond the pavement are open meadows with a small lake, Little Hawes Water, surrounded by alder carr, and unusual in being on calcareous marl. Take care in woodland on hidden pavement.
NATURE CONSERVANCY COUNCIL

F:10 HAMPSFIELD FELL & EGGERSLACK WOOD★
Near Grange-over-Sands; *park at Grange and walk up B5271; consult Landranger or Pathfinder map: extensive footpaths. Take any through Eggerslack Wood on to the fell. Keep to footpaths.*

■ Grassy limestone pavement, coppiced oak/hazel/sycamore.

■ Pavement area on fell for special ferns. Woodland is an example of old coppiced oak with remains of tanning pits; good ground flora. Best Jun-Aug. **Plants** Limestone fern, rigid buckler-fern, lemon-scented fern. **Butterflies** Pearl-bordered fritillary, holly blue.

F:11 HUTTON ROOF CRAGS & FARLETON KNOTT★
Near Burton-in-Kendal; *go N from Burton on A6070, turn right at Clawthorpe Hall along minor road; continue to top of hill – roadside parking. Footpaths leave either side to the sites; keep to footpaths; permit required for CTNC reserve mentioned below, apply CTNC, Church Street,* Ambleside, Cumbria LA22 0BU.

■ Elevated limestone pavement.

■ Nationally important both geologically and for flora. A lower wooded section of Hutton Roof Crags is CTNC entry by permit only. **Plants** Limestone fern, rigid-buckler fern, green spleenwort, lesser meadow-rue, angular Solomon's seal.

F:A LEIGHTON MOSS
Silverdale, near Carnforth; *from M6 or A6 at Carnforth, follow signposts to Silverdale and turn N along unclassified road just E of Silverdale Station. Some areas accessible from rights of way, but most need permit bought on site.*

■ Reed-bed on fen, carr, salt-marsh, woodland, scrub.

■ This reserve is centred on a *Phragmites* fen with willow and alder carr plus large areas of salt-marsh. It is an important breeding site for bittern, and has a rich flora and invertebrate fauna. Breeding birds include shoveler, pochard, tufted duck, greylag goose, black-headed gull, water rail and bearded tit. In winter, teal and mallard numbers reach treble figures.

① The reserve centre provides permits and reports as well as latest sightings.

② Public hides are provided on this causeway which carries a public footpath. The hides overlook the northern pool which is favoured by diving ducks, pochard, tufted, goldeneye, also surface ducks and coot, often in good numbers. Passage terns and osprey also favour this end of the reserve. The bracket fungus *Daedaleopsis confragosa* grows on willow here.

③ These hides are accessible to RSPB members, or with a permit. They overlook areas where passage waders and breeding birds are more easily seen. Peregrine and sparrowhawk are regular, and recently marsh harrier has bred successfully. Herons are often present and may be accompanied by rarities such as spoonbill. Otters, red and roe deer are often seen. A notable feature is a huge starling roost, with attendant raptors, well worth seeing at dusk. Migrants include garganey, wood and green sandpipers, greenshank and spotted redshank.

④ The N end of the reserve is good for plants, invertebrates and breeding passerines. Large tussocks of tufted-sedge are a feature and marsh marigold is conspicuous in spring. *Odonata* are best seen in this area. *Lepidoptera* include high brown and pearl-bordered fritillaries, holly blue, mother shipton and many day-flying Pyralid species. Redpolls

and grasshopper and *Sylvia* warblers breed here. In winter, siskins join redpolls on the alders and birches and thrush flocks are regular.

⑤ Two hides overlook the salt-marsh and newly made scrapes here. Gulls, terns, raptors, wigeon, goosander, red-breasted merganser, teal, pintail and shelduck are regular with smew and whooper swans occasional. Waders include ruff, godwits, ringed plover, greenshank, curlew sandpiper. A flock of greylag geese is present in winter with pink-footed, bean, brent and barnacle less frequent.
ROYAL SOCIETY FOR THE PROTECTION OF BIRDS

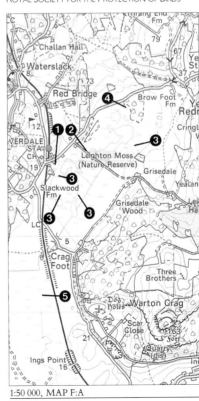

1:50 000, MAP F:A

The **high brown fritillary** (above), locally
common in the Lake District, is now largely
confined to isolated colonies in Wales and the
West Country. It is a strong flyer, soaring high
into the woodland canopy to roost at night and
in dull weather, but descending to feed on
bramble blossom and thistles.

Adult male **black grouse** (right), is instantly
recognized by its lyre-shaped tail and glossy
black plumage. Early each morning during Mar
and Apr, up to 12 males gather to perform a
courtship display called a lek. Traditional flat
areas of moorland or arenas are used – but
afforestation is now destroying many ancient
mating sites.

Slightly larger than a mistle thrush, the
merlin (left) is a rare and elusive bird of the
heather-clad moors of western and northern
Britain. Small birds form the main source of
prey and are caught as the diminutive falcon
quarters the moorland in rapid, low-level flight.

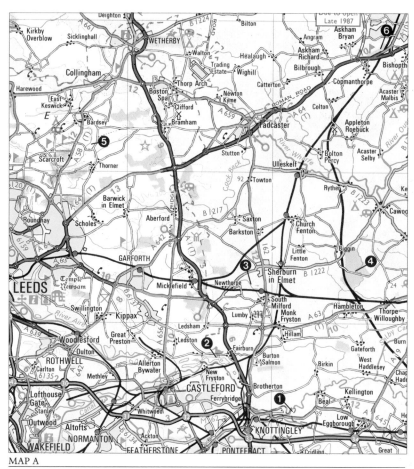

MAP A

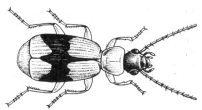

Beetle, Dromius sigma – see A:6, below.

A:6 ASKHAM BOGS★
Near York; *N of A64, park on roadside before railway bridge. Keep out of far wood section of reserve.*
■ Open fen, raised bog, oak/birch/alder/ woodland.
■ Remnant of a large swampy area. Of national importance for its insect life; varied ground flora and birds. **Insects** Beetles such as *Dromius sigma* and *Agabus undulatus;* fen square-spot moth. **Plants** Bog myrtle, sedges, royal fern, water-violet. **Birds** Grasshopper warbler. **Mammals** Water vole.
YORKSHIRE WILDLIFE TRUST

B:1 BOLTON WOODS & THE STRID
Near Skipton; *from A59 turn N at Bolton Priory on to B6180 to Bolton Abbey. Small fee for nature trail W of river at The Strid.*
■ Upland river with rapids, deciduous woodlands.
■ Rich woodland ground flora and birds including dipper, kingfisher, common sandpiper, grey wagtail, redstart, pied flycatcher, wood warblers, nuthatch, treecreeper, great spotted woodpecker.
BOLTON ESTATES

B:2 GRASS WOOD★
Near Grassington; *park by wood, one mile (1.5 km) N.*
■ Ash woodland, limestone pavement, consolidated scree.
■ An example of ash wood on great scar limestone with a number of plants and animals with a restricted distribution, encouraged by SW-facing slope above the River Wharfe. Important for *Lepidoptera*. There is a Brigantian fort and Iron Age settlement in the reserve. **Plants** Lily-of-the-valley, burnet rose, blue moor-grass, guelder-rose. **Birds** Nuthatch, treecreeper, marsh tit, warblers.
YORKSHIRE WILDLIFE TRUST

A:1 WILLOW GARTH★
Knottingley; *into Trundles Lane by canal bridge, sharp right by narrow footbridge, canal on left, fence on right; reserve 220 yards (200 metres) at end of fence.*
■ Open water, marsh, willow carr.
■ This flood plain area is criss-crossed by ditches, has a high water table and was formerly a commercial osier bed – now partly maintained as a result of mining subsidence. The range of habitats favours a number of less common plants, birds and mammals, the outstanding feature being the large number of harvest mice present. **Birds** Greenshank, redshank, common and green sandpipers.
YORKSHIRE WILDLIFE TRUST

A:2 FAIRBURN INGS★★
Near Castleford; *reached from Fairburn village off A1 or by causeway and footpath from village. Good views from lay-bys. Footpath to public hides. Information centre, toilets and boardwalk for wheelchairs at weekends.*
■ Shallow lakes, marsh, scrub, subsidence pools, riverside deciduous woodland.
■ Major wetland complex for birds, including wintering wildfowl, passage birds and some nesting species, including rarities. Number of dragonfly species associated with water edge and a rich marshland flora. Large swallow roost in autumn. **Birds** (Winter) whooper swan, goosander, goldeneye; (passage) little gull, black, Arctic and common terns; (nesting) little ringed plover, great crested and little grebes, redshank, snipe.
ROYAL SOCIETY FOR THE PROTECTION OF BIRDS

A:3 SHERBURN WILLOWS
Near Sherburn in Elmet; *from centre of village take A162 Ferrybridge Road, turn right into New Lane, reserve at end. Park where lane passes school and housing estate. Take farm track, turn left through farm gates.*
■ Calcareous grassland, quarry, marsh, stream.
■ Reserve on magnesian limestone important for a range of uncommon flora and *Lepidoptera*, with scrub and rich calcareous wetland at base of steep, dry slope. **Plants** Purple milk-vetch, pale St John's-wort, sainfoin.
YORKSHIRE WILDLIFE TRUST

A:4 BISHOPS WOOD
Near Sherburn in Elmet; *take B1222 from Sherburn to A162, turning S on to minor road to Wistow. FC leaflet available.*
■ Mixed woodland.
■ Open woodland with a nature trail mainly of ornithological interest at most times of year. Birds include tree pipit, woodcock, coal tit, jay with warblers in summer. Siskins and bramblings in winter.
FORESTRY COMMISSION

A:5 HETCHELL WOOD★
Near Leeds; *park in villages of Rowley Grange or Thorner. Footpaths to reserve.*
■ Alder carr, marsh, acid oak woodland, hawthorn woods, calcareous grassland.
■ Mixture of habitats on grits with magnesian limestone capping, old quarries and Roman encampment. Reserve noted for insect populations. **Plants** Toothwort, sanicle, greater tussock-sedge.
YORKSHIRE WILDLIFE TRUST

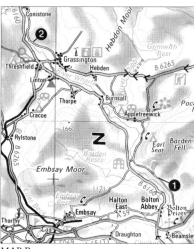

MAP B

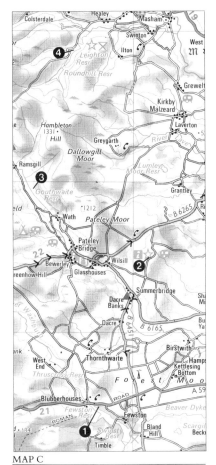

MAP C

C:1 WASHBURN VALLEY★
Near Patley Bridge/Otley; good views from road running S from Greenhow HIll on A6265 to Blubberhouses on A59 and on to Fewston and B6451 to Otley.
■ A series of large reservoirs, coniferous plantations, deciduous woodland, farmland, moorland.
■ Good conditions for a wide range of birds, easily seen from the roads at all times of the year. **Birds** (High ground) red grouse, ring ouzel, dipper, wheatear, curlew; (reservoirs of Thruscross, Fewston, Swinsty and Lindley Wood) whooper and Bewick's swans, great crested grebe; (lower Washburn valley) pied flycatcher, redstart.

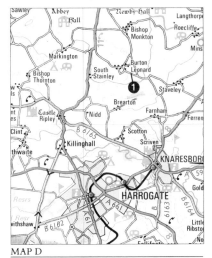

MAP D

Pine fruit – seen at C:1, Washburn Valley.

C:2 BRIMHAM ROCKS★
Near Patley Bridge; between B6265 Ripon-Patley Bridge road and B6165 Harrogate to Patley Bridge road. Fee for car park; no cars allowed on to area outside parking.
■ Dry upland heath.
■ Main interest is in the fretted, eroded pillars of millstone grit which protrude from the bedrock for over 20 feet (6 m) forming unique geological features.
NATIONAL TRUST

C:3 GOUTHWAITE RESERVOIR★
Near Patley Bridge; good views from road W of water, in upper Nidderdale. No entry to reserve.
■ Freshwater lake, moorland, woodland, plantation.
■ This large reservoir was created in a glacial lake basin. It is an important breeding and overwintering site for wildfowl, but many other bird species nest or pass through. The upper, shallower end is particularly varied and over 200 species have been recorded. Good all year, but winter is most rewarding.
YORKSHIRE WATER AUTHORITY

C:4 LEIGHTON RESERVOIR
Near Masham; good views from road W of Masham to Lofthouse which skirts reservoir.
■ Reservoir, moorland.
■ This large stretch of water is noted for its population of overwintering goosander. Pintail, shoveler, teal and gulls also present.
YORKSHIRE WATER

D:1 BURTON LEONARD QUARRIES
Near Ripon; ½ mile (0.8 km) S of Burton Leonard village, approached from A61 Harrogate-Ripon road. Park in village. Keep to paths – dangerous cliffs.
■ Exposed limestone floors, cliffs.
■ Magnesian limestone quarries with varied flora, and a wide range of native shrubs and trees. **Plants** Squinancywort, burnet rose, common rock-rose.
YORKSHIRE WILDLIFE TRUST

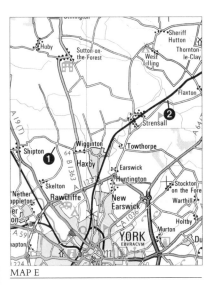

MAP E

E:1 MOORLANDS
Near York; from A19 turn through Skelton; reserve in 2 miles (3 km). Park on verge near entrance. Fee (also members) for 8 weeks in spring.
■ Mixed woodland, small ponds.
■ Impressive forest trees, with a variety of conifers. More than 50 bird species recorded; rich (planted) ground flora with colourful show of daffodils, narcissi, azaleas and rhododendrons. **Trees** Spruce, firs, pines, larch, hemlock, Norway maple, tulip-tree, tree-of-heaven, *Acers*.
YORKSHIRE WILDLIFE TRUST

E:2 STRENSALL COMMON★
Near York; from Strensall take Flaxton Road to cattle grid. Park here or further along, but not over railway line.
■ Lowland wet/dry heath.
■ Remnant of lowland heath once common on the glacial clays in the vale of York. Uncommon plants and rich insect fauna. **Plants** Marsh gentian, heath dog-violet, cross-leaved heath, cottongrass, mat-grass. **Moths** Orange underwing.
YORKSHIRE WILDLIFE TRUST

F:1 WHARRAM QUARRY
Near Malton; turn off B1248 into Wharram le Street, towards Birdsall. Signposted S of road.
■ Calcareous turf, long grass, scrub.
■ SW-facing quarry in chalk with flat floor and steep faces deliberately hollowed out for variety. Numbers of lime-loving plants with a range of butterflies. **Plants** Bee orchid, restharrow, quaking-grass.
YORKSHIRE WILDLIFE TRUST.

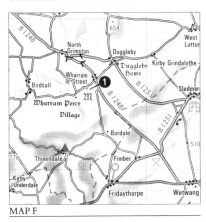

MAP F

143

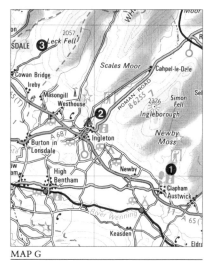

MAP G

G:1 CLAPHAM WOODS

Near Ingleton; N of Clapham village, just off A65 between Settle and Ingleton. Small fee.

■ Mixed woodland, lake, limestone pastures, cave.

■ Mixed limestone habitats (with some overlying acid soil) support a range of planted species such as rhododendrons and bamboos. Important for a range of birds, in-

cluding woodcock, dipper, grey wagtail and wheatear.

G:2 INGLETON WATERFALLS

Near Ingleton; immediately N of Ingleton village on A65. Reached by surfaced footpaths and bridges.

■ Mixed woodland, upland stream, open moorland.

■ Attractive valley walk showing some classic geological exposures of the ancient basement rocks of the Pennines. Range of birdlife, including common sandpiper, grey wagtail, dipper, curlew and other waders.

G:3 LECK FELL

Near Kirkby Lonsdale; parking at Bullpot Farm. Keep to well-used tracks – danger of potholes.

■ Heather moorland, upland watercourse.

■ Tracks lead across heather moor past limestone potholes surrounded with limestone plants, to Ease Gill which, running over limestone, is often dry. The course of the gill is rich in interesting plants, especially ferns with as many as ten species in 50 yards (49 m). Moorland birds and insects add to the variety. **Plants** Rigid buckler-fern, limestone fern, lemon-scented fern, brittle bladder-fern, green spleenwort, hoary whitlowgrass, hairy rock-cress, sanicle. **Birds** Merlin, wheatear. **Moths** Fox and emperor.

H:1 RIBBLE VALLEY★

Near Settle; A682 from Settle to Long Preston; views.

■ Moorland, upland river (floodland in winter).

■ Valley lies on main migration route and is best known for flocking waders in late summer and autumn; also an important nesting area for many upland birds. **Birds** (Nesting) golden plover, oystercatcher, curlew; (winter) whooper and Bewick's swans; (passage) black-tailed godwit, ruff, little stint and other waders.

H:2 GLOBEFLOWER WOOD

Near Settle; from town take B6479 to Lancliffe in Ribblesdale, turn right into Arncliffe. Reserve at second junction about one mile (1.5 km) W of Malham tarn. Parking very restricted. No entry to reserve; view from road.

■ Marshy meadow.

■ Lies on old rocks periodically flushed with lime-rich water from surrounding Great Scar. Chief interest is in the succession of flowers, including globeflower, melancholy thistle and wood crane's-bill. Best in Jun.

YORKSHIRE WILDLIFE TRUST

H:3 CRAVEN UPLANDS

Near Settle; on to open moors from Littondale road and Stainforth to Halton Gill road.

H:A MALHAM★★

Near Skipton; keep to marked routes, including Pennine Way, part of which is nature trail.

■ Lake, calcareous marsh, fen, limestone pavement, scree, woodland.

① Malham Tarn, lying on impervious Silurian rocks, but spring-fed from surrounding limestone, is the highest lime-rich lake in the country. Best seen, along with (2) and (3), from nature trail. Parking at Low Trenthouse and Chapel Fell.

② Parts of Tarn have silted up giving rise to mire, swamp, fen and bog with rich plant communities including sedges and horsetails.

③ Wilderness woodland flanking tarn. Much of land private, owned by Field Studies Council whose aim is to protect these unique habitats – please respect this.

④ Malham Cove, and all other sites mentioned here, are best reached by parking in Malham village and following signposted walks. This ice- and water-eroded amphitheatre in the limestone is one of the few natural nest sites for house martins and rare plants such as Pennine whitebeam, *Sorbus rupicola.*

⑤ Watlowes dry valley, created by glacial meltwater; present stream, in common with many others in area, disappears below ground into solution caves in limestone. Many classic pot holes in this area.

⑥ Limestone pavements here are among the best examples of 'Glaciokarst' scenery in the world. Scoured clean by ice and acidic rain water, then dissolved along the cracks. Eroded depressions known as grikes, blocks between as clints. Shady grikes often contain rare, woodland-type ground flora.

⑦ Janet's Foss wood, a good example of limestone woodland.

⑧ Gordale Scar – winding gorge eroded through thickly-bedded limestone by glacial meltwater. Dissolved limestone redeposited as yellowish tufa lower down the valley.

⑨ Ancient field patterns around Malham village evidence of man's modifying lowland

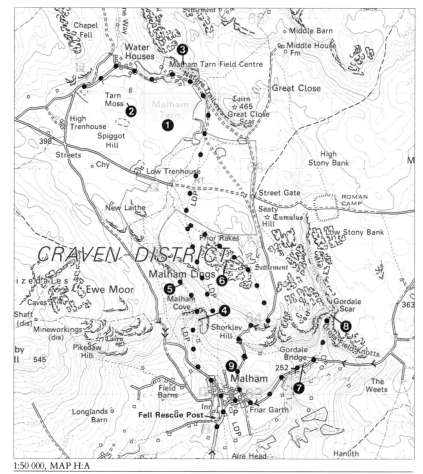

1:50 000, MAP H:A

areas for centuries; contrasts with bare limestone faces.

Plants Alpine bartsia, orpine, alpine cinquefoil, avens, mountain pansy, bloody

crane's-bill, bird's-eye primrose, northern bedstraw, hoary whitlow grass.

NATIONAL TRUST/PRIVATE OWNERSHIP/ FIELD STUDIES COUNCIL

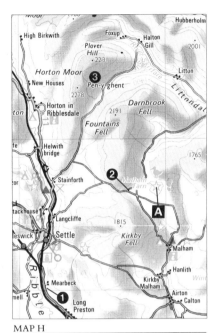

MAP H

■ Moorland, calcareous grassland, limestone pavement.

■ The high limestone hills around Pen-y-Ghent carry a varied flora and, most important, are of value to a range of breeding birds. **Birds** Raven, buzzard, dipper, golden plover. **Plants** Mountain pansy, bird's-eye primrose, meadow saxifrage, mountain-everlasting, bird's-eye primrose, moonwort.

I:1 GARBUTT WOOD & SUTTON BANK★★

Near Thirsk; *pathways from car park and information centre, at top of Sutton bank on A170.*
■ Calcareous pasture, scrub, inland cliff, scree, mixed woodland, lake, plantation.
■ The massive cliff features and the areas below them carry a range of habitats which can be seen well from the nature trail. On the limestone pastures, rock-rose and bloody crane's-bill grow. On the steeper grit, sandstone and limestone slopes there is woodland dominated by birch, with oak, ash, elm, sycamore and rowan with hazel coppice. Wood-sorrel and moschatel grow on the wood floor. Lake Gormire lies in a glacial

overflow channel dammed at one end by a landslip. **Plants** Tufted loose-strife, marsh cinquefoil, bog bean. **Mammals** Fallow, red and roe deer, badger, bats.
YORKSHIRE WILDLIFE TRUST/FORESTRY COMMISSION

I:2 ASHBERRY WOOD AREA★

Near Helmsley; *park in village and walk, crossing river by road bridge at Ashberry Farm. Entrance to reserve by permit only from chairman of management committee.*
■ Mixed deciduous woodland, limestone grassland, wet acid/calcareous grasslands.
■ This hilltop and valley bottom complex in the River Rye valley gives a wide range of flora and fauna, particularly some invertebrates which, in this warm, calcareous area, are at the N limit of their range.
In the ash woods, baneberry, fly orchid and lily-of-the-valley grow. On more acid conditions are oak/birch woods. Some caves are used by long-eared, Daubenton's and whiskered bats, and harvest mouse breeds.
YORKSHIRE WILDLIFE TRUST/PRIVATE OWNERSHIP

I:3 KIRKDALE & LOWER BRANSDALE★

Near Kirkbymoorside; *minor road from A170 Kirkbymoorside to Kirkdale or minor road into Sleightmolmedale from Fadmoor. Parking limited (extremely narrow, dead-end roads). Keep to bridle-paths and footpaths.*
■ Mixed deciduous woodland, neutral grassland, fen.
■ In this limestone valley, the stream is swallowed into the limestone in summer, producing a dry limestone bed with pools important for caddis flies. Floods occur in winter. The woodland is dominated by pedunculate oak, ash, wych elm, lime, hazel, field maple and bird cherry. Lily-of-the-valley, herb Paris and columbine grow. Alder is found in wetter areas, with great burnet, devil's-bit scabious, betony and adder's-tongue. The Kirkdale Caves, which contained remains of ancient cold and warm faunas – including rhinocerous, elephants and lion – may be seen in the quarry wall.

I:4 FARNDALE★

Near Kirkbymoorside; *minor roads from town and Hutton le Hole. Parking limited. Best to park in Low Mill or Church Houses and use riverside footpaths.*

■ River, marsh, deciduous woodland, unimproved pasture, heather moorland.
■ The main interest in this large local nature reserve is the spectacular display of wild daffodils which carpet the riverside marsh in spring. The alder-lined river banks are frequented by dipper and water vole. Birds include red grouse, whinchat, stonechat and ring ouzel. Adder and common lizard are found on the moors.
'PRIVATE OWNERSHIP, DESIGNATED BY NORTH YORK MOORS NATIONAL PARK COMMITTEE

J:1 ELLERBURN BANK *(map on next page)*

Near Pickering; *turn N in Thornton Dale on A170, follow forest drive for about one mile (1.5 km). Track to right leads to reserve. Park on verge of forest drive, not on tracks. Fee for forest drive. Permit needed from chairman of reserve committee.*
■ Limestone pasture, plantation.
■ Varied flora on shallow calcareous soils, with a fauna associated both with limestone pastures and woodland edge, including slow-worm. Flowering communities throughout the growing season.
YORKSHIRE WILDLIFE TRUST/FORESTRY COMMISSION

J:2 FORGE VALLEY & RAINCLIFFE WOODS★

Near Scarborough; *from town, follow Lady Edith's Drive, or from A170 in East Ayton, take minor road for Hackness. Car parks at site; avoid roadside. Keep to footpaths and bridle-paths.*
■ Mixed deciduous woodland, river, marsh, fen.
■ In the wet valley floor there is alder and willow with butterbur, pendulous sedge, opposite- and alternate-leaved golden-saxifrage. The middle slopes carry ash, wych elm, hazel, field maple, spurge-laurel, ramsons, wood anemone, sanicle, toothwort, and broad-leaved helleborine. On the top slopes are pedunculate oak and rowan with bilberry, heather and great wood-rush.
NATURE CONSERVANCY COUNCIL/ SCARBOROUGH BOROUGH COUNCIL

J:3 DALBY FOREST★

Near Pickering; *car parks with FC information centre at Dalby village. Fee for private road.*
■ Plantation, fen, marsh, pond, acid/calcareous pastures, heather moorland, stream, woodland.
■ The drive has been established to show various aspects of large-scale afforestation. In addition to large blocks of trees at various stages of growth, there are unplanted areas, streamside mixed deciduous woodlands, man-made ponds and pockets of moorland. The forest covers a range of rocks, from limestones to grits and shales, giving an enormous variety of both land form and habitat. **Plants** Narrow-leaved marsh-orchid, grass-of-Parnassus, bee, fly and fragrant orchids, dropwort, bog pimpernel. **Mammals** Bats.
FORESTRY COMMISSION

J:4 BRIDESTONES

Near Pickering; *reached along Dalby forest drive N of Thornton Dale. Park by Staindale lake. Fee for forest road.*
■ Heather moorland, woodland, upland pasture.
■ Much of the area is underlain by siliceous grits, topped by harder passage beds which

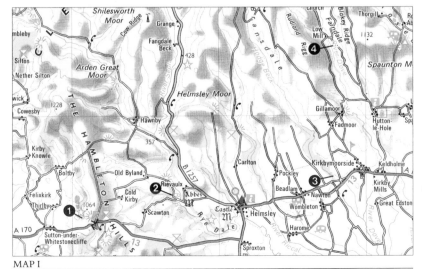

MAP I

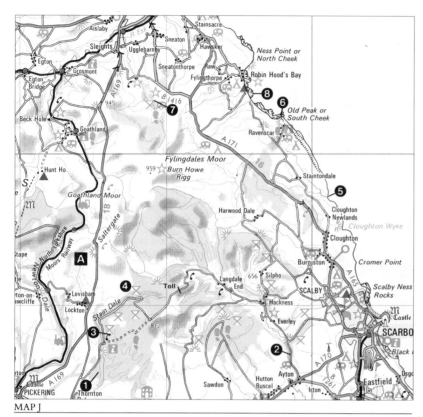

MAP J

MAP K

have weathered into pillars of sometimes spectacular shapes. In Dovedale Griff the soils become damper and there is a range from the very dry, bracken-covered slopes to the wetter cross-leaved heath and cotton-grass areas.
YORKSHIRE WILDLIFE TRUST/NATIONAL TRUST

J:5 HAYBURN WYKE
Near Scarborough; Ravenscar road from A171 in Cloughton village. Track to reserve about 1¼ miles (1.5 km) N of Cloughton. Park on track or near hotel; small fee for hotel car park.
■ Scrub oak woodland, coastal cliff, beck.
■ Noted for beetles, wide range of birds and varied flora including mosses and liverworts. Lias shales with fossil plant remains exposed along the stony beach.
YORKSHIRE WILDLIFE TRUST/NATIONAL TRUST

J:6 RAVENSCAR★
Near Whitby; minor roads off A171. Ample parking in Ravenscar village. Keep to footpath when crossing golf course.
■ Quarries, cliff, scrub woodland, foreshore.
■ There is a marked geological trail providing excellent views across Robin Hood's bay. There are quarries associated with alum working, dogger beds of ironstone and limestone over shales which form the so-called 'mermaids tables' on the rocky foreshore. The complex system of the peak fault may be seen in the rocks by the Raven Hotel. In the sandstones, fossil horsetails, ripple marks and even dinosaur footprints may be seen. In the shales, ammonites, belemnites and oysters *Gryphea* are common.
NATIONAL TRUST/PRIVATE OWNERSHIP

J:7 MAY BECK & FALLING FOSS★
Near Whitby; clearly signposted along B1416.

Car park at May Beck and Falling Foss.
■ Heather moorland, broad-leaved woodland, plantation.
■ Trails cover moorland which is managed by burning strips of land in rotation to generate new heather growth for red grouse and sheep. The main plant species on the moor are heather, crowberry, bilberry, cowberry and bracken. Adder and common lizard are often seen.
Plantations are of Japanese larch and lodgepole pine, the most recent providing a habitat for nightjars.
FORESTRY COMMISSION

J:8 ROBIN HOOD'S BAY★
Near Whitby; park at top of bank signposted from A171 Whitby to Scarborough road.
■ Cliffs, wave-cut platform.
■ One of the finest examples of a wave-cut platform and glacial till cliffs. Cliffs show a classic section through lower Jurassic rocks, where there are numerous fossil ammonites. Varied rock pool fauna and seaweeds. Best at lowest tides.
NATIONAL TRUST/PRIVATE OWNERSHIP

Japanese larch – see J:7, this page.

K:1 SEMER WATER★
Near Bainbridge; approached from two minor roads leading S from Bainbridge on A684. Fee for car parks. A footpath runs along the edge of the reserve giving good views; no access to the marsh. Keep to footpaths.
■ Lake, upland river, marsh, calcareous pastures.
■ The largest natural lake in Yorkshire has a rich flora and fauna; especially valuable for overwintering birds such as wigeon and whooper swan. Passage birds include goldeneye, shelduck and teal. Curlew, lapwing and snipe breed. Associated with the river are trout, crayfish, rare mayflies. Orchids are found on the steep limestone banks.
YORKSHIRE WILDLIFE TRUST

K:2 YELLANDS MEADOW
Near Richmond; close to Muker village on B6270. Permission needed from management committee to enter meadow Mar-Jul. Keep to marked route.
■ Dales hay meadow.
■ Reserve managed by hay cutting and light winter grazing. Its range of flora and fauna typify a limestone-based meadow.
Plants Wood crane's-bill, giant bellflower, primrose. **Insects** Mayflies, stoneflies.
YORKSHIRE WILDLIFE TRUST

K:3 TAN HILL
Near Richmond; minor roads from Reeth up Arkengarthdale (off B6270) to Tan Hill and Barras, from Keld in Swaledale.
■ Heather moor, acid grassland, bog, upland streams, plantation.
■ Superb bird-watching country from the open road or the Pennine Way, with colonies of black-headed and lesser black-backed gulls, red and black grouse, golden plover, lapwing, curlew, dipper, common sandpiper, wheatear, short-eared owls and merlin.

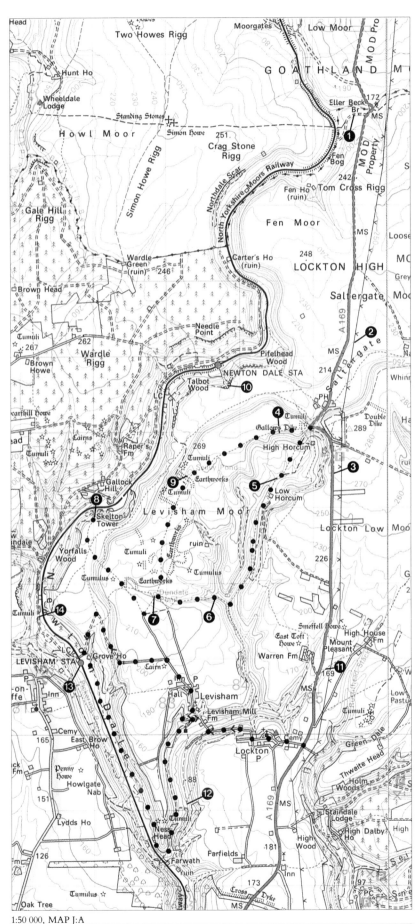

Hen harrier.

J:A LEVISHAM MOOR**
Near Pickering; *reached by A169 Whitby to Pickering road. Car park at top of Saltersgate brow convenient to bridle-paths. Also good access from road to Levisham station. Keep to footpaths and bridle-paths. Keep dogs on lead.*

■ Moorland, mixed woodland, traditional pastures, valley bogs, plantation.

① Fen Bog Yorkshire Wildlife Trust reserve car park off A169. Valley bottom mire at head of glacial drainage channel. Of national importance. Plants include sundew, butterwort, bog asphodel, bog myrtle and various orchids. Peat up to 11 yards (10.5 m) deep in places. Noted for dragonflies. Birds include redstart, whinchat.

② Small valley bog created by silting up of old drainage channels on Nab farm. Good display of cottongrass in summer. Observe from road only.

③ Main car park. Views across Levisham moor and reclaimed moorland on E side of A169.

④ Open heather moor on scarp of calcareous grits. To N are wetter mixed moors; to S the Hole of Horcum, a huge hollow caused by water and perhaps ice action. Experiments with heather management seen on both sides of track.

⑤ Hole of Horcum shows contrast between improved farmland and bracken-covered areas on its floor. Moorland rim famous for arctic-alpine relict plants such as dwarf cornel and bearberry. Traditional pastures carry many butterfly species and plants such as small-white orchid, adder's-tongue, pignut, fragrant orchid, betony.

⑥ Dundale Griff – deeply eroding channel characteristic of the area's unstable geology. Creeping willow grows nearby.

⑦ Dundale pond important for dragonflies and mayflies.

⑧ Skelton Tower provides views along the glacial drainage channel of Newtondale and FC plantations of Cropton Forest. Harriers and merlin may be seen and badgers are active.

⑨ Seavy pond valuable for breeding dragonflies, such as *Cordulguester boltoni*; *Genista* grows close by.

⑩ Cliffs in Newton Dale are site of medieval falconry. Valley bottom best seen from train; several routes on foot from Newton Dale Halt.

⑪ Old limestone quarries with rich calcareous flora.

⑫ Hagg Wood Marsh (YWT reserve). Park in Levisham village and use bridle-path to W of beck. Wetter woodland with alder; drier with oak, birch, ash, and guelder-rose. Valley floor with tussock-sedge, globeflower, ragged-robin.

⑬ Levisham Station gives access to beck. Several traditional hay meadows along valley.

⑭ Forestry plantation; look for signs of roe deer, fox, badger and mink.

NORTH YORK MOORS NATIONAL PARK
AUTHORITY/PRIVATE OWNERSHIP

CUMBRIA

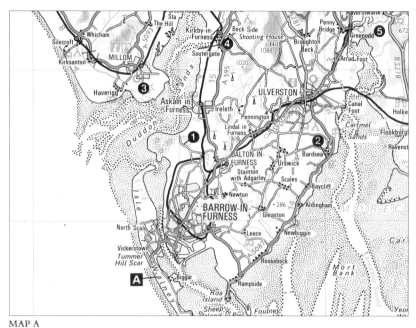

MAP A

A:1 SANDSCALE HAWS★★

Near Dalton-in-Furness; *from Roanhead continue to car park at end of road. Space limited, early start advised. Contact warden for advice.*
■ Dunes, dune slacks, sandy shore.
■ Extensive calcareous and dune and slack system over clay. A walk along the shore reveals fore-dune formation from pioneers, and over the main fixed dune ridge, plant diveristy increases to a rich slack flora. Around 200 species of plant have been recorded. Sea holly, Portland spurge and sand sedge are prominent among the stabilizers after the marram.
NATIONAL TRUST

A:2 BARDSEA

Near Ulverston; *approach on A5087 S from Ulverston.*
■ Shore, offshore scar, oak/beech woodland.
■ A country park consisting of a 1½-mile (2.5-km) stretch of coastline with views of the high tide wader roost at Wadhead Scar. Notable specimens of wild cherry occur in Sea Wood above the shore; many fine oaks, too. Rising or falling tide best for wader viewing.
CUMBRIA COUNTY COUNCIL

A:3 HODBARROW LAGOON★

Near Millom; *from A5093 near station, at SD 174791, take track on left – some parking space or park in Millom; tracks on foot. As it is a new reserve, contact warden (currently Doug Radford of 129, Port Haverigg Holiday Village, Millom). Status of some areas may change.*
■ Freshwater lagoon, scrub, calcareous grassland.
■ New reserve on site of old mine with developing flora on waste land. Fresh lake by sea good for wind-blown migrants and wintering wildfowl.
RSPB

A:4 DUDDON SANDS

Near Broughton in Furness; *approached from A595 at various points.*
■ Estuarine sand banks, salt-marsh, stream.
■ Important wader site; also wildfowl.

Kirkby Pool for *Odonata.* Only venture on to sands with local advice – some areas are dangerous.

A:5 ROUDSEA WOOD & MOSSES★

Near Haverthwaite; *turn off B5278 just S of Leven Bridge at Low Wood; track leads to reserve entrance with parking opposite. NCC permit needed. Map and leaflet available.*
■ Oak woodland on contrasting rock, valley mire, raised bog.
■ An NNR consisting of a band of oak woodland on carboniferous limestone separated by a narrow valley mire from oak woodland on acidic Bannisdale slates. The plants in each community illustrate the contrast well, while the diversity of habitat results in a rich invertebrate fauna. The raft spider occurs on the mosses, and notable *Lepidoptera* include clouded ermine, large heath butterfly, marsh oblique-barred snout, scarce prominent, silver hook and red-necked footman. Notable plants include large yellow-sedge, lesser tussock-sedge, lily-of-the-valley, columbine, fly orchid, bird's-nest orchid, bog-rosemary. **Reptiles** Adder, grass snake. **Mammals** Dormouse, red squirrel, roe deer.
NATURE CONSERVANCY COUNCIL

B:1 WHITBARROW SCAR & WITHERSLACK WOODS★★

Near Kendal; *paths on to the Scar from Row, The Howe, Mill Side or Witherslack Hall; also from car park at quarry by Raven's Lodge. CTNC permit required for Hervey Reserve.*
■ Mixed woodland, limestone grassland, weathered limestone pavement.
■ The Scar is a prominent, low limestone ridge. The W side comprises cliffs above high forest situated on limestone and, in Witherslack Woods, siliceous rocks. Much of this can be viewed from adjacent roads and footpaths. The woodland, notable for the mature oaks and ash, are also well known for *Lepidoptera.*

The top of the Scar is largely a CTNC reserve forming a gently sloping open grassland zone with scrub juniper, birch and ash. The limestone outcrops as barely fissured pavement which has weathered into a loose scree. Blue moor-grass is dominant, with abundant common rock-rose and, on the W side, hoary rock-rose. Hard shield-fern and rigid buckler-fern occur in hollows. *Lepidoptera* include high-brown and pearl-bordered fritillary, holly blue and grayling.

The woodland is mixed with open scrubby areas and limestone outcrops. Rich fungus flora.
CUMBRIA TRUST FOR NATURE CONSERVATION

B:2 SCOUT SCAR & CUNSWICK SCAR★

Near Kendal; *approach on footpaths from Kendal-Underbarrow road.*
■ Limestone scarps, cliffs, grassland.
■ Easy access to rich limestone flora. Blue moor-grass dominant over shattered pavement, cliffs covered with common and hoary rock-rose. **Plants** Lesser butterfly-orchid, bloody crane's-bill, small scabious, pale St John's-wort, squinancywort, fingered and bird's-foot sedge.

B:3 GRIZEDALE FOREST

Near Satterthwaite; *information centre marked on map.*
■ Woodland, tarns, becks.
■ Deer watching and photo hides. **Birds** Goshawk, crossbill, buzzard, woodcock, sparrowhawk, redpoll.
FORESTRY COMMISSION

B:4 CLAIFE HEIGHTS★

Near Hawkshead; *footpaths from Far Sawrey or Red Nab (car parks).*
■ Mixed woodland, small mires, tarns.

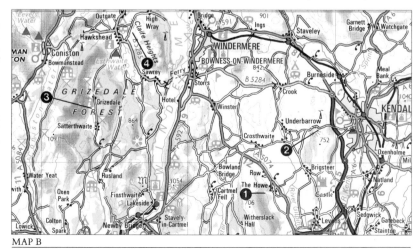

MAP B

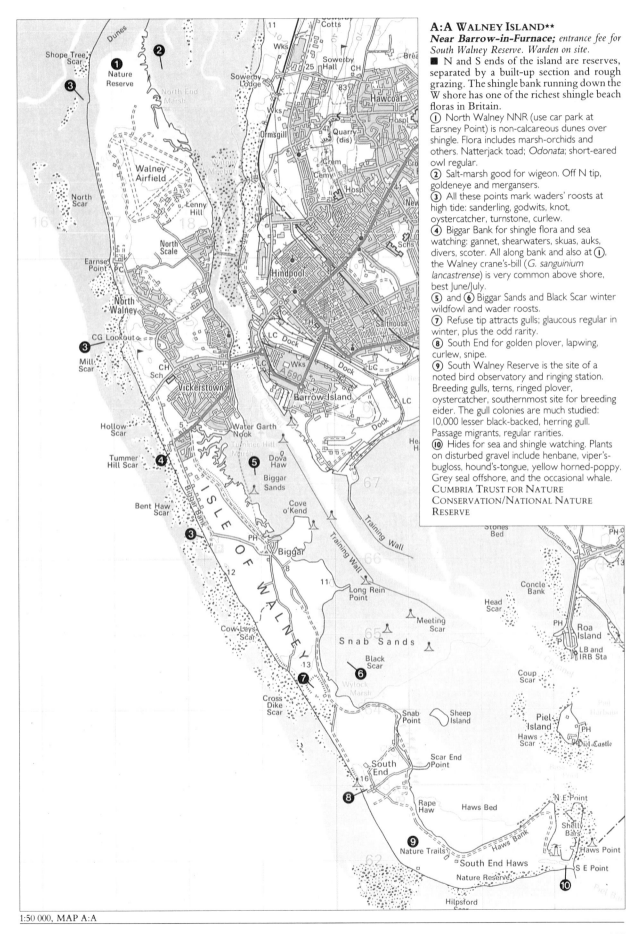

A:A WALNEY ISLAND**

*Near **Barrow-in-Furnace;** entrance fee for South Walney Reserve. Warden on site.*

■ N and S ends of the island are reserves, separated by a built-up section and rough grazing. The shingle bank running down the W shore has one of the richest shingle beach floras in Britain.

① North Walney NNR (use car park at Earsney Point) is non-calcareous dunes over shingle. Flora includes marsh-orchids and others. Natterjack toad; *Odonata*; short-eared owl regular.

② Salt-marsh good for wigeon. Off N tip, goldeneye and mergansers.

③ All these points mark waders' roosts at high tide: sanderling, godwits, knot, oystercatcher, turnstone, curlew.

④ Biggar Bank for shingle flora and sea watching: gannet, shearwaters, skuas, auks, divers, scoter. All along bank and also at ①, the Walney crane's-bill (*G. sanguinium lancastrense*) is very common above shore, best June/July.

⑤ and ⑥ Biggar Sands and Black Scar winter wildfowl and wader roosts.

⑦ Refuse tip attracts gulls; glaucous regular in winter, plus the odd rarity.

⑧ South End for golden plover, lapwing, curlew, snipe.

⑨ South Walney Reserve is the site of a noted bird observatory and ringing station. Breeding gulls, terns, ringed plover, oystercatcher, southernmost site for breeding eider. The gull colonies are much studied: 10,000 lesser black-backed, herring gull. Passage migrants, regular rarities.

⑩ Hides for sea and shingle watching. Plants on disturbed gravel include henbane, viper's-bugloss, hound's-tongue, yellow horned-poppy. Grey seal offshore, and the occasional whale.

CUMBRIA TRUST FOR NATURE CONSERVATION/NATIONAL NATURE RESERVE

1:50 000, MAP A:A

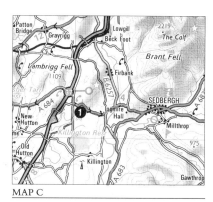

MAP C

■ Birdwatching in open woodland, also on tarns in winter; mires and meres good for insects. *Odonata* well represented. **Birds** Lesser spotted woodpecker, pied flycatcher, siskin, goldeneye. **Mammals** Red squirrel. **Insects** Downy emerald, black darter.
NATIONAL TRUST

C:1 KILLINGTON RESERVOIR
Near Sedbergh; approach and view on minor road S from A684, just E of M6 junction 37.
■ Lake with islands.
■ Good birdwatching, especially passage migrants; large resident flock of Canada geese. Best spring, autumn and winter. **Birds** Barnacle and greylag geese, whooper swan, red-breasted merganser, goosander.

MAP D

D:1 DRIGG DUNES & IRT ESTUARY★
Near Ravenglass; cross railway at Drigg; park at Drigg foreshore. CCC permit required for reserve. Or view from Ravenglass.
■ Sandy estuary, dunes, salt-marsh.
■ Passage waders and wintering wildfowl, breeding gulls and terns, dune flora and insects. Check high tide roost along the Irt. **Birds** Godwits, little stint, sanderling, green sandpiper, red-breasted merganser, kingfisher, grey plover, greenshank, turnstone.
CUMBRIA COUNTY COUNCIL

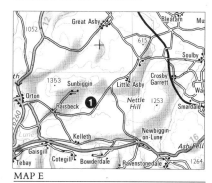

MAP E

E:1 SUNBIGGIN TARN & MIRES★
Near Tebay; park on road near tarn; view from road.
■ Calcareous mire complex with tarns.
■ A nationally important site: water rises through calcareous rock and forms slightly alkaline springs rich in dissolved ions. Calcicole plants thrive beside those typical of the acidic soils all round on the glacial drift. Some rare snails. **Plants** Bird's-eye primrose, grass-of-Parnassus, fragrant, marsh- and spotted-orchids. **Birds** Ruff, whimbrel, gadwall, greenshank, green sandpiper, raptors.

F:1 ST BEES HEAD
Near Whitehaven; park in St Bees; footpath along cliff top.
■ Coastal cliff.
■ Sea-bird cliffs with the only English mainland colony of black guillemot. Sea-watching and spring passage of note. **Birds** Puffin, razorbill, guillemot, fulmar, kittiwake, terns, passerines on passage.
ROYAL SOCIETY FOR THE PROTECTION OF BIRDS

G:1 GRUNE POINT
Near Silloth; approach by Dicktrod Lane, Skinburness.
■ Shingle bank, estuarine sands, scrub.
■ The point projects into the entrance of Moricambe Bay giving view over the flats and salt-marshes of Skinburness. The shingle bank and Silloth promenade offer good sea-watching; passage passerines in the scrub. Best Sep-May. **Birds** Shearwaters, terns, waders, gannet, raptors, owls.

G:2 CARDURNOCK FLATTS & MORECAMBE BAY
Near Bowness-on-Solway; minor road W of Carlisle follows shore of Solway Firth after Burgh by Sands, continuing to Anthorn.
■ Estuarine shores.
■ Bird-watching points at Bowness, Herdhill Scar, Cardurnock Flatts, and from aerials beside Morecambe Bay. River Wampool can be viewed from Anthorn. Best Sep-May. **Birds** Divers, godwits, ruff, sanderling, grey plover, short-eared owl, raptors.

G:3 DRUMBURGH MOSS
Near Carlisle; track SW from Drumburgh centre, reserve in 0.8 mile (one km) on left, just past Moss Cottage. CTNC permit required.
■ Raised bog, heath and *Sphagnum*, open pools.
■ Unspoilt remnant of Solway raised bogs. **Birds** Merlin, short-eared and barn owls, redshank, curlew, snipe. **Plants** Lesser butterfly- and spotted-orchids, cranberry, white beak-sedge. **Reptiles** Adder. **Insects** Large heath, black darter.
CUMBRIA TRUST FOR NATURE CONSERVATION

G:4 BOWNESS-ON-SOLWAY RESERVE
Near Bowness-on-Solway; about 1¼ miles (2 km) W of Bowness, entrance by Campfield Marsh. CTNC permit required.
■ Gravel pit workings, pools, scrub.
■ Pits now densely colonized by plants with a rich insect fauna. Drier zones are habitat for heath plants. **Plants** Greater spearwort, marsh- and spotted-orchids. **Birds** Water rail. **Amphibians** Smooth and great crested newts. **Insects** Four-spotted chaser and other *Odonata*.
CUMBRIA TRUST FOR NATURE CONSERVATION

G:5 LONGTOWN GRAVEL PITS
Near Gretna; view from A6071, and minor road by Dicktree Cottage.
■ River, open water.
■ Taken with the River Esk this is a good bird-watching site, with passage migrants and wildfowl. Rarities often reported. Best Sept-May. **Birds** Peregrine, merlin, little gull, ruff, spotted redshank, water rail, pink-footed goose, migrant swans.

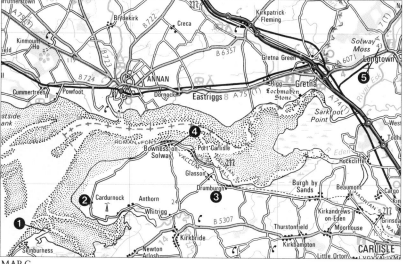

MAP G

A:1 GOD'S BRIDGE

Near Bowes; *park off the A66 and walk S along Pennine Way for around 270 yards (245 m).*

■ Carboniferous limestone intruding into millstone grits.

■ The finest example of a natural bridge in Britain. Look out for moorland birds, including merlin. Brittle bladder-fern can be found growing on the limestone of the bridge. The Stainmore pass is frequently blocked in winter: ring local forecasts for up-to-date information.

A:2 BRIGNALL BANKS*

Barnard Castle; *limited parking at Greta Bridge (NZ 086132, Brignall church (NZ 073133), the track past Moor House Farm (NZ 050173) and the bridge at NZ 035121.*

■ Deciduous woodland, some plantation, limestone gorge.

■ The Greta Valley is wooded on both sides; the plantations of conifers are of limited interest to the naturalist but there is some fine deciduous woodland. The Brignall side is the better, as it gets more sun and has fewer stretches of plantation. The best section is the middle where herb Paris grows under trees covered with oak-moss and *Usnea subfloridana.* Lichen buffs should not miss the old churchyard below Brignall village (abandoned after the Great Plague). Red squirrel, roe deer, redstart, slow-worm and

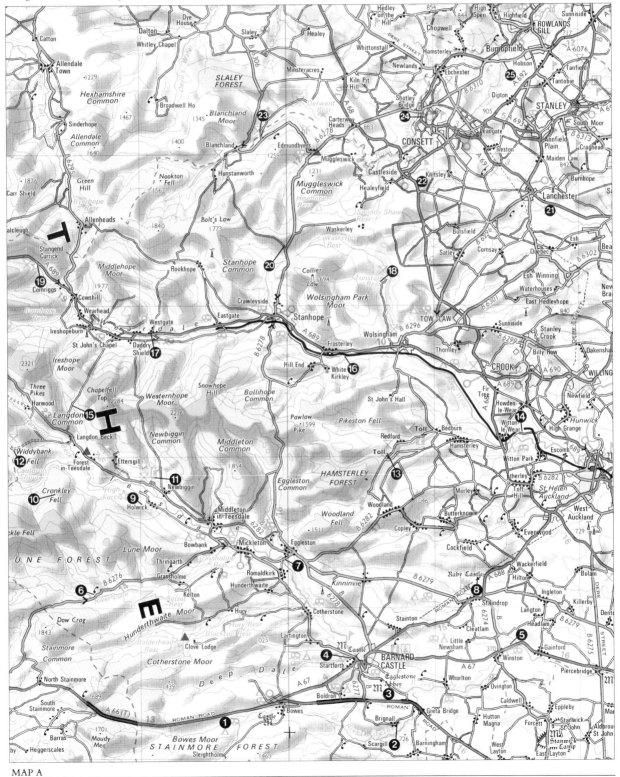

DURHAM

other species typical of the best northern woods are common. The upstream end of the valley is a glacial boulder field with meadow saxifrage and mountain pansy growing among boulders of shap granite.

A:3 EGGLESTONE ABBEY BRIDGE
Barnard Castle; take minor road past Bowes Museum, then first right down to river.
■ Bridge, carboniferous limestone gorge, mixed woodland.
■ The bridge supports a colony of Daubenton's bats which can be seen skimming low over the river at dusk in summer. The river banks are managed as a country park and support an attractive woodland flora (best in May).

A:4 DEEPDALE
Barnard Castle; park on B6277 Lartington road about ½ mile (0.8 km) after Barnard Castle bridge.
■ Deciduous woodland.
■ A pleasant area of managed woodland, mainly oak and beech. Visit in late spring to see good display of commoner woodland flowers; also roe deer, redstart, treecreeper.

A:5 GAINFORD SPA WOOD
Near Gainford; park in lay-by on A67 just E of Winston.
■ Mixed deciduous woodland, upland river.
■ One of the most accessible of the Teesbank woodlands, a pleasant stroll at any time even though it has now lost its wych elms. **Plants** (Mar) yellow star-of-Bethlehem; (Jul) martagon lily; goldilocks buttercup, wood forget-me-not. **Trees** Bird cherry.

A:6 GRAINS O'TH' BECK
Near Middleton in Teesdale; park on B6276 at NY 872212 – don't obstruct entrance to Closehouse Mine – and view from road.
■ Moorland, upland pasture, two upland streams with extensive gravel fans.
■ All the beauty of the moors with none of the effort, good in Apr for breeding birds and in late Aug for colour, scenery and post-breeding flocks.

A:7 SHIPLEY & GREAT WOODS★
Eggleston; keep to footpaths S from bridge at Eggleston (NY 997232), SE from Romaldkirk (NY 996220), N from Cotherstone (NZ 013202).
■ Ancient woodland on acid and limestone rocks.
■ The steep valley sides have prevented commercial exploitation and natural regeneration in clearings has been encouraged by fallen trees. The flora and fauna include many typical woodland species such as red squirrel, woodpeckers and (rare in the North) nuthatch. Herb Paris, wood forget-me-not, goldilocks buttercup, carpets of spring flowers and an impressive lichen flora are all indicators of the wood's antiquity. Molluscs include *Azeca goodalli* and several of the *Limax* slugs. Best in spring or early summer for the flora, high summer for the insects, winter for the mammals.

A:8 RABY CASTLE
Near Staindrop; N off A688; open easter-autumn (entrance fee).
■ Parkland, castle.
■ Spectacular herds of deer in the park and beautiful flora growing on the castle ramparts. The whole estate is good for bats; look

out for moth wings in the main gateway which is used as a feeding roost. **Mammals** Red and fallow deer; pipistrelles, long-eared, whiskered and natterer's bats.

A:9 HOLWICK HAY MEADOWS★
Middleton in Teesdale; follow footpath from Holwick (NY 904270) to Wynch Bridge (NY 903279), then along the river. Don't leave the path.
■ Hay meadow, river, gravels.
■ The hay meadows of Upper Teesdale have never been 'improved' for agriculture and now rank with the machair as the finest left in the country. They are at their best just before the hay is cut, in late Jun or early Jul. Typical species include yellow rattle and great burnet in the drier areas and marsh-orchids and ragged-robin in the damper parts. Melancholy thistle and globeflower are also quite common. Look out for the upland species of bumble-bee, *Bombus monticola* and *B. jonellus*. Expert botanists can find eight species of lady's mantle, including two species found nowhere else in Britain. Shrubby cinquefoil still grows on gravel banks in the Tees, 300 years after John Ray saw it there and first recognized the importance of Upper Teesdale.

Other good places from which to see the Teesdale hay meadows are on the roadside near Langdon Beck Youth Hostel (NY 860304), and the footpaths running SW from Dale Chapel (NY 871294) and from Widdybank Farm (NY 837298).

A:10 CRONKLEY FELL★★
Near Middleton in Teesdale; follow Pennine Way from Holwick or park at Dale Chapel (NY 871294), cross Cronkley Bridge and follow river upstream under Cronkley Scar to the broad path leading up to the fell top. Don't enter enclosures.
■ Sugar limestone grassland, heather moor, hay meadows.
■ This unique site, best visited in summer, has Arctic/Alpine plant species growing alongside southern species, and the fences on the fell top contain hoary rock-rose, thyme, spring sandwort, northern bedstraw and several other rarities. The fences are to keep sheep, walkers and naturalists off an extremely fragile habitat. Even the grasses are special: blue moor-grass and crested hair-grass are important components of the sward. Other upland wildlife include red grouse and emperor moths in the heather. The block scree of Cronkley Scar supports ring ouzels, wheatears and parsley fern.

A longer return route following the river takes you through some of the finest juniper in Britain.
NATURE CONSERVANCY COUNCIL

A:11 BOWLEES & GIBSON'S CAVE
Near Middleton in Teesdale; signpost on B6277 to car park and picnic site; visitors centre open 9-5.
■ Disused quarry, limestone grassland, upland stream.
■ The visitor centre provides an excellent introduction to the natural history of Teesdale. In the old quarry, look for redstart, palmate newts and butterwort. Good calcareous grassland flora on the walk up to Gibson's Cave and waterfall includes greater butterfly orchid and the bright yellow fungus, *Tricholoma sulphureum*.
DURHAM COUNTY CONSERVATION TRUST/
DURHAM COUNTY COUNCIL

A:12 WIDDYBANK FELL & CAULDRON SNOUT★★
Near Middleton in Teesdale; car park at Cow Green Reservoir. Keep to metalled path, unless permit obtained.
■ Sugar limestone grassland/flushes, heather moor, whin sill cliffs, lead-rich spoil.
■ Widdybank Fell, together with the spectacular Cauldron Snout waterfall, is one of the most exciting botanical sites in Britain. The reason lies in the unique soil, a coarse, crumbly marble known as sugar limestone. This well-drained, calcareous soil is the home of spring gentians and hair sedge. Lead-rich spoil from old mines allows Alpine penny-cress and spring sandwort to thrive in the absence of competition. Flushes support Scottish asphodel and the unique Teesdale sandwort.

Most of the Teesdale rarities (usually at their best around the end of May) can be seen from the metalled nature trail. **Birds** Red grouse. **Beetles** *Agonum ericeti*.
NATURE CONSERVANCY COUNCIL

A:13 HAMSTERLEY FOREST★
Wolsingham; access via toll road from E leads to large car park with both FC and Durham County Council visitor information centres.
■ Coniferous plantation, deciduous woodland, open grassland, hay meadow, upland becks, moorland.
■ There are more rare animals here than anywhere else in Durham, yet the wood still makes a profit. The key to success has been conservation of blocks of old woodland and other natural habitats. The Bedburn Beck and its tributaries provide a network of corridors for wildlife. You have to be up early for roe deer and very observant to see hawfinch, but redstart, wood warbler, pied flycatcher and red squirrel are easy to find. Hamsterley has the longest list of fungi of any site in the county. **Birds** Nightjar, hawfinch, redstart, pied flycatcher, wood warbler, woodpeckers. **Mammals** Red squirrel, roe deer. **Insects** Small pearl-bordered and dark green fritillaries. **Reptiles** Adder, slow-worm. **Molluscs** Lemon slug, ash-black slug. **Beetles** Green tiger beetle.
FORESTRY COMMISSION

A:14 WITTON-LE-WEAR★
Near Bishop Auckland; open access to individuals during daylight hours; parties by appointment; track to reserve signposted one mile (1.5 km) E of Witton-le-Wear village.
■ Disused and flooded gravel workings, willow scrub, alder carr, river gravels.
■ Popular with local naturalists because the variety of habitats ensures that there is always something to see. The large expanse of water (an uncommon habitat in the North) attracts a variety of wildfowl including mute swan and gadwall, and supports good populations of frogs and toads, as well as nine species of dragonfly and damselfly, water spiders and smooth newts. Grey wagtail and common sandpiper both breed.
DURHAM COUNTY CONSERVATION TRUST

A:15 LANGDON COMMON
Near Middleton in Teesdale; take minor road from St John's Chapel to Langdon Beck and park on roadside above first cattle grid.
■ Grass moor, heather moor with upland pasture, small conifer plantation.
■ One of the few places to watch black grouse without disturbing them – provided

you stay in your car. Best times are early morning or evening, Apr–early Aug.

A:16 HAREHOPE QUARRY
Frosterley; cross Tilcon bridge on E side of Frosterley, bear left and park beyond farmhouse. Permits fron Tilcon, Portobellow Rd, Birtley, Tyne & Wear.
■ Disused carboniferous limestone quarry, upland beck; limestone grassland, willow scrub.
■ An enormous site with good populations of breeding waders along the stream and an impressive limestone flora. Frosterley Marble, a coral-rich limestone, was mined here and large boulders can still be seen. *Please do not attempt to chip at them.*
TILCON

A:17 SLIT WOODS
Westgate; take minor road running N, and follow footpath along beck.
■ Beck, deciduous woodland, shallow ponds on carboniferous limestone.
■ A fine example of an oak/ash wood with some interesting pools created by former lead mines. Watch out for hidden mine shafts. **Mammals** Badger, mink. **Birds** Grey wagtail. **Plants** Ivy-leaved bellflower.

A:18 TUNSTALL RESERVOIR & BLACKSTONE BANK
Wolsingham; turn off A689 on to minor road by Wolsingham Grammar School, and park by side of reservoir. Walk across dam for access to Blackstone Bank.
■ Reservoir, oak woodland, moorland.
■ The open water is important for breeding toads in spring and frequently persuades ospreys to stay in late summer. Blackstone Bank is a fine example of an upland sessile oak wood; it leads out on to the heather moor of Salter's Gate. **Birds** Wood warbler, redstart, osprey. **Reptiles** Adders. **Butterflies** Green hairstreak.
NORTHUMBRIAN WATER AUTHORITY

A:19 UPPER WEARDALE
Near Cowshill; take A689 to Killhope Wheel and park on roadside.
■ Upland stream, hay meadows, lead-rich spoil, moorland.
■ Killhope Wheel, a major industrial archaeological tourist attraction (well worth a visit to see its lead ore processing machinery) is a good starting point to explore this area, best visited in early summer. Though not as spectacular as those in Teesdale, the Weardale hay meadows are still very interesting. The spoil heaps round Killhope Wheel are botanically interesting and the surrounding moorland holds a wide variety of upland birds. A splendid overthrust fault, the Burtreeford Disturbance, is visible in the beck at Cowshill. **Plants** Spring sandwort, Alpine penny-cress (on soil heaps), moonwort, wood crane's-bill, early-purple orchids, *Alchemilla acutiloba* (hay meadows).

A:20 MUGGLESWICK COMMON
Near Consett.
■ Heather moorland, small acid pools.
■ Typical Pennine Moors; even the bluebottles are upland species. If visiting in Aug or Sep (best time for the heather), go on a Sunday to avoid the grouse shoots. **Birds** Red grouse, merlin, oystercatcher, dunlin, golden plover, curlew, wheatear. **Insects** Golden-ringed dragonfly, *Bombus monticola* and *B. jonellus*. **Plants** Long-leaved sundew.

A:21 MALTON
Near Lanchester; park at picnic site signposted off A691.
■ Birch scrub, mature willows and elms, beechwood, upland stream, gorse scrub, low/herb/lichen heath on shale, pond.
■ Best visited in Apr and May for birds and Jul for flowers and butterflies. **Birds** Redstart, dipper, tree pipit, sparrowhawk, warblers, woodpeckers. **Plants** Northern marsh-orchid, lesser skullcap. **Mammals** Noctule, pipistrelle, Brandt's bats, roe deer, badger. **Butterflies** Dingy skipper.
DURHAM COUNTY COUNCIL

A:22 KNITSLEY RAVINE
Near Consett; park at Rowley car park. Follow old railway line, drop down beside viaduct to enter ravine.
■ Alder/birch carr in valley bottom, oak/birch wood with holly on slopes.
■ The valley bottom carr is the best example in Durham, carpeted with marshmarigolds interspersed with globeflower and tussock-sedge (best in late May and Jun). The drier woodland has red squirrel, sparrowhawk and substantial numbers of the commoner woodland birds.

A:23 DERWENT RESERVOIR
Near Consett; car parks at Pow Hill and Carricks. Lay-bys along NW edge.
■ Open water with rough grazing, upland stream, acid bog with heather, conifers.
■ Watch birds from the road rather than the hide (early winter is best). Explore the bog on foot (in summer) avoiding adders (May onwards). **Birds** Goosander, red-breasted merganser, siskin, dipper, heron. **Plants** Bog asphodel. **Insects** Bumble-bees.
NORTHUMBRIAN WATER AUTHORITY

A:24 ST CUTHBERT'S CHURCHYARD, BENFIELDSIDE
Consett; drive up the steep and narrow Church Bank from Shotley Bridge Post Office.
■ Undisturbed grassland on clay.
■ The unusual nature and management of the churchyard has preserved a unique area of grassland with field garlic and marshorchids. You need a strong engine and an efficient handbrake to visit this site which is best in Jun. **Plants** Northern marsh-orchid, wild raspberry, fox-and-cubs.
CHURCH COMMISSIONERS

A:25 PONT BURN WOOD
Near Rowlands Gill.
■ Mixed deciduous woodland.
■ One of the best blocks of woodland – mainly oak with beech and some smallleaved lime, with a good understorey of hazel and holly left in the Derwent Valley, rich in species which demonstrate the wood's ancient origins. **Birds** Nuthatch. **Plants** Sanicle, woodruff. **Mammals** Red squirrel, badger, noctule. **Invertebrates** Lemon slug, Durham slug, pygmy woodlouse (*Trichoniscus pygmaeus*).
WOODLAND TRUST

B:1 HARDWICK HALL COUNTRY PARK
Near Sedgefield; signposted off A177 just outside Sedgefield.
■ Parkland, lake, alder carr, deciduous woodland, conifers.
■ Often over-run, this country park is still a rich site for pond life and species which like old trees in open surroundings. Particularly important for dragonflies, and the boardwalk through the carr is an experience not to be missed.
DURHAM COUNTY COUNCIL

B:2 HURWORTH BURN & CROOKFOOT RESERVOIRS
Near Hartlepool; park at S edge of Hurworth Burn on minor road running E from Trimdon. Follow footpath and old railway track on foot. View Crookfoot from the private road S from NZ 438322; otherwise a permit required.
■ Open water, grassland.
■ The best places to watch winter wildfowl, including rarer visitors, in Durham. The *Typha* swamp to the S of Hurworth Burn is also worth investigating for water rail and turtle dove in the surrounding trees.
HARTLEPOOL WATER

B:3 HARTLEPOOL HEADLAND ROCKS & FOSSIL FOREST
Hartlepool; park along roadsides near coastguard's lookout.
■ Limestone headland, peat beds.
■ Important landfall for passerine winter migrants, easily observed from headland. Submerged peat beds yield sub-fossil plants, Neolithic artefacts. **Birds** Yellow-browed warbler, bluethroat, wryneck, pied flycatcher, redstart, ring ouzel, skuas, divers, terns, sea duck, auks, gulls. **Plants** Seamilkwort, sea fern-grass, sea-spurrey, buck's-thorn plantain, fucoid seaweeds.

B:4 ROSA SHAFTOE
Near Spennymoor; enter Tudhoe village from B6288, head NW and turn first left after leaving village. Park where road widens and follow footpath into reserve. Bear right after stream.
■ Mixed plantation, hazel understorey.
■ One of the best displays of spring flowers in mid-Durham. **Birds** Wood and grasshopper warblers. **Butterflies** White-letter hairstreak.
DURHAM COUNTY COUNCIL
CONSERVATION TRUST

B:5 CRIMDON DENE MOUTH
Near Hartlepool; ignore the caravan park; park and walk down to the shore. Turn N to look at the magnesian limestone cliffs, S to dunes.
■ Dunes, brackish pools, magnesian limestone cliffs.
■ Rich sand dunes with five species of spotted- and marsh-orchids (late Jun), burnt orchid and the only known sand-dune colony of the rare giant millipede *Cylindroiulus londinensis* (late May). The brackish pool attracts waders, particularly sanderling, and gulls (Jul onward) including little gulls from B:6 and wintering Mediterranean gull.

B:6 CASTLE EDEN DENE*
Near Peterlee; enter from Castle Eden Church (NZ 428384) or the visitor centre at Oakeshott Lodge (signposted). For access to Dene Mouth, park by A1086 and walk under viaduct.
■ Mixed woodland, magnesian limestone, cliff-top grassland.
■ The wooded denes which cut through the magnesian limestone of the the Durham coast between Sunderland and Hartlepool are a feature unique to the county. Castle Eden Dene is the largest and has been popular with visitors since it was first opened to the public in 1850. The dene is now an NNR and the information centre at Oakeshott Lodge provides background information.
NATURE CONSERVANCY COUNCIL

DURHAM

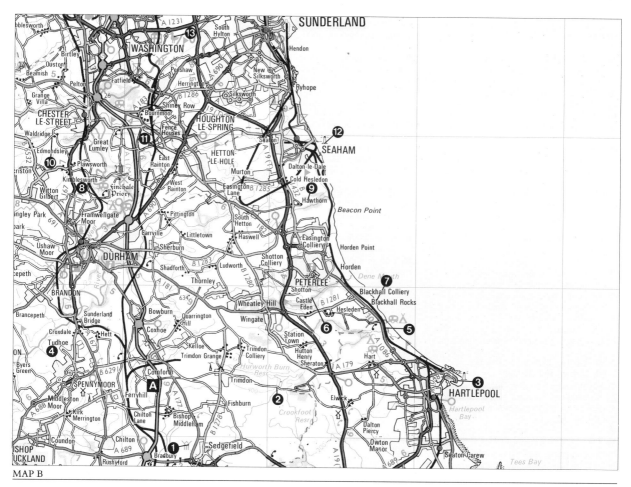

MAP B

B:7 BLACKHALL ROCKS★

Near Peterlee; use County Council cliff-top car park. Walk N to find best areas.

■ Magnesian limeston para-maritime grassland, magnesian limestone cliffs.

■ Looking down from the cliff top on to a beach black with coal waste, then turning round to view a mono-culture of cereals, it is easy to see the precarious nature of para-maritime magnesian limestone grassland. Fertilizer run-off has turned some flower-rich gulleys into beds of hogweed and nettles, but there is still much to see. Headlands support bloody crane's-bill, rock-rose and burnet rose. Each gulley is different: one supports yellow flag, another holds bird's-eye primrose. The most interesting area is Blue House Gill where round-leaved wintergreen, grass-of-Parnassus, butterwort and creeping willow are found. Northern brown argus and cistus forester moths both occur along the cliff top and sea spleenwort grows on the cliff-face at its only Durham station.

DURHAM COUNTY CONSERVATION TRUST

B:8 BRASSIDE PONDS

Durham; park carefully by bus-turning circle outside Frankland Prison. Walk down track W of prison until you see water on your left. View from old railway line or obtain permit from Durham County Conservation Trust to enter reserve.

■ Clay pits, damp birch woodland.

■ The old clay pits provide an aquatic habitat otherwise rare in mid-Durham, making one of the best breeding spots close to the city, good in winter and late spring. The pond is important for aquatic insects, espe-cially dragonflies, and for a unique brown algae (*Pleurocladia palustris*).

B:9 HAWTHORN DENE★

Near Peterlee; follow track from NE end of Hawthorn village. Leave car at reserve entrance (please park considerately).

■ Mixed woodland on magnesian limestone, magnesian limestone grassland, cliffs.

■ The second largest of the Durham denes, famous for its snowdrops in early spring, and in many ways more natural than Castle Eden Dene. Although some alien trees have been planted in the past, these are steadily being removed. The least disturbed and most natural parts of the reserve lie in the valley bottom. The grassland supports snails, including the local *Cernuella virgata*.

DURHAM COUNTY CONSERVATION TRUST

B:10 WALDRIDGE FELL

Near Chester-le-Street; several car parks between Waldridge and Edmondsley.

■ Lowland heath, bog, birch scrub, ash/alder carr, pond.

■ An important relict of once widespread habitat. The moths have been extensively surveyed. The pond contains 20 species of waterbeetle, and there are at least eight species of bumble-bee. **Plants** Royal fern, cowberry, bogbean. **Moths** Emperor moth, orange underwing, ruddy highflyer, toadflax pug, neglected rustic, northern drab, dark spectacle, red carpet, marsh pug.

DURHAM COUNTY COUNCIL

B:11 JOE'S POND

Near Houghton-le-Spring; park on road-side by bridge over stream at Chilton Moor; track signposted Joe's Pond. Keep to paths.

■ Open water, tall fen, neutral grassland, hawthorn scrub.

■ An old brick pit now an important oasis in an area dominated by agriculture and in-dustry. Best when sunny. **Mammals** Water vole. **Birds** Water rail, great crested and little grebes, owls. **Plants** Sea club-rush. **Insects** Southern hawker. **Amphibians** Toad, smooth newt. **Invertebrates** Water spider.

DURHAM COUNTY CONSERVATION TRUST

B:12 SEAHAM HARBOUR & RYHOPE DENE

Seaham; park in Seaham car park and walk along beach to Ryhope Dene.

■ Coastal rocks, cliff, dene.

■ The rocks of Seaham Harbour are famous for the Seaham Formation (Permian limestones) and for their waders such as purple sandpipers and turnstones; visit at low tide. Ryhope Dene is well worth a visit for migrant birds (in autumn) when the conditions are right. **Birds** Mediterranean gull. **Invertebrates** Giant millipede (Ryhope Dene). **Molluscs** Blue-rayed limpet.

FORESHORE/LOCAL AUTHORITY

B:13 WASHINGTON WILDFOWL PARK

Washington; fee to non-WT members.

■ Wader scrapes, ponds, reed-bed, hawthorn scrub.

■ There is more to Washington than the wildfowl collection: the wild areas attract waders; 136 species of *Lepidoptera* recorded.

WILDFOWL TRUST

B:A MAGNESIAN LIMESTONE GRASSLAND: A SERIES OF SITES

① THRISLINGTON PLANTATION★★

Near Ferry Hill; *park on minor road heading S from W Cornforth to Bishop Middleham. Footpath starts about 300 yards (275 m) S of Stob Cross. Permit needed off the footpath.*

■ Magnesian limestone, grassland, scrub.

■ This NNR is the finest area of magnesian limestone grassland in Britain, the only large primary area left unploughed, thanks to a (fortunately unsuccessful) attempt at the turn of the century to establish a larch plantation. Look out for blue moor-grass and other northern species such as dark-red helleborine and mountain-everlasting, growing happily alongside southern species such as columbine, fragrant orchid and perennial flax. These, added to calcareous species – salad burnet, quaking grass, kidney vetch – and neutral grassland species – yellow rattle, cowslip – make this a wonderfully colourful habitat, at its best in Jun and Jul.

As well as enjoying the plants, look out for northern brown argus, snails (abundant rather than diverse) and glow-worms.

STEETLEY MAGNESITE

② BISHOP MIDDLEHAM QUARRY★★

Sedgefield; *roadside parking. Permit required by non-Trust members.*

■ Disused magnesian limestone quarry.

■ Not a primary habitat, but some original grassland left round about, so that it has been colonized by characteristic magnesian lime-stone species. It is the best place in Britain to see dark-red helleborines (in Jul). Other interesting plants are northern marsh-, common spotted- and fragrant orchids and spiny restharrow; and, to N end of quarry, crested hair-grass and blue fleabane. Look out also for northern brown argus and the attractive heath snail, seldom found in northern Britain.

DURHAM COUNTY CONSERVATION TRUST

③ RAISBY QUARRY★

Near Coxhoe; *take B6291 E, then minor road to right. Parking by wood. Permit required for non-Trust members.*

■ Disused magnesian limestone quarry, calcareous dunes, elm wood.

■ Another good dark-red helleborine site but most notable for the bee and frog orchids on the valley floor and the attractive flora of the enormous 'dunes' of fine limestone waste: musk thistle, viper's-bugloss, blue fleabane and others.

Watch out for pied flycatcher and little owl (both breed in the area), stoat and, among the wych elms, white-letter hair-streak butterflies.

Nearby, at ④, is a roadside bank with an attractive flora which includes sanfoin at its absolute northern limit.

DURHAM COUNTY CONSERVATION TRUST

⑤ TOWN KELLOE BANK★

Just E of Town Kelloe; *park on verge. Access is through gate 200 yards (180 m) on right* down track to Carr House Farm. Permit required by non-Trust members.

■ Magnesian limestone bank with flushes.

■ The biggest display of birds'-eye primroses in Britain (late May-Jun), growing with butterwort and glaucous sedge. Look out for wild gooseberry.

DURHAM COUNTY CONSERVATION TRUST

⑥ WINGATE QUARRY

Near Wheatley Hill; *signs from B1278.*

■ Disused magnesian limestone quarry, old grassland, hawthorn scrub, ponds.

■ One of the best magnesian limestone sites for animals: the hawthorn scrub attracts thrushes in the autumn and blackcaps in winter; two ponds support four species of damselfly and great crested newts; and butterflies – common blues, large skippers, small heaths – make up in number for their lack of diversity.

DURHAM COUNTY COUNCIL

⑦ CASSOP VALE

Thornley; *park opposite club; take footpath down into vale.*

■ Magnesian limestone grassland, ash/elm woodland, pond.

■ Of particular interest because of the woodland along the southern edge which hides globe flower and the pond, trapped in a clay bowl at the bottom of the vale, which is good for dragonflies and covered with a raft of bogbean in summer.

NATURE CONSERVANCY COUNCIL

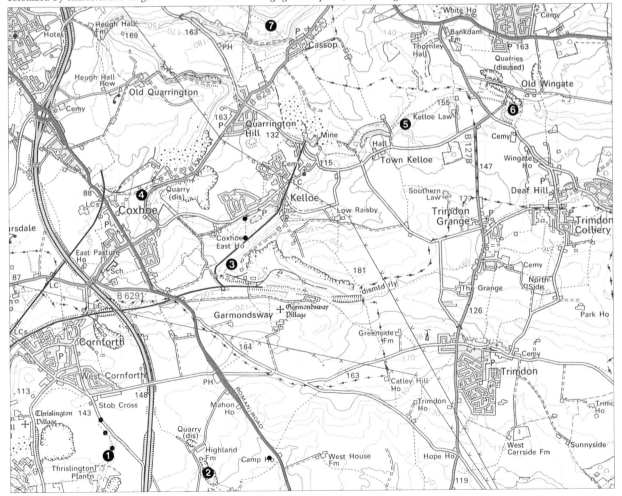

Piebald **oystercatchers** (above), with their
loud piping whistle, are familiar birds around
Britain's coastline, feeding on cockles, mussels
and crabs. Vast flocks winter on estuaries and
mudflats, dispersing in spring to breed on
sandy, shingle or rocky shores. Visitors
unwittingly disturb some beach-nesting birds,
but in the last 20 years many oystercatchers
have started using river shingle banks as
alternative nesting habitats.

Harvest mice (right) live in coarse grass,
often at the base of hedgerows, invading corn
fields in summer to feed. Weighing 1/5 oz
(6-7gm), they are one of Europe's smallest
mice and are very agile, climbing among plant
stems using their tail as an extra limb to grasp
the stalks. Their main breeding period is Aug-
Sep, when a spherical nest woven from grass
leaves is built well off the ground.

CLEVELAND

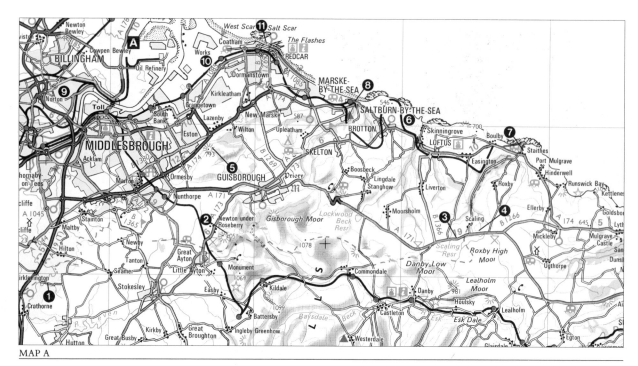

MAP A

A:1 RIVER LEVEN VALLEY

Near Yarm; *limited parking at river bridge on road from Yarm to Middleton-on-Leven. Keep to footpaths.*

■ Ash/elm/hazel wood, stream, old pasture.

■ Attractive valley flanked by floristically rich woods; good riverine and woodland bird communities. Castle Hill has herb-rich grassland and associated invertebrates. **Plants** Toothwort, early-purple orchid, betony.

A:2 ROSEBERRY TOPPING*

Near Great Ayton; *car park just S of Newton village under Roseberry. Care needed on steep paths.*

■ Moorland, inland cliff face, deciduous woodland.

■ Classic geological site in middle of Jurassic rocks containing fossil plant beds, good example of acid woodland with wet and dry phases in ground flora.
NATIONAL TRUST

A:3 SCALING RESERVOIR

Near Staithes; *access to Waupley Moor and Scaling Reservoir from A171 by Scaling Dam. Access to woodland by footpaths at intervals along minor road from Scaling to Staithes.*

■ Reservoir, moorland, ash/elm/oak woodland.

■ Two becks run through ancient deciduous woodland dene full of wildlife/conservation interest. Best Apr-Sep. **Plants** Bogbean, marsh-orchids, cottongrass, sedges, ferns, bryophytes. **Mammals** Roe deer, fox, squirrel. **Insects** Woodland moths, beetles, dark green fritillary, green hairstreak.

A:4 SCALING DAM*

Near Guisborough; *car park at E end of reservoir, immediately off the Guisborough-Whitby road. Keep to footpath which runs part way round reservoir.*

■ Reservoir, heather moorland, plantation.

■ Important overwintering site for many wildfowl. Part of bank is CTNC reserve.

Fine flora in spring and summer.
NORTHUMBRIAN WATER AUTHORITY/
CLEVELAND TRUST FOR NATURE
CONSERVATION

A:5 ESTON NAB

Normanby; *park at Normanby and Ormesby brickworks picnic site, Flatts Lane, off A171 and follow footpath.*

■ Heather moorland, birch woodland, *Sphagnum/Juncus* mires.

■ An outlier of the N York moors. In the dry grassland and *Sphagnum/Juncus* mires invertebrates and amphibians abound. The fringes of the moor adjoin areas supporting a diverse range of birds. This has been a popular spider-hunting site since the discovery in 1909 of a North American species. *Hypselistes florens.* To date some 190 species have been recorded.

Many fossils and some jet can still be found in the jurassic rock shales of the area's mines and spoil heaps.
CLEVELAND COUNTY COUNCIL

A:6 KILTON WOODS

Loftus; *footpath runs from Loftus to Liverton Mills. Access to Hagg Wood by path from Moorsholm.*

■ Broad-leaved woodland, river valley.

■ This wooded dene runs inland from Loftus, splitting into two arms following Kilton and Hagg becks. It is varied deciduous woodland for most part, elm and ash near the stream, with alder-dominated herb-rich damp flushes characterized by pendulous sedge, ramsons, golden-saxifrage and ferns.

The steep valley sides are very damp and covered in ferns and bryophytes. The dene has a woodland bird community and numerous invertebrates. Of note are the ash-black slug, the snail *Zenobiella subrufescens* and green and white-letter hairstreaks.
WOODLAND TRUST/CLEVELAND COUNTY
COUNCIL/PRIVATE OWNERSHIP

A:7 CLEVELAND
HERITAGE COAST**

Saltburn-Staithes; *park at Saltburn, Skin-*

ningrove or Staithes and follow marked rights of way. Descend cliffs only at proper steps. Foreshore may be cut off by tide.

■ Coastal cliffs, quarries, grassland.

■ The coastal path takes in the highest cliffs in northern England at 650 feet (200 m) on Bouby Head, with large colonies of kittiwake and cormorant, and cliff-nesting house martin.

Waders feed on the rocks below the cliffs at low tide; in autumn the passage of seabirds is best seen from the cliffs. Migrant passerines such as black redstart and ring ouzel shelter in the quarries and hollows of the cliff top, especially in spring and autumn. The disused alum quarries bear fossil-rich Jurassic rock; ammonites are common and fossil marine reptiles have been found. The coastal strip exhibits a mix of heath and herb-rich grassland plants.
CLEVELAND COUNTY COUNCIL

A:8 SALTBURN WOOD
& SKELTON BECK

■ Ancient broad-leaved woodland denes.

■ Rich variety of trees, understorey and spring/summer ground flora. Ancient woodland indicator invertebrates. **Plants** Ferns, fungi.
CLEVELAND NATURE CONSERVANCY
TRUST/PRIVATE OWNERSHIP

A:9 BILLINGHAM
BOTTOMS

Billingham; *park at picnic site signposted off old A19/A139 roundabout.*

■ Beck, water meadows.

■ Watermeadows with a natural wildlife corridor of considerable conservation value. Many marsh plants and insects. **Plants** Pepper-saxifrage, marschp-orchids, valerian. **Birds** (Winter) water rail, jack snipe; grasshopper warblers.
CLEVELAND COUNTY COUNCIL

A:10 SOUTH GARE
& COATHAM SANDS*

Near Redcar; *car park in Tod Point Road at Warrenby or enar Locke Park. Access along*

foreshore from Coatham. CNTC permit required to visit hides on Coatham Marsh.
■ Freshwater marsh, dune slacks, dunes, shore.
■ Wintering wildfowl and waders; staging post for migrants. Dunes and slacks rich in summer flora and invertibrates. **Birds** Sanderling, purple sandpiper, knot, terns, gulls.

Plants Hare's-ear, marsh-orchids, sea-lavender. **Invertebrates** Spiders, harvestmen beetles, flies.
BRITISH STEEL CORPORATION/CLEVELAND NATURE CONSERVATION TRUST

A:11 REDCAR ROCKS
Redcar: park along Redcar seafront and espla- nade. The rocks are submerged at high tide.
■ Intertidal rock exposures, tide pools.
■ Fossiliferous exposures of Jurassic rock in foreshore reefs support communities of marine plants and animals which attract considerable numbers of waders in winter. **Invertebrates** Swimming crabs, sea-lemon, sea-squirts, sea-anemones.

A:A SEAL SANDS & TEES MOUTH**
Adjacent to A178 Port Clarence to Hartlepool road. Access restricted to hides and footpaths.
■ Estuarine mudflats, freshwater pools, dunes, dune slacks.
① Park in Seaton Carew to visit Seaton Dunes and Common, one of the best examples of natural dunes remaining between the Tweed and the Humber. Look out for bloody crane's-bill and purple milk-vetch.
② Extensive growth of sea-buckthorn, food and cover for migrant birds in spring and autumn. In winter, dunes near North Gare attract flock of snow buntings, usually more than 100, and sometimes including Lapland buntings and shore larks. From the breakwater, look for wintering sea duck, divers and auks and, late Jul-late Sep, passage of sea-birds.
③ Dune slacks and freshwater marsh support enormous population of marsh-orchids, including narrow-leaved. Sheltered, sandy

foreshore important for feeding and resting waders in winter.
④ Small car park leads on to Cowpen Marsh NR, used by large numbers of waders and wildfowl, viewed from the raised hide. Greatham Creek's banks support an interesting mixture of salt-marsh and slag-colonizing plants.
⑤ Public hide for viewing the tidal pool, approached along footpaths to S of road.
⑥ Take footpath along creek to Teesmouth Bird Club hide with its commanding view over the intertidal mudflats of Seal Sands. Look for grey and common seals, also many and varied waders and wildfowl; up to 5 per cent of Europe's shelduck can be seen here in winter.
⑦ Pools and scrub along Long Drag attract passerines, waders and wildfowl. Reed-beds are developing: bittern, reed warbler and water rail are now regular.
⑧ From disused allotments approach freshwater pools and reed-beds of Haverton

Hole, one of the few areas of extensive reed-bed in N England and regionally no notable for breeding water rails and reed warblers, and roosting swallows and yellow wagtails. Bitterns, bearded tit, spotted crake and spoonbill are regular visitors. Also an important breeding site for amphibians.
⑨ Saltholme Pool, best viewed from your car with a telescope, has attracted 34 species of wader to date.
⑩ Dorman's Pool is a complex of pools of varying depths. Vegetated areas attract rails; shallow pools are good for waders and deeper water encourages marsh terns to linger. Conditions change quickly, so follow the lead of local bird-watchers. Above all, if they stay in their cars do the same or you may scare off a national rarity.
CLEVELAND COUNTY COUNCIL/
CLEVELAND NATURE CONSERVATION TRUST

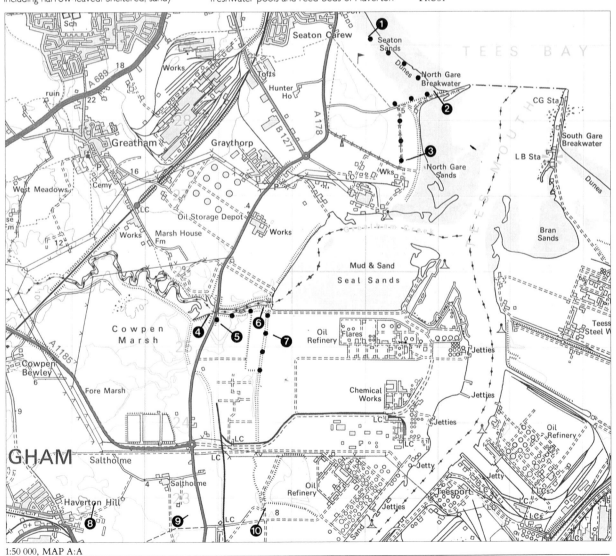

TYNE & WEAR

MAP A

A:1 Shibdon Pond

Blaydon; follow nature trail from Blaydon Baths.

■ Open water, reedmace, reed canary-grass/hairy willowherb marshes, dry neutral grassland.

■ Shibdon Pond is fed by constant temperature water draining from a colliery, so it never freezes solid, making it important for wildfowl. The marsh communities are host to a wide variety of plants, birds, mammals and invertebrates. **Mammals** Water vole, water shrew.

Gateshead Metropolitan Borough Council/Durham County Conservation Trust

A:2 Boldon Flats

Near East Boldon; view from B1299 between East Boldon and Cleadon, and from Moor Lane, which skirts the S edge of Flats.

■ Ancient pasture, water meadow, pools, drainage ditches.

■ Important area of ancient grassland and water meadow supporting an impressive list of plants, birds and wetland insects. **Birds** Jack snipe, curlew, passage waders, wintering ducks, geese and swans, sandpiper. **Plants** Tubular water-dropwort, adder's-tongue, thread-leaved water-crowfoot. **Insects** Dragonflies, water-beetles.

Church Commissioners

A:A Derwent Walk Woodlands*
Near Rowlands Gill.

■ The Derwent Valley has long been a favourite with naturalists. Access used to be by the Derwent Valley branch line; it was closed in 1962, but is now reincarnated as the Derwent Walk.

① Start looking at the natural history of the Derwent Valley at the Thornley Woodland Centre (open daily 9-5): displays and helpful wardens; trails into Thornley and Paddock Hill

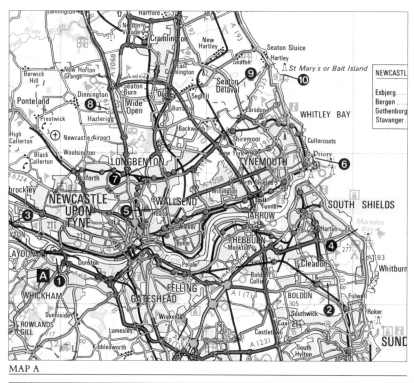

1:50 000, MAP A:A

Woods. These are mature mixed deciduous woods on sandstone. The flora is generally acidic with wood melick, bilberry, common cow-wheat. The trees are mature enough to support red squirrel, wood warbler, nuthatch and woodpeckers. The acidic soil limits the snail fauna, but the slug list is impressive with Durham slug, ash-black slug and lemon slug.
② A crack under Lockhaugh Viaduct is the unusual home of a colony of noctules.
③ Red squirrels are easy to see in the treetops of the avenue leading from Gibbside Chapel and at least three species of bat breed in the area. Gibbside is also an important site for centipedes, millipedes and beetles.
④ Strother Hills is wetter than the other Derwent Valley woods and the woodland floor has some impressive mires. The dominant species are pendulous sedge and marsh-marigold. The site is under-recorded and much remains to be discovered.
⑤ Chopwell Wood is a Forestry Commission plantation on the site of a much older wood. Because the conifers were planted as soon as the previous deciduous woods were felled, woodland species such as bluebell and ash-black slug manage to survive. The Luftwaffe dug some ponds at Chopwell during the Second World War and these are important for amphibians and dragonflies, particularly brown hawker. *Lepidoptera* include triple-spotted and oak-tree pugs.
⑥ Lintzford gives access to the river: kingfisher, water vole and water shrew. Look out for dipper from the Ink Works bridge. As you climb up towards the Derwent Walk, watch for wood melick, tall brome and roe deer. Bear left where the ascending path divides, turn right at the railway and return to the Ink Works by descending when you reach the old station. If you continue on the Derwent Walk you cross into Co. Durham where a pair of impressive viaducts take you to the bottom end of Pontburn Wood.

Gateshead Metropolitan District Council

TYNE & WEAR

A:3 RYTON WILLOWS

Ryton; park on village green. Follow footpath signposted Ryton Willows.

■ Mixed woodland, ponds, salt-marsh, para-maritime grassland.

■ An excellent site at the upper limits of the tidal range of the Tyne. Visit at low tide for salt-marsh plants, high tide for wintering duck. **Birds** Dipper; (wintering) kingfisher, goosander, goldeneye. **Plants** Sea aster, thrift, frog-bit. **Amphibians** Frogs, newts. **Fish** Salmon. **Insects** Dragonflies, old lady moth, water beetles.
GATESHEAD METROPOLITAN BOROUGH COUNCIL

A:4 TYNE & WEAR HERITAGE COAST*

Near South Shields; parking at South Bents, Lizard Point, Marsden Rick, Trow Point. Stay clear of cliff edges.

■ Magnesian limestone cliffs, maritime grassland, rocky/sandy shores.

■ The magnesian limestone meets the North Sea here to produce some impressive cliff scenery and one of Britain's most accessible sea-bird colonies – Marsden Rock. Purple sandpiper and turnstone are common along the rocky shores and sanderling and plovers frequent the sandier shores in winter. Marsden Quarry, long known to botanists for perennial flax, is fast acquiring a reputation amongst birders for migrant passerines. The cliffs near Souter Lighthouse are good for watching silver Y's, painted ladies and other migrant insects fly in off the sea. Fossil sand-dunes at the base of the Permian are exposed at Frenchman's Bay, and as you walk S from there, you walk forward in time on to the Lower magnesian limestone. The snail *Candidula gigaxii* occurs on one of its few northern stations at Trow Point. **Birds** Shearwaters, skuas, fulmar, kittiwake, purple sandpiper; (on migration) woodchat, yellow-browed warbler, bluethroats, red-breasted flycatcher. **Plants** Perennial flax. **Molluscs** *Candidula gigaxii, Pyramidula rupestris.*
GATESHEAD METROPOLITAN BOROUGH COUNCIL

A:5 GOSFORTH PARK

Near Newcastle upon Tyne; approach from A189 N out of Newcastle. Entry by permit only: apply Natural History Society of Northumbria, Hancock Museum, Newcastle upon Tyne (sae).

■ Mixed woodland, open water, reed-bed.

■ One of the most northerly reed-beds in England: 194 species of *Lepidoptera* are recorded.
NATURAL HISTORY SOCIETY OF NORTHUMBRIA

A:6 TYNEMOUTH*

Near Newcastle upon Tyne; park on front for Priory Park or Whitley Bay Cemetery. For fish quay follow signs off A193. Strictly no access to Priors Park – viewed only from car park. Ask one of the uniformed officials. Access to fish quay is open if quay is not busy.

■ Urban tree and shrub plantations, fish quay, sewer outfall, rocky coastline.

■ Tynemouth is of greatest interest to birders in spring and autumn. When the wind is from the E in autumn, nearly every shrub in every garden is worth inspecting, but the favourite spots are Prior's Park (strictly no admittance – view from car park) and Whitley Bay Cemetery (*discreet* bird-watchers tolerated). Tynemouth Priory is over-shadowed by other sea-watching sites further up the coast, but it is still good for skuas and terns in Aug. The fish quay at North Shields and adjacent sewage outfall are a winter Mecca for gulls and those who watch them. Glaucous and ivory gulls join breeding species each winter and the Mediterranean gull is a frequent visitor. **Birds** Iceland gull, migrant warblers, bluethroat, flycatchers, waders.

A:7 JESMOND DENE

Newcastle upon Tyne; approach from A1058 (E-bound only) or several side streets in Jesmond and Heaton.

■ Mature woodland, stream.

■ Go past the pet's corner and walk up into the heart of the Dene. The impressive artificial waterfall is popular with kingfisher and grey wagtail. Avoid at weekends.
NEWCASTLE CITY COUNCIL

A:8 BIG WATERS

Wide Open; in Wide Open turn down metalled track to car park at Ca'Canny pub. Permit required for non-NWT members; apply Hancock Museum, Newcastle.

■ Subsidence pond, old grassland, willow/alder carr, reedmace.

■ The largest subsidence pond in SE Northumberland with an interesting mixture of ancient grassland and swamp flora. Primarily a birdwatcher's reserve, it is best worked from the hides. Best in winter or during migration. **Birds** Whooper swan,

Nuthatch – see A:A, Derwent Walk Woodlands, opposite page.

goldeneye, great crested grebe. **Plants** Early-purple orchid, great burnet.
NORTHUMBERLAND WILDLIFE TRUST

A:9 HOLYWELL POND

Near Seaton Delaval; turn E off A192 in Holywell village, on right-angled bend. Park on E side of housing estate. Follow path N to reserve. Access restricted 1st Apr-31st Jul. Permit required for non-NWT members; apply Hancock Museum, Newcastle.

■ Open water, mixed woodland edge.

■ A regularly wintering flock of whooper swans.
NORTHUMBERLAND WILDLIFE TRUST

A:10 SEATON SLUICE & ST MARY'S ISLAND*

Whitley Bay; St Mary's Island: park in Council car park and walk across causeway (check tide times); Seaton Sluice: park near King's Arms, and follow footpath N (do not turn right after bridge). Sea watch tower accessible only to members of Northumberland and Tyneside Bird Club.

■ Rocky shore, open sea, rough grassland.

■ St Mary's Island is wonderful in autumn as the wader roost starts to build up, terns loiter off the shore and unusual passerines stop off in the cottage gardens. The rocks round the lighthouse are quite rich in shore-life including squat lobster and blue-rayed limpet. Walk up the coast in winter as flocks of snow and Lapland buntings are often disturbed from the rough grassland by hen harriers, merlin and short-eared owls. At New Hartley, head inland along Holywell Dene for passerines, or up the coast to the coast look-out at Seaton Sluice for sea-birds.

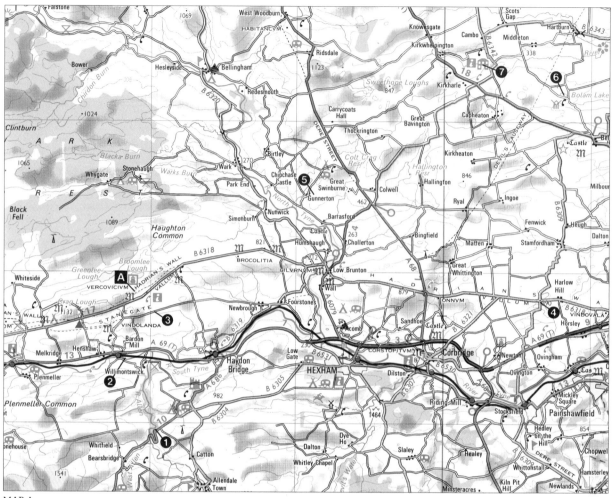

MAP A

A:1 ALLEN BANKS★

Near Hexham. *Turn off A69 one mile (1.5 km) E of Bardon Hill, signposted after ¼ mile (0.5 km), park in NT car park.*

■ Stream, plantation.

■ The whole of the lower Allen Valley is worth a visit. If the NT park is full, explore the middle section (Briarwood Banks) from Plankey Mill or follow the stream down from Cupola Bridge.

The NT has signposted woodland and riverside walks where you can see many woodland birds. The richest areas are the untouched ancient woodlands, in particular Briarwood Banks. These will be of greatest interest to botanists, but the conifer plantations also provide continuous food and cover for a surprising variety of species of mammals and birds. **Birds** Hawfinch, redstart, hawfinch, woodpeckers, spring migrants. **Mammals** Dormouse, red squirrel, roe deer, badger. **Lepidoptera** Purple hairstreak, sprawler. **Plants** Meadow saxifrage, bird's-nest orchid, toothwort, oak fern, broad-leaved helleborine, opposite-leaved golden saxifrage, woodruff.

NATIONAL TRUST/NORTHUMBERLAND WILDLIFE TRUST

A:2 BELTINGHAM SHINGLES★

Near Hexham; *park on roadside ½ mile (0.5 km) W of Beltingham or cross footbridge from Bardon Mill and follow S bank downstream; access at W end of reserve. No dogs, camping, radios. Do not attempt to cross to island.*

■ River with shingle islands, grassland, alder/birch scrub, carr.

■ One of the best examples of metal-rich shingles in England which provides botanists with easily accessible examples of mountain species. High concentrations of lead and zinc, probably washed down as a result of mining in the Pennine dales, prevent lowland species from colonizing, but seeds of plants otherwise found only on mountain tops or the coast are also washed down and thrive.

The shingle banks provide nest sites for a variety of waders and the scrub holds important populations of warblers, including grasshopper and sedge, which are local in the North Country. Goosander is frequent, and the South Tyne is noted for its salmon and brown trout. **Plants** Mountain pansy, Alpine scurvy grass, Alpine pennycress, spring sandwort, melancholy thistle, thrift, monkey flower, northern bedstraw. **Birds** Goosander, oystercatcher, redshank, common sandpiper, dipper, woodcock, warblers. **Fish** Salmon, brown trout. **Lepidoptera** 163 species including large ear, streamer, puss moth, sallow kitten.

NORTHUMBERLAND WILDLIFE TRUST

A:3 MUCKLE MOSS

Near Hexham; *park at E end of plantation. Follow woodland edge S, into bog in corner of field. Permit required: apply NWT.*

■ Acid bog, heath, 'patterned mire'.

■ Patterned mire unique in Britain; rests on impervious shale and supports the rare bog-moss *Sphagnum majus*. The site is well known for insects – beetles, flies and dragonflies. Uneven ground; watch out for adders. **Plants** Bog-rosemary, sundew. **Dragonflies** Black darter, golden-ringed, keeled skimmer. **Lepidoptera** Large heath, scarce silver-lines, wood tiger, emperor moth, Manchester treble-bar. **Flies** Giant horsefly *Tabanus sudeticus*.

NORTHUMBERLAND WILDLIFE TRUST

A:4 WHITTLE DENE RESERVOIR

Near Corbridge; *view from Military Road (B6318) and B6309; roadside parking on B6309.*

■ Reservoir, grassland.

■ An important and easily accessible birdwatching site along the Tyne Valley flyway. Regular smew in winter. **Birds** (Winter) smew, red-breasted merganser, goosander, passage waders.

NEWCASTLE AND GATESHEAD WATER COMPANY

A:5 GUNNERTON NICK★

Near Hexham; *park in Gunnerton, walk E on rough lane, through gate into reserve. Permit required; apply NWT.*

■ Disused quarries.

■ The juxtaposition of whinstone and limestone grasslands supports an exciting range of plants. The interface between the Whin Sill and fossil-rich limestone is of great geological interest. The quarry faces are

dangerous. Look out for the sandy carpet moth and an uncommon woodlouse, *Porcellio spinicornis*. **Plants** (Whinstone) knotted and hare's-foot clovers, petty whin, dyer's greenweed, parsley fern, crow garlic, crested hair-grass; (limestone) meadow saxifrage, hoary plantain, six species of crane's-bill, rock-rose.
NORTHUMBERLAND WILDLIFE TRUST

A:6 BOLAM LAKE
Near Belsay; follow minor road N from Belsay, park in County Council car parks.

■ Open water, mixed woodland, grassland.
■ Bolam is noted for its hungry, hand-tame birds, which hop around the car in winter. Because of the variety of woodland habitats it is also good for fungi. The lake supports waterfowl and is the only site in Britain for the American water hog-louse *Asellus communis*. An exceptional site for the photographer. **Birds** Nuthatch, finches, buntings, six species of tit, great crested grebe. **Beetles** *Pterostichus aethiops*.
NORTHUMBERLAND COUNTY COUNCIL

A:7 WALLINGTON HALL
Near Cambo/Ponteland; follow NT signposts from A696 and B6342.
■ Parkland.
■ A great place to watch the birds and bats that appreciate old, mature trees. The Hall houses an intriguing collection of marine shells and it is worth looking round the gardens for interesting plants such as false thorow-wax. **Birds** Hawfinch, nuthatch, woodcock. **Mammals** Noctule, whiskered bat, pipistrelle. **Plants** False thorow-wax.
NATIONAL TRUST

A:A HADRIAN'S WALL
& THE BORDER LOUGHS★
Near Haltwhistle; permit required to approach edge of all loughs.
■ Whinstone crag, oligtrophic lakes, poor fen, whinstone/carboniferous limestone grassland.
① Start at Housesteads Fort. When the Romans built their wall from the Tyne to the Solway they made maximum use of the Great Whin Sill, a massive dolerite dyke.
Head W along the wall through the sycamore wood; from here you can see the Whin Sill thrusting through the waves of limestone escarpments that run parallel to the wall. Crag Lough lies ahead; it can be approached from this direction, but if time is limited, retrace your steps.
② Crag Lough (NT) can be reached ③ on foot from the Military Road (B6318) or from Steel Rigg car park. Like all the Border loughs, it is a shallow glacial lake trapped on shale.

The basic habitat is poor fen and swamp carr with reed, bottle sedge, common spike-rush, marsh-marigold and marsh cinquefoil. Enrichment, due to run-off from surrounding limestone, encourages the growth of bogbean, ragged-robin, skullcap and marsh lousewort.
Crag Lough is noted for caddisflies, water-beetles and the mud snail *Lymnaea glabra*.
④ At Grindon Lough (NWT) you can watch teal, wigeon, shoveler, whooper swans and bean, greylag and pink-footed geese from the car.
⑤ The hay meadows at Crindledykes can be viewed from the footpath. Look out for yellow rattle, fairy flax and autumn gentian. The quarry is a NWT nature reserve (permit required) for its limestone flora and the fold and fault features it exposes.
⑥ Halleypike Lough may be reached on foot by the track from Sewing Housesteads or on the roadside. These two smaller loughs do not attract the larger wildfowl as often as their larger neighbours.

⑦ View Broomlee from the track to the S, best approached from Housesteads. It attracts wildfowl in winter and is stocked for fishing but is still important for pond life, including water beetles.
⑧ Greenlee Lough is the largest and the best for whooper swan in winter. It can be reached by the footpath between Cragend and Bonny Rigg Hall; park at Housesteads or Steel Rigg.
⑨ Follow the wall W to Cawfields Crag car park and picnic site. This is an old whinstone quarry, dominated by a superb section through the Whin Sill dyke. Look out for toads in the deep, steep-sided pond, orchids and other whinstone grassland plants.
⑩ Walk up to Walltown Crags, from Carvoran Museum and look out for the wild chives. Legend says these were introduced by the Romans, but the plants are indigenous. The impressive coppery click-beetle *Ctenicera pectinicornis* can be found here.
NATIONAL TRUST/NORTHUMBERLAND WILDLIFE TRUST/NATIONAL PARK

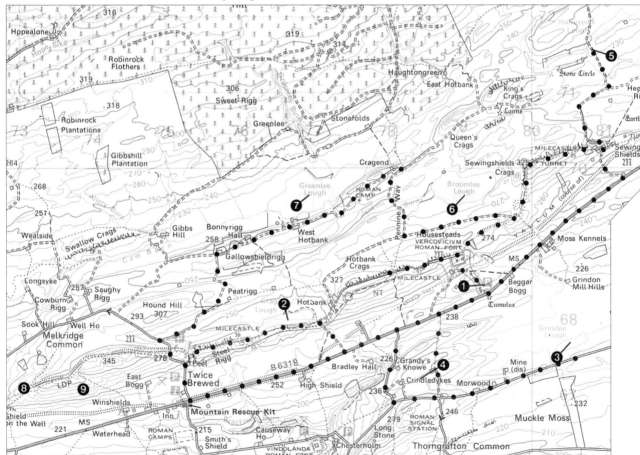

1:50 000, MAP A:A

NORTHUMBERLAND

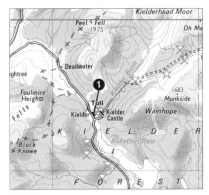

MAP B

B:1 KIELDER*

Near Hexham; car parks and a forest drive (toll) are signposted. Permit required for Kielderhead Moor: apply Northumberland Wildlife Trust.

■ Dense coniferous plantation, open moorland, open water.

■ The few specialist species that live in the monotonous plantation are interesting but frustratingly elusive.

The flooding of the North Tyne valley created in Kielder Reservoir the largest manmade lake in Europe; goosander and pochard are regular visitors.

Kielderhead Moor is wild and rough, with cloudberry, merlin, short-eared owl and red and black grouse. Feral goats roam.

The Forest Drive is chassis-shattering after the first 2 miles (3 km). Best in late spring/summer. **Birds** Goshawk, merlin, black and red grouse, crossbill, owls, siskin, goosander. **Mammals** Pine marten, otter, red squirrel, roe deer. *Lepidoptera* 241 species including coronet, brindled ochre, golden-rod brindle.

NORTHUMBRIAN WATER AUTHORITY/ FORESTRY COMMISSION

C:1 HARBOTTLE CRAG

Near Rothbury; park at information hut , mile (0.5 km) W of Harbottle.

■ Heather moorland, oligtrophic lake, sandstone cliffs, high-level birch/rowan/ oak woodland.

■ A well-managed upland grouse moor, topped by broken crags of Carboniferous fell sandstone above a natural, acid lough. This site provides a microcosm of the Pennine habitats with wildfowl on the lough in winter and a wealth of birds, insects and flowering plants in summer.

Visit in summer or year-round in fine weather, since it is rough and wet underfoot.

NORTHUMBERLAND WILDLIFE TRUST

C:2 CRAG SIDE

Near Rothbury; from which it is signposted.

■ Mature gardens/plantations, lakes.

■ Although Cragside is artificial, in that 150 years ago it was open moorland, it is now mature and provides an attractive alternative to the surrounding uplants. A drive links a series of view points and round walks; there is a good collection of conifers, and rhododendrons are fine in Jun. It is good for fungi, birds (great crested grebe) and the ponds are important for dragonflies (10 species) and water beetles. Visit summer and early autumn.

NATIONAL TRUST

C:3 THRUNTON WOOD

Near Rothbury; park in FC car park and follow trails.

■ Conifer plantation, Carboniferous limestone crags.

■ An under-worked site, best in spring, which will pay dividends for anyone prepared to walk, then sit and listen. **Plants** Crowberry, cowberry. **Birds** Birds of prey, grouse, crossbills. **Mammals** Roe deer. **Insects** *Altica britteni* (a blue or green flea beetle on heather); 8 species of bumble-bee. *Lepidoptera* 87 species recorded.

FORESTRY COMMISSION

C:4 HULNE PARK

Alnwick; take B6346 N; bear left at church, and park in road by gate. Keep to footpath. Permit required: apply estate office or entrance to Alnwick Castle; open weekdays 11 am to sunset.

■ Mature woodland, parkland, river.

■ Hulne Park is enormous and complete exploration would be a long day. But it can also provide a pleasant stroll with opportunity to see some of the typical birds of a

northern estate. **Birds** Hawfinch, redstart, wood warbler, chiffchaff, woodpeckers. **Reptiles** Common lizard. **Plants** Giant bellflower.

DUKE OF NORTHUMBERLAND

C:5 INGRAM VALLEY

Near Rothbury; follow minor road W through Ingram. Park on roadside and follow footpath to Linhope Spout and (for experienced hill walkers) the Cheviot beyond.

■ Upland stream, steep-sided valley, woodland.

■ One of the many pleasant roads leading high into the Cheviot, which is heather covered, while surrounding lavas are covered with mat grass. **Birds** Ring ouzel, siskin, dipper, common sandpiper, green and great spotted woodpeckers; (on the tops) grouse, dotterel. **Plants** Cloudberry, upland plants. *Lepidoptera* Broad-bordered white underwing, northern dart.

D:1 CRESSWELL POND

Near Ashington; view from minor road between Cresswell and Druridge.

■ Pond.

■ This shallow pond, about 55 yards (50 m) from the sea, attracts a wide variety of waders on passage, also wildfowl in winter. **Birds** (Spring/autumn) wood sandpiper, whimbrel, curlew sandpiper, stints; (winter) whooper swan, wigeon.

ALCAN

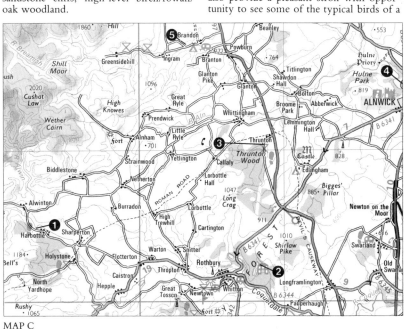

MAP C

MAP D

D:2 DRURIDGE BAY*

Near Ashington; park at Cresswell or in NT car park near Druridge.
■ Dunes, sand shore, submerged sub-fossil forest.
■ One of the most extensive dune systems in E England and usually deserted.

The dunes are noted for their orchids in Jul, particularly dune helleborine, with marsh helleborine in the slacks, and for many coastal moths. The bay is popular with terns once they have finished breeding on the Farne Islands (Aug) and skuas (Sep).

In winter, flocks of snow and Lapland buntings can be found in the dunes and red-necked grebe and sea-duck in the bay.

A low tide following a winter storm is the best time to look at the sub-fossil forest. These peat deposits, dating from 7500 to 3000 BC, reveal stumps and branches, bones and antlers of deer and even Mesolithic implements. Make the most of it – Druridge is the proposed site of a nuclear power station.
NATIONAL TRUST

D:3 HADSTON LAKE

Near Amble; turn off A1068 at Red Row on to minor road. Through East Chevington look for entrance road with large double gates. Park on roadside.
■ Open water, mixed woodland, grassland.

■ A new habitat which is already proving popular with wintering wildfowl. **Birds** Smew, red-breasted merganser, pintail, goldeneye, little stint.
NORTHUMBRIAN WATER AUTHORITY

D:4 HAUXLEY

Near Amble-by-the-sea; access via track from High Hauxley to Low Hauxley road. Permit required: apply Northumbria Ringing Group for access to ringing station; keys to hides from NWT HQ in Newcastle or warden in Low Hauxley.
■ Lagoon reclaimed from open-cast coal site, open foreshore, dunes.
■ Hauxley is situated at the top end of the Druridge dunes, immediately opposite Coquet Island. Jutting out into the North Sea, it is good for migrating birds as well as migratory insects. **Birds** Red-breasted flycatcher, bluethroat, black redstart, terns (including roseate) jack snipe, godwit; (offshore) grebes, divers, scoter, scaup, eider.
NORTHUMBERLAND WILDLIFE TRUST/
NORTHUMBRIA RINGING GROUP (RINGING STATION)

D:5 WARKWORTH GUT

Warkworth; leave Warkworth N, turn E just over the Coquet, follow signs to beach and cemetery; park and follow the Gut on foot. Return along beach. View river also from A1068.

■ Estuary, dune and foreshore, scrub.
■ The estuary always holds something exciting; fishing terns (including the odd roseate tern from Coquet Island) in summer, divers in winter. The Gut is the old course of the river, of interest for sheltering passerines in winter. **Birds** Grebes, divers, terns, snow bunting, twite, short-eared owl, stonechat.

D:6 BOULMER HAVEN

Near Alnwick; park at Boulmer and walk out over exposed rocks. Check tides and watch for slippery seaweed. Dress suitably – you are bound to get wet.
■ Rocky shore.
■ Best in spring and autumn, Boulmer Haven is probably the most interesting site at low tide for rock pool life in NE England. Extensive flats break the face of the waves and, coupled with long, deep pools, give shelter to a wide range of species. The outgoing tide rushes through channels in the rock and dextrous net work can trap a whole variety of fish and other marine creatures – for inspection only. **Fish** Goldsinny, ballan wrasse, poor cod, butterfish, viviparous blenny, two-spot goby, long- and short-spined sea scorpions, Montague's sea-snail, northern rockling.

Pine marten outside den – see B:1, Kielder, opposite.

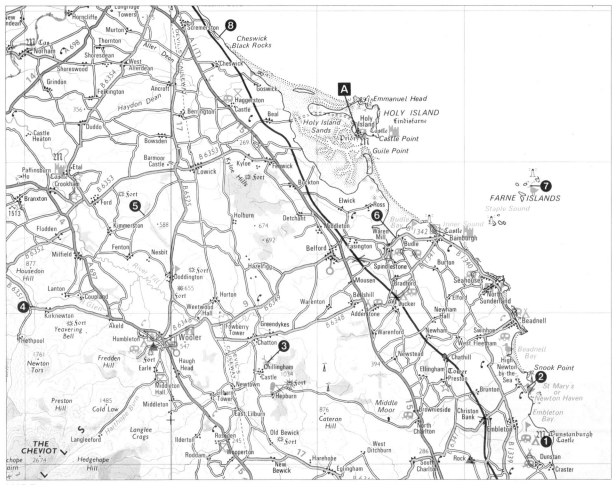

MAP E

E:1 DUNSTANBURGH CASTLE & EMBLETON LINKS

Near Alnwick; castle closed Sun morning, Christmas, Boxing and New Year's Day, and Thur, Fri and Sun mid-Oct to mid-Mar. Walk across links from Embleton or up coast from Craster.

■ Whinstone cliffs, whin, limestone, dune grassland.

■ Dunstanburgh Castle is built on a whinstone promontory. Fulmar, kittiwake and eider nest on and around the castle, and puffin and other auks frequent the sheltered bay at the northern end in summer. It is a good place for sea-watching and the surrounding close-grazed whin and limestone grasslands support an attractive variety of flowers.
NATIONAL TRUST

E:2 LOW NEWTON

Near Alnwick; car park at top of village; follow path S to two hides (one has access for wheelchairs).

■ Dunes, freshwater pool.

■ The proximity of fresh water and the sea attracts an interesting variety of birds including passage migrants in spring and autumn, wildfowl in winter. **Birds** Spotted crake.
NATIONAL TRUST

E:3 CHILLINGHAM PARK★★

Wooler; regular tours with warden.

■ Ancient deer park.

■ The Chillingham wild cattle are justly famous – they have been enclosed at Chil-

lingham since just after the Norman Conquest. Debate rages as to whether they are feral or truly wild. **Mammals** Wild white cattle, fallow deer.

E:4 COLLEGE VALLEY

Near Wooler; take B6351 to W Kirknewton, turn S on to minor road. park at Hethpool; continue on foot.

■ Upland stream, birch/oak/alder woodland, heather moorland.

■ Perhaps the easiest way to tackle The Cheviot. The lower valley track is quite safe, but if you want to make for the fell top, make sure you go well equipped. Choose good weather in late spring to early autumn. The obvious hills of the yellow meadow ant can be found here at one of its very few Northumbrian stations. **Birds** Dotterel, black and red grouse, dipper, golden plover. **Plants** Lesser twayblade, starry saxifrage. **Arachnids** Upland harvestman (*Mitopus ericaeus*). **Reptiles** Slow-worm.

E:5 ROUGHTING LINN

Near Wooler; take minor road W to Milfield off B6525 one mile (1.5 km) SW of Lowick; park on roadside in 2 miles (3 km). Roughting Linn is the scrub area to the N.

■ Scrub grassland, stream.

■ This is one of the largest carved prehistoric slabs in Britain and its historical interest has preserved the surrounding scrub.

E:6 BUDLE BAY★

Near Bamburgh; view Budle Bay from

B1342 between Warren Mill and Bamburgh; approach Ross Links and Ross Back Sands on foot from Ross Farm. Footpath to dunes and foreshore.

■ Mudflats, dunes.

■ At the right tide in winter Budle Bay is covered with wigeon, shelduck and other wildfowl. Take a telescope since the bay is nearly one mile (1.5 km) wide; you may see distant pintail or even whooper swan. Look carefully for light-bellied brent goose from the tiny Svalbard population.

If you have time, park at Ross Farm and walk across the links to the coast. Keep your eyes open for orchids, moths and solitary wasps in summer and for buntings, twite, shore larks and short-eared owls in winter. The coast holds numbers of waders.
NATIONAL TRUST

E:7 FARNE ISLANDS★★

Seahouses; regular half-day trips from Seahouses in summer; arrange longer excursions and winter trips with the boatman. Landing not allowed Oct-Mar and mid-May to mid-Jul.

■ Flat, grassy and steep rocky islands.

■ The Farne Islands were Britain's first nature reserve: St Cuthbert passed an edict protecting the eider duck 1,300 years ago. They provide a wildlife experience equalled only by sites like the Camargue and Ngorongoro crater. When you land on the low, grass-covered Inner Farne, the air is white with terns which try to see you off. Common tern flies low, but Arctic tern may peck as they fly past, so take a hat. You will find

Lindisfarne Castle – see E:A, below.

the birds so approachable that a telephoto lens is sometimes a nuisance. Look out for the jumping spider, *Sitticus pubescens*, on the walls of St Cuthbert's Chapel.

Staple Island is more rocky and provides nest sites for guillemots, razorbills and puffins. Grey seals haul out on Browsman and a pod of orcas regularly visits the Farnes to feed on them in autumn.

In winter, you can get very close to red-necked grebe, velvet scoter and long-tailed duck. **Mammals** Common porpoise.
NATIONAL TRUST

E:8 COCKLAWBURN DUNES

Near Berwick-upon-Tweed; turn off A1 at Scraneston and follow signs to Cocklawburn Beach, road ends at N end of reserve.
■ Limestone spoil, foredunes, shore.
■ An old quarry and lime kiln reclaimed by nature, this site supports many insects and attractive calcicole plants; it is the southernmost mainland station for Scot's lovage.
NORTHUMBERLAND WILDLIFE TRUST

E:A LINDISFARNE (HOLY ISLAND)★★

Near Berwick-upon-Tweed; follow minor road from A1 through Beal to causeway. Not accessible at high tide; the island is cut off for 5 hours out of 12. Open access except farmland where keep to footpaths. Castle and Priory, open to public, give added visitor interest.
■ Dunes, rocky shore, mudflats, shallow pools, hedgerows.
① Tide tables: safe crossing times displayed; ignore at your peril.
② Pull in on bridge (space limited) to look over flats. Whooper swan and light-bellied brent goose in winter; waders all year, especially bar-tailed godwits.
③ Pull off road into dunes – safe except at highest tides – if there is seaweed on road, do not risk it.
④ Dunes and dune slacks important for dune and marsh helleborines; snails abundant, especially *Cernuella virgata*.

⑤ Walk down to The Snook. The cottage is inhabited, but the garden is an important focus for autumn migrants: regular pied flycatcher, black redstart, red-backed shrike and other Scandinavian species.
⑥ Use car park in village and look E over pool, an oasis for waders and good for raptors in winter.
⑦ The hedged lane, known locally as a lonnen, is the largest collection of trees on Lindisfarne and the best place for migrants in autumn. Early arrivals of redwings and fieldfares; passage birds such as red-breasted flycatcher and yellow-browed warbler; best in early Oct.
⑧ The dunes are best in summer; acres of grass-of-Parnassus grow alongside some permanent slacks. Rich in orchids, including dune helleborine; drier areas dominated by pirri-pirri burr. Insects include grayling and dark green fritillary.
⑨ Castlehead Rocks: basking grey seal and

eider offshore. Check the bay to the W for waders.
⑩ The pyramid at Emmanuel Head is a useful point for sea-watching; gannets from Bass Rock can often be seen fishing offshore; the passage of terns in Aug is followed by skuas, Arctic are annual and great and pomarine are regular.
⑪ The pool is another attraction for migrants. Little grebe breeds.
⑫ Look along the limestone shore at low tide for squat lobster and turnstone.
⑬ Fulmar breeds on the castle. Thrift, sea campion and biting stonecrop dominate the natural rock garden below. In winter look over the water for divers, (all three occur regularly), sea duck, great crested and red-necked grebes.
⑭ Waders at low tide.
⑮ A sheltered shore in contrast to ⑫. Look out for 'St Cuthbert's Beads': fragments of fossil sea-lilies.
NORTHUMBERLAND
COUNTY COUNCIL

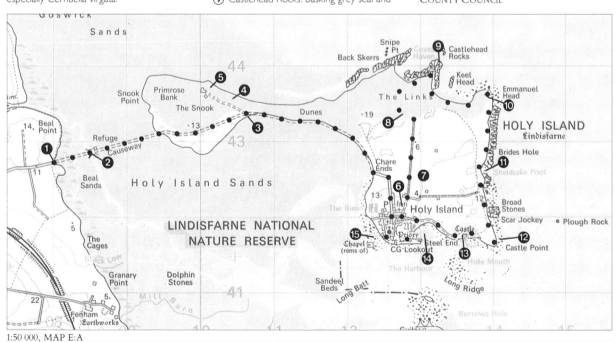

1:50 000, MAP E:A

WALES

The mountain flanks of Wales are dissected by woods (left), valleys and moorland bogs. Large areas of Wales are still wilderness, providing sanctuary for shy and rare animals, including polecat and pine marten. The steep 'hanging' oak-woods of south Central Wales are the last refuge of the red kite.

The **silver–studded blue butterfly** (above) has become rare throughout Britain but colonies survive on heathlands of North Wales and sand dunes of South Wales. Frequently alighting on heather to mate, the male reveals silvery-blue upper wings, with broad black edges. Females are brown with orange crescents on the upper wings, and both sexes live in discrete colonies.

WEST GLAMORGAN

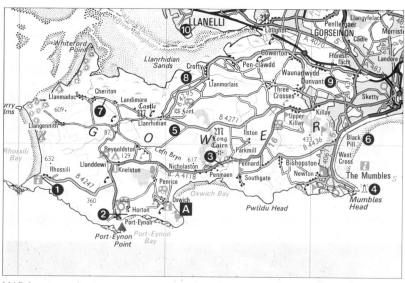

MAP A

A:1 RHOSSILI★★

Near Swansea; A4118 W from town, then B4247. Car park. Consult tide tables; avoid being cut off on Worm's Head.

■ Sandy/rocky shore, cliffs, acid grassland.

■ Area of exceptional interest for shells. Bivalves predominate on sandy shores, gastropods on rocky ones with sheltering crevices and pools.

Carboniferous limestone rocks provide crevices for shelter and there are many large rockpools with sea-slugs. Also, whelks, dog-whelks, limpets, winkles, top-shells and chitons. Snails outnumber bivalves on most rocky shores.

Flowering plants on headland include golden-samphire, rock samphire and rock sea-lavender. Birdlife consists of gulls, kittiwakes, puffins, guillemots, razorbills, shag, fulmar. Manx shearwaters and gannets, common scoter and purple sandpiper in winter.

A:A OXWICH★★

Near Swansea; unclassified road off A4118 W of town. Car park and information centre with leaflets. National Nature Reserve. Keep to paths on dunes.

■ Rocky/sandy shores, sand dunes, wetlands, saltmarsh, deciduous woodland, limestone grassland, cliffs, limestone walls.

① Follow path through dunes to beach. Sand dunes stabilized by marram. Some areas fenced to prevent trampling. Look for specialized dune plants – marram, sea couch, sand sedge, sea-holly, sea rocket and sandwort.

② Walk along sandy beach, rich in seashells washed in from offshore including live cockles, trough shells, carpet shells and tellins. Also look for casts and exposed tubes of polychaete worms and empty tests of heart urchin or sea-potato. Seaweed (*Porphyra umbilicalis*) used for Welsh laverbread grows here. Curlew, ringed plover, oystercatcher and gulls feed on the sands at low tide.

③ Oxwich church, reached by footpath from beach. Wall is habitat for yellow whitlowgrass, a Gower speciality which flowers in March.

④ Follow path through Oxwich wood to Oxwich Point. Wood is of sycamore, oak and ash and has its own rookery. Woodland herbs flower in May.

⑤ Follow coastal path out of wood to track leading to Oxwich green. Gorse and bluebells colouful in spring. The calcicole round-mouth snail lives here. From green, follow road back down hill to car park.

Inland of car park are freshwater marshes and salt-marshes with wigeon, sedge and reed warblers.

NATURE CONSERVANCY COUNCIL

Clean air here good for lichens; look on tombstones and splash zone at Worm's Head.

NATIONAL TRUST

A:2 PORT-EYNON & SOUTH GOWER★★

Near Swansea; A4118 W from town; park in Port-Eynon. Keep to footpaths.

■ Rocky/sandy shores, limestone cliffs, grassland, "chalk" heath.

■ Fine S-facing cliffs with exceptional variety of wildflowers; yellow whitlowgrass and small restharrow as specialities. Good for birds including raven, jackdaw and cliff-nesting species like kittiwakes and razorbills. **Plants** Bloody crane's-bill, spring squill, broomrape, early-purple orchid, spurges, madder, golden-samphire, rockrose. **Birds** Gannet, Manx shearwater, sanderling, ringed plover.

NATURE CONSERVANCY COUNCIL/ NATIONAL TRUST/GLAMORGAN WILDLIFE TRUST

A:3 PARKMILL TO THREE CLIFFS BAY

Near Swansea; A4118 W from town. Limited parking at Parkmill. Footpath along stream to Pennard Burrows and Three Cliffs Bay.

■ Wooded valley, dunes, salt-marsh, sandy bay.

■ Plant life and abundance of snails reflect calcareous soil. Late spring and early summer best for dune flowers. There is a Spartina-Salicornia salt-marsh in Three Cliffs Bay.

NATIONAL TRUST/PENNARD GOLF CLUB

A:4 MUMBLES★★

Swansea, W of bay; A4067 along town seafront, then B4433 to Mumbles Head car park. Limited parking at pier head. Consult tide tables.

■ Rocky shore, limestone cliffs.

■ Headland with islands and caves rich in marine life. The rocks have many crevices and a good seaweed cover.

Various sponges and sea anemones attach to rock; sea-mats and sea-firs form sedentary colonies on seaweeds. Marine worms live on rocks and in pools. Crabs, barnacles, mussels (and the starfish which eat them) are present.

Highlight of limestone headland's interesting wildflowers, is the stock (Matthiola incana.) Species typical of location include thrift, spring squill, rock samphire, golden-samphire, sea beet.

Good for observing migrant birds. Also look for turnstone, oystercatcher, redshank, ring plover and purple sandpiper.

SWANSEA CITY COUNCIL

A:5 BROAD POOL

Near Swansea; on unclassified road leading off B4271 at Cillibion.

■ Pool, bog, moorland.

■ Pool supports waterfowl and wetland birds, with dragonflies and interesting flora in surrounding bog. Notable for fringed water-lily which threatened to take over. Animal life includes frogs, toads, newts, rudd, water snails, leeches and many aquatic insects. **Plants** Lesser bladderwort, round-leaved sundew, marsh St John's-wort, bog myrtle, marsh violet, bog mosses.

GLAMORGAN WILDLIFE TRUST

A:6 SWANSEA BAY AT BLACK PILL★

Swansea; parking at points along sea-front on

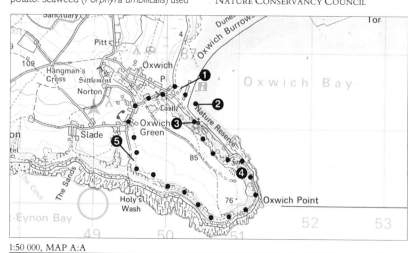

1:50 000, MAP A:A

A4067. Consult tide tables. Beware quicksand.
■ Sandy/mudflats.
■ Muddy sandy shore rich in marine life – over 30 species of seashells. Birds feed on invertebrates at low tide.

A:7 HAMBURY WOOD
Near Swansea; *B4271 W to Llanrhidian, then W on minor road towards Landimore. Parking by Weobley Castle.*
■ Oak/hazel coppice with standards.
■ Deciduous woodland on steep slopes of Carboniferous limestone escarpment. Coppicing to be re-introduced to this new reserve. Trees include oak, ash, sycamore, elm, hazel, holly and field maple. Buzzards nest in the wood.
GLAMORGAN WILDLIFE TRUST

A:8 LLANRHIDIAN MARSH
Near Swansea; *W of town by A4118 and B4271; them minor Crofty – Llanrhidian road. Consult tide tables.*
■ Salt-marsh, sand/mudflats.
■ Site of the famous cockle fishery of the Burry inlet; now much in decline (fishermen blame the oystercatchers). Over 100 species of birds recorded here, with mudflats good for waders.

Tidal salt-marsh above is common land, grazed by sheep and ponies for centuries. Lower salt-marsh community dominated by glassworts and cord-grass. Thousands of Pennant's spire shells living near surface provide food for birds.

Landward, stability of marsh and diversity of flora increases. Saltmarsh turf is mostly common saltmarsh-grass with glasswort, herbaceous seablite, thrift, sea aster, sea-lavender and sea-purslane. Creeks cutting into marsh are fringed with sea-purslane. In the algae of salt-pans are minute sea-slugs.

A:9 CWMLLWYD WOOD
Near Swansea; *NW of town, from A4218 take unclassified road off Waunarlwydd Road at Cockett.*
■ Oak woodland, bracken grassland, marsh.
■ Wood on coal measures dominated by sessile and pedunculate oak which hybridize. Interesting marshland species grow on valley floor along stream and around old coal workings. **Plants** Alder buckthorn, rowan, heath spotted-orchid, bog asphodel, ragged robin.
WEST GLAMORGAN COUNTY COUNCIL

A:10 MACHYNYS PONDS★
Near Llanelli; *take road S from town towards racecourse – ponds to the left of road.*
■ Open ponds, damp slacks.
■ One of the best sites in Dyfed for dragonflies (13 recorded species). The ponds also support a number of rare plants, such as frogbit. In the adjoining damp slacks, royal fern can be found together with marestail and plants associated with sand dunes. For the botanist seeking the unusual, the waste ground nearby supports a number of introduced weeds and adventives.

The nearby Burry Estuary is very important for wintering wildfowl, and excellent

Ragged Robin – see A:9, Cwmllwyd Wood, this page.

views of mud- and sand flats may be obtained from the Machynys area and from Morfa Bacas a short distance upstream.

Summer best for plants and insects, winter for wildfowl.
LLANELLI BOROUGH COUNCIL

B:1 SWANSEA
CANAL
Near Pontardawe; *2 miles N of town; park on Cilmaengwyn Road or in layby on A4067 + mile (0.8 km) beyond Glenafon Hotel. WGCC leaflet.*
■ Towpath walk along canal with range of aquatic and waterside plants; dipper and grey wagtails resident. **Plants** (Wetland) Heath spotted-orchid.
WEST GLAMORGAN COUNTY COUNCIL

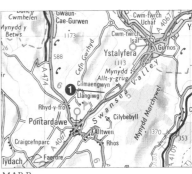

MAP B

WALES

MID GLAMORGAN

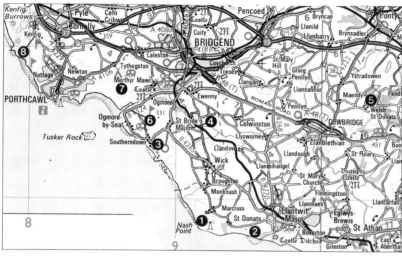

MAP A

A:1 NASH POINT & CWM MARCROSS
Near Llantwit Major; car park at headland. *Well-marked footpaths and nature trail.*
■ Grassland, limestone cliffs, deciduous wood, limestone boulder beach.
■ Variety of plants and animals typical of lime-rich soil; interesting geology and fossils on the beach. Many butterflies and varied birdlife. **Butterflies** Grayling, dingy skipper.
SOUTH GLAMORGAN COUNTY COUNCIL

A:2 LLANTWIT MAJOR
& COL-HUW VALLEY*
Llantwit Major; beach road to car park on shore. Many public footpaths. Check tides and beware rock falls. SGCC leaflet available.
■ Limestone cliffs, rocky shore, old limestone walls, hedges, stream.
■ Beach consists of rocky ledges and pools, colonized by some seaweed, beadlet anemones and molluscs. Look for limestone rocks with tunnels made by rock-boring bivalves.
Vertical cliffs (alternating layers of limestone and shale) support maritime plants such as rock sea-lavender, samphire, thrift and wild carrot. Birds of the the cliff-tops include stonechat and meadow pipit.
Wild madder, stinking iris and many other flowers grow in Col-Huw valley; bloody-nosed beetles on paths in summer.
Inland, old limestone walls, home to snails, are colonized by red valerian, wall pennywort and yellow stonecrop as well as ferns, mosses and lichens.
SOUTH GLAMORGAN COUNTY COUNCIL

A:3 SOUTHERNDOWN
& DUNRAVEN BAY*
Near Bridgend; S of town on B4524. Two large car parks.
■ Sandy beach, rocks, limestone cliffs, wooded valleys.
■ Winkles, limpets, top-shells and common dog whelks live on rocks with anemones and crabs. Wildflowers include snowdrops, primroses, spurge-laurel and stinking hellebore. Turf kept short by rabbits is good for wrinkled and banded snails.
MID GLAMORGAN COUNTY COUNCIL

A:4 COED-Y-BWL
Near Bridgend; on unclassified road off A4265; limited parking.
■ Ash/elm/field maple woodland.

■ Reserve known particularly for daffodils. Snails abundant on the lime-rich soil. **Plants** Moschatel, wood anemone, pignut, sedges, spindle, yellow archangel, wild privet, wood melick grass, hart's-tongue fern, lesser celandine.
GLAMORGAN WILDLIFE TRUST

A:5 HENSOL FOREST
Near Welsh St Donats; from A4222 Llantrisant road, turn right as Ystrad Dowen. Two car parks at site.
■ Larch, conifer, deciduous plantation, rides, glade.
■ Birdlife.
FORESTRY COMMISSION

A:6 OGMORE RIVER
Near Bridgend; S of town on B4524. Car park on river inland of Ogmore-on-Sea. Footpath to estuary mouth.
■ Estuarine salt-marsh/mudflats.
■ The tidal reaches of the Ogmore river estuary provide attractive feeding grounds for wading birds. Good all year.
MID GLAMORGAN COUNTY COUNCIL

A:7 MERTHYR MAWR*
Near Bridgend; SW of town on B4524. Park at Candleston Castle.
■ Sand dune system, slacks.
■ Mature dune turf with usual range of specialized plants and ground nesting birds. Slacks dominated by creeping willow and valleys with thickets of sea buckthorn. The uncommon sandhill snail and tiny wall whorl snail occur.
MERTHYR MAWR ESTATE

A:8 KENFIG**
Near Porthcawl; unclassified road off B4283 and A48. Car park and visitor centre; hide (restricted opening times); leaflets available.
■ Sand dunes, dune slacks, pool.
■ Large area of open water, rich in aquatic animals, breeding place for frogs, toads and newts and resort for water birds, species varying with the season. Damselflies and dragonflies on the wing in summer.
Dune slacks support rich flora including marsh and fen orchids and creeping willow. Hind dunes show great range of flowering plants, mosses and lichens, with brambles and dewberry on stable sand. Dune system as a whole stabilized by marram. **Birds** (Pool) whooper, Bewick's and mute swans,

goldeneye, great crested grebe, teal, redshank; (dunes) peregrine, merlin, short-eared owl, stonechat.
KENFIG CORPORATION PROPERTY/MID GLAMORGAN COUNTY COUNCIL

B:1 GLAMORGAN
NATURE CENTRE & CWM RISCA
Near Bridgend; NW of town on Fountain Road, off B4281; car park.
■ Man-made pond, marsh, oak wood.
■ Headquarters of GWT with exhibitions on wildlife and conservation.
Close to centre are two small reserves; Park Pond is a man-made habitat managed to show plant succession from open water through marsh to wet woodland.
Diverse flora of wetland plants includes saw-wort, marsh orchid, hemlock water dropwort, creeping willow, ragged robin. Frogs, damselflies and dragonflies breed, and about 15 species of butterflies have been recorded.
Birds include siskin, water rail, goldcrest, spotted flycatcher.
GLAMORGAN WILDLIFE TRUST

B:2 BRYNGARW
Near Bridgend; N of town (off A4063 or A4064; leaflet available.
■ Ornamental woodland, stream, upland grassland, coal measures sandstone.
■ The 113 acres of landscaped grounds include ornamental gardens, wilder wet woodland, coppiced woods, meadows and pasture. Good range of woodland and wetland wildflowers, ferns and mosses, also birds and butterflies. **Birds** Great tit, jays, buzzard, grey heron.
ORWR BOROUGH COUNCIL

B:3 MARGAM
Near Port Talbot; off A48, 3½ miles (5.6 km) SE of town; car park. Guide books available. Closes at 7 pm, last entrance 5 pm.
■ Country park with herd of fallow deer, foxes, badgers and small mammals. Adders sun themselves in grassy places. Birds include predators and water species.
WEST GLAMORGAN COUNTY COUNCIL

B:4 AFAN ARGOED
Near Port Talbot; on A417, 6 miles NE of town. Guide book available on site.
■ Sessile oak woodland, stream, acid soil, valleys.
■ Some of site reclaimed from disused colliery works. Mosses, lichens and pearly everlasting grows on spoil tips. **Birds** Re-

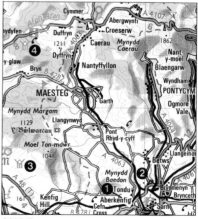

MAP B

172

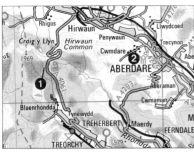

MAP C

dstart, stonechat, nuthatch, raven, grey wagtail, goldcrest.
WEST GLAMORGAN COUNTY COUNCIL/
FORESTRY COMMISSION

C:1 BLAENRRHONDDA WATERFALLS
Near Treherbert; car park on A4061 on top of Mynydd Ystradfernol between town and Hirwaun. Leaflet available.
■ Upland grassland, upland streams, plantations, rocky boulders, waterfalls.
■ Open country has plants typical of acid soils. Native trees are ash, rowan, sallow and birch. Streams frequented by grey wagtail and dippers, while grey heron fish in reservoir. **Birds** Buzzard kestrel, sparrowhawk, raven. **Plants** Mat grass, heath rush, purple moor grass, sheep's fescue, sheep's sorrel, heath bedstraw, heath violet, milkwort, tormentil bilberry, foxgloves, gorse, bracken, woolly hair moss.
FORESTRY COMMISSION/MID GLAMORGAN COUNTY COUNCIL

Milkwort

C:2 DARE VALLEY
Near Aberdare; W of town off B4275 and A4059. Two car parks and visitor centre. Leaflet, waymarked trails, special activities organized by rangers.
■ Upland grassland, alder wood, lakes, stream, reclaimed land.
■ In the 480 acres of woodland and upland grassland, much of which is secondary colonization from a derelict coal mining site, ornithological specialities are ring ousel and peregrine.
CYNON VALLEY BOROUGH COUNCIL

SOUTH GLAMORGAN

A:1 LAVERNOCK POINT
Near Penarth; S of town off B4267 towards Sully. Public footpath across meadow S of Lavernock Point Lane.
■ Limestone grassland, scrub, cliff top.
■ Reserve supports rich limestone flora and good range of butterflies and moths. A diversity of habitat from grassland to scrub. Old wartime concrete structures are a resting station for migrating birds. **Plants** Adder's-tongue, bee orchid, butterfly-orchid, early-purple orchid, common twayblade, common spotted-orchid, yellow-

wort, salad burnet, hairy violet. **Birds** Auks, gannets, gulls, waders.
GLAMORGAN WILDLIFE TRUST

A:2 COSMESTON LAKES
Near Penarth; on Lavernock Road (B4267) towards Sully.
■ Lakes, reed-beds, limestone grassland, wooded area.
■ Country park site quarried until 1970 so plant life still developing. Lakes supplied by underground springs. The flora and fauna reflect the calcareous habitat.
SOUTH GLAMORGAN COUNTY COUNCIL/
VALE OF GLAMORGAN BOROUGH COUNCIL

A:3 PENARTH FLATS
Cardiff; dockland reached by esplanade and Penarth Terrace at S end of Butetown. Views across Taff estuary from sea-wall. Keep off mudflats.
■ Salt-marsh, estuarine mudflats.
■ Good point to watch wading birds as they feed on exposed mud; exceptionally low tides in Bristol Channel. Should Severn barrage be built, area would be flooded and no longer tidal.
CARDIFF CITY COUNCIL

A:4 BUTE PARK
Cardiff; entrance by Cardiff Castle. Car park in civic centre.
■ Parkland, ornamental gardens, river, canal, castle moat.
■ Sheltered valley site along river Taff with network of paths on both sides. Interesting aquatic life and waterside plants in castle moat.
CARDIFF CITY COUNCIL

A:5 GLAMORGAN CANAL & LONG WOOD
Near Whitchurch; from town turn into Velindre Road from roundabout, right at T junction. Park in Forest Farm Road near reserve entrance. Keep to footpaths. CCC leaflet available.
■ Canal, banks, alder carr, deciduous woodland.
■ Local nature reserve and SSSI incorporating a stretch of derelict canal. Living in calcareous canal water are freshwater sponges, water snails and a varied fauna of aquatic insect larvae and fish. There are also water voles, kingfishers, damselflies and dragonflies. Notable plants are arrowhead and floating liverworts.
Long Wood (flanking canal to one side) is pedunculate oak, beech, ash and sycamore, with alder at foot of slope. In spring see bluebells, wood anemone and violets as well as the parasitic toothwort.
The reserve supports about 100 species of birds. Woodland examples are lesser spotted woodpeckers; nuthatches; treecreepers and tits. Visitors to the canal include water rail and kingfisher. Warblers are present in summer while siskin, redpoll and thrushes move in during winter.
CARDIFF CITY COUNCIL

A:6 TY'N-COED, CREIGIAU
NW of Creigiau, unclassified road off A4119 towards Llantrisant.
■ Deciduous/coniferous plantation.
■ Waymarked forest walk with viewpoints and old limestone quarry. More than 70 species of birds (notably owls and warblers) and a range of mammals including badgers and foxes.
FORESTRY COMMISSION

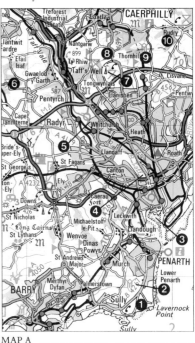

MAP A

A:7 WENALLT
Near Cardiff; unclassified road off A469 N of town; car park.
■ Oak/beech/ash woodland, open heath, acid soil.
■ Mixed deciduous woodland on S edge of coalfield with good distant views. Woodland wildflowers in spring; site also good for birds.
CARDIFF CITY COUNCIL

A:8 CAERPHILLY MOUNTAIN & COMMON
Near Caerphilly; S of town on A469 Cardiff road. Car park. Cardiff City Council booklet available.
■ Upland grassland, acid soil.
■ An area of high ground with fine views. The summit on Caerphilly Common is 888 ft (271 metres).
Moorland on acid coal measures sandstones is characterized by heather, bell heather, bilberry and bracken. Wet soil in lower coal measures colonized by wet heathland plants like marsh pennywort and cross-leaved heath. The carboniferous limestone is instantly recognized from change in vegetation: a useful indicator plant is traveller's-joy.
MID GLAMORGAN COUNTY COUNCIL

A:9 CEFN ONN
Near Cardiff; N of town on A469; car park.
■ Ornamental wooded garden, pools.
CARDIFF CITY COUNCIL

A:10 COED LLWYNCELYN, RUDRY
Near Cardiff; unclassified roads off A468 (Newport-Caerphilly) or B4562 (Llanishen-St Mellons); car park.
■ Broad-leaved/coniferous plantation.
■ One of several FC woods with public access in the Rudry-Draethen area. Waymarked walks with good views. A range of birds can be seen, especially tits; woodland flowers along grassy rides and butterflies (most spectacular is silver-washed fritillary) where the woods are not too mature.
FORESTRY COMMISSION

DYFED

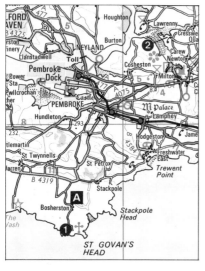

MAP A

A:1 CASTLEMARTIN/ ELEGUG STACKS/STACK ROCKS★

Near Pembroke; from Pembroke follow B4319 S, then through Bosherston village to car park. When firing is taking place on the eastern range (check local press and notices), the road from Bosherston, the car park and the footpath are closed.

■ Coastal limestone cliffs.

A:A STACKPOLE/BOSHERSTON★★

Near Pembroke; approach from D4319; car parks at Stackpole Quay, Bosherston and Broad Haven. Many footpaths.

① From Stackpole Quay (historic artefacts, old quay, harbour) there is access to the rocky shore, clear waters and colourful marine life. The Pembrokeshire Coast Path leads W to Barafundle Bay.

② Behind the bay, sand dunes are colonized by sea-buckthorn.

③ Stackpole Warren is a cliff-top complex of sand dunes and grassland. Much modified by past agriculture, this area supports an unusual

■ Towering cliffs plunge vertically into the sea here. The maritime limestone flora is especially colourful in spring. The stacks, just offshore, provide nesting sites for a range of sea-birds; peregrines nest on the cliffs.

MINISTRY OF DEFENCE

A:2 WEST WILLIAMSTON★

Near Pembroke; from A4075 take road to West Williamston. From car park footpath crosses fields to the reserve.

■ Limestone quarries, salt-marsh, grassland, scrub.

■ The varied habitat produces an exceptional diversity of plants and invertebrates, including many rare species.

The salt-marsh supports a broad belt of cordgrass with glasswort, seacouch, marsh mallow, thrift and red fescue. Sea aster, seamilkwort, sea plantain and sea arrowgrass grow on the mudflats. Between areas of scrub and the quarries limestone grassland supports a rich flora with yellow-wort, carline thistle, autumn gentian and salad burnet. Large numbers of waders and wildfowl frequent the salt-marsh and mudflats. **Plants** Columbine, bee orchid, tutsan, stinking iris; (salt-marsh) lax-flowered sea-lavender, rock sea-lavender, English scurvy-grass.

WEST WALES TRUST FOR NATURE CONSERVATION

mixture of maritime cliff and sand dune plants.

④ Broad Haven's sweeping beach, backed by sand dunes, behind which the dry warm sand of the Mere Pool Valley is rich in insect life.

⑤ Bosherston Ponds, artificial lakes, are mainly spring-fed and hardly ever freeze. Their famous water-lilies are a magnificent display in summer. They also support the uncommon alga stonewort. The sheltered water provides a winter refuge for wildfowl including unusual species in most years. One of the most important SW sites for otter.

Surrounding woods: diverse flora.

NATIONAL TRUST

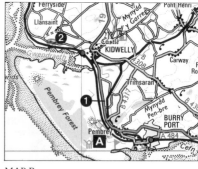

MAP B

B:1 FFRWD FEN★

NW of Burry Port; from the B4137 (Pembrey to Pinged), access along footpath; or walk the canal footpath which forms the fen's N boundary.

■ Open water, ditches and pools, reed-beds, relict dunes.

■ The botany of Ffrwd Fen is extremely rich. The most significant rarity is the marsh pea, known at only one other site in the country and normally associated with the East Anglian marshes. In the recently re-created open water there are rarities such as frogbit and floating club-rush. During spring a wide range of birds associated with fens and reed-beds can be seen, including the water rail. In winter, bittern, marsh harrier and wildfowl arrive. The reserve is also rich in dragonflies and butterflies. **Plants** Tubular water-dropwort, marsh lousewort, bogbean. **Insects** Hairy dragonfly, short-winged conehead.

WEST WALES TRUST FOR NATURE CONSERVATION

B:2 GWENDRAETH ESTUARY/ CEFN SIDAN SANDS★

S and W of Kidwelly; access to Kidwelly Marsh from near the junction of A484 and minor road to Pinged. The N side is best viewed from Salmon Scar Point 2 miles (3 km) from Kidwelly on the St Ishmaels road. Access to S part of Cefn Sidan from Pembrey Burrows. The S side of the estuary is in MoD control and cannot be visited.

■ Mud/sand flats, marsh, sand dunes.

■ The mud- and sand flats and the marshes are important wintering, passage and feeding grounds for a wide range of waders and wildfowl. Birds of prey such as peregrine, merlin, hen harrier and short-eared owl are regularly seen hunting. **Plants** Fen orchid, dune gentian. **Birds** (Regular visitors) velvet and common scoter, red-breasted merganser, eider, golden plover; (more rarely) avocet, spotted redshank, ruff, whimbrel, green sandpiper, litte stint.

MINISTRY OF DEFENCE/COMMON LAND

C:1 SKOKHOLM ISLAND★★

Island 3 miles (5 km) from Marloes peninsula. Details from WWTNC. One-week study courses available. Day visits on Mon only.

■ Old Red Sandstone, maritime grassland.

■ The island is composed entirely of Old Red Sandstone which supports a rare example of rabbit-maintained maritime grassland. The sward is dominated in different areas by thrift, sea campion and grasses with buck's horn plantain and bracken. Skokholm is particularly important for its population of Manx shearwater (36,000 pairs) and storm petrel (6,000 pairs). Apart from the rabbit, the house mouse is the only other resident mammal; the only reptile is the slow-worm. There are rare

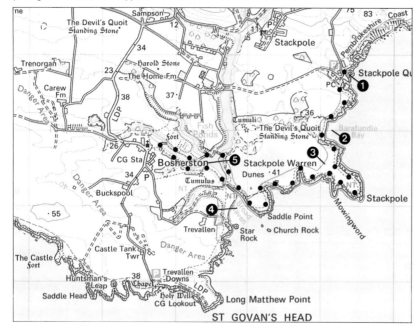

1:50 000, MAP A:A

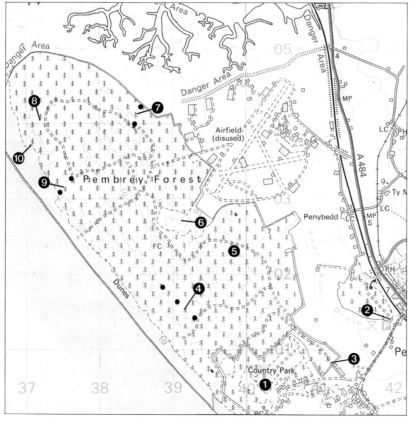

1:50 000, MAP B:A

B:A PEMBREY COUNTRY PARK, BURROWS & FOREST★★

Near Llanelli; entry fee; keep strictly to rides and footpaths.

① The country park area supports a diverse flora and is extremely rich entomologically.

② Look for bloody crane's-bill at Penybedd Wood. Butterflies include skippers, blues, graylings, brown argus, marbled whites and silver-washed fritillaries.

③ At the forest entrance a scrubby area is of value to small birds which feed on its abundant insects and fruit.

④ The 'butterfly ride' has a rich and varied flora: 32 species of butterfly.

⑤ The main forest road with its broad edges supports a very diverse flora including rarities.

⑥ In the large clearing are species of bee and wasp which live in the sandy soil. Also important for butterflies, grasshoppers and bush-crickets.

⑦ Along the narrow ride may be found rare species of soldier-fly and longhorn beetle.

⑧ The small pond has dragonflies and damselflies; also unusual plants such as stoneworts and lesser water-plantain.

⑨ This ride is a regular site for scarlet tiger moth and silver-washed fritillaries.

⑩ Dune slack: Bee orchids grow in fluctuating numbers with pyramidal, fragrant and green-winged orchids among the other interesting flora. **Plants** Marsh helleborine, fen orchid, dune helleborine, broad-leaved helleborine, autumn lady's-tresses, moonwort, adder's-tongue, twiggy mullein, round-leaved wintergreen, yellow bartsia, rock sea-lavender. **Birds** Goshawk, crossbill, siskin.
LLANELLI BOROUGH COUNCIL

---

beetles and moths. Skokholm is renowned for its great number of visiting migrant birds. **Plants** Tree mallow, lesser skullcap, marsh St John's-wort, rock sea-spurrey, sea fern-grass, allseed, mudweed, shoreweed. **Birds** (Breeding) Puffins, razorbills, guillemots, lesser and greater black-backed gulls, herring gulls; (visiting migrants) hobby, great skua, little gull, black tern, hoopoe, wryneck, bluethroat, firecrest, Lapland bunting.
WEST WALES TRUST FOR NATURE CONSERVATION

C:2 MARLOES MERE

Marloes; park in Marloes Sands car park, where a track leads to the reserve. WWTNC permit needed.

■ Wet acidic pasture, flooded mere in winter.

■ Wintering wildfowl include large flocks of wigeon, with pintail, shoveler, teal, jack

snipe and snipe. Peregrine, merlin and buzzard present. **Plants** Three-lobed crowfoot, tubular water-dropwort. **Invertebrates** Marsh fritillary, emperor dragonfly, great green bush-cricket, medicinal leech.
WEST WALES TRUST FOR NATURE CONSERVATION

C:3 MARLOES SANDS★

Marloes; parking available; leaflet from WWTNC.
■ Cliff, beach.

■ The cliffs contain many fossils, crossbeds, ripple marks, scour structures and burrows. The nature trail passes through rich cliff-top maritime heath. **Birds** Chough.
WEST WALES TRUST FOR NATURE CONSERVATION

C:4 GANN ESTUARY★

Near Milford Haven; excellent views from

B4327 Dale road; keep to footpaths.

■ Mudflats, sandbanks, shingle bank, brackish lagoon, islands.

■ This diverse estuary has a rich variety of marine invertebrates, the only mature shingle vegetation in the district and numerous rare salt-marsh plants. The site is noted for its 30 species of hydroid and five species of sea anemone. Among terrestrial invertebrates, bush-crickets are most prominent. The principal ornithological feature is wintering waders.
DYFED COUNTY COUNCIL

C:5 GRASSHOLME ISLAND★★

Island 6 miles (10 km) from Marloes peninsula; details from WWTNC, 7, Market Street, Haverfordwest, SA61 1NF. Boat crossings limited to favourable conditions; no visits before 15 June.

■ Rocky basalt island, maritime grassland.

■ The foreshore and sub-littoral zone around the island is of outstanding interest, being one of the most tide- and wave-exposed habitats in Britain. But Grassholme supports little vegetation, the sward of red fescue grass having been modified by the activities of many breeding birds. Once, far more extensive turf supported up to 100,000 pairs of breeding puffins; these rapidly declined following colonization of the island by gannets which now number about 28,500 pairs, the third largest colony in the world. Grey seals can often be seen close to the island or on the shingle beaches. **Birds** (Breeding) Kittiwake, guillemot, razorbill, herring gull, great black-backed gull, shag. **Plants** Buck's-horn plantain, tree mallow.
ROYAL SOCIETY FOR THE PROTECTION OF BIRDS

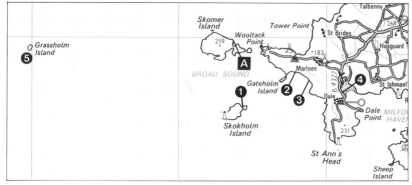

MAP C

DYFED

C:A SKOMER ISLAND★★

St Bride's Bay; park at Martin's Haven and take ferry. Open daily except Mon, March to Sep, 10-6.

■ One of the most important sea-bird sites in southern Britain. Among the principal nesting species are Manx shearwater (100,000 pairs), storm petrel and fulmar, puffin (6,500 pairs), razorbill and guillemot, kittiwake and lesser black-backed gulls (15,000 pairs).

① North Haven has many Manx shearwater and puffin breeding burrows: birds present April to early August.

② Views of South Haven and the Neck, left undisturbed for research.

③ South Stream Valley, sheltered and damp, supports a wide range of plants and nesting sites for small birds.

④ Welsh Way offers views of lesser black-backed and herring gull nesting colonies.

⑤ High Cliff supports a dense and noisy colony of kittiwakes with razorbills.

⑥ The Wick, a magnificent cliff panorama, supports thousands of breeding sea-birds.

⑦ South Ridge, an exposed rock ridge with nesting greater black-backed gull and wheatears.

⑧ Tom's House offers magnificent coastal views, and is a site for breeding storm petrels.

⑨ Skomer Head, an exposed headland on which few plants survive.

⑩ Pigstone Bay: sea campion dominates; seals frequently seen.

⑪ Bull Hole is a fine maritime heath dominated by old heather.

⑫ Garland Stone is the best place to view seals, frequently basking on the rocks and swimming in the channel between the stone and the cliff. Chough and raven.

⑬ North Stream Valley: toads and frogs breed in the wet hollows. Stonechats nest in the shrub. Short-eared owls hunt up and down the valley.

⑭ East Fields: part of the old farm.

Plants Lanceolate spleenwort, three-lobed water crowfoot, tree mallow, Portland spurge, sea stork's bill, rock sea-lavender, chaffweed. **Birds** Peregrine, chough, little owl, waders. **Insects** Glow-worm.

WEST WALES TRUST
FOR NATURE
CONSERVATION

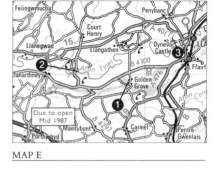

MAP E

from many parts of the world. The mixed flora beneath these trees include lower plants such as mosses, lichens and fungi. Birdlife is abundant including treecreepers, woodpeckers, redstarts, buzzards. Badgers live in the woodlands as do many smaller mammals. There are about a hundred fallow deer. **Reptiles** Slow-worm, grass snake, adder, common lizard.

DYFED COUNTY COUNCIL

E:2 GWEUNYDD DRYSLWYN★

Between Carmarthen and Llandeilo; leave A40 between Llanegwed and Llangathen and follow B4297 to Dryslwyn. Best views from Dryslwyn Castle or bridge, or from the bridge at Llangathen.

■ Riverside meadows, ponds.

■ Dryslwyn Meadows is an important wildfowl sites, comprising relatively undisturbed, damp, low-lying fields occasionally flooded by the River Tywi. These provide over-wintering grounds for many wildfowl and waders. **Birds** (Wintering) Siberian white-fronted goose, wigeon, golden plover, teal.

CADW

E:3 CASTLE WOODS/ DYNEFWR DEER PARK

Near Llandeilo; follow the A40 to the outskirts of Llandeilo; park at the ambulance station. Walk through Penlan Park to the reserve. Keep to marked footpaths.

■ Mixed broad-leaved woodland, woodland pasture, flood plain.

■ The mature, mixed woodland consists mainly of oak, ash, beech and sycamore. Active management will ensure perpetuation of the woodland through planting and natural regercnation, and elms will be replaced.

The deer park is one of the finest Welsh examples of woodland pasture, with oak trees of immense size and age. The lichen communities here and in the woodlands are of considerable importance. The woods and park are important habitats for a range of invertebrates, particularly beetles, spiders, and snails. Badgers are present. **Plants** (Woodlands) tutsan, toothwort, buckthorn, alder buckthorn; (western part) bladderwort, bladder sedge, pondweeds. **Butterflies** Silver-washed fritillary. **Birds** Pied flycatcher, redstart, wood warbler, woodpeckers, peregrine; (wildfowl) Siberian white-fronted goose.

WEST WALES TRUST FOR NATURE
CONSERVATION

F:1 RAMSEY ISLAND★

Separated from mainland near St David's by the one-mile (1.5 km) Ramsey Sound; boats from St Justinian daily, Jun to Sept; landing fee: inquire at the landing stage.

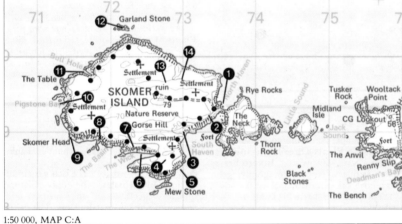

1:50 000, MAP C:A

D:1 SCOLTON MANOR★

Near Haverfordwest; take B4329 NE – Scolton is signposted in about 7 miles (11 km).

■ Varied artificial and natural habitats, including arboretum and butterfly garden.

■ Mature deciduous woodland mingles with conifers and exotic trees, each supporting its own characteristic web of plant and animal life. The butterfly garden provides the widest possible range of flowers and food plants that will attract butterflies, and for as long as possible during each season.

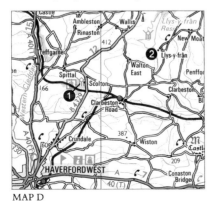

MAP D

DYFED COUNTY COUNCIL

D:2 LLSYFRAN COUNTRY PARK★

Near Haverfordwest; Daily or seasonal fishing permits obtainable from the Welsh Water Authority, Haverfordwest.

■ Reservoir surrounded by woodland and grassland.

■ Large reservoir in a wooded valley at the base of the Preseli Hills with fine views, attractive walks, a rich variety of wildlife and a lakeside perimeter path of 7½ miles (12 km). During the winter and on passage, large numbers of wildfowl waders spend time in the park. The park supports polecat, badger, fox, weasel, stoat, and smaller mammals. It is also a good site for insects, particularly butterflies. **Birds** Whooper and Bewick's swans, Siberian white fronted goose, divers, goldeneye, wigeon.

DYFED COUNTY COUNCIL

E:1 GELLI AUR/GOLDEN GROVE★

Near Llandeilo; information from warden.

■ Mixed woodlands, arboretum, gardens, deer park.

■ Gelli Aur mansion is surrounded by 90 acres of woodland and parkland. The arboretum contains a large collection of broadleaved and coniferous trees and shrubs

Scarlet tiger moth

■ Igneous rock, rugged cliffs, maritime heath.
■ Because of its erosion-resistant igneous rocks, Ramsey is more rugged and hilly than Skomer or Skokholm. Maritime heath dominates those areas not being farmed and the spring flora (spring squill, gorse and thrift) is impressive. The island is grazed by sheep and a herd of 90 red deer.

Ramsey is well known for its breeding choughs, as well as for guillemot, razorbill,

MAP F

kittiwake, Manx shearwater and fulmar (best viewed from the sea). The presence of the rat precludes the use of the island by burrow nesting birds.

Here is also the largest breeding colony of grey seals in SW Britain, with up to 300 pups born annually on beaches and in caves. Large numbers of adults regularly haul out on selected beaches. **Plants** Yellow centaury, subterranean cover, lanceolate spleenworth, floating water-plantain, juniper. **Birds** (Breeding) chough, short-eared and little owl.

F:2 DOWROG COMMON★
Near St David's; *from St David's take A487, then first left on to B4583. Then shortly take minor road N at a sharp bend. Park on roadside.*
■ Lowland wet heath, fen, willow carr, river, pool.
■ Over 350 species of flowering plant have been recorded at this extremely diverse site, a nationally important example of oceanic lowland heath. The principal components are grey willow, gorse, heather, cross-leaved heath and purple moor-grass. The pools contain bog pondweed, marsh St John's-wort, bulrush, water horsetail, marsh cinquefoil and bogbean.

Breeding birds include coot, moorhen, water rail, sedge warbler, buzzard, kestrel and sparrowhawk. Pintail, pochard, teal, tufted duck, wigeon, whooper and Bewick's swan, hen harrier and merlin are frequently seen during the winter months. There are 17 species of butterfly and 14 of dragonfly. **Plants** Pillwort, sundew, pennyroyal, wavy St John's-wort, yellow centaury, fibrous tussock sedge, three-lobed crowfoot. **Birds** Short-eared owl, grasshopper warbler. **Insects** Green hairstreak, small red damselfly.
WEST WALES TRUST FOR NATURE CONSERVATION

F:3 ST DAVID'S HEAD★
Near St David's; *parking available. Pembrokeshire Coast footpath goes around headland.*
■ Sea cliffs, maritime heath, scrub.
■ Sea birds abound, together with chough, raven and buzzard. The many gulleys, inlets, coves and beaches provide sites for seals to haul out. Fine cliff walking.
Plants Orpine, hairy greenweed, English stonecrop, heath pearlwort, saw-wort, rock sea-spurrey.

177

G:1 PEMBROKESHIRE COAST PATH★★

Cardigan to Amroth; *access at many points along the length of the waymarked path.*

■ Cliffs, beaches, dunes, grassland, maritime heath.

■ The Pembrokeshire Coast Path passes through impressive coastal scenery; cliffs on a grand scale with offshore islands, maritime heath and grass, coastal woodland, beach and dune. Botanical variety is dictated by habitat changes from hard rock heath to lush freshwater marsh. There are breeding sea-bird colonies and many unusual migrants make their landfalls here. The clear waters of the Irish Sea are a rich feeding ground for seals, which are frequently observed; dolphin and porpoise also visit. **Plants** Perennial centaury, dune gentian. **Birds** Chough, gannet, puffin, common scoter.

G:2 GWAUN VALLEY WOODLAND★

Near Fishguard; *take B4313 to Narberth from Fishguard, then follow signs to Cwm Gwaun. The woodland occupies the valley sides for about 5 miles (8 km). Car parks at Picton Mill and Sychbant picnic site. Extensive footpath network.*

■ Mature and coppice oak, damp alder and willow woodland.

■ Sessile oak dominates on the slopes; mixtures of ash, hazel and holly, and some beech, sycamore and wych elm. The woodlands support a rich bird fauna, as well as ferns and more than a hundred species of bryophytes, and 100 lichens on record.
PEMBROKESHIRE COAST NATIONAL PARK AUTHORITY

G:3 GOODWICK MOOR★

Fishguard; *park in sea front car park, walk along A40 towards Fishguard. Just after the hotel, take footpath on right. A circular footpath traverses the reserve.*

■ Reed-beds, flood-plain mire, alder and willow carr, ditches and ponds.

■ A splendid mixture of wetland habitats. The reed-bed is dominated by common reed, with sea rush, and sea asters present on the seaward side. On the flood-plain mire, the reed gradually gives way to a greater variety of marsh plants.

In the shade of the willow and alder carr, the sparse ground flora is dominated by several ferns. The ponds and ditches support bogbean and bog pondweed and provide an ideal breeding ground for frogs and toads. **Plants** Royal fern, bog myrtle, cottongrass, devil's-bit scabious, glaucous club-rush. **Birds** Stonechat, snipe, siskin, buzzard, kestrel, sparrowhawk. **Butterflies** Dark green fritillary.
WEST WALES TRUST FOR NATURE CONSERVATION

G:4 COED TY CNOL★

Near Newport; *Extensive footpath network from Pentre Ifan farm or burial chamber. Permit required to stray off footpaths.*

■ Woodland, boulder-strewn heathland, rock outcrops.

■ The lichen flora is outstanding – 22 of the 310 species are ancient woodland indicators. In addition, 130 species of bryophyte have been recorded. **Plants** Wilson's filmy-fern, Tunbridge filmy-fern, hay-scented buckler-fern, many-stemmed spike-rush, Devil's-bit scabious, western gorse, cottongrass. **Mammals** Dormouse, polecat. **Insects** Purple hairstreak and silver-washed fritillary butterflies, keeled skimmer dragonfly.
NATURE CONSERVANCY COUNCIL

G:5 PENGELLI FOREST

Near Eglwyswrw; *access N of A487, from the unclassified Velindre to Eglwyswrw road. Park on verge. Footpaths, and four marked trails.*

■ Sessile oak woodland, mixed damp deciduous woodland.

■ Pengelli Forest is part of the largest block of ancient oak woodland in west Wales. **Mammals** Badger, dormouse, polecat, fox. **Birds** Pied flycatcher, redstart, wood warbler, tawny owl, sparrowhawk, woodcock, buzzard, woodpeckers. **Insects** Dark and speckled bush-crickets, purple- and white-letter hairstreaks, silver-washed fritillary butterflies, oil beetle.

WEST WALES TRUST FOR NATURE CONSERVATION

G:6 STRUMBLE HEAD★

Near Fishguard; *follow lanes to Strumble Head lookout. The Pembrokeshire Coast Path traverses the cliff.*

■ Cliffs, maritime grassland, heath.

■ Dramatic cliffs rise 450 feet (124 m) above the sea. This is one of the most geologically complex sections of coast in Britain, with Cambrian and Ordovician strata and intrusive and extrusive rocks. The geological diversity is matched by the variety of flowering plants and ferns. Habitat ranges from exceedingly exposed grassland and heath, to sheltered scrub, and the site is of national importance for its sea cliff vegetation. Strumble Head is also noted for its breeding sea-birds; grey seals breed in caves and on the beaches.

G:7 COEDYDD A CHORSYDD ABER TEIFI★

Near Cardigan; *much of the steep and marshy Teifi gorge is inaccessible. Stay on footpaths starting at Llechryd, Cilgerran, or at points between Cilgerran and Cardigan. Keep to footpaths.*

■ Estuary marshes, gorge woodlands. **Plants** Wild service-tree, dotted sedge. **Birds** (Wintering) black-tailed and bar-tailed godwit, woodcock.

G:8 CARDIGAN ISLAND

At mouth of the Teifi; *take B4548 road from Cardigan to Gwbert, and park. The cliff walk to Carreg-lydan point gives views across the narrow strait. Landing is difficult; contact Trust office for details of boat trips.*

■ Maritime grassland, low rock cliffs, foreshore.

■ Excellent habitat for breeding sea-birds. This undisturbed island supports a large colony of herring gulls, with greater and lesser black-backed gulls, fulmar, shag.
WEST WALES TRUST FOR NATURE CONSERVATION

Opposite: Tawny owl – see G:5.

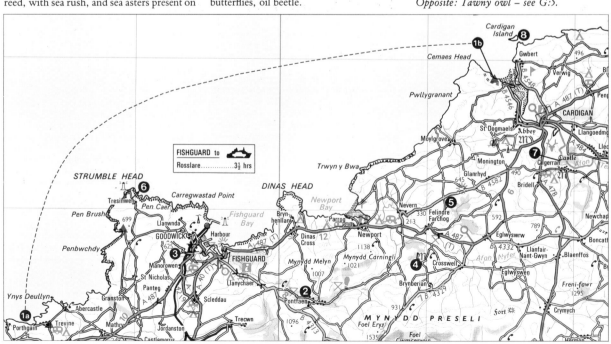

MAP G

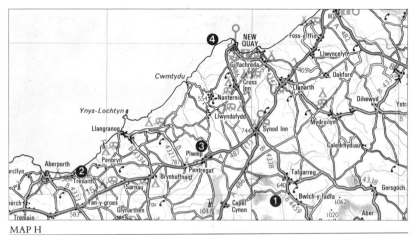

MAP H

maritime species such as thrift, sea plantain and sea campion occur with English stonecrop and Portland spurge. **Plants** Ivy broomrape, sheep's-bit, pyramidal orchid, wild madder, wood spurge, sea bindweed.
NATIONAL TRUST

H:3 RHOS PIL-BACH
Near Cardigan; N of Plwmp on A487; park about ½ mile (0.8 km) from village, at end of track leading to reserve.
■ Lowland wet heath, sedge-rich pasture.
■ The extremely species-rich damp meadow is a superb example of ancient ridge-and-furrow pasture. The site is important for its marsh fritillary butterflies. **Plants** Meadow thistle, bog asphodel, heath spotted-, northern marsh- and common spotted-orchids.
WEST WALES TRUST FOR NATURE CONSERVATION

H:4 CRAIG YR ADAR★
Near New Quay; one mile (1.5 km) W of New Quay; access on foot from New Quay, along the cliff path.
■ High precipitous cliffs.
■ An important sea-bird breeding site. Grey seals haul out on the foreshore and breed nearby.
CEREDIGION DISTRICT COUNCIL

H:1 RHOS LLAWR CWRT
Near Talgarreg; one mile (1.5 km) S of Talgarreg on B4459, turn right; entrance in one mile (1.5 km). NCC permit required.
■ Unimproved sedge-rich grassland and peatland, pingos (glacial features).
■ Wetland flora with cottongrass, bogbean, mare's-tail and cross-leaved heath; grassland is dominated by a variety of grasses, sedges and rushes. Large colony of marsh fritillary butterflies. **Plants** Cran-

berry, bog asphodel, bitter vetch, heath milkworth, lousewort, several bog mosses (Sphagnum).
NATURE CONSERVANCY COUNCIL

H:2 CREIGIAU PENBRYN★
Near Cardigan; leave A487 at Sarnau, take unclassified road to Penbryn. Keep to footpaths.
■ Sea cliffs, sand dunes, beach.
■ Crumbly cliffs support a rich and diverse flora in a wide range of habitat. Typical

I:1 DINAS & GWENFFRWD★★
Near Llandovery; open access to Dinas information centre. RSPB permit required to enter more remote Gwenffrwd area.
■ Steep valley woodlands, moorland and mountain grassland, wet flushes and mire.
■ The smaller Dinas area is mainly hanging oakwood with some alder carr and marsh. Grazing has reduced the understorey and ground flora, but it is still quite diverse in the less accessible areas. Characteristic woodland birds include abundant nuthatches, treecreepers, woodpeckers, flycatchers, redstarts and wood warblers. Buzzard, peregrine and red kite may be seen hunting in the area.

Gwenffrwd is essentially moorland with some hanging oakwood. Swift-flowing river valleys provide an additional habitat. Its principle bird species include red grouse, wheatears, whinchats, ravens and merlins in addition to the list for Dinas.

Throughout the reserve ferns and bryophytes are abundant. Foxes are numerous and there are several badger setts; red and grey squirrel and polecat are present.
ROYAL SOCIETY FOR THE PROTECTION OF BIRDS

I:2 ALLT RHYD Y GROES★
Near Llandovery; take the turning which crosses the river Tywi, proceed to the bailey bridge and park. NCC permit required to visit areas off the public footpath.
■ Oak woodland, crag, scree/mountain grassland, damp meadows.
■ The close-canopied woodland is dominated by sessile oak. Grasses and ferns dominate the ground flora but the most striking feature is the abundance of bryophytes. The adjoining meadows are much more herb-rich.

On the rock, scree and mountain grassland more than 130 species of flowering plant and 20 ferns have been recorded. In addition to many breeding bird species, the red kite is a frequent visitor. Polecats and otters are present though seldom seen. **Plants** Globe-

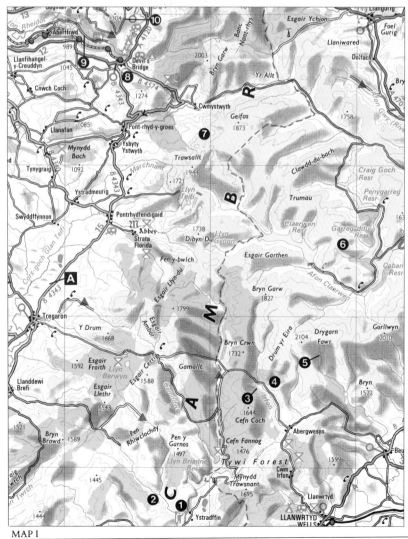

MAP I

flower, orpine, parsley fern, Wilson's filmy-fern, oak fern, clubmosses.
NATURE CONSERVANCY COUNCIL

I:3 NANT IRFON*
Near Llanwrtyd Wells; *cross river from unclassified road NW of Abergwesyn.*
■ Acid upland grassland, rocky outcrops, hanging oakwood.
■ Nant Irfon is a typical example of upland habitat in this part of Wales. The outcrops of Silurian rocks support a diverse lichen flora. The woodlands are important for breeding birds, and contain rich moss and lichen communities. Small blanket mires and boggy flushes support rushes, cottongrass and bogbean. **Plants** Globe-flower. **Birds** Pied flycatcher, ring ouzel, redstart, golden plover, whinchat.
NATURE CONSERVANCY COUNCIL

I:4 CRAIG IRFON*
Near Llanwrtyd Wells; *2 roadside parking and access. The site is exposed and subject to sudden changes of weather.*
■ Upland grassland, heather moorland, blanket bog, crags, screes.
■ Predominantly sheep-grazed grassland. On the less accessible crags and ledges, heather and bilberry flourish. Boggy areas support a greater variety of vegetation with purple moor-grass, cross-leaved heath and bog mosses. The rocky outcrops are rich in lichens and the crevices shelter a variety of ferns, as well as providing nesting sites for

mountain birds. **Plants** Round-leaved sundew, lesser skullcap, cranberry, marsh lousewort, bog asphodel, oak fern. **Birds** Ring ouzel, wheatear, stonechat, whinchat, dipper, raven, buzzard.
BRECKNOCK WILDLIFE TRUST

I:5 DRYGARN FAWR A GORLLWYN*
Near Llanwrtyd Wells; *access on foot from the unclassified Beulah to Tregaron road, NW of Abergwesyn, or from Rhayader to Claerwen reservoir road. Unenclosed land can be boggy; keep to footpaths crossing the site.*
■ Upland grassland, moorland, peat bogs; rocky outcrops, cliffs, screes, sessile oak woodland, wooded gorges.
■ Some of the least disturbed upland in Wales; blanket peat is drained by a network of streams. Purple moor-grass dominates large areas, with cotton-grasses, marsh violet and several species of *Sphagnum* moss. Better drained areas support bilberry and heath bedstraw among the mat-grass and fescues. Where peat has begun to erode into haggs, heather and Cladonia lichens become prominent.
Upland birds include stonechat and whinchat. Birds of prey are easy to observe. **Plants** Sundew, butterwort. **Birds** Red kite, goshawk, peregrine, hen harrier, merlin, short-eared owl, red grouse, golden plover, dunlin, ring ouzel, wheatear, raven.

I:6 ELAN VALLEY*
Near Rhayader; *access from B4518 SW from*

Ring ouzel – see 1:3, 1:5.

Rhayader, then on foot from unclassified roads round reservoirs.
■ Grassland, rocky outcrop, scree, peat bog, open water.
■ In the steep catchment of the Elan Valley reservoirs sessile oak woodland has developed, and large areas have been planted with conifers. The deciduous woodland has a lush epiphytic flora of lichens and mosses, and a remarkable variety and volume of springtime birdsong. The mixed woodlands of the lower valley may hold up to 50 breeding species of birds. Waders, wildfowl and birds of prey are present on the boggy areas and the reservoirs. Summer insects include the yellow-ringed dragonfly and the black and

I:A CORS CARON**
Near Lampeter; *access to reserve at Ty Coed; to railway at Maesllyn.*
■ Cors Caron is among the finest example of a raised mire in England and Wales. It was formed by the action of ice during the last major glacial period. Two walks are available: the longer one (permit required, apply warden) crosses the bog and returns along the disused railway. The short walk (open access) follows the disused railway to the excellent observation tower, returning along same route.
① The Lagg: Nutrient-rich water draining off surrounding land gives a lush marginal strip containing a profusion of water-loving plants.
② The gently sloping sides of the raised bog are better drained than the centre and support a wet heath vegetation.
③ Peat is formed from the partially humified remains of *Sphagnum* mosses, and these still dominate the vegetation at the central 'growing complex' of the bog. Spectacular lichens on the drier hummocks.
④ The flood plain, irrigated with nutrient-rich water supports a vegetation community not found elsewhere in the reserve. Where it is ungrazed, reed canary grass is dominant but in other areas look for rushes, purple moor grass, sedges and various grasses.
⑤ These meanders, cut off when an artificial bed was cut for the river, have formed lakes supporting water lilies; attractive to wildfowl.
⑥ The clean and unpolluted River Teifi supports a rich aquatic flora and is also the breeding ground of salmon, trout, many large pike, and vast numbers of eels, the favourite food of the otter. Signs of this elusive mammal, in the form of spraints' are often on riverside mounds; footprints may be seen in soft mud.
⑦ Open water flashes form where main drains meet the river; still backwaters used by wildfowl and other water birds.

⑧ The willow carr has developed in abandoned peat cuttings. Nutrient-rich water supports a diverse flora.
⑨ Observation tower, with fine, long views of reserve; hide ideal for winter birdwatching. Dippers, wildfowl.
⑩ Returning along the railway, further fine views of this part of the reserve, supporting a flora and a different insect community of its own. The pools beside the track have a range of water plants.
⑪ Farm section, dominated by arable weeds; probably the best area for butterflies.
⑫ Sheltered cutting; on warm days in spring and summer, many butterflies, grasshoppers and lizards. Small rodents, weasels, polecats

and adders are often found here. The remaining section of track is mostly scrub; pied flycatchers and warblers.
⑬ The pond at Maesllyn is á kettle hole', formed by a huge piece of ice which became detached from the receding glacier and melted into the large hole it created. Swans and wildfowl in winter.
More than 40 bird species breed on the reserve, and many more are recorded in winter or on passage. They include red kite, peregrine, harriers, merlin and buzzard. The reserve is also rich in invertebrates, most notable and easily observed being dragonflies and damselflies.
NATURE CONSERVANCY COUNCIL

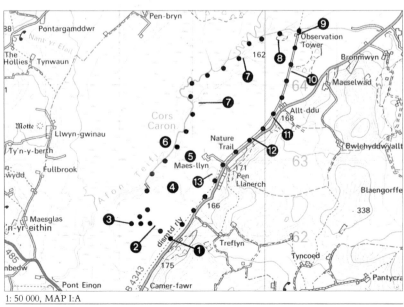

1: 50 000, MAP I:A

shiny dor beetle.
WELSH WATER AUTHORITY

I:7 ELENYDD★★

Near Devil's Bridge; the minor mountain road from Cwm Ystwyth to Rhayader passes through N part of the site. A minor road from Pontrhydfendigaid goes to Teifi pools at S end. Open country with complex ownership including the Crown. Open access, but with respect.

■ Blanket bog, acid grassland, open freshwater, rivers.

■ A vast upland site and one of the most important for nature conservation in Wales. Most of the plateau is covered by bog and acid grassland. The blanket bogs are of three main types, characterized by heather/cottongrass; heather/deer-grass; or purple moor-grass. The areas of pool and hummock bog are of great botanical and ornithological importance.

The area supports the largest known breeding populations of golden plover and dunlin in Wales. It is within the feeding range of the red kite and also supports a very high population of ravens and buzzards. **Birds** Peregrine, hen harrier, merlin, short-eared owl, red grouse, ring ouzel, redstart, pied flycatcher, wood warbler, wheatear.

I:8 COEDYDD A CHEUNANT RHEIDOL★

Near Devil's Bridge; access to woodland footpaths from end of classified road from Capel Bangor to Rheidol Falls, from Devil's Bridge, and from Parson's Bridge. Permit required to stray off footpaths.

■ Deep valley and gorge, oak woodland, river.

■ The deep and precipitous gorge of the River Rheidol is hazardous away from the footpaths. The woodland consists of even-aged sessile oak, with a light mixture of birch and rowan. Wetter areas have developed a more mixed woodland type, and a more diverse field layer with globeflower, Welsh poppy and forked spleenwort. **Birds** Red kite, pied flycatcher, redstart, wood warbler, tree pipit, woodpeckers, buzzard.
NATURE CONSERVANCY COUNCIL

I:9 CWM RHEIDOL★

Near Aberystwyth; leave reception centre near dam.

■ Sessile oak woodland, open water, boggy flushes.

■ The Cwm Rheidol nature trail follows a 2½ mile (4 km) route around an artificial lake. The oak woodland is principally of coppice origin. It is rich in woodland birds such as treecreepers, warblers, buzzards and ravens.
CENTRAL ELECTRICITY GENERATING BOARD

I:10 BRYN BRAS★

Near Aberystwyth; leave A44 W of Ponterwyd and take unclassified Ystumtuen road. Park on roadside.

■ High acid moorland, basin mires, upland grassland.

■ Dwarf shrub heath predominates on the N and W facing slopes with mainly heather, bilberry, bell heather and crowberry, while the warmer S and E slopes support acid grassland and western gorse. Basin mires and wet flushes of higher base status are notable for their mosses and liverworts. **Plants** Bog orchid, parsley fern, clubmosses, bryophytes, lichen.

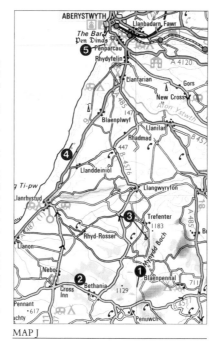

MAP J

J:1 CORS LLYN FARCH & LLYN FANOD

Near Tregaron; roadside parking either end of lake. No permit required but visitors are requested to keep strictly to the shoreline of Llwyn Fanod.

■ Lake, basin mire, poor fen.

■ A succession from open water communities, through reed swamp, willow and birch carr to acid bog; rich in invertebrates, particularly dragonflies, damselflies, caddisflies and lepidoptera. **Plants** Water lobelia, quillwort, awlwort, shoreweed, bogbean.
WEST WALES TRUST FOR NATURE CONSERVATION

J:2 CORS CARANOD

Near Aberystwyth; follow B4577 from Aberarth. Cors Caranod is N of this road a short distance E of Cross Inn.

■ Valley mire.

■ The mire supports a fen community. The catchment has well-developed heathland. A small area of modified raised bog is also present, with infilled peat cuttings and herb-rich wet pasture. **Plants** Crowberry, white sedge, bottle sedge, cottongrasses, bog mosses, lichens.

J:3 LLYN EIDDWEN

Near Aberystwyth; leave A485 near Bronant and take minor road towards Trefenter. Park on road.

■ Natural upland lake, unimproved upland grassland.

■ The unpolluted waters of the lake support a remarkably diverse flora. Cottongrass, sedges and water horsetails dominate the edge while the true aquatics include water lobelia, shoreweed, quillworts, awlwort and floating water-plantain. Wintering wildfowl and about 30 whooper swans often use the lake. Wide variety of invertebrates, particularly dragonflies and caddisflies. S and N of the lake are actively growing basin mires with vegetation grading into drier heathland-grassland communities. **Plants** Round-leaved sundew, cranberry, bog asphodel. **Dragonflies** Keeled skimmer.
WEST WALES TRUST FOR NATURE CONSERVATION

J:4 PENDERI HANGING OAKWOOD/ CREIGIAU PEN Y GRAIG

Near Aberystwyth; access on foot from Pen y Graig farm, signposted from A487 road.

■ Sea cliffs, hanging oak woodland.

■ The sessile oaks are stunted and wind pruned but the woodland still supports a good selection of characteristic plants. Seabirds breed on the cliffs and it is an important site for choughs. **Birds** Chough, shag, fulmar, cormorant, raven. **Mammals** Grey seal.
WEST WALES TRUST FOR NATURE CONSERVATION

J:5 ALLT WEN A TRAETH TANYBWLCH

Aberystwyth; access along track from the S side of the harbour pier. A track traverses the site.

■ Cliffs, sand and shingle spit/beach, saltmarsh, dune.

■ The seaward side of the shingle ridge is uncolonized while the landward side supports sea campion, sea herb-robert and red fescue. In the sandy areas sea holly, sea rocket, sea purslane and sea couch are present.
CEREDIGION DISTRICT COUNCIL

K:1 YNYS EIDIOL – YNYS HIR★★

Near Machynlleth; leave A487 at Eglwysfach and follow signs. Permit required, available on site.

■ Salt-marsh and mudflats, peatland, freshwater marsh, broad-leaved woodland.

■ A complex mixture of habitats. Ynys Eidiol possesses a rich wetland flora; Ynys Hir peatland contains all three species of sundew, with bog rosemary and ivy-leaved bellflower. The woodlands are of sessile oak, beech and ash, with a base-rich flora of sanicle and yellow archangel. The 31 species of butterfly include green hairstreak, grayling and five of fritillary; the site is equally rich in dragonflies, damselflies and moths. **Plants** Royal fern, heath spotted-orchid, butterwort, bog pimpernel, lesser skullcap,

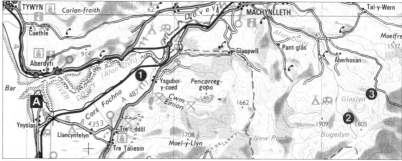

MAP K

bog asphodel, white beak-sedge. **Birds** Nightjar, peregrine, hen harrier, merlin, pied flycatcher, woodpeckers, red-breasted merganser, dunlin.
ROYAL SOCIETY FOR THE PROTECTION OF BIRDS

K:2 PUMLUMON*
Between Newtown and Aberystwyth; access from A44 between Ponterwyd and Llangurig, or from unclassified road to Geufron and Staylittle and roads through Hafren Forest. Park on roadside. The area is bleak, remote and subject to sudden changes in the weather; dress appropriately, and take a large-scale map.
■ Acid grassland, blanket bog, dwarf shrub heath, open water, rivers, streams.
■ The mountain is managed as traditional sheep walk and contains the sources of the Rivers Wye and Severn. Soils range from acid brown earths in the better-drained areas to deep blanket peat. The acid grassland is an unusual mixture of sheep's fescue and bilberry. The dwarf shrub heath supports a mixture of heather, bilberry and crowberry. **Plants** Starry saxifrage, fir clubmoss, alpine clubmoss. **Birds** Ring ouzel, red grouse, golden plover, common sandpiper, kestrel, buzzard, merlin, short-eared owl, red kite, hen harrier, peregrine, wheatear, whinchat, teal, Greenland white-fronted goose.

Bog pimpernel – see K:1, opposite page.

K:3 GLASLYN*
Near Machynlleth; access from unclassified road. Park on roadside, follow footpath to the reserve.
■ Heather moorland, river gorge, open water.
■ One of the last remaining areas of unspoilt heather moorland, including part of Glaslyn Lake, a large river gorge and spec-

tacular upland views for walkers. Moorland plants include heather, bilberry, crowberry, cottongrass, sedges, rushes and a variety of bog mosses. The reserve and lake are exciting for their birdlife, the moorland and gorge provide nesting sites for a variety of species. **Birds** Red kite, peregrine, merlin, red grouse, ring ouzel, golden plover, wheatear, whooper swan.
MONTGOMERY TRUST FOR NATURE CONSERVATION

K:A DYFI**
Near Aberystwyth; beach parking at Ynyslas. Permit required (apply warden) for Cors Fochno, open access to other areas.
■ Sand dunes, estuarine mudflats, saltmarsh, raised bog.
■ An estuary of outstanding physiographic interest with an exceptional range of habitats including the raised bog at Cors Fochno. A permit is required to visit this (apply warden). Visitors may be diverted to Cors Caron (I:A) in order to alleviate pressure.
① Reception centre open Easter-Sept.
② The shingle beach is unstable below high tide line: constant movement of pebbles inhibits colonization. Elsewhere, it is quickly colonized by lichens, and flowering plants such as sea campion, sea beet and scurvy grass take root between the stones.
③ At the top of the ridge, sand accumulates around tide-borne debris at high water mark, and under favourable conditions, sea rocket and prickly saltwort begin to stabilize the sand. If they survive the winter storms, these embryo dunes are colonized by sand couch and marram grasses, which create increasingly stable conditions, and the yellow dune ridges begin to support a wider range of plants. Red fescue grass and sand sedge are typical, with mosses, lichens and colourful fungi, all of which leave organic residues which further help to bind the sand. Tiny spring ephemerals such as little mouse-ear, and rue-leaved saxifrage which grow, flower and set seed before the summer drought, are peculiar to this demanding habitat.
④ Further from the sea, older 'grey dunes', the organic content of the sand increases and the sand has complete vegetation cover. The area is important for dune butterflies including grayling and dark green fritillary.
Snails are a key component of the dune ecosystem: discarded shells witness their value as food to birds.
⑤ Dune slacks are damp, low lying areas between the grey dunes. Ynyslas is noted for its orchids in early summer.

⑥ When the tide retreats, the exposed sand and mud seem barren, but plankton, shrimps, crustaceans, marine snails, bivalves and worms all live here.
The countless millions of invertebrate animals in the estuary provide food for predatory fish entering with the tide; birds benefit from the rich harvest when the tide is low. Waders such as ringed plover and curlew are numerous; bar-tailed godwit, grey plover and greenshank less frequent. Shelduck feed on the estuarine snails; goldeneye and merganser feed on fish at high tide.
⑦ In higher parts, less scoured by the tide, the mudflats become stabilized and colonized by green plants. Green algae and glasswort are among the first colonizers of bare mud, but the dominant vegetation is cord-grass, which can

withstand long periods of immersion in sea water.
Salt-marsh is unsuitable for waders, but ducks and geese thrive here. Greenland white-fronted geese winter on the salt-marsh and birds of prey take advantage of these large concentrations of passerines, waders and duck.
⑧ The raised bog is a gently undulating mosaic of hummocks and hollows. Low shrubs such as bog-myrtle, heather and cross-leaved heath dominate the hummocks. The hollows are green lawns of bog mosses. Birdlife is notable: hen harriers, short-eared owls, passing merlin and peregrine are prominent. Abundant dragonflies, whose numbers have increased due to good management. One of the most southerly locations for the large heath butterfly.
NATURE CONSERVANCY COUNCIL

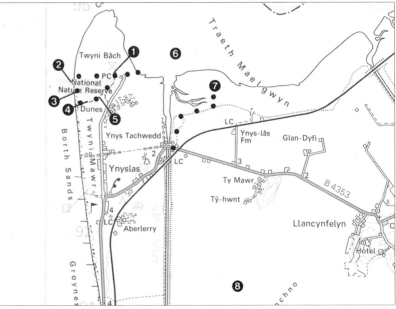

1:50 000, MAP K:A

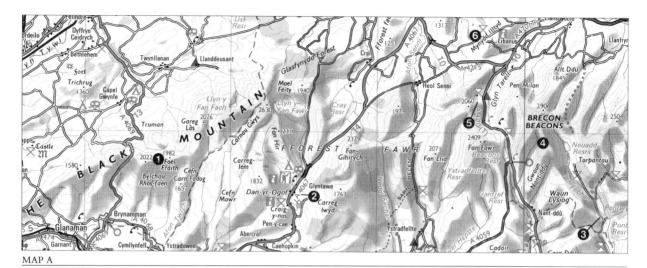

MAP A

A:1 MYNYDD DU*

At the head of the Swansea valley; access to footpath network from many points on A4067, A4068, A4069 nearby roads and minor roads. The site is exposed and subject to sudden changes in weather.

■ Upland limestone grassland, open water, cave systems.

■ Large area of exposed limestone with rock ledge and upland plant communities. Features include two corrie lakes and a 4-mile (6.5 km) escarpment of Old Red Sandstone. **Plants** Northern bedstraw, roseroot, dwarf willow, cowberry.

BRECON BEACONS NATIONAL PARK

A:2 OGOF FFYNNON DDU*

Near Abercraf; from A4067 just N of Abercraf, take unclassified road to Penwyllt, and park.

■ Grassland, crags, limestone pavement, cave systems.

■ Heather moorland dominates the plateau. The limestone grassland is floristically richer while the pavement areas support shade-tolerant and relict woodland species. An extensive cave system goes many miles into the mountain and is one of the largest, deepest and best studied systems in Britain. **Plants** Green spleenwort, lily-of-the-valley, mossy saxifrage, mountain everlasting, small scabious, limestone bedstraw, mountain melick, autumn gentian. **Birds** (Breeding) ring ouzel, wheatear.

NATURE CONSERVANCY COUNCIL

A:3 PENTWYN RESERVOIR*

Near Merthyr Tydfil; access from unclassified road traversing the W side of Taf Fechan and Pentwyn reservoirs. Park at the Pentwyn dam. Permit required: apply BWT, Lion House, Lion Street, Brecon, Powys, LD3 7AY.

■ Reservoir, exposed mud and marsh, woodland and scrub, disused railway.

■ Seasonally used by a good selection of wildfowl and waders. The surrounding woodlands add to the diversity of flora and fauna.

BRECKNOCK WILDLIFE TRUST

A:4 BRECON BEACONS**

Between Brecon and Merthyr Tydfil; access from various points along the A470. Park on roadside.

■ Upland/montane grassland and blanket bog; dwarf shrub heath; broadleaved woodlands; precipitous slopes, rock outcrops/ledges; river/stream valleys.

■ The limestone and Old Red Sandstone of the plateau has been weathered into huge escarpments which provide wide vistas. The grazed grasslands contrast with the rich, rock ledge flora, while both support an abundance of upland birds. **Plants** Globeflower, purple and mossy saxifrage, Wilson's filmy fern, green spleenworth. **Birds** Peregrine, merlin, ring ouzel, buzzard, wheatear.

A:5 CRAIG CERRIG GLEISIAD*

Between Merthyr Tydfil and Brecon; access on foot from lay-by on A470. Keep to footpaths. Crags and gullies dangerous – do not climb. The site is exposed and subject to sudden changes in weather: as with all upland sites, dress appropriately and take a large-scale map.

■ Upland grassland and dwarf shrub/heath; crags, rocky outcrops, gullies.

■ Two crags dominate the reserve, separated by a broad ridge extending N to the rocky outcrops of Fan Frynych. The upland vegetation is dominated by bilberry and mat-grass.

On the crags and in the gullies a number of unusual Arctic-Alpine plants survive at the S limit of their range in Britain. Of the 60 bird species recorded, 30 are known to breed, including peregrine, raven, red grouse and ring ouzel. **Plants** Purple saxifrage, globeflower, green spleenwort, Wilson's filmy fern, northern bedstraw, Welsh poppy, parsley fern. **Birds** Merlin, dipper, redstart, buzzard, wheatear, grey wagtail, tree pipit.

NATURE CONSERVANCY COUNCIL

A:6 ILLTYD POOLS & TRAETH MAWR*

Near Brecon; access on footpaths from A4215 or from unclassified road between A470 and A4215. Mires deep and dangerous; keep to footpaths. BWT permit required: apply Lion House, Lion Street, Brecon, Powys, LD3 7AY.

■ Pools, swamp/peat-filled hollows, damp grassland, heath.

■ Some of the pools on the summit ridge of Mynydd Illtyd are fed by base-rich water and support rare calcareous plants; others are more acidic with floating mats of vegetation. In the peat, well-developed hummocks and hollows have formed with bog mosses, cross-leaved heath, bog pimpernel and cottongrass. The site supports waders, wildfowl, heathland and woodland birds, a number of rare aquatic insects and spiders. **Plants** Lesser marshwort, shoreweed, great fen-sedge, slender sedge, star sedge.

BRECKNOCK WILDLIFE TRUST

B:1 CRAIG Y CILAU*

Near Crickhowell; access from unclassified Llangattock to Blaen Onneu road; park on roadside. Keep clear of the caves and crags, which are very dangerous.

■ Limestone escarpment topped by dry millstone grit moorland, grassland slopes on Old Red Sandstone, extensive cave system.

■ The reserve is extremely important for its flora, with over 250 species. The crags support a number of uncommon trees which include large- and small-leaved lime and five species of whitebeam.

Extensive caves and underground galleries lie under the mountain. Public access is permitted to Eglwys Faen.

The hawthorn scrub on the screes provides a nesting habitat for redstart, wood warblers, pied flycatchers and tree pipits. Badger breed here and the caves are important roosts for bats. A small raised bog supports cottongrass, cross-leaved heath and sundew. **Trees** Whitebeams. **Plants** Angular Solomon's seal, limestone polypody, Alpine enchanter's nightshade, mossy saxifrage, brittle bladder-fern. **Birds** Peregrine, ring ouzel, dipper, raven, wheatear, whinchat, buzzard, grey wagtail.

NATURE CONSERVANCY COUNCIL

MAP B

B:2 SUGAR LOAF*

Near Abergavenny; *minor road from A40 and A465 bounds the area; roadside parking. Keep to footpaths.*
■ Upland grassland, bracken/bilberry heath, broad-leaved woodland.
■ Old red sandstone upland supporting acid grassland and heath, grading down to oak, beech and damp alder woodland. The area includes the St Mary's Vale Nature Trail. **Plants** Bryophytes, lichens. **Birds** Kestrel, buzzard.
NATIONAL TRUST

B:3 STRAWBERRY COTTAGE WOOD

Near Abergavenny; *park near the Stanton-Forest coal pit road junction. Footbridge across the Honddu; cross the fields, turn left through gate by Strawberry Cottage.*
■ Hanging sessile oak woodland.
■ The woodland grows on the side of a steep old red sandstone bluff and supports some unusually well-grown oaks, both sessile and pedunculate.
GWENT TRUST FOR NATURE
CONSERVATION

B:4 TALYBONT RESERVOIR*

Near Brecon; *leave A40 Brecon to Abergavenny road and follow signs to Talybont. Through the village, unclassified road S leads to reservoir. Signposted parking on road on W shore of lake. Footpaths around the lake. BWT permit required for nature reserve only.*
■ Open water, damp meadows.
■ Particularly interesting for wintering wildfowl. At S end dabbling and wading birds feed in muddy shallows, and marshy area floods in winter supporting interesting flora. **Birds** Bewick's and whooper swans, green and common sandpipers, greenshank, goosander, wigeon, teal. **Plants** Needle spike-rush, brown sedge.
WELSH WATER AUTHORITY

C:1 BLACK MOUNTAINS**

Near Hay-on-Wye; *take minor road to head of Olchon Valley (SO 263337). Follow footpath up stream and on to hilltops.*
■ Upland.
■ The Black Mountains are an extensive upland massif with deep steep-sided valleys frequently bounded by cliffs. Although they cover a large area, the hills occupying the English/Welsh border are representative of the range as a whole. There is a magnificent series of cliffs, the Darrens, along the border. The higher ground has extensive areas of purple moor-grass, heather, bilberry with a good deal of cowberry and crowberry in places. Large blanket mires with the three cottongrasses – common, hare's-tail and broad-leaved – are found over extensive areas. The mountain flora is rich, especially on the more calcareous cliffs such as the Darrens. Notable are globeflower, mossy saxifrage, lesser skullcap, green spleenwort, shoreweed, brittle bladder, limestone, beech and oak fern, fir and stag's-horn clubmoss, bee orchid. There is a good selection of upland birds including red grouse and peregrine.

C:2 PWLL Y WRACH*

Near Talgarth; *park at entrance to reserve, one mile (1.5 km) SE of Talgarth. Keep to footpaths.*
■ Broad-leaved woodland, wet flushes, small river.
■ This steep woodland above the River Enig is of considerable botanical interest,

Great crested grebe – see C:4.

arising from variations in bedrock, soil chemistry and drainage. Upper parts of the valley support sessile oak woodland over a ground flora of acid-loving species such as heather and hard fern. Lower down, nutrients from the slopes encourage ash and elm woodland with hazel, holly, spindle, dogwood and field maple. Ground flora is dominated by bluebell, wood sorrel and enchanter's nightshade. The path leads to a waterfall, which supports a rich diversity of ferns, mosses and liverworts. **Plants** Herb Paris, toothwort, adder's-tongue, alternate-leaved golden saxifrage, early-purple orchid. **Butterflies** Silver-washed fritillary, speckled wood. **Birds** Dipper, nuthatch, treecreeper, grey wagtail.
BRECKNOCK WILDLIFE TRUST

C:3 LLANDEILO – GRABAN ROADSIDE*

Near Builth Wells; *leave A470 one mile (1.5 km) NW of Erwood or at Llanstephan to the S. Cross river at either point. Access at former Erwood station and Llanstephen Halt.*
■ Woodland, meadow, marsh, disused railway.

■ Old Red Sandstone and Upper Silurian rocks support a varied flora, including deep woodland in the Bach Howey Brook ravine and the old railway's grassland. The site is also rich in butterflies and other insects including glow-worm and has a diverse bird population. **Amphibians** Great crested newt.
HEREFORDSHIRE & RADNORSHIRE NATURE
TRUST

C:4 LLYN BWCH-LLYN LAKE*

Near Builth Wells; *located to N of B4594. Approach from unclassified road N of the lake. H&RNT permit required.*
■ Open freshwater, fringing marsh.
■ The largest natural lake in Radnor, though modified for water abstraction, with aquatic and freshwater marsh vegetation. An important site for winter wildfowl, breeding water birds and passage migrants. **Plants** Greater spearwort, lesser bulrush, skullcap. **Birds** Great crested grebe, teal, dunlin, sandpipers.
HEREFORDSHIRE & RADNORSHIRE NATURE
TRUST

C:5 RHOS GOCH COMMON*

Midway between Newchurch and Pain-scastle; *park in Rhosgoch village; access from track at S end of site. Permit required from NCC Warden.*
■ Raised mire, poor fen swamp; well-developed willow/birch carr.
■ The surface of the raised mire consists of numerous wet hollows or pools separated by drier ridges which are dominated by purple moor-grass, heather, cross-leaved heath, bilberry and cottongrass. The hollows contain abundant bog mosses with bogbean and bog asphodel.

A carr is mainly common sallow and birch, with some pedunculate oak, rowan and guelder-rose. Sedges and common reed are most prominent in the ground flora, but royal fern also occurs.

The poor-fen swamp is dominated by a rush-sedge community with horsetails and ragged-robin. **Plants** Meadow thistle, greater spearwort, marsh fern, marsh speedwell, lesser skullcap, petty whin.
NATURE CONSERVANCY COUNCIL

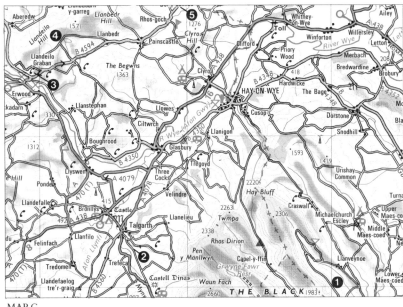

MAP C

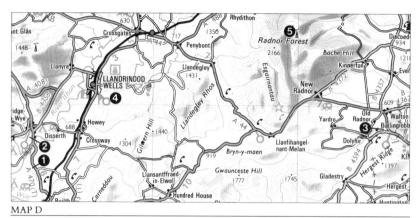

MAP D

D:1 CORS Y LLYN

Near Newbridge-on-Wye; turn off A470 S *of Newbridge-on-Wye and follow narrow road to small reserve car park. NCC permit required.*

■ Basin mire, birch/willow carr, pine woodland, acid grassland.

■ Cors y Llyn is a small composite basin mire lying in an irregular glacial hollow. The lagg community is dominated by birch which supports the rare epiphytic lichen Cetraria sepincola. **Plants** Sundew, cranberry, bog asphodel, crowberry, white beaked-sedge, meadow thistle, petty whin, dyer's greenweed, heath spotted-orchid.

NATURE CONSERVANCY COUNCIL

D:2 ABERITHON

Near Newbridge-on-Wye; take A470 S *from Newbridge on Wye, then turn right on to unclassified Brynwern road. Access through gate 200 yards (180 m) from junction.*

■ Peat bog, fen and fringing willow carr, old meadowland.

■ Peat cutting ceased about 50 years ago, and the area quickly filled with water. Since then, there has been little interference from man. The present flora is a mixture of bog and fen plants with areas of common reed and bulrush, and with willow which is now invading the fen areas. The surrounding herb-rich meadows support a wide range of plants, including a few large old Scots pine. The birch trees support the rare lichen Cetraria sepincola which is known only on a few sites in England and Wales. The birds and insect life is abundant and varied. **Plants** Lesser bladderwort, meadow thistle, bogbean, marsh cinquefoil, Dyer's greenweed, ivy-leaved bellflower, floating club-rush.

HEREFORDSHIRE & RADNORSHIRE NATURE TRUST LTD

D:3 STANNER ROCKS*

Near Kington; site adjoins A44 at junction with B4594. Limited parking on roadside. NCC permit, available from the warden, is required to visit areas away from the quarry floor.

■ Mixed deciduous woodland, scrub, grassland; rocky outcrops; scree; abandoned quarry face.

■ Situated on doleritic cliffs, this small reserve contains several botanical species of Continental, European or Mediterranean distribution. The cliff grassland is subject to summer drought and the woodlands and cliffs are important for lichens and bryophytes. **Plants** Sheep's-bit, sticky catchfly, perennial knawel, rock stonecrop, common rock-rose.

NATURE CONSERVANCY COUNCIL

D:4 LAKE WOOD*

Near Llandrindod Wells; roads from town centre lead to the lake and wood. Park around the lake. Keep to footpaths.

■ Sessile oak woodland.

■ The species-rich mature oak woodland illustrates the variation in vegetation of free-draining and waterlogged soils. The upper wood has well-developed understorey of hazel, blackthorn and hawthorn while the nutrient-rich lower slopes are dominated by alder and willow.

RADNOR DISTRICT COUNCIL

D:5 MYNYDD FFOESIDOES

Near Knighton; take B4357 and B4372 to Kinnerton. Take the road NW to Fieldstile Farm, turn left to the field gate where parking is available. Follow the fence on foot for 1/2 mile (0.8 km) to the reserve. Access may be restricted during periods of fire danger.

■ Upland heather moorland, blanket bog, pools.

■ The site is on the summit plateau of Radnor Forest and is a fine example of submontane heath dominated by heather, moorland grasses and mosses. Peaty hollows and pools support cottongrass and purple moor-grass, and the reserve is important for upland birds.

HEREFORD & RADNORSHIRE NATURE TRUST LTD

E:1 SHROPSHIRE UNION CANAL, MONTGOMERY SECTION**

Newtown to Tan-y-Fron; access to towpath where canal is adjacent to road. See also F:1.

■ Waterway, fringing vegetation, reedbed, grassland, woodland.

■ This section of the Shropshire Union Canal has not been legally open to traffic since 1944. However, it has been maintained as a waterway, and its restoration in the 1970s has greatly benefitted the flora and fauna. Its aquatic and emergent plant communities are species-rich in a way unmatched by any comparable habitat in the area. Dragonflies, damselflies and caddisflies are abundant; the site is noted for molluscs and the rare flatworm Bdellocephala punctata. **Plants** Flowering rush, frogbit, floating water-plantain, greater and fat duckweed, water dock, unbranched bur-reed, cyperus sedge. **Birds** Kingfisher, grey heron, wagtails, reed warbler, reed bunting. **Mammals** Otter, water vole.

BRITISH WATERWAYS BOARD

E:2 ROUNDTON HILL*

Near Montgomery; from Church Stoke take unclassified road to Old Church Stoke and the foot of the hill.

■ Hill grassland, open woodland, scrub, scree, rock outcrop, wet flushes.

■ The ancient hill grassland – never ploughed, reseeded or fertilized – is of great botanical interest. Summer drought results in a number of unusual species adapted to such a condition.

The lower slopes are well-wooded, while streamsides and wet flushes add another dimension with characteristic plants. Mosses and lichens include a number of rarities among the hundred or so species recorded. An ancient rabbit warren provides habitat for a number of mammals. Several species of bats hibernate here. **Plants** Mountain pansy, upright chickweeds, shepherd's cress, lesser chickweed, early forget-me-not. **Mammals** Polecat, badger, stoat, weasel. **Birds** Redstart, woodpeckers, raven, buzzard.

MONTGOMERY TRUST FOR NATURE CONSERVATION

E:3 LLYN MAWR*

Near Newtown; access from A470 to Machynlleth. Exit N of Pontdolgoch, follow unclassified road past Bwlch y Garreg to end. Footpaths radiate from here.

■ Upland lake, acid grassland, wet heath, marsh.

■ The lake lies in a narrow basin on an upland plateau. The lakeside vegetation is dominated by rushes and extensive areas of willow carr. Quillwort and yellow water-lily are present in the lake. The marsh and wet heath areas are species-rich and contain bog mosses and marsh cinquefoil.

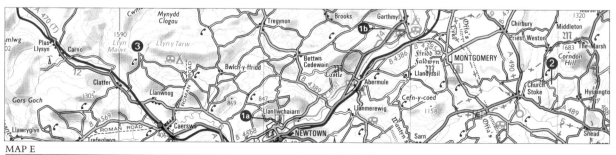

MAP E

Surveys of aquatic invertebrates have revealed a wide range of characteristic species. The uncommon caddis Molanna palpata has been recorded here. **Plants** Sundew, butterwort, bog asphodel, northern marsh-orchid, marsh lousewort. **Birds** (Winter) Greenland white-fronted goose, whooper swan, goosander, great crested grebe, wigeon, goldeneye; (summer) stonechat, whinchat.
MONTGOMERY TRUST FOR NATURE CONSERVATION

F:1 SHROPSHIRE UNION CANAL, MONTGOMERY SECTION★★
Berview to Vyrnwey Aqueduct; see E:1 for access, habitat, general information and species list.
■ The section between Maerdy Bridge and Tanhouse Bridge supports a particularly rich and diverse flora.
BRITISH WATERWAYS BOARD

F:2 BREIDDEN HILL★
Near Welshpool; from A485 turn left at Trewern and follow either of two unclassified roads which traverse base of hill. Many footpaths cross the site. Visitors must not enter quarry workings currently in use; the abandoned quarry faces are dangerous.
■ Broad-leaved/conifer woodland, grassland, rocky outcrop, scree, abandoned quarry faces.
■ The extremely complex geological structure of this igneous outcrop creates conditions suitable for both acid- and lime-loving plants. The rock outcrops support a diverse lichen, moss and liverwort flora, while the steep broad-leaved woodlands add to the diversity. **Plants** Spiked speedwell, sticky catchfly.

F:3 LLANYMYNECH HILL
Near Oswestry; take A483 S to Pant. Turn right to the base of the hill.
■ Extensive grassland/woodland, natural rock faces/screes, abandoned quarries.
■ The site's many limestone plants are dominated by grasses but there are also

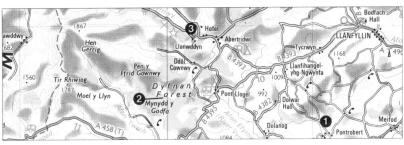

many rarities. The screes are notable for mosses and liverworts, and the rare whitebeam, Sorbus anglica, occurs on the cliffs. **Plants** Frog, green-winged and fragrant orchids, autumn lady's-tresses, mountain everlasting, stemless thistle, small scabious, knotted hedge parsley, autumn gentian.
MONTGOMERY TRUST FOR NATURE CONSERVATION

G:1 COED PENDUGWM★
Near Welshpool; from A495 take unclassified road NW through Pontrobert to Pendugwm.
■ Mature broad-leaved woodland.
■ Ancient oak and beech woodland with some birch and ash, and an understorey of rowan, hawthorn, hazel and holly. The ground flora is rich in wildflowers, especially bluebell, primrose, dog violet, wood anemone and wood sorrel. **Plants** Bird's-nest and early-purple orchids, yellow pimpernel, sanicle, cow-wheat, broad-leaved helleborine. **Birds** Pied flycatcher, redstart, wood warbler, dipper, nuthatch. **Mammals** Red squirrel.
MONTGOMERY TRUST FOR NATURE CONSERVATION

G:2 GWEUNYDD DYFNANT
Near Lake Vyrnwy; access from B4393 SE of Llanwddyn. Take unclassified road to Ddol Conwy and turn left through Dyfnant forest to the meadows.
■ Unimproved acid pasture with dry and damp areas, sloping steeply to the S.

Wild polecat – see E:2, Roundton Hill, opposite page.

■ **Plants** Burnet-saxifrage, tawny sedge, cross-leaved heath, bog asphodel.
MONTGOMERY TRUST FOR NATURE CONSERVATION

G:3 LAKE VYRNWY★★
Near Oswestry; take A495 and A490 from Oswestry to Llanfyllin and then B4393 to Llanwddyn. Nature trails and hides on site; information centre in summer.
■ Open water, scrub woodland, small meadows, deciduous woodland, conifer forest, heather moorland.
■ There is an enormous variety of habitats in this reserve. It is principally noted for its birds – almost 140 species have been recorded including rarities like great grey shrike, hawfinch, nightjar, quail, goshawk and osprey. Unusual plants include globeflower, and three species of clubmoss. Lichens, mosses, liverworts and ferns are abundant in the damp, deciduous woodlands.

The red squirrel, otter and polecat are resident mammals. The reserve supports many species of butterfly including silver-washed, high brown, pearl-bordered and small pearl-bordered fritillaries and purple and green hairstreaks. **Plants** Lesser twayblade, greater butterfly-, heath spotted- and southern marsh-orchids. **Birds** Red-breasted merganser, goosander, merlin, red and black grouse, whimbrel, long-eared owl, woodpeckers, dipper, ring ouzel, redstart, pied flycatcher, firecrest, siskin, crossbill, brambling.
ROYAL SOCIETY FOR THE PROTECTION OF BIRDS

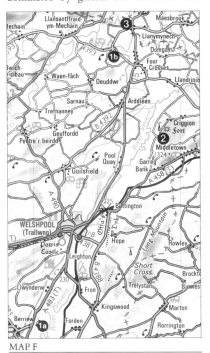

MAP F

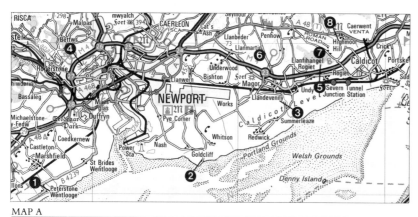

MAP A

A:1 Peterstone Wentlooge*

Near Cardiff; footpath past Peterstone Church to sea wall.

■ Mudflats, salt-marsh, maritime grassland, ditches and dykes.

■ The most important site in Gwent for variety of birds; best in winter. **Birds** Avocet, wood sandpiper, little stint, ruff, long-tailed duck, common scoter, little ringed and grey plovers, knot, shoveler, shelduck, dunlin. **Plants** Spiny rest-harrow, bristly oxtongue.

Gwent Trust for Nature Conservation

A:2 Goldcliff & Magor Pill*

Near Newport; footpath from Goldcliff to Goldcliff Point, or follow footpath along foreshore to Magor Pill.

■ Mudflat, salt-marsh, reclaimed grassland, reeds.

■ Foreshore for passage and winter waders and wildfowl; reclaimed land for birds and invertebrates; salt-marsh at Magor Pill for locally rare plants. **Birds** Peregrine, short-eared owl, merlin; (breeding) redshank.

Gwent Trust for Nature Conservation

A:3 Magor Marsh*

Near Newport; immediately S of Magor on Redwick road turn left over railway bridge; car park in 200 yds (180 m) on right.

■ Fenland, damp grassland, scrub, lake, reed-beds, marsh, meadow.

■ The only remaining fenland in Gwent, with a wide range of fen and marsh communities from abandoned wet meadows to fringing reed and open water. The sparse scrub, willow pollards and reed are excellent for associated bird species, and it is an important site for migrants. **Plants** Flowering rush, frogbit, arrowhead, marestail, spearwort, marsh-marigold, bulrush, purple-loosestrife. **Birds** Garganey, water rail, shoveler, reed and grasshopper warblers.

Gwent Trust for Nature Conservation

A:4 Allt-yr-Yn Nature Park

In Newport; on NE side of town, between residential area and M4. Roadside parking.

■ Semi-natural and coppice woodland.

■ An urban nature park under development: no striking rarities, but potential.

Gwent Trust for Nature Conservation

A:5 Burness Castle Quarry

Near Caldicot; M4, exit 23, cross M4 to disused quarries on N side. Permit required: apply GTNC.

■ Limestone quarry.

■ This disused quarry has been colonized by a rich flora with a number of herbaceous species which are of limited distribution in the county. More than 90 plant species have been recorded; mosses are plentiful, too. **Plants** Star of Bethlehem, viper's-bugloss. **Reptiles** Adders.

Gwent Trust for Nature Conservation

A:6 Penhow Woodlands*

Near Newport; roadside parking and access to circular walk within the main woodland, Coed Wen; no right of way across farmland to the smaller detached blocks of woodland (The Knoll and West Lone), but footpaths run close by. No permit required for Coed Wen.

■ Mixed woodland.

■ This small nature reserve comprises three areas of ancient woodland growing on carboniferous limestone and calcareous drift. The two blocks known as Coed Wen and West Lone have developed on fertile deep soils and support trees of greater stature than the Knoll which has developed on a much thinner soil. The woodlands generally contain a rich mixture of native tree species and many plants characteristic of mixed woodland. The parish boundaries are marked by ancient pollarded oaks and limes.

In 1980 a considerable area of Coed Wen was felled following an attack of Dutch elm disease, and the coppice regrowth has been highly successful. Future management, aimed at diversity of species and age, will be achieved by further coppicing. **Plants** Upright (or Tintern) spurge, bird's-nest orchid, green hellebore, wild daffodil, lesser periwinkle.

Nature Conservancy Council

A:7 Hardwick Wood

Near Caldicot; at Highmoor Hill enter woodland on FC track beside telephone box. Turn right on to footpath and right again where it forks: the reserve is on left.

■ Mixed deciduous woodland.

■ Half-acre remnant of mixed deciduous wood amid extensive forestry developments, still supporting a rich ground flora of lime-loving plants. **Plants** Greater and lesser butterfly- and early-purple orchids, marsh and broad helleborine, common twayblade.

Gwent Trust for Nature Conservation

A:8 Brockwell's Meadows

Near Caldicot; adjoins road junction at Brockwell's Farm. Permit required, from GTNC, Monmouth, normal office hours.

■ Pasture.

■ A fine example of unimproved grassland on a lime-rich soil supporting a rich variety of herbaceous plants now of limited distribution in the county. Also interesting for a variety of insects. **Plants** Green-winged orchid, autumn lady's-tresses, large thyme.

Gwent Trust for Nature Conservation

B:1 Henllys Bog

Near Cwmbran; from Henllys village go to Pandy Mawr Farm; walk from there, entering reserve over stile and footbridge.

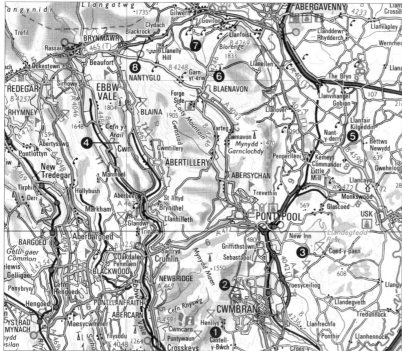

MAP B

■ Wetland, damp grassland.
■ A small site, but over 85 plant species have been recorded, including some of limited distribution. **Plants** Marsh helleborine, sundews.
GWENT TRUST FOR NATURE CONSERVATION

B:2 FIVE LOCKS CANAL★
Near Cwmbran; access from Five Locks, Pontnewydd, to Bevan's Bridge.
■ Canal, farmland.
■ An important habitat for aquatic plants, invertebrates and amphibians. Over 120 plant species have been recorded, dragonflies abound, and the alder trees harbour an interesting range of birds, summer and winter. **Plants** Water-milfoil, pondweeds, monkeyflower. **Birds** Twite, kingfisher, siskin, redpoll.
GWENT TRUST FOR NATURE CONSERVATION

B:3 LLANDEGFEDD RESERVOIR★
Near Pontypool; parking close to dam, from which various circular walks.
■ Reservoir, woodland, steep valley, open hill.
■ A large reservoir which has become one of the three most important sites in the region for wintering wildfowl; some notable migrants. **Birds** Goosander, great crested grebe, migrating terns, goldeneye, wigeon, teal, pochard.
WELSH WATER AUTHORITY

B:4 CWM MERDDOG
Near Ebbw Vale; from A4064 S of Ebbw Vale at Cwm cemetery, walk E to the reserve.
■ Mainly beech/oak woodland, scrub.
■ The wet stream-side flushes have a rich flora. **Birds** Pied flycatcher, redstart.
GWENT TRUST FOR NATURE CONSERVATION

B:5 PRIORY WOOD★
Near Usk; roadside parking.
■ Broad-leaved woodland.
■ The finest remaining example of ancient semi-natural woodland on the Silurian rocks of the Usk inlier, containing a variety of woodland types. **Trees** Pedunculate and sessile oak, silver birch. **Birds** Pied flycatcher.
GWENT TRUST FOR NATURE CONSERVATION

B:6 BLORENGE★
Near Blaenavon; approach on B4246, or unclassified road from Blaenavon to Llanellen; roadside parking.
■ Sub-montane heath, calcareous grassland.
■ Sub-montane heath is rare in south Wales: large areas of heather. Best in summer. **Plants** (Heath) crowberry, cowberry; (grassland) hairy violet, wild thyme, fairy flax, salad burnet.
BRITISH COAL

B:7 GILWERN HILL
Near Brynmawr; approach from unclassified road between Blaenavon and Gilwern; roadside parking.
■ Limestone grassland, old quarries, ash wood.
■ Carboniferous limestone landscape supporting a characteristic grassland community, including several locally rare species. Beware disused mine shafts and natural

swallow holes. **Plants** Autumn gentian, brittle bladder-fern.
BRITISH COAL

B:8 CWM CLYDACH★
Near Brynmawr; footpath from Clydach village or from minor road between A465 and Daren Felen; roadside parking at both points.
■ Beech wood, calcareous grassland, gorge, damp areas.
■ The Carboniferous limestone and millstone grit of the gorge give rise to both acidic and base-rich conditions and support mature beech woodland. The areas of broken canopy and the woodland edge support a range of grasses and sedges, together with violets and wild thyme; under the canopy itself, look for two species of saprophytic plants, yellow bird's-nest and bird's-nest orchids. In the damp, shady gorge, ferns and lower plants abound. **Plants** Soft-leaved sedge, whitebeam (Sorbus porrigentiformis), early dog violet, large thyme. **Birds** Dipper, grey wagtail, redstart, raven, nuthatch, treecreeper, green and great spotted woodpeckers, tawny owl, sparrowhawk.
NATURE CONSERVANCY COUNCIL

C:1 LLWYN-Y-CELYN BOG
Near Shirenewton; from crossroads on B4235 N of Shirenewton, continue N about one mile (1.5 km); roadside parking. Permit required from GTNC, Monmouth, normal office hours.
■ Lowland bog.
■ Only just over an acre in area, the reserve supports a wide range of marsh plants. Colourful in early summer. **Plants** Monkshood, marsh lousewort, lesser skullcap, marsh-mallow, bogbean, water avens.
GWENT TRUST FOR NATURE CONSERVATION

C:2 LOWER WYE VALLEY WOODLANDS★★
Near Chepstow; approach from N along Offa's Dyke Path from Brockweir; or via Lan-

caut. *Park on verge ½ mile (0.8 km) after village. Keep to footpaths.*
■ Woodland, salt-marsh, river, cliffs.
■ These woods occupy the steep valley slopes and cliffs along the E bank of the River Wye, stretching for about 4 miles (6.5 km) from Brockweir to Chepstow. They lie on limestone, are structurally diverse, rich in trees and shrubs and support many rare species.
Below Lancaut is a salt-marsh of botanical interest, grading naturally into valley woodland, one of the few examples of this transition in Britain. A number of cliff ledges and old quarries add diversity: nest sites for birds and some interesting geological exposures. The richest and most diverse part of all is at Lancaut, where the whole range of habitats is illustrated. **Plants** Narrow-leaved helleborine, ivy broomrape, wild service-tree, green hellebore, pale St John's-wort, upright spurge, sea and subterranean clovers, rock stonecrop, lesser calamint, wood stitchwort, fiddle dock, fingered sedge.
FORESTRY COMMISSION/GLOUCESTER TRUST FOR NATURE CONSERVATION

C:3 LOWER WYE GORGE★★
Near Chepstow; parking and access from various points along A466. There is a 16-mile (25.5 km) waymarked walk between Chepstow and Monmouth, a reception centre and picnic centre at Tintern, and a nature trail at Wyndcliff. Keep to footpaths.
■ Broad-leaved woodland, river gorge.
■ The once-turbulent waters of the river Wye have carved a spectacular gorge through the local strata of carboniferous limestone and sandstone rocks which now support lime- and acid-loving floras respectively, and have evolved an enormous range of plants and some of the most important woodlands left in Britain. This deep section of the river is now tidal, and in its lower reaches becomes increasingly brackish.
The enormous diversity of woodland is a

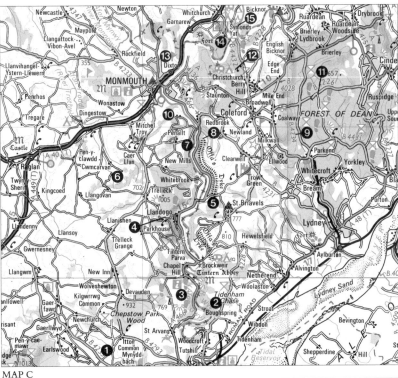

MAP C

GWENT

product of varying conditions of soil, rock, slope and drainage, and includes oak and beech woods on the old red sandstone; ash, small-leaved lime, field maple, wych elm, whitebeam and yew on the limestone, and alder on the damp river sides. The ground flora is equally diverse and includes a large number of extremely rare species. In turn there is also a great wealth of insects, particularly butterflies. **Plants** Upright spurge, herb Paris, giant bellflower, yellow bird's-nest, crane's-bill, narrow-leaved bittercress, toothwort, common wintergreen, spurge-laurel, fingered sedge, ploughman's-spike-nard, marjoram. **Butterflies** Silver-washed fritillary, purple and green hairstreak, holly blue, speckled wood. **Mammals** Greater horseshoe bat, yellow-necked mouse.

C:4 CLEDDON SHOOTS*
Near Llandogo; small parking area at N end of reserve; follow sign to Cleddon Falls.
■ Deciduous woodland, glacial spillway.
■ Located on old red sandstone and limestone, the valley comprises nearly 25 acres of ancient semi-natural woodland. Falls and flushes form an additional habitat with a diverse bryophyte community. **Trees** Wild cherry, holly, yews. **Birds** Pied flycatcher, redstart, wood warbler, green and great spotted woodpeckers, grey wagtail, buzzard.
GWENT TRUST FOR NATURE CONSERVATION

C:5 BIGSWEIR WOOD*
Near Lydney; leave the A466 on unclassified road E of Bigsweir Bridge; enter wood on Offa's Dyke Path in about ½ mile (0.8 km).
■ Woodland.
■ An acidic oak/ash/beech wood with areas of small-leaved lime/beech coppice and typical flora. **Birds** Hawfinch, pied flycatcher, redstart, buzzard.
WOODLAND TRUST

C:6 CROES ROBERT WOOD
Near Monmouth; from Trellech on B4239, take unclassified road W. Take the first right fork; park where woodland adjoins road on right. Contact GTNC, Monmouth office, normal office hours, before visiting.
■ Coppiced broad-leaved woodland.
■ A steeply sloping wood dominated by ash and wych elm. The acid soils produce a mixed and varied flora encouraged by coppice management; an interesting range of bryophytes and birdlife.
GWENT TRUST FOR NATURE CONSERVATION

C:7 PRISK WOOD
Near Monmouth; from crossroads at Penallt, continue ¾ mile (1 km); park where woodland meets road on right.
■ Semi-natural ancient broad-leaved woodland.
■ On side of Wye Gorge, this woodland supports an enormous diversity of trees and shrubs. Birds and insects are abundant. **Trees** Ash, wych elm, cherry, small leaved lime. **Birds** Pied and spotted flycatchers, sparrowhawk, woodcock.
GWENT TRUST FOR NATURE CONSERVATION

C:8 HIGHBURY WOOD*
Near Monmouth; On Offa's Dyke Path, , mile (0.5 km) S of Lower Redbrook; keep to footpaths.

■ Woodland.
■ This National Nature Reserve is a fine example of the rich ancient semi-natural woods of the Wye Valley. Situated on limestones which occupy the steep valley sides, it contains some old lime kilns indicating man's long use of the site. It is structurally diverse, with a rich variety of trees and shrubs – more than 30 species including wild service-tree, whitebeam, spurge-laurel and yew. It supports an interesting range of unusual small-leaved lime communities. The ground flora is rich and is mainly composed of calcicole species including tutsan, broad-leaved helleborine, woodruff and a variety of ferns. The diverse birdlife includes hawfinch, wood warbler and buzzard.
NATURE CONSERVANCY COUNCIL

C:9 NAGSHEAD*
Near Cinderford; enter reserve off B4431 immediately after leaving Parkend.
■ Woodland, streams.
■ An area of mature oakwood lying within the Forest of Dean, supporting a largely acidic flora. An impressive breeding bird population. **Mammals** Fallow deer. **Birds** Pied flycatcher, redstart, wood warbler, dipper, grey wagtail. **Butterflies** White admiral.
ROYAL SOCIETY FOR THE PROTECTION OF BIRDS

C:10 PENALLT OLD CHURCH WOOD
Near Monmouth; the reserve lies below the road leading to Penallt old church.
■ Deciduous woodland.
■ Oak woodland on old red sandstone supporting a wide range of woodland herbs; diverse birdlife. **Plants** Moschatel, wild daffodil. **Birds** Flycatchers, nuthatch, tree pipit, sparrowhawk.
GWENT TRUST FOR NATURE CONSERVATION

C:11 FOREST OF DEAN**
Near Lydney; many roads cross the forest – good access from B4226, B4431, B4234. Speech House (SO 620120) and Cannop (SO 608110) are particularly good areas.
■ Woodland.
■ A former royal deer country forest, this is a vast area of woodland. There has been replanting with conifers but extensive tracts of predominantly oak with occasional beech remain. Most of the forest is on acid soils. The understorey of holly, birch and rowan is sparse and the ground flora is dominated by creeping soft-grass, bracken, bilberry and heather. Mixed oak/beech/lime/ash wood occupies the more lime-rich parts. The stream valleys, ponds and small bogs are particularly interesting.
The finest and oldest oaks are in the Speech House area; they support an exceptionally rich lichen and moss epiphytic community. **Birds** Pied flycatcher, siskin, redstart, crossbill, wood warbler, dipper, woodcock. **Plants** White helleborine, stinking hellebore, bog asphodel, common wintergreen, bog pimpernel, stag's-horn clubmoss, ivy-leaved bellflower, few-flowered spike-rush.
FORESTRY COMMISSION

C:12 LADY PARK WOOD*
Near Monmouth; park on forest road in Mailscot Wood or at Symonds Yat. From Mailscot Wood, path leads to suspension bridge across river and network of tracks.

■ Mixed broad-leaved woodland, limestone cliffs, river.
■ The spectacular, wooded meandering gorge of the River Wye here cuts through rocks of Old Red Sandstone and carboniferous limestone. Lady Park Wood and Mailscot Wood extend from the summit of a 600-foot (180-m) ridge down to the river, and the network of steep and physically demanding paths provide some of the most spectacular woodland walks in the district. These are some of the best examples of mixed deciduous woodland in Britain, supporting a diverse flora including some rarities, a wide selection of birds, and a vast range of insects.
From Symonds Yat, there are spectacular views of the limestone cliffs of the gorge and, in most years, sightings of nesting peregrine falcons. **Trees** Beech, small- and large-leaved lime, wild service-tree, hazel, wych elm, oak, ash, yew. **Plants** Yellow bird's-nest, herb Paris, spurge-laurel, common wintergreen, fingered sedge, thin-spiked wood sedge, ploughman's-spike-nard, woodruff, yellow archangel, marjoram. **Birds** Wood warbler, redstart, raven, grey wagtail, green and great spotted woodpeckers, nuthatch, sparrowhawk, tawny owl.
FORESTRY COMMISSION/NATURE CONSERVANCY COUNCIL

C:13 DIXTON EMBANKMENT
Near Monmouth; park by A449 at Dixton; follow path from church.
■ River.
■ The reserve follows the course of the Wye and supports a very wide range of lime-loving plants and numerous invertebrates. **Plants** Bee orchid. **Insects** Marbled white and ringlet butterflies; ants.
GWENT TRUST FOR NATURE CONSERVATION

C:14 LORD'S WOOD*
Near Monmouth; at Whitchurch, take B4164 off A40, follow to river and park at wood adjoining to S. Keep to footpaths; beware of cliffs and old lime shafts.
■ Woodland, cliffs, river.
■ This fine ancient semi-natural woodland clothes the W bank of the magnificent Wye Gorge near Symonds Yat. It adjoins the Wye, itself a prime wildlife habitat. The luxuriant river vegetation holds nationally important invertebrate communities including such notable species as the club-tailed dragonfly. The wood, being on the limestone, is rich in trees and shrubs, including wild service-tree, large- and small-leaved lime and whitebeams. The diversity of the wood is increased by a series of limestone cliffs with a rich calcareous flora. **Birds** Dipper, kingfisher. **Fish** Salmon, lamprey, allis shad. **Plants** White and narrow-leaved helleborine, bee orchid, bloody crane's-bill, yellow bird's-nest, heath cudweed, pale St John's-wort, small scabious, narrow-leaved bittercress, wild madder.
WOODLAND TRUST/PRIVATE OWNERSHIP

C:15 SYMONDS YAT ROCK*
Near Monmouth; park in Forestry Commission car park off B4432 and follow steep hill to river at SO 563159. Cross road to rock and viewpoint; follow footpaths through woods.
■ Woodland, cliff, river.
■ Symonds Yat Rock has commanding views over the Wye Valley and is now famous as a watch point for a peregrine's

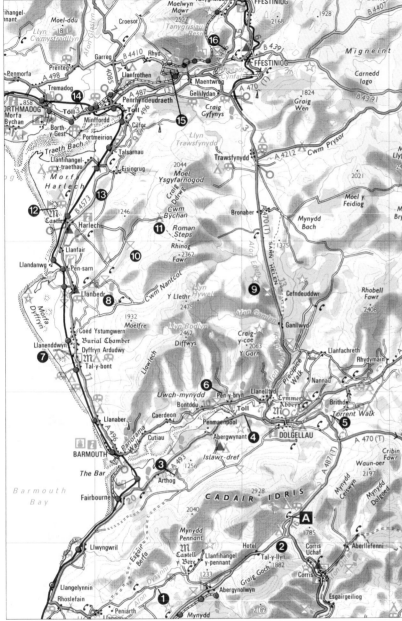

MAP A

eyrie. The woodlands below the rock are rich in species. **Birds** Peregrine, pied flycatcher, buzzard. **Plants** Herb Paris, wild service-tree, whitebeam, hutchinsia, early-purple orchid.

A:1 CRAIG ADERYN

Near Tywyn; park on public road around SH 641069. View from road only.
■ Large rock outcrop.
■ Dramatic rock sticking up on S side of Dysynni valley is well known for its inland nesting cormorant colony. Chough, peregrine and wild goats may also be seen.

A:2 TAL-Y-LLYN

Near Dolgellau; park along S side of lake as convenient (mid-point at SH 721100). View from road only.
■ Acidic lake.
■ Large natural lake at foot of spectacular Talyllyn pass under ramparts of Cadair Idris; accessible place to watch waterfowl in

winter. Common sandpipers and dipper can be seen in summer.

A:3 LLYNNAU CREGENNEN/ CREGENNEN LAKES

Near Dolgellau; car park at SH 656143.
■ Stony, acid mountain lakes, grassland, bog.
■ Mountain lake set in spectacular country on N side of Cadair Idris. Aquatic/bog plants of considerable interest. Best in summer. **Plants** Water lobelia, marsh cinquefoil, quillwort, shoreweed, marsh St John's-wort, bogbean.
NATIONAL TRUST

A:4 MAWDDACH ESTUARY

Near Dolgellau; car park at Penmain Pool Information Centre one mile (1.5 km) outside town on A493. Centre open end May-mid Sep, 11.30am-5.30pm. Leaflets available.
■ Estuarine river, woodland, bog, scrub, grazing land.

■ One of the most beautiful estuaries in Britain. Converted signal box houses information centre. Best in spring and autumn. **Birds** Red-breasted merganser, common sandpiper, goldeneye, cormorant, wigeon, red warbler, teal.
ROYAL SOCIETY FOR THE PROTECTION OF BIRDS

A:5 TORRENT WALK

Near Dolgellau; entrance to walk and parking at SH 762182.
■ Mixed woodland, stream, gorge.
■ Well-maintained walk through beautiful wooded gorge notable for its trees, flowering plants and especially ferns. Alternating bands of acid and basic rocks give rise to a highly varied flora. **Plants** Small-leaved lime, hornbeam, Tunbridge filmy-fern, beech fern, wood fescue.
SNOWDONIA NATIONAL PARK AUTHORITY

A:6 COED GARTH GELL

Near Dolgellau; public footpath at SH 687191 from A496 on N side of estuary near tollbridge. Reserve signposted.
■ Sessile oak/birch woodland, stream, gorge.
■ Steep ungrazed woodland overlooking beautiful Mawddach estuary; well marked path adjacent to dramatic stream gorge and ruined mine. Best in spring and summer. **Birds** Pied flycatcher, redstart, wood warbler, buzzard, dipper, grey wagtail.
ROYAL SOCIETY FOR PROTECTION OF BIRDS

A:7 MORFA DYFFRYN

Near Harlech; at Llanbedr, SH 585267 drive W to lagoon edge and park or at Llanddwywe, SH 586224 drive W to car park at end of road.
■ Calcareous dunes, slacks, salt-marsh, foreshore.
■ Dune flora rich in late spring and summer; foreshore and estuary interesting for birds in spring, autumn and winter. **Plants** Green-flowered helleborine, seaside centaury, marsh-orchids, houndstongue, sharp rush, sea spurge. **Birds** Whimbrel, ringed plover.
NATURE CONSERVANCY COUNCIL

A:8 COED LLETYWALTER

Near Harlech; leave A496 at Llanbedr, drive up valley to SH 603275 and park by access gate. NCC permit required.
■ Rocky oak woodland, carr woodland, marsh, lake.
■ An ungrazed western oak wood with bilberry, wood anemone, bluebells and common cow-wheat in spring, and some interesting bryophytes. Damp areas and lily-covered lake add variety. Characteristic birds are pied flycatcher, redstart, wood warbler, tree pipit, buzzard.
NATURE CONSERVANCY COUNCIL

A:9 COED Y BRENIN★

Near Dolgellau; turn off A470 W (about half way to Trawfynydd and park at Maesgwm Visitor Centre.
■ Conifer forest, broad-leaved woodland, streams, rivers, moorland, upland pasture, rocky outcrops, bogs.
■ Diverse forest worth exploring in detail. Facilities include hide (for fallow deer), nature trails, walking trails and leaflets. **Plants** Globeflower, orchids, alder buckthorn, spring sandworth, thrift. **Mammals** Polecat, red squirrel, fallow deer.
FORESTRY COMMISSION

A:10 COED CRAFNANT★

Near Harlech; car park at SH 629296. Reserve entrance on path from Pont Crafnant at SH 628289.

■ Sessile oak wood, streams, rock outcrops.

■ Ancient NW-facing wood gets little sunlight and has high humidity, giving rise to a bryophyte flora of international importance, and interesting ferns and lichens. **Plants** Filmy-ferns; liverworts, mosses, lichens.

NORTH WALES NATURALISTS' TRUST

A:11 RHINOG★★

Near Harlech; park at E end of Llyn Cwm Bychan at SH 647315. Take footpath up ancient steps over Bwlch Tyddiad. Difficult and dangerous walking away from path.

■ Mountain, blanket bog, flushes.

■ One of the most dramatic and intractable areas of mountain country in Wales. A huge jumble of block-littered slopes on Cambrian grits with rank, ungrazed heather sheltering interesting bryophytes.

NATURE CONSERVANCY COUNCIL

A:12 MORFA HARLECH★★

Near Harlech; for estuary at SH 598354 follow road on to open saltings and park off road; for dunes and beach use car park at SH 574317. NCC permit required off beach and rights of way. Keep off tidal flats.

■ Calcareous dune system, foreshore, salt-marsh, mudflats.

■ Salt-marsh and mudflats at N end good for waders, wildfowl and plants. The large undamaged dune system with grassland, mobile dunes and slacks has a rich flora and fauna, all with magnificent backdrop of Snowdonia mountains. **Birds** Ducks, waders. **Plants** (Dunes) marsh helleborine, pyramidal and green-winged orchids. **Butterflies** Dark-green fritillary, grayling, dingy skipper. **Mammals** Polecat.

NATURE CONSERVANCY COUNCIL

A:13 COED LLECHWEDD

Near Harlech; footpath into wood from B4573 at SH 598326.

■ Oak wood.

■ Situated on steeply sloping former sea cliff overlooking dunes and salt-marsh, this diverse woodland has both acid and basic elements to its flora which includes ramsons and heather. Best in spring and summer.

WOODLAND TRUST

A:14 GLASLYN MARSHES★

Near Porthmadog; use stile by gate on minor road at SH 592385. Cross field and stile on opposite side into reserve. Excellent bird-watching also from Porthmadog Cob. Permit needed from NWNT. Wet underfoot.

■ Fresh/brackish marshland, wet grassland, alder woodland.

■ Estuarine marshes noted for wintering wildfowl and wader, with good flowering plants including orchids and the rare Welsh mudwort. **Birds** Whooper swan, red-breasted merganser, pintail, goldeneye, shoveler, wigeon.

NORTH WALES NATURALISTS' TRUST

A:15 COEDYDD MAENTWROG★

Near Ffestiniog; leave A487 at Oakley Arms' hotel and take B4410 to Llyn Mair car park in one mile (1.5 km). Areas apart from Coed Llyn Mair (nature trail) at SH 652413 require NCC permit.

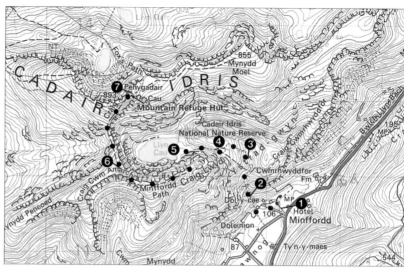

1:50 000, MAP A:A

A:A CADAIR IDRIS★★

Near Dolgellau; car park W of A487 junction adjacent Minffordd Hotel.

① From car park, enter reserve following steep path up the mountain into Cwm Cau.

② Remnant oak wood on thin acid soil with frequent outcrops of moss-covered rocks. Abundance of lichen indicates lack of atmospheric pollution. Native trees along path include wild pear and wild cherry. Breeding birds include pied flycatcher, wood warbler, redstart, tree pipit.

③ Upland bog here adjacent to stream is dominated by bog moss and cottongrass which rarely flowers as buds are devoured by sheep. Ruined buildings near path were once shepherd's summer residence. Green hairstreak butterflies and emperor moths seen here in summer.

④ Magnificent, glacier-carved scenery of Cwm Cau. Stonechat and whinchat on lower slopes; ring ouzel and raven higher up, with some peregrines and merlins hunting.

⑤ The corrie lake at Llyn Cau is extremely cold and deep. Bordering alkaline outcrops, safe from sheep, grow green spleenwort, brittle bladder-fern, mossy and starry saxifrage and roseroot as well as damp woodland species.

⑥ Here the path follows a watershed draining N, S and W. Wind-pruned heather predominates. Parsley ferns grow on scree.

⑦ Summit known as Penygadair stands at 2,928 ft (893 m). Spectacular views – sometimes to the Irish coast – but little bird or animal life, and low creeping mat of gale-resistant vegetation including clubmosses and thrift. Mountain rescue hut by summit cairn. Return to car park by same route or down N side if transport arranged below.

NATURE CONSERVANCY COUNCIL

■ Sessile oak wood, grassy glades, wet grassland, heath.

■ This reserve runs for about 2 miles (3 km) along the N slopes of the vale of Ffestiniog. Acid soils and heavy rainfall make this typical of the sessile oak woods once widespread in N Wales valleys. In the lower parts the ground flora is largely a mixture of grasses; higher up mosses prevail. The wood has a good selection of liverworts and lichens, including lungwort, an indicator of ancient woodland with little or no atmospheric pollution. Glades and marshy grassland add to the diversity of plants and animals. Preservation of oak is hampered by damage from feral goats. **Birds** Pied flycatcher, wood warbler, buzzard, nuthatch. **Mammals** Badger, feral goat.

NATURE CONSERVANCY COUNCIL/NORTH WALES NATURALISTS' TRUST

A:16 COED CYMERAU

Near Ffestiniog; reserve entrance at SH 690424, reached by footpath from A496 at Rhyd-y-sarn. NCC permit required off rights of way.

■ Sessile oak woodland, river ravine.

■ Oak wood on thin acid soils in humid ravine with extreme oceanic climate favours ferns and bryophytes, some uncommon western species including Wilson's filmy-fern, Tunbridge filmy-fern and ivy-leaved bellflower.

NATURE CONSERVANCY COUNCIL

B:1 LLYN TEGID/BALA LAKE★

Bala; lakeside car park just S of town. Various access points around lake.

■ Lake, swampy/gravelly shore, willow/alder carr.

■ Located in glacial-cut basin Llyn Tegid is the largest natural lake in Wales. The fish fauna is particularly rich with perch, pike, roach, grayling, brown trout and others plus the unique gwyniad, a sub-species of the European whitefish, only found here. (However, seven similar are in other U.K. lakes and lochs.) Aquatic and marginal vegetation also has scarce species.

Red-breasted merganser and goosander breed and other aquatic species are present in winter and on passage. **Plants** Globeflower, floating water-plantain, shoreweed, Welsh poppy, marsh cinquefoil, water sedge, stamened waterwort.

SNOWDONIA NATIONAL PARK AUTHORITY

MAP B

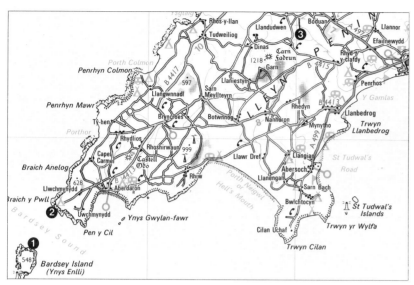

MAP C

MAP D

C:1 YNYS ENLLI/BARDSEY ISLAND★★
Off the Lleyn Peninsula; *boats from Pwllheli. Accommodation in observatory must be booked through Stan Baber, 38, Walthew Avenue, Holyhead, Anglesey or (cottages) through David Thomas, 0766 522239.*
■ Maritime grassland, heath, rocky/sandy coast, foreshore, rich offshore waters.
■ Separated from the mainland by 2 miles (3 km) of water, Ynys Enlli is a conspicuous punctuation mark at the tip of the Lleyn peninsula, set in waters that are of special interest for their diverse and undisturbed marine life. The island's heath and grassland is dominated by fescues, western gorse and heathers, with a rich lichen flora (more than 350 species recorded).

An observatory and field centre aid the study of birdlife. The most significant species is the Manx shearwater, 4,000 pairs of which nest in grassland burrows. Smaller numbers of other sea-birds nest in suitable cliff sites around the coast; as do several pairs of choughs. A few pairs of little owls have established the unusual habit of nesting in disused burrows. Grey seals are regular in the coves and around the coast. **Plants** Wilson's filmy-fern, spring squill, Danish scurvygrass. **Birds** Auk, gulls, migrants (including rarities).
BARDSEY ISLAND TRUST

C:2 MYNYDD MAWR/ ABERDARON HEAD
Near Pwllheli; *take A499 then B4413 from town; minor roads to tip of Lleyn peninsula. Rights of way only at Porth Mendwy.*
■ Coastal heath, rocky headland, valley.
■ Interesting plants and birds are in a wonderful location passages. Scrub-filled valley leading up from Porth Mendwy noted for scarce migrant birds during late spring and autumn. **Birds** Chough, peregrine, shearwater.
NATIONAL TRUST

C:3 CORS GEIRCH
Near Pwllheli; *leave B4415 at SH 312353, turn N at Bodgadle and park at SH 317356. Entry by NCC permit only.*
■ Fen, open water, alder carr.
■ Narrow valley mire, drained in part, divided into three remaining areas of rich fen, some of which has reverted to carr. Brook lamprey and sea trout in river. **Plants** Narrow-leaved, lesser and intermediate bladderwort, great fen-sedge.
NATURE CONSERVANCY COUNCIL

D:1 CORS GYFELOG
Near Porthmadog; *park as convenient at farm, SH 458476. NCC permit needed.*
■ Neutral fen, river, willow carr.
■ Extensive basis mire with fen vegetation ranging from open water to carr supports an interesting range of plants and animals, notably dragonflies.
NATURE CONSERVANCY COUNCIL

E:1 YR WYDDFA/SNOWDON★★
Near Caernarfon; *from Pen y pass car park at SH 647556 follow miner's track. Take due care. No entry to enclosed woodland and experimental plots.*
■ Montane grassland, cliffs, crops, sub-Arctic heath, streams, lakes.
■ The highest peak S of the Scottish Highlands and part of the extensive mountain complex of Eryri which makes up central Snowdonia. Plant life reflects the complex geology consisting of acidic slates, grits, rhyolite and granite interspersed with calcareous pummice tuff and dolerite, the latter supporting lime-loving Arctic/Alpine species, relicts of glacial times. Sheep grazing has modified the upland heaths to grasslands and confined the less tolerant plants to inaccessible ledges and cliffs. On ledges with deeper soil a luxuriant growth of tall herbs includes roseroot, mountain sorrel, Alpine saw-wort, Welsh poppy and globeflower. The rainbow leaf-beetle is a glacial relict.
NATURE CONSERVANCY COUNCIL

E:2 GWYDYR FOREST★★
Near Betws-y-coed; *y Stablau information centre in Betws-y-coed for details, leaflets, maps.*
■ Conifer/mixed woodland, remnant oakwood, scrub, lakes, streams, bogs. Open hill land, rocky mountain site.

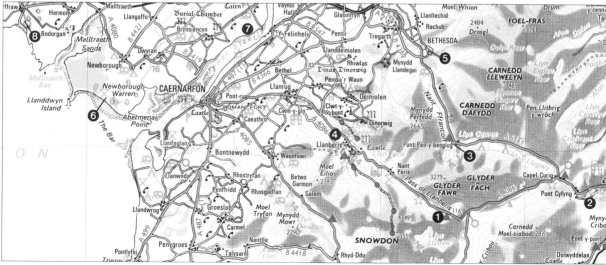

MAP E

■ Wonderful range of habitats and wildlife set in the beautiful scenery of the Snowdonia National Park. Great variety of walks, trails and features.
FORESTRY COMMISSION

E:3 CWM IDWAL**
Near Bangor; *car park by Ogwen cottage at SH 649604. Take footpath S into reserve. Only skilled climbers should leave paths.*
■ Cliffs, crags, upland lake, streams, montane pasture.
■ Gouged out by the action of ice 12,000 years ago this is one of the best examples of a corrie in Wales. The geology is a mixture of acidic slates and rhyolite interspersed with calcareous pummice tuff where grow the Arctic/Alpine plants for which Cwm Idwal is known. Sheep-free ledges with rich soil support thrift, sea campion and globeflower (a hint of the botanical richness to be found on Welsh mountains before sheep became so plentiful). The lake has a particularly good selection of montane aquatic plants. **Plants** Snowdon lily, moss campion, purple and mossy saxifrage, mountain avens, awlwort, water lobelia, quillwort, roseroot.
NATURE CONSERVANCY COUNCIL

E:4 COED DINORWIG
Near Caernarfon; *take A4086 to Llanberris and signs to Padarn Country Park.*
■ Upland sessile oakwood.
■ Wood unusual in having been long ungrazed, allowing for well developed under-storey and ground flora. **Birds** Pied flycatcher, redstart, wood warbler.
GWYNEDD COUNTY COUNCIL

E:5 CARNEDDAU**
Near Bethesda; *at Tal-y-bont, use car park near Llyn Eigiau for access to summit. Caution essential; suitable only for properly equipped and experienced mountain walkers.*
■ Montane plateau, grasslands, cliffs, crags, screes, streams, lakes, upland heath.
■ Wild and remote with many peaks over 3,000 ft (917 m): interesting montane plants and birds and active polygon arrangement of stones caused by frost heave. **Plants** Snowdon lily, mountain sorrel, globeflower, roseroot. **Birds** Chough, peregrine, ring ouzel.
NATIONAL TRUST

E:6 NEWBOROUGH WARREN/ NEWBOROUGH FOREST**
Near Llanfairpwllgwyngyll; *car park just above track at SH 405634. NCC permit needed off prescribed routes (see NCC leaflet).*
■ Dunes, foreshore, salt-marsh, brackish pool, rocky headland, conifer forest.
■ A fine range of coastal habitats with a highly varied flora and fauna. The dune system is one of the biggest in Britain and includes the conifer plantation. Since the decline of rabbits much of the warren has become stabilized and bare sand conditions are scarce away from the foredunes. Many scarce plants such as grass-of-Parnassus and round-leaved wintergreen are abundant in the lush sward.
Ynys Llanddwyn, a small rocky headland, supports such plants as spring squill and golden-samphire, and has a colony of nesting cormorants and shaps on offshore rocks. Saltmarsh species include sea aster and glasswort. **Plants** (Dune) meadow saxifrage, dune helleborine, butterwort.
NATURE CONSERVANCY COUNCIL

E:7 COED PORTHAMEL
Near Menai Bridge; *leave A4080 Llanfairpwllgwyngyll-Brynsiencyn road turning S at signs to Motl y Dou. After ¾ mile (one km) turn right by post box into lane marked 'no through road'. Turn left at first T junction and right at second before reaching reserve gate. Obtain key from Porthamel Old Farm House 100 yards (90 m) to N. NWNT permit needed. Hidden debris.*
■ Broad-leaved woodland.
■ Woodland dominated by sycamore/elm in one area, ash in another; ground flora augmented by unusual number of garden escapes, also interesting for invertebrates.
NORTH WALES NATURALISTS' TRUST

E:8 TYWYN ABERFFRAW/ ABERFFRAW DUNES
Near Llangefni; *take A4080 to Aberffraw and park adjacent to dunes just E of village. Access for reserve only by permit from: The Agent, Meyrick Estate Management Ltd, Estate Office, Bodorgan, Anglesey LLB2 5LP, Gwynedd.*

F:A HOLY ISLAND COAST**
Near Holyhead; *take road W from Holyhead to South Stack, car park SH 210820.*
① Walk from car park to RSPB information centre (mid-Apr-mid-Sep, 11 am-5 pm). Excellent facilities for viewing cliff-nesting birds. Wonderful sea-bird colonies with rare vagrants such as red-footed falcon, bee-eater and honey buzzard sometimes seen.
② S of Elling Tower along cliffs look for choughs and peregrines. Attractive cliff plants – thrift, sheep's-bit – abound; green tiger beetles scuttle across bare path. Return to car park along road to S Stack, branching off right towards Holyhead mountain.
③ Acid heathland plants carpet thin soil between rocky outcrops, with marsh species in wetter areas. The beautiful and very rare spotted rock-rose grows here. Return to car park and walk round cliffs to Penrhos Feilw common or drive round and walk from car park out towards cliffs.
④ Superb maritime heath dominated by heather, bell heather and western gorse assumes wave-like formations in response to salt-laden winds. Attractive grassland species by cliffs include rare field fleawort. Common blue, silver-studded blue grayling, small pearl-bordered, dark green and marsh fritillary butterflies seen. Sea-watching from point.
⑤ Cliffs and rocks here are natural rock gardens in June-July, with colourful species such as bloody cranesbill and sea campion attracting butterflies. Avoid trampling tall vegetation due to be cut for hay.
⑥ Walk round the cliffs or drive round to car park at Porth Dafarch.
ROYAL SOCIETY FOR THE PROTECTION OF BIRDS

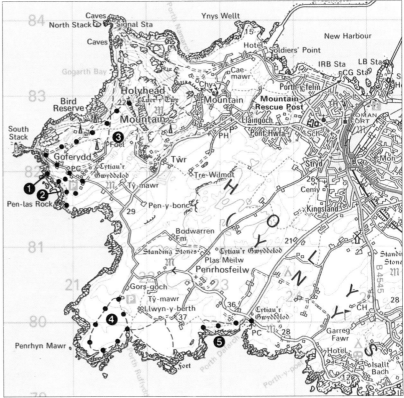

MAP F

MAP F:A

■ Calcareous dunes system, foreshore, tidal river mouth.
■ Compact, relatively undamaged dune system with particularly fine dune grassland, some of it closely grazed by rabbits and livestock. Flowering plants and bryophyte flora are of note in spring and summer.
MEYRICK ESTATE

G:1 CORS BODEILIO*

Near Llangefni; park as convenient on B5109 N of Talwrn at SH 497774. NCC permit needed.
■ Fen vegetation, hedgerows.
■ Small basin mire with excellent variety of plants; dragonflies include the variable damselfly. **Plants** Narrow-leaved marsh-, fly and lesser butterfly-orchids; greater spearwort, great fen-sedge.
NATURE CONSERVANCY COUNCIL

G:2 RED WHARF BAY

Near Menai Bridge; view S side of bay from end of road running N from Pentrarth village at SH 535799.
■ Sandy bay.
■ Good for common waders and spring passage. Best at high tide. Common scoter flock a special mid-winter feature. **Birds** Whimbrel, common scoter, sanderling.

G:3 CEFNI RESERVOIR

Near Llangefni; on B5111 2 miles (3 km) N of town. Car park at site. Signposted bird hide.
■ Reservoir, spruce forest.
■ Good views of waterfowl at N end of site from the hide. When water levels are low in late summer waders feed on mud. Siskins in surrounding spruce trees.
WELSH WATER AUTHORITY

G:4 CORS ERDDREINIOG**

Near Benllech; turn W off B5110 4 miles (6.5 km) N of Llangefni and park at SH 478809. NCC permit needed.
■ Fen, flushes, acid heathland.
■ Large rich fen with fine assemblage of flowering plants, notably spring flush areas. Insects and birds also well represented. **Plants** Narrow-leaved marsh-orchid, marsh helleborine. **Insects** (Butterflies)

Whooper swans – winter visitors at G:8, Cemlyn, this page.

Small pearl-bordered fritillary, dark green fritillary, dingy skipper; hairy dragonfly, variable damselfly. **Mammals** Harvest mouse.
NATURE CONSERVANCY COUNCIL

G:5 CRAIG WEN*

Near Llangefni; park (very limited) on B5108 at SH 504817. Farm track to marked entrance, SH 494804. NWNT permit needed.
■ Dry/wet acid heath, streams.
■ Reserve mainly to protect marsh gentian, declining in Wales. Good variety of other plants in areas flushed with calcareous water.
NORTH WALES NATURALIST'S TRUST

G:6 CORS GOCH*

Near Benllech; park in lay-by N of reserve entrance, SH 504817. NWNT permit needed. Keep to board walk and paths.
■ Fen, acid heath, limestone grassland, lake, willow carr.
■ A ridge of limestone almost divides this

fine valley mire, rich in flora, into two halves: the E end with sedges, and common reed communities; the W end with its lake. Bog myrtle fringes the mire.
There are 19 species of butterflies recorded including fritillaries and dingy skipper and 250 moths. Wildfowl pass through or overwinter. **Plants** Marsh helleborine, early and northern marsh-orchids; frog, green winged, fragrant and lesser butterfly-orchids; grass-of-Parnassus, common and lesser butterwort, lesser water-plantain. **Birds** Marsh harrier, bittern.
NORTH WALES NATURALISTS' TRUST

G:7 LLYN ALAW*

Near Llangefni; signposted from B5112 toward Llanerchymedd. Information Centre and hide.
■ Reservoir.
■ Large reservoir attracting good variety of wildfowl. In late summer dropping water levels expose mud used by passage waders.
WELSH WATER AUTHORITY

G:8 CEMLYN**

Near Amlwch; signposted from A5025 at Tregele. Car parks either side of bay. Avoid crest of shingle ridge.
■ Brackish pools, storm beach, foreshore, scrub.
■ The nature reserve consists of a large brackish lagoon impounded by a fine storm beach at the head of Cemlyn bay. The pool has great ornithological interest for breeding, wintering and migrant birds. Terns and black-headed gulls nest on islands in the main pool. The shingle ridge has strand-line species of plants such as spring squill, able to stand the battering of high tides and shifting pebbles. **Birds** Common, Arctic and Sandwich terns; (winter) whooper and Bewick's swans, waders.
NORTH WALES NATURALISTS' TRUST

G:9 POINT LYNAS*

Near Amlwch; take road to Llaneilian from A5025 or Amlwch and park near lighthouse. Walk to end of point.
■ Rocky headland.
■ Probably the best sea-watching place in N Wales for skuas, terns, gulls and auks. Sabine's gull almost annual; pomarine skuas sometimes in spring. Best in May and autumn.

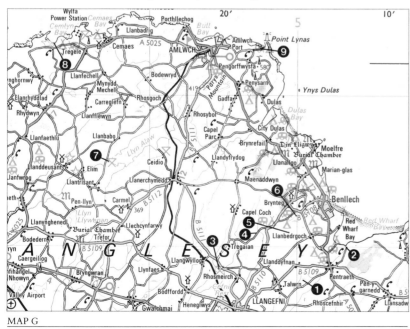

MAP G

GWYNEDD

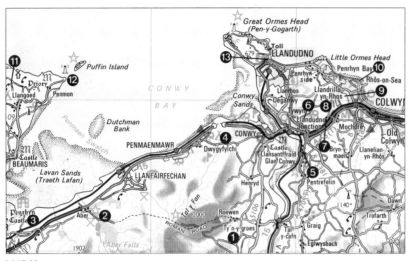

MAP H

H:1 COED GORSWEN

Near Conwy; *turn off B5106 for Roewen at SH 774706. Park at Pont Gorswen 1½ miles (2.5 km) on. Walk W to site beyond farm. NCC permit needed.*

■ Oak woodland, streams, bog margins.

■ Wide variety of trees and flowers on soils unusually rich for area; substantial shrub layer. Best in spring and autumn.

NATURE CONSERVANCY COUNCIL

H:2 COEDYDD ABER*

Near Bangor; *at Aber village, SH 655727 drive S up valley to car park at reserve entrance. NCC permit needed off rights of way.*

■ Deciduous woodland, stream and falls, open grassland.

■ The reserve is distinguished by the diversity of the woodland complex, reflecting differences in soil types and past management. Higher parts are typical dry sessile oak; lower it grades into mixed deciduous types with ash, wych elm, birch and abundant hazel on base-rich soils. On flatter waterlogged ground are patches of alderwood with a swampy floor. Around the falls the cliffs support a luxuriant field layer including some scarce Atlantic mosses, liverworts and rare lichens.

NATURE CONSERVANCY COUNCIL

H:3 TRAETH LAFAN/
LAVAN SANDS*

Near Bangor; *view from Llanfairfechan seafront off A55 or Spinnies reserve.*

■ Tidal flats, foreshore.

■ The huge expanse of sand and mud flats is host to 10-14,000 waders of 10 or more species and large numbers of wildfowl from late summer through to early spring. In mid-winter one per cent of the British population of oystercatchers, dunlin, curlew and redshank feed and roost here. It is nationally important for late summer moult of hundreds of great crested grebes and red-breasted mergansers. Some overwinter, joined by black-necked and Slavonian grebes and divers. Ducks can be viewed from the excellent hide at the Spinnies, waders from Llanfairfechan sea-front.

NORTH WALES NATURALISTS' TRUST

H:4 BWLCH SYCHNANT/
SYCHNANT PASS

Near Conwy; *about 2 miles (3 km) W of town on road to Dwygyfylchi.*

■ Upland heath, pools, streams, rocky slopes.

■ Popular and accessible with a characteristic heath and bog flora and a particularly rich moth and dragonfly fauna.

H:5 GLAN CONWY

Near Conwy; *view from end of road under railway in Glan Conwy village or from lay-by on W side of A470 S of Llandudno junction at SH 803766. Keep off mudflats.*

■ Estuarine mudflats.

■ Good for common waders with more interesting species including ruff, black-tailed godwit, greenshank and knot on autumn passage.

H:6 MARLE HALL WOODS*

Near Llandudno Junction; *enter wood from road at SH 805793. Keep off cliffs.*

■ Mixed woodland, species-rich grassland, limestone pavement, cliff.

■ Large, structurally diverse woodland partly on steep carboniferous limestone. Rich ground flora, especially where small glades, rock outcrops and cliffs increase range of habitat.

WOODLAND TRUST

H:7 COED BRON GARTH

Near Llandudno Junction; *enter wood from road W of Mochdre at SH 822789.*

■ Mixed woodland, limestone scarp.

■ Good structural diversity, largely ungrazed and dominated by ash, wych elm, sycamore and oak, with hornbeam, small-leaved lime, yew, wild cherry and spindle.

WOODLAND TRUST

Razorbill and grey seal – see H:12.

H:8 BRYN PYDEW*

Near Colwyn Bay; *park at SH 818797. Reserve to SW either side of Wiga cottage path. NWNT permit needed.*

■ Limestone pavement, quarries, grassland, woodland.

■ One of the richest limestone pavement sites in Wales with a fine flora and fauna, including the glow-worm. **Plants** Bloody cranesbill, green-winged orchid, autumn lady's-tresses, rue-leaved saxifrage, lily-of-the-valley, juniper. **Insects** Brown argus and dingy skipper butterflies; Cistus Forester moth.

NORTH WALES NATURALISTS' TRUST

H:9 BRYN EURYN*

Near Colwyn Bay; *3eave A55 at SH 835795. Nature trail starts at Llys Euryn on left of junction of Tan y Bryn Road with Rhôs Road. Nature trail guide from CBC.*

■ Limestone grassland, ash/sycamore woodland, limestone crags.

■ Prominent hill above Colwyn Bay with panoramic views. Woodland and grassland on carboniferous limestone rich in plant species and interesting butterflies. **Plants** Green-winged orchid, hoary-rock rose, Nottingham catchfly, St John's-wort, bloody crane's-bill, dropwort, juniper.

COLWYN BOROUGH COUNCIL

H:10 RHÔS POINT

Near Colwyn Bay; *view from Rhôs-on-Sea sea-front and foreshore.*

■ Foreshore, sea.

■ Good for winter sea watching and waders on musselbeds on point. Auks and gannets on passage in spring and autumn.

H:11 MARIANDYRYS*

Near Beaumaris; *take B5109 to Glan-yr-afon village. Park beyond Bodfryn villa where road widens. Reserve signposted. NWNT permit needed.*

■ Limestone grassland, heath, limestone quarry.

■ Prominent hilltop with rich assemblage of plants and insects; superb views of Irish coast and Isle of Man.

NORTH WALES NATURALISTS' TRUST

H:12 PENMON POINT*

Near Beaumaris; *toll road from Penmon. Park near coastguard station, walk to point.*

■ Rocky limestone headland.

■ Overlooks Puffin Island (noted for cormorant colony); excellent for sea watching. Breeding song birds in scrub and limestone flora add variety. **Birds** Razorbill, guillemot, kittiwake, puffin, fulmar; (in scrub) stonechat, grasshopper warbler, lesser whitethroat. **Mammals** Grey seal.

H:13 GREAT ORME**

Near Llandudno; *car park at Information Centre on summit of marine drive from town. Leaflet available.*

■ Limestone cliffs, pavement, grassland.

■ This massive headland is famous for its limestone plants, best seen in the rocky, less heavily grazed areas. Southerly, northern and maritime elements combine to make the flora especially interesting; this is the only station for the wild cotoneaster in Britain. Butterflies occur, notably special forms of grayling and silver-studded blue. There are modest colonies of sea-birds on the cliffs, and peregrines may be seen.

ABERCONWY BOROUGH COUNCIL

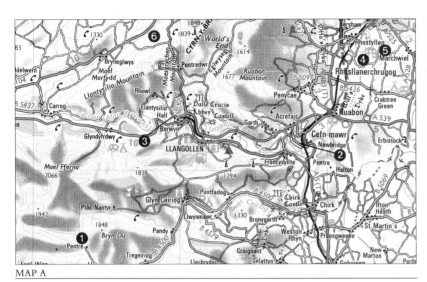

MAP A

MAP B

A:1 BERWYN MOUNTAINS*
Near Chirk; park on roadside 3 miles (5 km) W of Llanarmon Dyfryn Ceiriog. Keep to public rights of way only. Managed grouse moors – shooting sometimes in progress.
■ Blanket bog, upland heath, streams, flushes.
■ High quality upland vegetation dominated by heather, cottongrass and bog mosses on deep peat, with cowberry and cranberry; starry saxifrage by stream. Best in summer and autumn.

A:2 TY MAWR
Near Wrexham; turn off W from A483 at SJ 283420. Country Park signposted.
■ Grassland, scrub, woodland, river.
■ Small, accessible country park with a good range of grassland and woodland wildlife. Excellent for children. **Plants** Toothwort, herb Paris, moschatel.
WREXHAM MAELOR BOROUGH COUNCIL

A:3 LLANGOLLEN CANAL
Llangollen; walk E along towpath from Llangollen Wharf at SJ 215422.
■ Canal, boggy margins, woodlands, scrub, farmland.
■ Quiet canal meanders through attractive country from Llangollen passing under limestone cliffs. A variety of plants, birds and animals to be seen, such as pied flycatchers, wood warblers and water voles.

A:4 HAFOD WOOD
Near Wrexham; at SJ 323493 go S one mile (1.5 km) to NT Erddig Estate. Park at Plas Grano. Enter reserve on right at SH 323477. NWNT permit needed.
■ Alder carr, marsh, open water, mixed broad-leaved woodland.
■ Views from boardwalk of very wet woodland with considerable floristic interest. Drier woodland and stream add diversity. **Mammals** Badger, including sandy-coloured and melanic animals.
NORTH WALES NATURALISTS' TRUST

A:5 SONTLEY MOOR
Near Wrexham; at SJ 337473, park on roadside. Footpath from T-junction to reserve. NWNT permit needed.
■ Dry/wet grassland, swamp, alder carr, blackthorn scrub, stream, drainage ditches.
■ Complex of mainly wetland habitats, particularly the tall herb communities

becoming increasingly scarce as areas are drained for agriculture. Polecats sometimes seen.
NORTH WALES NATURALISTS' TRUST

A:6 LLANTYSILIO MOUNTAIN*
Near Llangollen; park at caf at SJ 192481. Walk W along ridge track.
■ Heather moorland.
■ Prominent and accessible ridge of a type of moorland now scarce in Wales, with magnificent views of Mynydd Eglwyseg. **Birds** Red grouse, wheatear, whinchat, peregrine, merlin.

B:1 CLOCAENOG FOREST
Near Ruthin; take B5105 SW from town. Visitor centre signs at SJ 038510 in forest.
■ Coniferous forest.
■ A stronghold of red squirrels many of which use the boxes put up for tawny owls. FC nature trail provided. Black grouse, crossbills and pine martin also live here. Best in spring and autumn.
FORESTRY COMMISION

B:2 BRENIG RESERVOIR
Near Denbigh; turn off A543 Petrepoelas to Denbigh road on to the B4501 near Sportsmans Arms.
■ Moorland, blanket bog, open water, conifer forest.
■ The mixture of habitats surrounding the reservoir provides a good variety of upland wildlife. Hide (suitable for wheelchairs), information centre and nature trail. Summer is best.
WELSH WATER AUTHORITY

B:3 HIRAETHOG MOOR
Near Denbigh; drive in any direction from road junction at SH 929568. View from road only.
■ Upland heath, blanket bog, acid grassland, flushes.
■ Rolling heather moors and bog-lands covered in cottongrass, once much more extensive in North Wales than now.

Peregrine at nest – see A:6, Llantysilio Mountain.

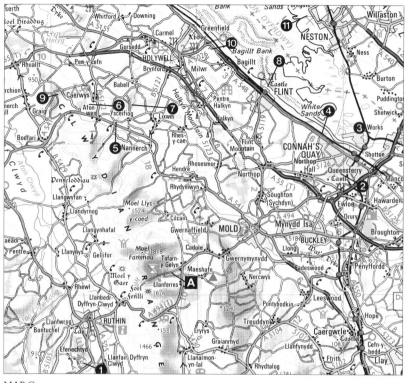

MAP C

C:1 CILYGROESLWYD WOOD★

Near Ruthin; *park at Pont Eyarth, SJ 127554. Recross A494 to reserve, SJ 125554.*

■ Yew/oak/ash woodland, limestone pavement, quarry.

■ The wood is distinguished by an extensive understorey of possibly-ancient yew and a rich flora. Hawfinch, a regional rarity,

breeds here. Best in spring and summer. **Plants** Bird's-nest orchid, lesser and greater and butterfly-orchids, fragrant orchid.
NORTH WALES NATURALISTS' TRUST

C:2 WEPRE PARK

Near Connah's Quay; *car park at SJ 287673 NW of Ewloe.*

■ Dry oak woodland, alder/willow carr, stream, marsh, pools.

■ River with some ancient woodland, once part of a large estate; now run as country park with fine range of birds, insects and particularly plants.
ALYN AND DEESIDE DISTRICT COUNCIL

C:3 SHOTTON POOLS

Near Queensferry; *use main entrance to works off A550 N of town. Permit needed from Personnel Services Dept., Shotton Works, Deeside, Clwyd, CH5 2NH.*

■ Shallow pools, reed-beds, scrub, rough grassland.

■ Although not beautiful to look at, the old oxidation pools have long been famous for birdlife, with 150 pairs of common terns nesting on islands and rafts. Waders on passage, plant and insect life also interesting.
BRITISH STEEL

C:4 CONNAH'S QUAY★

Connah's Quay; *follow signs to power station entrance from A548. Permit needed from DNS. Ray Roberts, Melrose, Kelsperton Road, Connah's Quay, Clwyd.*

■ Salt-marsh, mudflats, freshwater/brackish pools, scrub.

■ This reserve, developed at the mouth of the Dee estuary, is noted for birds, with principal interest on the intertidal areas for wintering and passage wildfowl and waders. The pool complex, occasionally flooded by spring tides, is attractive to birds preferring freshwater, producing some interesting sightings. Raptors hunt the whole area in winter and storm driven vagrants are sometimes recorded. Surrounding scrub and woodland provide cover for small birds and add interest for botanists and entomologists.
CENTRAL ELECTRICITY GENERATING
BOARD/DEESIDE NATURALISTS' SOCIETY

C:A MOEL FAMAU & LOGGERHEADS★★

Near Mold; *country park signposted from A494 3 miles (5 km) W of town.*

① Information centre and start of Loggerheads nature trail. (Leaflets here for both parks).

② Shallow, fast-flowing part of river Alun, with river water-crowfoot, brown trout, dipper and grey wagtail.

③ Mixed woodland dominated by sycamore and ash with wych elm; lime-loving plants here include wayfaring-tree, spurge-laurel,

toothwort. Look for tawny owl, nuthatch, great spotted woodpecker, marsh tit and speckled wood butterflies.

④ Excellent limestone flora (best in July) around these rocks includes common rock-rose, wild thyme, lady's bedstraw, bloody cranesbill, field scabious, quaking-grass, lesser meadow-rue and salad burnet. Grizzled skipper and grayling butterflies feed from the flowers. Look W to see Moel Famau.

⑤ Beech/larch plantation leads back to main road and car park.

⑥ Moel Famau car park.

⑦ Dramatic, windswept, heather-covered hills E of Vale of Clwyd. Footpath along moorland slopes with bracken, hawthorn, heather and gorse harbouring linnet, whinchat and the day-flying Eggar moth.

⑧ Deeper peat at ridge top grows heather, bilberry, crowberry, with heath milkwort, and hard fern in the dwarf shrubs. Look for wheatear, raven and red and black grouse.

⑨ Magnificent views from ruined Jubilee Tower. Upper option of path back to car park preferable.
CLWYD COUNTY COUNCIL

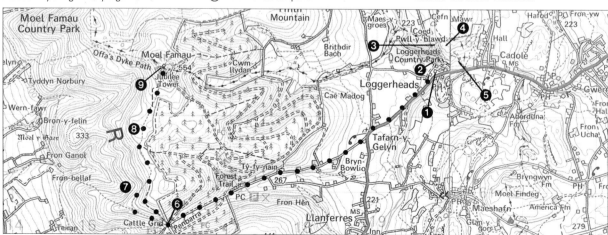

1:50 000, MAP C:A

C:5 DDOL UCHAF

Near Holywell; park on verge behind Ddol chapel. Best access is in NE corner. NWNT permit needed.

■ Disused marl pits, woodland, scrub, open grassland, pool, bare marl bank, stream.

■ There is an excellent range of conditions in this 10-acre reserve. The woodland is largely dominated by sycamore which shades out the ground flora; however open lime-rich grassland and damper areas, plus the rapidly colonizing area of bare marl, show an interesting variety of plants at different stages of colonization through to scrub. The reserve is rich in invertebrate species, particularly molluscs, lepidoptera and beetles, including four rare truffle-feeding species. **Plants** Grass-of-Parnassus, mare's-tail, ploughman's-spikenard.
NORTH WALES NATURALISTS' TRUST

C:6 PWLL-GWYN WOOD

Near Denbigh; park near pub on A541 at SJ 127717 and take footpath ½ mile (0.8 km) to wood.

■ Oak/ash/sycamore woodland.

■ Prominent hill wood looking S over valley of river Wheeler to Clwydian hills. Some replanting since Dutch elm disease.
WOODLAND TRUST

C:7 COED TYDDYN HALEN

Near Holywell; use footpath from road at SJ 153720 N of Ysceifiog and walk NW into site at SJ 154724.

■ Mixed woodland, stream.

■ Small, quiet woodland in secluded valley with rich ground flora and good variety of trees and shrubs.
WOODLAND TRUST

C:8 FLINT CASTLE*

Flint; car park at castle, SJ 247734. Walk SE along embankment by rugby field.

■ Estuarine mud, sand flats.

■ Excellent for viewing swirling flocks of waders and wildfowl characteristic of Dee Estuary. Birch wood near rugby field good for winter flocks of brambling and redpoll.
Birds Black-tailed godwit, sanderling, knot, pintail, wigeon.

C:9 COED Y GLYN

Near Holywell; enter from road N of A541 at SJ 104730.

■ Alder coppice, oak/ash woodland, hazel coppice, flushes.

■ Steep valley woodland with interesting wet areas. Rich ground flora, best in spring and summer.
WOODLAND TRUST

C:10 GREENFIELD VALLEY

Near Holywell; access point and car park off A548 at SJ 196776. Closed Christmas.

■ Woodland, grassland, streams, lakes.

■ Country park with fine industrial archaeological sites, also interesting for wildlife particularly along the old railway line and around the lakes and streams. A good place to take children.
DELYN BOROUGH COUNCIL

C:11 GAYTON SANDS**

Near Heswall; car park at Parkgate approached via B5139. No access to salt-marsh: best birdwatching point is Parkgate Quay (SJ 280780).

■ Salt-marsh, mudflats, estuary.

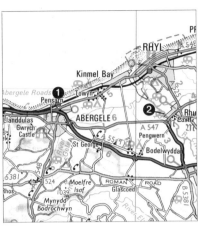

MAP D

■ At high tide many waders and waterfowl which congregate on the Dee Estuary seek shelter on the mudflats and salt-marsh at its margins. The largest single block of un-reclaimed salt-marsh on the estuary is Gayton Sands. As well as waders and waterfowl, smaller birds such as water pipit, brambling and finches also find food and shelter on the more mature marsh. Hen harrier, merlin, short-eared owl and occasional peregrine hunt the area. Since the Second World War, the shore at Parkgate has changed from sandy beach to salt-marsh dominated by cord grass. Habitat management is being implemented.
ROYAL SOCIETY FOR THE PROTECTION OF BIRDS

D:1 PENSARN*

Near Abergele; take road over railway at SH 946787 to foreshore.

■ Shingle ridge, sandy grassland, foreshore.

■ Shingle and adjacent grassland with characteristic flora including yellow horned-poppy, sea rocket and restharrow, orchids; foreshore good for sanderling and winter sea-watching.

D:2 CLWYD ESTUARY

Near Rhyl; park on outskirts of Rhyl or Rhuddlan and use footpaths parallel to either side of river.

■ Salt-marsh, mudflats, river, marine lake.

■ Botanical interest in salt-marsh plants (best W side); good for wintering and passage waders (best E side).

Black-tailed godwit – see C:8, Flint Castle.

Shore lark – see E:3, Point of Ayr.

E:1 GRAIG FAWR*

Near Prestatyn; leave A547 at SJ 056802 and park adjacent to hill. NT leaflet available.

■ Limestone crags, grassland, scrub.

■ Steep-sided outcrop supporting a range of calcicole plants, including some uncommon species such as hoary rock-rose, Nottingham catchfly and wild madder (N edge of its range). Interesting insect fauna, particularly butterflies and moths, including the cistus forester.
NATIONAL TRUST

E:2 PRESTATYN HILLSIDE

Near Prestatyn; park on minor road toward Gwaenysgor Park at base of hill behind town and follow footpath S along escarpment. Keep to footpaths.

■ Limestone grassland, heath, broadleaved woodland.

■ Dramatic escarpment on Carboniferous limestone with interesting flora such as columbine and tutsan; butterflies. Includes initial section of Offa's Dyke Path; fine views N and W.

E:3 POINT OF AYR

Near Prestatyn; park at end of Station Road out of Talacre.

■ Salt-marsh, intertidal sand/mudflats, sand dunes, freshwater pools, scrub.

■ This huge area of intertidal flats at the mouth of the Dee estuary is of great importance as a feeding and nesting ground for waders and wildfowl, both overwintering and on passage. In late summer the passage of terns is impressive, with up to 3,000 birds. In winter snow bunting, shore lark and sometimes water pipit occur on and around the spit. Common passerines find shelter in the scrub and around pools, and predators hunt along the shoreline. Wild winter weather can bring storm-driven vagrants such as petrels and Sabine's gull.
ROYAL SOCIETY FOR THE PROTECTION OF BIRDS

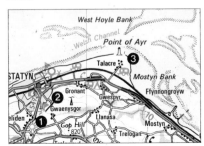

MAP E

SCOTLAND

Many glens of Argyll (left) contain fragments
of old native pine-woods and deciduous forests,
but much of Scotland has become afforested with
conifers smothering hillsides where native
woodland once occurred. Crossbill, goldcrest and
siskin breed in the new plantations and black
grouse on moorland fringes.

Mature Scots pine woods are the favourite
habitat of the **red squirrel** (above), although
they breed in northern England, upland Wales,
Ireland and East Anglia. Trees are their
natural environment: they are equipped with
sharp claws to grip tree trunks and branches
where few predators can catch them. In
summer, the fur is chestnut brown, becoming
greyer in winter with well developed ear tufts.

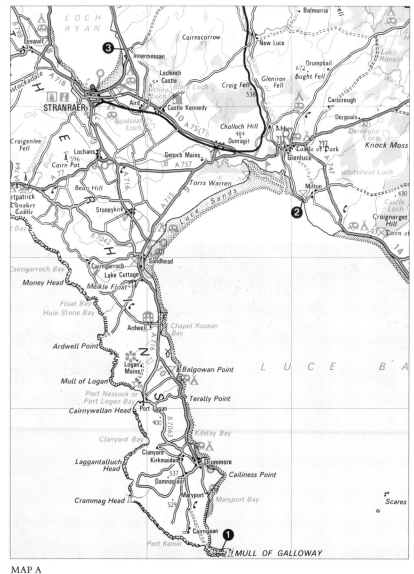

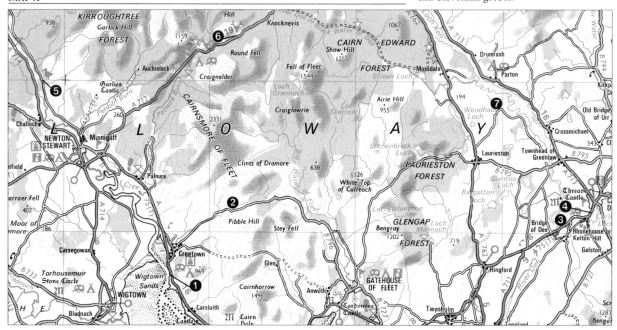

MAP A

MAP B

A:1 MULL OF GALLOWAY*

Near Stranraer; *take B7041 from Drummore, then minor road; park just before lighthouse entrance at NX 156303. The cliff edge is dangerous.*

■ Cliff, cliff-top grassland.

■ Although the sea-bird colony is small by Scottish standards, the dramatic scenery adds greatly to the site, best seen to the W of the car park. The point S of the lighthouse is a good sea-watching site and gives a distant view of the Scar Rocks gannetry (formed 1939, 770 nests 1984/5). **Birds** (Breeding) black guillemot, guillemot, razorbill, kittiwake, shag, fulmar, cormorant. **Plants** Scots lovage and roseroot are at their southernmost site; golden and rock samphire at their northernmost, spring squill, purple milk-vetch.

ROYAL SOCIETY FOR THE PROTECTION OF BIRDS

A:2 LUCE BAY

Near Stranraer; *best views from minor road, signposted on A75 just W of Glenluce, and picnic area at Stairhaven (NX 309537). Also from A747 NW of Port William, or follow signposted track to bay through Forestry Commission plantation at Torrs Warren. Access forbidden to Torrs Warren – it is used as a bombing range.*

■ Muddy/rocky estuary, dunes.

■ In autumn and winter there are numbers of sea-duck and waders on passage. Torrs Warren is an interesting sand-dune system. **Birds** Common scoter, pintail, red-breasted merganser; (river mouth) great crested grebe, wigeon.

A:3 LOCH RYAN

Near Stranraer; *view from A718 W side, or A77 on E; from lay-by and picnic area just N of Stranraer, and from ferry to Larne.*

■ Estuary.

■ Small areas of mud on S shore from Stranraer to Leffnoll Point, and at the Wig, S of Kirkcolm, are most productive. To find occasional rarities such as king eider, work around the roads, stopping to scan the shore. **Birds** Red-breasted merganser, scaup, eider, goldeneye; (occasional) black-necked and Slavonian grebes.

DUMFRIES & GALLOWAY

B:1 WIGTOWN BAY
Wigtown; roadside views from A75 S of Creetown (esp lay-by at NX 472576); also of Fleet Bay, SE of Gatehouse of Fleet. Views over River Cree and Wigtown Sands from minor road N of Wigtown. No entry to private farmland; beware of wildfowlers.
■ Sandy/muddy estuary.
■ The site is a proposed local nature reserve. Thousands of pink-footed goose and a few whooper swan roost on the flats, especially in Feb and Mar, and feed in nearby fields, but cord-grass is spreading and reducing the feeding. **Birds** Pintail, knot, golden plover, wigeon.

B:2 CAIRNSMORE OF FLEET
Near Gatehouse of Fleet; follow B796 NW, turn right on track to Dromore Farm (NX 554638). Enter reserve from there by Clints of Dromore or forestry track about ½ mile (0.8 km) NE of farm; no paths in reserve. Further information from warden, Falbrae Cottage, Falbrae, Creetown.
■ Grass/heather moorland.
■ Exploration of this NNR consisting of undulating moorland rising to the great granite dome of Cairnsmore of Fleet, 2,332 feet (711 m), is only for the serious naturalist or hill walker. Rewarding views of golden eagle, golden plover and red deer. **Birds** Merlin, red grouse, raven. **Mammals** Mountain hare, feral goat. **Reptiles** Adder, common lizard. **Butterflies** Scotch argus, pearl-bordered fritillary, large heath. **Plants** Great sundew, pale butterwort, few-flowered sedge; (high tops) stiff sedge.
NATURE CONSERVANCY COUNCIL (SW Scotland)

B:3 THREAVE WILDFOWL REFUGE★
Near Castle Douglas; three hides accessible off A75 at Lodge of Kelton Farm (NX 742608); best is Lamb Island hide (NX 736606); two more hides from Kelton Mains Farm (NX 746617). Hides closed 31 Mar–1 Nov). Parking limited; leaflet from Threave Garden Visitor Centre, signposted off A75 at NX 753605. Access to other parts of refuge only with warden (not Mons), fee. Contact warden, Kelton Mill, Castle Douglas, Dumfries and Galloway, DG7 1RZ.
■ Flood marshes.
■ Greylag goose (up to 1,500) are the main attraction; Greenland white-fronted goose may turn up, with bean goose occasionally on Hightae Drum, which can be viewed from the entrance to Hightae Farm at NX 753612 (park with care).
NATIONAL TRUST FOR SCOTLAND

B:4 CARLINGWARK LOCH
Castle Douglas; view from caravan site in Castle Douglas (NX 765617) or park at edge of town and walk along A75. View Gelston marsh (NX 7660) from B736.
■ Open water, marshland.
■ The loch holds good numbers of wildfowl. Gelston marsh is used by a small flock of bean geese – under 30 birds – best viewed in Jan and Feb when they fly in to roost at dusk.

B:5 WOOD OF CREE
Newton Stewart; pull off on grass alongside minor road from Minigaff, at NX 382708; take track to wood. Warden at Gairland, Old Edinburgh Road, Minigaff, Newton Stewart.
■ Broad-leaved woodland, river.
■ Fine woodland, mainly old coppice of

sessile oak, birch, hazel, ash and rowan. Good flora and birdlife in the wood in spring and summer, dippers and grey wagtails by the river. **Lepidoptera** Scotch argus, dark green fritillary.
ROYAL SOCIETY FOR THE PROTECTION OF BIRDS

B:6 GALLOWAY FOREST PARK
Near Newton Stewart; well signposted from A714 or A712. Details from Recreation Forester, Glentrool Forest, Bargrennan, Newton Stewart.
■ Coniferous plantation, open hillside.
■ Recreation is an important aspect of the management of this 250 square mile (648 square km) forest, and there are many attractive areas with clearly marked trails, although some may be closed for forestry works. At Craigdews a herd of feral goats in a large enclosure is best seen from the roadside at NX 491721. Red deer roam in a wild moorland enclosure on Brockloch Hill, signposted from the car park at NX 522732, a 110-yard (100-m) walk up a grassy path. There is a deer museum at Clatteringshaws on the A712 (NX 551763), closed Oct-Mar.
FORESTRY COMMISSION

B:7 KEN-DEE MARSHES★
Near New Galloway; roadside views from A713 of Loch Ken, and from minor road off B795 at Glenlochar W of Townhead of Lochar. Access to RSPB reserve only in escorted parties by written arrangement with the Warden, Midtown, Laurieston, nr Castle Douglas, Dumfries and Galloway, DG7 2PP (fee for non-members).
■ Marsh, meadow, farmland, deciduous woodland.
■ Freshwater marshes and wet meadows in two sections: around Kenmure Holms beside Kenmure Castle at NX 638765, and the loch shore at NX 695964. Greenland white-fronted goose (around 300) is most common in winter on pasture E of the A713 N of Crossmichael (NX 721683), or on rough grazing beside the minor road S of Mains of Duchrae (NX 702683), which is also good for about 80 whooper swans. Explore the Cairn Edward Forest for siskin, redpoll, crossbill and even black grouse.
ROYAL SOCIETY FOR THE PROTECTION OF BIRDS

C:1 ROCKCLIFFE COAST
Near Dalbeattie; park just before Rockcliffe village at NX 852536; walk into village; at the Merse a signed path leads to Castlehill Point, about one mile (1.5 km). Details from the NTS Representative, Threave House, Castle Douglas, Dumfries and Galloway, DG7 1RX.
■ Rocky coastline, tidal mudflats.
■ The bay at Rockcliffe is well worth exploring for waders, including greenshank. It overlooks Rough Island, a 20-acre bird sanctuary and NTS reserve, closed in May and Jun when birds are nesting, but otherwise accessible at low tide.
NATIONAL TRUST FOR SCOTLAND

C:2 SOUTHWICK COAST WILDLIFE RESERVE
Near Dalbeattie; entrance opposite minor road signed Nether Clifton at NX 914562 (park in rough lay-by up hill to SW). Follow track through rock called Needle's Eye. Details from Reserve Office, SWT. Beware dangerous cliff edges.
■ Ancient oakwood, sea cliff, fen, salt-marsh.
■ Overlooks Mersehead Sands; many geese, ducks and waders visit the salt-marsh and sands in winter. The woodland has a shrub layer of hazel and holly, and a rich ground flora. Unusual flowers of the base-rich areas include sticky catchfly. The dramatic rock pillars known as Lot's Wife and the Needle's Eye provide geological interest.
SCOTTISH WILDLIFE TRUST

C:3 DRUMMAINS REED-BED WILDLIFE RESERVE
Dumfries; park at side of A710 at Drumburn opposite cottage called 'Criffel Bank' (NX 980608); follow overgrown and muddy track to the shore. Contact Reserves Office, SWT, prior to visit (bird and plant lists available; sae please).
■ Salt-marsh, reed-bed.
■ A hide is available (no key required) to the left at the foot of the entrance track. Visit in winter for wildfowl and waders, with numerous shelduck. Variety of salt-marsh flowers.
SCOTTISH WILDLIFE TRUST

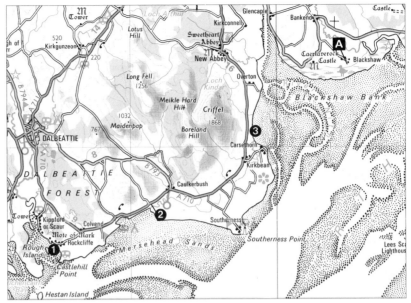

MAP C

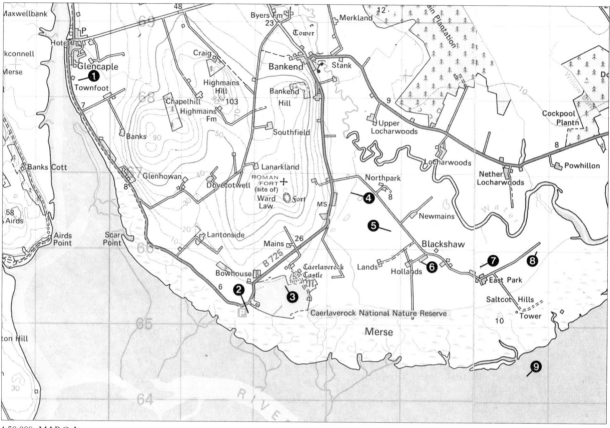

1:50 000, MAP C:A

C:A NORTH SOLWAY COAST★★
Near Dumfries.
Caerlaverock NNR: no access to sanctuary area at mouth of Lochar Water.
East Park Wildfowl Refuge: ample parking, lavatories, visitors admitted daily from 16th Sept to 30th Apr, 9.30 am to 5 pm (closed 24th and 25th Dec). Admission fee. concessions for parties booked in advance – apply Wildfowl Trust, East Park Farm, Caerlaverock, Dumfries.
① Roadside views across the Nith to Kirkconnel Merse, where whooper swan feeds in winter.
② At corner of road is a car park and picnic area with views over the merse (salt-marsh) to the mudflats of Blackshaw Bank. In winter,

barnacle and pink-footed geese feed on the merse, and large numbers of waders may gather. It is possible to walk W along the merse, but it can be wet underfoot.
③ A feral group of Canada goose lives in the moat of Caerlaverock Castle; don't confuse with barnacle goose.
④ and ⑤ Large numbers of barnacle goose feed in the fields here in winter.
⑥ The NCC warden is based here, but general enquiries should be in writing please (Tadorna, Hollands Farm Road, Caerlaverock, Dumfries.)
⑦ Entrance to the Wildfowl Trust's Refuge. The heated Observatory offers one of the finest wildlife spectacles in Scotland, with 17

species of wildfowl, various waders, and occasionally even hunting peregrines on view.
The entire Spitsbergen population of barnacle geese (more than 10,000 in 1986/7) winters in the area, together with more than 200 whooper swans and large numbers of wigeon, pintail and other duck. Waders regularly hunted by peregrine falcon.
⑧ From the Trust's tower hide, vast flocks of barnacle goose can be seen feeding in winter, with pink-footed goose and whooper swan.
⑨ No access to the sanctuary area which stretches from here to beyond the Lochar Water.
NATURE CONSERVANCY COUNCIL (SW Scotland)/THE WILDFOWL TRUST

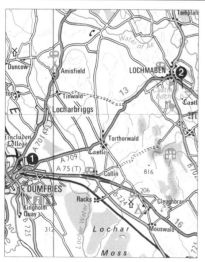

MAP D

D:1 FOUNTAINBLEAU & LADYPARK
Dumfries; *between A701 and A709 at NX 986772. Park on Marchmount Avenue; path leads NE to the wood, over several stiles. Permit required: apply Reserves Office, SWT. Keep to marked paths.*
■ Wet birch woodland.
■ A well laid out board walk leads through this attractive reserve, which frequently floods. The rotting, waterlogged birches are rich in fungi, and dead stumps provide nest sites for willow tits which are a speciality.
Plants Marsh cinquefoil, marsh penny-wort, sedges.
SCOTTISH WILDLIFE TRUST

D:2 CASTLE & HIGHTAE LOCHS★★
Near Lochmaben; *Castle Loch: views from A709, car parks at NY 090819 and at castle at NY 088812. Hightae Loch: park at nature re-serve sign on right of B7020 at NY 087799; walk to loch. No access to main bird breeding areas.*
■ Open water, reed-bed, alder carr.

■ These lochs, an LNR, are remarkably rich in wildfowl in winter. The goose roost, especially at Castle Loch, has 1,000 or more greylag, up to 13,000 pink-footed geese and the occasional bean, white-fronted, barnacle or brent goose. Mallard, wigeon and pochard use both lochs, with goosander at Castle Loch. A small flock of whooper swan winters here, while in summer a few great crested grebe breed; there is a resident feral flock of Canada goose. In dry summers, ex-posed mud at the SE corner of Castle Loch can be good for waders, including green-shank, dunlin and ringed plover. Check the plantation around Hightae Loch in winter for tits, siskin and redpoll, and in summer for breeding warblers.
All in all an outstanding amount of in-terest bearing in mind that the lochs are easily accessible from Lochmaben, and are not far from the A75 Euroroute to Stranraer.
ANNANDALE & ESKDALE DISTRICT COUNCIL

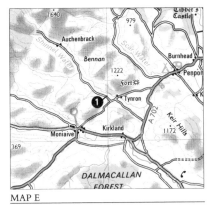

MAP E

E:1 TYNRON JUNIPER WOOD
Near New Galloway; *view from above A702 about 6 miles (10 km) E of Moniaive, at NX 829930. Permit required: apply Warden, Tadorna, Hollands Farm Road, Caerlaverock, Dumfries; entrance only for those with a specialist interest.*
■ Juniper woodland.
■ One of the best surviving remnants of juniper woodland in the area. The fenced stand covers some 12 acres. The juniper is in many growth forms, from low bushes to tall columns, some almost 16 ft (5 m) high. **Plants** Ash, wild cherry; wood sorrel, honeysuckle. ***Lepidoptera*** Juniper carpet, juniper pug moths.
NATURE CONSERVANCY COUNCIL (SW Scotland)

F:1 GREY MARE'S TAIL★
Near Moffat; *park off A708 at NT 185145. A path W of Tail Burn gives close views of waterfall; the steep, rocky path E of the burn leads to Loch Skeen and moorland. Details of ranger-led walks from NTS headquarters.*
■ Moorland, cliffs, open water, waterfall.
■ By the spectacular 190-foot (60-m) waterfall grow roseroot, dog's mercury and wood sage, but the more unusual Arctic/Alpine plants require a longer, harder walk. **Birds** (Breeding) dipper, grey wagtail, common gull. **Mammals** Feral goat. **Plants** (Arctic/Alpine) 3 species of saxifrage, Alpine lady's-mantle, cloudberry.
NATIONAL TRUST FOR SCOTLAND

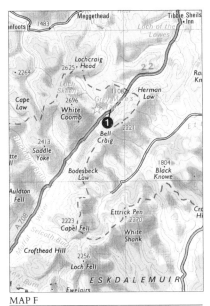

MAP F

MAP A

BORDERS

A:1 DAWYCK BOTANIC GARDEN
Near Peebles; *clearly signposted off B712 at NT 1633537; ample parking, admission fee, closed Oct-Mar and daily 5 pm-10 am. No dogs.*
■ Mature woodland, river.
■ In an arboretum more than 300 years old, underplanted with flowering shrubs. Woodland birds abound, and wild flowers and ferns thrive, as do red squirrels. The herd of Sika deer, brought from Japan in 1908, has gone wild and flourished.
ROYAL BOTANIC GARDEN, EDINBURGH

Sika deer – see A:1.

A:2 RIVER TWEED WALK
Peebles; *car parks by bridge over River Tweed on B7062 at NT 250403. Public access S of bridge to footpath only. Route card from Ranger Service, BRC, Newton St Boswells.*
■ River, woodland, farmland.
■ The walk follows S bank to Old Manor Bridge (NT 229394), then back along N bank past Neidpath Castle. **Birds** Goosander, dipper. **Mammals** Red squirrel.
BORDERS REGIONAL COUNCIL

A:3 GLENTRESS FOREST
Near Peebles; *follow signs off A72; four walks 1-4½ miles (1.5-7 km) in length are marked from the car park.*
■ Coniferous plantation, moorland.
■ Many typical woodland birds can be seen in this 17-square mile (44-sq km) forest of spruce, larch, pine and Douglas fir.
FORESTRY COMMISSION

A:4 MOOR FOOT HILLS
Near Dalkeith; *roadside views from B709 and B7007 N of Innerleithen. No access to private farmland.*
■ Heather/grass moorland.
■ Despite their proximity to Edinburgh, these hills seem wild and remote and provide a breeding refuge for peregrine, merlin and golden plover. **Birds** Peregrine, merlin, red grouse, golden plover, short-eared owl, wheatear, curlew. **Plants** Cloudberry.

B:1 LINDEAN RESERVOIR★
Near Selkirk; *turn first left after B653 on right of A699; park E of reservoir at NT 506293, where there is an explanatory board. A muddy footpath leads around the reservoir. Information from Ranger Service, BRC, Newtown St Boswells.*
■ Base-rich disused reservoir, meadow, coniferous woodland.

■ This 20-acre reservoir is rich in freshwater invertebrates – many species of waterbeetle, several damselflies and dragonflies. The surrounding meadows are good for plants and butterflies; whinchat, reed bunting and linnet are among the breeding birds. In winter, water fowl and whooper swan gather here and can be seen from the small hide. **Plants** Northern and early marsh-orchids, skullcap, grass-of-Parnassus. **Birds** Slavonian grebe, black-throated diver, water rail, black tern; (winter) smew, whooper swan, goldeneye, teal.
BORDERS REGIONAL COUNCIL

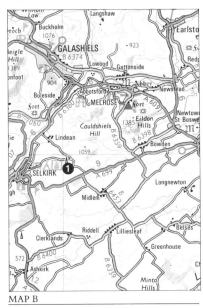

MAP B

BORDERS

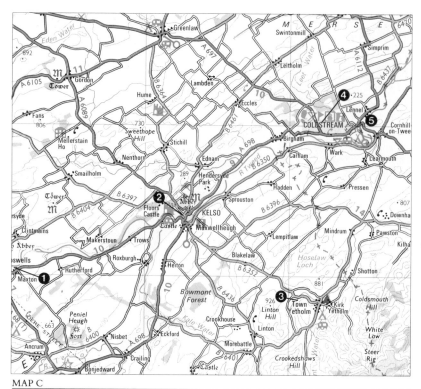

MAP C

C:1 RIVER TWEED WALK★

Newtown St Boswells; park beside auction mart at NT 577316; limited parking by Maxton Church. Public access to footpath only, all surrounding land is private; route card from Ranger Services, BRC, Newton St Boswells.

■ River, mixed woodland, farmland.

■ Route cards, picking out local features of interest, add greatly to the enjoyment of the attractive Tweed and Teviot walks, arranged with the co-operation of the local landowners, whose privacy should be respected. This walk is particularly attractive for the woodland through which it passes. **Birds** (Riverside) goosander, dipper, grey wagtail, oystercatcher; (woodland) blackcap, willow warbler, chiffchaff. **Plants** (Riverside) water avens; (woodland) meadow saxifrage, goldilocks buttercup, moschatel, few-flowered leek, leopard's-bane.
BORDERS REGIONAL COUNCIL

C:2 RIVER TEVIOT WALK

Kelso; limited off-street parking in town. Public access to footpath; route card to Kalemouth (NT 709274) from Ranger Service, BRC, Newton St Boswells.

■ River, woodland, farmland.

■ The best place to see duck is at Hogarth's Mill opposite the junction of the rivers Tweed and Teviot (NT 726338). In summer, riverside plants and woodland birds abound. When sunny, beware the dangerous sap of giant hogweed.
BORDERS REGIONAL COUNCIL

C:3 YETHOLM LOCH

Near Kelso; rough track leads to parking area at NT 804284, off B6325 just before town of Yetholm. No permit required, but contact Reserves Office, SWT, in advance; keep out of marsh during breeding season.

■ Freshwater loch, fenland.

■ In summer great crested grebe, shoveler and teal breed in the marsh, and greater spearwort flowers among the bottle sedge.

The reserve's major interest is in autumn and winter when more than 1,000 mallard gather together with teal, wigeon, pochard, up to 700 greylag geese, shovelers, tufted duck, goldeneye and goosander.
SCOTTISH WILDLIFE TRUST

C:4 THE HIRSEL★

Coldstream; signposted off A697; car park, lavatories and picnic area at museum, from which a full bird list can be obtained. Entrance by dona- tion during seasonable daylight hours. Further information and walk leaflets from Estate Office, The Hirsel, Coldstream, TD12 4LP.

■ Lake, woodland, river.

■ Three walks: around Hirsel Lake, through century-old Dundock Wood, or along the Leet, a tributary of the Tweed. The lake (with a hide) has breeding grebes in summer, and whooper swan, pink-footed and greylag geese and a major mallard roost in winter. **Birds** (Woodland) pied flycatcher; (riverside) dipper, kingfisher; (winter) whooper swan, greylag and pink-footed geese, goosander, teal.
LORD HOME OF THE HIRSEL/DOUGLAS AND ANGUS ESTATES

C:5 RIVER TWEED

Berwick-upon-Tweed; access to harbour: follow signs to Spittal and Tweedmouth on S side of river; to pier: follow signs to Nessgate on N side of river; to river: at Coldstream, Norham, Horncliffe and Berwick.

■ Estuary, river, mixed woodland.

■ The Tweed Estuary is famous for salmon, swans and many other wildfowl in winter. The S side of the river is accessible by footpath as far as Coldstream and the stretch running upstream from Norham is particularly attractive in summer. Berwick Pier provides excellent sea-watching. **Birds** (Winter) whooper and mute swans, divers, grebes, goldeneye; (autumn) gannet, skua; (river) goosander, dipper, grey wagtail. **Mammals** Mink.

D:1 DUNS CASTLE

Duns; park at Castle Road, or off B6365 at N end of reserve (NT 784561). Open entry to reserve and hide; details from Reserves Office, SWT.

■ Mixed woodland, open loch, meadow.

■ A variety of attractive walks lead through the woodland, which is full of flowers and breeding birds in spring. The artificial loch,

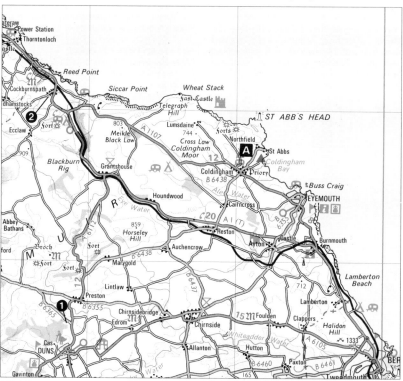

MAP D

Mink – see C:5, opposite page.

unromantically called the Hen Poo, has many flowers and some wildfowl. **Birds** (Breeding) pied flycatcher, redstart, marsh tit, chiffchaff. **Plants** (Lochside) toothwort, bogbean, common wintergreen, common twayblade.

SCOTTISH WILDLIFE TRUST

D:2 SOUTHERN UPLAND WAY

Near Dunbar; start at market cross in Cockburnspath, or ½ mile (0.8 km) N take minor road E to Cove; park overlooking harbour.

■ Coastal grassland, sessile oak/ash/elm woodland, coniferous plantation.

■ From the cliffs, with superb scenery (and nesting fulmar, passing gannets, house martin, kittiwake and guillemot), the route moves inland through Pease Dean; a steepsided wooded valley with typical woodland flowers and butterflies. Turn and retrace steps where way meets railway line and A1, or continue beyond Blackburn Farm or to Abbey St Bathans, 10 miles (16 km).

COUNTRYSIDE COMMISSION FOR SCOTLAND

Dipper – see C:1, C:4 and C:5, opposite page.

D:A ST ABBS HEAD**

Near Eyemouth; details and leaflet from Ranger, Northfield, St Abb's, Borders.

■ Cliffs, coastal grassland, loch.

① The harbour at St Abbs is good for gulls and sea-duck, and is the base for diving expeditions into the marine nature reserve.

② The reserve (this is an NNR) car park is signposted left off the main road, just before Northfield Farm. The path into the reserve follows the road, then leaves on the left at ③. On quiet days, parking may be available at ④ follow road past Northfield Farm.

⑤ The cliff at White Heugh has guillemot, kittiwake and a few razorbill.

⑥ This area is good for flowers, including common rock-rose and purple milk-vetch.

⑦ The rock stacks seen from the point here are crammed with guillemots, kittiwakes, razorbills and a few puffins, with shags below. Roseroot and Scots lovage grow on the cliffs.

⑧ Kittiwakes bathe in the Mire Loch, and little grebe, sedge warbler, and whitethroat nest around the edge.

⑨ Coldingham Bay has sand dunes, and rocks with thrift, sea campion and sea milkwort.

Mar–Jul best for seabirds, Sep–Oct for sea watching.

Wheatear and rock pipit nest in the grasslands, while in spring and autumn migrants land in the shrubs around Mire Loch. Large numbers of gannets pass the Head, and there are passages of skuas and shearwaters in autumn.

NATIONAL TRUST FOR SCOTLAND/ SCOTTISH WILDLIFE TRUST

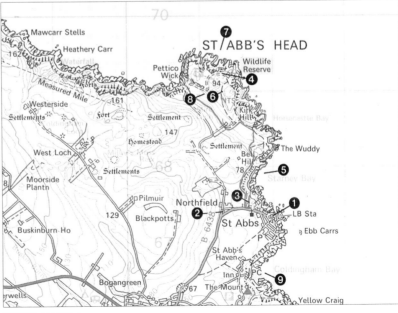

1:50 000, MAP D:A

MAP A

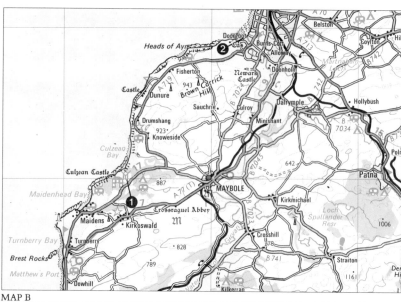

MAP B

A:1 BALLANTRAE SHINGLE BEACH*

Near Girvan; car park, signposted from Ballantrae, next to shore at NX 082825; walk out to the spit from here. No access to fenced areas in breeding season. Details of guided walks from Reserves Office, Scottish Wildlife Trust.

■ Shingle spit, brackish lagoons.

■ This shingle spit provides a nesting place for Arctic and little terns, and many waders use the lagoons. Eider duck gather offshore and gannets are often seen fishing against the spectacular backdrop of their breeding site on Ailsa Craig. **Birds** Little, Sandwich and Arctic terns, red-breasted merganser, ringed plover. **Plants** Oysterplant, sea campion, thrift, common scurvy-grass.

SCOTTISH WILDLIFE TRUST

A:2 AILSA CRAIG**

Day trips by boat from Girvan; contact Tourist Information Centre, Bridge Street, Girvan (0465-4950) for name of boatman. Crossing: about 1¼ hrs. Permit required to stay on island: apply Marquis of Ailsa, Blanefield House, Kirkoswald, Strathclyde. Keep away from foot of cliffs (falling stones).

■ Rocky island with rough grassland, boulder shore.

■ The massive gannetry (22,800 nests in 1985) on the W cliffs can best be appreciated from the shore below, but a six-hour boat trip (allowing 3½ hours ashore) is essential for this. Walk around the S shore from the pier, but note that Stranny Point (at NX 016994) is cut off at high tide, and do not attempt within two hours of this (check tide times with boatman). **Birds** Peregrine, black guillemot, puffin, gannet, razorbill, guillemot, fulmar, kittiwake, raven, wheatear, rock pipit. **Plants** Sea spleenwort, tree mallow, sea campion, sea radish, rock seaspurrey, common scurvy-grass, thrift, navelwort.

B:1 CULZEAN*

Near Ayr; signposted off A719; parking (fee payable) in several car parks, the best is at the Park Centre (closed Oct-Mar; castle closed Nov-Mar). Admission on foot to Park free all year 9 am-sunset. Further details from The Administrator, Culzean Country Park, Maybole, Strathclyde, KA19 8LE.

■ Mixed woodland, rocky and sandy shores, streams, ponds, parkland, farmland.

■ This lowland estate and country park, centred on its 18thC castle, offers a full programme of ranger-guided walks and talks, as well as leaflets on birds, seashore life, and rocks and scenery. **Fish** (Rock pools) rock goby. **Invertebrates** (Rock pools) hermit, crabs, chitons, sea urchins, brittle star, seahare, sea-slugs. **Seaweeds** (Shore) channelled and knotted wrack, oarweed. **Birds**

Four-spotted chaser – see C:2, opposite page.

(Breeding) sparrowhawk, ringed plover, woodcock, heron, little grebe; (winter) Slavonian grebe, whooper swan, purple sandpiper.

NATIONAL TRUST FOR SCOTLAND

B:2 DOONFOOT BAY

Near Ayr; turn off towards the coast at roundabout on A719 S of Doonfoot; park near coast and walk to shore.

■ Rocky and muddy shore, open sea, farmland.

■ The bay is used in winter by many waders and wildfowl, and has a gull roost which often contains northern species such as Iceland and glaucous gulls, or even the southern Mediterranean gull. In summer, gannets from Ailsa Craig, common and Arctic terns feed offshore. **Birds** (Winter) red-breasted merganser, scaup, eider duck, goldeneye, ringed plover, wigeon, curlew.

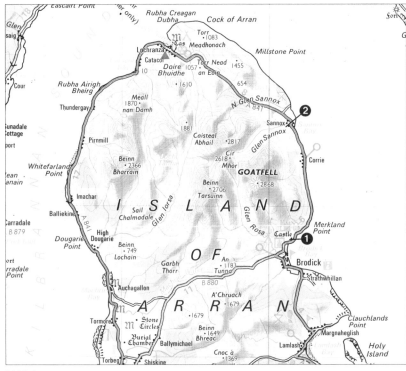

MAP C

C:1 BRODICK
COUNTRY PARK, ARRAN★
Brodick, Island of Arran; ferry from Ardrossan to Brodick; entry to Country Park from A841; free parking. Park open 9.30 am-sunset daily; castle closed mid-Oct to mid-Apr; fee for admission to castle and gardens.
■ Mixed deciduous woodland, garden.
■ Breeding birds in the mature woodland include chiffchaff, wood warbler, goldcrest, spotted flycatcher, crossbill and barn owl, and nightjars may be heard at dusk – Scotland's largest population. Park rangers lead regular guided walks and run the Arran biological records centre, so the Park is well documented (checklist from Park Centre). **Birds** Tawny owl, buzzard, sparrowhawk, kestrel, woodcock, treecreeper. **Mammals** Red squirrel, brown hare, pipistrelle and long-eared bat. **Plants** Bluebell, ramsons, dog's mercury, beech fern, royal fern, Tunbridge filmy-fern, Arran whitebeams, *Sorbus pseudofennica* and *Sorbus arranensis*.
NATIONAL TRUST FOR SCOTLAND/
CUNNINGHAM DISTRICT COUNCIL

C:2 GOATFELL, ARRAN
Near Brodick, Island of Arran; the most popular path, following the Cnocan burn, starts in the Country Park at NS 005382; other routes from Glen Rosa, Corrie or Glen Sannox.
■ Grass and heather moorland, mountain heath.
■ The massive granite peaks of Goatfell and its neighbours show many classical glaciation features (corries, hanging valleys, moraines) and provide dramatic hill walking. On the tops, golden plover, ring ouzel, peregrine falcon, raven, and Britain's most southerly population of ptarmigan all breed, and with luck you may see a golden eagle. **Plants** Dwarf willow, mountain everlasting, starry saxifrage, mountain sorrel, heath spotted-orchid, fir clubmoss. **Dragonflies** Common aeshna, golden-ringed, four-spotted chaser, highland darter, large red

and common blue damselflies. **Mammals** Red deer, brown hare.
NATIONAL TRUST FOR SCOTLAND

D:1 SHEWALTON SANDPITS
Near Irvine; about one mile (1.5 km) S on A737, take minor road E to Dreghorn; park on left beyond houses, at NS 326370. Enter reserve

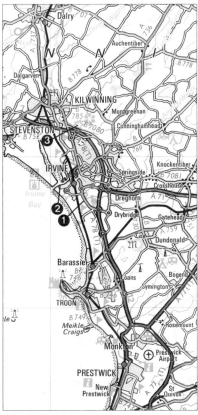

MAP D

E of there, or recross A737 and enter opposite road junction.
■ Pools, lagoons, grassland, scrub, river.
■ Fashioned from worked-out sand and gravel pits, these pools show clearly how valuable wildlife habitats can be created from industrial wasteland. A wide variety of birds uses the pools including bar-tailed godwit, greenshank and ruff on autumn migration and teal, wigeon, tufted duck, and whooper swan later in the winter, while the surrounding grassland has many insects in summer. **Plants** Round-leaved sundew, creeping willow, sand sedge. **Mammals** Badger, fox, stoat. **Insects** Grayling butterfly, green tiger beetle.
SCOTTISH WILDLIFE TRUST

D:2 BOGSIDE FLATS★
Irvine; follow signs for Magnum Leisure Centre, park by by harbour. View from harbour wall (NS 310382), road to harbour bar, or from Bogside race course.
■ Mudflats, salt-marsh.
■ In winter, these flats are one of the best sites in Ayrshire for waders, including golden plover, knot, and oystercatcher, sometimes hounded by a stooping peregrine or hunting merlin. A small flock of whooper swan is regularly present in winter, and rarities recorded here include little stint and spoonbill.

D:3 EGLINTON
COUNTRY PARK
Near Irvine; access road from A78 at Eglinton Interchange, off A737; at NS 319419 are car park, toilets, tearooms, Visitor Centre (closed 4.30 pm-10 am; closed Oct-Mar).
■ Mixed deciduous woodland, plantation, loch, river, marsh, garden, farmland.
■ This attractive area has many common woodland birds and flowers. A full summer programme of ranger-guided walks. **Birds** (Woodland) barn and tawny owls, great spotted woodpecker; (riverside) dipper, kingfisher. **Mammals** Roe deer, mink.
IRVINE DEVELOPMENT CORPORATION

E:1 AYR GORGE
Near Ayr; park in lay-by beside A758 at Failford; enter reserve by track E of railway bridge (NS 455261) which runs E to the river, then downstream on W bank.
■ Steep-sided gorge with sessile oak/birch woodland.
■ The woodlands with a sparse scrub layer of holly, hazel and rowan, shelter many woodland birds, such as great spotted woodpecker, treecreeper and blackcap, as well as red squirrel, roe deer and badger.
SCOTTISH WILDLIFE TRUST

MAP E

STRATHCLYDE

F:1 STRATHCLYDE COUNTRY PARK
Near Motherwell; *enter from roundabout on A725 beneath junction 5 of M74, or from A723 E of junction 6; park by Water Sports Centre (NS 733565) or E of loch; Visitor Centre at NW corner (NS 716584). Permit required for hides and sanctuary: apply Park Director, Strathclyde Country Park, 366 Hamilton Road, Motherwell, ML1 4ED.*
■ Artificial loch, mixed deciduous woodland, pasture, marsh, pond, river.
■ Although primarily created for water sports, the loch, with the adjoining ponds and marshes of Hamilton Low Parks, is much used by wildfowl in winter. Unusual birds recorded include smew and more than a hundred goosander in hard weather. There is a heronry within the Park. **Birds** (Winter) pintail, whooper and mute swans, goldeneye; (resident) heron, treecreeper, great spotted woodpecker. **Mammals** Fox, mink.
STRATHCLYDE REGIONAL COUNCIL

F:2 BARONS HAUGH★
Motherwell; *turn E off M74 on to the A723 at Junction 6; after about ½ mile (0.8 km) turn right into Airbles Road, then right into Adele Street, opposite Motherwell Civic Centre. Enter reserve by lane at NS 755554. School groups contact Warden, 9 Wisteria Lane, Carluke, ML8 5TB.*
■ Marsh, pool, mixed deciduous woodland, scrub, meadow, parkland.
■ 'Haugh' is the local name for a wet meadow, and this marshy area by the Clyde is visited by a wide range of wildfowl in winter, including up to 50 whooper swans. In summer little grebe, redshank, water rail and sedge and grasshopper warblers nest around the marshes, garden warbler, tree pipit and whinchat in scrub, and kingfisher and common sandpiper by the river. Pools have been dug, water levels raised, and a number of hides built by the RSPB. **Birds** (Passage migrants) osprey, little ringed plover. **Mammals** Red and grey squirrels, roe deer, badger.
ROYAL SOCIETY FOR THE PROTECTION OF BIRDS

F:3 NETHAN GORGE
Near Lanark; *park at side of A72 at Nethan-foot Bridge, NS 824471; alternative access from track to Craignethan Castle; a rough footpath connects the two.*
■ Ancient deciduous woodland, river gorge.
■ This fine remnant woodland is set on the gorge below the ruined 16th-C castle. Oak and birch grow on the acid soils at the top of the ravine, ash and wych elm on the richer, less stable slopes, and alder by the river. **Plants** Bird's-nest orchid, great horsetail, wood anemone, ramsons. **Birds** (Woodland) great spotted woodpecker, treecreeper; (riverside) dipper, kingfisher, grey wagtail.
SCOTTISH WILDLIFE TRUST

F:4 FALLS OF CLYDE★★
Lanark; *from A73 take minor road signposted New Lanark: park on right just below main street; path leads from SWT Visitor Centre (signposted) to reserve. Rangers lead guided walks. Visitor Centre closed until 1 pm weekends; Easter-Oct closed 5 pm-11 am weekdays; closed winter.*
■ Broad-leaved woodland, river, coniferous plantation.
■ This reserve is worth visiting for its scenery alone, including the 100-foot (30-m) waterfall of Corra Linn. In the fine woodland by the Clyde are wood anemone, bluebell and dog's mercury, with less common species, such as wood vetch, northern bedstraw, common cow-wheat and purple saxifrage, at an unusual site on rocks by the waterfall; many woodland and river birds are to be found. The display in the Visitor Centre is excellent. **Mammals** Red squirrel, roe deer, badger, mink, Natterer's bat.
SCOTTISH WILDLIFE TRUST

F:5 CLYDE VALLEY WOODS
Near Lanark; *park at side of A706 about 2 miles (3 km) E of Lanark; footpath enters reserve over Mouse Water at NS 904453. Permit required to leave path: apply NNC (SW Scotland)*
■ Elm/ash/oak/alder woodland, river.
■ Known locally as Cleghorn Glen, this 60-acre NNR resembles other remnants of native woodland on steep riversides in this area, but has several locally uncommon species including herb Paris, stone bramble

and rough horsetail. **Birds** (Woodland) treecreeper, great spotted woodpecker; (riverside) dipper, kingfisher, grey wagtail.
NATURE CONSERVANCY COUNCIL

G:1 GREAT CUMBRAE ISLAND
Near Largs; *ferry service to Cumbrae slip. The A860 gives frequent access to the shore; best enjoyed by bicycle, hired on island.*
■ Rocky and sandy shore, farmland, rough grassland.
■ Studies of the marine life of the island have been made by the marine research station at Keppel, at NS 175545, and the aquarium there is worth a visit. White Bay in the N (NS 176591) has some of the best rock pools and is a good place for watching seabirds. **Birds** (Coast and shore) gannet, eider duck, Sandwich, Arctic and common terns, ringed plover, curlew, rock pipit; (inland) raven.

G:2 MUIRSHIEL
Near Lochwinnoch; *about 5 miles (8 km) along minor road following River Calder signposted off B786; car park, Information Centre (closed 7 pm-9 am daily, and Oct-Mar) at NS 313632; three trails (½-one hour) start here.*
■ Mixed woodland, moor, river.
■ The Country Park is former estate woodland, set high in the Calder valley amid rolling moorland; on Windy Hill red grouse, curlew, wheatear, skylark and occasionally short-eared owl and hen harrier can be seen. **Birds** (Resident) dipper, grey wagtail,; (summer) chiffchaff; (winter) common crossbill, siskin. **Mammals** Roe deer. **Plants** (River) musk, monkeyflower.
STRATHCLYDE REGIONAL COUNCIL

G:3 LOCHWINNOCH
Near Glasgow; *entrance to nature centre and reserve N of A760 opposite Lochwinnoch railway station at NS 359581. Reserve, Information Centre, observation tower and shop open 10 am-5.15 pm daily. School parties book with Warden, Nature Centre, Large Road, Lochwinnoch.*
■ Shallow loch, sedge fen, alder/willow scrub, mixed deciduous woodland.
■ There is much here to attract school parties and plenty for the casual visitor to see from the three hides and observation tower, linked by a nature trail. The reserve is in two parts: Barr Loch S of the main road, and Aird Meadow to the N. It is a breeding stronghold for great crested grebe (up to 11 pairs) and other birds in summer, and in winter, up to 3,000 duck, greylag goose and whooper swan use the Barr Loch area. **Birds** (Breeding) wigeon, shoveler, grasshopper warbler; (winter) goosander. **Amphibians** Palmate newt, common toad, frog. **Mammals** Roe deer. **Plants** Greater butterfly-orchid, bird's-nest orchid, bogbean, broad-leaved helleborine.
ROYAL SOCIETY FOR THE PROTECTION OF BIRDS

G:4 LUNDERSTON BAY
Near Greenock; *car park, toilets, off A78, 2 miles (3 km) N of Inverkip at NS 204742. No boats allowed unless 'car-topped'. School groups contact ranger at Carnalees Bridge.*
■ Sea shore (rock, sand, pebbles), field, woodland.
■ Situated near the mouth of the Clyde Estuary, the coastal walk and bay are part of the proposed Clyde-Muirshiel Regional Park. The bay is surprisingly unpolluted and is an excellent site for sea-shore studies. In

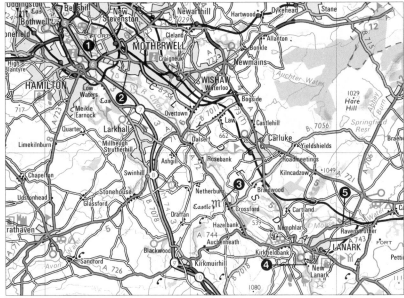

MAP F

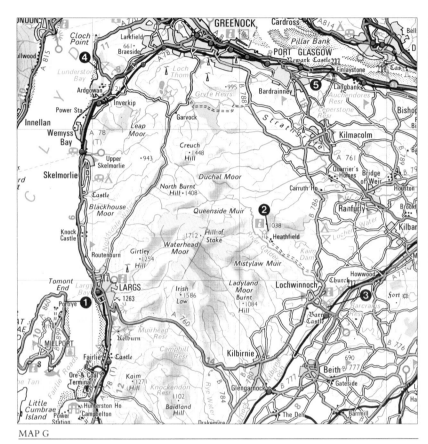

MAP G

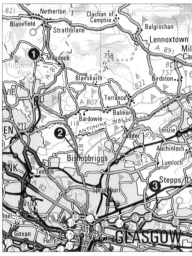

MAP H

- Fen, loch, birch/willow scrub, damp grassland.
- Almost surrounded by industry and housing, Possil Marsh and loch are a wildlife haven in the city. In winter many waterfowl visit the loch. Great crested grebe, water rail and redshank are less frequent visitors. Orchids and bell heather are found in the grassland, and marsh cinquefoil grows around the loch. Water creatures include leopard-spotted flatworm, lake limpet and great ram's-horn snails. Keep to the path on the edge of the reservoir, the centre is extremely marshy.
SCOTTISH WILDLIFE TRUST

H:3 HOGGANFIELD LOCH
Glasgow; entrance S of Cumbernauld Road (A80), about ½ mile (0.8 km) N of Junction 12, M80; car park, tea room, and lavatories on SW shore at NS 638672.
- Artificial loch with wooded island.
- A boating lake in summer, the loch is worth visiting in winter for the comforting sight of wildfowl close to Glasgow city centre. **Birds** (Winter) goldeneye, wigeon, teal, mute swan, resident feral greylag goose and Canada goose, occasional whooper swan, gadwall.
CITY OF GLASGOW PARKS & RECREATION DEPARTMENT

winter the shore is good for waders and wildfowl. **Birds** (Winter) bar-tailed godwit, grey and ringed plover, eider, goldeneye, wigeon, turnstone. **Invertebrates** (Rock pools) hermit crab, grey sea-slug, sea urchin, starfish.
STRATHCLYDE REGIONAL COUNCIL

G:5 CLYDE SHORE, LANGBANK TO ERSKINE
Near Glasgow; minor road to sea wall at West Ferry (NS 400730) from roundabout at M8, junction 31; also access N from A726 E of M898 to pier at NS 463722.
- Muddy shore and estuary.
- Despite heavy industry nearby, these mudflats are remarkably rich in waders and duck in winter, with up to 8,000 redshank (8 per cent of the British population), and more than 20,000 black-headed gulls roosting off West Ferry. Rarities such as smew, green and curlew sandpiper are always possible. Beware of soft mud. **Birds** (Winter) red-throated and black-throated diver (occasional), scaup, red-breasted marganser, pintail, eider, greenshank, turnstone.

H:1 MUGDOCK COUNTRY PARK
Near Milngavie (pronounced 'Mull-gai'); main approach road signposted off A81; main car park and visitor centre are in NW corner at NS 546780. Alternatively, walk N along West Highland Way from Milngavie railway station.
- Parkland, ancient oak woodland, small loch, marshland.
- This park, so close to the Glasgow conurbation, is valuable for informal education. The ranger service (tel 041-956-6100 for details) runs regular summer walks (everything from 'Birds Before Breakfast' to 'Wild Food for Free'), the WATCH club for chil-

dren and regular activities for youngsters and schools. **Birds** Great spotted woodpecker; (winter) whooper swan. **Plants** Frog, greater butterfly- and common spotted- orchids. **Fish** Pike, perch.
CENTRAL REGIONAL COUNCIL

H:2 POSSIL MARSH*
Lambhill, N Glasgow; park in Skirsa Court on Skirsa Street (leave no valuables in car); turn W at traffic lights just N of bridge over Forth to Clyde canal; cross Balmore Road (A879), enter by stile at NS 584695. Details of summer walks from Reserves Office, Scottish Wildlife Trust.

Wheatear – see G:2, opposite page.

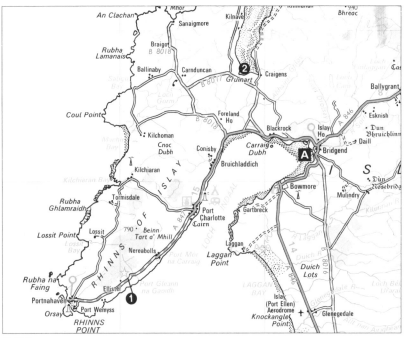

MAP I

I:1 ELLISTER WILDFOWL COLLECTION, ISLAY

Near Port Charlotte, Islay; *situated at Easter Ellister (NR 201535) on A847; fee; limited opening in winter.*

■ Wildfowl collection.

■ One of the best places for close views and photographs of some of the rarer duck (smew, long-tailed, king eider and ruddy duck), without disturbing wild birds. The owner is also founder of the Islay Natural History Trust, whose field centre in Port Charlotte has a useful public reference room (closed after one pm).

I:2 LOCH GRUINART, ISLAY★★

Near Bridgend, Islay; *park at Aoradh farm (NR 276673) and view from B8017 where it bends W across Gruinart flats. Don't enter fields; avoid disturbing geese and livestock.*

■ Improved pasture, salt-marsh, sea loch.

■ In winter 17,000 barnacle goose feed on the clover-rich mix of the flats, which are overlooked by a hide. Greenland white-fronted geese prefer the rushier fields west of Aoradh Farm. Hen harrier, merlin, buzzard, kestrel and sparrowhawk all hunt around here, and roe deer venture on to the flats. The minor road on the west of the loch gives good views of the geese roosting at dusk,

and turnstone on the shore. Walk along the track to Killinallan (NR 315724) for the chance sight of chough, golden eagle and peregrine.
ROYAL SOCIETY FOR THE PROTECTION OF BIRDS

J:1 WEST LOCH TARBERT★

Near Tarbert; *view from A83 opposite West Loch Hotel and pier at NR 844673, or causeway to Kennacraig ferry terminal; also from B8024 around Achaglachgach; or from Caledonian McBrain ferry to Islay.*

■ Sea loch with muddy shore.

■ This sheltered loch is excellent in winter for divers, sea-duck and waders. Slavonian grebe often swim close to the pier. In the outer waters of the loch are all three species of diver, red-breasted merganser, eider duck and goldeneye. Barnacle goose may visit Eilein Traighe, near the loch mouth, in spring. A large flock of Greenland white-fronted goose feeds in winter in the pastures between the A83 and the sea at Rhunahaorine Point, often with greylag goose, while the Sound of Gigha beyond is good for common and velvet scoter (view from the pier at NR 694467). **Birds** Black guillemot, long-tailed duck; (Tarbert harbour) Iceland and glaucous gull.

K:1 ARGYLL FOREST ROAD

Near Dunoon; *details of walks – ½-10 miles (0.8-16 km) – from forest offices at Ardgarten near Arrochar on A83 (NN 272034), Glenbranter on A815 (NS 112977), or Kilmun on A880 (NS 160825). Kilmun Arboretum at NS 165822; admission free. Forest Guide from HMSO.*

■ Coniferous plantation, some mixed broad-leaved woodland, sea lochs.

■ This massive Forest Park encompasses some 240 square miles (622 sq km) of the Ardgarten, Glenbranter and Benmore Forests) and includes the 'Arrochar Alps' on Beinn Ime. Wood warbler most often seen in the few areas of oak woodland. **Birds** (Woodland) capercaillie, black grouse, crossbill, siskin, buzzard, sparrowhawk, goldcrest. **Mammals** Red and grey squirrels, sika and roe deer. **Plants** Beech and oak fern.
FORESTRY COMMISSION

K:2 ARDMORE POINT

Near Helensburgh; *park on shore just beyond Ardmore Farm (NS 325786) on minor road from A814. Nature trail across meadow to coast and around Ardmore Point; no access to fenced fields; warden in summer.*

■ Mudflats, rocky shore, salt-marsh, wet heathland, scrub.

■ Of interest geologically for the non-conformity in the old red sandstone rocks. The rocky shore has excellent rockpools with viviparous blenny and butterfish. The mudflats in winter share many of the ducks and waders of the Clyde Estuary. **Birds** (Winter) whimbrel, bar-tailed godwit, red-breasted merganser, scaup, greenshank, golden plover; (summer in scrub) whinchat. **Plants** Bog asphodel, marsh cinquefoil, common meadow-rue, yellow rattle.
SCOTTISH WILDLIFE TRUST

K:3 BALLOCH CASTLE

Near Dumbarton; *main entrance off B854 through Balloch just E of Balloch Central Station; Visitor Centre, car park, lavatories, caf.*

■ Mixed woodland, arboretum, walled garden, grassland, including orchid meadow.

■ At the S end of Loch Lomond, this country park is most notable for its exotic trees, including tulip-tree, Indian bean-tree, Californian redwoods and weeping ash. There is an active rookery, typical woodland birds, and grey squirrels abound. **Birds** Wood warbler, treecreeper, great spotted woodpecker. **Plants** Greater butterfly-orchid, yellow rattle, ramsons.
DUMBARTON DISTRICT COUNCIL

MAP J

MAP K

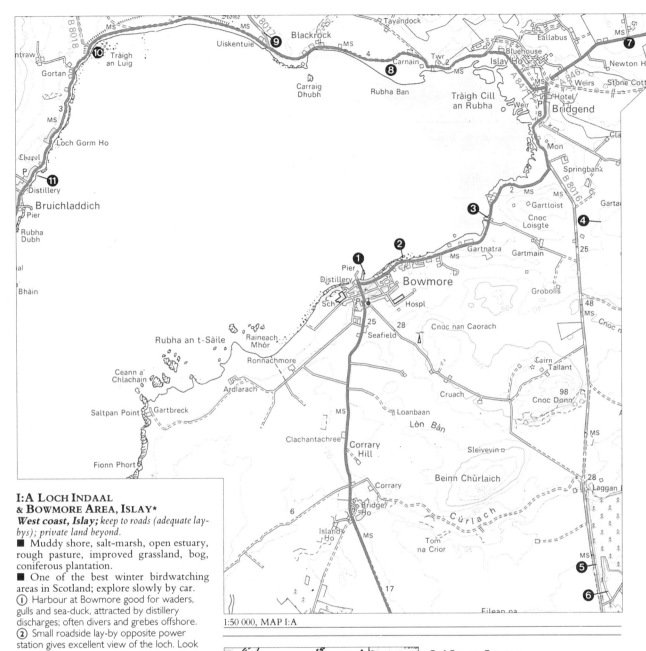

1:50 000, MAP I:A

I:A Loch Indaal & Bowmore Area, Islay★

West coast, Islay; keep to roads (adequate lay-bys); private land beyond.

■ Muddy shore, salt-marsh, open estuary, rough pasture, improved grassland, bog, coniferous plantation.

■ One of the best winter birdwatching areas in Scotland; explore slowly by car.

① Harbour at Bowmore good for waders, gulls and sea-duck, attracted by distillery discharges; often divers and grebes offshore.

② Small roadside lay-by opposite power station gives excellent view of the loch. Look for large flock of scaup (over 1,000) usually in middle of loch, with goldeneye, eider, and a few common scoter. Waders on shore.

③ Rough lay-by on north side of small bridge is best place to watch feeding barnacle goose in early morning, or roosting flocks at dusk (20,000 on Islay, especially early winter); Slavonian grebe just offshore; wigeon, pintail, shelduck, curlew, and bar-tailed godwit feeding on the mud.

④ Barnacle and Greenland white-fronted goose (5,000 on Islay) in fields here.

⑤ View to Duich Moss: major white-fronted goose roost; possibly peregrine and hen harrier over moor.

⑥ Black grouse in plantation. Continue south for more small flocks of white-fronted goose, especially in rough fields near Leorin Farm (NR 349484), and roe deer on moor.

⑦ A846 E good for white-fronts.

⑧ Often barnacle goose near shore.

⑨ Road to Loch Gruinart.

⑩ Good area for waders on shore.

⑪ Often sea-duck off distillery.

MAP L

L:1 Loch Sween

Near Lochgilphead; view from B8025 between Tayvallich and Keillmore, or minor road signposted Kilmore and Castle Sween on E of Loch; or from shore.

■ Sheltered sea loch with muddy and rocky shores.

■ On the E shore, there is a good chance of seeing otters in daylight; herons feed here, buzzard is common over the hills; and the woods S and E of Kilmory are exceptional for their many large wood ants' nests. Linne Mhuirich and Loch na Cille S of Tayvallich on the W coast are wildfowl haunts, and Eilean Mor off the mouth of the loch is a winter roost for barnacle geese. **Birds** Whooper swan, red-breasted merganser, eider.

L:2 Taynish

Near Lochgilphead; park in Tayvallich or take minor road off B8025 just S of village; public road ends near Lochan Taynish at NR 737853 (room for two cars); pedestrian access only on

213

footpath through reserve to end of peninsula.

■ Oak woodland, bog, grass and heather moorland, rocky and muddy shore.

■ One of the larger remnants of native deciduous woodland in Scotland, this NNR is notable for luxuriant mosses, liverworts and lichens. The wood is also very attractive, with Scotch argus butterflies, dragonflies, and northern marsh-orchids in boggy clearings, bilberry, wood sorrel and bugle beneath the trees, and many woodland birds. **Birds** Redstart, wood warbler, siskin, tree pipit, great spotted woodpecker. **Mammals** Otter, sika and roe deer. **Plants** Hay-scented buckler-fern, scaly male-fern, oak fern.

NATURE CONSERVANCY COUNCIL (SW Scotland)

L:3 KNAPDALE FOREST

Near Lochgilphead; access from B841; walks start at Forest Office at Cairnbaan (NR 831907); at Crinan Harbour (NR 784943 -- car park); and three beside Loch Barnluasgan (parking at NR 790911). Leaflet from Forest Office or Tourist Centre, Lochgilphead. Trails closed during foresty operations.

■ Coniferous plantation, small areas of oak woodland, lochs.

■ There is a good chance of seeing roe deer or introduced Sika deer, which have colonized this area. The walk from Crinan is good for sea-birds, including black guillemot, and possibly otters; the one beside Loch Coille-Bharr for wildfowl in winter. **Birds** Hen harrier, buzzard, wheatear. **Mammals** Wildcat, pine marten, otter, red squirrel, grey seal, red deer.

FORESTRY COMMISSION

M:1 ISLE OF COLONSAY★

S of Mull; ferries sail three days a week from Oban (crossing time: 2½ hrs); check timetable with Caledonian MacBrayne Ltd, The Ferry Terminal, Gourock, Strathclyde, PA19 1QP. Open access to many areas, but do not disrupt farming activities; Good bird guide available locally or from bookshops in Oban.

■ Muddy, sandy and rocky shores, cliffs, farmland, mixed deciduous plantation, rough grasslands.

■ Colonsay's charm is its small size and accessibility. The 'Strand' (tidal mudflats between Colonsay and Oronsay, crossable on foot at low tide) is the best site for waders,

while on Oronsay hen harriers and buzzard may be seen over the 14thC priory. Fields near Kiloran may have white-fronted, barnacle or Canada goose in winter, and perhaps a calling corncrake in summer. Kiloran dunes, and fields near Balnahard Farm (keep to track) are good for chough. Loch Fada nearby is worth checking for teal, goldeneye, red-throated divers and, in winter, whooper swan. **Birds** (Strand) greenshank, bar-tailed godwit, ringed plover; (coast) black guillemot, long-tailed duck, great northern diver, fulmar, common scoter; (moor/scrub) stonechat, whinchat, wheatear. **Mammals** Otter, feral goat, grey and common seals.

N:1 GRAVELLACH ISLANDS

In Firth of Lorn, S of Mull; organized trips, May-Aug, good weather only, by boat from Cullipool on the island of Luing (accessible by ferry). The boat can carry 12 people and must be booked by hour: contact Lachlan MacLachlan, Jubilee, Cullipool, Luing, by Oban.

■ Rocky islands, relict ash/wych elm/birch/rowan/alder woodland.

■ The trip to these 'Isles of the Sea', with a 9thC monastery and beehive cells, offers close views of common seal (with pups in summer), grey seal, fulmar, black guillemot, oystercatcher, red deer on the shore and golden eagle on the cliffs. Limestone ridges and cliffs on some islands are botanically rich with plants such as mountain avens and hoary whitlow-grass.

O:1 OBAN BAY

Oban; park in town; explore harbour area (NM 857298) and promenade along N bay (boat trips depart from here). The minor coastal roads to Ganavan and Gallanach are worth walking.

■ Sheltered sea bay with rocky and gravel shore.

■ Common seal regularly come in close to the main fishing pier in search of discarded fish and offal, and black guillemot, shag and eider duck are often seen. The seals breed on

MAP N

islets W of Kerrera which can be visited by boat. **Birds** Rock pipit. **Plants** Sea and black spleenworts.

O:2 GLEN NANT★

Near Oban; B845 S of Taynuilt runs through the reserve, giving good views: nature trail starts in car park W of road at c NN 019273.

■ Ash/hazel or oak/birch woodland.

■ Ash and hazel are the main trees on the richer soils of this NNR, with sanicle, ramsons, primrose, dog's mercury, and oak, beech and lemon-scented ferns. On the poorer soils, sessile oak and birch dominate, with bilberry, heather and bell heather, cow-wheat and tormentil beneath. Interesting historical association with the restored Bonawe iron furnace at Taynuilt (NN 009318). **Birds** Redstart, wood warblers, tree pipit. **Mammals** Wild cat, roe deer.

FORESTRY COMMISSION/NATURE CONSERVANCY COUNCIL (SW Scotland)

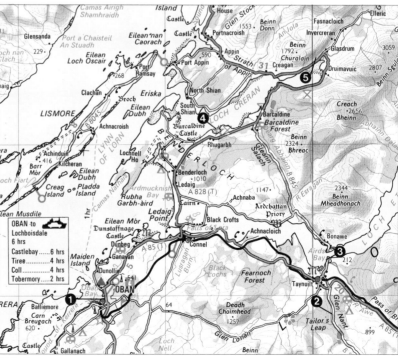

MAP M

MAP O

O:3 LOCH ETIVE

Near Oban; view from A85 for 3 miles (5 km) E of Connel, esp at NM 935345; also from minor road from N end of Connel Bridge to Ardchattan. Boat trips from pier at Taynuilt (NN 010327) -- phone Taynuilt 280 for details.

■ Sea loch with rocky and muddy shore.

■ This sheltered sea loch has numbers of sea-duck in winter, with Scots lovage, sea-milkwort and sea arrow-grass along the shore, and cormorants, herring and lesser black-backed gulls breeding on small islands. A 3¾-hr cruise to the inaccessible parts of the loch gives close views of many of these, and also the chance of seeing golden eagle over the hills.

O:4 SEALIFE CENTRE

Near Oban; clearly signposted off A828 at Barcaldine; large car park, caf and lavatories; admission fee. Closed Oct-Easter.

■ Marine aquarium.

■ One of the best ways to view the rock-pool and undersea life of this part of the west coast, since all specimens are locally caught (and returned to the sea at the end of the season). Other tanks show flatfish on the sea bed, herring shoaling in the ocean, salmon and cod, and common seals swimming underwater.

SEALIFE CENTRE

O:5 GLASDRUM WOOD

Near Oban; view reserve (between Inver, NM 995451, and St Mary's Church, NN 009462) from lay-bys on A828. Permit required to enter reserve: apply NCC (SW Scotland).

■ Deciduous woodland.

■ This NNR is a 'hanging' ashwood, with sessile oak, birch, hazel and alder, on the steep south-facing slopes of Beinn Churalain, 30–600 feet (10–180 m) above sea level. There are no paths in the reserve, but many typical birds and flowers can be seen from the road along the N shore. **Plants** Lemon-scented fern, common cow-wheat, lichens, mosses.

NATURE CONSERVANCY COUNCIL (SW Scotland)

P:1 ARDMEANACH, MULL

West coast; view from B8035 (Salen – Glen More); explore unfenced hillside S and W of road on foot with care. Do not disrupt farming activities.

■ Rough grassland, cliff, rocky shore, mountain heath, relict hazel/oak woodland.

■ The road gives views of Loch na Keal and S to Ben More, where there is a good chance of seeing golden eagle; yellow saxifrage and moss campion grow almost at the roadside in places. The hills around Beinn na Sreine have rich grasslands with montane species such as mountain avens, mountain sorrel, roseroot, mossy cyphel and hairy stonecrop. **Plants** (Relict woods) rock whitebeam (*Sorbus rupicola*), tutsan. **Butterflies** (Grassland below cliffs) Dark green fritillary, grayling.

P:2 LOCH NA KEAL, MULL

W coast; view from shore or roadside; pull off B8035 S of loch or B8073 N; do not obstruct passing places on single track road.

■ Sea loch with rocky and muddy shore.

■ Numbers of great northern diver build up at the head of this loch from September, peaking at about 25. Red- and black-throated divers and Slavonian grebes also winter here, with goldeneye off the river mouth. Eider and red-breasted merganser

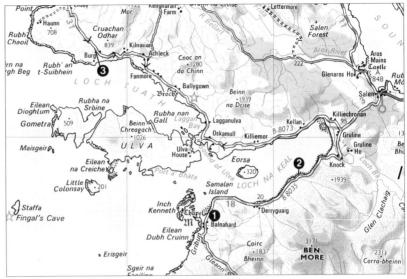

MAP P

can be found all year, Manx shearwaters and gannets in summer. **Birds** Black guillemot, kittiwake.

P:3 BURG, MULL

W coast; turn W off B8035 beside Kilfinichen Bay (NM 492286) on to track and park at Tiroran Hotel (NM 478278). Leaflet available from NTS representative at Burg Farm (NM 427266). Allow a full day.

■ Rough grassland, cliff, rocky shore, open sea.

■ A hard 5-mile (8-km) walk along the coastal path leads to a famous fossil tree at NM 403278, which may be 50 million years old. Fine coastline with magnificent views to the Ross of Mull, Staffa and the Treshnish islands. **Birds** Golden eagle, peregrine, buzzard, raven, golden plover, sparrowhawk, sea-birds. **Mammals** Otter, feral goat, red deer, roe deer, grey seal.

NATIONAL TRUST FOR SCOTLAND

Q:1 ISLE OF TIREE*

W of Mull; ferries from Oban 3 or 4 times a week; check with Caledonian MacBrayne; daily plane from Glasgow (not Sunday); details from Loganair Ltd, Glasgow Airport, Paisley, Strathclyde. Much of the island can be seen from roads or the shore; treat crofting land with respect.

■ Sandy beaches, machair, wet machair, moorland, shallow lochs, farmland, both crofted and in small holdings.

■ White shell-sand from west-coast beaches is blown inland to form rich machair grasslands. Those around Barrapol and Bal-

levullin in the south-west are particularly good for waders and lime-loving plants. Nearby, Loch a'Phuill (view from B8065, B8067 and several tracks) has wintering and breeding wildfowl, with marsh cinquefoil on its margins. Sea-birds breed on the cliffs at Ceann a'Mhara (NL 9340), and the Reef near the airport has a few breeding little tern and a winter flock of Greenland white-fronted goose. Tiree is a stronghold for corncrake (around 80 calling birds).

R:1 ISLE OF COLL

W of Mull; ferries from Oban; this service also allows crossing to and from Tiree. Much of the island can be viewed from the road or coast; keep out of crofting and farming land.

■ Sandy and rocky beaches, rocky grass moorland, machair, lochs, crofted land.

■ Coll is slightly smaller than Tiree, and less populous (about 150 people, compared with 1,000 on Tiree), which means less disturbance for wildfowl: Greenland white-fronted geese on Coll have increased to over 400 in recent winters. Barnacle geese roost in winter on Gunna, S of Coll, and feed on Loch Breachacha, where snow goose has been recorded on passage (view from NM 159548). A few greylag geese breed, along with eider, shelduck, mute swan, about 30 pairs of Arctic skua and a few corncrake. The machair at Crossapol (NM 134533) is the best place for ringed plover and dune flowers in summer; unusual loch plants include pipewort, lesser water-plantain and great fen-sedge.

MAP Q

MAP R

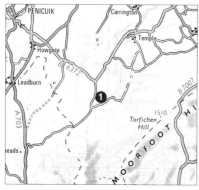

MAP A

A:1 GLADHOUSE RESERVOIR*

Near Edinburgh; *view from minor road on N side (NT 294540) or on S from rough car park on minor road to Moorfoot Farm (NT 294526). No access to shore.*

■ Reservoir, islands.

■ This LNR is a major roost for pink-footed goose in Oct-Nov, with around 5,000 regularly recorded and peak counts of more than 13,000 (15 per cent of the world population). Smaller numbers of greylag goose, duck and great crested grebe also use the reservoir, and more than 10,000 each of roosting black-headed and common gulls add to the frantic bird activity at dusk.

LOTHIAN REGIONAL COUNCIL

B:1 TAILEND MOSS

Near Bathgate; *view from roadside; park S of motorway bridge at NT 002676 on E of unclassified road between A89 and A70. Permit to enter reserve, details of open days and walks from Reserves Office, SWT. Deep Sphagnum pools in places. Warden in summer.*

■ Raised peat bog with pools.

■ One of the last areas of undrained peat

bog in the Lothians, covered in heather, with cross-leaved heath, cranberry, and hare's-tail cottongrass. Little grebe, reed bunting and sedge warbler breed near ponds and marshes; the larger pool is used in winter by whooper swans and greylag geese.

SCOTTISH WILDLIFE TRUST

B:2 ALMONDELL
& CALDER WOOD COUNTRY PARK

Livingston; *three entrances, each with free car park: main access signposted off A89 2 miles (3 km) S of Broxburn; also on B7015 off A71 W of Wilkieston, or 200 yards (183 m) along Mid-Calder to Pumpherston road; (access by car for disabled by prior arrangement). Tel Mid-Calder 882254 to check opening times of Visitor Centre.*

■ Mixed deciduous woodland, river.

■ This fine 'policy' woodland (amenity plantation) is rich in woodland and meadow flowers, including meadow and wood crane's-bill, betony, leopard's-bane and pink purslane. There are typical woodland birds and dipper, grey wagtail and heron by the river. The Visitor Centre has local wildlife displays and the rangers run a programme of guided walks.

WEST LOTHIAN DISTRICT COUNCIL

B:3 UNION CANAL

Edinburgh-N Falkirk section; *many access points to towing path from central Edinburgh to Falkirk; point 3 on map shows Ratho on B7030, with roadside parking and access at Bridge Inn (NT 149709).*

■ Canal, fringing grassland, woodland.

■ In quiet corners of this attractive canal, moorhen, mallard and mute swan breed, and toads spawn in the shallows. The stretch W of Ratho is particularly pleasing. **Plants** (Banks) water avens, wood avens and their hybrid; Pyrenean and common valerian, pink purslane.

BRITISH WATERWAYS BOARD

B:4 RED MOSS OF BALERNO

Near Edinburgh; *from A70 fork left into Balerno, turn left past Malleny House and Marchbank Hotel; straight over next junction; reserve and rough car park on right at NT 166638. Permit required to enter reserve: apply Reserves Office, SWT.*

■ Raised peat bog with birch/willow scrub.

■ Bog moss (*Sphagnum*) is the dominant plant, with round-leaved sundew, bog asphodel, and common cottongrass; there are deep *Sphagnum* pools. Heather and heath spotted-orchid add colour in drier areas. **Mammals** Roe deer. **Birds** Short-eared owl.

SCOTTISH WILDLIFE TRUST

B:5 COLINTON
& CRAIGLOCKHART DELLS

Edinburgh; *enter from Lanark Road beside Dell Inn W of Craiglockhart Avenue (NT 222707), or from car park under bridge on Bridge Road, Colinton (NT 214690); walkway continuous between these entrances, about 3 miles (5 km).*

■ Mixed woodland, river.

■ This walk partly follows an old railway line (complete with tunnel) beside the Water of Leith, where dipper and grey wagtail can be seen. **Plants** Goldilocks, pink purslane, leopard's-bane, hart's-tongue, ramsons. **Mammals** Badger, fox, stoat.

CITY OF EDINBURGH DISTRICT COUNCIL

B:6 HERMITAGE OF BRAID

Edinburgh; *best access from W gate on Braid Road at NT 244703; park at roadside on Hermitage Drive. Closed 6 pm or sunset-9 am.*

■ Elm/sycamore woodland, stream.

■ Fine woods planted in the 18th C. Hermitage House is the base for the Ranger Service and has local wildlife displays. **Plants** Few-flowered leek, sanicle, moschatel,

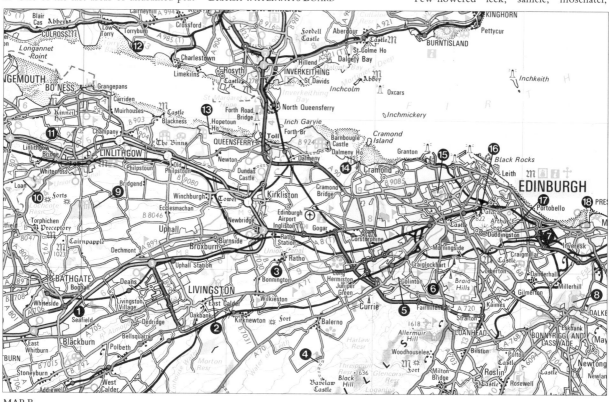

MAP B

wood anemone. **Birds** Great spotted and green woodpeckers, goldcrest; (summer) wood warbler; (winter) brambling.
CITY OF EDINBURGH DISTRICT COUNCIL

B:7 BAWSINCH
Holyrood Park, Edinburgh; park in Duddingston Road West (NT 285724) on SE corner of Park; enter by padlocked gate at corner of road behind barrier. Key to bird hide from Holyrood Park Visitor Centre. Permit required for rest of reserve: apply Reserves Office, SWT.
■ Mixed woodland, ponds, meadow.
■ In this remarkable reserve a wide range of plant and animal habitats have been created from waste ground. An Urban Nature Centre is proposed for the site, making it more readily accessible to the public. **Birds** (Summer) willow and sedge warblers, chiffchaff, whitethroat; (winter) redwing. **Mammals** Fox, grey squirrel. **Insects** Pond skaters, whirligig beetles, blue damselflies. **Butterflies** Small heath, cabbage white, red admiral.
SCOTTISH WILDLIFE TRUST

B:8 DALKEITH PARK
Dalkeith; enter by gate at E end of High Street, off A68 (NT 334676); nature trail of up to 4½ miles (7 km) begins in car park (small fee). Nature trail closed 6 pm (or sunset)-11 am weekdays Nov, Dec-Mar. Permit required for Old Oakwood: apply the Buccleuch Estates Ltd, Bowhill, Selkirk, TD7 5ES.
■ Mixed deciduous woodland, river, ancient remnant oakwood.
■ Fine estate woodland, with many unusual exotic trees, and riverside walks. Point 11 on the nature trail gives views of Dalkeith Old Wood, with some trees up to 300 years old, but little regeneration. **Plants** Western Hemlock, Wellingtonia. **Birds** Goldcrest, (but probably *not* firecrest or reed warbler as leaflet suggests); (river) dipper, grey wagtail, common sandpiper.
THE BUCCLEUCH ESTATES LTD

B:9 BEECRAIGS
Near Linlithgow; on unclassified road to Bathgate Hills 2 miles (3 km) S of town; follow signs to Park then Loch. Park Centre (guided walks), car park and lavatories are N of Beecraigs Loch at NT 007746.
■ Coniferous woodland, loch, meadow.
■ Of many marked paths, the walk around Beecraigs Loch, 1½ miles (2.5 km), is the most productive, especially in winter when many duck use the loch. The meadow at Balvormie (NS 998742) has displays of butterfly-orchids; keep to grass path through meadow or narrow path round the edge to avoid damaging orchids not in flower. **Birds** (Woodland) siskin, goldcrest, treecreeper. **Mammals** Roe deer, badger, captive red deer. **Reptiles** Slow-worm, adder.
WEST LOTHIAN DISTRICT COUNCIL

B:10 MUIRAVONSIDE
Linlithgow; car park, visitor centre, lavatories, picnic and barbecue areas signposted off B825. Visitor centre: closed 5 pm-9.30 am (Mon-Fri); 6 pm-9.30 am (Sat/Sun); Oct-Mar: weekends only, closed 4 pm-10 am.
■ Parkland, deciduous/coniferous woodland, gardens, shrubberies, river.
■ Guided walks provide an excellent opportunity for beginners to get to know a range of commoner birds and flowers. **Birds** (Breeding) dipper, grey wagtail, goldcrest, treecreeper. **Mammals** Roe deer,

badger. **Plants** Greater butterfly- and common spotted-orchids, broad-leaved helleborine.
FALKIRK DISTRICT COUNCIL

B:11 LINLITHGOW LOCH
Linlithgow; park beside entrance to Linlithgow Palace; follow path to loch.
■ Loch, reed-beds.
■ One of the best places in central Scotland to see the spectacular mating display of the great crested grebe in April; they nest in small reed-beds at corners of the loch, along with little grebe, coot, sedge warbler and reed bunting. Large numbers of wildfowl use the loch in winter, and cormorants regularly visit. **Plants** Dotted loosestrife.
HISTORIC BUILDINGS & MONUMENTS (SCOTTISH DEVELOPMENT DEPARTMENT)

B:12 CULROSS & TORRY BAY
Near Dunfermline; roadside viewing from B9037 E and W of Culross; also from minor road from Torryburn E of Torry Bay (NT 032846). No entry to ash lagoons at Culross.
■ Muddy shore, estuary.
■ Mergansers are particularly numerous along the shore, with wildfowl. The development of the settlement lagoons for ash from the Longannet Power Station has reduced the feeding area for waders, but many use the lagoons as a high tide roost. **Birds** Bar-tailed godwit, knot.

B:13 HOPETOUN HOUSE
Near South Queensferry; take minor road W from B924 underneath Forth Road Bridge W of Queensferry; follow shore for about 2 miles (3 km), entrance signposted to left. Closed mid-Sept-late May exc Easter (open 11 am-5.30 pm); fee; dogs on lead only.
■ Mixed woodland, shore.
■ A well-designed nature trail of 2½ miles (4 km) leads through woods, a park area with a captive herd of red deer, and down to the river, taking about 2½ hours. A ranger offers guided walks to view unusual plants on every afternoon during the open season; there is an exhibition room and picnic area. **Birds** Woodcock, treecreeper, sparrowhawk, many typical woodland birds. **Amphibians** Common toad. **Plants** Pink woodruff, female flowers of butterbur, Morinda Spruce, a 600-year-old yew.
HOPETOUN HOUSE PRESERVATION TRUST

B:14 CRAMOND FORESHORE & RIVER ALMOND
Edinburgh; car park signposted N of Cramond Glebe Road (NT 190770); walk to Esplanade, follow path W to river mouth, then S along river bank. Pedestrian access also from Old Cramond Brig (NT 179755).
■ Sandy and muddy shore, river, mixed deciduous woodland.
■ Surprisingly good birdwatching with knot, turnstone and ringed plover along the shore or at the river mouth; along the river are grey wagtail, dipper, and an occasional heron, as well as an alien saxifrage called pick-a-back plant. **Plants** (Shore) sea sandwort, sea rocket; (woodland) opposite-leaved golden saxifrage.
CITY OF EDINBURGH DISTRICT COUNCIL

B:15 ROYAL BOTANIC GARDEN
Edinburgh; park on Arboretum Road by W entrance (NT 244753); pedestrian access off Inverleith Row (E entrance). Closed sunset-9 am (11 am Sun).

■ Arboretum, gardens.
■ There is a systematic collection of Scottish native plants in the NW corner. At the SW corner of the garden meadow saxifrage is extensively naturalized and grey squirrel and many woodland birds, including hawfinch, can be seen. The pond in the middle of the garden is always worth checking, and the excellent Exhibition Hall often has displays of interest on local natural history. **Birds** Water rail, kingfisher. **Mammals** Badger, fox.
ROYAL BOTANIC GARDEN

B:16 HOLYROOD PARK★
Edinburgh; entrances at all four corners; park S of Palace of Holyroodhouse (NT 270737), beside Dunsapie Loch (NT 281731) or overlooking Duddingston Loch. Visitor Centre at Palace entrance sometimes closed in winter – check with Scottish Wildlife Trust. Park occasionally closed to traffic – check local press.
■ Hill grassland, crags, artificial lochs, lawns, planted trees.
■ This remarkably wild city-centre site is dominated by Arthur's Seat, the remnant of a volcano. On rough grassy slopes below the summit grow bell heather, bilberry and lady's bedstraw, while richer areas support purple milk-vetch, bloody crane's-bill and common rock-rose. Jackdaw and grey partridge are resident, and wheatear, stonechat and whinchat pass through in spring. St. Margaret's and Dunsapie Lochs have many wildfowl, and fulmar nests on Salisbury Crags. **Birds** (Winter) snow bunting, short-eared owl. **Plants** Maiden pink, viper's-bugloss.
HISTORIC BUILDINGS & MONUMENTS (SCOTTISH DEVELOPMENT DEPARTMENT)

B:17 DUDDINGSTON LOCH★
Edinburgh; park overlooking loch at SE entrance to Holyrood Park (NT 283726); access to shore. No access to rest of sanctuary; key to bird hide from Holyrood Park Visitor Centre.
■ Loch with fringing reed-bed, deciduous woodland.
■ Duddingston Loch has been a bird sanctuary since 1925. Reed-beds on the eastern and western shore provide nesting places for wildfowl, great crested and little grebes. They can be seen from the N shore, together with feral greylag geese. The loch lies in a glacial hollow.
HISTORIC BUILDINGS & MONUMENTS (SCOTTISH DEVELOPMENT DEPARTMENT)

B:18 MUSSELBURGH LAGOONS★
Musselburgh; access from minor road W of racecourse; park carefully at road-end at NT 347735. New Levenhall Links development (proposed wader scrape) is signposted off B1348 to the E.
■ Ash lagoons, open sea, muddy shore, reclaimed grassland, artificial lake(s).
■ The settlement lagoons for the fly ash from the nearby power station are used as a safe high-tide roost by thousands of waders; the sea-wall provides excellent views of waders feeding at the mouth of the Esk or sea-duck in the estuary. As the ash lagoons fill and are reclaimed, it is proposed to construct a purpose-built lagoon, with hides. **Birds** (Winter) long-tailed duck, snow bunting, red-throated diver, velvet and common scoter, eider, great crested grebe, bar-tailed godwit, grey, golden and ringed plovers.
EAST LOTHIAN DISTRICT COUNCIL

SCOTLAND

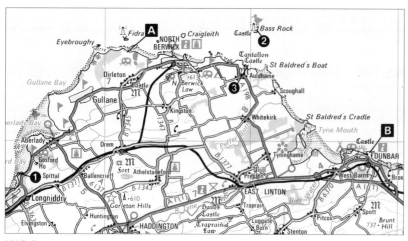

MAP C

C:1 GOSFORD BAY★

Near Edinburgh; car park at Ferny Ness on B198 N of Longniddry (NT 142775); view from the comfort of a car.

■ Open estuary, rocky shore.

■ Excellent birdwatching in winter with a peak count of more than 200 long-tailed duck, as well as red-breasted merganser, common, velvet and occasional surf scoters. Moulting flocks of great crested grebe in autumn are joined by red-necked and Slavo-nian grebes. Good numbers of red-throated diver build up in late afternoon (black-throated and great northern are possible, but not so likely). Bar-tailed godwit, grey plover and purple sandpiper feed along the shore. Glaucous, Mediterranean and little gulls have been recorded. **Birds** (Offshore in summer) Manx shearwater, gannet, Arctic and common terns. **Plants** (Summer) bloody crane's-bill.

EAST LOTHIAN DISTRICT COUNCIL

C:2 BASS ROCK★★

Near North Berwick; boat trips in summer from North Berwick harbour, check with boatman, Fred Marr, 24 Victoria Street, North Berwick, tel. 0620-2838); fee. Landing only for interested ornithologists and historians by prior arrangement with boatman.

■ Rocky island, cliffs, rough grassland.

■ Few birdwatching spectacles match a boat trip round Bass Rock in summer. Its 300-foot (90-m) cliffs throng with gannet, guillemots, kittiwake and razorbill. Better still is to land. The sound and the smell is overwhelming, with more than 20,000 sites 'occupied' by gannets on the rock from which they gained their scientific name, *Sula bassana*. **Birds** Rock dove, rock pipit, eider duck. **Plants** Tree mallow, sea campion, scurvy-grass.

C:3 TANTALLON CASTLE

Near North Berwick; signposted off A198 at NT 590850. Summer: closed 7 pm-9.30 am (Sun closed am); winter: usually closed 4 pm-9.30 am, check with HB&M; fee.

■ Sea-bird cliff, grassland, lawns.

■ This 14thC castle offers splendid views towards Bass Rock and its gannets, while the cliffs below are a nest site for fulmars. Cowslips, thyme, harebells and thrift grow in ditches around the castle.

HISTORIC BUILDINGS & MONUMENTS (SCOTTISH DEVELOPMENT DEPARTMENT)

C:A LOTHIAN COAST (1)★
Near Edinburgh.

■ Farmland, sandy and rocky shores, dunes, open sea, coniferous plantation.

① Large car park (fee). Walk over dunes (stabilized with sea-buckthorn, marram grass and lyme grass) to bay. In summer, early marsh-orchid in dunes. In winter, bay good for sea-duck and red-throated diver roost.

② Car park (fee) beyond caravan site. Nature trail leaflet available.

③ Good winter viewpoint for bar-tailed godwit, ringed plover, sanderling on shore, sea-duck offshore. In summer, many eider.

④ In summer; purple milk-vetch, spring vetch, Scots lovage, rue-leaved saxifrage and grass-of-Parnassus in dunes; spring beauty and yellow figwort in planation. View to Fidra Island (nesting kittiwakes, terns, puffins).

⑤ Walk along beach from North Berwick. Waders in winter; views of Lamb Island (nesting guillemots and cormorants) in summer.

⑥ Viewpoint for sea-duck and nesting puffins on Craigleith. Regular trips from harbour to Bass Rock and other islands.

⑦ and ⑧ Viewpoints to scan nearby fields for pink-footed goose. Over 10,000 feed on stubble fields in early winter and later on potatoes (Oct-Dec). Also whooper swan, greylag goose and occasionally bean, white-fronted and snow geese and Bewick's swan.

Birds (Winter) Slavonian and occasional red-throated grebes, long-tailed duck, red-breasted merganser, velvet and common scoter, eider, grey plover, purple sandpiper.

EAST LOTHIAN DISTRICT COUNCIL

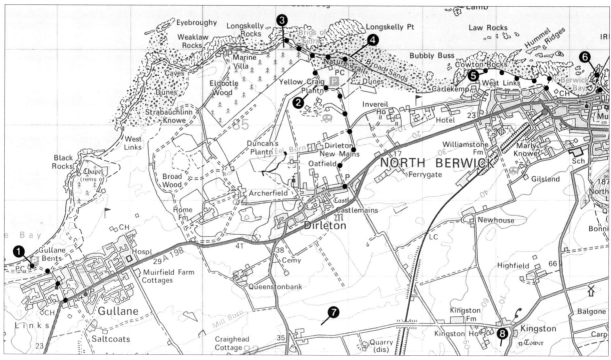

1:50 000, MAP C:A

C:B Lothian Coast (2)★
Near Edinburgh.
■ Rocky, sandy, muddy shores, open sea, farmland.

① Main car park (free) for John Muir Country Park. Follow green-topped posts through Park.

② Waders along muddy shore, ringed plover feeding beyond spit, terns feeding offshore in summer.

③ From shore in winter view high-tide wader roost, feeding area for wigeon, teal and other duck, up to 80 mute swans, and occasional goose roost.

④ Car park signposted at N end of High Street; access to harbour and cliff-top trail. Leaflets on Country Park and Barns Ness from Information Centre.

⑤ One of best nature trails in Scotland along cliff-top, with guide leaflet and display boards. Waders on rocky shore in winter. In summer, gannet, terns and kittiwake offshore, house martin nesting on cliffs, and meadow saxifrage, cowslip, and hoary cress in grassland.

⑥ Alternative car park for cliff-top walk. Viewpoint for gull roost, shelduck and waders by Biel Burn.

Gannet: dives from considerable height to take fish, and has a reinforced skull structure to withstand the impact.

⑦ In Dunbar harbour (summer), close views of kittiwake nests on ruined castle.

⑧ Barns Ness: geology trail shows origins of local limestones. Rich shore life described in guidebook. In winter, feeding waders along shore, and sea-duck and divers offshore. Bushes around lighthouse (just off map to E) excellent for migrants in spring and autumn.
LOTHIAN DISTRICT COUNCIL

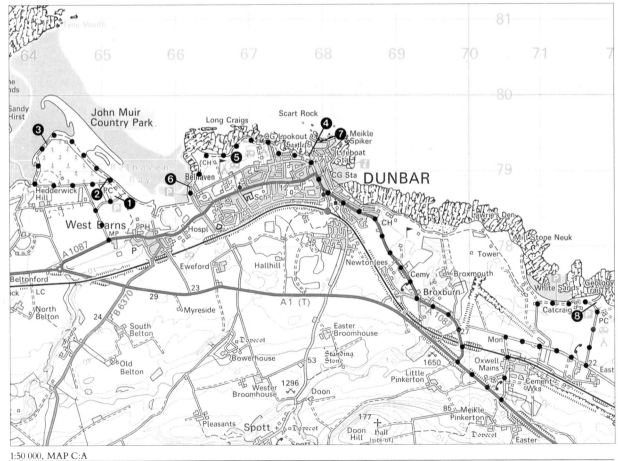

1:50 000, MAP C:A

CENTRAL

A:1 LOCH LOMOND

Near Dumbarton; access from Balmaha on the B837 (parking available); boat crossing to Inchcailloch; telephone Balmaha 215 to confirm. Prior booking for groups to NCC (SW Scotland office). Rest of reserve by permit only.

■ Open water, freshwater marsh, oak woodland.

■ The romantic appeal of Loch Lomond attracts many visitors, so only the more remote NE shore (see below), and the area around the mouth of Endrick Water are undisturbed. The latter is a sanctuary within the Loch Lomond NNR, where shoveler and shelduck breed and wildfowl gather in winter. The public are, however, welcome on Inchcailloch Island (best seen in spring and summer), which has a picnic area, camp site and 2-mile (3-km) nature trail through the island's oak woods. The winter wildfowl are best seen from Balmaha or the unclassified road N of Gartocharn. **Birds** (Winter) whooper swan, Greenland whitefronted goose, greylag; (breeding in woodland) redstart, tree pipit, great spotted woodpecker. **Plants** Sanicle, woodruff.

NATURE CONSERVANCY COUNCIL (SW Scotland)

A:2 BEN LOMOND

Loch Lomond; follow minor road N of Balmaha to car park and lavatories beyond Rowardennan Hotel (NS 360983). A rough track leads to the summit (7 miles (11 km), 3,100 feet (945 m). Allow at least 6 hours. Dogs must be kept on lead.

■ Moorland, mountain top.

■ This long hard walk, best in Jun-Aug, should be attempted only in fine weather and with adequate protective clothing.

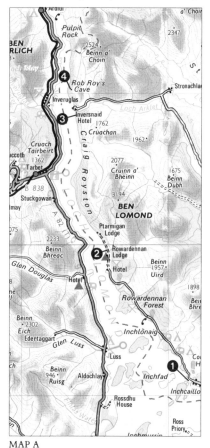

MAP A

Splendid views and a range of mountain vegetation and birds. **Plants** (Arctic/Alpine) cloudberry, mountain pansy, mossy cyphel, moss campion. **Birds** Ptarmigan, ring ouzel, raven. **Mammals** Mountain hare, red deer.

NATIONAL TRUST FOR SCOTLAND

A:3 WEST HIGHLAND WAY

Rowardennan to Inversnaid; follow minor road N of Balmaha to car park just beyond Rowardennan Hotel (NS 360983). Follow trail N from here. A descriptive guide and map are available from HMSO. Follow marked path and keep dogs on a lead.

■ Oak/birch woodland, loch.

■ Part of the 95-mile (153-km) route of the West Highland Way long-distance footpath, this section leads through attractive woodland on the E shore of the loch for just over 7 miles (11 km). It is rough going and wet underfoot; best May-Aug. Take insect repellant.

COUNTRYSIDE COMMISSION FOR SCOTLAND

A:4 INVERSNAID*

Inversnaid; follow B829 W from Aberfoyle, then minor road past Loch Arklet to Inversnaid Hotel (NN 337) car park, lavatories. In summer there may be passenger ferry crossings from Inveruglas on A82 W of the loch (confirm with Inversnaid Hotel).

■ Deciduous woodland/moorland, loch, mountain streams.

■ The West Highland Way leads gently along the E side of Loch Lomond among woodlands of ash, alder, oak and birch. In spring, wood-sorrel, anemone, ramsons, primroses and bluebells flower beneath the trees.

ROYAL SOCIETY FOR THE PROTECTION OF BIRDS

B:1 QUEEN ELIZABETH FOREST PARK

Aberfoyle; car park, picnic area, cafeteria, lavatories at the David Marshall Lodge, on A821, ½ mile (0.5 km) N of Aberfoyle at NN 518015. Open access to marked trails, exc during forestry operations. Further details: Forestry Commission District Office, Aberfoyle, FK8 3UX.

■ Coniferous plantation, moorland.

■ Sandwiched between Loch Lomond and the Trossachs, this 75,000-acre forest in the heart of tourist country is well provided with walks, picnic areas and caravan sites. It centres on the David Marshall Lodge from which radiate several forest walks, and an excellent geology trail explaining the effects

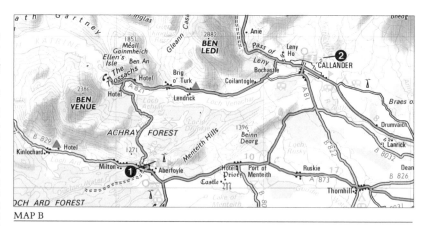

MAP B

of the Highland Boundary Fault. A project is under way to recreate a traditional coppiced oak wood, with information boards to guide the visitor through the area. The Park is wild enough in parts for capercaillie, crossbills, wild cats and even golden eagles to be found, and bats are worth looking out for at dusk around Aberfoyle. **Birds** Golden eagle, capercaillie, crossbill. **Mammals** Wild cat, bats.

FORESTRY COMMISSION

B:2 CALLANDER CRAIG & BRACKLINN FALLS

Callander; follow signs to Bracklinn Falls; car park at NN 638083, Walk ½ mile (0.8 km) E to the Falls; follow minor road ½ mile N; the path to the Craig is signposted on left.

■ Coniferous plantation, mixed deciduous woodland.

■ Bracklinn Falls are impressive, surrounded by oak, ash, and alder woodland, with typical woodland birds. The stiffish climb to the Queen Victoria Jubilee Cairn gives splendid views of hill grassland and grouse moors and distant mountains, perhaps with buzzard circling overhead.

FORESTRY COMMISSION/STIRLING DISTRICT COUNCIL

C:1 CAMBUS POOL

Near Alloa; follow unclassified road S of A907 through Cambus village, then right past the distillery. Park with consideration, cross bridge and follow track S along W bank of River Devon; the pool is at NS 847936.

■ Pond, wetland, islets.

■ This small wetland resulted from a breach in the flood bank of the River Forth and is managed by the Scottish Wildlife Trust as an informal wildlife reserve. It is used by nesting and feeding wildfowl and waders, many of which use the pool on migration, so best in spring and Aug-Oct. **Birds** (Regular) ruff, greenshank, green sandpiper; (occasional) black-tailed godwit, spotted redshank.

SCOTTISH GRAIN DISTILLERS

C:2 GARTMORN DAM*

Near Alloa; signposted off A908 at New Sauchie; clearly signposted car park at NS 911941. Follow path round loch anti-clockwise, passing visitor centre; closed dusk-9 am; further details are available here or from Countryside Ranger Service, 19 Mar Street, Alloa.

■ Reservoir, shoreline grassland/scrub, wooded island.

■ This LNR is also a country park, so it is well provided with facilities including a picnic area and bird hide, and the Ranger

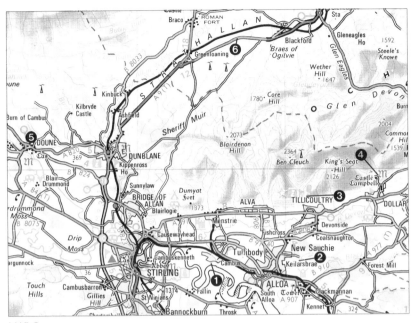

MAP C

Wild cat: see B:1, opposite page.

leads regular walks around the Dam. Aquatic plants and courting and nesting great crested grebe are among the summer attractions, but the real interest is in winter when large numbers of wildfowl gather. **Birds** Whooper swan, greylag goose.
CLACKMANNAN DISTRICT COUNCIL

C:3 MILL GLEN

Near Alloa; from A91 at W edge of Tilli-coultry, follow signs for car park near tourist information centre. Footpath beside stream into small park; gate leads into Mill Glen; trail is about one mile (1.5 km) and takes 1½ hours. Further details from Countryside Ranger Service, 19 Mar Street, Alloa.

■ Mixed woodland, open hill grassland.

■ This is a steep-sided glen on the edge of the Ochil Hills, marking the line of the Ochil Fault. The fast-flowing burn (stream) is clean and full of caddisfly, mayfly and stonefly larvae, which provide food for dipper.
CLACKMANNAN DISTRICT COUNCIL

C:4 DOLLAR GLEN

Dollar; follow signs to Castle Campbell on A91; park on edge of town and walk up towards castle, 1½ miles (2.5 km) on steep but well-maintained paths.

■ Oak/ash/wych elm woodland.

■ A spectacular walk along the bottom of this sheer valley leads up through the wood to the edge of the Ochil hills; the ground flora is rich.
NATIONAL TRUST FOR SCOTLAND

C:5 DOUNE PONDS

Doune; turn N on to unclassified road W of church in centre of town, then second left – car park and entrance are obvious (NN 725018). Keys for hides from grocer's shop, 36 Main Street, Doune.

■ Ponds, damp meadow, birch/willow scrub.

■ Created from a worked-out sand and gravel pit, these three ponds are used by commoner wildfowl, including breeding mute swans and coots, which may be seen from the two hides or the ½-mile (0.8-km) nature trail. The meadows have marsh orchids, ragged-robin and common valerian

in early summer with ringlet and common blue butterflies.
STIRLING DISTRICT COUNCIL

C:6 CARSEBRECK CURLING PONDS

Near Blackford; view from A9 about 2 miles (3 km) W of Blackford; also S of the minor road from Blackford -- A822; sometimes in fields N of Greenloaning. No access to private land.

■ Lochs, ponds, arable fields.

■ From Oct to Mar pink-footed and greylag geese (3,000-4,000 of each) roost on the ponds and feed in the fields nearby, with occasional barnacle, white-fronted or snow geese.

D:1 BEN LUI

Near Crianlarich; in dry weather only, approach from Forestry Commission car park in Glen Orchy (NN 238276); cross river and use the bridge under railway. The other approach is a long walk in along Glen Cononish from the A82 S of Tyndrum through private land. No permit required, but notify NCC, SW Scotland office, at Balloch. Attempt this only with stout shoes and full waterproof gear, map and compass.

■ Upland grassland, plant-rich crags.

■ Only for those with experience of the uplands and an interest in mountain flowers. The plant-rich crags of Ciochan Beinn Laoigh are not inaccessible, but need great care: the mists can close in at any time, even

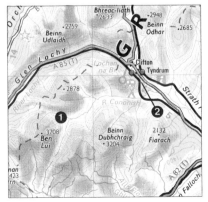

MAP D

in high summer. An NNR. **Plants** Alpine bartsia, globeflower, starry and yellow saxifrage, roseroot, mountain avens.
NATURE CONSERVANCY COUNCIL (SW Scotland)

D:2 WEST HIGHLAND WAY*

Inverarnan to Tyndrum; the marked path is signposted off A82 a short distance N of Inverarnan Hotel (NN 319188); parking is limited. The path can also be approached off A82 at Crianlarich, St Fillans, or S of Tyndrum. Keep dogs on lead. Guide and map from HMSO.

■ Moorland, oak/birch/pine woodland.

■ This stretch of the West Highland Way is never far from the safety of the main road, and will repay the effort of a keen walker. Good outdoor gear, map and compass essential. The 13 miles (21 km) can be broken at Crianlarich or only part attempted. The route leads from the oakwoods N of Loch Lomond, to birch wood, and, at the head of Glen Falloch, to remnant pine forest with red squirrels. A better remnant pinewood can be seen to the W of the path as it approaches Tyndrum, although this too is senile and overgrazed. On the open hill red grouse, red deer, and the local feral goats might be seen. **Birds** (Falloch gorge) dipper, buzzard; (moorland) red grouse. **Plants** (Wet moorland) bog asphodel, butterwort, cottongrass. **Mammals** Red squirrel.
COUNTRYSIDE COMMISSION FOR SCOTLAND

E:1 GLENOGLE TRAIL

Lochearnhead; car park on A85 in Lochearnhead, opposite water sports centre. Walk W to junction with A84, turn right, follow road, then turn left at sign for Lochearnhead Scout Station. No dogs in lambing season (Mar-May). Leaflet and route card available from local tourist information centres.

■ Moorland, hill pasture, birch scrub.

■ This is a 6-mile (9.5-km) walk (allow 4 hours) through a dramatic highland glen, partly following a disused railway line, closed 1964. All the birch scrub has regenerated since then. **Birds** (Moorland) whinchat, wheatear; (birch scrub) siskin, buzzard. **Plants** Yellow saxifrage, heath spotted-orchid.
STIRLING DISTRICT COUNCIL

MAP E

FIFE

A:1 LEVEN & LARGO BAYS★

Near Leven; best viewpoint from sea wall in Leven E of river (park at N0 383004); also view from harbour at Lower Largo (NO 416025).

■ Muddy and rocky shore, estuary.

■ With the reduction in numbers of sea-duck off Edinburgh since installation of a sewage scheme in 1980, this has become one of the best places to see them, often with more than 2,000 scaup, 500 or more common scoter, and a few velvet scoter. **Birds** (Winter) red-throated and black-throated diver, Slavonian, red-necked and great crested grebe, long-tailed duck, red-breasted merganser, glaucous and little gulls.

A:2 LETHAM GLEN

Near Leven; access from A915 at junction with A955; car park closed in winter. Nature trail leaflet available locally or from Dept of Leisure and Recreation, Kirkcaldy District Council.

■ Mixed broad-leaved woodland, stream.

■ A one-mile (1.5 km) trail, starting behind the pets' corner in the Park, leads up this pleasant glen, locally known as Spinkie Glen from the abundance of primroses (spinkies). Elm, ash, beech, oak, hawthorn, horse chestnut, wild cherry and Sitka spruce provide a home for a variety of birds including treecreeper and pied wagtail; sanicle and great woodrush grow under the trees.

KIRKCALDY DISTRICT COUNCIL

A:3 ELIE BAY

Near Leven; from Elie harbour, follow track to car park at NT 498996; walk to Elie Ness or park near golf course at Earlsferry (around NT 481996) and walk Kincraig Point to Shell Bay (NO 464004).

■ Rocky and sandy shore, estuary.

■ The bay shares many of the sea-duck of Largo Bay; glaucous gull sometimes visits Elie harbour, and little gull may pass in the autumn. Purple milk-vetch and common rock-rose grow on the cliffs W of Earlsferry, where short-eared owl hunts in winter. **Birds** (Winter) red-throated diver, great crested grebe, purple sandpiper; (summer) Arctic and common terns.

A:4 ISLE OF MAY★★

Off Crail; day boat trips take about one hour. Boatmen include: J. Smith (0333-50484); I.

Gatherum (0333-310860); R. Ritchie (0333-310697); or check with NCC. Limited accommodation in Observatory; book through Mrs R Cowper, 9 Oxgangs Road, Edinburgh, EH10.

■ Island with cliffs and rocky shore, rough grassland.

■ The Isle of May, an NNR, rises in the mouth of the Forth. Cliffs in the W are as high as 150 feet (45 m), with kittiwake, guillemot, razorbill, fulmar and shag nesting. Occupied puffin burrows are currently estimated at 12,000. Thrift, sea campion and breeding terns, are recovering as the result of a control programme. Grey seals are also increasing and rear 900 pups a year. But spring and autumn migrants are the special feature, with 15,000 goldcrest, 4,000 robin and 800 redwing on one day in October 1982. **Birds** (Breeding) eider duck, oystercatcher, lesser black-backed gull, rock pipit; (migrant) yellow-browed, barred and icterine warblers, ortolan and Lapland bunting, red-breasted flycatcher.

NATURE CONSERVANCY COUNCIL (SE Scotland)

A:5 CRAIGHALL GLEN

Near Cupar; W of Ceres on B939, take unclassified road S signposted to Largo; park at roadside in ½ mile (0.8 km); glen trail is one mile (1.5 km), allow 1-1½ hours. Nature trail leaflet on sale in Ceres Post Office.

■ Mixed broad-leaved woodland, stream.

■ An easy walk leads to a disused limekiln at the head of the glen. The woodland is of wych elm, sycamore, ash, beech, oak and alder, with silver birch, Scots pine and field maple in places.

NORTH-EAST FIFE DISTRICT COUNCIL

A:6 KILMINNING COAST

Near Crail; take minor road signposted Balcomie Golf Course and Fife Ness; turn right past disused airfield, follow signs to Kilminning, park near castle (NO 632086); or walk along coast from Crail harbour.

■ Raised beach with rocky shore, rough grassland, salt-marsh, blackthorn/bramble scrub.

■ Part of the Fife long-distance coastal footpath. The marshland contains sea milkwort, sea arrowgrass and marsh plants, including northern marsh-orchid. In spring and autumn, the scrub is worth checking for

migrants, and in winter the old airfield is good for golden plover.

SCOTTISH WILDLIFE TRUST

A:7 FIFE NESS

Near Crail; take unclassified road signposted Balcomie Golf Course and Fife Ness; park at non-golfers car park and pay fee at starter's office. Enter Fife Ness Muir only from E, by cottage on shore. Keep to road at golf course.

■ Rocky shore, rough grassland, scrub.

■ An excellent spot for sea-watching, esp in autumn, when shearwaters, skuas, terns and gannet pass offshore, and golden plover and whimbrel may rest on the rocks. Amongst the scrub of Fife Ness Muir, the SWT has planted trees to provide shelter for many migrant songbirds. **Birds** (Passage) sooty and Manx shearwaters, pomarine, Arctic and great skuas, little gull; (migrants, spring) red-backed shrike, wryneck, bluethroat, black redstart; (migrants, autumn) Radde's, yellow-browed, barred and icterine warblers, red-breasted flycatcher, great grey shrike.

SCOTTISH WILDLIFE TRUST

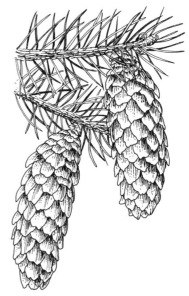

Sitka spruce needles and fruit – see A:2.

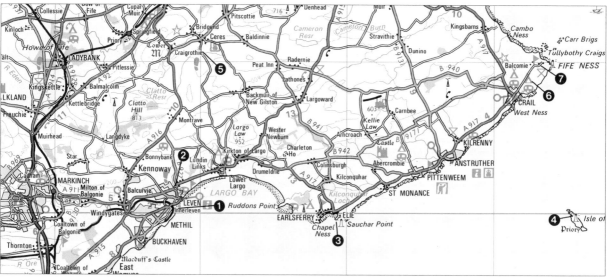

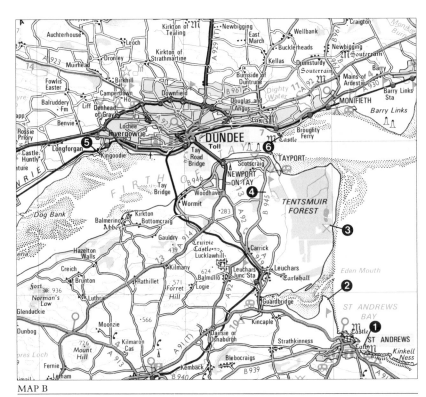

MAP B

duck that gather in the Tay in autumn.

On the way to the reserve, look for pink-footed goose in fields W of the forest, and capercaillie, crossbill, red squirrel and roe deer in the woods. **Birds** (Winter) long-tailed duck, common scoter, red-breasted merganser, bar-tailed godwit, sanderling, grey plover, curlew; (summer) Arctic and common terns. **Butterflies** Grayling, dark green fritillary.

NATURE CONSERVANCY COUNCIL (SE Scotland)

B:4 MORTON LOCHS★
Near St. Andrews; turn E off B945 about 2 miles (3 km) S of Tayport on to track, signposted Private Road; no access to beach at NO 453261; public hide and car park in one mile (1.5 km). Permit required for two more hides; apply NCC (SE Scotland).

■ Artificial lochs with islands, mixed woodland.

■ An artificial lagoon, originally created for fish-rearing, now an NNR. The loch S of the road has been mostly recolonized by rushes, and alder and willow carr (harbouring sedge and willow warblers), but the N loch was re-excavated in 1976. In spring, great crested grebe display and nest.

NATURE CONSERVANCY COUNCIL (SE Scotland)

B:5 TAY SHORE, KINGOODIE
Near Dundee; park on B958 at Kingoodie (NT 334294).

■ Muddy and sandy shore, estuary.

■ Large numbers of redshank and smaller numbers of bar-tailed godwit feed on the shore in winter, with goldeneye offshore. Greylag and pink-footed geese sometimes visit the sandbanks.

B:6 TAY SHORE, BROUGHTY FERRY
Near Dundee; park on shore by castle (NO 464304).

■ Sandy, rocky and muddy shore, estuary.

■ From Oct to May, numbers of goldeneye, bar-tailed godwit, redshank and curlew can be seen along the shore, with red-breasted merganser and goosander by the sewage outflows. Many eider duck are present, from the flock of over 10,000 in the outer Firth of Tay.

B:1 ST ANDREWS BAY
St Andrews; West Sands: take road past R & A golf clubhouse to Out Head; East Sands: reached from St Andrews harbour (NO 516166). Parking at both.

■ Sandy and rocky shores, open sea.

■ Up to 3,000 common scoter have been counted here, large numbers of velvet scoter, occasional surf scoter, red-throated and black-throated divers, and great crested and Slavonian grebes. The N end of West Sands is the best viewpoint, while the rocky shore at the castle and harbour is good for purple sandpiper and turnstone.

B:2 EDEN ESTUARY★★
Near St Andrews; follow minor road to car park at Out Head (NO 495197) and walk; or park in Guardbridge lay-by on A91 at NO 454188. No access to three sanctuary areas (see display notice at Out Head). Details from Ranger, Craigtoun Country Park, St. Andrews, Fife.

■ Sand- and mudflats, open estuary, farmland.

■ This LNR is internationally important for the numbers of shelduck, bar-tailed godwit and redshank that gather in winter (over 1,000 of each) and up to 350 grey plover and 180 black-tailed godwit – unusual in Scotland. It is also one of the most convenient estuaries for seeing wildfowl and waders in winter: the mudflats can be seen from the lay-by at Guardbridge. The road to Out Head gives views of scoter, long-tailed duck, eider, grebes and divers near the mouth of the Eden, and the grey and common seals on sandbanks in the estuary. **Birds** (Mainly autumn/winter) brent goose, greylag goose, red-breasted merganser, pintail, ringed and golden plover, goldeneye; (passage) Kentish plover, spotted redshank, Arctic skua, whimbrel, ruff.

NORTH-EAST FIFE DISTRICT COUNCIL/NE FIFE RANGER SERVICE

B:3 TENTSMUIR POINT★★
Near St. Andrews; at NO 467234 follow minor road NE from Leuchars; park at Kinshaldy near shore (NO 498242); walk N along beach. No access to Abertay Sands, but view from shore near point.

■ Dunes, sandy shore.

■ Tentsmuir is a rapidly growing sand-dune system (and an NNR), having extended 800 yards (730 m) in 40 years. Marram and lyme grass and purple milk-vetch grow on the dunes, with coralroot orchid, grass-of-Parnassus and Baltic rush in damp hollows. Butterflies are common in summer. In winter, the shore is alive with waders. Common and grey seals haul out on Abertay Sands. Large groups of sea-duck offshore include many of the 10-15,000 eider

Capercaillie (hen) – Scottish coniferous forests.

MAP A

A:1 LOCHORE MEADOWS

Near Cowdenbeath; access to Park Centre and E end from B920 (NT 178959); to hide and nature reserve at W end from B996 (NT 151948). Centre closed 5 pm-9 am (8.30 pm-9 am Apr-Sept).

■ Artificial loch, grassland, young broadleaved plantation.

■ Created from coal mining dereliction, the Park – and especially the nature reserve – is rapidly growing in attractiveness and

A:A LOCH LEVEN★★
Kinross.

■ Loch, muddy shore, farmland, coniferous plantation.

■ This NNR has, in Loch Leven, the largest eutrophic (nutrient-rich) lake in Britain. It is also one of the richest for wildfowl, with huge numbers of geese, swans and ducks in winter, and many breeding duck in summer.

① Kirkgate Park (park by road): good view of displaying great crested grebes (spring) and duck (all year).

value to wildlife as the reed-beds and planted trees mature. There is a 2-hour nature trail. FIFE REGIONAL COUNCIL

A:2 VANE FARM★

Near Kinross; at S end of Loch Leven (NT 160991) see Landranger map below; car park, nature centre, observation room, hide. Limited opening Jan-Mar; phone 0577-62355 to check.

■ Lagoons, marshes, loch, grass/heather moorland, birch woodland, farmland.

■ The main purpose of Vane Farm is education (school parties should contact the Teacher-Naturalist, Vane Farm Nature Centre, Kinross, KY13 7LX), and a nature trail on to Benarty Hill provides an attractive introduction to bird-watching. ROYAL SOCIETY FOR THE PROTECTION OF BIRDS

B:1 KINNOULL HILL

Near Perth; off A93, park in Quarry car park (NO 135235) or Jubilee car park (NO 144237).

■ Mixed deciduous woodland, coniferous plantation.

② Burleigh Sands: NCC car park at roadside, then short path through plantation (crossbills in winter) to shore: mute swan, grebe, duck.
③ Pink-footed goose and whooper swan sometimes in fields by airfield.
④ Findatie: public car park and picnic site; short walk along shore (marsh orchids in grassland). View to St Serf's island. In winter, goldeneye and whooper swan in corner of loch.
⑤ RSPB Vane Farm Reserve (see above): car park and local information.
⑥ RSPB hide (access from Vane Farm)

MAP B

■ A nature walk, children's walk and forest walk lead over Kinnoull Hill, with views to the River Ray, and on into the Foresty Commission woods. **Mammals** Red squirrel, roe deer. PERTH & KINROSS DISTRICT COUNCIL

overlooking artificial lagoons; good for wigeon, shelduck, redshank, and occasional rarer waders. Best view of St Serf's island (nests of 500 tufted duck, 400 mallard: 30 gadwall and teal in summer; winter, pink-footed goose roost); and of loch (goldeneye, greylag and pink-footed geese, whooper and Bewick's swans in winter).
⑦ and ⑧ Pink-footed and greylag geese feed in fields; don't obstruct road. NATURE CONSERVANCY COUNCIL (SE Scotland)/ROYAL SOCIETY FOR THE PROTECTION OF BIRDS

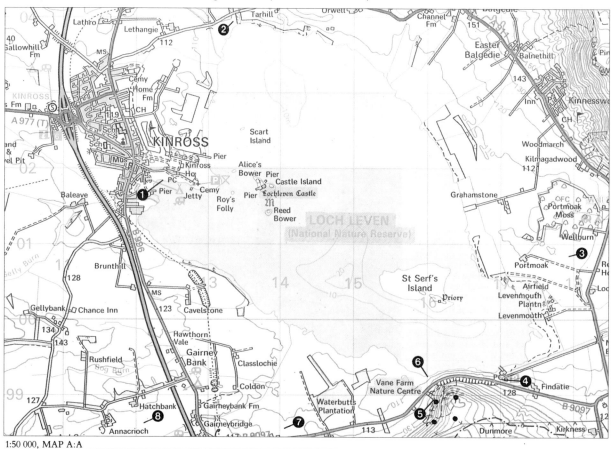

1:50 000, MAP A:A

C:1 DRUMMOND HILL FOREST
Near Aberfeldy; walk begins from Dalerb car park and picnic site at NN 762453 on A827; viewpoint at Black Rock (NN 763457) is signposted.
■ Mature larch/spruce plantation, loch.
■ One of the best places to see capercaillie, reintroduced here from Sweden in 1837. **Birds** (Woodland) pied flycatcher, siskin, goldcrest; (loch) goosander, wigeon. **Mammals** Red squirrel, roe deer.
FORESTRY COMMISSION

C:2 KELTNEYBURN
Near Aberfeldy; from B846, take minor road to Keltneyburn, then steep lane past Balchroich to meadow (NN 774495); park by track (or in village). Permit required; apply Reserves Office, SWT; also leaflet, guided walks.
■ Ash/hazel/elm woodland in steep-sided gorge, herb-rich meadow, pond.
■ The wooded gorge is wet and extremely difficult underfoot, but the Balchroich Meadow is delightful in high summer with common spotted-, greater butterfly-, small-white and fragrant orchids, fairy flax, spignel, globeflower, Alpine bistort, and chickweed wintergreen. **Butterflies** Scotch argus, small pearl-bordered fritillary.
SCOTTISH WILDLIFE TRUST

C:3 BLACK WOOD OF RANNOCH*
Loch Rannoch; take minor road S of loch; park in lay-by at Dall (NN 591568) and follow path beside Dall Burn or Blackwood Cottage (NN 561564), or at NN 573565.
■ Native pine wood, open heather moorland.
■ The FC trail through pine plantations at Carie (NN 617573) gives fine views W over the Black Wood, but that is no substitute for a close view of the fine old granny' pines – some over 300 years old – that make this wood special. The fragrance of pine and the spring of moss underfoot are the main sensations, but you may also find pinewood flowers or insects like the Rannoch looper moth, or catch a glimpse of capercaillie, black grouse, crossbill, goldcrest, siskin, red squirrel or roe deer. Also one of the classic sites for ancient pine-wood insects. **Plants** Lesser twayblade, juniper, intermediate, serrated and chickweed wintergreens, wood crane's-bill. **Birds** Redstart, tree piper. **Insects** Beetles, flies, bugs associated with old pines.
FORESTRY COMMISSION

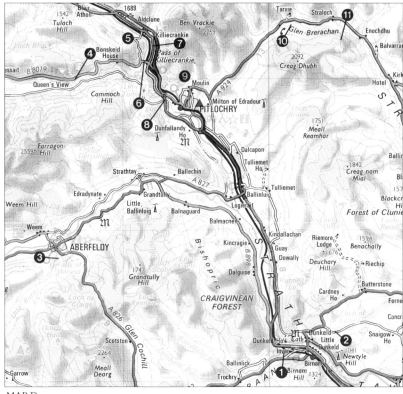

MAP D

D:1 THE HERMITAGE
Near Dunkeld; signposted off A9, car park is at NO 012422; paths lead W from here. Open access. Fee for car park (honesty box). Further information from Pass of Killiecrankie Visitor Centre (see below).
■ Mixed conifer and broad-leaved woodlands.
■ Towering Douglas fir are the main trees in these plantations, and willow warbler or chaffinch the only birds to be heard above the roar of the waterfall at Black Linn. An FC walk leading beyond this begins with a Douglas Fir 201 feet (61 m) tall in 1983, possibly the tallest tree in Britain.
NATIONAL TRUST FOR SCOTLAND/
FORESTRY COMMISSION

D:2 LOCH OF LOWES*
Near Dunkeld; take minor road signposted off A923; visitor centre, hide and car park at NO 044434. Hide open all year. Visitor Centre closed Oct-Easter.
■ Loch, woodland, marsh.
■ The comfortable hide (with access for the disabled) provides tranquil views throughout the year. The main attraction is the ospreys which first bred here in 1969 and usually nest here late Mar-Sep. In winter, resident ducks are joined by goldeneye, pochard and flocks of greylag.
SCOTTISH WILDLIFE TRUST

D:3 BIRKS OF ABERFELDY*
Near Aberfeldy; car park signposted off A826 S; track leads along the burn. A nature trail leaflet is available from a dispenser in the car park.
■ Birch/oak/wych elm/hazel/ash/rowan woodland, river gorge.
■ A 3-mile (5-km) path, taking in the spectacular Falls of Moness, leads through the 'birks' or birchwoods. Birds include redstart and wood warbler **Plants** Shady horsetail, bird's-nest orchid, wood vetch, wood crane's-bill, chickweed and common wintergreens, oak and beech ferns.
PERTH & KINROSS DISTRICT COUNCIL

D:4 TUMMEL FOREST
Near Pitlochry; four walks (3/4 hour to 3 hours) begin from the Allean car park (NN 858601) on B8019 W of Garry Bridge. Details from Queen's View Information Centre at NN 865598 (closed Oct-Easter).
■ Coniferous plantation.
■ Three walks climb the hill overlooking Loch Tummel; the fourth, leading steeply down to the loch has explanatory posts. **Birds** Capercaillie, black grouse, crossbill, redstart, wood warblers, buzzard.
FORESTRY COMMISSION

D:5 KILLIECRANKIE
Near Pitlochry; from A9 take B8097 to Killiecrankie; turn W over bridge; fork right within

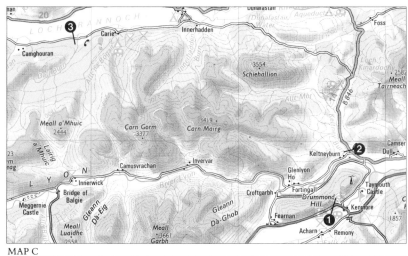

MAP C

½ mile (0.8 km) to warden's house at Balrobbie Farm (NN 907627); open access to waymarked trails. Escorted visits by arrangement with warden (Balrobbie Farm, Killiecranke, Pitlochry, Tayside, PH16 5LJ).

■ Sessile oak/birch woodland, marsh, limestone grassland, pasture, heather moorland.

■ The reserve overlooks the Pass of Killiecrankie; wood warbler, redstart, tree pipit and pied flycatcher are among its specialities, and the limestone outcrops on the hill support a rich grassland and marsh flora.
ROYAL SOCIETY FOR THE PROTECTION OF BIRDS

D:6 LINN OF TUMMEL*
Near Pitlochry; turn W off A9 on to B8019 Kinloch Rannoch road; car park at W end of Garry Bridge (NN 914609); guide available from dispenser.

■ Oak/birch/beech/hazel/Scots pine/larch woodland, river bank, meadow.

■ This attractive wooded site lies along the Rivers Garry and Tummel, and connects N with the Pass of Killiecrankie (see D:7), and S with the River Tummel walks (see D:8). The path runs beneath the bridge, S to the Tummel and W to the Coronation Bridge at NN 903602 (allow at least one hour). The woodland is rich in birds and plants and gives views of river birds.
NATIONAL TRUST FOR SCOTLAND

D:7 PASS OF KILLIECRANKIE
Near Pitlochry; Visitor Centre (closed mid-Oct-Apr), access to woods and car park just S of Killiecrankie village (NN 917626).

■ Sessile oak/birch/ash/wych elm/alder/hazel woodland, river gorge.

■ The fine woods, with rich ground flora, lie on the slopes leading down to the gorge of the River Garry.
NATIONAL TRUST FOR SCOTLAND

D:8 RIVER TUMMEL WALKS
Pitlochry; walks begin from car park at Faskally hydro-electric dam (NN 936578) or by boat harbour (NN 929587); booklet from Tourist Information Centre.

■ Mixed woodland, coniferous plantation, loch, river, farmland.

■ Paths on either side of Loch Fascally and the River Tummel meet the paths of sites D:6 and D:7 beyond; all sites share the same birds and mammals.
PERTH & KINROSS DISTRICT COUNCIL

D:9 CRAIGOWER HILL
Near Pitlochry; turn left off A924 just past Moulin Inn, turn left again to car park at Balnacraig (NN 936594); path marked from here.

■ Norway and Sitka spruce/larch plantation.

■ The path up to the beacon hill owned by the NTS leads through FC plantations rich in fungi in late summer and autumn, and continues as the circular Dunmore Trail (yellow waymarks; allow 1½ hours). Here and there by the track are grass-of-Parnassus, yellow saxifrage and Scottish asphodel.
NATIONAL TRUST FOR SCOTLAND/
FORESTRY COMMISSION

D:10 BRERECHAN MEADOW*
Near Pitlochry; S of A924 at NO 015638; park in lay-by near small bridge and view from roadside. Permit required to enter meadow; apply Reserves Office, SWT.

■ Herb-rich meadow.

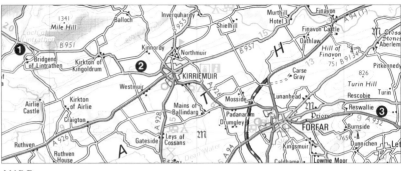

MAP E

■ In Jun this 2-acre meadow is yellow with marsh marigold and globeflower, wood crane's-bill adding a touch of purple; lapwing displays overhead and common sandpiper calls by the burn; by Jul, the colours are the purple of melancholy thistle and cream of meadowsweet. **Plants** Spignel, bog myrtle.
SCOTTISH WILDLIFE TRUST

D:11 KINDROGAN WOODS
Near Pitlochry; walks start at Kindrogan Field Centre (NO 055629) S of A924, approached from Enochdhu (NO 064628).

■ Mixed broad-leaved woodland, river, coniferous plantation.

■ The short Victorian Trail leads along the River Ardle (trail guide from Centre); the longer hill walk leads into FC (guide map). Field courses at Centre range from general Highlands natural history to fungi, mountain flowers or spiders.
FORESTRY COMMISSION/SCOTTISH FIELD STUDIES ASSOCIATION

E:1 LOCH OF LINTRATHEN*
Near Kirriemuir; S of B951; minor roads circling the loch give views. Key on deposit, giving access to hide and car park at NW corner of loch from Reserves Office, SWT.

■ Loch, coniferous plantation.

■ This deep loch, a major water supply for Dundee, is internationally recognized under the Ramsar Convention as a site of importance for wildfowl. Greylag goose predominates, with over 3,000 on occasions.
SCOTTISH WILDLIFE TRUST

E:2 LOCH OF KINNORDY*
Near Kirriemuir; N of B951; roadside car park at NO 361539, path to hide. Sundays only Sep-Nov; closed Dec-Mar.

■ Fresh water marsh, flood pools, willow/alder scrub.

■ The remains of a loch drained last century, the reserve is an open marsh, flooding regularly, with a fen plant community including bogbean and mare's-tail. Among the birds nesting in the marshes are 6,000 pairs of black-headed gull; also ruddy duck – which first bred in Scotland here in 1979.
ROYAL SOCIETY FOR THE PROTECTION OF BIRDS

E:3 BALGAVIES LOCH
Near Forfar; N side of A932 to Friockheim, with roadside viewing platform at NO 534507. Car park and hide (NO 529519) open first Sunday each month, or with key on deposit (contact Reserves Office, SWT).

■ Loch, fen, mixed woodland.

■ Perch, pike and trout in the loch provide food for cormorant, heron and otter, and great crested grebe nest in the reed-beds. In winter large skeins of greylag and pink-footed geese often flight in to roost.
SCOTTISH WILDLIFE TRUST

F:1 SEATON CLIFFS*
Arbroath; park at roadside E of Arbroath promenade at NO 656412; a path leads to cliffs and Carlingheugh Bay.

■ Red sandstone cliff, rocky shore.

■ Lime-loving plants including purple milk-vetch, clustered bellflower and carline thistle grow on the rich grassland.
SCOTTISH WILDLIFE TRUST

F:2 MONTROSE BASIN**
Montrose; view from A935 (N) and A92 (S); Montrose station; minor road to Inchbraoch (NO 706568); path from Bridge of Dun (NO 706568) to Montrose pier. Permit required for access to hides from Ranger, 4 Dunrossie Crescent, Taoch, Montrose, DD10 9LS.

■ Tidal mudflats, farmland.

■ Conservation measures by the SWT and local wildfowlers have greatly increased goose numbers on this LNR, and up to 12,000 pink-footed and 2,000 greylag geese now roost on the mudflats. Over 2,000 knot, dunlin, redshank, duck and many whooper swans also use the basin, encouraged by a feeding programme designed to prevent damage to surrounding farms. Autumn passage waders include ruff, spotted redshank, curlew and green sandpiper, greenshank and black-tailed godwit.
SCOTTISH WILDLIFE TRUST

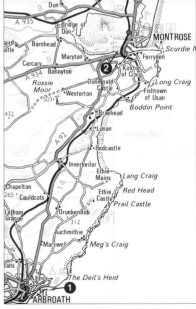

MAP F

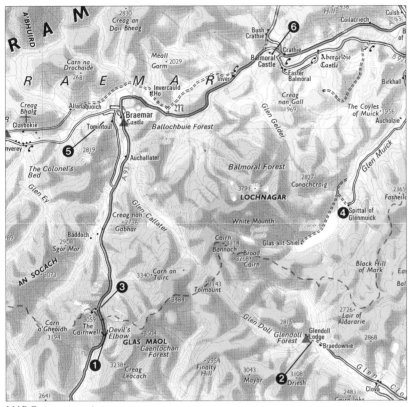

MAP G

A:1 Caenlochan**

Near Braemar; car park off A93 at Cairnwell (NO 143776); follow ski track over Meall Odhar to Ghlas Maol; or take Monega path from Tulchan Lodge, Glen Isla (NO 149800). Permit required for access other than paths to Ghlas Maol; apply Jun-Oct NCC (SE Scotland).

■ Mountain heath, crags, grass and heather moorland.

■ This NNR is probably the finest site in Britain for Arctic/Alpine plants, and access is restricted in order to protect its flora and avoid disruption to deer stalking. There are no obvious paths on Ghlas Maol and the cliffs can be very dangerous (contact NCC, SE Scotland, for information), but dotterel, ptarmigan, dunlin and golden plover breed here. On the high tops plants include mountain crowberry, dwarf willow, stiff sedge, three-leaved rush, dwarf cudweed, yellow, purple, starry, mossy and Alpine saxifrages, mountain avens, moss campion, rock speedwell, Alpine meadow-rue, holly and parsley ferns and many more. **Birds** Golden eagle, ring ouzel. **Mammals** Mountain hare, red deer.

A:2 Glen Clova & Glen Doll**

Near Kirriemuir; park in FC car park at NO 284762; paths lead from here into Glen Doll (Jock's Road) and to Coire Fee (permit required Aug-Oct; apply NCC (SE Scotland).

■ Grass and heather moorland, plant-rich crags, coniferous plantation.

■ Black grouse, capercaillie, and red deer may all be seen on the road up the glen. Mountain pansy grows in the grass by the car park, and globeflower, melancholy thistle and wood crane's-bill by the forest trail, with the alien lady's-mantle, *Alchemilla conjuncta,* by the burn. Continuing up Jock's Road to the shelter (NO 233778), you may find Alpine bistort, Alpine lady's-mantle,

northern bedstraw, yellow saxifrage, cloudberry and dwarf cornel, with the chance of sighting golden eagle, peregrine or ring ouzel around the crags. But the most impressive path is into Coire Fee, a classic glacial corrie, where, in Apr, purple saxifrage flowers. In summer the crags are worth exploring for roseroot, mountain sorrel, Alpine meadow-rue, Alpine saw-wort, moss campion, Alpine cinquefoil, wood vetch, starry and Alpine saxifrages, early-purple orchid, green spleenwort and holly ferns and many more. **Mammals** Mountain hare, roe deer, fox.

FORESTRY COMMISSION/NATURE CONSERVANCY COUNCIL (SE Scotland)

A:3 Cairnwell**

Near Braemar; car park A93 on Tayside/Grampian border. Chairlift operates Jun-Aug and in ski-ing season; do not venture far in shooting/stalking season (from Aug).

■ Mountain grassland, exposed summit ridge.

■ The grassland around the car park (at over 2,000 feet (610 m) and the chair lift has many Arctic/Alpine flowers: starry saxifrage, cloudberry, Alpine lady's-mantle, Alpine meadow-rue; also chickweed wintergreen and frog orchid. There are snow buntings here in winter. Climb on up, looking for red grouse, mountain hare and dwarf cornel, or take the chairlift to the exposed summit ridge, on which grow dwarf birch, trailing azalea and fir clubmoss. In the craggy area along the ridge are ptarmigan, ring ouzel and purple saxifrage. Before the path rises again to Carn Aosda, at about NO 127787, a rough track leads back down to the car park. Do not stray from path leading from chairlift upper terminal along ridge to Carn Aosda.

INVERCAULD ESTATE

A:4 Glen Muick & Lochnagar Wildlife Reserve*

Near Ballater; park at Spittal of Glenmuick (NO 310851); details of walks from Visitor Centre signposted beyond. Keep to paths in stalking season.

■ Pine and birch woodland, moorland, mountain top.

■ Red deer are attracted close to the Visitor Centre by winter feeding. The gullies and corries of 'dark Lochnagar' with their rare Arctic/Alpine flowers are only suitable for experienced hill walkers, but there is much of interest on the moorland: crowberry, bearberry, petty whin, common lizard, emperor and northern eggar moths, red grouse, snipe, mountain hare and stoat, perhaps with distant golden eagle and peregrine.

SCOTTISH WILDLIFE TRUST/ROYAL ESTATE OF BALMORAL

A:5 Morrone Birkwood*

Near Braemar; take minor road signposted Linn of Dee; past police station fork left (Chapel Brae); park by loch at NO 143911. No dogs; keep to tracks; deer-stalking 1 Sep-20 Oct.

■ Birch/juniper woodland, open fen.

■ Scientifically, this birchwood (an NNR) on the side of Morrone Hill is said to resemble the woods of Dovrefjord in Norway, but the casual visitor will be more impressed by the sheer beauty of the wood and its open aspect N to the Cairngorms. Red deer graze the wood heavily and can be seen even in mid-summer. Small enclosures have been built to allow regeneration of the wood; check the one behind the cairn at NO 142908 for globeflower, wood crane's-bill and spignel. Rich flushes beside the track have Scottish asphodel, yellow saxifrage, fragrant and early marsh-orchids, but are delicate, so view from the edge. **Birds** Black grouse (occasional), ring ouzel, siskin, tits. **Insects** Wood ants.

NATURE CONSERVANCY COUNCIL

A:6 Royal Deeside

Near Braemar; view from A93 N of River Dee or S from B976 Banchory-Braemar. Private land off road, but walkers welcomed in many areas; shooting/stalking season from Aug.

■ Remnant pine woodland/plantation, birch woodland, moorland, farmland.

■ Centred on Balmoral Castle, this is an area of great beauty with much mature woodland beside the meandering river, and a good chance of seeing capercaillie, black grouse, woodcock, siskin and Scottish crossbill, with chickweed wintergreen and creeping lady's-tresses on the woodland floor. Hen harrier, peregrine, sparrowhawk, buzzard, and perhaps even a distant golden eagle over the tops. Common sandpiper, dipper, grey wagtail and goosander on the river. Bearberry, petty whin, and wintergreens on the moorlands.

Red grouse – see A:3, Cairnwell.

227

MAP B

B:1 FOWLSHEUGH*

Near Stonehaven; *park at Crawton, sign-posted off A92 at NO 876805 and walk N along cliff-top footpath.*

■ Old red sandstone sea-bird cliff.

■ Guillemot and kittiwake (30,000 nests each), plus smaller numbers of razorbill, fulmar, herring gull, shag and puffin, make this one of the largest sea-bird colonies in Britain. There are views from the cliff top, with eider and grey seal offshore.

ROYAL SOCIETY FOR THE PROTECTION OF BIRDS

C:1 GLEN TANAR*

Near Aboyne; *take minor road off B976; car park and visitor centre at Braeloine (NO 481965), not as shown on Landranger map (closed Oct-Mar).*

■ Pine forest, heather moorland.

■ Some of the pine trees in this NNR, a remnant of the Old Caledonian forest, are over 240 years old. Red deer have been excluded by a fence since 1936, resulting in active regeneration of the pines, among which are siskin, Scottish crossbills, capercaillie and black grouse. Under the trees grow creeping lady's-tresses, wintergreens, and the delicate little twinflower.

NATURE CONSERVANCY COUNCIL (NE Scotland)

C:2 MUIR OF DINNET*

Near Aboyne; *access from car park at Burn o'Vat on the A97 at NO 429998; view Loch Davan from A97 at NJ 437013. Excellent guide from NCC.*

■ Heather moorland, pine/birch woodland, bog, open water.

■ A flat glacial plain, the Muir (or Moor) is attractive in any season. In winter skeins of greylag and pink-footed geese flight into

MAP C

MAP D

Loch Davan. In summer and autumn bearberry, with its pink flowers and red berries, is unusually common among the heather, along with intermediate wintergreen, petty whin, bitter vetch, and lesser twayblade. The nature trail to Meikle Kinord illustrates the plants and the glacial features, which include meltwater channels and kettleholes. Otters can be seen on the lochs, especially in the early morning. An NNR.

NATURE CONSERVANCY COUNCIL (NE Scotland)

D:1 CRATHES ESTATE

Near Banchory; *signposted off A93; car park, lavatories, restaurant, Visitor Centre (trail leaflet available; closed Nov-Easter, w/e only Oct). Picnic area. Admission fee.*

■ Oak/sycamore/silver birch/rowan/wild cherry woodland, coniferous plantation, ponds.

■ Five woodland trails from 1½ miles (2.5 km) to 6 miles (10 km) round this estate centred on a late 16th C castle; there is a short ¼ mile (0.5 km) trail for the disabled. **Mammals** Otter (rare), red squirrel, roe deer.

NATIONAL TRUST FOR SCOTLAND

D:2 DRUM

Near Aberdeen; *signposted off A93; well-marked woodland walks start from car park. Admission by donation.*

■ Oak woodland, deciduous and coniferous plantation, arboretum.

■ In the grounds of this late-13th C tower

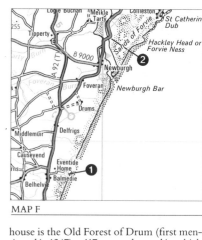

MAP F

house is the Old Forest of Drum (first mentioned in 1247), a 117-acre oakwood in which 500 pairs of rooks nest, together with red, great spotted woodpecker, treecreeper, and spotted flycatcher in nestboxes.

NATIONAL TRUST FOR SCOTLAND

D:3 LOCH OF SKENE

Near Aberdeen; *view from A944 N of loch; private land beyond.*

■ Loch.

■ Often over 1,000 greylag geese roost here in winter, together with smaller numbers of whooper swan and goosander, especially before Jan. The greylag feed on fields and wet meadows around the River Dee to the S.

E:1 BENNACHIE

Near Inverurie; access from minor roads off B993, or B9902; guidebook and map available at Donview Centre (NJ 672191). Approach 'Mither Tap' from Esson's car park at NJ 701217.

■ Coniferous plantation, moorland.

■ A little hill (highest point 1,730 ft (528 m), with a big reputation. The granite tops have Alpine and fir clubmosses, and bearberry, cloudberry, and crowberry grow on the open moors, where there are red and black grouse, short-eared owl and mountain hare. In the forest are roe deer, red squirrels, woodcock, capercaillie, great spotted woodpecker and chickweed wintergreen.

FORESTRY COMMISSION

E:2 LEITH HALL

Near Huntly; *off B9002; car park at NJ 541298, with signposted trails. Admission to grounds by donation, all year round; closed sunset-9.30am; no dogs in certain areas.*

■ Coniferous and deciduous plantation, open grass moorland, farmland.

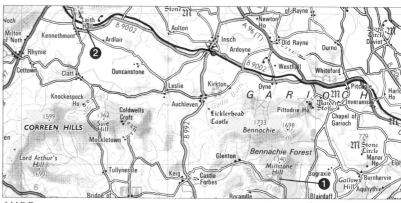

MAP E

■ Two nature trails, each about 1½ miles (3 km) long, lead through the wooded grounds of this 17th C mansion. The Kirkhill Trail (the more interesting) passes an old turf meadow, rich in butterflies in late summer, and two ponds, one with a hide. **Plants** Pink purslane, leopard's-bane.
NATIONAL TRUST FOR SCOTLAND

F:1 BALMEDIE BEACH
Near Aberdeen; signposted off A92; Visitor Centre and car park at NJ 777182, with access to beach on duckboard path.
■ Sandy beach, dunes.
■ Balmedie is the central access to the sand-dune system running S from the Sands of Forvie. In winter, sanderling, snow bunting, dunlin, and ringed plover can be seen along the shore; in summer common, Arctic and little terns, also gannet fly past.
GRAMPIAN REGIONAL COUNCIL

F:2 SANDS OF FORVIE & YTHAN ESTUARY*
Near Aberdeen; on A975 N of Newburgh; Reserve Centre and car park on B9003 (at NK 035290); view estuary from near bridge at NK 003268. Permit required for access off paths; apply NCC (NE Scotland). No access to tern breeding areas; no dogs.
■ Sandy shore, dunes, estuary, salt-marsh.
■ In summer, the dunes of this NNR hold the largest breeding concentration of eider duck in Britain (up to 2,000 pairs), as well as nesting shelduck and Arctic, common, Sandwich and little terns. Creeping lady's-tresses, heather, crowberry, curved sedge and stag's-horn clubmoss grow among the dunes. In winter, sanderling scuttle along the shore, common scoter, long-tailed duck and divers gather out to sea, and curlew, turnstone, redshank, and bar-tailed godwit visit the estuary. In autumn, 6,000 pink-footed and 1,000 greylag geese roost here or at Miekle Loch farther N on the A975.
NATURE CONSERVANCY COUNCIL (NE Scotland)

Curlew.

G:1 LONGHAVEN CLIFFS
Near Peterhead; take minor road off A975 and park in Blackhill Quarry (NK 116393); follow cliffs N.
■ Granite cliff, coastal heathland.
■ Numerous guillemot and kittiwake, with razorbill, shag, puffin, herring gull and fulmar, are the main attraction on these sheer, 200-foot (60-m) cliffs. Roseroot and sea campion cling to the cliffs, and devil's-bit scabious, bell heather and grass-of-Parnassus colour the heathland beyond.
SCOTTISH WILDLIFE TRUST

G:2 PETERHEAD BAY
Peterhead; view from breakwater of S harbour or A952 (South Road).
■ Open sea.
■ The many harbours and points from Peterhead round the Buchan coast to Nairn, are worth searching for sea-birds. The har-

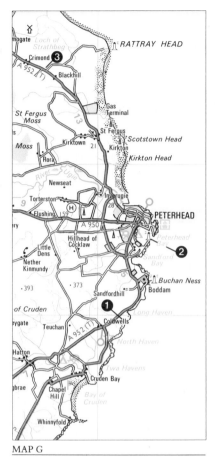

MAP G

bour offers views of skua passage in late summer, with Iceland and glaucous gulls in winter. Eider, common scoter, and occasionally great northern diver frequent the bay.

G:3 LOCH OF STRATHBEG**
Near Peterhead; view from minor road S of loch; entry off A952 S of Crimond at NK 063564. Permit required: apply Warden, Crimonmogate, Lonmay, Fraserburgh, AB4 4UB.
■ Shallow loch, dunes, marsh, woodland.
■ Once the estuary of the Rattray Burn, the Loch was cut off from the sea by a sandstorm in the 18th C. Today, its main attraction is a huge gathering of up to 35,000 wildfowl, among them flocks of greylag and pink-footed geese. A hundred or more whooper swans may be on the loch in Nov, and goldeneye, goosander and occasional smew can be seen; osprey and marsh harrier regularly pass through in spring. Rattray Head, E of the loch, is a good sea watching

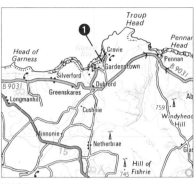

MAP I

point, with divers and autumn passages of skuas. **Plants** (Dunes) lesser butterfly- and coralroot orchids.
ROYAL SOCIETY FOR THE PROTECTION OF BIRDS

H:1 BURGHEAD POINT*
Near Elgin; take B9089 to Burghead harbour, or view from shore at Findhorn end of B9011.
■ Open sea.
■ In Feb, up to 6,000 long-tailed duck may roost in the bay; smaller numbers remain all winter. Several hundred scoter, (mostly common, but 10 per cent velvet) and more rarely great northern, black-throated and red-throated divers, black-necked, red-necked and Slavonian grebes, and red-breasted mergansers can be seen.

H:2 SPEY BAY**
Near Elgin; take B9015 to Kingston and walk W along the shore; or view from Spey Bay or Branderburgh harbour.
■ Open sea, sand and shingle beach.
■ In winter, the bay holds common scoter (5,000) and velvet scoter (1,800). There are numbers of eider duck and scaup, a few red-breasted merganser and red-throated diver, and rarities such as the king eider and surf scoter can turn up. The mouth of the Lossie at Branderburgh has dunlin, oystercatcher and ringed plover, while the rocky shore E of Portgordon is a good place to see purple sandpiper, turnstone, and golden plover.

I:1 DARNAWAY FOREST
Near Forres; details of walks/guided tours from Darnaway Farm Visitor Centre at Tearie; (NH 989569), closed late Sept-May. Admission fee; keep to paths.
■ Pine and beech plantations.
■ The walks lead through attractive woodland with typical birds and flowers alongside the dramatic gorge of the River Findhorn.
MORAY ESTATES

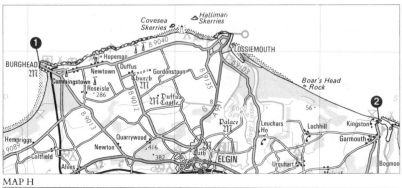

MAP H

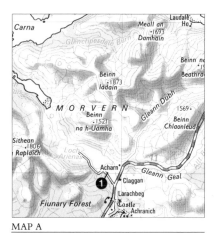

MAP A

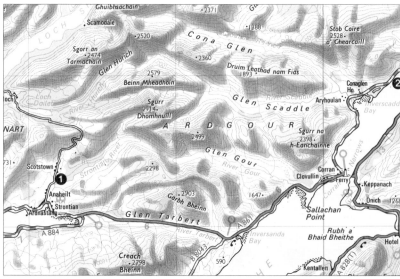

MAP C

A:1 RAHOY HILLS

Corran Ferry, Morvern peninsula; *car parking and access at entrance to Black Glen (NM 703505) on N side of A884 at Acharn; can be viewed from road. Permit required to enter reserve; apply Reserves Office, SWT.*

■ Grass moorland, bog, mountain heath and crags, lochs, oak woodland.

■ The reserve is dominated by the basalt-topped peak of Beinn na h-Uamha, whose crags have many montane plants including roseroot, globeflower, Alpine meadow-grass, northern rock-cress and Arctic sand-wort. Golden eagle hunts over the hills, greenshank breed on the moors and red-throated diver on the lochs. **Mammals** Red deer, wildcat, pine marten. **Plants** (Crags) purple, mossy, Alpine and yellow saxifrages, Alpine lady's-mantle, moss campion, holly fern.

SCOTTISH WILDLIFE TRUST

B:1 GLEN COE★

Near Fort William; *car park and Visitor Centre at NN 127565 E of Ballachulish on A82; fee. Lost Valley and other walks best begun from lay-by S of A82 at NN 171568. Details from Visitor Centre; closed 5.30 pm-10 am (6.30 pm-9 am Jul/Aug) and late Oct-early Apr.*

■ Grass moor, mountain heath, cliffs, river, loch.

■ The brooding valley of Glen Coe is set in some of Scotland's most magnificent scenery. The awe-inspiring Aonach Eagach ridge walk is only for the experienced, but gentler walks are described in a booklet from the Visitor Centre. On the walk by Loch Achtriochtan look for dipper, heron, common sandpiper, cormorant and perhaps black-throated diver. The walk up to Coire Ghabhail (Lost Valley) is steep, but safe if care is taken. Cross the bridge at NN 173564, and follow the path over the lip of

MAP B

the hanging valley (with Wilson's filmy fern in the rocks below); continue part way up N side of the valley for moss campion, starry, mossy and yellow saxifrages, and parsley fern. **Birds** (High tops) golden eagle, dotterel, ptarmigan, peregrine, buzzard, raven; (S end of glen) black and red grouse, golden plover. **Mammals** Pine marten, otter, red deer.

NATIONAL TRUST FOR SCOTLAND

C:1 LOCH SUNART WOODLANDS

Near Fort William; *turn off A861 in Strontian, towards Polloch; after one mile (1.5 km) fork right on to rough track to car park and picnic area; acess on foot only. Note: former nature trail up to lead mines is closed; walk ends at second reserve sign.*

■ Oak woodland, with ash/wych elm/alder/sallow.

■ Centred on Ariundle Wood, this NNR contains attractive remnants of west-coast oak woodland; the unpolluted atmosphere means that it is rich in mosses, liverworts, and lichens. **Plants** Grass-of-Parnassus, common cow-wheat, wood anemone. **Birds** Redstart, wood warbler, buzzard, great spotted woodpecker. **Butterflies** Scotch argus, small pearl-bordered fritillary, green hairstreak. **Mammals** Pine marten, roe deer.

NATURE CONSERVANCY COUNCIL (NW Scotland)

C:2 DOIRE DONN

Near Fort William; *view from A861 7 miles (11 km) N of Corran Ferry; park at roadside at NN 045695 or NN 057708. Permit required to enter wood: apply Reserves Office, SWT.*

■ Oak woodland with birch.

■ This rich wood is managed to produce clearings with abundant wild flowers, in particular to encourage the chequered skipper butterfly at the centre of its local distribution. **Mammals** Wild cat, pine marten, red squirrel, red and roe deer. **Plants** Sanicle, woodruff, wood anemone.

SCOTTISH WILDLIFE TRUST

D:1 EIGG★

Ferry service from Mallaig; *day trips (Tues, Thur) in summer from Arisaig on Shearwater; confirm with Murdo Grant, Arisaig Harbour, Highland, PH39 4NH. No cars; for camp-*

ing apply: Isle of Eigg Estate, Maybank, Udny, Ellon, Aberdeenshire. Permit required for some areas: apply Mrs Hay at above address, tel 06513 2367.

■ Grass moorland, mountain heath, rocky shore, farmland, coniferous plantation.

■ Three areas of the island are reserves. The Sgurr, a dramatic ridge of pitchstone lava has dwarf willow and Wilson's filmy-fern. Moss campion, roseroot and Arctic sand-wort grow on Beinn Buidhe at N of the island, and there is a small Manx shearwater colony above Cleadale. The third reserve, above Laig Farm, includes two wooded ravines and an area of bog. Visitors should acquire the SWT's leaflet and if possible contact the summer warden, who takes guided walks (ask about both at the pier tearoom). Book ahead, accommodation is limited. **Birds** Golden eagle, peregrine, black guillemot, Arctic skua, golden plover, stonechat, buzzard, wheatear, sparrowhawk.

ISLE OF EIGG ESTATE/SCOTTISH WILDLIFE TRUST

D:2 SOUND OF EIGG★

E of Eigg; *view from minor road SW of Arisaig (NM 627852); or S of Morar on A830, park on roadside at NM 664917 and walk to Camusdarach beach; or view from cruise boat or ferry.*

■ Open sea.

■ The boat trip offers close views of massed Manx shearwater, guillemot, fulmar, and occasional puffin and great skua, against the superb backdrop of Rhum and Eigg. **Mammals** Common dolphin.

Golden eagle – see B:1 and D:1.

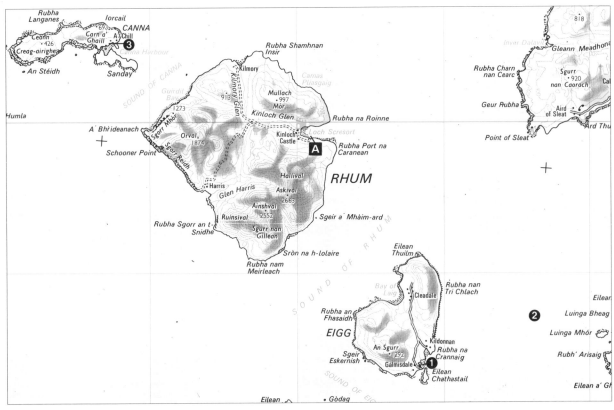

MAP D

D:3 CANNA⋆

NW of Rhum; *ferry from Mallaig, occasional cruises from Arisaig: contact Murdo Grant, Arisaig Harbour, Highland, PH39 4NH.*

■ Sea-bird cliffs, rocky shore, crofting farmland.

■ One of the most beautiful and unspoilt of the Hebridean islands. Canna's sea-birds have been well studied, and various reports are worth seeking out to enhance a visit (try the Scottish Ornithologists' Club, 21 Regent Terrace, Edinburgh, EH7 5BT enclosing an sae). Hay fields and beds of yellow iris still harbour corncrake. **Birds** (Summer) Corncrake, Manx shearwater (about 1,000 pairs), black guillemot, puffin, razorbill, guillemot, kittiwake, fulmar, shag.

NATIONAL TRUST FOR SCOTLAND

D:A RHUM⋆⋆

Ferry service from Mallaig; *not Tue, Thu, Sun; day visits only on Sat; check with Caledonian MacBrayne, Ferry Terminal Gourock, PA19 1QP, or in summer (Tues/Thur) day trips from Arisaig (2-4 hours ashore; confirm with Murdo Grant, Arisaig Harbour, Highland, PH39 4NH). Best time May/Jun; after that midges make life impossible (insect repellants essential at any time). To stay on island, book in advance with Chief Warden, White House, Kinloch, Isle of Rhum, via Mallaig, Highland.*

■ Grass and heather moorland, mixed planted woodland, coastal cliffs, mountain tops. An NNR.

① Watch for black guillemot, eider duck, red-breasted merganser, red-throated and perhaps great northern divers in Loch Scresort.

② Nature trail leaflet from warden's office; check no-access areas here.

③ South Side nature trail: on open moor look for three sundew species, Wilson's filmy-fern on shady rocks, common seals and perhaps otters in the bay, dark green fritillary butterfly and emperor and fox moths.

④ Trail ends here: common and lesser black-backed gulls nest in ruined village; oystercatchers, common sandpipers and herring gulls on shore.

⑤ Eider duck, oystercatcher, curlew, heron and sea-milkwort on shore; common gull at river mouth; grey wagtail and common sandpiper by river; wood and willow warblers, whitethroat, chiffchaff and cuckoo in trees.

⑥ Kinloch Glen nature trail: large area replanted with native trees in last 20 years and red deer excluded.

⑦ Beyond deer fence, watch for red deer and red grouse. Path continues N to Kilmore Glen (red deer study area) and SW to Harris (feral goats), passing cages from which 82 white-tailed eagles from Norway were released 1975-85, now rarely seen on island.

⑧ Coire Dubh path (hard walking) leads to ridge with moss campion, stone bramble and northern rock-cress, and beyond to Hallival and Askival where 130,000 Manx shearwaters nest (best visited overnight, but arrange with warden).

NATURE CONSERVANCY COUNCIL (NW Scotland)

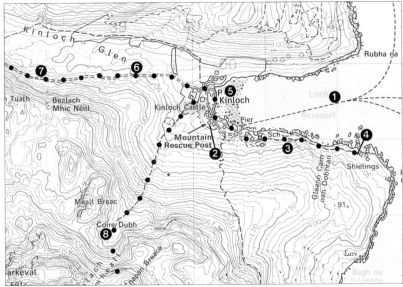

1:50 000, MAP D:A

HIGHLAND

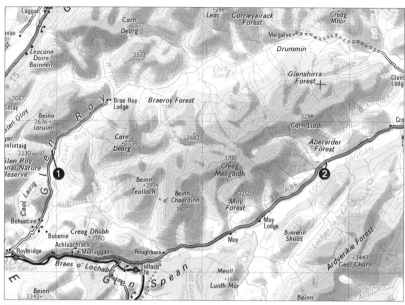

MAP E

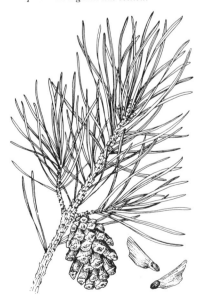

MAP G

E:1 GLEN ROY
Near Spean Bridge; on unclassified road sign-posted to Bohuntine off A86 on W side of River Roy; car park and viewpoint at NN 297854. Descriptive booklet from NCC (NW Scotland).
■ Grass moorland, with ridge features.
■ This NNR was established to protect a series of pronounced terraces on the hillside. Although called 'parallel roads' and shown as such on many maps, they were actually created by successive levels of a glacier-dammed lake. Typical moorland birds and plants.
NATURE CONSERVANCY COUNCIL (NW Scotland)

E:2 CREAG MEGAIDH
Near Spean Bridge; park in lay-bys on A86 or at road end at Aberarder (NH 483873); follow track N past birchwood. In stalking season (usually from August) check with NCC, Achan-toul, Aviemore (Aviemore 810477).
■ Plant-rich crags, grass moorland, bog, birch woodland, pine plantation.
■ The slopes of this rugged mountain, 3,700 feet (1,128 m), were bought by the NCC, largely to prevent afforestation. The crags behind Lochan a' Choire and Moy Corrie have interesting Alpine plants, but should only be tackled by experienced walk-ers. An NNR. **Birds** Golden eagle, pere-grine, greenshank, golden plover. **Plants** (Moorland) Alpine lady's-mantle, yellow saxifrage, crowberry, bilberry; (crags) Alpine speedwell, highland cudweed, Alpine chickweed, downy willow, melan-choly thistle, Alpine cat's-tail grass, wood vetch.
NATURE CONSERVANCY COUNCIL (NE Scotland)

F:1 COILLE THOGABHAIG
Near Ord, Skye; on minor road leading W from A851. Park on roadside at NG 618132 where road turns S, and walk along road.
■ Birch/ash woodland, limestone gorge.
■ Sometimes anglicized as Tokavaig Wood; this sheltered woodland, (an NNR), is dominated by birch on the poorer soils and ash where the limestone outcrops. Its main interest is botanical, with many ferns, mosses and lichens and with herb-Paris,

stone bramble, and dark-red helleborine in the more inaccessible parts of the limestone gorge. Take care, the gorge is very steep.
Plants Lesser and common twayblade and frog orchids, melancholy thistle, hay-scented buckler-fern.
NATURE CONSERVANCY COUNCIL

F:2 STRATHSUARDAL★
Near Broadford, Skye; park in lay-by on A881 opposite church of Cill Chriosd (NG 617207), or continue down track to NG 593202 and park overlooking Camas Malag at NG 573193.
■ Limestone grassland, limestone pave-ment, deciduous woodland, rocky shore.
■ The soft, gentle limestone landscape of Strathsuardal is in dramatic contrast to the scree-covered peaks of the Red Cuillin to the north. The limestone pavements below Ben Suardal (around NG 614204), provide a refuge for stone bramble, twayblade, glo-beflower and herb-Paris. In Coille Gaireal-lach are bluebell and early-purple orchid,

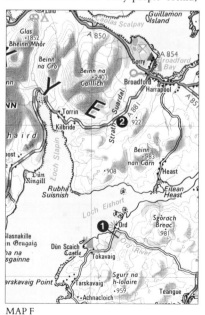

MAP F

along with montane species including bear-berry, Alpine meadow-rue and mountain avens. On the limestone outcrops S of Camas Malag this last grows a few yards from the sea, along with frog orchid and dark-red helleborine. Red-throated diver often display in the bay.
DEPT OF AGRICULTURE & FISHERIES FOR SCOTLAND

G:1 OLD MAN OF STORR★
Near Portree, Skye; an obvious path leads from the FC car park on W side of A855; walk 2½ miles (4 km); allow 2 hours.
■ Cliffs, rock stacks, grassland with open gravel, heather moorland and bog, conife-rous plantation.
■ The steep, well-defined path leads up through coniferous woodland planted in 1970. Where a boardwalk crosses a small bog, look for bogbean and round-leaved sundew. then scramble a further 300 yards (274 m) to the base of the Old Man of Storr, an isolated rock pinnacle, 160 feet (50 m) high. At its base, several montane plants grow at unusually low altitude, including northern rock-cress, moss campion, Alpine lady's-mantle, and roseroot. A ring ouzel may sing from its summit or another nearby pinnacle. In the gravel nearby, and in the magnificent Coire Scamadal to the N, look for the very local Iceland-purslane, mossy and starry saxifrage, mossy cyphel, and three-flowered rush. Best in early summer; midges are a torment later.
FORESTRY COMMISSION

Scots pine – throughout this section.

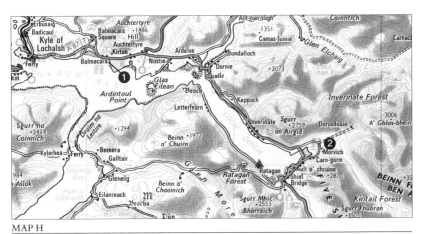

MAP H

H:1 BALMACARA

Kyle of Lochalsh; clearly signposted at Balmacara on A87; park in village. Details of walks from information kiosk at Coach House (closed 1-2 pm, Sun, and 1 Oct-31 May). Woodland garden open all year 9-sunset; fee.

■ Deciduous plantation, heather moorland, rocky seashore and islands, lochs, crofted farmland.

■ This NTS property covers 5,616 acres of the Kyle and Plockton peninsula, with diverse habitats from rocky islets to low heather-clad hills. The woodland garden beside Lochalsh House at Balmacara provides pleasant walks, and there are guided walks around the area. Woodland, moorland and shore birds. Mammals include otter, wild cat, and grey and common seals.

NATIONAL TRUST FOR SCOTLAND

H:2 KINTAIL & MORVICH

Kyle of Lochalsh; Countryside Centre at Morvich Farm (NG 961201) on minor road off A87. Access to hills from Gleann Lichd, S of Centre, or from bridge at Glenshiel battleground (NG 990132); roadside parking at NH 007136. Countryside Centre closed 5.30 pm-9 am, and to 1.30 pm Sun; closed Oct-end May; admission by donation.

■ Grass moorland, mountain heath.

■ The Five Sisters of Kintail reach 3,505 feet (1,068 m) at Sgurr Fhuaran. The breathtaking ridge walk is steep and rugged; and should not be tackled without the advice of the ranger/naturalist at Morvich. **Birds** Ptarmigan, merlin, black-throated diver, greenshank, golden plover. **Mammals** Mountain hare, feral goat, red deer. **Plants** Alpine and starry saxifrage, dwarf willow, dwarf cudweed, cloudberry, greater and lesser butterfly-orchids, fragrant orchid.

NATIONAL TRUST FOR SCOTLAND

I:1 INSH MARSHES★

Near Kingussie; car park and information centre at NH 775998, ½ mile (0.8 km) E of Ruthven on B970. Limited access to reserve: details from Information Centre or Warden, Ivy Cottage, Insh, Kingussie, PH21 1NT.

■ River marsh, pools, willow scrub, birch woodland, meadow.

■ In winter, the marshes hold up to 200 whooper swans (10 per cent of the British population), greylag goose, wigeon, goldeneye. Goosander, red-breasted merganser and grasshopper warbler breed. Spotted crake and water rail are often heard and in Apr-Aug osprey hunt over the river marshes, where water sedge is a speciality. Tree pipit and redstart breed in the woodland. The grasslands have the hybrid between wild and mountain pansy, the Tromie meadow small-white orchid and more than 5,000 spikes of fragrant orchid. **Birds** (Summer) wood and common sandpipers; (all year) hen harrier, buzzard, sparrowhawk. **Mammals** Otter, roe deer, stoat. **Butterflies** Scotch argus, small pearl-bordered fritillary. **Insects** Kentish glory, Rannoch sprawler and chimneysweeper moths; bee beetle, golden-ringed dragonfly.

ROYAL SOCIETY FOR THE PROTECTION OF BIRDS

I:2 GLENFESHIE

Near Aviemore; from Feshiebridge follow minor road S to Achlean, roadside parking at NN 852977; or take minor road off B970 S from Insh House, park at Balnascriten (NN 841997). Keep to footpaths, especially in deer-stalking season (from 1st Aug).

■ Heather moorland with remnant pine trees, river, riverside shingle.

■ The best walk is from Achlean S along River Feshie, crossing the bridge at Carnachuin (NN 846937), then following the private road N down W side of the river, crossing back at the bridge at NN 851965, about 6 miles (9.5 km). Check river shingles (especially the Allt Garbhlach stream at NN 851954) for Alpine plants washed down from the hills, including starry and mossy saxifrage, mountain sorrel, and Alpine pearlwort. **Plants** Lesser twayblade, Alpine lady's-mantle, mountain everlasting, bearberry. **Birds** Scottish crossbill; (shingle) golden eagle, peregrine, hen harrier. **Mammals** Mountain hare, red and roe deer.

GLENFESHIE ESTATE

I:3 ROTHIEMURCHUS★

Near Aviemore; take B970 to Inverdruie; Visitor Centre on left at NH 903108; from here take road signposted Feshiebridge, turn left on to minor road to Loch an Eilein, park at NH 897086; restrictions during stalking season (Sep-Oct).

■ Pine plantation with some remnant Caledonian pinewood, loch, heather moorland.

■ Details of guided walks and the many paths through the estate from the Visitor Centre at Inverdruie (or phone Aviemore 810858); another centre at Loch-an-Eilein sells a guide leaflet to the path around the loch. There is a real possibility of seeing Scottish crossbill, crested tit, siskin and red

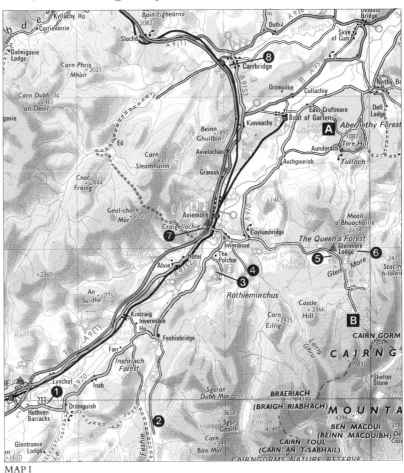

MAP I

squirrel in the pine trees. Beneath the trees are petty whin, common and chickweed wintergreen, and common rock-rose. Osprey may fish the loch, and there are often whinchats on the path to the moor at NH 906076.
ROTHIEMURCHUS ESTATE

I:4 WHITEWELL★

Near Aviemore; at Inverdruie on B970 take right fork signposted Blackpark and Tullochgrue; after one mile (1.5 km), fork left, park at end of public road at around NH 915089.
■ Grass and heather moorland, remnant juniper woodland, single pine trees.
■ A breathtaking view to the Cairngorms and Lairig Ghru, and, in summer, moorland and pinewood flowers: abundant small white and fragrant orchids, heath spotted and lesser twayblade orchids, petty whin, mountain everlasting and oak fern. **Birds** Osprey, Scottish crossbill, black grouse, wheatear.
ROTHIEMURCHUS ESTATE

I:5 GLENMORE FOREST PARK

Near Aviemore; park at Glenmore FC car park (NH 977097). Local forest trail guide available from camp-site office opposite or from Aviemore tourist office. Trails from 1¼ to 11 miles (2 to 18 km).
■ Coniferous plantation around remnants of native pine woodland.
■ This forest has been developed with its scenic value and recreational potential much in mind. The Pinewood Trail (white) takes in pine trees up to 250 years old, with typical pinewood plants and animals.
FORESTRY COMMISSION

I:6 PASS OF RYVOAN

Near Aviemore; Forestry Commission car park at Glenmore (NH 977097); follow metalled road past Glenmore Lodge, then track beyond for 3 miles (5 km).

I:A LOCH GARTEN & ABERNETHY FOREST★★

Near Aviemore; from A95 turn into Boat of Garten, E over River Spey, left on to B970, then

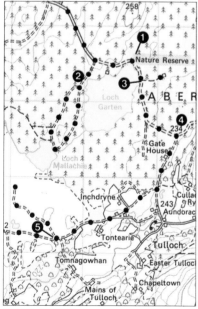

1:50 000, MAP I:A

■ Native pine woodland, open heather moorland.
■ Situated on an old drove road used as a public right-of-way to Braemar, the Pass of Ryvoan is an attractive remnant of ancient Caledonian pine forest, and forms part of several Glenmore Forest Park waymarked routes, allowing a return along the steep but beautiful blue trail, or the even steeper green trail which climbs to the imposing summit of Meall a'Bhuachaille (Shepherd's Hill). **Plants** (Pine forest) juniper, petty whin, chickweed, common wintergreen, moschatel, crowberry. **Birds** Golden eagle, peregrine, capercaillie, crested tit, Scottish crossbill, black grouse, siskin, redstart. **Mammals** Wild cat, pine marten, red squirrel, red deer.
SCOTTISH WILDLIFE TRUST

I:7 CRAIGELLACHIE

Aviemore; park in Aviemore Centre, follow path from S end past small lake, and under A9 to reserve entrance; keep to paths. Leaflet from Information Centre.
■ Birch woodland.
■ The birch woodland NNR is somewhat degraded, but a well-built nature trail, taking about 45 minutes, still makes a pleasant walk with commoner birds and a few flowers on display. The main attraction is the very public peregrine eyrie on Craigellachie crag, where jackdaws also nest.
NATURE CONSERVANCY COUNCIL (NE Scotland)

I:8 LANDMARK PINEWOOD TRAIL

Carrbridge; on S outskirts on B9153, car park, exhibition, restaurant; nature trail accessible to wheelchairs. Admission fee. Open every day from 9.30 am (closing 9.30 pm Jun-Aug; 5 pm or 6 pm rest of year).
■ Native Scots pine woodland.
■ This trail of 1½ miles (2.5 km) includes a board walk level with the tops of the great

first right on to minor road; roadside parking near Loch Garten. Restricted access to parts of Abernethy forest; check with NCC office at Achantoul, Aviemore (Aviemore 810477).
■ Pine woodland, open heather moorland, loch, bog.
① Park in lay-by. Views across Loch Garten (common sandpiper, teal, goldeneye with young in summer; greylag goose, whooper swan, goldeneye, and goosander in winter). Walk back along road to obvious track on left.
② Clear looped track to Loch Mallachie good for crested tit, crossbill, siskin, and spotted flycatcher. Look for dingy skipper butterfly and creeping lady's-tresses by track in Jul; also common, serrated and chickweed wintergreen and common cow-wheat.
③ Park at roadside and walk to hide, sited for nesting ospreys (usually present early Apr to Aug); also views of crested tit and capercaillie. Open 10 am-8 pm; closed from late Aug to late Apr. Information displays and sales desk.
④ Abernethy Forest NNR stretches E from here. No facilities for visitors although limited access to tracks; check with RSPB Warden, Grianan, Tulloch, near Nethybridge.
⑤ Park at roadside and follow track to Tulloch Moor; bearberry, wheatear, roding woodcock at dusk.
ROYAL SOCIETY FOR THE PROTECTION OF BIRDS/NATURE CONSERVANCY COUNCIL (NE Scotland)/ABERNETHY FOREST LODGE ESTATE

MAP J

pine trees, some of which are 250 years old. Crossbill, coal and crested tits and red squirrel can often be seen.
LANDMARK VISITOR CENTRE

J:1 GLEN AFFRIC★

Loch Ness; A831 to Cannich, then SW on minor road to Glen Affric. Park at Dog Falls; river walks begin from car park beyond Loch Beinn a'Mheadhoin at NH 201233.
■ Native pine woodland.
■ Glen Affric has extensive remnants of native pine woodlands, best seen from the river walk. FC route cards.
FORESTRY COMMISSION

I:B CAIRNGORMS★★

Near Aviemore; Do not enter clearly marked re-seeded areas on Cairngorm. Access restricted on parts owned by Rothiemurchus Estate during stalking season.
■ Heather/bilberry/crowberry moorland, mountain top, pine woodland, coniferous plantation. An NNR.
① Access to Lairig Ghru, long-distance walk, 22 miles (35 km), through rugged moor and mountain landscape.
② Many pinewood walks available in Rothiemurchus estate.
③ Common sandpiper and dipper by busy Loch Morlich and occasional fishing osprey; for surrounding Glenmore Forest see I:5.
④ Reindeer House; ask here about daily visits to see reindeer, introduced to Cairngorm in 1952. Metalled road S of House leads to Pass of Ryvoan.
⑤ Pass of Ryvoan; see I:6.
⑥ Shingle banks beside the Allt Mor (burn) are good for Alpine plants washed down from mountain, including yellow and starry saxifrages.
⑦ Car park at ski development with café, lavatories, exhibition of Cairngorm wildlife; ranger base. Useful leaflet available, *Journey to Cairngorm Summit.* Snow bunting around car park in winter. Take chairlift to summit; heather gives way to bilberry and crowberry.
⑧ Ptarmigan restaurant: views. Follow the obvious 'motorway' to summit only if carrying proper clothing; watch for snow bunting.
⑨ Summit area devastated by feet, but, a few yards away, good chance of seeing ptarmigan, snow bunting and mountain hare. Naturally sparse vegetation on granite gravel, includes dwarf willow, fir clubmoss, three-leaved rush, thrift, trailing azalea and *Racomitrium* moss.
⑩ Walk SW from main car park across initially boarded path for good range of 'peat Alpine' plants, including cloudberry, dwarf cornel, bog bilberry and interrupted clubmoss.
NATURE CONSERVANCY COUNCIL (NE Scotland)/WEST HIGHLAND WOODLANDS/HIGHLANDS & ISLANDS DEVELOPMENT BOARD/ROTHIEMURCHUS ESTATE

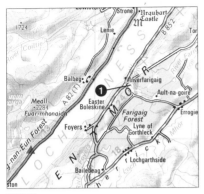

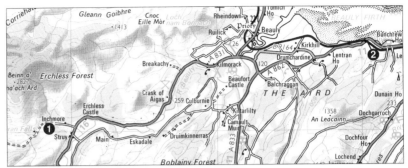

MAP K

MAP L

K:1 FARIGAIG FOREST

Near Loch Ness; on minor road from Inverfarigaig off B852 on S shore; information centre and forest trail at NH 523237. Permit required for SWT reserve: apply Reserves Office, SWT.

■ Birch/oak/alder/aspen/willow woodland, fir/spruce plantation, river gorge.

■ The trail leads about 1¼ miles (2 km) through a plantation to a viewpoint over Loch Ness and the gorge of the Farigaig River, an SWT wildlife reserve.

FC/SCOTTISH WILDLIFE TRUST

L:1 STRATHFARRAR

Near Beauly; turn W off A831 on minor road on N bank of River Farrar for ½ mile (0.8 km), park at roadside and walk along track. Foot access W of Inchmore only (permit required for access by car from Gatekeeper's House at NH 395406). Groups should contact Warden, Eilean Aigas Bungalow, Hughton, by Beauly.

■ Native pinewood, birch woodland, heather moorland, bog.

■ Fragments of native pinewoods that once covered much of the Scottish highlands.

NATURE CONSERVANCY COUNCIL (NW Scotland)

L:2 BEAULY FIRTH

Near Inverness; view S shore from A862; from causeway of Caledonian canal at Clachnaharry (NH 634467) or minor road along Longman Bay off A96. View N shore from Kessock Bridge (A9) or minor road, North Kessock-Milton.

■ Mudflats, salt-marsh.

■ Most notable for goosander (exceeding 1,000 in early winter) and red-breasted merganser (up to 2,000); over 1,500 greylag geese can be present in Apr, and a growing number of Canada geese visit from N England in Jul and Aug to moult.

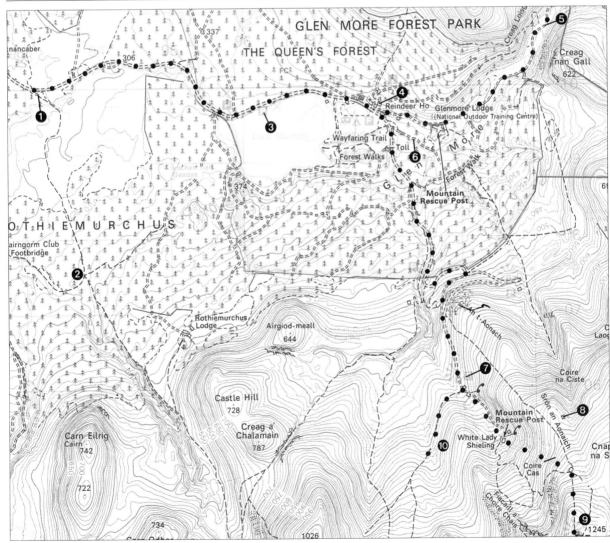

1:50 000, MAP I:B

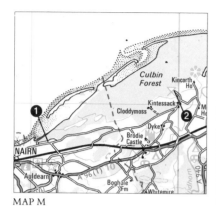

MAP M

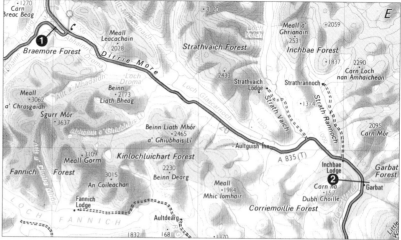

MAP O

M:1 CULBIN SANDS

Near Nairn; *take minor road past golf course to Kingsteps; park on unsignposted track on left, walk to shore.*

■ Sand, salt-marsh, shingle bars and spits.
■ The main attractions of the shore here are sea-duck, with large concentrations of common and velvet scoter and long-tailed duck offshore, and the chance of great northern, red-throated and black-throated divers. Waders include knot, ringed plover and bar-tailed godwit. **Birds** (Breeding) eider duck, ringed plover, oystercatcher.
ROYAL SOCIETY FOR THE PROTECTION OF BIRDS

M:2 CULBIN FOREST★

Near Forres; *park at Cloddymoss (NJ 982599) or Wellhill (NH 998614) and explore forest tracks to shore; or follow the shore W to Culbin Bar.*

■ Coniferous plantation on dunes.
■ This Corsican/Scots pine forest has been planted to stabilize one of Britain's largest sand dune systems. A variety of woodland birds survive, while beneath the trees and on the open dunes and shore a remarkable collection of flowers is recorded. **Birds** (Forest) capercaillie, crested tit, long-eared owl. **Plants** (Woodland) coralroot, lesser tway-

blade, creeping lady's-tresses, one-flowered, common and serrated wintergreens; (shore) sea-milkwort, sea rocket; (dunes) Scots lovage.
FORESTRY COMMISSION

N:1 RASSAL ASHWOOD

Near Loch Carron; *on A896 NW of Loch-carron village; park in lay-by at NG 843433, walk to woodland on E hillside; Allt Mor Gorge is ½ mile (0.8 km).*

■ Ash wood, heather and grass moorland.
■ This northernmost British ashwood (an NNR) is heavily grazed by sheep; only in the fenced enclosures or the sides of Allt Mor Gorge can the woodland and limestone plants flower.
NATURE CONSERVANCY COUNCIL

N:2 TORRIDON★

Near Loch Maree; *The NTS Visitor Centre (details of walks available) is at the junction of A896 and unclassified road to Diabaig (NG 905556). Also parking and viewpoints on roads N and S of Loch Torridon.*

■ Heather and grass moorland, bog, mountain top.
■ The 12,000-acre Torridon Estate includes two sandstone hills, Liathach, 3,456 feet (1,054 m) and Beinn Alligin, 3,232 feet (985 m). Common moorland heaths and grasses grow on the poor soils low on the hills with scattered pine and birch trees. The tops have Arctic/Alpine flowers, ptarmigan and golden eagle. The visitor centre offers an audio-visual programme on local wildlife, and a deer museum lies 600 yards (550 m) along gravel track to the Mains.
NATIONAL TRUST FOR SCOTLAND

N:3 BEINN EIGHE★

Near Kinlochewe; *Aultroy Visitor Centre is ½ mile (0.8 km) NW at NH 019630; guide leaflet available. Restricted access 1 Sep-21 Nov. Visitor centre closed weekends and Oct-Apr.*

■ Heather moorland, mountain top, remnant pine forest.
■ The scree-covered Beinn Eighe – pronounced Ben-ay – 3,313 feet (1,010 m), with its 7 summits of sandstone and quartzite, dominates this, the first National Nature Reserve in Britain, established primarily to protect a fine remnant pinewood at Glas Leitire. One trail leads through the wood (globeflower, melancholy thistle, siskin, tree pipit, crossbill), and another to 1,700 feet (518 m) on the mountainside (look out for trailing azalea, dwarf cornel, ptarmigan, golden eagle, buzzard and merlin). Both start from the car park beside Loch Maree at NH 001650. Red deer are abundant, wild cat and pine marten more elusive.
NATURE CONSERVANCY COUNCIL (NW Scotland)

O:1 CORRIESHALLOCH GORGE★

Near Ullapool; *signposted at Braemore near junction of A835 and A832 (NH 204777); woodland paths, viewpoint; view gorge from suspension bridge.*

■ Mixed deciduous woodland, river gorge.
■ The primary interest of this NNR is the geomorphology and the scenery: the river gorge, 200 feet (61 m) deep in places, with the River Abhainn Droma plunging 150 feet (46 m) over the Falls of Maesach. The woodland is of birch, rowan, oak, hazel, wych elm, aspen, bird cherry, and Scots pine, with interesting flora; ravens nest on a ledge opposite the viewpoint.
NATIONAL TRUST FOR SCOTLAND/NATURE CONSERVANCY COUNCIL (NW Scotland)

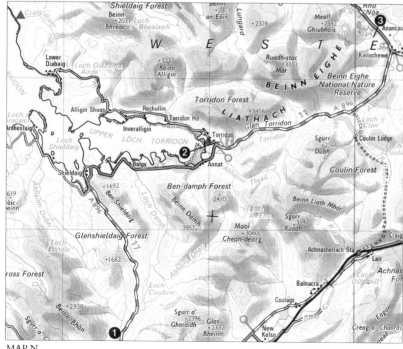

MAP N

O:2 BEN WYVIS

Near Dingwall; park at roadside near Garbat cottage (NH 413679) on A835. Gate in forest fence marks start of well-used path across Bealach Mor moor to An Cabar and Glas Leathad Mor. Care required during stalking season (from Aug).

■ Heather moorland, mire, mountain top, moss-sedge heath.

■ The 10-mile (16-km) walk to the summit ascends through 2,500 feet (762 m), and should be tackled only by experienced hill walkers; but the old drove road across Bealach Mor shows many plants of lower peatlands, including bearberry, cloudberry, dwarf birch and Alpine bearberry. Screes below the summit of gneiss have parsley fern and Alpine lady-fern; the summit is dominated by stiff sedge and the moss *Racomitrium lanuginosum*. An NNR.
NATURE CONSERVANCY COUNCIL (NW Scotland)

P:1 CROMARTY FIRTH

View from sea-front at Dingwall; lay-bys on A862 and A9 on N shore, B817 Alness-Invergordon: B9163 on S shore.

■ Mudflats, salt-marsh, cliff.

■ The extensive mudflats are significant for wildfowl and waders (esp redshank numbers). The Sutors – cliffs at the mouth of the Firth – have a few cormorants and often provide good views of dolphin.

P:2 NIGG & UDALE BAYS*

Cromarty Firth; view Nigg Bay from Invergordon E on B817 and unclassified road from Nigg along E side of Bay; view Udale Bay from B9163 near Jemimaville, or park opposite ruined chapel at NH 706658 and walk along shore to Newhallpoint.

■ Mudflats, salt-marsh.

■ Nigg is the richer of these two bays (an NNR), despite the industrial development nearby, with up to 10,000 wigeon feeding on the abundant eelgrass, and goldeneye, mute and whooper swan, especially around the distillery outfalls. More than 1,000 pink-footed geese may roost here in late winter, with occasional greenshank along the shore. Keep off mud, which is dangerous in places.
NATURE CONSERVANCY COUNCIL (NW Scotland)

P:3 DORNOCH FIRTH

Near Tain; view from lay-bys on A9, or from Meikle Ferry; S at Ferry Point (NH 732859) or N at Newton Point (NH 729870).

■ Mudflat, salt-marsh.

■ In winter this estuary holds many wigeon, teal, pintail, scaup, shelduck, mute swan and waders. The coast beyond the mouth (view from Tarbat Ness, Dornoch or Embo) is good for long-tailed duck, common and velvet scoter.

P:4 LOCH FLEET*

Near Golspie; park on Ferry Links at Littleferry, walk E along shore, then N. Or view unclassified minor road S of Loch signposted Skelbo, or at Embo. Warden leads walks in summer. Permit required for access off paths in Ferry Links Wood; apply Reserves Office, SWT.

■ Tidal mudflats, dunes, coastal heath, pine plantation, sandy shore.

■ Many sea-duck feed in this almost land-locked estuary in winter: up to 800 wigeon, common scoter, shelduck, oystercatcher, curlew and knot. In spring, 1,000 long-tailed duck may gather at Littleferry; off the coast at Embo, all three divers, common scoter,

MAP P

velvet scoter, an occasional surf scoter and a rare king eider may be seen. In summer, eider and common seal gather in the estuary, and terns fish. The mature pine plantation at Balbair Wood has a range of woodland birds and flowers, also roe deer.
SCOTTISH WILDLIFE TRUST

P:5 MOUND ALDERWOOD

Near Golspie; no access to wood; view from Mound embankment on A9 at head of Loch Fleet

Common alder – see P:5.

(esp from railway bridge at NH 775983), or from minor road W to Torboll.

■ Wet alder woodland, fen, estuary.

■ Since this embankment was built in 1815, stopping tidal flow, a dense alder wood has developed, which shelters a variety of woodland birds and plants. Salmon gather inland of the sluice gate in the embankment as the tide ebbs, waiting for it to open, while the embankment itself is a useful viewpoint for Loch Fleet. An NNR.
NATURE CONSERVANCY COUNCIL (NW Scotland)

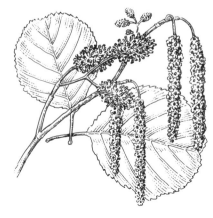

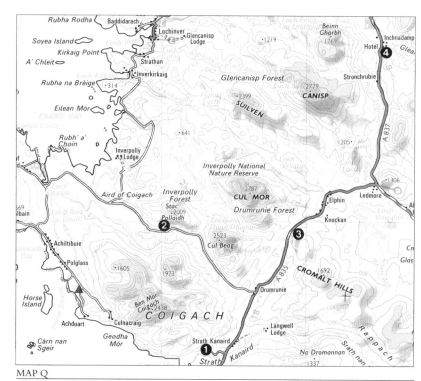

MAP Q

MAP R

Q:1 BEN MORE COIGACH*

Near Ullapool; view from unclassified road to Blughasary off A835 in Strath Kinaird (car park at NC 135015); or from minor road Drumrunie-Achiltibuie. Leaflet from SWT.

■ Grass and heather moorland, mountain top, lochs, rocky coast, crofted farmland.

■ The drive to Achiltibuie gives spectacular views of Ben More Coigach and much wildlife can be seen: abundant red deer, divers on the small lochans, and red grouse, twite, golden plover, greenshank, and distant raven and golden eagle on the moor.

SCOTTISH WILDLIFE TRUST

Q:2 INVERPOLLY*

Near Ullapool; view from unclassified road W from Drumrunie, parking S of Stac Pollaidh at NC 108095; or from Knockan Visitor Centre signposted off A835 at NC 187092. Access restricted 1 Sept-21 Oct for deer stalking; check with Knockan Visitor Centre or warden (Lochinver 204 or Elphin 234).

■ Grass moorland, bog, lochs, mountain-top heath, birch/hazel woodland remnants.

■ The sandstone peaks of Cul Mor, Cul Beag, and Stac Pollaidh form the centrepiece of this 26,000-acre NNR. Golden eagle can be seen, and deer roam freely. Golden plover, greenshank and stonechat are on the moors in summer, and bogbean, greater sundew, common and pale butterwort flower. The tops have ptarmigan, ring ouzel, dwarf willow, three-leaved rush, and, at one spot, the rare Norwegian mugwort. In the woodland fragments are wood warbler, melancholy thistle, hay-scented buckler fern and Wilson's filmy-fern.

NATURE CONSERVANCY COUNCIL (NW Scotland)

Q:3 KNOCKAN CLIFF*

Near Ullapool; trail starts from car park at Knockan Centre, signed off A835 at NC 187092.

■ Limestone cliff, heather moorland.

■ Knockan was one of the places where

massive earth movements (in this case, the Moine thrust) were first demonstrated in the mid-19thC. One trail guide explains this phenomenon in a dramatic way; another, using the same route, details local flora, fauna and land-use.

NATURE CONSERVANCY COUNCIL

Q:4 INCHNADAMPH

Near Ullapool; entrance beside Inchnadamph Hotel on A837; take the track by Traligill Burn. Approach Stronchrubie Cliffs from parking places on A837. Permission required during deer stalking (15 July-15 Oct): apply Assynt Estates (Lochinver 203). No dogs allowed.

■ Limestone cliffs, limestone grassland, grass moorland.

■ The limestone landscape, complete with swallow-holes, dry valleys, caves and dramatic cliffs, is the main interest of this NNR. One cave held relics of human occupation just after the last Ice Age, when Arctic fox, reindeer and lemming roamed the area. Golden plover, ring ouzel, red grouse, or peregrine falcon are today's inhabitants. The flora of the limestone grassland is a reminder of the Arctic conditions which once prevailed. The cliffs display dark-red helleborine, the meadow beside the burn, heath spotted-, fragrant, small-white and lesser butterfly-orchids and globeflower.

NATURE CONSERVANCY COUNCIL

R:1 LOCH A'MHUILINN

Near Scourie; park on minor road off A894 at NC 169399, or at W end of Loch a'Chreagain Daraich at NC 167394.

■ Birch woodland, bog, lochans, rocky seashore.

■ The predominantly downy birch woodland of this NNR includes the most northerly remnants of oak woodland in Britain (intermediate between sessile and pedunculate oak); primrose, bluebell, wood anemone and yellow pimpernel grow in the wood, in which 177 species of lichen and 9 species of dragonfly have also been recorded.

NATURE CONSERVANCY COUNCIL (NW Scotland)

R:2 HANDA ISLAND**

Off Scourie; by private boat from Tarbet (boatman: William MacRae, Scourie; Scourie 2156). Boat service not operational Sun or from mid-Sep to end of Mar. Landing fee for non-members of RSPB. Keep to marked paths; no access in bad weather.

■ Sandstone cliffs, sandy coves, sheep pasture, peat bog.

■ There is a mass of sea-birds in early summer: approaching 50,000 pairs of guillemot; 16,000 razorbills; nearly 11,000 pairs of kittiwake; also fulmar, puffin, shag, herring and great black-backed gulls; plus black guillemot. A small colony of great and Arctic skuas is slowly increasing. In the centre of the island pale butterwort and royal fern are among the less common plants. The boat crossing can offer sight of black- and red-throated divers, porpoise and common dolphin. The boatman sometimes also runs trips up the coast from Tarbet.

ROYAL SOCIETY FOR THE PROTECTION OF BIRDS

Raven – see Q:1.

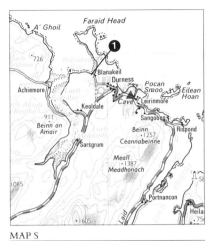

MAP S

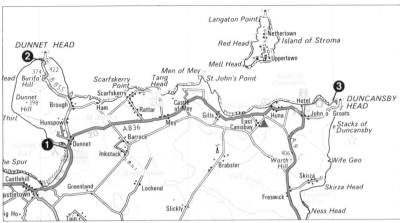

MAP U

S:1 DURNESS★★

Durness; *park at Balnakeil sands (NC 392687), walk to Faraid Head; for Clo Mor cross Kyle of Durness by passenger ferry from Keoldale (NC 377652); minibus service to Kearvaig, then walk. Avoid crofting land.*

■ Limestone grassland, Dryas-heath, cliffs, sandy beaches, dunes, heather moorland.

■ Mountain avens, signifying limestone, is abundant, with other mountain plants emphasizing the sub-Arctic habitat. Lochs in the area may have breeding tufted duck, gadwall, and red-throated diver. Beyond the marram dunes of Balnakeil Bay (long-tailed duck and great northern diver offshore in spring), the cliffs of Faraid Head have some 1,800 puffin burrows on the grassy E slopes and are a good sea-watching point in autumn for passing shearwaters. The great sandstone cliff of Clo Mor ('the great web of cloth', from its striated appearance), is the highest mainland cliff in Britain, 921 feet (280 m), and has spectacular sea-bird colonies including razorbill, black guillemot, and the largest mainland puffin colony.

T:1 INVERNAVER★

Bettyhill; *park where A836 and minor road to Invernaver meet at NC 707599; walk past houses into reserve, or take rough path from Torrisdale (NC 681612).*

■ Heath, dunes, shingle, mudflats, hazel/birch scrub, heather moorland.

■ Blown sand produces rich hillside soils in which montane species thrive at low altitudes; mountain avens, purple oxytropis, dark-red helleborine, moss campion, yellow and purple saxifrages, Alpine bistort, dwarf

Arctic skua – see U:3, Duncansby Head.

juniper. Buzzard nests on crags, snipe and greenshank on boggy moorland, which is the only British locality for the moss *Brachythecium erythrorrhizon*. An NNR.

NATURE CONSERVANCY COUNCIL (NW Scotland)

T:2 STRATHY POINT

Near Bettyhill; *park near lighthouse and walk to cliffs; an obvious path from graveyard (NC 838656) leads to Strathy Bay.*

■ Coastal grassland, cliff.

■ The delicate Scottish primrose flowers here in May-Jun and again in late Jul; Strathy Point also has Scots lovage, spring squill and northern scurvy-grass on the cliffs. The dunes beside Strathy Bay have purple oxytropis, globeflower, grass-of-Parnassus, field gentian, and abundant twayblade.

U:1 DUNNET LINKS

Thurso; *park at caravan site on A836 (ND 219705) or near Burn of Midsand (ND 216688).*

■ Dune, dune grassland, sandy beach, open sea, marsh, fen.

■ Several montane plants grow in this NNR at unusually low altitude; a few Arctic terns breed; great northern divers are common in summer and are joined by red- and black-throated divers, common scoter and long-tailed duck in winter.

NATURE CONSERVANCY COUNCIL

U:2 DUNNET HEAD★

Near Thurso; *park at Easter Head just before lighthouse (ND 202764). Care at cliff edge.*

■ Old Red Sandstone cliffs, cliff-top grassland, heather moorland.

■ These 400-foot (120-m) cliffs have a large breeding population of sea-birds: 15,000 pairs of kittiwake, guillemot, razorbill, puffin, fulmar, and a few great skua which rarely breed successfully. Cliff tops receiving salt spray support Scottish primrose and spring squill; cliffs have roseroot, Scots lovage and Alpine saw-wort.

U:3 DUNCANSBY HEAD

Near John o'Groats; *park just before lighthouse (ND 404734); keep out of lighthouse grounds. Care at cliff edge.*

■ Old Red Sandstone cliffs and stacks, heather moorland.

■ Duncansby Head is Scotland's 'land's end', with 260-foot (80-m) cliffs on which nest guillemot, kittiwake, razorbill, fulmar and puffin. Small numbers of great and Arctic skuas may breed on the moor and can be seen from the cliff top as they harry the other sea-birds for food. **Plants** Spring squill, Scots lovage.

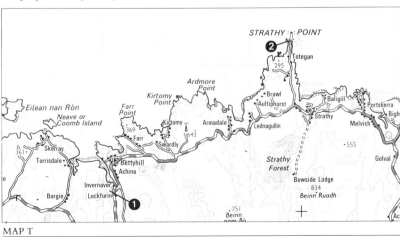

MAP T

Buzzard – see T:1, Invernaver.

WESTERN ISLES

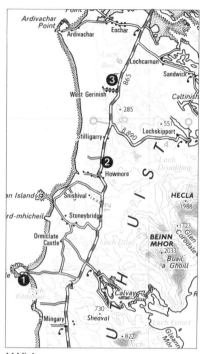

MAP A

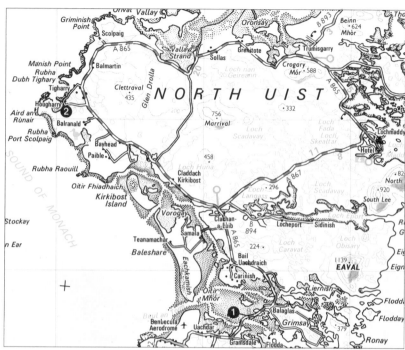

MAP B

A:1 SOUTH UIST MACHAIRS★★

On the island's W coast; access points include
Kilpheder (NF 735202), Peninerine (NF
736346) and Howmore (NF 753364). Best site
is Rudha Ardvule (NF 710300), a little-used
artillery range; no entry when red flag flies.

■ Rich grassland, crofted farmland, marsh.

■ Machair is grassland, enriched by the
white shell sand blown in from the west
coast, and maintained by traditional crofter
farming. It supports a glorious array of
flowers, and waders breed at exceptional
densities, up to 600 pairs per sq km in parts.
Lapwing, dunlin, redshank and over 25 per
cent of the breeding ringed plover in Britain
nest here, with snipe in damper areas, and
corncrake in the wet machair marshes inland. Keep to paths and tracks, so as not to
disturb the birds. **Plants** (Dry machair) red
and white clovers, kidney vetch, eyebright,
lady's bedstraw, yellow rattle, tufted vetch,
harebell, red bartsia, lesser meadow-rue,
scentless mayweed; (ploughed land)
bugloss, knotgrass, fumitory, corn marigold; (wet machair) ragged robin, yellow
iris, early-purple orchid. **Butterflies** Common blue, meadow brown, large heath.

A:2 LOCH DRUIDIBEG

On South Uist; view from A865 around Stilligarry, or from B890 to Loch Skipport (good for
water plants). Permit required for entry during
breeding season: apply NCC (NW Scotland).

■ Loch, islands, grass and heather moorland, machair, plantation.

■ Up to 65 pairs of greylag geese – 30 per
cent of the wild birds breeding in Britain –
breed around the loch, which is an NNR.
After the young hatch they move to Lochs
Stilligarry and Grogarry, where 200-250
adult greylag gather to moult in June and
July. **Birds** (Loch) red-breasted merganser,
tufted duck, mute swan, red-throated diver;
(plantation) greenfinch, goldcrest, merlin,
peregrine, sparrowhawk. **Plants** Water
lobelia, floating club-rush, royal fern.
NATURE CONSERVANCY COUNCIL (NW
Scotland)

A:3 LOCH BEE, SOUTH UIST

At the N end of the island; view from A865
causeway across loch, parking in lay-by at N or S
end.

■ Shallow fresh water loch.

■ This vast loch supports 300-400 mute
swans, mainly non-breeding adults,
throughout the year, one of the largest
gatherings in Scotland. In winter, 30 or so
whooper swans and small numbers of
wigeon and goldeneye visit.

B:1 NORTH FORD, BENBECULA★

At the S end of the island; view from A865
causeway connecting Benbecula, Grimsay and
North Uist, park in lay-bys near either end; or
from end of track S of Carinish to Rubha nan Ron
(NT 818590). Beware fast-flowing tide.

■ Sandy and muddy shore, estuary.

■ This large area of sand and mud (and
smaller area of South Ford) is excellent for
waders in winter, with large numbers of
grey plover, bar-tailed godwit and dunlin,
and even a little stint or curlew sandpiper in
autumn. The shore at Balivanich often has
glaucous and Iceland gulls, and little tern
breeds at the airport. **Birds** Oystercatcher,
ringed plover, knot, redshank, greenshank,
curlew.

B:2 BALRANALD, NORTH UIST★★

In the island's NW; from A865 take minor
road signposted Hougharry (not Balranald), bear
left after one mile (1.5 km), to reception cottage at
NF 706707. View loch from S of cemetery (NF
707705). Keep to marked paths in breeding season.

■ Lochs, marshes, machair, sandy and
rocky shore.

■ Waders abound in the machair, early
summer; dunlin, ringed plover, lapwing and
oystercatcher nest at high densities among a
riot of machair flowers. Snipe nest in the
damp areas, and shoveler, gadwall, teal and
wigeon by Loch nam Feithean. Whooper
swan and greylag goose visit in winter, and
an odd whooper may stay on all summer.
Stray visitors include blue-winged teal, little

egret and black tern. Early and northern
marsh orchids and ragged robin flower in
the marshes, and, from the beds of yellow
iris, 10 or more corncrakes may call. On the
white sandy bays are more waders, sea sandwort and Scots lovage. Aird an Runair is a
superb sea-watching point: 1,000 Manx
shearwaters an hour in autumn, and many
less common birds. **Birds** (Breeding) buzzard, little and Arctic terns, twite, wheatear,
eider duck; (regular visitors) buzzard, hen
harrier, short-eared owl; (passage) gannet,
sooty, great and Cory's shearwaters, great,
Arctic, pomarine and long-tailed skuas,
Leach's and storm petrels, glaucous gull.
ROYAL SOCIETY FOR THE PROTECTION OF
BIRDS

C:1 SOUTH HARRIS

Near Tarbert; take A859 down W coast; S of
Rodel take unclassified road to Finsbay; return up
E coast (allow time for slow roads).

■ Sandy and rocky shores, sheltered bays,
open sea.

■ Many waders feed along the sandy W
shores: the E coast is more water than land,
with myriad lochs with divers and geese.
From Leverburgh pier (NG 012864) watch
for great northern diver, and in winter for

Long-tailed skua – see B:2.

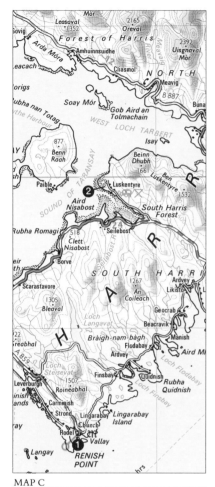

MAP C

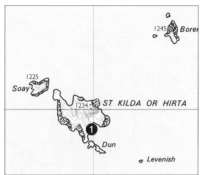

MAP D

MAP E

greylag and barnacle geese on offshore islands. **Birds** (Shore) ringed plover, dunlin, oystercatcher, redshank, curlew, turnstone, black guillemot, Arctic skua; (moorland) buzzard, merlin, golden eagle. **Mammals** Grey and common seals, otter.

C:2 SOUND OF TARANSAY★

W coast of Harris; from A859 take unclassified road signposted Luskentyre; park by graveyard at NG 068993 and walk over dunes to shore.

■ Mudflats, salt-marsh, estuary, open sea.

■ This sound holds up to 700 common scoter in early winter, with a few velvet and surf scoters, 300 or more eider duck, long-tailed duck, Slavonian grebe and red-breasted merganser out to sea, and numbers of waders on the salt-marsh. **Birds** (Winter) shelduck, wigeon, Brent goose, barnacle goose (Taransay), oystercatcher, redshank, ringed plover, dunlin, knot, greenshank, grey plover, sanderling, spotted redshank.

D:1 ST KILDA★★

W of Harris; details from NTS on week-long work parties; otherwise commercial companies run tours, usually based on sailing boats; check advertisements in specialist magazines. Permission required to stay on island; apply NTS.

■ Rocky islands, cliffs, grass moorland.

■ This NNR is the most remote site in the *Nature Atlas* – 41 miles (66 km) NW of North Uist – and certainly one of the most exciting, although the drone of generators from the army camp shatters all illusion of solitude. The gannetry on Boreray, Stac an Armin

and Stac Lee is the largest in the world with more than 50,000 occupied sites; landing is impossible but good views can be had from a boat. Puffins once numbered two million; numbers crashed in the sixties, but have recovered to around 300,000 pairs. There are vast colonies of other sea-birds, grey seal around the coast, feral Soay sheep, endemic races of wren and wood mouse, and some interesting flowers – ample rewards for the effort to get here. **Birds** (Breeding) guillemot, black guillemot, razorbill, fulmar, Manx shearwater, Leach's and storm petrels, great skua, golden plover. **Plants** Roseroot, purple saxifrage, moss campion, honeysucks, primrose, wild angelica, sea mayweed, sweet vernal grass, lady fern. NATURE CONSERVANCY COUNCIL (NW Scotland)/NATIONAL TRUST FOR SCOTLAND

E:1 THE MINCH

E of the Western Isles; excellent views from all ferry crossings to Western Isles; Oban to Lochboisdale (South Uist); Uig (Skye) to Lochmaddy (North Uist) or Tarbert (Harris) or Ullapool to Stornoway (Lewis). Details of timetables from Caledonian MacBrayne, Ferry Terminal, Gourock, Strathclyde, PA19 1QP.

■ Open sea.

■ The Minch can be one of the stormiest waters in the world, but the ferry crossing is a superb way to see the birds of the high seas; particularly in autumn there is a good chance of seeing sooty shearwater and long-tailed skua on passage. **Birds** Gannet, fulmar, guillemot, razorbill, black guillemot, puffin, kittiwake, Manx shearwater, herring gull, lesser and greater black-backed gulls, Arctic and great skuas. **Mammals** Common and white-sided dolphins, killer whale (occasional).

E:2 STORNOWAY WOODS (LEWIS CASTLE GROUNDS)

Stornoway, Isle of Lewis; main entrance on A857, opposite junction of Bayhead, Matheson and Macaulay roads, at NB 424335. Nature trail leaflet available from the Tourist Information Office and local stationers. No access to immediate grounds of Lewis College.

■ Mixed woodland, parkland, moorland.

■ Planted in the late-19thC, these woods of elm, sycamore, ash, beech and exotic species, with dense thickets of *Rhododendron ponticum*, are one of the few homes on Lewis for woodland plants, although the presence of pink purslane and Welsh poppy attests that these too are planted. A rookery of 150 nests is the only one on Lewis, and many woodland birds breed. **Plants** Lesser celandine, wood cranesbill, primrose, ramsons, wood sorrel, bluebell, green hellebore,

marsh marigold, Himalayan knotweed. **Birds** (Breeding) blue and great tits, tree sparrow, spotted flycatcher, mistle thrush, treecreeper, goldcrest, willow warbler; (occasional) grasshopper warbler, great spotted woodpecker, common crossbill. STORNOWAY TRUST

E:3 BROAD BAY, LEWIS★

Stornoway, Isle of Lewis; view from shore S of Tong on B895 (NB 450357), or Steinish on minor road at NB 447341, or from A866 at Branahuie Banks (car park at NB 478323).

■ Sandy and muddy shore, sheltered sea bay.

■ Eider duck, long-tailed duck, red-breasted merganser, common scoter, great northern and black-throated diver can all be seen in winter, and greylag geese, wigeon and shelduck feed on the salt-marsh at the mouth of the River Laxdale. In summer, Arctic and great skuas breed on moorland NW of the Bay, and common, Arctic and little terns on the Melbost sands.

F:1 BUTT OF LEWIS

On North Lewis; take B8013 or B8014 to Europie, then minor road to lighthouse; car park at NB 520665.

■ Sea-bird cliffs of greiss, coastal grassland.

■ A few fulmar and kittiwake nest on the cliffs and black guillemot on the rocks below, but its real attraction is as a sea-watching point, with many gannets from the Sula Sgeir colony; pomarine and long-tailed skua in autumn. **Birds** (Breeding) rock dove; (passage) Manx, great and sooty shearwaters, great and Arctic skuas. **Plants** Thrift, sea campion, roseroot, common scurvy grass, Scots lovage.

MAP F

241

ORKNEY

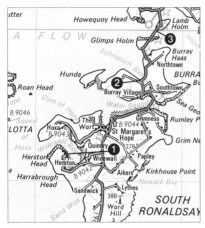

MAP A

ORKNEY ISLANDS**

Car ferry Scrabster (near Thurso) to Stromness (P&O Ferries, Jamieson Quay, Aberdeen, AB9 8DL); passenger ferry in summer John o'Groats-Burwick (Thomas & Bews, Ferry Office, John o'Groats); regular flights by British Airways and Loganair with connections to most British airports. Further information from Orkney Tourist Board, Kirkwall, Orkney, KW15 1NX.

■ Archipelago of 67 islands.

■ Most of the Orkney islands are fertile, undulating farmland, although Hoy is more rugged, reaching a height of 1,565 feet (477 m). Birds are very much a feature of this mostly tree-less landscape, with many curlew and common gull, short-eared owl hunting over the fields and hen harrier over the moors. Coastal cliffs abound with fulmar, kittiwake, guillemot and puffin, sometimes hounded by piratical great or Arctic skua. Terns, otter and grey and common seals also occur. Scots primrose grows on several cliff tops, with spring squill, roseroot and Scots lovage, while a few gravelly shores have oysterplant.

A:1 WIDEWALL BAY

On W coast of South Ronaldsay; view S shore from B9042, esp beside Kirkhouse Mill at ND 434915; N shore from B9043; continue to Hoxa Head (ND 410935) for views over Scapa Flow.

■ Estuary, rocky islands, muddy shore.

■ Common seals often haul out on a low skerry in the Oyce of Quindry at the head of the bay, with redshank, dunlin and oystercatcher along the shore in summer. In winter, long-tailed duck, goldeneye, and perhaps divers from Scapa Flow feed here.

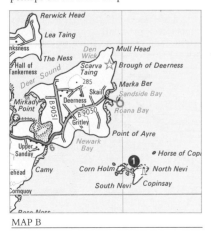

MAP B

A:2 ECHNA LOCH

On W coast of Burray; view from natural causeway between the loch and the sea on A961; park in lay-by at S end (ND 473967).

■ Fresh water loch, sea bay with sandy shore.

■ Tufted duck, mute swan and red-breasted merganser breed on the fresh water loch, with 30 or so pochard in winter. The bay NW of the road holds numbers of goldeneye, eider, red-breasted merganser, and long-tailed duck (esp in late winter), and is good for velvet scoter.

A:3 CHURCHILL BARRIERS

Southern Isles; view from A961 connecting Lamb Holm, Glimps Holm, Burray and South Ronaldsay; picnic area overlooking Barrier No.4 at ND 481954.

■ Rocky and sandy shores, open sea.

■ These causeways, built in World War II to protect the approaches to Scapa Flow, now provide excellent views of sea-duck in the sheltered waters of the Flow, including up to 2,000 long-tailed duck. In summer, black guillemot and otters, great and Arctic skuas can be seen, terns nest near the Italian chapel on Lamb Holm, and shags rest on the wrecked ships by Causeway No. 2.

B:1 COPINSAY**

Off E coast of Mainland Orkney. Day trips by boat from Skaill (Deerness peninsula, Mainland, HY 589064); book in advance with boatman (S. Foubister, tel: 085-674-252): contact RSPB Orkney Officer, Smyril, Stenness, Stromness, KW16 3JX, to book limited basic overnight accommodation.

■ Old Red Sandstone cliffs, rocky shore.

■ A mile of sheer cliffs up to 250 feet (76 m)

on the SE coast, packed with sea-birds: 30,000 guillemots, 10,000 kittiwake nests, razorbill, fulmar, and smaller numbers of shag, puffin, and black guillemot. Migrants, in spring and autumn, include black redstart, bluethroat and scarlet rosefinch.
Plants Oysterplant, sea aster (beach).
ROYAL SOCIETY FOR THE PROTECTION OF BIRDS

C:1 HOBBISTER

Near Kirkwall, Mainland Orkney; track S of A964 at HY 396070, or minor road S at HY 381068, with car park overlooking Waulkmill Bay at HY 383065. Access at all times to land between A964 and sea, but keep to footpaths.

■ Heather moorland, bog, fen, sandy shore, open bay, salt-marsh.

■ Typical Orkney moorland birds (hen harrier, short-eared owl, merlin, red grouse, curlew, snipe, red-throated diver, twite) all nest here, although they can be elusive in summer. Fulmars, red-breasted merganser, black guillemot, red-throated diver, goldeneye and Arctic tern can all be seen in Waulkmill Bay, while sea-milkwort, sea arrowgrass, salt-marsh rush, salt-marsh flatsedge and long-bracted sedge grow in the salt-marsh at its head.
ROYAL SOCIETY FOR THE PROTECTION OF BIRDS

C:2 LOCHS OF HARRAY & STENNESS*

Near Stromness, Mainland Orkney; view from B9055; car park at HY 296134; view Stenness also from Bridge of Waithe.

■ Salt water (Stenness) and fresh water (Harray) lochs.

■ Large numbers of wildfowl in winter:

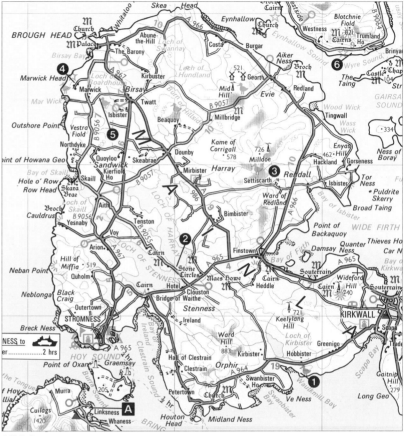

MAP C

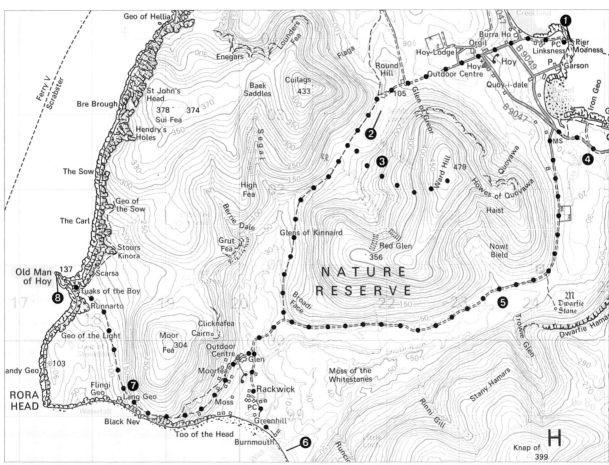

1:50 000, MAP C:A

C:A NORTH HOY★★

SW of Stromness; passenger ferry, Strom-ness-Maness pier; car ferry Houton (A965 S of Stromness) to Lyness (S Hoy); details from Ork-ney Tourist Board.

■ Heather and grass moorland, sea cliffs, rocky shore, mountain heather.
① Moness pier; RSPB display in Hoy Inn.
② Sandy Loch, on well-marked, easy track to Rackwick, has red-throated divers (do not disturb). Great skuas bathe and breed on moor nearby (1,500 pairs on Hoy). Perhaps golden eagle overhead.
③ Possible detour to climb Ward Hill -- about

3 hrs: steep, grassy slope with great and Arctic skuas. Golden plover, mountain hare, common and Alpine bearberry, dwarf willow, and bog bilberry on summit ridge.
④ If driving from Lyness, take B9047 N, watching for Arctic skuas and red-throated divers in Lyrawa Bay (view from road at ND 293986).
⑤ Drive along minor road to Rackwick (hen harrier, stonechat on gorse, and yellow mountain saxifrage by road).
⑥ Rackwick Bay; rough car park at end of road. Wild scenery with gulls on small pool and evening gathering of Manx shearwaters. Sand

and curved sedge in wet areas behind beach.
⑦ Rough path signposted from Rackwick to Old Man of Hoy, past Loch of Stourdale (breeding greater black-backed gulls). Beware dangerous cliff edge.
⑧ Old Man of Hoy; dramatic rock stack with nesting fulmar.

Birds (Cliffs) guillemot, kittiwake, razorbill, puffin; (moors) snipe, dunlin, wheatear, twite, peregrine, merlin, kestrel. **Plants** Purple saxifrage, Alpine saw-wort, stone bramble.
ROYAL SOCIETY FOR THE PROTECTION OF BIRDS

long-tailed duck, scaup, eider, merganser, wigeon, tufted duck and goldeneye use Stenness; Harray has over 1,000 pochard, tufted duck, wigeon and greylag goose; mute and whooper swans on both.

C:3 BIRSAY MOORS & COTTASGARTH★

Near Kirkwall, Mainland Orkney; Cot-tasgarth: turn W off A966 N of Norseman Garage on to minor road, turn right to Cottas-garth farm at NY 368187. Burgar Hill: sign-posted off A966 at Evie (NY 358266). Dee of Durkadale: from minor road S of Loch of Hun-dland, turn S to ruined farm at Durkadale (NY 299248).

■ Heather moorland, bog.

■ Hides at Cottasgarth and on Burgar Hill allow views of many moorland birds, esp hen harriers (also to be seen from minor road W of Cottasgarth or B9057 E of Dounby). Lowrie's Water, seen from Burgar Hill hide,

has breeding red-throated divers and teal. **Birds** Merlin, kestrel, great and Arctic skuas, oystercatcher, golden plover, curlew, dunlin, stonechat, wheatear, short-eared owl, lesser black-backed, herring and com-mon gulls. **Plants** Bog whortleberry, lesser twayblade orchid (Cottasgarth); heath spotted, northern marsh and early marsh orchids, bottle and bog sedges (Dee of Dur-kadale).
ROYAL SOCIETY FOR THE PROTECTION OF BIRDS

C:4 MARWICK HEAD★★

Near Marwick, Mainland Orkney; park at end of unclassified road S of Marwick (HY 229242); or one mile (1.5 km) N take unclassi-fied road to Cumlaquoy and Marwick, and park at end of track, HY 232252. Walk to cliff top at around HU 224252. Take care on cliff edge.

■ Old Red Sandstone cliff, rocky bay, wet meadow.

■ This one-mile (1.5-km) stretch of cliffs is the most accessible sea-bird colony in Ork-ney, and a must for any summer visitor. The approach from Marwick is the most pleas-ing, with Scots lovage and sea sandwort on the rocks, and common or grey seals in the bay. The wet meadow E of the bay has breeding waders. The cliff path is gentle, and leads to the rocky promontory at Chol-dertoo (NY 224249) where razorbills, puf-fins and fulmars allow close approach. To the N, the 280-foot (85-m) cliffs below the Kitchener Memorial are alive with birds: 35,000 guillemots, nearly 10,000 kittiwake nests, fulmar and razorbill, great and Arctic skuas on patrol out to sea, and thrift, spring squill and sea campion on the cliff. **Birds** Wheatear, rock dove, rock pipit, raven; (meadow) redshank, curlew, snipe, lapw-ing, oystercatcher.
ROYAL SOCIETY FOR THE PROTECTION OF BIRDS

ORKNEY

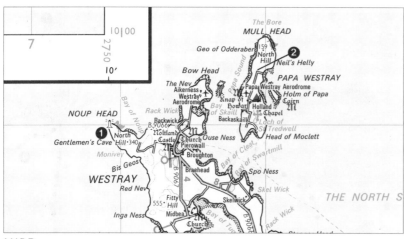

MAP D

C:5 THE LOONS*

Near Marwick, Mainland Orkney; *just beyond Twatt, turn W off A986 on minor road to Marwick; hide is S of road at NY 246242. Access at all times to hide; no access into reserve.*

■ Marsh, loch.

■ Duck and waders breed in this attractive marshland site, as well as common and black-headed gulls and Arctic terns; corncrakes can be heard from the iris beds or hayfields nearby. A regular winter flock of Greenland white-fronted goose reached record numbers (79) in 1986/7.

ROYAL SOCIETY FOR THE PROTECTION OF BIRDS

C:6 TRUMLAND, ROUSAY

NE of Mainland Orkney; *passenger ferry from Tingwall. Reserve is N of Rousay Pier; enter by track W of Trumland House (HY 427276). Access at all times, but visitors from Apr to Aug must contact the summer warden (Trumland Mill Cottage) who will escort them.*

■ Heather moorland, crags, small loch.

■ The reserve takes in the island's highest point, Blotchnie Fiold, with superb views N. Moorland birds include hen harrier (Orkney has 10 per cent of the British population), merlin, short-eared owl, golden plover, red-throated diver, great and Arctic skuas. **Mammals** Orkney vole, otter.

RSPB

D:1 NOUP CLIFFS, WESTRAY*

NW of Mainland Orkney; *passenger ferry Kirkwall-Pierowall or flights (2-3 weekly) from Kirkwall; take minor road past Noltland Castle to Noup Farm; follow track to lighthouse (HY 392500), about 4 miles (6.5 km).*

■ Sandstone cliff, maritime heath.

■ On 1½ miles (2.5 km) of cliff S of the lighthouse is one of the largest sea-bird colonies in Britain, with over 40,000 guille-

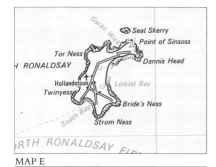

MAP E

mots, some 25,000 pairs of kittiwakes, and smaller numbers of razorbill, fulmar, puffin and shag. Grey seal and occasionally porpoises and dolphins can be seen offshore. **Plants** Sea campion, thrift, spring squill.

ROYAL SOCIETY FOR THE PROTECTION OF BIRDS

D:2 NORTH HILL, PAPA WESTRAY**

N island of Orkney group; *passenger ferry Kirkwall-Papa Westray or flights (2-3 weekly) from Kirkwall. From mid-Apr to mid-Aug contact warden (c/o Gavrie, Papa Westray, KW17 2BU) in advance for guided tour.*

■ Maritime heath, rocky shore, low sandstone cliffs.

■ Allow two days to visit Papa Westray. Spend one on North Hill in summer, when it throngs with birds, including the largest colony of Arctic terns in Britain (6,210 pairs in 1985). Enter the reserve at N end of road (HY 496538), turn W to the coast and continue clockwise. Keep to the coast to avoid disturbing the terns (and to escape divebombing by terns and 100 pairs of Arctic skuas). Black guillemots are numerous among the flagstones, Scots primrose

flowers in the coastal heath, and razorbill, kittiwake, and guillemot on the low cliff at Fowl Crag are well seen from a rock platform at HY 508544. The adjoining island of Holm of Papay is also good for birds (the farmer is the boatman). **Birds** (Fowl Craig) guillemot, razorbill, kittiwake; (heath) oystercatcher, ringed plover, lapwing, dunlin, curlew, snipe; (fields S of reserve) corncrake. **Plants** (Heath) grass of Parnassus, Alpine meadow-rue, awl-leaved pearlwort, Alpine bistort, frog orchid.

ROYAL SOCIETY FOR THE PROTECTION OF BIRDS

E: NORTH RONALDSAY**

Access by ferry or plane from Kirkwall, mainland Orkney; *keep off farm and crofting land; shut gates to prevent sheep straying.*

■ Rocky shore, maritime heath, crofted farmland, loch, marsh.

■ In Sep and Oct there are huge passages of shearwaters and petrels (view from the old beacon; HY 788556), and migrants' fall' in large numbers, including rarities like yellow-browed warbler and bluethroat. Serious birdwatchers should contact Kevin Woodbridge, Bird Observatory, Twingness, North Ronaldsay, KW17 2BE. A perimeter wall keeps the unique North Ronaldsay sheep to the shore and coastal grasslands.

There are no large sea-bird colonies, but black guillemot, Arctic tern, fulmar and a few Arctic skua nest around the coast, duck on the lochs, and many waders in the damper meadows. A few corncrakes lurk in iris beds or hayfields. **Birds** (Summer) common gull, Sandwich tern, curlew, redshank, ringed plover, oystercatcher, snipe, lapwing, shoveler, teal, shelduck, eider, gadwall, pintail, mute swan, twite, skylark, wheatear; (skerry off lighthouse) cormorant. **Plants** (Roadside) meadow cranesbill, sweet cicely, perennial sowthistle; (meadows) ragged robin; (maritime heath) ling and bell heather, devil's-bit scabious.

Below: thrift – see D:1, Noup Cliffs, and many other coastal sites in the Atlas. Opposite, guillemots – see Shetland.

SHETLAND

SHETLAND★★

Daily car ferry Aberdeen-Lerwick (not Sun; 14 hr crossing; P&O Ferries, PO Box 5, Jamieson's Quay, Aberdeen, AB9 8DL). Regular British Airways flights from Aberdeen, Loganair from Edinburgh. Further information from Shetland Tourist Organization, Information Centre, Lerwick, Shetland, ZE1 0LU.

■ Archipelago of about a hundred islands, with more than 3,000 miles (5,000 km) of coastline.

■ Peat is the dominant feature of the Shetland landscape, interspersed with many small lochs, but these support important bird populations.

Shetland has around 80 per cent of whimbrel breeding in Britain, 96 per cent of great skuas, 70 per cent of Arctic skuas, and 60 per cent of red-throated divers, all easily seen from the roads. The vast coastline supports some 10 per cent of British breeding seabirds. By contrast, woodland birds and flowers are restricted to a few poor plantations. The northern latitude makes for a limited but often showy flora: deep red Shetland red campion and flowery plants of tufted vetch are notable on roadsides. The inter-island ferries are cheap, so a multi-centre holiday to explore all the islands is recommended.

A: FAIR ISLE★★

Southernmost of Shetland Group; plane from Tingwall on Mon, Fri and Sat in summer (Loganair, Tingwall Airport, Gott, Shetland); passenger boat, Tues (and Sat May-Sept); 2½ hr crossing (J.W. Stout, Skerryholm, Fair Isle, Shetland). Day visits (7 hrs) may be possible by plane Mons in summer; otherwise book accommodation with Bird Observatory, Fair Isle, ZE2 9JU.

■ Cliffs, crofted farmland, grass moor.

■ Magnificent sea-bird colonies, including storm petrels and 138 pairs of gannets in 1985, but the biggest attraction is migrant birds in May, Jun and early Oct: golden oriole, bluethroat, barred and yellow-browed warblers, red-breasted flycatcher, Lapland bunting, great grey shrike. **Birds** (Breeding) fulmar, shag, kittiwake, common and Arctic terns, puffin, guillemot, black-guillemot, razorbill, great and Arctic skuas, pipits, wheatear, Fair Isle wren. **Plants** Roseroot, sea pink, spring squill, frog orchid, moonwort and adder's-tongue ferns.

NATIONAL TRUST FOR SCOTLAND

B: FOULA★★

W of Mainland Shetland; in summer, boat from Walls, Shetland (HU 240489) Tue, Fri (boatman: Mr Holbourn, Burns, Isle of Foula); weekly flights (details from Tourist Organization). No day visits; essential to book accommodation in advance.

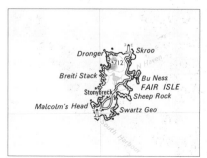

MAP A

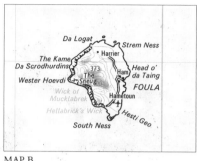

MAP B

■ Cliffs, crofted farmland, grass moorland.

■ Sandstone cliffs rising to 1,220 feet (370 m) harbour 125,000 pairs of sea-birds, including 2,500 pairs of great skuas (1986) – 30 per cent of northern hemisphere population – Arctic skua (180 pairs), Arctic tern (200 pairs), fulmar (40,000 pairs), puffin (35,000 pairs), guillemot, razorbill, black guillemot, shag, kittiwake, Manx shearwater, storm and Leach's petrels, gannet (210 nest sites in 1985).

C:1 SUMBURGH HEAD

Mainland Shetland; pull off road just before lighthouse at HU 408082; keep out of lighthouse grounds.

■ Cliffs.

■ Views of cliff-nesting fulmar, kittiwake, shag and puffin from the lee of the wall beside lighthouse gate. Good sea watching Aug-Oct from below the lighthouse, with sooty shearwater, pomarine and long-tailed skua among the rarer species that may be picked out through a telescope.

C:2 LOCH OF SPIGGIE

Mainland Shetland; near Scousburgh take minor road off B9122 signposted Spiggie; view from beside RSPB hut at HU 373176. No entry to reserve.

■ Shallow fresh water loch, marsh.

■ Teal, shelduck, oystercatcher and curlew nest around the loch, and great and Arctic skuas and kittiwake bathe there in summer.

MAP C

In winter 300 whooper swans and other wildfowl gather on the loch; in spring long-tailed duck display before migrating N to breed. **Invertebrates** Water cricket, water spider, horse leech, freshwater shrimp. **Plants** Bogbean, marsh marigold, mares-tail; (meadow) northern marsh orchid, grass-of-Parnassus.

ROYAL SOCIETY FOR THE PROTECTION OF BIRDS

C:3 MOUSA★

SE of mainland Shetland; day trips by boat. Advance booking essential, contact boatman: Tom Jamieson, Leebitton, Sandwick, Shetland.

■ Sheep-grazed island, fresh water loch, sea lagoon, rocky shore.

■ Storm petrels nest in the superb Pictish broch tower and on the storm beach below (the boatman may be prepared to arrange a late-night trip to hear the petrels). The West Pool at HU 464236 often has both common and grey seals, black guillemots and ringed plover. **Birds** (Moor) great skua; (loch) red-throated diver, kittiwake; wheatear, twite, skylark, meadow pipit; (offshore) gannet; (shore) Arctic tern. **Plants** Frog orchid, thrift.

HISTORIC BUILDINGS & MONUMENTS (SCOTTISH DEVELOPMENT DEPARTMENT)

Razorbills – see Fair Isle.

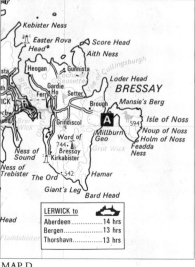

MAP D

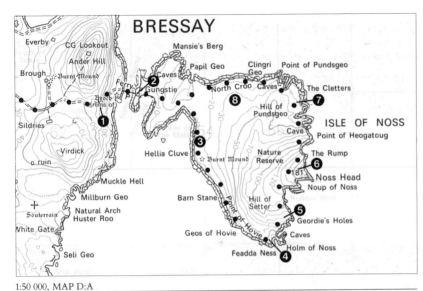

BRESSAY

1:50 000, MAP D:A

D:A ISLE OF NOSS★★

Off Bressay; regular ferry Lerwick-Bressay; 3-mile (5-km) drive across island (or book taxi). No ferry to Noss if stormy; check with Tourist Office (Lerwick 3434) or coastguard; closed Mon, Thur and end Aug-mid May; last ferry 5 pm. An NNR.

■ Rocky coast, cliffs, grass and heather moorland.

① Small car park at road end; walk down track to ferry point. Crossings to Noss by inflatable dingy (fee); not operating if red flag flies on Noss. Wait on rocks and watch terns, skuas, gannet, and perhaps porpoises in channel.

② Gungstie Cottage: NCC displays; guide leaflet; lavatory. Allow 3-4 hours to walk anti-clockwise round coast.

③ Fulmar nests on low, sandy cliff. Black guillemots and seals offshore.

④ View to Cradle Holm: Old Red Sandstone

eroded to horizontal ledges, packed with kittiwakes and guillemots until mid-July; shags low on rocks and puffins on slope beside stack.

⑤ Charlie's Holm: close views of massed puffins beside stack to E. Ledge gives superb view N to the Noup of Noss with over 5,000 gannet nests, guillemot and kittiwake.

⑥ Superb views from Noup. Twite and the sub-species, Shetland wren, in old wall.

⑦ Whiggie Geo: rocky inlet with sea pink, mayweed, roseroot and fulmar.

⑧ No access to skua breeding area. Arctic skua declining to only 18 pairs as great skua increases (about 400 pairs).

Birds (Breeding) herring and greater black-backed gulls, razorbill, red-throated diver, oystercatcher, ringed plover, snipe, rock dove, skylark, meadow and rock pipits, raven. **Mammals** Otter, rabbit, brown rat, common and grey seals.

NATURE CONSERVANCY COUNCIL

MAP E

E:1 RONAS HILL

Mainland Shetland; access on foot from private road to Collafirth Hill at HU 353836; bona fide visitors may be able to take cars with permission from NATO FSS (Shetland), Maybury, Virkie, Shetland.

■ Mountain heath.

■ Particular interest: geomorphological features, for example solifluction terracing. Low altitude Arctic environment: open granite boulder field with Arctic/Alpine plants such as stiff sedge, Alpine lady's-mantle, Alpine bearberry, Alpine clubmoss and bog bilberry; snowy owls and snow buntings are recorded. **Birds** Dotterel, great skua, golden plover. **Plants** Mountain everlasting, sea plantain, Alpine sawwort, dwarf juniper, fir clubmoss, and the moss *Racomitrium lanuginosum*.

BUSTA ESTATE

F:1 FETLAR★★

NE island of Shetland group; ferry from Gutcher (North Yell) or Belmont (Unst) three times daily in summer; book cars in advance telephone Burravoe 259 or 268). Warden's house is 2½ miles (4 km) from ferry at HU 604916 (roadside parking). No access to sanctuary in summer without warden (Bealance, Fetlar, ZE2 9DJ).

■ Grass and heather moorland, bog, cliff, sandy and rocky coast, loch, pools.

■ About a hundred people live on this small island, making their living from crofting and farming. The RSPB manages 1,700 acres of moorland, rising to the summits of Vord Hill and Stackaberg, as a bird sanctuary. Arctic skua, whimbrel and Arctic tern breed here in nationally important numbers, with great skua, golden plover, dunlin, and merlin. Snowy owls bred here from 1969 to 1975, and an odd female may still remain. Red-throated divers on some of the lochs; Loch of Funzie is a good site to see red-necked phalarope (view from car at roadside at HU 654901). **Mammals** Common and grey seals, otter, rabbit, hedgehog, house and field mice. **Plants** Moonwort, frog orchid, dwarf race of goldenrod.

RSPB

F:2 LUMBISTER, YELL

N of Shetland group; car ferry from Toft (N Mainland) to Ulsta (S Yell). View to W of

A968 from Mid Yell. Limited access to reserve from lay-by at HU 509974; no paths. Do not disturb breeding birds.

■ Heather moorland, bog, lochs, rocky shore.

■ The main function of this reserve is to protect nesting sites of such birds as whimbrel, red-throated diver, great and Arctic skua, golden plover and dunlin, from any development (including commercial peat extraction), all of which can be seen better from the roadside elsewhere. **Birds** Curlew, snipe, red-breasted merganser, merlin, skylark, meadow pipit, wheatear; (cliffs) fulmar, puffin, black guillemot, shag, raven. **Plants** Lesser twayblade orchid.

ROYAL SOCIETY FOR THE PROTECTION OF BIRDS

F:3 HERMA NESS★★

N tip of Unst; park at roadside at HP 614147, follow path to cliffs; shelter, with latest bird news, on path at HP 608172. Keep to marked paths and cliff top (very slippery).

■ Cliff, rock stacks, grass moor.

■ This NNR provides some of Shetland's most exciting birdwatching. Over 800 pairs of great skua nest on the moorland heart of the peninsula, and attack anyone who leaves the path. (Hold a stick above your head to keep them at bay.) They share their habitat with dunlin, golden plover and a few Arctic skua. The coast has over 14,000 gannet nest sites, on Muckle Flugga, Clingra Stack (view from HP 601178) and Saito (HP 597165). Near Clingra are masses of puffins, while Saito was the home from 1972 of a lone black-browed albatross from the southern hemisphere, which finally may have disappeared in July 1987. **Birds** Guillemot, razorbill, puffin, kittiwake, fulmar, red-throated diver, whimbrel, twite, Shetland wren.

NATURE CONSERVANCY COUNCIL

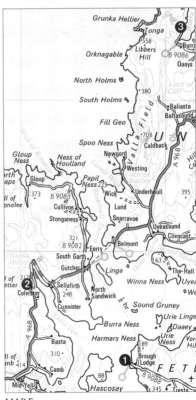

MAP F

IRELAND

The panoramic Lady's View (left) looking north from the Ring of Kerry across the Killarney Valley, is typical of Ireland's mountains, lake and woodland scenery and famous worldwide as one of the country's most beautiful regions.

Otters (above) are rare and declining animals over much of Great Britain, but Ireland has more otters than any comparable area of Europe. Webbed feet (rarely glimpsed) rapidly propel the long, muscular, streamlined body through the water. The ears, eyes and nostrils are set high on the head to assist surface swimming and stiff whiskers provide sensory perception when diving along muddy river beds.

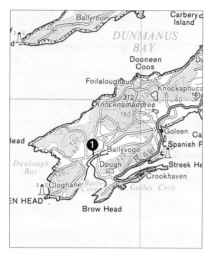

MAP A

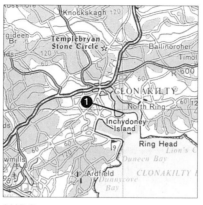

MAP C

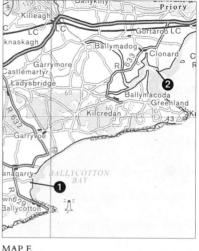

MAP E

A:1 LISSAGRIFFIN LAKE

Near Skull; from Skull take Barley Cove road and turn right after Goleen.

■ Lake, salt-marsh, sand dunes.

■ Shallow sandy lake important for wildfowl and waders. American waders in autumn.

B:1 CLEAR ISLAND★★

Off Baltimore; boat from Baltimore; accommodation available on island; bird observatory building.

■ Marine island, cliffs, bog.

■ Breeding sea-birds including fulmar and black guillemot; choughs; rare passerines; extensive offshore sea-bird movements. Interesting bog vegetation.

Common grey sea slug – see B:2.

B:2 LOUGH HYNE

Near Baltimore; best access on S shore.

■ Sea inlet, rocky shore.

■ This NNR is a deep land-locked bay, joined to the Atlantic by a narrow, shallow channel, so that tides are reduced to 3 feet (one m) or so. Bathymetrical telescoping encourages deep-water animals such as sea slugs, sponges, and sea urchins living close to water surface. The concentration of the intertidal zone and the warmth and shelter of the waters combine to produce a rich fauna. Extremely large forms of eel grass. Best Apr-Oct.
WILDLIFE SERVICE

C:1 CLONAKILTY BAY

Clonakilty; extensive area with multiple access points.

■ Mudflats, salt-marsh, dunes.

■ Large numbers of waders (up to 10,000) and wildfowl use the estuary. Interesting flowers on sand dunes. **Plants** Frosted orache, teasel, mullein, viper's-bugloss.

D:1 LOUGH BEG

Near Ringaskiddy; parking outside Pen chemicals factory; Irish Wildbird Conservancy observation hide.

■ Mudflats, salt-marsh.

■ Mudflats important for wildfowl and waders. Unusual plants on shingle bank with grassland. **Plants** Fluellen, round-leaved crane's-bill, pepperwort.

D:2 WHITEGATE MUDFLATS

Whitegate; adjacent road makes useful viewpoint.

■ Mudflats.

■ Easy views of waders and wildfowl characteristic of Cork Harbour – dunlin, wigeon, knot, oystercatcher. Best Oct-Apr.

MAP D

D:3 ROSTELLAN LAKE

Near Aghada; adjacent road makes useful viewpoint.

■ Lake with brackish water.

■ Impounded lake with alder scrub at E end. Good birdlife and aquatic vegetation. Best Oct-Apr.

E:1 BALLYCOTTON BAY

Ballycotton; multiple access points.

■ Coastal marsh, lagoons, salt-marsh.

■ Important wetland area for wildfowl and waders. Interesting marsh plants. **Birds** Rare American waders, black-tailed and bar-tailed godwits.

E:2 BALLYMACODA, CLONPRIEST & PILLMORE

Near Youghal; multiple access points.

■ Grassland, mudflats, salt-marsh.

■ Extensive open wetland habitat for wintering wildfowl. **Birds** Rare American waders, black-tailed and bar-tailed godwits.

F:1 KILCOLMAN BOG

Near Buttevant; contact Kilcolman Wildfowl Refuge (022) 24200.

■ Lake, fen, typha reed-bed.

■ Site of former lake, now partially covered over by marsh and fen. Important wildfowl sanctuary with good viewing facilities. **Birds** Bewick's and whooper swans, Greenland white-fronted goose. **Plants** Greater spearwort, bogbean, marsh willowherb, ragged robin.

MAP B

MAP F

MAP A

A:1 GREAT SKELLIG*

Off Valencia Island; access by boat from Valencia Island: contact Des Lavelle, 0667 6124. Great Skellig is closed to allow repairs to monastic settlement – except by special arrangement.

■ Marine island, sea-bird cliffs.
■ Great Skellig has a large colony of nesting sea-birds with upwards of 10,000 pairs of storm petrel and 5,000 pairs of Manx shearwater. There are up to 6,000 pairs of razorbill and fulmar with lesser numbers of puffin, kittiwake and guillemot. The remains of the monastic settlement are of archaeological importance.
NATIONAL PARKS & MONUMENTS SERVICE

A:2 PUFFIN ISLAND*

Off Valencia Island: access by boat from Valencia Island: contact Des Lavelle, 0667 6124. No permit required for day visit. Contact IWC, 8 Longford Place, Blackrock, Co. Dublin, to arrange a longer visit.

■ Marine island, grassland, sea-bird cliffs.
■ Puffin Island has probably the largest colony (about 7,000 pairs) of Manx shearwater in Ireland. There are also at least 3,000 pairs of puffin and 1,000 pairs of storm petrel, with razorbill, guillemot, kittiwake, fulmar, common gull, shag and three other gull species. Best Apr–Aug.
IRISH WILDBIRD CONSERVANCY

B:1 LAMB'S HEAD

Near Caherdaniel; take coast road to Lamb's Head, park on roadside and walk.

■ Rocky headland, bog, heath.
■ Typical blanket bog flora with the rare Kerry lily and juniper in drier areas.

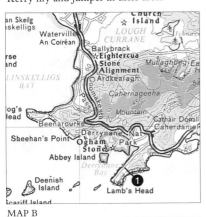

MAP B

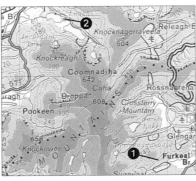

MAP C

C:1 GLENGARRIFF WOODLAND

Near Glengarriff; easy access from Glengariff to Kenmare road.

■ Oak woodland.
■ Woodland with birch and rowan and a well-developed holly understorey; strawberry-tree, filmy-ferns; rich fern, moss and liverwort ground-flora. Best Apr–Oct.
WILDLIFE SERVICE

C:2 URAGH WOOD & CLOONEE LOUGHS

Near Kenmare; car park.

■ Oak wood, lake, bog.
■ Typical shallow soil oak wood with small trees and holly understorey. Interesting aquatic vegetation. An NNR. **Plants** Quillwort, pipewort, waterwort, filmy-ferns, strawberry-tree, juniper.
WILDLIFE SERVICE

D:1 DERRYCUNIHY & GALWAY'S WOODS

Near Killarney; approach from road at Galway's bridge.

■ Oak/holly wood.
■ A classic oak wood with abundant mosses, ferns and lichens. Rich bird- and insect life. **Mammals** Red deer. **Plants** Lesser twayblade, white helleborine, filmy-ferns.
NATIONAL PARKS SERVICE

D:2 TORC CASCADE

Near Killarney; park by roadside and approach on foot.

■ Upland stream.

MAP D

■ Luxuriant growth of mosses, liverworts and ferns, including filmy-ferns, on rocks by stream. Rich insect and mollusc fauna.
NATIONAL PARKS SERVICE

D:3 MUCKROSS WOOD

Near Killarney; access from Muckross House (worth a visit – folk museum).

■ Yew/oak woodland.
■ Contrasting woodland with yew and whitebeam to E on limestone and oak and strawberry-tree on W sandstone section.
NATIONAL PARKS SERVICE

D:4 ROSS ISLAND

Near Killarney; road access.

■ Ash/yew wood.
■ Woodland on carboniferous limestone with a herb-rich ground flora.
NATIONAL PARKS SERVICE

D:5 TOMIES WOOD

Near Killarney; on W side of Lough Leane: approach from N.

■ Oak wood.
■ A comparatively open oak wood with some birch. Grazed by Sika deer and almost free from rhododendron.
NATIONAL PARKS SERVICE

E:1 ROSSBEHY

Near Glenbeigh; car park.

■ Sand dunes, salt-marsh, mudflats.
■ A sand and shingle spit enclosing salt-marsh and mudflats. Interesting flora and wintering wildfowl. **Birds** Chough. **Plants** Yellow-wort.

E:2 CARAGH LAKE

Near Glenbeigh; many access points by road around lake.

■ Lake, oak wood.
■ A rich aquatic flora, both submerged and visible. Oak wood patches on slopes. **Plants** Quillwort, pipewort, waterwort, flexible naiad.

E:3 INCH SPIT & MUDFLATS*

Near Anascaul; car park N end of dunes; walk into dunes from here.

■ Sand dunes, dune slacks, salt-marsh, mudflats.
■ The spit holds the finest dune belt in the country with a representative W coast dune flora. The salt-marsh to the E grades into extensive mudflats with large areas of eelgrass. Large numbers of wintering wildfowl: wigeon, pintail, shoveler, teal and pale-breasted brent goose. Flowers include field gentian, sea pansy, corn salad. **Amphibians** Natterjack toad.

MAP E

MAP F

F:1 LOUGH GILL★
Near Castlegregory; access at many obvious points.
■ Lake, sand dunes, reed-bed.
■ The Castlegregory spit which extends N to link some of the Maharee Islands is a large tombolo (see page 13). Lough Gill occurs in its centre, a shallow lake with rich feeding for fish and birds. There are up to 4,000 teal, 2,000 tufted duck, 1,500 shoveler and 100 gadwall. Choughs are frequently seen. The dune flora is one of the richest in the county.

G:1 AKERAGH LOUGH★
Near Ballyheige; walk along dunes S of Ballyheige: views down into lough.
■ Shallow brackish lagoon, salt-marsh, sand dunes.
■ The lagoon lies behind a line of lush dunes. Fresh and salt water plant communities show interesting transition. The large number of wintering wildfowl include teal, gadwall and curlew. Probably the best place in Ireland for American waders during autumn. Flora includes strawberry clover, water-dropwort, sea club-rush, grey club-rush and sea rush.

LIMERICK

A:1 LOUGH GUR★
Near Bruff; road on S shore gives access.

MAP G

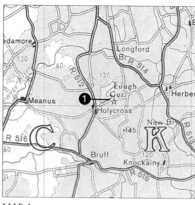

MAP A

■ Lake, marsh, fen.
■ Eutrophic lake important for rich flora and invertebrate fauna which provide food for large wintering wildfowl population. Also important for sub-fossil remains of giant Irish elk. Best Oct-Apr.

Chough – see F:1. Not difficult to separate from other crows – the down-curved bill is unmistakable, as are the red feet in close views.

B:1 SHANNON ESTUARY – AUGHINISH/ASKEATON
Near Askeaton; access on numerous unclassified roads. Respect the farmland.
■ Mudflats, grassland.
■ Probably the third most important section of the Shannon estuary for wildfowl and waders. Best Oct-Apr. **Birds** Bar-tailed godwit, scaup, wigeon, curlew, teal.

MAP B

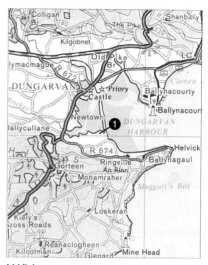

MAP A

WATERFORD

A:1 DUNGARVAN HARBOUR
Dungarvan.
■ Mudflats, shingle spit.
■ Extensive intertidal mudflats important for wintering wildfowl. Largest wader flocks in county. Best Oct-Apr. **Birds** Black-tailed godwit, paled-breasted brent goose, grey plover, knot.

B:1 TRAMORE DUNES & MUDFLATS
Tramore; park at beach and walk to dunes.
■ Sand dunes, mudflats.
■ Well-developed dune system with interesting flora. Mudflats behind dunes important for wintering wildfowl. **Plants** Sea knotgrass. **Birds** Grey plover.

B:2 COOLFIN MARSHES
Near Portlaw; park on roadside just after turning to Portlaw from Waterford (L26).
■ Grassland.
■ Wet grassland beside River Suir. Main site in Munster for wintering greylag goose, present Oct-Apr.

MAP B

TIPPERARY/KILKENNY

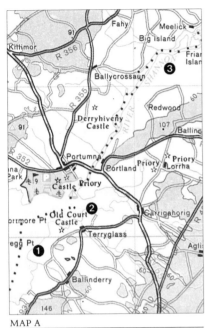

MAP A

TIPPERARY

A:1 CORNALACK WOOD
*Near **Ballinderry** track to wood and lake shore.*
■ Yew/juniper wood.
■ Well-developed woodland on limestone soil; rich ground flora.

A:2 LOUGH DERG – SLEVOIR BAY & GORTMORE POINT*
*Near **Terryglass**; approach on coast road.*
■ Reed-bed, lakeshore, hazel/ash woodland.
■ Large bay at head of Lough Derg with extensive reed-beds and a diversity of habitats. Rich birdlife.

A:3 REDWOOD BOG
*Near **Portumna**; road access.*
■ Raised bog.
■ A well-developed wet raised bog crossed by several eskers (see page 13). Best Oct-Apr. **Birds** Greenland white-fronted goose.

Waders – see A:1, opposite page. High tide is usually the best time to view wader flocks because they tend to be concentrated along the high water mark.

KILKENNY

A:1 OAKPARK
*Near **Carlow;** from Carlow take Athy road (L18) N; turn right in 1½ miles (2.5 km) to Oak Park.*
■ Lake, reed-bed, mixed woodland.
■ Largest area of standing water in county, good for wildfowl and woodland birds.
AGRICULTURAL RESEARCH INSTITUTE

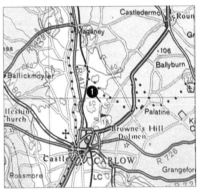

MAP A

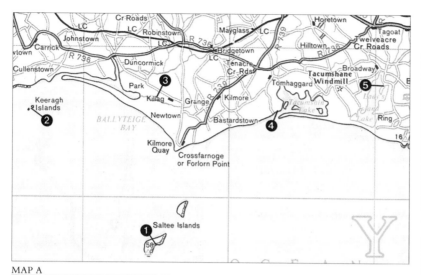

MAP A

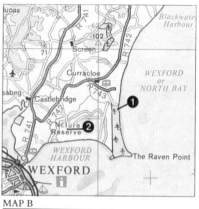

MAP B

A:1 GREAT SALTEE ISLAND★★

Kilmore Quay; from N25 turn right for Kilmore Quay signposted 4 miles (6 km) out of Wexford. Enquire at Kilmore Quay about boat trips to the island, daily during summer. As a courtesy to the owner, write for permission to visit to Prince Michael Neal, 2 Green Park, Orwell Park, Rathgar, Dublin 6.

■ Marine island.

■ One of the most important breeding sea-bird colonies in Ireland, with 11 species, including Manx shearwater. Occasional chough, peregrine and raven. Easy to observe all sea-birds. Important bird migration observation and ringing station, many rarities recorded.

Bird observatory is now closed, but operated informally. Details from Oscar Merne, Wildlife Service, Sidmonton Place, Bray, Co. Wicklow, 01-867751. Best Mar-Oct. **Birds** Gannet, puffin, razorbill, guillemot, kittiwake, shag. **Plants** Sea spleenwort, golden-samphire.

A:2 KEERAGH ISLANDS

Near Kilmore Quay; contact warden, Jim Hurley, Grange, Kilmore, Co. Wexford. 053-29671.

■ Marine island, shingle/rocky shore, grassland.

■ Formerly important breeding site for common, Arctic and little tern. Five per cent of the national cormorant population breeds here. Best Apr-Sep. **Birds** Sandwich tern, shag, ringed plover.
IRISH WILDBIRD CONSERVANCY

A:3 BALLYTEIGE SAND DUNES★

Near Wexford; from N25 turn right for Kilmore Quay, signposted about 4 miles (6 km) out of Wexford. Park at Kilmore Quay; walk into dunes.

■ Sand dunes, dune slack, mudflats, salt-marsh.

■ Extensive sand dune system stretching 6 miles (9 km) W of Kilmore Quay. Interesting vegetation, invertebrates and birds. Only Irish locality for lichen, *Fulgensia subbracteata* and a rich invertebrate fauna. An NNR. **Plants** Wild asparagus, Portland spurge, red goosefoot, perennial glasswort.

A:4 TACUMSHIN LAKE★

Near Tomhaggard; take turning to Ballyhealy at Kilmore Quay road; continue to W end of Tacumshin.

■ Salt-marsh, mudflats, dunes.

■ A drained lake with interesting tidal mudflat vegetation and large populations of waders, wildfowl and other birds. **Plants** Sea-blite, sea orache, glasswort, eelgrass, tasselweed. **Birds** Pale-breasted brent goose, pintail, shoveler, wigeon. **Molluscs** Cockles, mussels and sand gaper.

A:5 LADY'S ISLAND LAKE★

Near Rosslare Harbour; signposted Lady's Island from N25.

■ Brackish lake, islands, reed-bed, shingle shore.

■ Large, shallow, brackish lake of botanical and ornithological interest. **Plants** Cottonweed, pondweeds, stoneworts. **Birds** Sandwich and roseate terns, wigeon, rare waders.
WILDLIFE SERVICE

B:1 THE RAVEN

Near Wexford; from Wexford to Gorey road 2, miles (3.5 km) N of Wexford take turning signposted Curracloe. Follow road to nature reserve; parking.

■ Sand dune, dune slack, Corsican pine plantation.

■ Best example of sand dune system with

Gannet with young – see A:1.

dune slacks in County Wexford; an NNR. **Birds** Long-eared owl, sparrowhawk. **Mammals** Irish hare, red squirrel, badger. **Invertebrates** Woodlouse *Armadillidium album*, beetle *Eury nebria complanata*.
WILDLIFE SERVICE

B:2 WEXFORD WILDFOWL RESERVE★★

Near Wexford; signposted from Wexford to Gorey road, 3 miles (5 km) N of Wexford; car park; open all year.

■ Grassland (reclaimed estuary mudflats), drainage channels, reed-beds, farmland.

■ Ireland's premier wildfowl reserve; look over embankment wall for waders, divers, grebes and common scoter. Watch geese flighting at dawn from harbour roost to North Slobs.

Check main channel for shoveler, pintail, scaup, pochard, goldeneye and Bewick's swan.

Views from observation tower of Greenland white-fronted goose grazing pasture. Up to 1,500 pale-breasted brent geese can also occur here. Rarer species are small transatlantic Canadian, snow, barnacle, pink-footed and Russian white-fronted geese. Good for birds of prey, too.

For the intrepid only: walk along sea wall keeping your body outline below horizon: waders feeding on mudflats. Work your way to Raven Point, good for sea-birds.
WILDLIFE SERVICE/IRISH WILDBIRD CONSERVANCY/PRIVATE OWNERSHIP

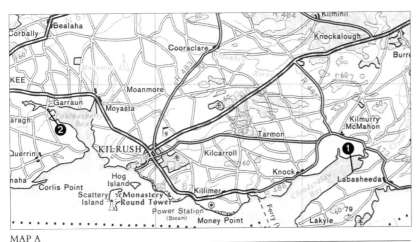

MAP A

A:1 CLONDERALAW BAY
Near Kilrush; turn off L51 outside Labasheda to bay shore.
■ Mudflats, salt-marsh.
■ Bay off Shannon estuary important especially for wildfowl. Best Oct–Apr.

A:2 POULNASHERRY BAY
Near Kilrush; on Kilrush-Kilkee road (N67), turn S at W end of bay to Querrin.
■ Mudflats, salt-marsh.
■ Bay off Shannon estuary important for wildfowl. Best Oct–Apr. **Birds** Pale-breasted brent goose, waders.

MAP B

B:1 CLIFFS OF MOHER★★
Near Ennistimon; from Ennistimon take coast road to Liscannor; cliffs are signposted; car park, visitor centre.
■ Sea-bird cliffs.
■ Vertical cliffs with unsurpassed views of breeding sea-birds: razorbill, guillemot, puffin, kittiwake, fulmar.

C:1 LOUGH ATEDAUN
Near Corrofin park in Corrofin and walk.
■ Lake.
■ Limestone lake important for wintering wildfowl. Best Oct–Apr. **Birds** Bewick's and whooper swans, waders.

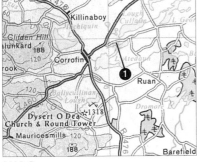

MAP C

MAP D

D:1 CAHERMURPHY WOODLAND
Near Gort; from N18 wood is 2 miles (3 km) N.
■ Oak woodland.
■ Intact oak woodland with sound structure and ground communities. An NNR. **Mammals** Badger.
WILDLIFE SERVICE

E:1 MULLAGH MORE★★
Near Corrofin; from the Corrofin to Killinaboy road, turn right at Killinaboy, then take second right fork: a rough, narrow road.
■ Turlough, limestone pavement, hazel/elm wood.
■ Burren flora and a diversity of habitats: folded carboniferous limestone on hill. Best May–Aug. For explanation of turlough see page 13. **Mammals** Pine marten. **Plants** Maidenhair fern, dense-flowered orchid, shrubby cinquefoil.
NATIONAL PARKS SERVICE/PRIVATE OWNERSHIP

E:2 POULAVALLAN & GLEN OF CLAB★
Near Carran; from Carran take Kinvara road 2½ miles (4 km). Park at woodland site on left and walk up wood to Poulavallan.
■ Hazel/ash wood.
■ Best woodland of its kind in Burren. Curious and dramatic land depression (doline). Abundant ferns and mosses. Best May–Aug.

E:3 BLACK HEAD★★
Near Ballyvaghan; follow coast road W from Ballyvaghan, stop at headland and park in lay-by.
■ Calcareous grassland, limestone pavement.
■ Unique assemblage of plants: spring gentian, mountain avens, bloody crane's-bill, mossy saxifrage, bearberry, wintergreen. Best May–Aug.

E:4 POULSALLAGH★
Near Lisdoonvarna; from Lisdoonvarna take Black Head road; park where it meets coast.
■ Calcareous grassland, limestone pavement.
■ Typical Burren flora with high species density. Purple sea urchins in rock hollows on shore. Best May–Aug. **Plants** Pyramidal bugle, spring gentian, orchids.

E:5 FANORE DUNES★
Near Lisdoonvarna; on coast road from Lisdoonvarna to Black Head, dunes are 2½ miles (4 km) before Black Head; car park.
■ Sand dunes, exposed limestone pavement.
■ The only large sand dunes in the Burren, also the only surface river. Best May–Aug.

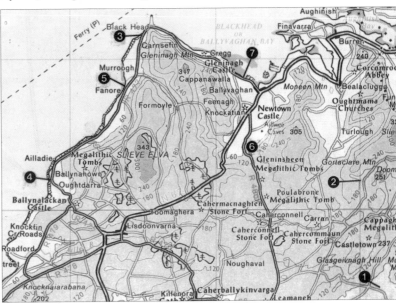

MAP E

Oak flowers – see F:3.

Plants Lady's-tresses, lesser dodder. **Birds** Chough, waders.

E:6 AILWEE CAVE★★
Near Ballyvaghan; signposted from Bally- vaghan. Car park, visitor centre.
■ Cave.
■ Best single tunnel cave in Ireland with full range of cave features (including calcite curtains and brown bear remains).

E:7 BALLYVAGHAN BAY
Ballyvaghan.
■ Salt-marsh, shingle spit, mudflats.
■ Estuarine habitat for wildfowl and wad- ers. **Birds** Pale-breasted brent goose, terns. **Mammals** Grey seal.

F:1 LOUGH BUNNY★
Near Gort; on Corrofin to Boston road.
■ Lake, limestone pavement.
■ Calcareous lake with washed up shells forming small beaches; Burren flora. Best May-Aug. **Plants** Orchids, dropwort.

F:2 SLIEVECARRAN WOOD★
Near Kinvara; from Kinvara take Carran road. Wood at cliff base in 4 miles (6.5 km).
■ Hazel/ash wood.
■ One of the most natural tracts of wood- land in the Burren. An NNReserve. Best May-Aug.
WILDLIFE SERVICE

F:3 GARRYLAND & COOLE
Near Gort; signposted on N18 from Gort.
■ Oak/ash woodland, turlough.
■ Woodland on limestone with one of the few semi-natural stands of pedunculate oak in Ireland. Best Apr-Oct. For explanation of turlough, see page 13. **Birds** Whooper swan. **Mammals** Pine marten.
WILDLIFE SERVICE

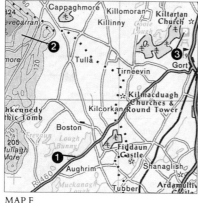

MAP F

MAP A

GALWAY

A:1 RAHASANE TURLOUGH★
Craughwell; on the Loughrea to Galway road: turn first left after railway level crossing outside Craughwell.
■ Grassland, lake.
■ The last remaining turlough (see page 13) in the country with a permanent river, the Dunkellin, flowing through it. The fairy shrimp, *Tanymastrix,* occurs. Damp grass- land extends out from the water body to limestone outcrops, sometimes covered by blackthorn and hazel scrub, a habitat for in- teresting butterflies.

Rahasane Turlough is one of the most im- portant wildfowl wetlands in Ireland and is unique in Europe. Bewick's and whooper

MAP B

swans, shoveler, wigeon, teal and Green- land white-fronted goose. Up to 20,000 waders (mostly golden plover) occur at times. Rare waders have been recorded. However, unless winter water levels are low, Rahasane can be a disappointing visit. Best Oct-Apr.

B:1 GENTIAN HILL & LOUGH RUISIN
Near Galway.
■ Mudflats, beech wood, grassland.
■ Lough Ruisin is important for wintering wildfowl and waders. Gentian Hill has cal- careous soils with a flora similar to the Bur- ren, including spring gentian.

B:2 LOUGH CORRIB: S END
Near Galway; best viewed from marble quarry at Menlough, N of Galway.
■ Lake, reed-beds.
■ Major autumnal staging area for diving waterfowl with up to 10 per cent of NW Europe's pochard population. Best Oct- Apr.

B:3 LOUGH CORRIB: MOUNT ROSS INLET
Near Headford; take road to Annaghdown for some 5 miles (8 km) S of Headford and continue to Corrib shore.
■ Lake inlet, reed-beds.
■ Important summer and winter wildfowl habitat. **Birds** Greenland white-fronted goose (on offshore island), great crested grebe, shoveler.

C:1 AILLEBRACK★
Near Ballyconneely; approach on coast road from Doon Hill.
■ Calcareous grassland, sand dunes.
■ An extensive low-lying area of sand dunes with dune slacks, calcareous grassland and an area of salt-marsh. The rich flora con- tains many Burren species which flourish here because of the calcium content of animal and plant remains. Irish eyebright, squinancywort, lady's-tresses, pyramidal and dense-flowered (*Neofinea intacta*) orchids. Breeding area for ringed plover, dunlin and lapwing. Terns on offshore islands. Check nearby Bunowen Castle for nesting chough. Best Apr-Oct.

D:1 ERRISBEG BLANKET BOG★
Near Roundstone; best access is by road across bog from Toombeola to Ballinaboy. Take care –

MAP C

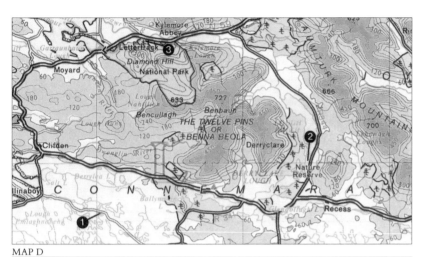

MAP D

and drive around lough.

■ Oak wood, lake.

■ Old, semi-natural oak wood with rich communities of lichen and invertebrates. Interesting aquatic vegetation. An NNR. Best Apr-Oct. **Plants** Pillwort, awlwort, pipewort.

WILDLIFE SERVICE

D:3 CONNEMARA NAT. PARK**
Near Letterfrack; *signposted on Clifden to Letterfrack road (N59); car park and visitor centre, open all year.*

■ Blanket bog, heath, mountain, oak woodland, acid grassland.

■ The visitor centre has an audio-visual display. See also the herd of red deer and pure-bred Connemara ponies. From here take the woodland nature trail.

On the blanket bog you will find cross-leaved and bell heather, sundews, louse-wort, cottongrass, bog asphodel and bog myrtle. St Dabeoc's heath is a speciality.

Where peat has been cut for fuel, pine stumps, up to 4,000 years old, are often exposed. Up to 15 feet (4.5 m) of peat lie on top of granite, boulder clay and gravels.

Birds of prey include peregrine, merlin, kestrel and sparrowhawk. Meadow pipit, stonechat, snipe and woodcock breed. Mammals of the park include badger, stoat and fox. Bats are often seen.

Best from Easter to the end of Sep.

NATIONAL PARK SERVICE

the bog is very wet.

■ Blanket bog, oak/holly woodland on islands, lakes, exposed rock.

■ Outstanding example of lowland blanket bog extending N of Errisbeg with patches of heath on rocky outcrops. Numerous small lakes have interesting aquatic flora with oak/

Bloody crane's-bill, a rare native perennial found on dry rocky places, sand dunes and on limestone, including some of the Burren sites on these pages.

holly woodland surviving on islands. Some tree-nesting cormorants. Many heather species including the Dorset heath, Mackay's heath and Mediterranean heath. Merlin and common lizard frequently seen. Landing site of transatlantic fliers Alcock and Brown nearby.

D:2 DERRYCLARE WOOD & LOUGH INAGH
Near Clifden; *take the Letterfrack turning off the Maam Cross to Clifden road. Walk to wood*

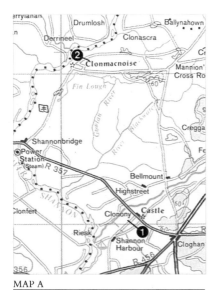

MAP A

OFFALY

A:1 LITTLE BROSNA RIVER★★
Near Birr; several minor roads on either side of river.
■ River, grassland, marsh, flooded pasture.
■ The river flood plain and associated marshes form one of Ireland's most outstanding areas for wintering wildfowl and waders. Numbers fluctuate with degree of flooding on the callow lands. There are large numbers of Greenland white-fronted goose, black-tailed godwit, golden plover, pintail, wigeon, shoveler, teal. Best Oct–Apr.

A:2 MONGAN'S BOG★★
Near Clonmacnoise; best access near a lay-by on road at W end of bog; as a matter of courtesy seek permission to visit from An Taisce, Tailor's Hall, Dublin 8.
■ Raised bog.
■ One of the best examples of raised bog in Ireland with well-developed hummock and pool system. It lies between two eskers (see page 13) close to the monastic settlement at Clonmacnoise (also worth a visit). The bog is well and regenerating. All characteristic species of raised bog are found. Greenland white-fronted goose roosts regularly.
AN TAISCE (NATIONAL TRUST FOR IRELAND)

Top, pintail; above, shoveler – see A:1, Offaly.

B:1 CLARA BOG★★
Near Clara; the road to Rahan, 1¼ miles (2 km) S of Clara, bisects the bog.
■ Raised bog.
■ One of the largest raised bogs in Ireland and the only one with a well-developed soak system consisting of a series of interconnecting lakes which are rich in minerals. Around the lakes can be found marsh-orchids, royal fern, marsh pennywort, bogbean and cottongrass. Shrubs include crowberry and cranberry. There is a swampy birch woodland with willow, bilberry and bog myrtle.
WILDLIFE SERVICE

B:2 KILTOBER ESKER
Near Tullamore; S of Kiltober on road to Tullamore via Murphy's Bridge; roadside parking.
■ Hazel/ash woodland.
■ The esker (see page 13) supports probably the most natural woodland in the county on such a site. Interesting ground flora.

MAP A

LAOIS

A:1 TIMAHOE ESKERS★
Near Timahoe; approach on roads N or E of Timahoe; park and walk to ridges.
■ Eskers, mixed woodland.
■ One of the best examples of eskers (see page 13) in the country showing branching and other characteristic features. W part is covered by hazel woodland but is being excavated. E ridge partly planted by western hemlock, Japanese larch and spruce species. Hazel, oak and some ash also occur. Good for birds. An NNR.

Common hazel nuts – see A:1.

B:1 SLIEVE BLOOM MOUNTAINS★
Near Kinnitty; take Kinnitty to Mountrath road and park car at highest point on mountain. Walk to summit.
■ Blanket bog.
■ Fine example of upland blanket bog with typical flora. **Plants** Bog asphodel, fir clubmoss, crowberry, deergrass. **Birds** Red grouse, merlin.
WILDLIFE SERVICE

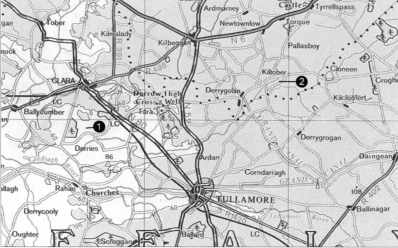

MAP B

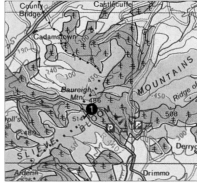

MAP B

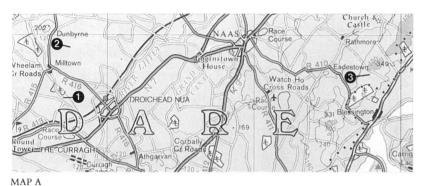

MAP A

KILDARE

A:1 POLLARDSTOWN FEN*
Near Newbridge; take Rathagan road from Newbridge, park close to fen and walk in.
■ Fen.
■ Best developed fen in Ireland with largest area of great fen-sedge in western Europe. **Plants** Black bog-rush, fly, marsh-, spotted- and butterfly-orchids.
WILDLIFE SERVICE/PRIVATE OWNERSHIP

A:2 MOULD'S BOG*
Near Newbridge; many access points from neighbouring roads.

Lesser butterfly orchid – see A:1, above.

■ Raised bog.
■ An extensive and well-preserved raised bog. Deep *Sphagnum* moss with much cottongrass, crowberry and cranberry. Some of the surface bog pools remain open. Drier parts of bog have tall heather. Good examples of bog 'regeneration' with alternating hummocks and hollows. **Birds** Red grouse, stonechat.

A:3 REDBOG
Near Blessington; take Rathmore road from Blessington.
■ Lake.
■ Lake lying between morainic ridges, with extensive floating vegetation comprised of bogbean.

MAP A

WICKLOW

A:1 RATHDRUM WOODS
Near Rathdrum; on Laragh road one mile (1.5 km) N or Rathdrum.
■ Oak woodland.
■ Mixed wood with highest proportion oak in central part of wood. Well-developed ground flora. **Plants** Sanicle, yellow pimpernel.
FOREST SERVICE

A:2 GLENDALOUGH VALLEY**
Near Laragh; signposted from adjacent roads; car park, nature trail and picnic tables.
■ Oak woodland, marsh, lake, heath, heather moor.
■ A fine glaciated valley with well-developed mixed woodlands: oak, hazel, birch and Scot's pine. Ground flora include woodrush, bell heather, cross-leaved heath and hard fern.
  Marsh at W edge of upper lake is dominated by common reed with bottle sedge, marsh St John's-wort and marsh violet. White water-lily, broad-leaved pondweed and bulbous rush in lake. Shore of lower lake is just as interesting. The early Christian monastic settlement is also worth a visit.
NATIONAL PARKS AND WILDLIFE SERVICE/ PRIVATE OWNERSHIP

B:1 BRITTAS BAY & BUCKRONEY MARSH
Near Arklow; take the coast road, turning right off L29 (Arklow to Wicklow) just outside Arklow and continue 5 miles (8 km) to Buckroney Marsh. Continue to sand dunes.
■ Sand dunes, fen, grassland.
■ Extensive dune system with well-developed plant communities. Buckroney Marsh lies at the S end of the dunes. **Plants** Marsh fern, meadow saxifrage, sharp rush.

B:2 GLEN OF THE DOWNS
Near Bray; 5 miles (8 km) S of Bray on Wicklow road; car park and nature trail.
■ Oak woodland.
■ Nationally important oak woodland with rich ground flora set in a glacial overflow channel. Best Apr-Oct. **Plants** Sanicle, pignut, spindle, ramsons.
WILDLIFE SERVICE

B:3 THE MURROUGH**

Near Newcastle; take rough road at New-castle E to Six Mile Point. Park car thoughtfully on roadside at railway line.

■ Coastal marsh, lagoons, fen, reed-beds, sand dunes, shingle beach, grassland.

■ A remarkable mosaic of habitats stretching 9½ miles (15 km) along coastline, rich with birds and flowers.

Walking N beside the railway track, on shingle beach, note the sea rocket and pur-slane. Look for hottentot-fig, dwarf spurge, common broomrape and lesser toadflax between railway and dunes. Further N, little tern breed on beach. Three birds of prey breed in area.

Further N still, greylag goose, whooper swan, wigeon, teal, dunlin, golden plover and pintail are present in winter.

At least 23 species of rare flowering plants occur in the area.

Bearded tits have nested in reed-beds S of Six Mile Point.

Sea-birds offshore include black guille-mot, common tern, kittiwake and several gull species.

MAP B

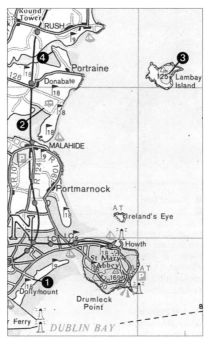

MAP A

DUBLIN

A:1 NORTH BULL ISLAND*

Near Dublin; best access across causeway. Park near visitor centre where there is an educa-tional display.

■ Mudflats, salt-marsh, sand dunes, dune slack, grassland, sandy beach.

■ A unique assemblage of habitats, and the best place to observe wildfowl and waders in Dublin: up to 25,000 birds of 15 species with the highest densities in the country. Pale-breasted brent goose, pintail, shoveler, shel-duck and wigeon are notable. One of the best places to see the Irish hare, common on the grassland and salt-marsh. Alder carr in dune slack with orchids and other plants. DUBLIN CORPORATION

A:2 MALAHIDE ESTUARY

Malahide; several road access points for upper and lower parts; go to golf club for access to dunes.

■ Estuary, sand dunes, salt-marsh, grass-land, brackish lake.

■ Important for wintering wildfowl. Dune system is best developed and most natural in county. Best Oct-Apr. **Birds** Red-breasted merganser, great crested grebe, goldeneye.

A:3 LAMBAY ISLAND

Off Donabate; boat from Donabate can be arranged. Essential to obtain permission from Lord Revelstoke, Lambay Island, Co. Dublin.

■ Offshore island, grassland, sea-bird cliff.

■ Important sea-bird populations, winter-ing greylag and barnacle geese. Best Apr-Oct. **Birds** Cormorant, razorbill, guille-mot, shag, kittiwake. LORD REVELSTOKE

A:4 ROGERSTOWN ESTUARY

Near Donabate; best access on road due N of Donabate to estuary shore which makes a useful viewing point.

■ Estuary, mudflats.

■ Second most important estuary for wild-fowl in county. Best Oct-Apr. **Birds** Brent goose, pintail, teal, wigeon, shelduck.

MAP A

WESTMEATH

A:1 SCRAGH BOG*

Near Mullingar; take main road (N4) from Mullingar to Sligo. After level crossing take second right; continue one mile (1.5 km). No right of way to fen. Permission to cross fields must be sought from local farmer.

■ Pond, fen.

■ An extremely small wet quaking fen with several rare plants and insects. **Plants** Large wintergreen, slender cottongrass, downy-fruited and lesser tussock-sedges. IRISH PEATLAND CONSERVATION COUNCIL

A:2 LOUGH DERRAVARAGH

Near Mullingar; best access at W end of lough, by bridge over Inny River.

■ Lake.

■ Raised bog and extensive flat grasslands at W end, but also important for wintering wildfowl. Best Oct-Apr. **Birds** Whooper swan, goldeneye, wigeon.

A:3 LOUGHS KINALE & DERRAGH

Near Granard; park at W side Lough Kinale and walk shore line.

■ Lake, reed-beds.

■ Large numbers of wintering wildfowl. There are freshwater mussels on the shore of Lough Derragh.

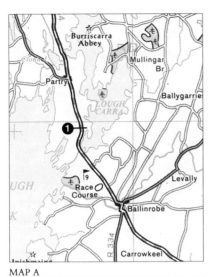

MAP A

MAYO

A:1 LOUGH CARRA**
Near Ballinrobe; many access roads.
■ Limestone lake, fen, limestone grassland and pavement, ash/hazel woodland.
■ Best example in the country of a spring-fed limestone lake with extensive marl deposition and great ecological interest. **Birds** Gadwall, goldeneye, shoveler. **Plants** Spring gentian, dense-flowered orchid.

B:1 OLD HEAD WOOD**
Near Louisburgh; park at Oldhead Harbour and walk into wood.
■ Oak wood.
■ A rare example of Atlantic oak wood with rich growth of lichens such as lungwort, and interesting birdlife. A NNR. **Birds** Nightjar, redstart, woodcock.
WILDLIFE SERVICE

B:2 CLARE ISLAND**
Near Louisburgh; regular boat service from Roonah Quay. Check departure times with post office at Louisburgh. Worth spending whole day on island, even two.
■ Marine island, acid grassland, bog, seabird cliffs.
■ Large diverse island of wide natural history interest, especially birds and plants. **Birds** Chough, gannet, puffin, razorbill, kittiwake, fulmar.

MAP C

C:1 PONTOON WOODS**
Pontoon; from road by Pontoon, further N at Corryosla Bridge and along shore to E.
■ Oak/holly woodland.
■ Excellent example of an Atlantic oak/holly woodland, species-rich in trees, shrubs, herbs and lower plants. **Plants** Spindle. **Birds** Common scoter, treecreeper, sparrowhawk.
WILDLIFE SERVICE

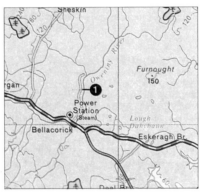

MAP D

D:1 BELLACORICK FLUSH**
Near Crossmolina; call at Bord na Mona headquarters, Bellacorick, to arrange visit.
■ Freshwater marsh in blanket bog.
■ A small marsh with a unique plant community, marsh saxifrage with great fen-sedge and marsh cinquefoil.
AN TAISCE (NATIONAL TRUST FOR IRELAND)

MAP E

E:1 MOY ESTUARY
Near Ballina; several access roads on W and E sides of estuary.
■ Mudflats, salt-marsh, sand dunes.
■ Extensive estuary, important for wildfowl and waders. **Plants** Flat-sedge.

Spindle – see C:1, Pontoon Woods.

F:1 TERMONCARRAGH LAKE*
Near Belmullet; approach from Annagh or Corclogh. Extensive walking in vicinity of lake.
■ Brackish lake, calcareous grassland.
■ Richest and most productive lake on the Mullet, important for wintering and breeding wildfowl and waders. **Plants** Clubrushes, bogbean, yellow rattle. **Birds** Whooper swan, barnacle goose, golden plover, red-necked phalarope.
IRISH WILDBIRD CONSERVANCY/PRIVATE OWNERSHIP

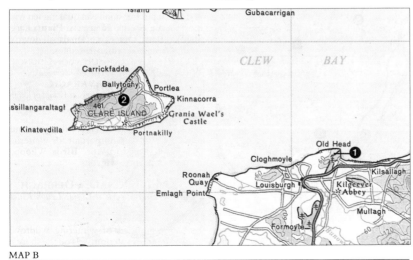

MAP B

MAP F

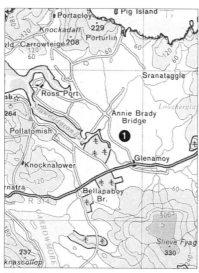

MAP G

G:1 GLENAMOY BOG

Near Glenamoy; turn on to Portacloy road at Glenamoy Bridge and park on roadside.
■ Blanket bog.
■ One of the best examples of lowland blanket bog in Ireland with many open surface pools. Wet spots are dangerously soft. **Plants** Bladderwort, bogbean. **Mammals** Irish hare. **Reptiles** Common lizard.

Irish hare – see G:1, Glenamoy Bog.

H:1 DOWNPATRICK HEAD*

Near Ballycastle; road continues almost to headland.
■ Carboniferous sandstone, sea-bird cliffs.
■ Spectacular scenery and sea-bird nesting site. **Birds** Chough, razorbill, guillemot, kittiwake, fulmar.

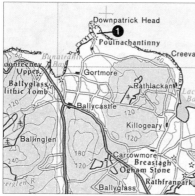

MAP H

MAP A

ROSCOMMON

A:1 LOUGH FUNSHINAGH**

Near Athlone; road access to S and E shore.
■ Turlough, reed-beds, lake.
■ This turlough (see page 13) lies in a deeper basin than most and so never dries out completely. Common clubrush dominates open water in large clumps. Common reed is more localized. Typical turlough flora in shallower parts. Important area for breeding water birds and wintering wildfowl: Greenland white-fronted goose, whooper swan, wigeon and grebes.

B:1 LOUGH REE*

Near Athlone; several access points.
■ Lake, woodland, reed-beds.
■ Many different habitats at SE end of lough – Meehan Wood, Killinure Lough and Coosan Lough. **Birds** (Wintering) whooper swan, wigeon. **Plants** Marsh fern, frogbit.

B:2 LOUGH REE: BALLY BAY*

Near Athlone; drive to Hodson's Bay and walk.
■ Lake, marsh, fen.
■ The most sheltered bay on the Roscommon shore of Lough Ree. Extensive reed-beds; important for breeding and wintering wildfowl.

B:3 LOUGH REE: YEW POINT*

Near Athlone; access from Hodson's Bay.

MAP B

MAP C

■ Hazel/ash woodland.
■ Dry, young woodland on limestone drift. Rich ground flora and interesting woodland birds. **Plants** Water germander.

B:4 LOUGH REE: BARLEY TO PORTANURE LODGE*

Near Lanesborough; access difficult – best take road to Barley Harbour and walk S along shore.
■ Lake, reed-beds.
■ Excellent wildfowl habitat and limestone shore good for flowers.

B:5 ST JOHN'S WOOD*

Near Athlone; approach on road from Lecarrow to Blackbrink Bay.
■ Oak/hazel wood on thin limestone soils.
■ The largest and least-managed wood in the Irish midlands; several rare woodland plants; rich birdlife. **Plants** Bird's-nest orchid, toothwort, woodruff.
WILDLIFE SERVICE/PRIVATE OWNERSHIP

C:1 BRIERFIELD, CASTLEPLUNKET & MULLYGOLLAN*

Near Castleplunket; shore road gives access to all three sites.
■ Turlough.
■ Three areas important for wintering wildfowl; best Oct-Apr. For definition of a turlough, see page 13. **Birds** Bewick's and whooper swans, pintail, shoveler, wigeon, teal.

D:1 LOUGH GARA

Near Frenchpark; road access to S shore and along peninsula into lake.
■ Lake.
■ Important for wintering wildfowl, but most occur on the N section (in County Sligo). Best Oct-Apr. **Birds** Bewick's swan, Greenland white-fronted goose.

MAP D

MAP A LONGFORD

MAP B

LONGFORD

A:1 CLOONDARA BOG
Near Longford; approach on Cloondara-Killashee road and park close to Begnagh Bridge.
■ Raised bog.
■ A fine example of a midland raised bog with a typical flora and well-developed hummock and pool flora. **Plants** Bog-rosemary, crowberry, deergrass, cottongrass.

SLIGO

A:1 BALLYSADARE BAY
Near Ballysadare; multiple viewing points from several roads around bay.
■ Mudflats, salt-marsh.
■ Important area for wintering wildfowl, best Oct-Apr. **Birds** Shelduck, goldeneye, bar-tailed godwit, teal, pale-breasted brent goose.

A:2 AUGHRIS HEAD
Near Ballysadare; walk along cliff top from Aughris village.
■ Sea-bird cliffs.
■ Good exposure of upper carboniferous strata. Breeding sea-birds include razorbill, guillemot, fulmar and kittiwake.

A:3 CUMMEEN STRAND
Near Sligo; best access to S shore.
■ Mudflats.
■ Important area for wintering wildfowl. Best Oct-Apr. **Birds** Pale-breasted brent goose, wigeon, oystercatcher.

A:4 LISSADELL★★
Near Sligo; approach on road alongside field and view from car. Hide at N end of field.
■ Grassland, pond.

Barnacle geese: unlike any other true goose, the whole face is white.

■ A large grass field with small pond which floods in winter. The largest mainland wintering flock of barnacle geese (up to 1,300) occurs here. Wigeon, teal, redshank, oystercatcher, curlew and other waders also use the pond. An NNR. Best Oct-Apr.
WILDLIFE SERVICE

B:1 INISHMURRAY★★
Off Mullaghmore; access by boat from Mullaghmore.
■ Marine island, bog, grassland.
■ A low-lying island of sandstone covered by wet acidic grassland and some bog. Apart from interesting archaeological remains, the eider duck breeds in large numbers. Oystercatcher, shag, gulls and occasionally Arctic tern also nest. During winter, there are large numbers of barnacle geese.

B:2 BUNDUFF LOUGH★
Near Mullaghmore; well served by roads.
■ Lake, reed-beds, marsh.
■ Important for population of wintering wildfowl. **Birds** Whooper swan, Greenland white-fronted goose.

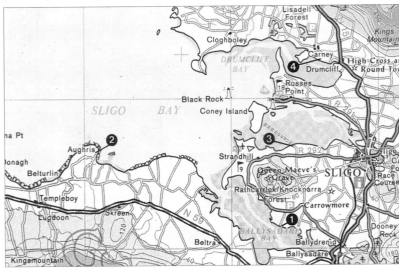

MAP A SLIGO

LEITRIM/CAVAN/MONAGHAN

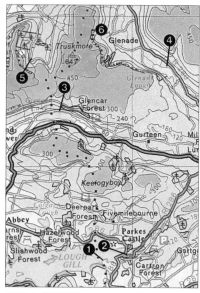

MAP A LEITRIM

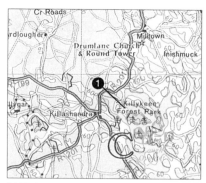

MAP A CAVAN

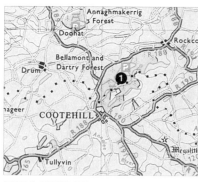

MAP A MONAGHAN

LEITRIM

A:1 BONET RIVER WOOD
Near Dromahair; park on road.
■ Ash/hazel woodland.
■ Woodland on limestone and alluvial soil which changes sharply in character as acid rocks appear in the W. Rich ground flora. **Plants** Bird's-nest and early-purple orchids, goldilocks.

A:2 LOUGH GILL WOODS
Near Dromahair; take road to E end of Lough Gill, park and walk into woods.
■ Ash woodland.
■ Semi-natural ash woodland with hawthorn, willows and wych elm on thin limestone soil with a rich ground flora.

A:3 GLENCAR WATERFALL
Near Manorhamilton; park on roadside, walk up to falls.
■ Rock outcrops, woodland.
■ The waterfall area has a rich bryophyte flora with several rare species.

A:4 GLENADE LOUGH
Near Manorhamilton; park beside lough and walk perimeter.
■ Lake.
■ Well-developed aquatic vegetation.

A:5 BENBULBIN & GLENIFF★★
Near Sligo; take road up to mine, park at top.
■ Cliffs.
■ Best developed high-level plant communities in Ireland. Many Arctic/Alpine species on N-facing cliffs. Sandwort and clustered Alpine saxifrage have their only Irish stations here. Golden-saxifrage, yellow saxifrage, Alpine meadow-rue and purple saxifrage are also present. Summit of plateau covered by heather, bell heather with crowberry and cowberry. Take extreme care if walking close to cliff edge.

A:6 GLENADE CLIFFS
Near Manorhamilton; park close to cliff, continue, taking due care, on foot.
■ Limestone cliff, grassland.
■ Many Arctic/Alpine species: rich flora, especially willowherb; ferns, mosses and lichens.

CAVAN

A:1 LOUGH OUGHTER
Near Cavan; off L15, Cavan-Crossdoney road.
■ Lake, mixed woodland.
■ Best example of flooded drumlin landscape in Ireland. **Birds** Whooper swan, great crested grebe. **Plants** Starwort, large bitter-cress, Cyperus sedge.

Corncrake – see C:1, opposite page.

MONAGHAN

A:1 DROMORE LAKES★
Near Cootehill; choice of several approach roads to lakes and woodland.
■ Open water, coniferous woodland.
■ Three interconnecting lakes lying amongst drumlins and surrounded by extensive coniferous woodland. Wintering wildfowl and woodland animals. **Mammals** Pine marten, red squirrel, fallow deer.

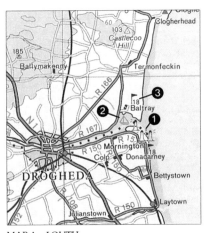

MAP A   LOUTH

LOUTH

A:1 MORNINGTON SAND DUNES*
Near Drogheda; car park close to dunes. Walk S through dunes.
- Sand dunes, grassland, dune slack.
- Highly calcareous dunes and grassland. Well-developed at N end. Some rare plants, and a colony of the rare snail, *Theba pisana.*
Plants Viper's-bugloss, adder's-tongue.

A:2 BOYNE ESTUARY*
Near Drogheda; take road from Drogheda E to Baltray – easy views of mudflats from road.
- Estuarine mudflats.
- Important area for waders and wildfowl. Best Oct-Apr; visit at high tide. **Birds** Black-tailed godwit.

A:3 BALTRAY DUNES
Near Drogheda; take road E from Drogheda to dunes.
- Sand dunes.
- Well-developed, highly calcareous stable dunes with interesting plants, and the Mediterranean snail, *Theba pisana.*

B:1 DUNDALK BAY*
Dundalk; take road from Dundalk E to Soldiers Point, park and walk S. Or drive to Marsh South and park.
- Salt-marsh, mudflats.
- One of the most important areas in Ireland for wintering and migrating waders: up to 48,000 recorded. Best Oct-Apr; visit at high tide. **Birds** Bar-tailed godwit, knot, golden plover, oystercatcher, curlew, dunlin, redshank.

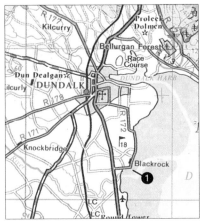

MAP B

MAP A   DONEGAL

DONEGAL

A:1 BIRRA LOUGH
Near Ballintra; access from Ballintra-Rossnowlagh road.
- Lake, reed-beds.
- Wintering wildfowl, present Oct-Apr. **Birds** Whooper swan.

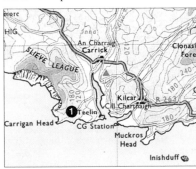

MAP B

B:1 SLIEVE LEAGUE*
Near Carrick; take Carrick to Teelin road, drive up hill and park. Follow footpath to summit; take great care – dangerous cliffs.
- Blanket bog, moorland, cliffs.
- Quartzite cliffs, highest in Ireland, with well-developed heath at summit. Intact blanket bog. Back wall of Lough Agh corrie supports the richest Arctic/Alpine flora in Ireland. **Plants** Mountain avens, yellow mountain, purple saxifrage, holly fern.

C:1 SHESKINMORE LOUGH*
Near Ardara; from Ardara take the Naran road and in 3½ miles (5.5 km) turn left; roadside parking.
- Lake, reed-beds, wet calcareous grassland.
- Valuable for wintering wildfowl, which include Greenland white-fronted goose and barnacle goose; also for summer-breeding waders: dunlin, lapwing and redshank.

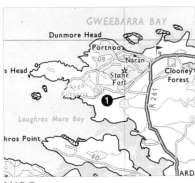

MAP C

Look for corncrake and chough, too. Rare plants, including several orchids, are summer features. Warblers in reed-beds.
IRISH WILDBIRD CONSERVANCY

D:1 LOUGH NACUNG
Near Gortahork; from Gortahork-Bunbeg road (N56), turn left before power station; park and walk the shore.
- Lake, bog.
- Several rare plant species: waterwort and blue-eyed-grass in water/wet spots with Mackay's heath in bog around lake margin.

D:2 GLENVEAGH NATIONAL PARK**
Near Letterkenny; visitor centre and car park off L77 at NE end of Lough Veagh; open all year.
- Moorland, lake, bog, oak/birch woodland.
- Visit audio-visual displays and exhibits, and take the Derrylahan nature trail.

Take minibus from visitor centre to Glenveagh Castle (built 1870) 5 miles (8 km) along shore. Castle garden has delicate plants from Chile, Madeira and Tasmania.

Take track towards head of glen. The oak/birch woodland supports a luxuriant growth of mosses and filmy-fern. Look for treecreepers, redstarts, wood warblers and siskins.

On open moorland, red deer roam within a 28-mile (45-km) fence. Raven, peregrine, merlin, stonechat and grouse may be seen. Tormentil and bog asphodel add colour to heather and purple moor-grass.

E:1 BLANKET NOOK**
Near Newtown Cunningham; on N13 from Letterkenny to Derry, turn left just before Newtown Cunningham, then right. Park beside embankment and walk.
- Brackish lake, reed swamp, marsh.
- Wildfowl wetland with rare plants. **Birds** Whooper swan, ducks, waders. **Plants** Sea and grey club-rush.

MAP D

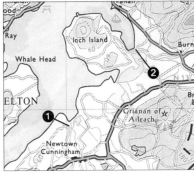

MAP E

265

E:2 INCH LOUGH★★
Near Burnfoot; cross causeway to Inch Island; park and proceed on foot.
■ Brackish lake.
■ The most important wildfowl wetland in the county. The lough is highly productive with abundant food for large populations of wildfowl. Up to 1,500 whooper swans visit in autumn, with smaller numbers of mute swan, pochard, wigeon and coot.

Breeding birds include Sandwich tern and plentiful redshank and snipe.

Occasional Greenland white-fronted and greylag geese occur. Over the sea wall, to the N, pale-breasted brent goose, shelduck and many waders can be seen.

F:1 CREESLOUGH WOOD
Near Creeslough; the woodland is close to the village.
■ Birch woodland.
■ Small woodland, rich in birdlife.

F:2 DUNFANAGHY★★
Near Dunfanaghy; from Dunfanaghy drive N across low sand dunes; soon park and walk.
■ Lake, sand dunes, dune slacks, grassland.
■ An important complex of habitats supporting diverse plants and birds.

Wintering wildfowl include Greenland white-fronted goose, wigeon, pochard, teal, mallard and whooper swan.

The large dune slack is dominated by common sedge, creeping bent, creeping willow with marsh pennywort and silverweed. In the drier parts are fairy flax, wild

Wood warbler – see A:6, opposite page.

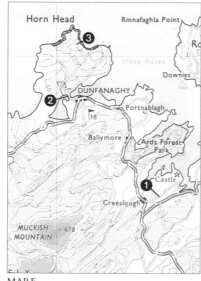

MAP F

thyme, thyme-leaved sandwort, field gentian and lesser clubmoss.

Choughs can sometimes be seen feeding on the grassland.

F:3 HORN HEAD★
Near Dunfanaghy; take Dunfanaghy road to Coastguard Hill; park and walk along cliffs.
■ Sea-bird cliff.
■ Quartzite cliffs with large colonies of sea-birds. **Birds** Puffin, razorbill, fulmar, kittwake.

FERMANAGH

A:1 REILLY & GOLE WOODS★
Near Lisnaskea; from Derrylin, ½ mile (one km) SE along A509. Take B127 E 2½ miles (4 km), then unclassified road SE 1¼ miles (2 km), unclassified road NE ¼ mile (0.5 km). Park on roadside. Access along concrete lane. Permit from warden, Castle Archdale Country Park, Lisnarric, Co. Fermanagh.
■ Oak woodland, mixed woodland.
■ Two wooded drumlins on heavy clay, on the shores of Upper Lough Erne, make up these woods, an NNR. It is thought that Reilly Wood has developed from a coppice with standards and since grazing of the woodland floor ceased, a luxuriant ground vegetation has grown up in the damp conditions. Gole Wood is a developing mixed deciduous wood, good for butterflies including silver-washed fritillary and purple hairstreak. Interesting plants to be found along the shore include blue-eyed-grass, marsh pea and cowbane; periods of low water level reveal fossilized coral and crinoids in the rock. An encounter with otters is always a real possibility. **Insects** Hairy dragonfly. **Mammals** Red and grey squirrels.
DEPARTMENT OF THE ENVIRONMENT (N Ireland) COUNTRYSIDE & WILDLIFE BRANCH

A:2 CUILCAGH SUMMIT★
Near Enniskillen; from Swanlinbar 2 miles (3 km) N along A32, turn W to car park at Gortalughany view point.
■ Moorland, blanket bog, sandstone cliffs.
■ The 3-mile (5-km) walk to the summit should be rewarded by views of red grouse, golden plover and perhaps a peregrine falcon or merlin. Arctic/Alpine plants found on cliffs near the top include dwarf willow and stiff sedge.
DEPARTMENT OF AGRICULTURE (N Ireland) FOREST SERVICE

A:3 DOOHATTY GLEBE★
Near Enniskillen; from Swanlinbar 3 miles (5 km) N along A32. Park on roadside. Foot access by forest track.
■ Limestone cliff, blanket bog, plantation.
■ The climb to the summit of Benaughlin mountain passes through state forest before reaching limestone scree slopes at the base of carboniferous limestone cliffs. A cairn adds archaeological interest. **Birds** Raven. **Plants** Mountain everlasting, adder's tongue.
DEPARTMENT OF AGRICULTURE (N Ireland) FOREST SERVICE

A:4 CROSSMURRIN★
Near Enniskillen; from Belcoo, go ⅓ mile (0.5 km) SW to Blacklion, then 1½ miles (2.5 km) SE to junction. Turn SW along Marlbank scenic loop 3½ miles (5.5 km). Park by roadside. Access by stone track to N. Permit only from warden, Castle Archdale Country Park, Lisnarrick, Co. Fermanagh.
■ Limestone pavement, limestone grassland, hazel scrub.
■ This NNR has fine examples of limestone pavement and swallow holes. Much of the exposed rock outcrops are fossiliferous with crinoids, corals and bivalves particularly plentiful. Today it is the plants favouring these shallow soils that are of interest – mountain everlasting, and mossy saxifrage, with blue moor-grass particularly abundant. Where blanket bog has formed on areas of

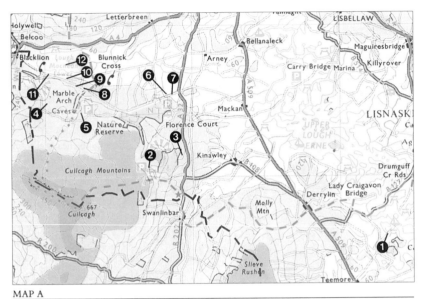

MAP A

poorly-drained ground, the acid-loving cottongrass and bog asphodel contrast markedly with the surrounding flora.
DEPARTMENT OF THE ENVIRONMENT (N Ireland) COUNTRYSIDE & WILDLIFE BRANCH

A:5 MARBLE ARCH CAVES★★

Near Enniskillen; from Belcoo go ⅓ mile (0.5 km) SW to Blacklion, then 1½ miles (2.5 km) SE to junction. Turn SW along Marlbank scenic loop 3¾ miles (6 km); car park at caves. Open daily Mar-Oct. Tours from 11 am daily. Entry by ticket only from reception centre on site. Advance reservations, tel 0365 82777.

■ Caves.

■ An extensive cave system formed by the action of three streams which run off the NW slopes of Cuilcagh mountain, joining deep underground to emerge at the Marble Arch.

Tours begin with a boat trip across an underground lake. A slope then leads to a dry chamber with rimstone pools and stalactites, followed by a fissure passage, straw stalactites, stalagmites and columns. Where the cave ceiling slopes, blades and translucent curtain formations may be seen. Flowstone sheets and cave cauliflowers climax in the uniqué Moses Walk' and a view of the 'Guardian Angel' stalagmite.
FERMANAGH DISTRICT COUNCIL

A:6 GLEN WOOD

Near Enniskillen; 2¾ miles (4.5 km) SW on A4 to junction with A32, then 3¾ miles (6 km) S along A32, turn W to Florence Court, and car park. Foot access S from here.

■ Mixed woodland, stream.

■ A 12-acre wood in a small glen where damp, shady stream sides provide perfect conditions for bryophyte growth. Wildlife includes wood warbler, red squirrel, Irish hare and badger.
DEPARTMENT OF AGRICULTURE (N Ireland) FOREST SERVICE

A:7 AGHATIROURKE★

Near Enniskillen; from Swanlinbar, 2 miles (3 km) N along A32. Turn W and park at Gortalughany viewpoint.

■ Blanket bog, limestone pavement, swallow holes.

■ Sheltered gullies and limestone pavement contrast markedly with adjacent acid bog on the mountain slopes. Birds of the uplands may be encountered. **Plants** Mountain everlasting, bog asphodel. **Birds** Hen harrier, merlin, red grouse, raven.
DEPARTMENT OF AGRICULTURE (N Ireland) FOREST SERVICE

A:8 MARBLE ARCH FOREST★★

Near Enniskillen; from Belcoo go ⅓ mile (0.5 km) SW to Blacklion, then 3¾ miles (6 km) SE to car park at bridge over Cladagh River.

■ Woodland, river.

■ See A:5. A deep gorge cut into the limestone shelf displays many landslip features on which a 'hanging' ash wood has developed. The woodland, with a very rich flora, supports silver-washed fritillary. Look for otter spraints by the river. An NNR.
DEPARTMENT OF THE ENVIRONMENT (N Ireland) COUNTRYSIDE & WILDLIFE BRANCH/DEPARTMENT OF AGRICULTURE (N Ireland) FOREST SERVICE

A:9 KILLESHER

Near Enniskillen; from Belcoo ⅓ mile (0.5 km) SW to Blacklion, then 2¾ miles (4.5 km) SE along concessionary road. Park, on public road. Access to reserve by track to S.

■ Ashwood.

■ A natural scrub woodland on base rich soils, with a typical dry limestone wood flora and a range of woodland birds.
DEPARTMENT OF AGRICULTURE (N Ireland) FOREST SERVICE

A:10 ROSSAA WOOD

Near Enniskillen; from Belcoo go ⅓ mile (0.5 km) SW to Blacklion, then 1½ miles (2.5 km) SE along concessionary road. Park at roadside. Access to S.

■ Ashwood, carboniferous limestone cliff.

■ A fine woodland rich in botanical and wildlife interest. Badger and fox dwell here, as well as the elusive pine marten. An NNR.
DEPARTMENT OF THE ENVIRONMENT (N Ireland) COUNTRYSIDE & WILDLIFE BRANCH/DEPARTMENT OF AGRICULTURE (N Ireland) FOREST SERVICE

A:11 CORRY POINT WOOD★

Near Enniskillen; from Belcoo ⅓ mile (0.5 km) SW to Blacklion, then one mile (1.5 km) E along concessionary road. Park on roadside. Foot access by track.

■ Woodland, shoreline vegetation.

■ Small reserve with a variety of habitats. Woodland with a fine display of wild flowers in spring, good selection of butterflies, dragonflies and wildfowl on the lough, including water rail and hairy dragonfly.
DEPARTMENT OF AGRICULTURE (N Ireland) FOREST SERVICE

A:12 HANGING ROCK★

Near Enniskillen; from Belcoo go ⅓ mile (0.5 km) SW to Blacklion, then 2¾ miles (4.5 km) SE along concessionary road. Park in lay-by at roadside. Midge repellent necessary. Boulders at cliff base very slippery.

■ Carboniferous limestone cliff, ash woodland.

■ The Hanging Rock is a prominent limestone knoll reef cliff. Here ravens and peregrine falcons can be seen regularly, while yew and juniper thrive on the cliff face. Lower down, the woodland has many interesting plants including Welsh poppy, tutsan and goldilocks buttercup. The harsh sound of the corncrake may be heard from the surrounding meadows and the woods support wood warbler, red squirrel and pine marten. Damp conditions favour a rich bryophyte growth. An NNR.
DEPARTMENT OF THE ENVIRONMENT (N Ireland) COUNTRYSIDE & WILDLIFE BRANCH

B:1 CROM CASTLE★★

Near Lisnaskea; from Newtownbutler, 3 miles (5 km) W on unclassified road. Park at Inisherk Lodge. No collecting.

■ Oak woodland, lough shore, swamp, fen meadows.

■ Excellent woodland, home to purple hairstreak and silver-washed fritillary, with many water birds and wildfowl along the shoreline and interesting plants including blue-eyed-grass. **Plants** Marsh pea, cowbane, frogbit, flowering-rush, greater water parsnip. **Mammals** Otter, red squirrel.
NATIONAL TRUST

B:2 CORNAGAGUE WOOD & LOUGH

Near Lisnaskea; 3 miles (5 km) SE on A34, then 5 miles (8 km) E on B36 to Mill Lough, ¾ mile (one km) S. Park on roadside.

■ Lough, scrub woodland.

■ Reed-fringed inter-drumlin lough; many water-birds breed here including the great crested grebe and water rail. Numerous dragonflies and damselflies found along the edge of the willow/alder dominated scrub.
DEPARTMENT OF AGRICULTURE (N Ireland) FOREST SERVICE

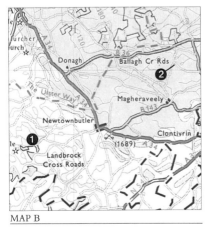

MAP B

The **golden plover**'s plaintive, monosyllabic flight call is one of the most beautiful sounds of upland Ireland and Britain during spring and early summer. Both male and female are striking birds, with speckled gold upper parts and white chest. In summer, the male has a distinctive black belly, clearly visible when it runs along the ground, between searching for food, which includes seeds, worms and insects.

The carboniferous limestone landscape of the Burren in County Clare, on Ireland's west coast, is the youngest landscape in Europe, with the most recent glaciation occurring 15,000 years ago. Much of the bare rock has a smooth flat surface, forming the famous limestone pavements, but towards late May the soil-filled crevices are filled with a profusion of colourful flowers. The flora is of international significance, with Arctic and Alpine species growing next to flowers normally found in the Mediterranean and the Azores.

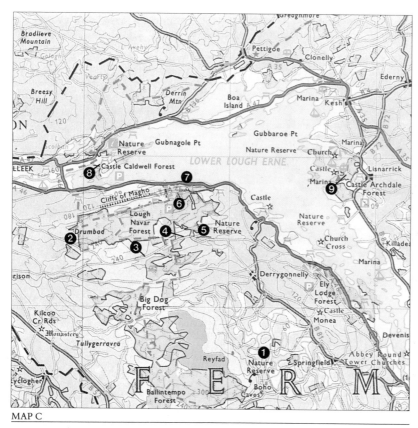

MAP C

Otter – see C:9.

C:1 ROSS LOUGH★

Near Enniskillen; *go 5 miles (8 km) NW on B81 to Monea, then 1, miles (2 km) SW. Park on roadside. Foot access by track. Avoid wildfowling season.*

■ Lough, swamp, fen.

■ Fen vegetation on the periodically flooded shoreline provides an area rich in plant and insect species. In winter the lough is visited by many wildfowl. An NNR.
DEPARTMENT OF AGRICULTURE (N Ireland) FOREST SERVICE/DEPARTMENT OF THE ENVIRONMENT (N Ireland) COUNTRYSIDE & WILDLIFE BRANCH

C:2 CARRICKNAGOWER★★

Near Belleek; *from Garrison 4¼ miles (7 km) E, then turn NW ½ mile (one km) and park on roadside. Access on foot.*

■ Blanket bog, lakes, cliff, marsh.

■ Reserve in two sections – to W, Carricknagower lake with associated marsh and sandstone cliff faces; to E, scarp and dip topography with typical wet moorland vegetation. Many notable plants including pale butterwort, lesser twayblade, Wilson's filmy-fern, serrated wintergreen, lesser wintergreen. **Birds** Hen harrier, merlin, raven. **Mammals** Red deer, Irish hare, badger.
DEPARTMENT OF AGRICULTURE (N Ireland) FOREST SERVICE

C:3 LOUGH NAMAN BOG★

Near Belleek; *from Garrison, 4½ miles (7.5 km) E. Park on roadside. Access across stile at E end of reserve. Permit from warden at Castle Archdale Country Park, Lisnarrick, Co. Fermanagh.*

■ Blanket bog.

■ This NNR is an excellent example of pool and hummock complexes, with mosses indicative of bog-building processes. Merlin

and golden plover in summer; Greenland white-fronted geese in winter.
DEPARTMENT OF THE ENVIRONMENT (N Ireland) COUNTRYSIDE AND WILDLIFE BRANCH

C:4 CONAGHER★

Near Belleek; *from Garrison, 7 miles (11.5 km) E. Park on roadside.*

■ Blanket bog, scarp and dip, lough.

■ An extensive area of upland vegetation with an interesting diversity added by the scarp and dip slope topography. Wildlife includes hen harrier, red grouse, merlin, raven, red deer, Irish hare and badger.
DEPARTMENT OF AGRICULTURE (N Ireland) FOREST SERVICE

C:5 CORREL GLEN FOREST★

Near Belleek; *from Garrison, 8 miles (13 km) E. Signposted Forest Scenic Drive. Car park.*

■ Mixed woodland, heath, river, lough.

■ An interesting vegetation has developed on this series of limestone escarpments supporting mixed deciduous woodland interspaced with sandstone dip slopes and their acid-loving heath communities.

In spring the woodland floor is a colourful carpet of lesser celandine, bluebells, woodsorrel and wood anemone. Among several uncommon plants are lesser twayblade, bird's-nest orchid and two wintergreens.

Speckled wood butterflies are conspicuous in sunny glades, with green hairstreaks on the heath. An NNR.
DEPARTMENT OF AGRICULTURE (N Ireland) FOREST SERVICE/DEPARTMENT OF THE ENVIRONMENT (N Ireland) COUNTRYSIDE & WILDLIFE BRANCH

C:6 BOLUSTY BOG

Near Belleek; *from Garrison 8 miles (13 km) E, signposted Forest Scenic Drive. Follow drive*

for 2 miles (3 km). Foot access by forest track.

■ Blanket bog, plantation.

■ A very damp area rich in such bog plants as great and round-leaved sundews, butterwort and cranberry. Nearby forest adds diversity with many common species of songbird.
DEPARTMENT OF AGRICULTURE (N Ireland) FOREST SERVICE

C:7 MAGHO★

Near Belleek; *8 miles (13 km) E along A46. Park on roadside.*

■ Carboniferous limestone cliff, scree, scrub.

■ Reserve straddles both sides of public road – lower scrub woodland fringes lough; above, extensive cliffs and slopes provide a fascinating diversity of animals and plants including mossy saxifrage, Tunbridge filmy-fern and juniper.
DEPARTMENT OF AGRICULTURE (N Ireland) FOREST SERVICE

C:8 CASTLE CALDWELL FOREST★★

Near Belleek; *4½ miles (7.5 km) E along the A47. Car park in forest grounds.*

■ Lough, reed-bed, fen, plantation, deciduous woodland.

■ A series of parallel limestone peninsulas stretching out into the waters of Lower Lough Erne forms sheltered bogs, some developing fine examples of reed-swamp, fen and carr vegetation. Mink and otter may be seen along the shore, where dunlin and common scoter are notable breeding birds.

A hide affords excellent views of many species of wildfowl. *Odonata* include ruddy darter and hairy dragonfly.
DEPARTMENT OF AGRICULTURE (N Ireland) FOREST SERVICE/ROYAL SOCIETY FOR THE PROTECTION OF BIRDS

C:9 CASTLE ARCHDALE COUNTRY PARK & ISLANDS★

Near Irvinestown; *signposted from Lisnarrick off B82. Car park, museum, lavatories.*

■ Mixed woodland, carr, lough, wooded islands.

■ The wide variety of habitats in this NNR affords a corresponding diversity of wildlife. The islands consist mainly of oak woodland; their isolation makes them particularly attractive for the nesting wildfowl. Coot, water rail and moorhen are all to be seen with reed bunting and sedge warbler proclaiming their territories in the carr. Otters also frequent the area.
DEPARTMENT OF THE ENVIRONMENT (N Ireland) COUNTRYSIDE & WILDLIFE BRANCH/DEPARTMENT OF AGRICULTURE (N Ireland) FOREST SERVICE

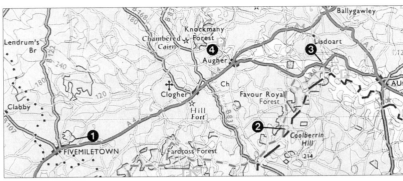

MAP A

A:1 Blessingbourne

Near Fivemiletown; just E along A4. Park in reserve. Permit required from UTNC, Belfast.

■ Reed-fringed lough, woodland.

■ Lough Fadda holds a variety of birds and in spring its shores display purple-loosestrife, marsh-marigold and yellow iris. Red squirrel may be seen foraging in surrounding woodland in autumn.

ULSTER WILDLIFE TRUST

A:2 Altadaven

Near Aughnachloy; from Augher, 3 miles (5 km) E along A28 then 2 miles (3 km) S to car park at St Patrick's Chair one mile (1.5 km) W of reserve.

■ Mixed woodland, moorland.

■ Old woodland enclosed by a stone wall; treecreeper resident. Surrounding open land has a typical moorland flora; fallow deer present.

DEPARTMENT OF AGRICULTURE (N Ireland) FOREST SERVICE

A:3 Favour Royal Forest

Near Aughnacloy; from Augher, 4¼ miles (7 km) E along A28. Car park in forest.

■ Mixed woodland.

■ A viewing platform is available to observe fallow deer which feed on the deer lawns. Best in Apr and Oct.

DEPARTMENT OF AGRICULTURE (N Ireland) FOREST SERVICE

A:4 Knockmany

Near Aughnacloy; from Clogher, 1½ miles (2.5 km) N along B83 to forest car park. Foot access by forest track. Closed Oct-Jan.

■ Reed-fringed lough, swamp.

■ Ardushin Lough is an important feeding and wintering area for several species of wildfowl. The swampy willow scrub has a typical flora.

DEPARTMENT OF AGRICULTURE (N Ireland) FOREST SERVICE

B:1 Drumlish

Near Dromore; 2 miles (3 km) N on un-classified road to B4. Park on roadside.

■ Mixed woodland, plantation.

■ Old woodland, mainly beech, particularly rich in fungi, with over 60 species recorded. Best Sep-Nov.

DEPARTMENT OF AGRICULTURE (N Ireland) FOREST SERVICE

C:1 Meenadoan★

Near Irvinestown; from Ederny, 4¼ miles (7 km) N along B72, then 1½ miles (2½ km) along unclassified road. Park at road side. Permit from warden, Castle Archdale Country Park, Lisnarick, Co. Fermanagh.

■ Ombrogenous/blanket bog.

■ Raised bog areas well preserved with an interesting mosaic of pools and hummocks, very rich in wetland flora and fauna.

DEPARTMENT OF THE ENVIRONMENT (N Ireland) COUNTRYSIDE & WILDLIFE BRANCH

C:2 Mullyfamore

Near Castlederg; from Killeter, cross Derg river at Aghyaran bridge, then W for 12¼ miles (20 km). Car park at Big Bridge. Foot access 3 miles (5 km) SE by forest track.

■ Ombrogenous bog.

■ A fine bog with well-developed pool and hummock complexes. Greenland white-fronted goose feeds on Rhyncospera alba during the winter, and raptors hunt.

DEPARTMENT OF AGRICULTURE (N Ireland) FOREST SERVICE

C:3 Killeter Forest Goose Lawns

Near Castlederg; from Killeter, cross Derg river at Aghyaran Bridge, then W for 12½ miles (20 km). Car park at Big Bridge. Foot access 3 miles (5 km) SE by forest track.

■ Blanket bog, plantation.

■ These feeding grounds for Greenland white-fronted goose are best seen in winter; the surrounding forest has good populations of songbirds.

DEPARTMENT OF AGRICULTURE (N Ireland) FOREST SERVICE

C:4 Killeter Forest★

Near Castlederg; from Killeter cross river Derg at Aghyaran Bridge, then W for 12½ miles (20 km). Car park at Big Bridge. Foot access 3 miles (5 km) SE by forest track.

■ Blanket bog, raised bog, forest.

■ Fine pool and hummock complexes with an associated rich flora, including intermediate bladderwort. Best in summer.

DEPARTMENT OF AGRICULTURE (N Ireland) FOREST SERVICE/DEPARTMENT OF THE ENVIRONMENT (N Ireland) COUNTRYSIDE & WILDLIFE BRANCH

White-fronted goose – see C:3.

MAP B

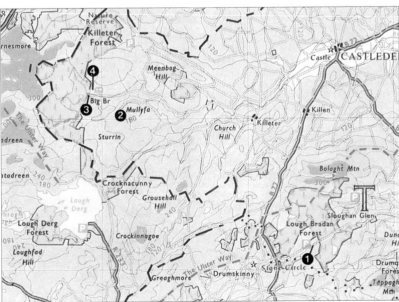

MAP C

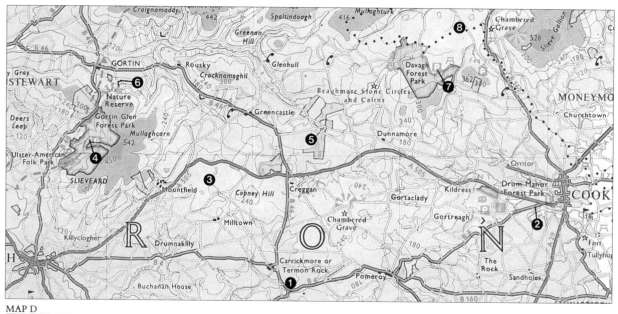

MAP D

D:1 TERMON GLEN

Near Omagh; *from Carrickmore, ½ mile (one km) SE on B4. Car park in estate. Permit from UTNC, Belfast.*

■ Wooded glen, lough.

■ Estate woodland with a variety of non-native trees; interesting birdlife and wild flowers, with 84 species of fungi recorded.

ULSTER WILDLIFE TRUST

D:2 DRUM MANOR★

Near Cookstown; *3 miles (5 km) W along A505. Car park.*

■ Mixed woodland, plantation.

■ Many species attracted to walled garden developed for butterflies. Plantation and estate woodland hold many breeding birds including heron and long-eared owl.

DEPARTMENT OF AGRICULTURE (N Ireland) FOREST SERVICE

D:3 THE MURRINS★

Near Omagh; *from Mountfield, 2 miles (3 km) E along A505. Park on roadside.*

■ Heath, lakes, bog.

■ Typical heath flora with tall bog-sedge occurring in damp boggy areas. The area is an example of an extensive glacial outwash feature. Best in spring.

DEPARTMENT OF THE ENVIRONMENT (N Ireland) COUNTRYSIDE & WILDLIFE BRANCH/DEPARTMENT OF AGRICULTURE (N Ireland) FOREST SERVICE

D:4 GORTIN GLEN FOREST★

Near Omagh; *from Gortin, 1½ miles (2.5 km) along B48, signposted Forest Drive.*

■ Plantation.

■ Good numbers of common songbirds, and more interesting species such as hen harrier, raven and red grouse. Deer enclosure with small herd of sika deer.

DEPARTMENT OF AGRICULTURE (N Ireland) FOREST SERVICE

D:5 BLACK BOG

Near Omagh; *from Greencastle, 2 miles (3 km) SE along B46. Park on roadside. Access across country to E.*

■ Raised bog.

■ A 118-acre reserve with fine pool and hummock complexes, small stream and ex-cellent bog flora. Good for butterflies, including marsh fritillary.

DEPARTMENT OF AGRICULTURE (N Ireland) FOREST SERVICE

D:6 BOORIN★

Near Newton Stewart; *from Gortin, one mile (1½ km) E along B46, turn S.*

■ Heath, mixed woodland.

■ An area of glacial deposition where a heath, possibly the best example in Northern Ireland, has formed on morainic material. The moraine itself has interesting kettle-hole lakes. A scrubby wood of oak and birch is found on the steep N side. An NNR.

DEPARTMENT OF THE ENVIRONMENT (N Ireland) COUNTRYSIDE & WILDLIFE BRANCH

D:7 SLAGHTFREEDEN

Near Cookstown; *3¾ miles (6 km) NW on B162, then 3¾ miles (6 km) W on unclassified road to car park in Davagh forest. Access on foot by forest track.*

■ Bog.

■ Two very damp low-lying areas with fine pool and hummock complexes. Hummocks of *Racomitrium lanuginosum*, pool hollows, hold range of *Sphagnum* species.

DEPARTMENT OF AGRICULTURE (N Ireland) FOREST SERVICE

D:8 TEAL LOUGH

Near Draperstown; *2¾ miles (4.5 km) SW*
on B47, 1½ miles (2.4 km) SW on unclassified road, then 1¼ miles (2 km) SE on unclassified road. Park on roadside. Foot access across country, ½ mile (one km) to SW.

■ Lough, bog.

■ Bog around lough displays good pool and hummock complex.

DEPARTMENT OF AGRICULTURE (N Ireland) FOREST SERVICE

E:1 MONEYGAL BOG

Near Castlederg; *2½ miles (4 km) NW. Park on public road.*

■ Raised bog.

■ A 116-acre dome raised bog rich in bog mosses. Many species of wildfowl and waders use the area including golden plover.

DEPARTMENT OF AGRICULTURE (N Ireland) FOREST SERVICE

E:2 STRABANE GLEN★

Near Strabane; *1¼ miles (2 km) NE along A5. Take B49 E, then first right turn. Park at end of track. Permit only, UTNC, Belfast.*

■ Mixed woodland, crags.

■ The steep-sided and wooded glen is a good place to observe red squirrels which feed on hazelnuts and acorns in the autumn. Badger, fox and stoat may be seen.

In the marshy clearing midway along glen, butterflies including wood whites and orange tips feed on the wild flowers.

ULSTER WILDLIFE TRUST

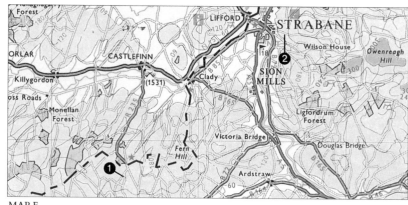

MAP E

A:1 MILFORD NATURE RESERVE★★

Milford; *footpath from village. Permit needed from UTNC, Belfast.*
■ Wood, damp grassland.
■ On fine summer days the grassy bank of this disused railway cutting is a splendid array of wild flowers and *Lepidoptera*. Unusual species include marsh helleborine and fragrant orchid; butterflies include silver-washed fritillary and wood white.
ULSTER TRUST FOR NATURE
CONSERVATION

A:2 KNOCKAGINNEY

Near Armagh; *from Caledon, 1¾ miles (3 km) W along A28, turn S 1¼ miles (2 km) along minor road. Park on roadside.*
■ Mixed woodland.
■ Small site with wide range of trees and shrubs. Fallow deer, fox, badger, stoat and many songbirds resident.
DEPARTMENT OF AGRICULTURE FOREST
SERVICE

A:3 THE ARGORY

Near Moy; *N 2 miles (3 km) along B106. Signposted. Use NT car park. Permit needed from UTNC, Belfast.*
■ Cut-over raised bog.
■ Reserve divided into a high and a low moss; heather the dominant cover. Six species of *Sphagnum* recorded and interesting moths including emperor, northern eggar, drinker, double dart and brindled green.
ULSTER TRUST FOR NATURE
CONSERVATION

A:4 PEATLANDS PARK★★

Near Dungannon; *E from M1 junction 13. Car park and interpretation centre.*
■ Cut-over bog, bog, woodland, lough.
■ From the car park and interpretation centre it is a short walk to bog garden transversed by a boardwalk. Views of typical plant species such as cottongrass, *Sphagnum* mosses bilberry, bog myrtle and the carnivorous bladderwort and sundews.
Don't miss the wet area of quaking bog, developed over a lake bed. At least 10 species of *Sphagnum* moss are found here along with bog-rosemary in its only readily accessible Northern Ireland site.
Derryadd Lough holds several species of duck, teal and mallard in summer with diving duck in winter. Many dragonflies are present, including the black hawker; emerald damselfly.
Annagarriff NNR, N of the Lough, comprises an area of woodland and uncut bog. Marsh fritillary and green hairstreak butterflies frequent the open areas with silver-washed fritillaries along the woodland edge.
Scattered through Annagarriff Wood are the large nests of the northern wood ant, *Formica aquilonia* in its only Irish site. Long-eared owl, sparrowhawk, jay and woodcock all nest within the wood.
W of Annagarriff Wood are several newly created ponds stocked with rudd and tench add a rich diversity to the park.
A second NNR within the Peatlands Park is known as Mulenakill. Its uncut bog is home to the large heath butterfly and emperor moth. Royal fern grows along the drainage ditches and marsh clubmoss, cranberry, bog asphodel and cow-wheat grow on the bog.
DEPARTMENT OF AGRICULTURE (N Ireland)
COUNTRYSIDE & WILDLIFE BRANCH

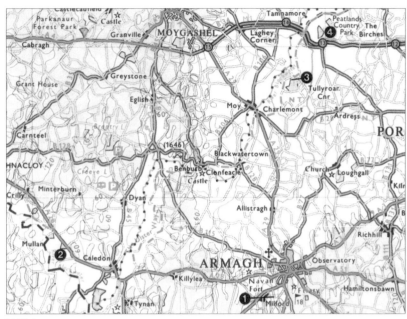

MAP A

B:1 BRACKAGH MOSS★

Near Portadown; *2 miles (3 km) along A27, then SE on to unclassified road ¼ mile (0.5 km). Park in lay-by. Access via N end of reserve. Keep to ramparts.*
■ Cut-over peat bog.
■ This 270-acre mosaic of pools, reed-swamp and open drainage ditches, with small areas of fen and bog, provides excellent breeding sites for dragonflies and damselflies; the ruddy darter and the scarce Irish damselfly, *Coenagrion lunulatum*, have been recorded here, while butterflies include green hairstreak, large heath and marsh fritillary. Of botanical interest are several orchid species, as well as royal fern, red bartsia, cowbane and bog asphodel. Woodcock and snipe breed; grasshopper warbler may be heard in spring.
DEPARTMENT OF AGRICULTURE (N Ireland)
COUNTRYSIDE & WILDLIFE BRANCH

B:2 CRAIGAVON LAKES★

Craigavon; *several car parks around lakes.*
■ Two man-made balancing lakes.
■ Many duck species use the lakes in winter, including goldeneye, shoveler and the occasional smew. A large flock of golden plover and lapwing may be observed in the grounds of the nearby Goodyear factory from late Aug.
CRAIGAVON BOROUGH COUNCIL

B:3 LURGAN PARK LAKE

Lurgan; *footpath from town centre car parks.*
■ Lake, parkland.
■ Excellent for close views of wildfowl which have become tolerant of disturbance.
CRAIGAVON BOROUGH COUNCIL

B:4 OXFORD ISLAND★★

Near Lurgan; *NW to M1 Junction 10. Signposted; an NNR.*
■ Lough, reed-beds, hay meadow, woodland.
■ A path leads round the peninsula. The recently created large pond W of Kinnegoe House has nesting tufted duck; also good for damselflies and dragonflies.
Hay meadows along the shoreline of Lough Neagh are species rich with much

yellow rattle, ragged-robin and common spotted-orchid.
Lough Neagh is the largest lake in the British Isles, listed in the Ramsar Convention for its international importance for wintering wildfowl. Bird hide at Kinnegoe gives excellent views of goldeneye, with occasional gadwall, shoveler, wigeon, teal, ruddy duck, scaup and smew. Reed-beds hide water rail, little and great crested grebe.
There are more hay meadows in the N half of the peninsula: listen for corncrakes in May and Jun. Irish hare is present, and well-worn fox pads criss-cross the meadows.
A bird hide overlooking The Closet gives views of the heronry on far shore. In spring, courtship display of great crested grebes is fascinating.
In the SW of the peninsula is a fringe of alder carr resulting from successive drainage schemes. Large mixed flocks of tits, finches and redpoll occur in winter. Otters known to frequent Closet Bay.
In autumn and winter large flocks of whooper and Bewick's swans graze on the fields to the S of the peninsula between Annaloist and Derrymacash. View from a discreet distance.
CRAIGAVON BOROUGH COUNCIL

MAP B

DOWN

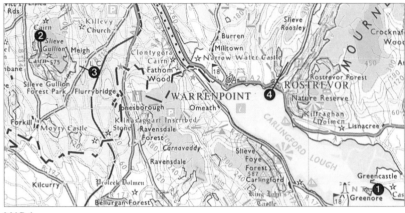

MAP A

A:1 GREEN ISLAND & GREENCASTLE POINT★

Near Kilkeel; *minor roads S of A2 to park at Greencastle Point. No access to islands.*
■ Sandy shore, island, mudflats.
■ Most noted for summer population of terns, but good bird watching all year. Mudflats host such winter species as pale-bellied brent goose, golden plover, dunlin and bar-tailed godwits. Dolphins and porpoises seen in the bay. **Birds** Roseate, Sandwich, Arctic and common terns, black guillemot, sanderling, knot.
NATIONAL TRUST/ROYAL SOCIETY FOR THE PROTECTION OF BIRDS

A:2 SLIEVE GULLION SUMMIT

Near Meigh; *SW along B113. Forest drive signposted. Parking at site.*
■ Heather moor, lough.
■ Commanding views from summit. Small lough near North Cairn holds a few wildfowl while skylarks and meadow pipits can be heard all over the mountain. Irish hares and feral goats may be seen.
DEPARTMENT OF AGRICULTURE (N Ireland) FOREST SERVICE

A:3 HAWTHORNE HILL

Near Meigh; *SW along B113, enter Slieve Gullion Forest and turn N to car park at site.*
■ Mixed woodland.
■ Red squirrels and Irish hares are plentiful here, where a mixture of habitats provides a diversity of common passerines and wild flowers including wood-sorrel, wood anemone, primrose and lords-and-ladies. Best in spring.
DEPARTMENT OF AGRICULTURE (N Ireland) FOREST SERVICE

A:4 ROSTREVOR FOREST★

Rostrevor; *½ mile (one km) E along A2. Car park at NW end of reserve. No access off paths.*
■ Oak woodland.
■ A 47-acre, mixed-age oak wood with luxuriant understorey, considered an example of primeval forest rare in Northern Ireland. Rings to the songs of many common passerines, including wood warbler. Badger, fox, and red squirrel present.
DEPARTMENT OF AGRICULTURE (N Ireland) FOREST SERVICE/DEPARTMENT OF THE ENVIRONMENT (N Ireland) COUNTRYSIDE & WILDLIFE BRANCH

B:1 BLOODY BRIDGE & MOURNE COASTAL PATH★

Near Newcastle; *3 miles (4.5 km) S along A2. Car park. Lavatories. No collecting.*
■ Sea-cliff, flushes, boulder beach, river, heathland.
■ In autumn and winter divers, grebes, terns, skuas and auks can be viewed from the car. Dippers along river and butterflies on sandy banks. **Plants** Oysterplant, pale butterwort, bog pimpernel, yellow horned-poppy.
NATIONAL TRUST

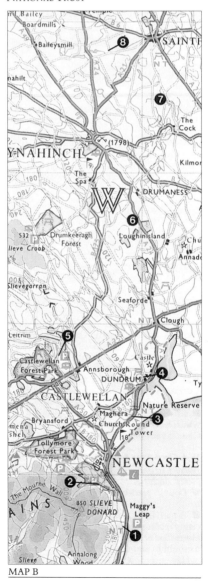

MAP B

B:2 DONARD PARK★

Newcastle; *car park at site, SW of town.*
■ River, plantation, scrub.
■ The Glen River tumbles through the park, at the base of Northern Ireland's tallest mountain, over an array of picturesque cascades and waterfalls. In the surrounding plantation common songbirds abound while several uncommon butterflies, such as silver-washed fritillary and grayling are seen on sunny days.
DEPARTMENT OF AGRICULTURE (N Ireland) FOREST SERVICE

B:3 MURLOUGH★★

Near Dundrum; *2 miles (3 km) SW along A2, turn E into NT car park. In summer access to part of reserve is by permit from warden only.*
■ Dunes, heath, scrub woodland, sandy shore, salt-marsh.
■ An extensive reserve of ancient sand dunes developed in late glacial times on raised storm beaches, with various dune heaths, rich in lichens. Many rare duneland plants on nearby grassland, including several species of orchid. Over 1,000 species of insects have been recorded, including 21 butterflies. In winter an extensive area of sea-buckthorn at the N end of the reserve attracts many passerines.
The bay offers excellent sea-watching with important numbers of sea duck and grebes; seals are always present.
NATIONAL TRUST

B:4 DUNDRUM INNER BAY & COASTAL PATH★

Dundrum; *park on hard shoulder of A2 one mile (1.5 km) S of town.*
■ Tidal estuary, mudflat, salt-marsh.
Neary land-locked site all but drained at low tide, attracting many waders and wildfowl. Best during migration periods. **Birds** Bewick's and whooper swans, brent goose, ruff, bar-tailed godwit, spotted redshank, greenshank, red-breasted merganser.
NATIONAL TRUST

B:5 CASTLEWELLAN FOREST PARK★★

Castlewellan; *forest car park, N off Main Street. Lavatories.*
■ Lake, plantation, national arboretum.
■ A mosaic of habitats with a remarkable diversity of wildlife, including sparrowhawk, otter, badger, fox, Irish hare and stoat.
DEPARTMENT OF AGRICULTURE (N Ireland) FOREST SERVICE

B:6 BOHILL WOOD★

Near Ballynahinch; *4 miles (6.5 km) SE along A24. Turn right on to unclassified road and park by forest.*
■ Scrub, plantation.
■ NNR established to protect the holly blue butterfly, rare in Northern Ireland. Many common songbirds here.
DEPARTMENT OF THE ENVIRONMENT (N Ireland) COUNTRYSIDE & WILDLIFE BRANCH/DEPARTMENT OF AGRICULTURE (N Ireland) FOREST SERVICE

B:7 BALLYDYAN RAILWAY CUTTING

Near Crossgar; *2 miles (3 km) W along B7, then N¾ mile (one km) along unclassified road. Park on roadside. Permit needed from UTNC, Belfast.*
■ Disused railway cutting, scrub wood.

■ Small wildlife refuge in an intensively farmed rural area. There are a variety of common birds, wild flowers and butterflies. ULSTER TRUST FOR NATURE CONSERVATION

B:8 LAUREL BANK FARM★

Near The Temple; one mile (1.5 km) E along B6, turn S on unclassified road, 1¼ miles (2 km) to farm. Park at roadside. Call at farmhouse to collect Nature Trail.
■ Scrub woodland, rough grazing, lough.
■ Diverse habitats with numerous common bird and plant species. Many butterflies including large colony of holly blues, rare here. Sparrowhawk and long-eared owl frequent the area.

C:1 ST JOHN'S POINT★

Near Killough; 2 miles (3 km) S, on unclassifed road. Park beside lighthouse.
■ Rocky shore, sea.
■ Protruding into the Irish Sea, the point is an important landfall for migrating birds and butterflies. Small passerines shelter in scrub around the lighthouse; offshore, gannets, razorbills and guillemots can be seen along with red-throated and great northern divers in winter. Sea-watching reveals common seals and occasional dolphins or porpoises. The seaweed-clad rocky beach deserves a careful look for marine other molluscs and invertebrates. **Birds** Manx shearwater, black redstart, Arctic skua, merlin, stonechat.

C:2 HOLLYMOUNT★

Near Downpatrick; 1½ miles (2.5 km) SW along the A25, turn NW for ½ mile (one km) on unclassified road. Access from forest track. Restricted access Oct-Jan.
■ Alder carr, fen.
■ Frequently flooded woodland provides suitable conditions for growth of many sedges; water violet occurs in wide drainage ditches. **Birds** Water rail, woodcock.
DEPARTMENT OF AGRICULTURE (N Ireland) FOREST SERVICE

C:3 BALLYQUINTIN POINT★

Near Portaferry; 4 miles (6.5 km) S, along coast road. Park at roadside. Contact warden, Quoile Centre, 5 Quay Road, Downpatrick, BT30 7JB.
■ Rocky shore, raised shingle beach, saltmarsh.
■ The extreme S end of the Ards peninsula, a first landfall for many migrating birds. Varied flora and mammals such as Irish hare, fox and badger.
DEPARTMENT OF THE ENVIRONMENT (N Ireland) COUNTRYSIDE & WILDLIFE BRANCH

C:4 QUOILE PONDAGE★★

Near Downpatrick; 1¼ miles (2 km) NE along A25. Car park in cul-de-sac running N. Access to S section on right bank only. Permit for remainder from warden, Quoile Centre, 5 Quay Road, Downpatrick BT30 7JB.
■ Lough, marsh, scrub woodland.
■ Due to artificial conversion of the estuary to a freshwater lake in 1957 subsequent successions have been of great interest to biologists. The shallow pondage has excellent conditions for invertebrates, providing food for fish and in turn attracting large numbers of birds and mammals. Otters occur but one is more likely to encounter birds, breeding in summer and sheltering in

MAP C

winter. Breeding species include various ducks, redshank and snipe. In late autumn and winter the shallow waters attract wildfowl, especially during inclement weather. Summer brings a rich insect fauna. **Birds** Barnacle goose, Greenland white-fronted goose, pink-footed goose, whooper swan, scaup, wood sandpiper.
DEPARTMENT OF THE ENVIRONMENT (N Ireland) COUNTRYSIDE & WILDLIFE BRANCH/DRAINAGE DIVISION DANI

C:5 CLOGHY ROCKS★

Near Strangford; 1½ miles (2.5 km) S on A2. Car park by roadside.
■ Foreshore, rocks.
■ In late summer, common seals haul out on rocks near the car park. The site also has exceptional marine and ornithological interest. **Birds** Gannet, terns, bar-tailed godwit, purple sandpiper, ringed plover.
DEPARTMENT OF THE ENVIRONMENT (N Ireland) COUNTRYSIDE & WILDLIFE BRANCH

C:6 GRANAGH BAY★

Near Portaferry; 1½ miles (2.5 km) SE. Park at roadside. Collecting by permit only.
■ Foreshore, rocky islands.
■ An area of outstanding marine biological importance with a gradation from rocky shore through mudflats to a poorly-developed beach. Unusual species include Devonshire cup coral, sea lemon and sea cucumber.
DEPARTMENT OF THE ENVIRONMENT (N Ireland) COUNTRYSIDE & WILDLIFE BRANCH

C:7 CASTLEWARD★★

Near Strangford; just SW along A25. Signposted. Use NT car park.
■ Mixed woodland, parkland, ponds, foreshore.
■ Diverse habitats in a relatively small area

with chance to see many sea and woodland bird species. Ponds contain various dragonflies and damselflies. **Birds** Roseate, Sandwich, Arctic and common terns, sanderling, buzzard, woodcock. **Mammals** Otter, badger.
NATIONAL TRUST

C:8 KEARNEY & KNOCKINELDER BAY★

Near Portaferry; S on coast road then E 2½ miles (4 km) across Ards peninsula. Car park by Knockinelder Bay. No collecting.
■ Rocky shore, sandy beach.
■ An excellent spot to view waders on the shore. During the winter months oyster-catcher, ringed plover, purple sandpiper and golden plover are present. Through the summer, three species of tern regularly fish the shallow waters for sand eels. Further offshore shags, cormorants and eider duck are present, with divers in winter. Both grey and common seals are seen, with otters frequent along the Ards coast. At low tide a large area of rocky shore is exposed. Particularly rich in flora and invertebrate fauna, it deserves close scrutiny.
NATIONAL TRUST

C:9 THE DORN★★

Near Portaferry; 3 miles (5 km) N along A20, turn NW towards Bishops Mill. Park on roadside. Collecting by permit only.
■ Tidal rapid, foreshore, mudflat, rock outcrops.
■ The bay's outlet is constricted, resulting in a fast-flowing salt water stream at most states of the tide. Tunicates, sponges, anemones and echinoderms occur in abundance.
DEPARTMENT OF THE ENVIRONMENT (N Ireland) COUNTRYSIDE & WILDLIFE BRANCH/NATIONAL TRUST

DOWN

C:10 KILLARD★★
Near Downpatrick; ½ *mile (one km) N from Ballyhornan. Park and walk to beach. Contact warden, Quoile Centre, 5 Quay Road, Downpatrick, BT30 7JB.*
■ Dune grassland, heath, foreshore, small cliffs.
■ Ballyhornan Beach is popular with waders; during winter, purple sandpiper, turnstone, golden and ringed plover present.

In autumn, surrounding fields host large flocks of linnet, chaffinch, greenfinch and skylark.

Red-breasted merganser, wigeon and teal present in winter on the bay on the S side of the peninsula. Shoreline plants include sea sandwort, sea rocket and frosted orache.

S and W of Killard Point is calcareous dune grassland with spring squill and lady's bedstraw, bee, frog, pyramidal, and green-winged orchids, early and northern marsh-orchids. In summer butterflies abound – common blue, grayling and painted lady with clouded yellow a rare visitor. Hummingbird and small elephant hawkmoths occur.

Seals regularly haul out on offshore rocks. In spring, the point is a first landfall for migrants. Look out for wheatear and black redstart.

There is more calcareous grassland inland and N of Killard Point. Irish hare races over short heath vegetation. Sand martin nests on cliffs and fulmar is always present. Good marine flora and fauna on foreshore.

Watch out for birds fishing – in winter, razorbills and guillemots; common, Arctic and Sandwich terns in summer. Occasionally, long-tailed duck and scoter may be seen, while shelduck nest in burrows at the cliff base.
DEPARTMENT OF THE ENVIRONMENT (N Ireland) COUNTRYSIDE & WILDLIFE BRANCH

D:1 BELSHAW'S QUARRY
Near Lisburn; NW along B101. Reserve signposted to W. Car park.
■ Disused quarry.
■ Many interesting geological features in a confined area, including dykes, a fault plane and an unconformity; Triassic marls, Pleistocene boulder clays, Cretaceous chalk, Tertiary basalt.
DEPARTMENT OF THE ENVIRONMENT (N Ireland) COUNTRYSIDE & WILDLIFE BRANCH

D:2 CASTLE ESPIE★★
Near Comber; ½ *mile (one km) SE along A22, turn SE along coast road, 2 miles (3 km) to car park and bird hide. Consult tide tables.*
■ Foreshore, mudflat, salt-marsh.
■ Excellent views from hide of many interesting birds which feed on the eelgrass and mudflats at low tide. Wide range of burrowing invertebrate fauna found in high densities. **Birds** Pale-bellied brent goose, sanderling, grey plover, knot, greenshank, golden plover.
NATIONAL TRUST

D:3 THE GIANT'S RING★
Near Belfast; just N of Ballylesson along unclassified road. Signposted. Car park.
■ Farmland.
■ The Giant's Ring is a 4,000-year-old dolmen or burial chamber surrounded by a 10-foot (3-m) grassed-over stone bank which encloses some 10 acres of grassland. Many common butterfly species found here.

D:4 COLLIN GLEN★
Near Belfast; W of town. Park on A501, N of reserve.
■ Mixed woodland, river.
■ In this steeply-sided, well-wooded river valley the vegetation comprises a semi-natural stand of ash/elm woodland with a diverse ground flora. Otter droppings have been found on the banks of Collin River and well-worn runs confirm the presence of badger. While there are no outstanding species of plant or bird here, there are good numbers of most common species. **Plants** Scaly male-fern, giant horsetail, wall-rue, pendulous, remote and wood sedges. **Birds** Dipper, kingfisher.
NORTHERN IRELAND CONSERVATION VOLUNTEERS

D:5 LAGAN MEADOWS
Near Belfast; follow signs for South Ring. Car park at Shaws Bridge. Access on foot on N bank of river Lagan.
■ Marsh, damp grassland.
■ Overgrown reservoir notable for many wild flowers and butterflies in close proximity to a built-up area.
BELFAST PARKS DEPARTMENT

D:6 LAGAN VALLEY REGIONAL PARK
Belfast; follow signs for South Ring. Car park at Shaw's Bridge.
■ River, mixed woodland.
■ The River Lagan is slow-moving here and a walk along the towpath will reveal such interesting birds as little grebe, kingfisher and coot. Otter, mink and fox are about.
BELFAST PARKS DEPARTMENT

D:7 MOUNT STEWART★
Near Greyabbey; 2 miles (3 km) NW along A20. Use NT car park. Open Apr-Sept.
■ Mixed woodland, conifer plantation, parkland.
■ Contrary to its name, a lowland area of diverse habitats rich in common bird species. Woodlands carpeted in wild flowers in spring. **Mammals** Red squirrel, fox, stoat.
NATIONAL TRUST

D:8 SCRABO COUNTRY PARK★★
Near Newtownards; one mile (1.5 km) W along A20, turn S 1¼ miles (2 km) on unclassified road to car park.
■ Quarry, mixed woodland
■ Scrabo Hill is made up of Triassic sandstones capped and protected from erosion by a dolerite sill formed during Tertiary vol-

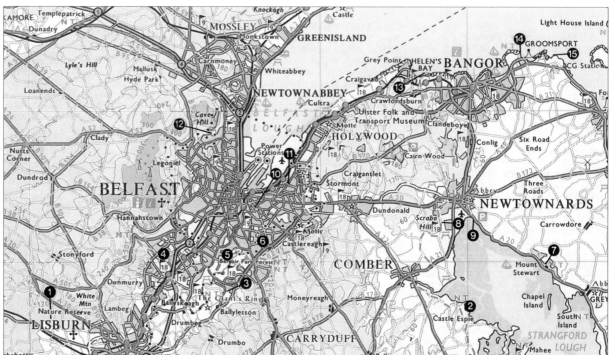

MAP D

Short-eared owl – see D:12.

canic intrusions. Two quarries on the site show geological successions from the Triassic era. Features such as stratification, beds and bedding-planes are present with ripple marks on the floor of the quarry. Igneous intrusions form sills and dykes, the latter displaying 'onion skin' weathering. Ice-age legacies are visible with scars scraped on to the sill indicating the direction of glacial flow. Wildlife includes peregrine, stonechat, feral goat and badger.
DEPARTMENT OF THE ENVIRONMENT (N Ireland) COUNTRYSIDE WILDLIFE BRANCH/ NATIONAL TRUST

D:9 NORTH STRANGFORD LOUGH★★
Near Newtownards; various access points from A20 to view mudflats around Strangford shore. Consult tide tables.
■ Mudflats.
■ Rising tides bring feeding birds closer to shore. Site is of international importance for several species. **Birds** Brent goose, whooper swan, red-breasted merganser, greenshank, pintail, golden and grey plovers.
NATIONAL TRUST

D:10 BEERSBRIDGE★
Belfast (East); Beersbridge Road off A20 2¼ miles (3.5 km) from city centre.
■ Pond, grassland, hedgerows.
■ Northern Ireland's first urban nature park and wildlife refuge, created in a disused railway cutting; it won first prize in the 1987 BBC1 wildlife awards.
NORTHERN IRELAND CONSERVATION VOLUNTEERS

D:11 VICTORIA PARK★
Belfast (East); from Park Avenue, enter park from underpass and park by bandstand.
■ Drained boating lake.
■ A high-tide roost for waders in the industrial heart of Belfast; up to 500 dunlin in winter, with oystercatchers seen on surrounding grass.
BELFAST PARKS DEPARTMENT

D:12 BELFAST CASTLE ESTATE & HAZELWOOD
Near Belfast; N along A6. Signposted. Car park.
■ Mixed woodland, cliffs.
■ Wide variety of common songbirds and fine springtime display of wild flowers on woodland floor. Ravens nest on cliffs; short-eared owls often present in winter.
BELFAST PARKS DEPARTMENT

D:13 CRAWFORDSBURN★
Near Bangor; from Crawfordsburn village, country park signposted. Car park, lavatories and interpretation centre. No collecting.
■ River, mixed woodland, foreshore, rocky shore.
■ An impressive cascade where damp shady conditions are ideal for growth of mosses and liverworts. Dipper and kingfisher are often seen along the river and the aerial display of hunting bats can be observed in the twilight over the lower reaches. On the foreshore there is an exposure of Permian rocks, one of only two such Irish sites, and Magnesian limestone contains the typical fossil fauna. Adding to the interest is an exposure of fossiliferous lower carboniferous black shales. The shore is excellent for viewing waders and sea-birds.
DEPARTMENT OF THE ENVIRONMENT (N Ireland) COUNTRYSIDE & WILDLIFE BRANCH

D:14 BALLYMACORMICK POINT★
Near Bangor; park in W Groomsport and walk W along beach.
■ Rocky headland, sandy bays, maritime grassland.
■ **Birds** Red-breasted merganser, Sandwich tern, shag, Arctic tern, purple sandpiper, turnstone, stonechat.
NATIONAL TRUST

D:15 GROOMSPORT HARBOUR & COCKLE ISLAND
Near Bangor; car park at harbour in Groomsport. No access to Cockle Island May-Aug.
■ Harbour, mudflats, island.
■ Island in the centre of the harbour has nesting Arctic terns and ringed plover. Best at low tide in autumn when many waders probe the mud for food. **Birds** Terns, turnstone, curlew, oystercatcher.
NATIONAL TRUST

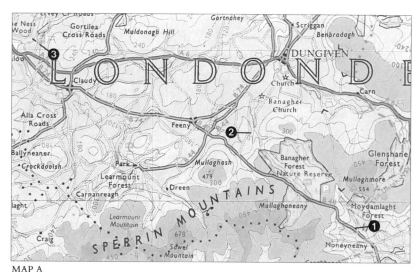

MAP A

A:1 CRAIG-NA-SHOKE

Near Maghera; from Moneyneany, one mile (1.5 km) NW along B40, take right fork. Park by roadside. Access by forest track to N.
■ Montane grassland, peat erosion.
■ Erosion has left 'peat hags' at high elevations, however a more typical moorland vegetation, including Alpine and fir clubmosses, occurs on the lower, drier slopes. Raptors include hen harrier and merlin.
DEPARTMENT OF AGRICULTURE (N Ireland) FOREST SERVICE

A:2 BANAGHER GLEN★

Near Dungiven; SW along A6 then B74 for 1¾ miles (3 km), then signs to Altnaheglish reservoir. Car park.
■ Wooded river valleys.
■ Reserve of three wooded glens, with red squirrel, crossbill and raven and an interesting selection of *Lepidoptera*, including silverwashed fritillary and poplar hawk moth.
DEPARTMENT OF THE ENVIRONMENT (N Ireland) COUNTRYSIDE & WILDLIFE BRANCH

A:3 NESS WOOD★

Near Londonderry; 5 miles (8 km) SE on A6, then 2 miles (3 km) E to Ervey Cross Roads, turn right to junction and right again to country park. Car park.
■ Mixed woodland, river, waterfall.
■ The Burntollet River, home to otters, flows through the steep and wooded gorge, tumbling over a spectacular waterfall within the park.
Red squirrel, badger and fox all breed.
In spring wildflowers carpet the woodland which rings to the chorus of wren, blackbird, robin, songthrush and chaffinch. Less numerous species include wood warbler, blackcap and treecreeper.
DEPARTMENT OF THE ENVIRONMENT (N Ireland) COUNTRYSIDE & WILDLIFE BRANCH

B:1 CREIGHTON'S WOOD★

Near Kilrea; ½ mile (one km) SW along B75, turn SE on to track to Kilrea Golf Club. Access by first tee. Permit only from UTNC, Belfast.
■ Coppice wood, cut-over bog.
■ Two wooded drumlins – one of hazel coppice, the other a small oak wood – are separated by a damp area of cut-over mire bog.
Both have a fine ground flora which in late spring provides a wonderful carpet of colour.

MAP B

Badgers, hedgehog and woodmice are very much at home here, with most common songbirds present. Rarities include large heath and the Irish damselfly, *Coenagrion lunulatum*.
ULSTER TRUST FOR NATURE CONSERVATION

C:1 ROE VALLEY★

Near Limavady; country park signposted S of town. Car park. Full visitor facilities.
■ River, mixed woodland.
■ Park stretches 3 miles (5 km) along the

river. Splendid flora, including toothwort and bird's-nest orchid, with many songbirds proclaiming their territories from the woodland. Wildlife includes otter, mink, fox and badger.
DEPARTMENT OF THE ENVIRONMENT (N Ireland) COUNTRYSIDE & WILDLIFE BRANCH

C:2 LOUGH FOYLE★★

Near Eglinton; from A2 by several unclassified roads N between Eglinton and Ballykelly.
■ Foreshore, mudflats.
■ Numbers peak in late autumn at this important staging post for migrating wildfowl; up to 26,000 wigeon and 1,500 pale-bellied brent geese can be seen, with lesser numbers of mallard, teal and pintail.
Waders are also found here in their thousands, and can best be observed near high tide. The rare gyr falcon has been seen occasionally in early winter, and peregrines are regular. **Birds** White-fronted and greylag geese, Bewick's and whooper swans, snow bunting, twite, brambling, whimbrel, spotted redshank.
ROYAL SOCIETY FOR THE PROTECTION OF BIRDS

C:3 ROE ESTUARY

Near Limavady; 2¾ miles (4.5 km) N along the B69, turn left on to minor road and park on roadside. Take care crossing the railway line.
■ River, mudflat, salt-marsh.
■ This NNR is an excellent feeding ground for many waders, ducks and geese, best observed at high tide throughout the winter months when the occasional rarity may be encountered. **Birds** Pale-bellied brent goose, Greenland white-fronted goose, whooper swan, gadwall.
DEPARTMENT OF THE ENVIRONMENT (N Ireland) COUNTRYSIDE & WILDLIFE BRANCH

C:4 BINEVENAGH★

Near Limavady; 5 miles (8 km) N along A2. Turn NE and follow road around Binevenagh Forest to car park. Access by arrangement with the warden, Portrush Countryside Centre, 8 Bath Road, Portrush.
■ Blanket bog, cliffs.
■ Mountain site with several interesting Arctic/Alpine plants including purple saxi-

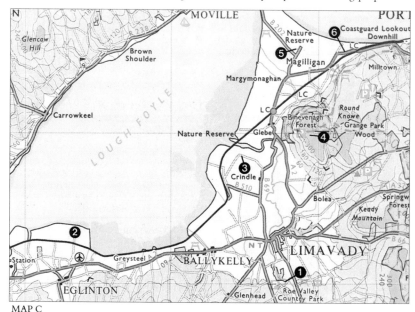

MAP C

frage and moss campion. Moorland birds include red grouse, raven and hen harrier. An NNR.

DEPARTMENT OF THE ENVIRONMENT (N Ireland) COUNTRYSIDE & WILDLIFE BRANCH

C:5 MAGILLIGAN POINT**

Near Coleraine; *from Downhill, 5, miles (8.5 km) SW along A2. Turn N on B202 past the prison to car park at the point. Part of reserve only open to public. Permit from DoE, Belfast.*

■ Dune system, sandy beach, mudflats.

■ A magnificent NNR with something to see at all times of the year. It shows a succession of dunes from mobile shifting sands near the beach through embryo dunes to the vegetated fixed dunes further back.

Interest begins out at sea; in winter a variety of auks and ducks can be seen off the point and good views of red-throated and great northern divers can be obtained, especially in spring as the birds take on their breeding plumage.

Little terns occasionally breed here at their only Northern Ireland station and there is an excellent collection of sea shells near the point.

In spring and summer the dunes bloom and the many rare and colourful species include grass-of-Parnassus, pearlwort and adder's-tongue.

DEPARTMENT OF THE ENVIRONMENT (N Ireland) COUNTRYSIDE & WILDLIFE BRANCH/MINISTRY OF DEFENCE

C:6 THE UMBRA**

Near Coleraine; *from Downhill, 2 miles (3 km) SW along A2. Park on roadside just after crossing railway. Permit only from UTNC, Belfast.*

■ Dune grassland, mixed woodland.

■ This fine duneland system on a windswept N coast displays a succession from mobile building dunes through to the established fixed dunes furthest from the sea. Dune slacks are flooded for most of the winter months and display a fascinating flora in summer when the site is at its best with butterflies, including marsh, dark green and silver-washed fritillaries and grayling. **Plants** Sea centaury, moonwort, creeping willow. **Birds** Peregrine, raven.

ULSTER TRUST FOR NATURE CONSERVATION

Peregrine – see C:6, above.

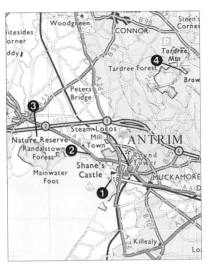

MAP A

ANTRIM

A:1 REA'S WOOD*

Antrim; *car park at confluence of Six Mile Water river and Lough Neagh.*

■ Mixed woodland, fen, lough shore.

■ Woodland reserve in frequently flooded area with extensive flora and diverse insect fauna. An NNR. **Plants** Spindle, wood club rush, summer snowflake, large bitter cress.

DEPARTMENT OF AGRICULTURE (N Ireland) FOREST SERVICE/DEPARTMENT OF ENVIRONMENT (N Ireland) COUNTRYSIDE & WILDLIFE BRANCH

A:2 SHANES CASTLE*

Near Antrim; *³/4 mile (one km) W along A6. Car park in grounds. Open Easter-Sep selected days. Winter visiting by arrangement with RSPB warden.*

■ Mixed woodland, lough, carr, reedbeds.

■ The reserve on the NE shore of the largest body of fresh water in the British Isles is chiefly of ornithological interest. The great crested grebes' spectacular courtship displays may be observed from the hide, and in winter large flocks of duck congregate with occasional whooper and Bewick's swans. Heron, sparrowhawk, long-eared owl and dipper all nest within the reserve. Otters are present, feeding on the lough's renowned eels. Other resident mammals include fallow deer, red squirrel and Irish hare.

PRIVATE OWNERSHIP/ROYAL SOCIETY FOR THE PROTECTION OF BIRDS

A:3 RANDALSTOWN FOREST*

Near Randalstown; *S of town, car park at reserve. Permit needed from Forest Service, Ballymena.*

■ Mixed woodland, plantation, fen, carr.

■ Various wetland habitats on regularly flooded areas of exposed shoreline host numerous wildfowl. Enclosure with viewing platform for watching fallow and red deer present in forest. An NNR.

DEPARTMENT OF AGRICULTURE (N Ireland) FOREST SERVICE/DEPARTMENT OF ENVIRONMENT (N Ireland) COUNTRYSIDE & WILDLIFE BRANCH

A:4 TARDREE FOREST

Near Kells; *3½ miles (5.5 km) SE on B98, then B59. Unclassified road to S. Car park in forest.*

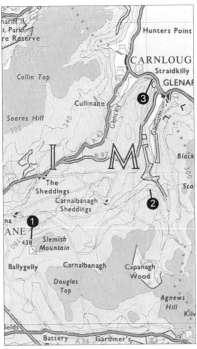

MAP B

■ Quarry.

■ Boulders of Tardree stone – acid lavas made up of rhyolites and glassy obsidian – are provided for easy sampling.

DEPARTMENT OF AGRICULTURE (N Ireland) FOREST SERVICE

B:1 SLEMISH*

Near Broughshane; *one mile (1.5 km) SE along B94, signposted. Car park.*

■ Crags.

■ A prominent dolerite plug rising high above the surrounding countryside, with views from summit well worth the climb. Raven and meadow pipit present.

B:2 UPPER GLEN, GLENARM**

Near Glenarm; *S ½ mile (one km) along B97. Track to left; park off track. By UTNC permit only.*

■ Woodland, deer park, marsh, river.

■ In this varied reserve, wood crane's-bill, Welsh poppy and tutsan grow, splendid specimens of adder's-tongue in the hazelwood. Moonwort grows on the dry grassy banks with twayblade and common spotted-orchids. Dipper, heron and sometimes otter are seen along the river, while badger, Irish hare and stoat inhabit upper reaches of the glen. Breeding birds include curlew, wood warbler, snipe and woodcock, and a rich insect fauna is present.

ULSTER TRUST FOR NATURE CONSERVATION

B:3 STRAIDKILLY

Glenarm; *NW along B97, then unclassified road ½ mile (one km) NW. Park at roadside. Access from track.*

■ Hazelwood, crag.

■ An excellent example of drier hazel thicket with a rich ground flora. Toothwort, bird's-nest and butterfly orchids grow here, with fulmar nesting on the crags. Best in spring.

DEPARTMENT OF THE ENVIRONMENT (N Ireland) COUNTRYSIDE & WILDLIFE BRANCH

ANTRIM

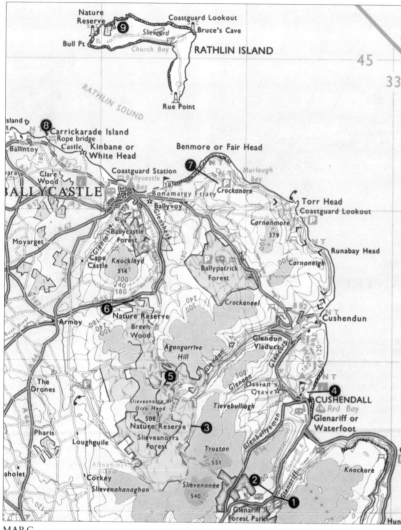

MAP C

C:1 GLENARIFF FOREST WATERFALLS★

Near Cargan; 3 *miles (5 km) NE along A43. Use forest car park.*

■ Gorge, river, mixed woodland.

■ Through this NNR the river drops from 750 to 200 feet (230 to 60 m) in a beautiful, wild series of waterfalls and cascades with intervening stretches of torrent. Foot-bridges, paths and catwalks make the humid gorge accessible – one of the finest sites for bryophytes in Ireland, notable for liverworts. The woodland is home to many birds, with raptors such as buzzard, peregrine and sparrowhawk regularly seen. DEPARTMENT OF THE ENVIRONMENT (N Ireland) COUNTRYSIDE & WILDLIFE BRANCH/DEPARTMENT OF AGRICULTURE (N Ireland) FOREST SERVICE

C:2 GLENARIFF LAKES★

Near Cargan; 3 *miles (5 km) NE along A43. Forest car park. Take track S towards Evish Hill.*

■ Blanket bog, loughs, plantation.

■ Upland site with varied wildfowl on three small loughs. Proximity of state forest allows for sightings of common woodland species and shelters Irish hare and fox. DEPARTMENT OF AGRICULTURE (N Ireland) FOREST SERVICE

C:3 SLIEVEANORRA MOOR★

Near Cushendall; 1½ *miles (2.5 km) NW along A2, then W along Glenaan for 4 miles (7 km). Park at roadside. Foot access from forest track. No dogs.*

■ Blanket bog, plantation.

■ A 555-acre reserve dedicated to conservation of red grouse, with other intresting birds to be seen including merlin, hen harrier, peregrine and raven. DEPARTMENT OF AGRICULTURE (N Ireland) FOREST SERVICE

C:4 CUSHENDUN

Near Cushendall; N *on A2, E on B92. NT car park in Cushendun.*

■ Rock outcrops.

■ A small granite boss with minor intrusions of pink quartz is of interest, as are the exposures of basal Old Red Sandstone conglomerates. Good all year. NATIONAL TRUST

C:5 SLIEVEANORRA FOREST★

Near Cushendall; 1½ *miles (2.5 km) NW along A2. Turn W along Glenaan 4 miles (7 km). Park at roadside. Foot access from forest park. No dogs.*

■ Blanket bog.

■ In this wild, barren, wet and windswept NNR several plots have been identified to highlight peat erosion, regeneration and development. At the summit wind and rain have stripped the mountain bare in places, but some recolonization is occurring; Alpine clubmoss may be found. Further down the mountain fine examples of blanket bog may be seen, home to several interesting beetles including the large ground-beetle *Carabus glabratus* and the stunning green and golden striped *C. nitens*. At the lowest site peat is regenerating – a fine example of a pool and hummock complex. Irish hare, red grouse, merlin, raven and hen harrier are typical in this terrain. **Plants** Lesser twayblade, cranberry, fir clubmoss, crowberry. DEPARTMENT OF AGRICULTURE (N Ireland) FOREST SERVICE/DEPARTMENT OF THE ENVIRONMENT (N Ireland) COUNTRYSIDE & WILDLIFE BRANCH

C:6 BREEN FOREST★

Near Armoy; 3 *miles (5 km) E along B15. Access by farm track S.*

■ Oak woodland.

■ This NNR is one of Northern Ireland's best examples of oak woodland, thought to be primeval. Acid soils restrict the ground flora somewhat, with great wood-rush predominating, but some interesting ferns occur, including Wilson's filmy. A small pond seethes with frogs in springtime – rich pickings for predators such as hen harrier, heron, otter and fox. Wood warblers are resident; buzzard and raven are frequently seen. Badger and Irish hare are present. DEPARTMENT OF AGRICULTURE (N Ireland) FOREST SERVICE/DEPARTMENT OF ENVIRONMENT (N Ireland) COUNTRYSIDE & WILDLIFE BRANCH.

C:7 FAIR HEAD & MURLOUGH BAY★

Near Ballycastle; 1½ *miles (2.5 km) E along A2. Take unclassified road NE. Car parks.*

■ Cliff, rocky shore, scrub woodland, moorland.

■ This impressive dolerite sill rises some 600 feet (220 m) from the rocky shore below, and with the bay exhibits geological successions from Dalradian through Trias to Cretaceous. Above the head is an area of moorland with three small loughs where whooper swan, snow bunting and twite are present in winter. Many raptors may be observed, while the characteristic calls of raven and chough may be heard. The mixed woodland on scree slopes is unique in Northern Ireland and holds many species of common passerine. Along the shore oystercatcher, curlew, redshank and turnstone are frequent while at sea auks, eider, shag and cormorant may be seen. NATIONAL TRUST

C:8 CARRICK-A-REDE ISLAND★★

Near Ballycastle; 5 *miles (8 km) W along coast road. Car park. Access possible only May-Sep, using rope bridge.*

■ Sea-bird cliff.

■ The island and mainland cliffs are remnants of an explosive volcanic vent. Many sea-birds nest here – kittiwake, guillemot and razorbill – on impossible ledges. Several pairs of puffin are present along with black guillemot, cormorant and shag. Many of these can be seen fishing for sand-eels in the waters below. The cliffs are home to raven and peregrine, with chough seen later in the season. A salmon fishery adds interest. NATIONAL TRUST

C:9 RATHLIN ISLAND★★

Near Ballycastle; daily boat crossings from town. From Church Bay 4 miles (7 km) W.
■ Sea-bird cliffs, grassland, heath, lake.
■ The features picked out below assume the island is toured in a clockwise walk, starting on unclassified road and continuing on cliff-top paths.

The unimproved grazing land holds many wild flowers, yellow rattle and eyebright; wheatear, stonechat and numerous meadow pipits.

Scrubby woodland provides shelter on this windswept island where common woodland species are present.

Cooraghy Bay gives access to shore; do not disturb nesting birds such as ringed plover and oystercatcher. Interesting marine fauna.

A small lake inland of Bull Point holds breeding wildfowl; kittiwake collect mud for nests.

At Bull Point colonies of kittiwake may be seen; watch for peregrine and chough, too.

Open grassland W of the small lake has heath spotted-, lesser butterfly- and fragrant orchids. Spring squill, harebell and bird's-foot trefoil add colour. Butterflies include dark green fritillary and grayling.

In the vicinity of West Lighthouse are excellent sea cliffs and sea stacks with amazing views of breeding kittiwake, razorbill and guillemot; puffin nests on grassy scree slopes.

Common spotted orchid – found at D:3, Portstewart Dunes.

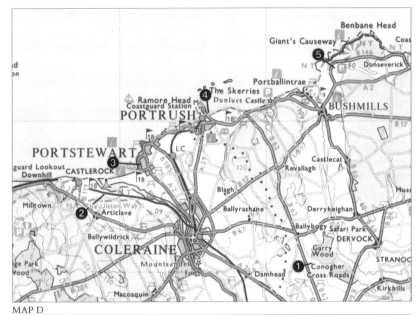

MAP D

Passerines are common in Kinramer Wood.

Loughnanskan, a small lake, has bogbean and yellow iris; snipe and reed bunting nest nearby.

There is an RSPB reserve inland from Skorriagh headland: more sea-bird cliffs; raptors. Watch for Ailsa Craig gannet and auks fishing at sea.

DEPARTMENT OF THE ENVIRONMENT (N Ireland) COUNTRYSIDE & WILDLIFE BRANCH/ROYAL SOCIETY FOR THE PROTECTION OF BIRDS/DEPARTMENT OF AGRICULTURE (N Ireland) FOREST SERVICE

D:1 GARRY BOG★

Near Ballymoney; 2 miles (3.5 km) N along B62. Park at roadside.
■ Raised bog.
■ Sixteen-acre lowland reserve with typical acid flora including bog asphodel and cranberry. Snipe, woodcock and Irish hare frequent this very wet site.
DEPARTMENT OF AGRICULTURE (N Ireland) FOREST SERVICE

D:2 BANN ESTUARY

Castlerock; car park in town. Reserve to E.
■ Estuary, mudflats.
■ Bird hide provides excellent views over the river with mudflats exposed at low tide. Renowned site for rarities during migration seasons when sea-watching can prove rewarding. **Birds** Great northern diver, red-throated diver, whimbrel, red-breasted merganser, curlew sandpiper, little stint, sanderling, eider, knot, great crested grebe.
NATIONAL TRUST

D:3 PORTSTEWART DUNES★

Portstewart; car park on W side of town.
■ Dune grassland.
■ The dune complex, progressing from mobile to fixed drier dunes the further one goes from the strand, holds a variety of interesting plants and insects, including orchids and cinnebar moth.
NATIONAL TRUST

D:4 PORTRUSH & RAMORE HEAD★

Portrush; park on NE side of town, access on foot to Ramore Head. No collecting.

■ Headland.
■ The headland's NE foreshore has exposures of the internationally famous Portrush rock. During the late 18thC geologists were divided into Neptunists, who believed that igneous rocks were the result of sedimentary processes, and Volcanists, who preferred the theory of volcanic origin. Here fossiliferous liassic shales were baked by the Portrush sill, resulting in a tough rock superficially similar to igneous, but containing many recognizable fossils, so Neptunists used it to argue their case. This NNR is also an ideal place for winter sea watching. Divers, storm and Leach's petrels, razorbill, black guillemot and possibly the little auk feed offshore.
DEPARTMENT OF THE ENVIRONMENT (N Ireland) COUNTRYSIDE & WILDLIFE BRANCH

D:5 THE GIANT'S CAUSEWAY & NORTH ANTRIM CLIFF PATH ★★

Near Ballycastle; from Bushmills, 2½ miles (4 km) N on A2 and B146. Car park.
■ Heath, cliff, grassland.
■ Path down past cliffs towards Great Stooken: fulmar and rock dove often seen. Lower grassland attracts butterflies, including grayling, which feed on the bright array of wild flowers.

The Giant's Causeway itself, designated a World Heritage Site in 1987, was formed by igneous intrusions during the Tertiary when prolonged cooling created an unusually perfect complex of predominantly hexagonal basalt columns.

The Giant's Organ columns of basalt are over 36 feet (12 m) tall. Look for fossils of *Lepedodendron* at the base.

Rock doves and chough may be seen along the cliff-top path.

At Port na Spaniagh oystercatcher, purple sandpiper, redshank and turnstone feel along the shore, rock pipits on the boulders.

On the heath, lizards are present, while healthy populations of pipits and skylarks often attract hunting peregrine falcons and sparrowhawks.

Benbane Head has excellent sea watching – fishing gannet, Manx shearwater, guillemot, razorbill and eider in summer with diver and many auk in winter.
NATIONAL TRUST

LOCATION INDEX

List of county names with
abbreviations used in these indexes

England

Avon	Avon
Bedfordshire	Beds
Berkshire	Berks
Buckinghamshire	Bucks
Cambridgeshire	Cambs
Cheshire	Ches
Cleveland	Cleve
Cornwall	Corn
Cumbria	Cumbr
Derbyshire	Derby
Devon	Devon
Dorset	Dorset
Durham	Durham
East Sussex	E.Susx
Essex	Essex
Gloucestershire	Glos
Greater London	G.Lon
Greater Manchester	G.Man
Hampshire	Hants
Hereford & Worcester	H&W
Hertfordshire	Herts
Humberside	Humbs
Isle of Wight	I of W
Kent	Kent
Lancashire	Lancs
Leicestershire	Leics
Lincolnshire	Lincs
Merseyside	Mers
Norfolk	Norf
North Yorkshire	N.Yks
Northamptonshire	Northnts
Northumberland	Northum
Nottinghamshire	Notts
Oxfordshire	Oxon
Shropshire	Shrops
Somerset	Somer
South Yorkshire	S.Yks
Staffordshire	Staffs
Suffolk	Suff
Surrey	Surrey
Tyne and Wear	T&W
Warwickshire	Warw
West Midlands	W.Mids
West Sussex	W.Susx
West Yorkshire	W.Yks
Wiltshire	Wilts

Wales

Clwyd	Clwyd
Dyfed	Dyfed
Gwent	Gwent
Gwynedd	Gwyn
Mid Glamorgan	M.Glam
Powys	Powys
South Glamorgan	S.Glam
West Glamorgan	W.Glam

Other Areas

Channel Islands	C.I
Isle of Man	I of M
Isles of Scilly	I of S

Region & Island Area Names
Scotland
Regions

Borders	Border
Central	Central
Dumfries & Galloway	D&G
Fife	Fife
Grampian	Grampn
Highland	Highl
Lothian	Lothn
Strathclyde	Strath
Tayside	Tays

Other Areas

Orkney	Orkney
Shetland	Shetld
Western Isles	W.Isles

Ireland
County names are printed in full.

This index lists places - generally towns -
used to locate sites in the *Atlas*. These are
usually the nearest town of any importance,
shown on Routemaster mapping by yellow
infill.

A

Abercraf (Powys) 184
Aberdare (M.Glam) 173
Aberdeen (Grampn) 228, 229
Aberfeldy (Tays) 225
Aberfoyle (Central) 220
Abergavenny (Gwent) 185
Abergele (Clwyd) 199
Aberystwyth (Dyfed) 182, 183
Aboyne (Grampn) 228
Aby (Lincs) 103
Aghada (Cork) 250
Ainsdale (Mers) 128
Aldeburgh (Suff) 119
Alderney (C.I.) 45
Aldershot (Hants) 68
Alford (Lincs) 103
Alloa (Central) 220, 221
Alnwick (Northum) 164, 165, 166
Alresford (Hants) 51
Alton (Hants) 51
Amble (Northum) 165
Amble-by-the-sea (Northum) 165
Amersham (Bucks) 78
Amlwch (Gwyn) 195
Ampthill (Beds) 81
Amroth (Dyfed) 178
Anascaul (Kerry) 251
Andover (Hants) 51
Anglesey Abbey (Cambs) 115
Antrim (Antrim) 279
Appley Bridge (Lancs) 128
Aboath (Tays) 226
Ardara (Donegal) 265
Arklow (Wicklow) 259
Armagh (Armagh) 273
Armoy (Antrim) 280
Arnside (Cumbr) 139
Arran, Island of (Strath) 209
Arundel (W.Susx) 52
Ashbourne (Derby) 98
Ashburton (Devon) 27
Ashford (Kent) 57, 58
Ashington (Northum) 164, 165
Askeaton (Limerick) 252
Athlone (Westmeath) 262
Attleborough (Norf) 119
Aughinish (Limerick) 252
Aughnacloy (Tyrone) 271
Avebury (Wilts) 65
Aviemore (Highl) 233, 234
Avonmouth (Avon) 43
Ayr (Strath) 208, 209

B

Bainbridge (N.Yks) 146
Bakewell (Derby) 106, 107

Bala (Gwyn) 192
Ballater (Grampn) 227
Ballina (Mayo) 261
Ballinrobe (Mayo) 261
Ballintra (Donegal) 265
Ballycastle (Antrim) 280, 281
Ballycastle (Mayo) 260
Ballyconneely (Galway) 256
Ballycotton (Cork) 250
Ballyheige (Kerry) 252
Ballymoney (Antrim) 281
Ballynahinch (Down) 274
Ballysadare (Sligo) 263
Ballyvaghan (Clare) 255, 256
Baltimore (Cork) 250
Bamber Bridge (Lancs) 130
Bamburgh (Northum) 166
Banbury (Oxon) 88
Banchory (Grampn) 228
Bangor (Gwyn) 194, 196
Bangor (Down) 277
Bardney (Lincs) 102
Barking (G.Lon) 72
Barnard Castle (Durham) 151, 152
Barnes (G.Lon) 72
Barnet (G.Lon) 73, 112
Barnstaple (Devon) 31
Barrow-in-Furness (Cumbr) 149
Barton-Le-Clay (Beds) 80
Barton upon Humber (Humbs) 134
Basildon (Essex) 109
Basingstoke (Hants) 66
Bath (Avon) 64
Bathgate (Lothian) 216
Battersea (G.Lon) 72
Battle (E.Susx) 56
Beaulieu (Hants) 49
Beauly (Highl) 235
Beaumaris (Gwyn) 196
Bebbington (Mers) 126
Bedford (Beds) 81, 82
Belfast (Antrim) 276, 277
Belleek (Fermanagh) 270
Belmullet (Mayo) 261
Belsay (Northum) 163
Bembridge (I of W) 47
Benbecula (W.Isles) 240
Benllech (Gwyn) 195
Benllech (Gwyn) 195
Bermondsey (G.Lon) 72
Berkhamsted (Herts) 80
Berview (Powys) 187
Berwick-upon-Tweed (Northum) 167, 206
Bethesda (Gwyn) 194
Bettws-y-coed (Gwyn) 193
Bettyhill (Highl) 239
Beverley (Humbs) 135
Bewdley (H. & W) 87
Bideford (Devon) 31

Billericay (Essex) 109
Billingham (Cleve) 158
Birkenhead (Mers) 126
Birmingham (W.Mids) 87
Birr (Offaly) 258
Bishop Auckland (Durham) 152
Bishops's Castle (Shrops) 94
Bishop's Stortford (Herts) 113
Blackford (Tays) 221
Blackpool (Lancs) 136
Blaenavon (Gwent) 189
Blagdon (Avon) 41
Blaydon (T&W) 160
Blessington (Kildare) 259
Bodmin (Corn) 23, 24
Bolton (G.Man) 131
Boscastle (Corn) 24
Boston (Lincs) 102
Bournemouth (Dorset) 37
Bowes (Durham) 151
Bowness-on-Solway (Cumbr) 150
Braemar (Grampn) 227
Bracknell (Berks) 68, 69
Brading (I.of W) 47
Brandon (Suff) 119
Braunton (Devon) 31
Bray (Wicklow) 259
Brecon (Powys) 184, 185
Brentwood (Essex) 109
Bressay (Shetld) 247
Bridgend (Islay, Strath) 212
Bridgend (M.Glam) 172
Bridgwater (Somer) 39, 40
Bridlington (Humbs) 135
Bridport (Dorset) 34
Brierley Hill (W.Mids) 87
Brighstone (I of W) 46, 47
Brighton (W.Susx) 53, 56
Bristol (Avon) 41, 42, 43
Bristol Channel (South Wales/South
 West England) 30
Broadford (Skye, Highl) 232
Brodick (Arran, Strath) 209
Brogborough (Beds) 81
Bromsgrove (H & W) 85, 87
Bromyard (H & W) 85
Broughshane (Antrim) 279
Broughton in Furness (Cumbr) 148
Broughty Ferry (Tays) 223
Brownhills (W.Mids) 96
Bruff (Limerick) 252
Brynmawr (Gwent) 189
Buckingham (Bucks) 79
Bude (Corn) 24, 25, 30
Budleigh Salterton (Devon) 29
Builth Wells (Powys) 185
Buntingford (Herts) 113
Burnfoot (Donegal) 266

Burnham-on-Sea (Somer) 40
Burray (Orkney) 242
Burry Port (Dyfed) 174
Burton-in-Kendal (Cumbr) 139
Burton upon Trent (Staffs) 106
Burwell (Cambs) 116
Bury (Lancs) 131
Bury St Edmunds (Suff) 118
Buttevant (Cork) 250
Buxton (Derby) 98, 107

C

Cadnam (Hants) 49
Caernarfon (Gwyn) 193, 194
Caerphilly (M.Glam) 173
Caherdaniel (Kerry) 251
Caldicot (Gwent) 189
Callander (Central) 220
Calne (Wilts) 64
Camberley (Surrey) 68
Camborne (Corn) 21
Cambridge (Cambs) 114
Camelford (Corn) 24
Cannock (Staffs) 96
Canterbury (Kent) 58, 60
Cardiff (S.Glam) 173, 188
Cardigan (Dyfed) 178, 180
Cargan (Antrim) 280
Carisbrooke (I of W) 46
Carlingwark Loch (D & G) 203
Carlisle (Cumbr) 150
Carlow (Carlow) 253
Carmarthen (Dyfed) 176
Carnforth (Lancs) 138, 139
Carran (Clare) 255
Carrbridge (Highl) 234
Carrick (Donegal) 265
Carrickfergus (Antrim) 277
Castle Combe (Wilts) 64
Castle Douglas (D&G) 203
Castlederg (Tyrone) 271, 272
Castlegregory (Kerry) 252
Castleford (W.Yks) 142
Castleplunket (Roscommon) 262
Castlerock (Antrim) 281
Castlewellan (Down) 274
Cavan (Cavan) 264
Chagford (Devon) 27
Chandler's Cross (Herts) 112
Channel Islands 44-5
Chatham (Kent) 59
Chatteris (Cambs) 116
Cheadle (Staffs) 97
Cheddar (Somer) 40, 41
Chelmsford (Essex) 111
Cheltenham (Glos) 75, 76
Chapstow (Gwent) 189

Chertsey (Surrey) 68
Chester-le-Street (Durham) 154
Chichester (W.Susx) 49, 52
Chirk (Clwyd) 197
Christchurch (Dorset) 37
Church Stretton (Shrops) 94
Churchtown, Southport (Mers) 129
Cinderford (Glos) 75, 190
Cirencester (Glos) 65, 74
Clacton (Essex) 111
Clara (Offaly) 258
Cleethorpes (Humbs) 103
Cleobury Mortimer (Shrops) 94
Clevedon (Avon) 42
Clifden (Galway) 257
Clitheroe (Lancs) 137
Clonakilty (Cork) 250
Clonmacnoise (Offaly) 258
Colchester (Essex) 110, 111
Coldstream (Border) 206
Coleraine (Londonderry) 279
Coleshill (Warw) 88
Colne (Lancs) 136
Colwyn Bay (Gwyn) 196
Comber (Down) 276
Compton (I of W) 46
Congleton (Ches) 98
Connah's Quay (Clwyd) 198
Consett (Durham) 153
Conwy (Gwyn) 196
Cookstown (Tyrone) 272
Corbridge (Northum) 162
Corby (Northnts) 93, 94
Corran Ferry (Highl) 230
Corrofin (Clare) 255
Coventry (Warw) 88
Cowdenbeath (Fife) 224
Cowshill (Durham) 153
Coxhoe (Durham) 155
Craigavon (Armagh) 273
Crail (Fife) 222
Craughwell (Galway) 256
Crawley (W.Susx) 56
Creeslough (Donegal) 266
Creigiau (M.Glam) 173
Creswell (Derby) 108
Crianlarich (Central) 221
Crickhowell (Powys) 184
Cricklade (Wilts) 65
Cromarty Firth (Highl) 237
Crossgar (Down) 274
Crossmolina (Mayo) 261
Crowborough (E.Susx) 56
Cromer (Norf) 124
Croxley Green (Herts) 73
Croydon (G.Lon) 71
Crystal Palace (G.Lon) 72

Cuffley (Herts) 112
Cupar (Fife) 222
Cushendall (Antrim) 280
Cwmbran (Gwent) 188, 189

D

Dalbeattie (D.&G.) 203
Dalkeith (Lothian) 205, 217
Dalton-in-Furness (Cumbr) 148
Daventry (Northnts) 88, 89
Dawlish (Devon) 29
Denbigh (Clwyd) 197, 199
Derby (Derby) 106
Devil's Bridge (Dyfed) 182
Devizes (Wilts) 64
Dingwall (Highl) 237
Diss (Norf) 119
Dolgellau (Gwyn) 191, 192
Dollar (Central) 221
Donabate (Dublin) 260
Doncaster (S.Yks) 132, 133
Dorchester (Dorset) 36
Dorking (Surrey) 71
Doune (Central) 221
Dover (Kent) 58
Downpatrick (Down) 275, 276
Draperstown (Londonderry) 272
Drogheda (Louth) 265
Droitwich (H.&W) 85
Dromahair (Leitrim) 264
Dromore (Tyrone) 271
Dublin (Dublin) 260
Dudley (W.Mids) 96
Dulverton (Somer) 38
Dumbarton (Strath) 212, 220
Dumfries (D.&G.) 203, 204
Dunbar (Lothian) 207
Dundalk (Louth) 265
Dundee (Tays) 223
Dundrum (Down) 274
Dunfanaghy (Donegal) 266
Dunfermline (Fife) 217
Dungannon (Tyrone) 273
Dungarvan (Waterford) 252
Dungiven (Londonderry) 278
Dunkeld (Tays) 225
Dunoon (Strath) 212
Duns (Border) 206
Dunsfold (Surrey) 70
Dunstable (Beds) 80
Durham (Durham) 154
Durness (Highl) 239
Durrington (Wilts) 61
Dursley (Glos) 74

E

Earls Barton (Northnts) 93
East Boldon (T.&W) 160
East Grinstead (W. Susx) 56
Eastbourne (E. Susx) 54
Easton on the Hill (Northnts) 94
Ebbw Vale (Gwent) 189
Eccleshall (Staffs) 96
Edinburgh (Lothian) 216, 217, 218, 219
Eggleston (Durham) 152
Eglinton (Londonderry) 278
Eglwyswrw (Dyfed) 178
Elgin (Grampn) 229
Ellesmere (Shrops) 95
Ellesmere Port (Ches) 126
Elstree (Herts) 112
Enniskillen (Fermanagh) 266, 267, 270
Ennistimon (Clare) 255
Epsom (Surrey) 71
Erskine (Strath) 211
Evesham (H.&W) 85
Exeter (Devon) 28, 29
Exmouth (Devon) 29
Eyemouth (Border) 207

F

Fakenham (Norf) 123
Falkirk (Lothian) 216
Fareham (Hants) 50
Farnborough (Surrey) 68
Farnham (Surrey) 70
Faversham (Kent) 60
Felixstowe (Suff) 117
Ferryhill (Durham) 155
Ffestiniog (Gwyn) 192
Filey (N.Yks) 135
Fishguard (Dyfed) 178
Fivemiletown (Tyrone) 271
Flamborough (Humbs) 135
Fleetwood (Lancs) 136
Flint (Clwyd) 199
Flitwick (Beds) 81
Folkestone (Kent) 58
Fordingbridge (Hants) 49
Forfar (Tays) 226
Formby (Mers) 127, 128
Forres (Grampn) 229, 236
Fort William (Highl) 230
Fowlmere (Cambs) 114
Framlingham (Suff) 118
Frenchpark (Roscommon) 262
Freshwater (I. of W) 46
Frodsham (Ches) 104
Frosterley (Durham) 153
Fulbourn (Cambs) 114

G

Gainford (Durham) 152
Galway (Galway) 256
Garstang (Lancs) 136
Gatehouse of Fleet (D.&G.) 203
Gerrards Cross (Bucks) 78
Girvan (Strath) 208
Glasgow (Strath) 210, 211
Glastonbury (Somer) 39
Glenamoy (Mayo) 262
Glenarm (Antrim) 279
Glenbeigh (Kerry) 251
Glengarriff (Kerry) 251
Gloucester (Glos) 75
Godalming (Surrey) 71
Godmanchester (Cambs) 115
Golspie (Highl) 237
Gort (Galway) 255, 256
Gortahork (Donegal) 265
Goulceby (Lincs) 102
Granard (Longford) 260
Grange-over-Sands (Cumbr) 139
Grantham (Lincs) 101
Grassington (N.Yks) 142
Great Ayton (N.Yks) 158
Great Gransden (Cambs) 82
Great Yarmouth (Norf) 122
Greenock (Strath) 210
Gretna (D.&G) 150
Greyabbey (Down) 276
Guernsey (C.I)
Guildford (Surrey) 70, 71
Guisborough (Cleve) 158

H

Hadleigh (Suff) 117, 118
Hailsham (E.Susx) 54
Halstead (Essex) 110
Haltwhistle (Northum) 163
Hampstead (G.Lon) 73
Harlech (Gwyn) 191, 192
Harlow (Essex) 113
Harris, Isle of (W.Isles) 241
Hartlepool (Cleve) 153
Harwich (Essex) 117
Haslemere (Surrey) 70
Hastings (E.Susx) 55, 56
Hauxley (Northum) 165
Haverfordwest (Dyfed) 176
Haverhill (Suff) 114
Haverthwaite (Cumbr) 148
Hawkhurst (Kent) 57
Hawkshead (Cumbr) 148, 149-50
Hay-on-Wye (Powys) 185
Hayle (Corn) 21
Haywards Heath (W.Susx) 56
Headford (Galway) 256
Heanor (Derby) 106
Hebden Bridge (W.Yks) 132
Helensburgh (Strath) 212
Helmsley (N.Yks) 145
Helston (Corn) 21
Hemel Hempstead (Herts) 112
Hendon (G.Lon) 73
Henley-on-Thames (Oxon) 78
Hereford (H&W) 84, 85
Herm 95
Hertford (Herts) 113
Heswall (Mers) 126, 199
Hexham (Northum) 162, 164
Hexton (Herts) 81
High Wycombe (Bucks) 78
Higham Ferrers (Northnts) 93
Highgate (G.Lon) 73
Hindhead (Surrey) 70
Hitchin (Herts) 81
Hockley (Essex) 109
Hoddesden (Herts) 113
Holt (Norf) 124, 125
Holyhead (Gwyn) 194
Holywell (Clwyd) 199
Horndeanm (Hants) 50
Hornsea (Humbs) 135
Horsham (W.Susx) 56
Horwich (G.Man) 130
Houghton Conquest (Beds) 81
Houghton-le-Spring (T&W) 154
Hounslow (G.Lon) 72
Hove (W.Susx) 52
Hoylake (Mers) 126
Hunmanby (N.Yks) 135
Hunstanton (Norf) 123
Huntingdon (Cambs) 115
Huntly (Grampn) 228

I

Ilfracombe (Devon) 31
Ingleton (N.Yks) 144
Inverarnan (Central) 221
Inverness (Highl) 235
Inversnaid (Central) 220
Inverurie (Grampn) 228
Ipswich (Suff) 117
Ironbridge (Shrops) 95
Irvine (Strath) 209
Irvinestown (Fermanagh) 270, 271
Islay, Island of (Strath) 212, 213
Islington (G.Lon) 72

J

Jersey (C.I) 44
John o'Groats (Highl) 239

K

Kells (Antrim) 279
Kelsall (Ches) 104
Kelso (Border) 206
Kendal (Cumbr) 148
Kenilworth (Warw) 88, 89
Kenmare (Kerry) 251
Kensington (G.Lon) 72
Kessingland (Suff) 119
Kettering (Northnts) 93
Kew (G.Lon) 72
Kidderminster (H&W) 86
Kidwelly (Dyfed) 174
Kielder (Northum) 164
Kilkeel (Down) 274
Killarney (Kerry) 251
Killough (Down) 275
Kilmore Quay (Wexford) 254
Kilnsea (Humbs) 134
Kilrea (Londonderry) 278
Kilrush (Clare) 255
Kingoodie (Tays) 223
King's Lynn (Norf) 121
Kingsbridge (Devon) 27
Kingsclere (Hants) 66
Kingston-upon-Thames (G.Lon) 71
Kington (H&W) 186
Kingussie (Highl) 233
Kinlochewe (Highl) 236
Kinnitty (Offaly) 258
Kinross (Tays) 224
Kinvara (Galway) 256
Kirkby Lonsdale (Cumbr) 138, 144
Kirkbymoorside (N.Yks) 145
Kirkwall (Mainland, Orkney) 242, 243, 244
Kirriemuir (Tays) 226, 227
Knighton (Powys) 186
Knottingley (W.Yks) 142
Knutsford (Ches) 105
Kyle of Localsh (Highl) 233

L

Lakenheath (Suff) 119
Lambhill (Strath) 211
Lampeter (Dyfed) 181
Lanark (Strath) 210
Lancaster (Lancs) 137, 138
Lanesborough (Longford) 262
Lanchester (Durham) 153
Langbank (Strath) 211
Laragh (Wicklow) 259
Largs (Strath) 210
Laxton (Humbs) 134
Leamington Spa (Warw) 88
Leatherhead (Surrey) 71
Ledbury (H&W) 84
Leeds (W.Yks) 142
Leek (Staffs) 98
Leicester (Leics) 99
Leigh (G.Man) 130
Leighton Buzzard (Beds) 81
Leominster (H&W) 86
Letterfrack (Galway) 257
Letterkenny (Donegal) 265
Leven (Fife) 222
Lewes (E.Susx) 55
Lewis, Isle of (W.Isles) 241
Limavady (Londonderry) 278
Limpsfield (Surrey) 57
Linlithgow (Lothian) 217
Lisburn (Antrim) 276
Lisdoonvarna (Clare) 255
Liskeard (Corn) 23
Lisnaskea (Fermanagh) 266, 267
Liverpool (Mers) 126
Livingston (Lothian) 216
Llandeilo (Dyfed) 176
Llandogo (Gwent) 190
Llandovery (Dyfed) 180
Llandrindod Wells (Powys) 186
Llandudno (Gwyn) 196
Llandudno Junction (Gwyn) 196
Llanelli (Dyfed) 171, 175
Llanfairpwllgwyngyll (Gwyn) 194
Llangefni (Gwyn) 194, 195
Llangollen (Clwyd) 197
Llantwit Major (S.Glam) 172
Llanwrtyd Wells (Dyfed) 181
Lleyn Peninsula (Gwyn) 193
Loch Carron (Highl) 236
Loch Lomond (Central/Strath) 220
Loch Maree (Highl) 236
Loch Ness (Highl) 234, 235
Loch Rannoch (Tays) 225
Lochearnhead (Central) 221
Lochgilphead (Strath) 213, 214
Lochmaben (D&G) 204
Lochwinnoch (Strath) 210
Loftus (Cleve) 158
London Colney (Herts) 112
Londonderry (Londonderry) 278
Longford (Longford) 263
Lorn, Firth of (Strath) 214
Lostwithiel (Corn) 23
Loughborough (Leics) 99, 100, 101
Loughton (Essex) 73, 113
Louth (Lincs) 103
Louisburgh (Mayo) 261
Low Bradfield (S.Yks) 107
Lowestoft (Suff) 120
Ludlow (Shrops) 86
Lurgan (Armagh) 273
Luton (Beds) 80
Lydford (Devon) 27
Lydney (Glos) 190
Lyme Regis (Dorset) 34
Lymington (Hants) 47
Lyndhurst (Hants) 48, 49
Lynton (Devon) 31, 33
Lytham St Anne's (Lancs) 136

M

Mablethorpe (Lincs) 103
Macclesfield (Ches) 98, 105
Machynlleth (Powys) 182, 183
Maghera (Londonderry) 278
Maidenhead (Berks) 69, 78
Maidstone (Kent) 59
Mainland (Orkney) 242, 243, 244
Mainland (Shetld) 246, 247
Maldon (Essex) 110
Malehide (Dublin) 260
Mallaig (Highl) 230, 231
Maltby (S.Yks) 133
Malton (N.Yks) 143
Malvern (H.&W) 76, 85
Manchester (G.Man) 107, 130
Manorhamilton (Leitrim) 264
Mansfield (Notts) 106
March (Cambs) 116
Market Weighton (Humbs) 134
Marlborough (Wilts) 64
Marloes (Dyfed) 174, 175
Marwick (Mainland, Orkney) 243, 244
Masham (N.Yks) 143
Matlock (Derby) 106
Meigh (Armagh) 274
Meltham (W.Yks) 132
Melton Mowbray (Leics) 101
Menai Bridge (Gwyn) 194, 195
Mere (Wilts) 61
Merthyr Tydfil (M.Glam) 184
Mexborough (S.Yks) 133
Middleton-in-Teesdale (Durham) 152
Midhurst (W.Susx) 70
Mildenhall (Suff) 119
Millford (Armagh) 273
Milford Haven (Dyfed) 175
Millom (Cumbr) 148
Milngavie (Strath) 211
Minehead (Somer) 38
Moffat (D&G) 205
Mold (Clwyd) 198
Monmouth (Gwent) 190
Montgomery (Powys) 186
Montrose (Tays) 226
Morecambe (Lancs) 136, 138
Motherwell (Strath) 210
Moy (Armagh) 273
Much Wenlock (Shrops) 94
Mull, Island of (Strath) 214, 215
Mullaghmore (Sligo) 263
Mullingar (Westmeath) 260
Musselburgh (Lothian) 217

N

Nailsea (Avon) 42
Nailsworth (Glos) 74
Nairn (Highl) 236
New Galloway (D&G) 203, 204
New Romney (Kent) 55
Newbridge (Kildare) 259
Newbridge-on-Wye (Powys) 186
Newbury (Berks) 66, 67, 69
Newcastle (Down) 274
Newcastle (Wicklow) 260
Newcastle upon Tyne (T&W) 161
Newchurch (Powys) 185
Newent (Glos) 76
Newmarket (Cambs) 115, 116
Newport (Dyfed) 178
Newport (Gwent) 189
Newport (IofW) 47
Newport (Shrops) 96
New Quay (Dyfed) 180
Newquay (Corn) 22
Newton Abbot (Devon) 28
Newton Stewart (D&G) 203
Newton Stewart (Tyrone) 272
Newtown (IofW) 47
Newtown (Powys) 183, 186
Newtown Cunningham (Donegal) 26
Newtown St Boswells (Border) 206
Newtownards (Down) 276, 277
Normanby (Cleve) 158
North Berwick (Lothian) 218
North Ronaldsay (Orkney) 244
North Uist (W.Isles) 240
Northampton (Northnts) 89, 92, 93
Northwich (Ches) 104
Norwich (Norf) 122
Nottingham (Notts) 108
Nuneaton (Warw) 88

O

Oakham (Leics) 100
Oban (Strath) 214, 215
Okehampton (Devon) 27
Oldham (G.Man) 131
Ollerton (Notts) 108
Omagh (Tyrone) 272
Ord (Skye, Highl) 232
Orford (Suff) 117
Orkney Islands (Scotland) 242-5
Ormskirk (Lancs) 128
Oswestry (Shrops) 95, 187
Otley (W.Yks) 143
Oundle (Northnts) 93
Ousefleet (Humbs) 134
Oxford (Oxon) 77

P

Padstow (Corn) 22
Painscastle (Powys) 185
Painswick (Glos) 75
Pangbourne (Berks) 67
Papa Westray (Orkney) 244
Parbold (Lancs) 128
Pateley Bridge (N.Yks) 143
Patrington (Humbs) 134
Peckham (G.Lon) 72
Peebles (Border) 205
Pembroke (Dyfed) 174
Penarth (S.Glam) 173
Penzance (Corn) 20, 21
Pershore (H.&W) 76, 85
Perth (Tays) 224
Peterborough (Cambs) 94, 116
Peterhead (Grampn) 229
Peterlee (Durham) 153, 154
Petersfield (Hants) 50, 51, 70
Petworth (W.Susx) 52, 70
Pewsey (Wilts) 64, 65
Pickering (N.Yks) 145, 147
Pilling (Lancs) 137
Pitlochry (Tays) 225
Pitsea (Essex) 109
Plymouth (Devon) 26
Pocklington (Humbs) 135
Pontardawe (W.Glam) 171
Ponteland (Northum) 163
Pontesbury (Shrops) 94
Pontoon (Mayo) 261
Pontypool (Gwent) 189
Poole (Dorset) 37
Porlock (Somer) 38
Port Charlotte (Islay, Strath) 212
Port Talbot (W.Glam) 172
Portadown (Armagh) 273
Portaferry (Down) 275
Porthcawl (M.Glam) 172
Porthmadog (Gwyn) 192, 193
Portishead (Avon) 42
Portlaw (Waterford) 252
Portree (Skye, Highl) 232
Portrush (Antrim) 281
Portsmouth (Hants) 49, 50
Portstewart (Antrim) 281
Portumna (Galway) 253
Prestatyn (Clwyd) 199
Preston (Lancs) 129
Princes Risborough (Bucks) 78
Pulborough (W.Susx) 52
Pwllheli (Gwyn) 193

Q

Queensferry (Clwyd) 198

R

Rainford (Mers) 127
Rainham (Kent) 59
Ramsey (Cambs) 115
Randalstown (Antrim) 279
Rathdrum (Wicklow) 259
Ravenglass (Cumbr) 150
Reading (Berks) 66, 67
Redcar (Cleve) 158, 159
Redditch (H.&W) 85
Redruth (Corn) 21
Rhayader (Powys) 181
Rhyl (Clwyd) 199
Richmond (N.Yks) 146
Richmond upon Thames (G.Lon) 72
Rickmansworth (Herts) 73
Ringaskiddy (Cork) 250
Ringwood (Hants) 48, 49
Ripon (N.Yks) 143
Rochdale (G.Man) 131
Rochester (Kent) 59, 60
Ropsley (Lincs) 102
Ross-on-Wye (H.&W) 76
Rosslare Harbour (Wexford) 254
Rostrevor (Down) 274
Rothbury (Northum) 164
Roundstone (Galway) 256
Rousay (Orkney) 244
Rowardennan (Central) 220
Rowlands Gill (T.&W) 153, 160
Royston (Herts) 114
Rufford (Lancs) 128
Rugby (Warw) 89, 92
Rugeley (Staffs) 96
Ruislip (G.Lon) 73
Ruthin (Clwyd) 197, 198
Rye (E.Susx) 56
Rye Street (H.&W) 76
Ryton (T.&W) 161

S

Saffron Walden (Essex) 114
St Andrews (Fife) 223
St Austell (Corn) 22
St Bride's Bay (Dyfed) 176
St David's (Dyfed) 176, 177
St Helens (Mers) 130
St Ives (Corn) 20, 21
St Just (Corn) 20
St Mawes (Corn) 21
St Neots (Cambs) 82, 114, 115
St Pancras (G.Lon) 72
Salisbury (Wilts) 61
Saltash (Devon) 26
Saltburn-by-the-sea (Cleve) 158
Sandbach (Ches) 104
Sandown (I. of W) 46
Sandwich (Kent) 59
Sandy (Beds) 82
Sark (C.I) 45
Satterthwaite (Cumbr) 148
Sawbridgeworth (Herts) 113
Saxmundham (Suff) 120
Scarborough (N.Yks) 145, 146
Scilly, Isles of 18-19
Scourie (Highl) 238
Seaford (E.Susx) 54
Seaforth, Crosby (Mers) 126
Seaham (Durham) 154
Seahouses (Northum) 166
Seaton (Devon) 34
Seaton Delavel (Northum) 161
Sedbergh (Cumbr) 150
Sedgefield (Durham) 153, 155
Selby (N.Yks) 134
Selkirk (Border) 205
Settle (N.Yks) 144
Sevenoaks (Kent) 57, 59
Shaftesbury (Dorset) 36, 61
Shalbourne (Wilts) 69
Sheffield (S.Yks) 107
Sherburn in Elmet (N.Yks) 142
Shetland Islands (Scotland) 246-7
Shirenewton (Gwent) 189
Sidcup (G.Lon) 72
Sidmouth (Devon) 29
Silloth (Cumbr) 150
Silverdale (Lancs) 139
Sittingbourne (Kent) 59
Sixpenny Handley (Dorset) 49
Skegness (Lincs) 102
Skipton (N.Yks) 142, 144

LOCATION INDEX

Skull (Cork) 250
Skye, Island of (Highl) 232
Sligo (Sligo) 263, 264
Slough (Berks) 78
Solihull (W.Mids) 88
South Molton (Devon) 31
South Ockenden (Essex) 109
South Queensferry (Lothian) 217
South Ronaldsay (Orkney) 242
South Shields (T&W) 161
South Thoresby (Lincs) 103
South Uist (W.Isles) 240
Southampton (Hants) 49, 50
Southend (Essex) 109
Southern Isles (Orkney) 242
Southport (Mers) 128, 129
Southwark (G.Lon) 72
Southwold (Suff) 119
Spean Bridge (Highl) 232
Spennymoor (Durham) 153
Stafford (Staffs) 96, 97
Staindrop (Durham) 152
Staines (Surrey) 72
Staithes (N.Yks) 158
Stalham (Norf) 123
Stanmore (G.Lon) 73
Stockbridge (Hants) 50
Stockport (G.Man) 130
Stoke-on-Trent (Staffs) 97
Stokenchurch (Bucks) 78
Stonehaven (Grampn) 228
Stornoway (Lewis, W.Isles) 241
Stourbridge (W.Mids) 96
Stourport-on-Severn (H&W) 85, 86
Strabane (Tyrone) 272
Strangford (Down) 275
Stranraer (D&G) 202
Street (Somer) 39
Stretton (Leics) 101
Stromness (Mainland, Orkney) 242, 243
Stroud (Glos) 74, 75
Studland (Dorset) 37
Sutton Coldfield (W.Mids) 88
Swaffham (Norf) 121
Swanage (Dorset) 35, 36
Swansea (W.Glam) 170, 171, 184
Swindon (Wilts) 65

T

Tadley (Hants) 66
Tain (Highl) 237
Talgarreg (Dyfed) 180
Talgarth (Powys) 185
Tamworth (Staffs) 88
Tan-y-Fron (Powys) 186
Tarbert (Strath) 212
Tarbert (Harris, W.Isles) 240
Tarporley (Ches) 104
Taunton (Somer) 39
Tavistock (Devon) 26, 27
Tebay (Cumbr) 150
Teifi, River (Dyfed) 78
Teignmouth (Devon) 28
Temple, The (Down) 275
Tenterden (Kent) 57
Terryglass (Tipperary) 253
Tewkesbury (Glos) 76
Thame (Bucks) 78
Thatcham (Berks) 66
Thetford (Norf) 119
Thirsk (N.Yks) 145
Thornley (Durham) 155
Thrapston (Northnts) 93
Thurso (Highl) 239
Timahoe (Laois) 258
Tiptree (Essex) 110
Tiverton (Devon) 30
Toddington (Beds) 80
Tollesbury (Essex) 110
Tomhaggard (Wexford) 254
Tonbridge (Kent) 57
Torbay (Devon) 28
Torpoint (Devon) 26
Totternhoe (Beds) 80
Town Kelloe (Durham) 155
Tramore (Waterford) 252
Tregaron (Dyfed) 182
Treherbert (M.Glam) 173
Tring (Herts) 80
Trowbridge (Wilts) 64
Truro (Corn) 21, 22
Tullamore (Offaly) 258
Tunbridge Wells (Kent) 57
Twickenham (G.Lon) 72
Tynemouth (T.&W) 161
Tywyn (Gwyn) 191

U

Ullapool (Highl) 236, 238
Ulverston (Cumbr) 148
Unst (Shetld) 247
Usk (Gwent) 189
Utterby (Lincs) 103

V

Valencia Island (Kerry) 251
Ventnor (I of W) 46
Vyrnwy Aqueduct (Powys) 187
Vyrnwy, Lake (Powys) 187

W

Wadebridge (Corn) 22, 23
Wakefield (W.Yks) 132
Wallingford (Berks) 67
Waltham Abbey (Essex) 113
Walton-on-the-Naze (Essex) 111
Wantage (Berks) 69
Wareham (Dorset) 36, 37
Warrington (Ches) 104
Warkworth (Northum) 165
Washington (T&W) 154
Watchet (Somer) 39
Watford (Herts) 112
Wath upon Dearne (S.Yks) 133
Watton (Norf) 121
Wellingborough (Northnts) 93
Wellington (Somer) 30, 38
Wells (Somer) 41
Wells-next-the-Sea (Norf) 124
Welsh St Donats (S.Glam) 172
Welshpool (Powys) 187
Welwyn Garden City (Herts) 112
Wem (Shrops) 95
Wendover (Bucks) 79
Wentbridge (N&W.Yks) 132
West Bretton (W.Yks) 132
West Bromwich (W.Mids) 96
West Derby, Liverpool (Mers) 126
West Kirby (Mers) 126, 127
West Wittering (Hants) 49
Westbury (Wilts) 61
Westerham (Kent) 57
Western Isles (Scotland) 241
Westgate (Durham) 153
Weston-super-Mare (Avon) 40, 42
Westray (Orkney) 244
Wexford (Wexford) 254
Weymouth (Dorset) 34, 35
Wheathampstead (Herts) 112
Wheatley Hill (Durham) 155
Whitby (N.Yks) 146
Whitchurch (S.Glam) 173
Whitchurch (Shrops) 95
Whitegate (Cork) 250
Whitehaven (Cumbr) 150
Whitley Bay (T&W) 161
Whitstable (Kent) 60
Whittlesey (Cambs) 116
Wide Open (T&W) 161
Widnes (Ches) 104
Wigan (G.Man) 128, 130
Wigtown (D.&G.) 203
Willoughby (Lincs) 103
Wilmslow (Ches) 105
Wimbledon (G.Lon) 72
Wimborne Minster (Dorset) 37, 48, 49
Winceby (Lincs) 102
Winchester (Hants) 50, 51
Windsor (Berks) 69
Wiveliscombe (Somer) 38
Woking (Surrey) 68
Wokingham (Berks) 68, 69
Wolsingham (Durham) 152, 153
Woodbridge (Suff) 117
Woodstock (Oxon) 77
Wool (Dorset) 35
Woolacombe (Devon) 31
Wooler (Northum) 166
Wombwell (S.Yks) 133
Worcester (H.&W) 85
Worksop (Notts) 108
Worthing (W.Susx) 53
Wotton-under-Edge (Glos) 74
Wrexham (Clwyd) 197
Wroughton (Wilts) 65
Wroxham (Norf) 122
Wye (Kent) 58
Wylye (Wilts) 61

Y

Yarm (Cleve) 158
Yarmouth (I. of W) 47
Yateley (Hants) 68
Yell (Shetld) 247
Yelverton (Devon) 26, 27
Yeovil (Somer) 38
York (N.Yks) 134, 142, 143
Youghal (Cork) 250

SITE INDEX

This index lists all the sites mentioned in the *Atlas.*

A

A Dyfi (Dyfed) 183
Abberton Reservoir (Essex) 110
Abbot's Wood (E.Susx) 54
Abbotstone Down (Hants) 51
Aberdaron Head/Mynydd Mawr (Gwyn) 193
Aberffraw Dunes/Tywyn Aberffraw (Gwyn) 194-5
Aberithon (Powys) 186
Abernethy Forest (Highl) 234
Abinger Roughs (Surrey) 71
Afan Angoed (W.Glam) 172-3
Agden Bog (S.Yks) 107
Aghagrefin (Fermanagh) 270
Aghatirourke (Fermanagh) 267
Aillebrack (Galway) 256
Ailsa Crag (Strath) 208
Ailwee Cave (Clare) 256
Ainsdale Sand Dunes (Mers) 128
Akeragh Lough (Kerry) 252
Alderley Edge (Ches) 105
Alice Holt Forest (Surrey) 70
Allen Banks (Northum) 162
Allerthorpe Common (Humbs) 135
Allt Rhyd y Groes (Dyfed) 180-1
Allt Wen a Traeth Tanybwlch (Dyfed) 182
Allt-yr-Yn Nature Park (Gwent) 188
Almond, River (Lothian) 217
Almondell & Calder Wood Country Park (Lothian) 216
Alresford Pond (Hants) 51
Alt Estuary (Mers) 127
Alton Water (Suff) 117
Altadeven (Tyrone) 271
Alvecote Pools (Warw) 88
Amberley Mount (W.Susx) 52
Annet (I.Scilly) 18
Ardmeanach (Mull, Strath) 215
Ardmore Point (Strath) 212
Argory, The (Armagh) 273
Argyll Forest Road (Strath) 212
Arlington Court (Devon) 31
Arlington Reservoir (E.Susx) 54
Arne Heath (Dorset) 37
Arnside Knott & Shore (Cumbr) 138-9
Arrowe Park (Mers) 126
Arundel Wildfowl Refuge (W.Susx) 52
Ashberry Wood Area (N.Yks) 145
Ashdown Forest (E.Susx) 56
Ashlawn Railway Cutting (Warw) 89
Ashleworth Ham (Glos) 76
Ashley Walk (Hants) 49
Ashridge (Herts) 80
Ashton Court Estate (Avon) 43
Ashworth Moor Reservoir (G.Man) 131
Askham Bogs (N.Yks) 142
Aston Rowant (Oxon) 78
Aston Woods (Bucks) 78
Attenborough Gravel Pits (Notts) 108
Aughris Head (Sligo) 263
Aust Rock (Avon) 43
Avon Floodmeadows, Ilsley (Hants) 48
Avon Forest (Hants) 49
Avon Gorge (Avon) 43
Avon, River (Wilts) 61
Avon Walkway (Avon) 43
Avon & Kennet Canal (Wilts) 62
Avon & Kennet Canal Towpath (Berks) 66
Axe Estuary (Devon/Dorset) 34
Axmouth Undercliffs (Dorset) 34
Aylesbeare Common (Devon) 29
Ayr Gorge (Strath) 209

B

Badby Wood (Northnts) 88
Bala Lake/Llyn Tegid (Gwyn) 192
Balgavies Loch (Tays) 226
Ballantrae Shingle Beach (Strath) 208
Balloch Castle (Strath) 212
Ballycotton Bay (Cork) 250
Ballydan Railway Cutting (Down) 274-5
Ballymacoda (Cork) 250
Ballymacormick Point (Down) 277
Ballyquinton Point (Down) 275
Ballysadare Bay (Sligo) 263
Ballyteige Sand Dunes (Wexford) 254
Ballyvaghan Bay (Clare) 256
Balmacara (Highl) 233
Balmedie Beach (Grampn) 229
Balranald (North Uist, W.Isles) 240
Baltray Dunes (Louth) 265
Banagher Glen (Londonderry) 278
Bann Estuary (Antrim) 281
Barbury Castle Country Park (Wilts) 65
Bardsea (Cumbr) 148
Bardsey Island/Ynys Enlli (Gwyn) 193
Barfold Copse (Surrey) 70
Barnes Common (G.Lon) 72
Barnwell Country Park (Northnts) 93
Barons Haugh (Strath) 210
Barrow Wake (Glos) 75
Barton Hills (Beds) 80
Basingstoke Canal Towpath (Hants/Surrey) 68
Bass Rock (Lothian) 218
Battersea Park (G.Lon) 72
Battery Point-Ladye Point (Avon) 42
Battery Rocks (Corn) 20
Bawsinch (Lothian) 217
Bayhurst Wood Country Park (G.Lon) 73
Beachy Head (E.Susx) 54
Beacon Hill (Leic) 99
Beauly Firth (Highl) 235
Bedgebury Pinetum (E.Susx) 57
Bedruthan Steps (Corn) 22
Beecraigs (Lothian) 217
Beechwood (Cambs) 114
Beechwoods (Glos) 75
Beer Wood (Somer) 39
Beersbridge (Antrim) 277
Beinn Eighe (Highl) 236
Belfairs (Essex) 109
Belfast Castle Estate & Hazel Wood (Antrim) 277
Belhus Woods (Essex) 109
Bellacorick Flush (Mayo) 261
Bellever Plantation (Devon) 27
Belshaw's Quarry (Antrim) 276
Belstone Cleave (Devon) 27
Beltingham Shingles (Northum) 162
Belvide Reservoir (Staffs) 96
Bembridge Ledges (I of W) 47
Bempton Cliffs (Humbs) 135
Ben Lomond (Central) 220
Ben Lui (Central/Strath) 221
Ben More Coigach (Highl) 238
Ben Wyvis (Highl) 237
Benacre (Suff) 119
Benbulbin (Leitrim) 264
Benfieldside (Durham) 153
Bennachie (Grampn) 228
Benthall Edge Wood (Shrops) 95
Berney Marshes (Norf) 122
Berrow Dunes (Somer) 40
Berry Head (Devon) 28
Berwyn Mountains (Clwyd) 197
Bewl Bridge (E. Susx) 57
Biddle Combe Nature Trail (Somer) 41
Big Waters (T&W) 161
Bigsweir Wood (Gwent) 190
Billingham Bottoms (Cleve) 158
Binevenagh (Londonderry) 278-9
Birkbank Bog (Lancs) 137
Birkdale Hills (Mers) 128
Birks of Aberfeldy (Tays) 225
Birra Lough (Donegal) 265
Birsay Moors (Mainland, Orkney) 243
Bishop Middleham Quarry (Durham) 155
Bishops Wood (N.Yks) 142
Black Bog (Tyrone) 272
Black Dam (Hants) 66
Black Down Nature Trail (Surrey) 70
Black Head (Clare) 255
Black Heath (Dorset) 36
Black Mountains (H&W/Powys) 185
Black Pill (W.Glam) 170-1
Black Rock Drove (Somer) 41
Black Ven (Dorset) 34
Black Wood of Rannoch (Tays) 225
Blackbrook Reservoir (Leic) 101
Blackbrook Valley (Derby) 98
Blackgrove Common (Herts) 113
Blackhall Rocks (Durham) 154
Blackmoor Copse (Wilts) 61
Blackmoorfoot (W.Yks) 132
Blackstone Bank (Durham) 153
Blackstone Rock (Avon) 42
Blacktoft Sand (Humbs) 134
Blackwater Estuary (Essex) 110
Blaenrrhondda Waterfalls (M.Glam) 173
Blagdon Reservoir (Avon) 41
Blakeney Point (Norf) 124
Blanket Nook (Donegal) 265
Blashford Gravel Pit (Hants) 48
Blatherwycke Lake (Northnts) 94
Bleaklow/Kinder (Derby) 107
Blean Woods (Kent) 60
Blenheim Park (Oxon) 77
Blessingbourne (Tyrone) 271
Blewbury Down (Berks) 67
Blithefield Reservoir (Staffs) 96
Bloody Bridge (Down) 274
Blorenge (Gwent) 189
Blunham Gravel Pits (Beds) 82
Bodmin Moor (Corn) 24
Bogside Flats (Strath) 209
Bohill Wood (Down) 274
Bolam Lake (Northum) 163
Bolderwood (Hants) 48
Boldon Flats (T&W) 160
Bolton Woods (N.Yks) 142
Bolusty Bog (Fermanagh) 270
Bonet River Wood (Leitrim) 264
Boorin (Tyrone) 272
Bordon Loughs, The (Northum) 163
Borthwood Copse (I of W) 46
Boscastle (Corn) 24
Bosherston (Dyfed) 174
Botanic Gardens, Cambridge University (Cambs) 114
Botanic Garden, Dawyck (Border) 205
Botanic Garden, Royal, Edinburgh (Lothian) 217
Botanic Gardens, Royal, Kew (G.Lon) 72
Botanic Gardens, Southport (Mers) 129
Bough Bank Reservoir (E.Susx) 57
Boulmer Haven (Northum) 165
Bovey Valley Woodlands (Devon) 28
Bowdown Woods (Berks) 66
Bowlees (Durham) 152
Bowmore Area (Islay, Strath) 213
Bowness-on-Solway Reserve (Cumbr) 150
Box Hill Country Park (Surrey) 71
Boyne Estuary (Louth) 265
Brackagh Moss (Armagh) 273
Bracklinn Falls (Central) 220
Bradenham Woods (Bucks) 78
Bradfield Woods (Suff) 118
Bradgate Park (Leic) 99
Brading Down & Marsh (I of W) 47
Bramley Bank (G.Lon) 71
Brancaster Manor (Norf) 123
Brand, The (Leic) 99
Brasside Ponds (Durham) 154
Braunton Burrows (Devon) 31
Brean Down (Somer) 40
Brecon Beacons (Powys) 184
Bredon Hill (H&W) 76
Breen Forest (Antrim) 280
Breidden Hill (Powys) 187
Brenchley Wells (E.Susx) 57
Brenig Reservoir (Clwyd) 197
Brent Reservoir (G.Lon) 72
Brerechan Meadow (Tays) 226
Bretton Lakes (W.Yks) 132
Breydon Water (Norf) 122
Bridestones (N.Yks) 145-6
Bridgwater Bay (Somer) 40
Brierfield (Roscommon) 262
Brighstone Down (I of W) 46
Brignall Banks (Durham) 151-2
Brigstock Country Park (Northnts) 93
Brimham Rocks (N.Yks) 143
Brimpton Gravel Pits (Berks) 66
Brittas Bay (Wicklow) 259
Broad Bay (Lewis, W.Isles) 241
Broad Colney Lakes (Herts) 112
Broad Pool (W.Glam) 170
Broadhead Clough (W.Yks) 132
Broadmoor Common (H&W) 84
Brock Valley (Lancs) 136
Brockadale (N&W.Yks) 132
Brockhoult Mount (E.Susx) 57
Brockley Combe (Avon) 42
Brockwell's Meadows (Gwent) 188
Brodick Country Park (Arran, Strath) 209
Brogbough Lake (Beds) 81
Brokerswood Woodland Park (Wilts) 61
Broomfield Hill & Walk (Somer) 39
Broomhill Flash (S.Yks) 133
Brown Clee Hill (Shrops) 94
Brown Moss (Shrops) 95
Brown's Folly (Avon) 64
Brownsea Island (Dorset) 37
Bryher (I of S) 18
Bryn Bras (Dyfed) 182
Bryn Euryn (Gwyn) 196
Bryn Pydew (Gwyn) 196
Bryngarw (M.Glam) 172
Bubwith Acres (Somer) 41
Buchan Park (E.Susx) 56
Bucklebury Common (Berks) 66-7
Bucklers Hard (Hants) 49
Buckroney Marsh (Wicklow) 259
Bude Canal & Marshes (Corn) 24-5
Budle Bay (Northum) 166
Bull's Cross (Glos) 75
Buncombe Wood (Somer) 39
Bunduff Lough (Sligo) 263
Bure Marshes (Norf) 122
Burg (Mull, Strath) 215
Burghead Point (Grampn) 229
Burham Marsh (Kent) 59

Burness Castle Quarry (Gwent) 188
Burnham Beeches (Bucks) 78
Burrator Reservoir (Devon) 26-7
Burrington Combe (Avon) 41
Burrough Hill (Leic) 101
Burton Dassett Country Park (Warw) 88
Burton Leonard Quarries (N.Yks) 143
Burton Mill Pond (W.Susx) 52
Bute Park (S.Glam) 173
Butt of Lewis (Lewis, W.Isles) 241
Buxton Country Park (Derby) 107
Buxton Heath (Norf) 122
Bwlch Sychnant/Sychnant Pass (Gwyn) 196

C

Cabin Hill (Mers) 127
Cadair Idris (Gwyn) 192
Cadbury Camp (Avon) 42
Caenlochan (Grampn) 227
Caerphilly Common & Mountain (M.Glam) 173
Cahermurphy Woodland (Galway) 255
Cairngorms (Highl) 234
Cairnsmore of Fleet (D & G) 203
Cairnwell (Grampn) 227
Calder Wood & Almondell Country Park (Lothian) 216
California Country Park (Berks) 68
Callander Craig (Central) 220
Cambridge University Botanic Gardens (Cambs) 114
Cambus Pool (Central) 220
Camel Estuary (Corn) 22-3
Camel's Cove (Corn) 22
Camley Street Nature Park (G.Lon) 72
Canna, Isle of (Highl) 231
Cannock Chase (Staffs) 97
Cantock Beach (Corn) 22
Cape Cornwall (Corn) 20
Capler Wood (H & W) 84
Caragh Lake (Kerry) 251
Cardigan Island (Dyfed) 178
Cardinham Woods (Corn) 23
Cardurnock Flatts (Cumbr) 150
Carlton Marshes (Suff) 120
Carnagh (Armagh) 272
Carneddau (Gwyn) 194
Carnkief Pond (Corn) 22
Carr Mill Dam (G.Man/Mers) 130
Carrick-a-Rede Island (Antrim) 280
Carricknagower (Fermanagh) 270
Carsebreck Curling Ponds (Tays) 221
Cassiobury Park (Herts) 112
Cassop Vale (Durham) 155
Castle Archdale Country Park & Islands (Fermanagh) 270
Castle Caldwell Forest (Fermanagh) 270
Castle Eden Dene (Durham) 153
Castle Espie (Down) 276
Castle Hill (W.Susx) 53
Castle Loch (D & G) 204
Castle Woods/Dynefwr Deer Park (Dyfed) 176
Castlemartin (Dyfed) 174
Castleplunket (Roscommon) 262
Castleward (Down) 275
Castlewellan Forest Park (Down) 274
Castor Hanglands (Cambs) 116
Catherington Down (Hants) 50
Cauldron Snout (Durham) 152
Cavenham Heath (Suff) 119
Cefn Onn (S.Glam) 173
Cefn Sidan Sands (Dyfed) 174
Cefni Reservoir (Gwyn) 195
Cemlyn (Gwyn) 195
Chaddesley Woods (H & W) 87
Chailey Common (E.Susx) 56
Chalkney Wood (Essex) 110
Chambers Wood (Lincs) 102
Chapel Wood (Devon) 31
Charnwood Forest (Leic) 99
Charnwood Lodge (Leic) 100
Chasewater (W.Mids) 96
Chawton Park Wood (Hants) 51
Cheddar Gorge (Somer) 40-1
Chedworth Railway Cutting (Glos) 75
Chee & Miller's Dale (Derby) 107
Cherhill Down (Wilts) 64
Chesham Bois Wood (Bucks) 78
Chesil Beach (Dorset) 34
Chew Valley Lake (Avon) 41
Chichester Gravel Pits (W.Susx) 52
Chichester Harbour (Hants) 49-50
Chilbolton Common (Hants) 51
Chillingham Park (Northum) 166
Chinnor Hill (Bucks) 78
Chippenham Fen (Cambs) 115
Chobham Common (Surrey) 68-9
Chudleigh Knighton Heath (Devon) 28
Church Wood (Bucks) 78
Church Wood (Kent) 60
Churchill Barriers (Southern Isles, Orkney) 242
Cilygroeslwyd Wood (Clwyd) 198
Cirencester Park (Glos) 74
Cissbury Ring (W.Susx) 53
Claife Heights (Cumbr) 148
Clapham Woods (N.Yks) 144
Clara Bog (Offaly) 258
Clare Island (Mayo) 261
Clatworthy Reservoir (Somer) 38
Cleddon Shoots (Gwent) 190
Clear Island (Cork) 250
Cleeve Common (Glos) 76
Cleveland Heritage Coast (Cleve) 158
Cley Marsh (Norf) 125
Cliffe Marshes (Kent) 59
Cliffs of Moher (Clare) 255
Cliveden (Berks/Bucks) 78
Clocaenog Forest (Clwyd) 197
Clodgy Point (Corn) 20
Cloghy Rocks (Down) 275
Clonakilty Bay (Cork) 250
Clonderlaw Bay (Clare) 255
Clonpriest (Cork) 250
Cloondara Bog (Longford) 263
Cloonee Loughs (Kerry) 251
Clougha Pike (Lancs) 137
Clouts Wood Nature Trail (Wilts) 65
Cloutsham Nature Trail (Somer) 38
Clowes Wood (Warw) 88
Clumber Park (Notts) 108
Clwyd Estuary (Clwyd) 199
Clyde Shore (Strath) 211
Clyde Valley Falls & Woods (Strath) 210
Coaley Wood (Glos) 74
Coast, Lothian (Lothian) 218, 219
Coast, Kilminning (Fife) 222
Coast Path (North Jersey, C.I.) 44
Coast Path (Devon) 31
Coastal Path, Dundrum (Down) 274
Coastal Path, Mourne (Down) 274
Coastal Path (Guernsey, C.I.) 44
Coastal Path, Pembrokeshire (Dyfed) 178
Coastal Trail (I of W) 47
Coate Water Country Park (Wilts) 65
Coatham Sands (Cleve) 158-9
Cockerham Moss (Lancs) 136
Cockey Down (Wilts) 61
Cocklawburn Dunes (Northum) 167
Cockle Island (Down) 277
Coed Bron Garth (Gwyn) 196
Coed Crafnant (Gwyn) 192
Coed Cymerau (Gwyn) 192
Coed Dinorwig (Gwyn) 194
Coed Garth Gell (Gwyn) 191
Coed Gorswen (Gwyn) 196
Coed Llechwedd (Gwyn) 192
Coed Lletywalter (Gwyn) 191
Coed Llwyncelyn (S.Glam) 173
Coed Pendugwn (Powys) 187
Coed Porthamel (Gwyn) 194
Coed Ty Cnol (Dyfed) 178
Coed Tyddyn Halen (Clwyd) 199
Coed y Brenin (Gwyn) 191
Coed-y-bwl (M.Glam) 172
Coed y glyn (Clwyd) 199
Coedydd a Cheunant Rheidol (Dyfed) 182
Coedydd a Chorsydd Aber Teifi (Dyfed) 178
Coedydd Aber (Gwyn) 196
Coedydd Maentwrog (Gwyn) 192
Coille Thogabhaig (Skye, Highl) 232
Col-Huw Valley (S.Glam) 172
Colemere Country Park (Shrops) 95
Colinton Dell (Lothian) 216
Coll, Isle of (Strath) 215
College Valley (Northum) 166
Collingwood (E.Susx) 57
Collin Glen (Antrim) 276
Collinpark Wood (Glos) 76
Collyweston Quarry (Northnts) 94
Colonsay, Isle of (Strath) 214
Colwick (Notts) 108
Common Hill (H & W) 84
Common Marsh (Hants) 50
Compton Bay (I of W) 46
Compton Down (Berks) 67
Compton Down (I of W) 46
Conagher (Fermanagh) 270
Conder Green (Lancs) 137
Connah's Quay (Clwyd) 198
Connemara National Park (Galway) 257
Constantine Bay (Corn) 22
Coole (Galway) 256
Coolfin Marshes (Waterford) 252
Coombe Abbey Country Park (Warw) 89
Coombe Hill (Bucks) 79
Coombe Hill Canal (Glos) 76
Coombes Valley (Staffs) 98
Cooper's Hill (Beds) 81
Cooper's Hill (Glos) 75
Cop Mere (Staffs) 96
Copinsay (Orkney) 242
Copperas Woods (Essex) 117
Coppetts Wood (G.Lon) 73
Corbet Wood (Shrops) 95
Cornagague Lough & Wood (Fermanagh) 267
Cornalack Wood (Tipperary) 253
Cornmill Stream (Essex) 113
Correl Glen Forest (Fermanagh) 270
Corrieshallcho Gorge (Highl) 236
Corry Point Wood (Leitrim) 267
Cors Bodeilio (Gwyn) 195
Cors Caranod (Dyfed) 182
Cors Caron (Dyfed) 181
Cors Erddreiniog (Gwyn) 195
Cors Geirch (Gwyn) 193
Cors Goch (Gwyn) 195
Cors Gyfelog (Gwyn) 193
Cors Llyn Farch (Dyfed) 182
Cors y Llyn (Powys) 186
Cosmeston Lakes (S.Glam) 173
Cotehele (Devon) 26
Cotswold Commons (Glos) 75
Cotswold Water Park (Glos/Wilts) 65
Cottasgarth (Mainland, Orkney) 243
Covehithe (Suff) 119
Covenham Reservoir (Lincs) 103
Crab Wood (Hants) 50
Crackley Woods (Warw) 88
Crag Side (Northum) 164
Craig Aderyn (Gwyn) 191
Craig Cerrig Gleisiad (Powys) 184
Craig Irfon (Dyfed) 181
Craig-na-Shoke (Londonderry) 278
Craig Sychtyn (Shrops) 95
Craig Wen (Gwyn) 195
Craig y Ciliau (Powys) 184
Craig yr Adar (Dyfed) 180
Craigavon Lakes (Armagh) 273
Craigellachie (Highl) 234
Craighall Glen (Fife) 222
Craiglockhart Dell (Lothian) 216
Craigower Hill (Tays) 226
Cramond Foreshore (Lothian) 217
Cranbourne Chase (Dorset) 36
Cranmere Pool (Devon) 27
Crathes Estate (Grampn) 228
Craven Uplands (N.Yks) 144-5
Crawfordsburn (Down) 277
Creag Megaidh (Highl) 232
Creeslough Wood (Donegal) 266
Cregennen Lakes/Llynnau Cregennen (Gwyn) 191
Creighton's Wood (Londonderry) 278
Creigiau Penbryn (Dyfed) 180
Creigiau Pen y Graig/Penderi Hanging Oakwood (Dyfed) 182
Cressbrook Dale (Derby) 107
Creswell Crags (Derby/Notts) 108
Cresswell Pond (Northum) 164
Crickley Hill Country Park (Glos) 75
Crimdon Dene Mouth (Durham) 153
Croal Irwell Valley (G.Man) 131
Croes Robert Wood (Gwent) 190
Croft Castle (H & W) 86
Crom Castle (Fermanagh) 267
Cromarty Firth (Highl) 237
Cromford Canal (Derby) 106
Cronkley Fell (Durham) 152
Crookfoot Reservoir (Cleve/ Durham) 153
Cropston Reservoir (Leic) 99
Crossmurrin (Fermanagh) 266
Crowdy Marsh & Reservoir (Corn) 24
Crowlink (E.Susx) 54
Crowthorne Wood (Berks) 68
Croxley Common Moor (Herts) 73
Croxteth Country Park (Mers) 126
Cuerdon Valley Country Park (Lancs) 130
Cuilcagh Summit (Fermanagh) 266
Culbin Forest & Sands (Highl) 236
Culross (Lothian) 217
Culzean (Strath) 208
Cummeen Strand (Sligo) 263
Cunswick Scar (Cumbr) 148
Cushendun (Antrim) 280
Cwm Clydach (Gwent) 189
Cwn Idwal (Gwyn) 194
Cwm Marcross (S.Glam) 172
Cwm Merddeg (Gwent) 189
Cwm Rheidol (Dyfed) 182
Cwm Risca (M.Glam) 172
Cwmllwyd Wood (W.Glam) 171

D

Daisy Nook Country Park (G.Man) 131
Dalby Forest (N.Yks) 145
Dalkeith Park (Lothian) 217
Danbury Ridge (Essex) 111
Dane Valley (Ches/Derby) 98
Danebury Ring (Hants) 51
Danes Moss (Ches) 105
Daneway Banks (Glos) 74
Dare Valley (M.Glam) 173
Darlands Lake (G.Lon) 73
Darnaway Forest (Grampn/Highl) 229
Daventry Country Park (Northnts) 89
Dawlish Warren (Devon) 29
Dawyck Botanick Garden (Border) 205
Ddol Uchaf (Clwyd) 199
Deepdale (Durham) 152
Deep Hayes Country Park (Staffs) 98
Deeside, Royal (Grampn) 227
Delamere Forest (Ches) 104
Denaby Ings (S.Yks) 133
Derbyshire Dales N.N.R./Monks Dale (Derby) 107
Derryclare Wood (Galway) 257
Derrycunihy Wood (Kerry) 251
Derwent Reservoir (Durham/ Northum) 153
Derwent Walk Woodlands (T & W) 160
Devil's Dyke (Cambs) 115
Devil's Dyke (W.Susx) 53
Devil's Punchbowl (Surrey) 70
Devil's Spittleful (H & W) 86
Devon North Coast Path (Devon) 31
Dibbinsdale (Mers) 126
Dimmings Dale (Staffs) 97
Dinas (Dyfed) 180
Dinas Head (Corn) 22
Dinton Pastures Country Park (Berks) 69
Ditchling Beacon (W.Susx) 53
Ditchling Common Country Park (E.Susx) 56
Dixton Embankment (Gwent) 190
Dodman Point (Corn) 22
Doffcocken Reservoir (G.Man) 131
Doire Donn (Highl) 230
Dolebury Warren (Avon) 41
Dollar Glen (Central) 221
Donard Park (Down) 274
Donna Nook (Lincs) 103
Doohatty Glebe (Fermanagh) 266
Doonfoot Bay (Strath) 208
Dorn, The (Down) 275
Dornoch Firth (Highl) 237
Doulton's Clay Pit (W.Mids) 87
Doune Ponds (Central) 221
Dove Point (Mers) 126
Dovedale (Derby/Staffs) 98
Downpatrick Head (Mayo) 262
Dowrog Common (Dyfed) 177
Doxey-Tillington Marshes (Staffs) 96
Draycote Water Country Park (Warw) 89
Draycott Sleights (Somer) 41
Drayne's Wood (Corn) 23
Drift Reservoir (Corn) 20
Drigg Dunes (Cumbr) 150
Dromore Lakes (Cavan/ Monaghan) 264
Dropshort Marsh (Beds) 80
Drum (Grampn) 228
Drum Manor (Tyrone) 272
Drumburgh Moss (Cumbr) 150
Drumlish (Tyrone) 271
Drummains Reed-Bed Wildlife Reserve (D & G) 203
Drummond Hill Forest (Tays) 225
Druridge Bay (Northum) 165
Drygarn Fawr a Gorllwyn (Dyfed) 181
Duckpool (Corn) 25
Duddingston Loch (Lothian) 217
Duddon Sands (Cumbr) 148
Duke of York Meadow (H & W) 76
Duncansby Head (Highl) 239
Dundalk Bay (Louth) 265
Dundrum Inner Bay & Coastal Path (Down) 274
Dundry Slopes (Avon) 43
Dunfanaghy (Donegal) 266
Dungarvan Harbour (Waterford) 252
Dungeness (Kent) 55
Dunkery Beacon (Somer) 38
Dunnet Head & Links (Highl) 239
Dunraven Bay (M.Glam) 172
Duns Castle (Border) 206
Dunstable (Beds) 80
Dunstanburgh Castle (Northum) 166
Dunwich Heath (Suff) 120
Durlston Country Park (Dorset) 36
Durness (Highl) 239
Dymock Woods (H & W) 84
Dynefwr Deer Park/Castle Woods (Dyfed) 176

E

Earl's Hill (Shrops) 94-5
Earlswood Lakes (Warw) 88
East Blean Wood (Kent) 60
East Dart River (Devon) 27
East Head (Hants) 49
East Wretham Heath (Norf) 119
Eastern Moors (Derby) 107
Eastham Country Park (Mers) 126
Eaves Wood (Lancs) 138
Ebbor Gorge (Somer) 41
Ebernoe Common (W.Susx) 70
Echna Loch (Burray, Orkney) 242
Eden Estuary (Fife) 223
Edgbarrow Woods (Berks) 68
Edge Hill (Warw) 88
Edinburgh Royal Botanic Garden (Lothian) 217
Eggerslack Wood (Cumbr) 139
Egglestone Abbey Bridge (Durham) 152
Eglinton Country Park (Strath) 209
Eigg, Isle of (Highl) 230
Eigg, Sound of (Highl) 230
Elan Valley (Powys) 181-2
Elegug Stacks (Dyfed) 174
Elenydd (Dyfed) 182
Elie Bay (Fife) 222
Ellerburn Bank (N.Yks) 145
Ellesborough Warren (Bucks) 79
Ellister Wildfowl Collection (Islay, Strath) 212
Elmley Marshes (Kent) 59
Elton Reservoir (G.Man) 131
Elvaston Castle Country Park (Derby) 106
Embleton Links (Northum) 166
Epping Forest (Essex) 113
Epsom Common (Surrey) 71
Errisbeg Blanket Bog (Galway) 256-7
Eston Nab (Cleve) 158
Etherow Country Park (G.Man) 130
Exe Estuary & Reed-Beds (Devon) 29
Eyebrook Reservoir (Northnts) 93
Eyeworth Pond (Hants) 49

F

Fair Head (Antrim) 280
Fair Isle (Shetld) 246
Fairburn Ings (N.Yks) 142
Fairhaven Lake & Shore (Lancs) 136
Falling Foss (N.Yks) 146
Falls of Clyde (Strath) 210
Fanore Dunes (Clare) 255-6
Farigaig Forest (Highl) 235
Farlesthorpe-Willoughby Railway Line (Lincs) 103
Farleton Knott (Cumbr) 139
Farley Mount Country Park (Hants) 50
Farlington Marshes (Hants) 50
Farmoor Reservoir (Oxon) 77
Farnborough Gravel Pit (Surrey) 68
Farndale (N.Yks) 145
Farne Islands (Northum) 166-7
Favour Royal Forest (Tyrone) 271
Felbrigg Woods (Norf) 124
Felmersham Gravel Pits (Beds) 82
Fernworthy Reservoir (Devon) 27
Ferry Meadows (Cambs) 116
Fetlar (Shetld) 247
Ffrwyd Fen (Dyfed) 174
Fife Ness (Fife) 222
Figsbury Ring (Wilts) 61
Filey Brigg & Dams (N.Yks) 135
Filsham Reedbeds (E.Susx) 55
Fingringhoe Wick (Essex) 111
Five Locks Canal (Gwent) 189
Five Pond Wood Trail (Somer) 39
Flamborough Head (Humbs) 135
Flatropers Wood (E.Susx) 56
Fleam Dyke (Cambs) 114
Fleet Pond (Hants) 68
Fleet, The (Dorset) 34
Flint Castle (Clwyd) 199
Flitwick Moor (Beds) 81
Folkestone Warren (Kent) 58
Forden Chalk Bank (Humbs/N.Yks) 135
Foremark Reservoir (Derby) 106
Formby Point (Mers) 128
Fordham Woods (Cambs) 115
Fore Wood (E.Susx) 56
Forest of Dean (Glos) 190
Forge Valley (N.Yks) 145
Fort Victoria Country Park (I of W) 47
Forvie, Sands of (Grampn) 229
Foula (Shetld) 246
Foulden Common (Norf) 121
Fountainbleau (D & G) 204
Fowlmere (Cambs) 114
Fowlsheugh (Grampn) 228
Fritillary Meadow (Suff) 118
Foxcote Reservoir (Bucks) 79
Foxton Mires (Devon) 27
Frampton Marshes (Lincs) 102
Freiston Shore (Lincs) 102
Frensham Country Park (Surrey) 70
Freshwater Marsh (I of W) 46
Frimley Gravel Pit (Surrey) 68
Friston Forest (E.Susx) 54
Fryent Country Park (G.Lon) 73
Fulbourn (Cambs) 114
Fyfield Down (Wilts) 64-5
Fyne Court (Somer) 39

G

Gainford Spa Wood (Durham) 152
Gait Barrows (Lancs) 139
Galley Hill (Beds) 80
Galloway Forest Park (D & G) 203
Galway's Wood (Kerry) 251
Gann Estuary (Dyfed) 175
Gannel Estuary (Corn) 22
Garbutt Wood (N.Yks) 145
Garden Cliff (Glos) 75
Garry Bog (Antrim) 281
Garryland (Galway) 256
Garston Wood (Hants) 49
Gartmoor Dam (Central) 220-1
Gayton Cottage Lane (Mers) 126
Gayton Sands (Mers) 199
Gelli Aur/Golden Grove (Dyfed) 176
Gentian Hill (Galway) 256
Giant's Causeway, The (Antrim) 281
Giant's Ring, The (Down) 276
Gibbet Hill (Surrey) 70
Gibraltar Point (Lincs) 102
Gibson's Cave (Durham) 152
Gillespie Road Open Space (G.Lon) 72-3
Gilwern Hill (Gwent) 189
Gisburn Forest (Lancs) 137
Glamorgan Canal (S.Glam) 173
Glamorgan Nature Centre (M.Glam) 172
Glan Conwy (Gwyn) 196
Glapthorne Cow Pasture (Northnts) 93
Glasdrum Wood (Strath) 215
Glaslyn (Dyfed) 183
Glaslyn Marshes (Gwyn) 192
Glebe Meadows (Beds) 81
Glen Affric (Highl) 234
Glen Clova (Tays) 227
Glen Coe (Highl) 230
Glen Doll (Tays) 227
Glen Glenain, Upper (Antrim) 279
Glen Muick & Lochnagar Wildlife Reserve (Grampn) 227
Glen Nant (Strath) 214
Glen of Clab (Clare) 255
Glen of the Downs (Wicklow) 259
Glen Roy (Highl) 232

Glen Tanar (Grampn) 228
Glen Wood (Fermanagh) 267
Glenade Cliffs & Lough (Leitrim) 264
Glenamoy Bog (Mayo) 262
Glenariff Forest Waterfalls (Antrim) 280
Glenariff Lakes (Antrim) 280
Glencar Waterfall (Leitrim) 264
Glendalough Valley (Wicklow) 259
Glenfeshie (Highl) 233
Glengarriff Woodland (Kerry) 251
Gleniff (Leitrim) 264
Glenmore Forest Park (Highl) 234
Glenogle Trail (Central) 221
Glenthorne Estate Walks (Devon) 31
Glentress Forest (Border) 205
Glenveagh National Park (Donegal) 265
Globeflower Wood (N.Yks) 144
Goatfell (Arran, Strath) 209
Goblin Combe (Avon) 42
God's Bridge (Durham) 151
Goldcliff (Gwent) 188
Goldsitch Moss (Derby) 98
Golden Cap (Dorset) 34
Golden Grove/Gelli Aur (Dyfed) 176
Gole Wood (Fermanagh) 266
Goodwick Moor (Dyfed) 178
Gortin Glen Forest (Tyrone) 272
Gosford Bay (Lothian) 218
Gosforth Park (T&W) 161
Goyt Valley (Derby) 98
Gouthwaite Reservoir (N.Yks) 143
Graban-Llandeilo Roadside (Dyfed/ Powys) 185
Grafham Water (Cambs) 115
Graig Fawr (Clwyd) 199
Grains O'th'Beck (Durham) 152
Granagh Bay (Down) 275
Grand Union Canal (Leic) 99
Grand Western Canal (Devon) 30
Grangelands (Bucks) 78-9
Gransden Wood (Cambs) 82
Grantham Canal (Leic/Lincs) 101
Grass Wood (N.Yks) 142
Grassholme Island (Dyfed) 175
Gratton Dale (Derby) 106
Gravellach Islands (Strath) 214
Great Bookham Common (Surrey) 71
Great Breach Wood (Somer) 39
Great Cumbrae Island (Strath) 210
Great Eau (Lincs) 103
Great Merrible Wood (Northnts) 94
Great Orme (Gwyn) 196
Great Skellig (Kerry) 251
Great Saltee Island (Wexford) 254
Great Wood (Durham) 152
Greatham Bridge (W.Susx) 52
Green Island (Down) 274
Greencastle Point (Down) 274
Greenfield Valley (Clwyd) 199
Greetham Meadows (Leic) 101
Grey Mare's Tail (D&G) 205
Grizedale Forest (Cumbr) 148
Groby Pool (Leic) 99
Groton Wood (Suff) 118
Groomsport Harbour (Down) 277
Grune Point (Cumbr) 150
Guernsey Coastal Path (C.I) 44
Gunnersbury Triangle (G.Lon) 72
Gunnerton Nick (Northum) 162-3
Gwaun Valley Woodlands (Dyfed) 178
Gwendraeth Estuary (Dyfed) 174
Gwenffrwd (Dyfed) 180
Gweunydd Dryslwyn (Dyfed) 176
Gweunydd Dyfnant (Powys) 187
Gwydyr Forest (Gwyn) 193-4

H

Hackhurst Down (Surrey) 71
Hadrian's Wall (Northum) 163
Hadston Lake (Northum) 165
Hafod Wood (Clwyd) 197
Haigh Hall Country Park (G.Man) 130
Haldon Woods (Devon) 28-9
Ham Hill (Wilts) 69
Ham Hill Country Park (Somer) 38
Ham Lands (G.Lon) 72
Ham Street Woods (E.Susx) 57
Hambury Wood (W.Glam) 171
Hampsfield Fell (Cumbr) 139
Hampstead Heath (G.Lon) 73
Hamstead Trail (I of W) 47
Hamsterley Forest (Durham) 152
Handa Island (Highl) 238
Hanging Bank (E.Susx) 57
Hanging Rock (Leitrim) 267
Harbottle Crag (Northum) 164
Hardwick Hall Country Park (Durham) 153
Hardwick Park (Derby) 106
Hardwick Wood (Gwent) 188
Harehope Quarry (Durham) 153
Haresfield Beacon (Glos) 75
Harlow Woods (Essex) 113
Harris, Isle of, South (W.Isles) 240-1
Harrold-Odell (Beds) 82
Harrow Weald Common (G.Lon) 73
Hartland Moor (Dorset) 36
Hartland Point (Devon) 30
Hartlebury Common (H&W) 86
Hartlepool Headlands Rocks & Fossil Forest (Durham) 153
Hartshill Hayes Country Park (Warw) 88
Hastings Country Park (E.Susx) 55
Hatfield Forest (Herts) 113
Haugh Wood (H&W) 84
Havergate Island (Suff) 117
Hawke's Wood (Corn) 23
Hawksmoor Wood (Staffs) 97
Hawthorn Dene (Durham) 154
Hawthorne Hill (Armagh) 274
Hayburn Wyke (N.Yks) 146
Hayle Estuary (Corn) 21
Hayley Wood (Cambs) 82
Hayling Island (Hants) 49
Headley Heath (Surrey) 71
Heald Brow (Lancs) 138
Healey Dell (G.Man) 131
Heddon Valley Woods (Devon) 31
Helford River (Corn) 21
Hengistbury Head (Dorset) 37
Henllys Bay (Gwent) 188-9
Hensol Forest (S.Glam) 172
Hertford Heath (Herts) 113
Herma Ness (Unst, Shetld) 247
Hermitage, The (Tays) 225
Hermitage of Braid (Lothian) 216-17
Hesketh Park (Mers) 128
Hest Bank (Lancs) 138
Hetchell Wood (W.Yks) 142
Hexton Chalk Pit (Herts) 81
Heysham Harbour & Power Station (Lancs) 137
Hickling Broad (Norf) 123
Higham Ferrers Gravel Pits (Northnts) 93
Highbury Wood (Gwent) 190
Highgate Common (W.Mids) 96
Hightae Loch (D&G) 204
Hightown Dunes (Mers) 127
Hilbre Island (Mers) 127
Hilfield Park Reservoir (Herts) 112
Hindhead Common (Surrey) 70
Hiraethog Moor (Clwyd) 197
Hirsel, The (Border) 206
Hobbister (Mainland, Orkney) 242
Hockley Woods (Essex) 109
Hodbarrow Lagoon (Cumbr) 148
Hogganfield Loch (Strath) 211
Hogsmill Open Space (Surrey) 71
Holkham Meals (Norf) 124
Holland Haven (Essex) 111
Hollingworth Lake Country Park (G. Man) 131
Hollowell Reservoir (Northnts) 92
Hollymount (Down) 275
Holme Dunes (Norf) 123
Holme Pit (Notts) 108
Holt Heath (Dorset) 48
Holwell Quarries & Mineral Line (Leic) 101
Holwick Hay Meadows (Durham) 152
Holy Island/Lindisfarne (Northum) 167
Holy Island Coast (Gwyn) 194
Holyrood Park (Lothian) 217
Holywell Bay (Corn) 22
Holywell Marsh (Beds) 82
Holywell Pond (Northum) 161
Hook & Warsash Nature Reserve (Hants) 50
Hope's Nose (Devon) 28
Hopetoun House (Lothian) 217
Horn Head (Donegal) 266
Horner Wood (Somer) 38
Hornsea Mere (Humbs) 135
Horsell Common (Surrey) 68
Horton Country Park (Surrey) 71
Hothfield Common (Kent) 58
Hoveringham Gravel Pits (Notts) 108
How Hill (Norf) 122
Hoy, North (Orkney) 243
Hulne Park (Northum) 164
Humber Estuary (East) (Humbs) 134
Humber Wildlife Refuge (Humbs) 134
Hunstanton Cliffs (Norf) 123
Hurscombe (Somer) 38
Hurst Spit (Hants) 47
Hurworth Burn Reservoir (Durham) 153
Hutton Roof Crags (Cumbr) 139
Hyde Park (G.Lon) 72

I

Ibsley (Hants) 46
Ide Hill (E.Susx) 57
Illtyd Pools (Powys) 184
Inch Lough (Donegal) 266
Inch Mudflats & Spit (Kerry) 251
Inchnadamph (Highl) 238
Ingleton Waterfalls (N.Yks) 144
Ingram Valley (Northum) 164
Inishmurray (Sligo) 263
Inkpen Common & Hill (Berks) 69
Insh Marshes (Highl) 233
Invernaver (Highl) 239
Inverpolly (Highl) 238
Inversnaid (Central) 220
Iping Common (W.Susx) 70
Ipsley Alders Marsh (H&W) 85
Irchester Country Park (Northnts) 93
Irt Estuary (Cumbr) 150
Islay, Isle of (Strath) 213
Isle of Wight Coastal Trail (I of W) 47
Ivinghoe Beacon (Bucks) 80

J

Jenny Brown's Point (Lancs) 138
Jersey North Coast Path (C.I) 44
Jesmond Dene (T&W) 161
Joe's Pond (T&W) 154
Jones's Mill (Wilts) 64
Judge's Spring (Beds) 82
Jumbles Country Park (G.Man) 131
Juniper Hill (Glos) 75

K

Kearney Bay (Down) 275
Kelling & Salthouse Heath (Norf) 125
Kelsey Head (Corn) 22
Keltenyburn (Tays) 225
Kemsing Downs (Kent) 59
Kemyel Crease (Corn) 20
Ken-Dee Marshes (D&G) 203
Kenfig (M.Glam) 172
Kennet & Avon Canal (Wilts) 64
Kennet & Avon Canal Towpath (Berks) 66
Kerragh Islands (Wexford) 254
Kew, Royal Botanic Gardens (G.Lon) 72
Keyhaven Marsh (Hants) 47
Kilcolman Bog (Cork) 250
Killard (Down) 276
Killesher (Leitrim) 267
Killeter Forest & Forest Goose Lawns (Tyrone) 271
Killiecrankie (Tays) 225-6
Killiecrankie, Pass of (Tays) 226
Killington Reservoir (Cumbr) 150
Kilminning Coast (Fife) 222
Kiln Wood (Kent) 58
Kiltober Esker (Offaly) 258
Kilton Woods (Cleve) 158
Kinder/Bleaklow (Derby) 107
Kindrogan Woods (Tays) 226
Kingley Vale (W.Susx) 52
King's Cliffe (Northnts) 94
King's Wood (Beds) 81
King's Wood (Northnts) 93
Kingsbury Water Park (Warw) 88
Kingsmill Lake (Devon) 26
Kinnoull Hill (Tays) 224
Kintail (Highl) 233
Kiplingcotes Chalk Pit (Humbs) 134
Kirkdale (N.Yks) 145
Knap Hill (Wilts) 65
Knapdale Forest (Strath) 214
Knapp & Papermill Nature Reserve (H&W) 85
Knettishall Heath (Suff) 119
Knitsley Ravine (Durham) 153
Knockaginney (Armagh) 273
Knockan Cliff (Highl) 238
Knockinelder Bay (Down) 275
Knockmany (Tyrone) 271

L

La Clare Mare (Guernsey, C.I) 45
Ladle Hill (Hants) 66
Ladye Point (Avon) 42
Lady Park Wood (Gwent/H&W) 190
Ladybower Reservoir (Derby) 107
Ladypark (D&G) 204
Lady's Island Lake (Wexford) 254
Lagan Meadows (Antrim) 276
Lagan Valley Regional Park (Antrim) 276
Lake Wood (Powys) 186
Lambay Island (Dublin) 260
Lamb's Head (Kerry) 251
L'Ancresse Common (Guernsey, C.I) 45
Landguard (Suff) 117
Landmark Pinewood Trail (Highl) 234
Land's End (Corn) 20
Langdon Common (Durham) 152-3
Langdon Hills (Essex) 109
Langford Heathfield (Somer) 38
Langstone Harbour (Hants) 50
Lanhydrock (Corn) 23
Largo Bay (Fife) 222
Lathkill Dale (Derby) 106-7
Laurel Bank Farm (Down) 275
Lavan Sands/Traeth Lafan (Gwyn) 196
Lavender Park (G.Lon) 72
Lavernock Point (S.Glam) 173
Le Couperon (Jersey, C.I) 44
Leck Fell (Cumbr) 144
Leckhampton Hill (Glos) 75
Leeds & Liverpool Canal Towpath (G.Man/Lancs) 128
Leighton Moss (Lancs) 139
Leighton Reservoir (N.Yks) 143
Leith Hall (Grampn) 228-9
Lemsford Springs (Hants) 112
Lepe Country Park (Hants) 49
Les Quennevais (Jersey, C.I) 44
Les Mielles (Jersey, C.I) 44
Letham Glen (Fife) 222
Leven Bay (Fife) 222
Leven, River Valley (Cleve) 158
Levisham Moor (N.Yks) 147
Lewis Castle Grounds (Lewis, W.Isles) 241
Lickey Hills Country Park (W.Mids) 87
Lightwater Country Park (Surrey) 68
Lily Hill Park (Berks) 69
Lime Breach Wood (Avon) 42
Lindean Reservoir (Border) 205
Lindisfarne/Holy Island (Northum) 167
Lineover Wood (Glos) 75-6
Lings Wood (Northnts) 93
Linlithgow Loch (Lothian) 217
Linn of Tummel (Tays) 226
Lissadell (Sligo) 263
Lissagriffin Lake (Cork) 250
Little Brosna River (Offaly) 258
Little Budworth Common (Ches) 104
Little Paxton Gravel Pits (Cambs) 114
Liverpool & Leeds Canal Towpath (G.Man/Lancs) 128
Lizard, The (Corn) 21
Llan Bwlch-Llyn Lake (Powys) 185
Llandegfedd Reservoir (Gwent) 189
Llandeilo-Graban Roadside (Dyfed/Powys) 185
Llangollen Canal (Clwyd) 197
Llanrhidian Marsh (W.Glam) 171
Llantwit Major (S.Glam) 172
Llantysilio Mountain (Clwyd) 197
Llanymynech Hill (Powys/Shrops) 187
Llwyn-y-Celyn Bog (Gwent) 189
Llyn Alaw (Gwyn) 195
Llyn Eiddwen (Dyfed) 182
Llyn Fanod (Dyfed) 182
Llyn Mawr (Powys) 186-7
Llyn Tegid/Bala Lake (Gwyn) 192
Llynclys Common (Shrops) 95
Llynnau Cregennen/Cregennen Lakes (Gwyn) 191
Llysfran Country Park (Dyfed) 176
Loch A'Mhuilinn (Highl) 238
Loch Bee (South Uist, W.Isles) 240
Loch Druidibeg (South Uist, W.Isles) 240
Loch Etive (Strath) 215
Loch Fleet (Highl) 237
Loch Garten (Highl) 234
Loch Gruinart (Islay, Strath) 212
Loch Indaal (Islay, Strath) 213
Loch Leven (Tays) 224
Loch Lomond (Central/Strath) 220
Loch Na Keal (Mull, Strath) 215
Loch of Harray (Mainland, Orkney) 242-3
Loch of Kinnordy (Tays) 226
Loch of Lintrathen (Tays) 226
Loch of Lowes (Tays) 225
Loch of Skene (Grampn) 228
Loch of Spiggie (Mainland, Shetld) 246
Loch of Stenness (Mainland, Orkney) 242-3
Loch of Strathbeg (Grampn) 229
Loch Ryan (D&G) 202
Loch Sunart Woodlands (Highl) 230
Loch Sween (Strath) 213
Lochnagar & Glen Muick Wildlife Reserve (Grampn) 227
Lochore Meadows (Fife) 224
Lochwinnoch (Strath) 210
Lodge, The (Beds) 82
Lodmoor Country Park (Dorset) 35
Loe Bar & Pool (Corn) 21
Loggerheads (Clwyd) 198
Long Dale (Derby) 106
Long Mynd, The (Shrops) 94
Long Wood (S.Glam) 173
Longhaven Cliffs (Grampn) 229
Longshaw Estate (Derby) 107
Longtown Gravel Pits (D. & G) 150
Lopham Fen (Suff) 119
Loons, The (Mainland, Orkney) 244
Lord's Lot Wood (Lancs) 138
Lord's Wood (Gwent) 190
Lothian Coast (Lothian) 218, 219
Lough Atedaun (Clare) 255
Lough Beg (Cork) 250
Lough Bunny (Clare) 256
Lough Carra (Mayo) 261
Lough Corrib: Mount Ross Inlet (Galway) 256
Lough Corrib: southern end (Galway) 256
Lough Derg, Slevoir Bay & Gortmore Point (Tipperary) 253
Lough Derragh (Westmeath) 260
Lough Derrevaragh (Westmeath) 260
Lough Foyle (Londonderry) 278
Lough Funshinagh (Roscommon) 262
Lough Gara (Roscommon) 262
Lough Gill (Kerry) 252
Lough Gill Woods (Leitrim) 264
Lough Gur (Limerick) 252
Lough Hyne (Cork) 250
Lough Inagh (Galway) 257
Lough Kinale (Cavan/Longford/ Westmeath) 260
Lough Nacung (Donegal) 265
Lough Naman Bog (Fermanagh) 270
Lough Oughter (Cavan) 264
Lough Ree (Longford/Roscommon/ Westmeath) 262
Lough Ree: Bally Bay (Roscommon) 262
Lough Ree: Barley to Portanure Lodge (Longford) 262
Lough Ree: Yew Point (Roscommon) 262
Lough Ruisin (Galway) 256
Low Newton (Northum) 166
Lower Bransdale (N.Yks) 145
Lowestoft Ness (Suff) 120
Loynton Moss (Staffs) 96
Luccombe Chine (I of W) 46
Luce Bay (D&G) 202
Ludshott Common (Surrey) 70
Lugg Valley Meadows (H&W) 85
Lullington Heath (E.Susx) 54
Lulworth Cove & Range (Dorset) 35
Lumbistger (Yell, Shetld) 247
Lunderston Bay (Strath) 210-11
Lundsfield Quarry (Lancs) 138
Lundy (Devon) 30
Lune, River (Cumbr/Lancs) 138
Lurgan Park Lake (Armagh) 273
Luscombe Valley (Dorset) 37
Lydden Down (Kent) 58
Lydford Gorge (Devon) 27
Lyme Regis Undercliffs (Dorset) 38
Lyminge West Wood (Kent) 58
Lyn Valley Woodlands (Devon) 33

M

Machynys Ponds (Dyfed) 171
Maer Rocks (Devon) 29
Magho (Fermanagh) 270
Magilligan Point (Londonderry) 279
Magor Marsh & Pill (Gwent) 188
Maidenhead Thicket (Berks) 69
Maidscross Hill (Suff) 119
Malahide Estuary (Dublin) 260
Malham (N.Yks) 144
Maltby Low Common (S.Yks) 133
Malton (Durham) 153
Malvern Hills (H&W) 76
Malling Down (E.Susx) 55
Mallyadams Pond (E.Susx) 56
Manifold Valley (Staffs) 98
Mannington Hall (Norf) 124
Marazion Marsh (Corn) 21
Marble Arch Caves & Forest (Leitrim) 267
Marbury Country Park (Ches) 104
Margam (W.Glam) 172
Mariandyris (Gwyn) 196
Marle Hall Woods (Gwyn) 196
Marley Common (Surrey) 70
Marloes Mere & Sands (Dyfed) 175
Marshall Heath (Herts) 112
Marston Thrift (Beds) 81
Martham Broad (Norf) 122
Martin Mere (Lancs) 128
Martin's Pond (Notts) 108
Marton Mere (Lancs) 136
Marwick Head (Mainland, Orkney) 243
Maulden Wood (Beds) 81
May Beck (N.Yks) 146
May Hill (H&W) 76
May, Isle of (Fife) 222
Mawddach Estuary (Gwyn) 191
Medina Estuary (I of W) 47
Meenadoan (Tyrone) 271
Meldon Reservoir (Devon) 27
Mens, The (W.Susx) 70
Mere, The (Shrops) 95
Mere Sands Wood (Lancs) 128
Merthyr Mawr (M.Glam) 172
Middle Hope (Avon) 43
Milford Nature Reserve (Armagh) 273
Mill Glen (Central) 221
Miller's Dale (Derby) 107
Minch, The (W.Isles) 241
Minchinhampton Common (Glos) 74
Minsmere (Suff) 120
Moel Famau (Clwyd) 198
Molland Common (Devon) 31
Moneygal Bog (Tyrone) 272
Mongan's Bog (Offaly) 258
Monks Dale/Derbyshire Dales N.N.R. (Derby) 107
Monks Wood (Cambs) 115
Monkwood & Monkwood Green (H&W) 85
Montrose Basin(Tays) 226
Moor Foot Hills (Border/Lothian) 205
Moorlands (N.Yks) 143
Morecambe Bay (Cumbr/Lancs) 150
Morecambe Promenade (Lancs) 138
Morden Bog (Dorset) 36
Morfa Dyffryn (Gwyn) 191
Morfa Harlech (Gwyn) 192
Mornington Sand Dunes (Louth) 265
Morrone Birkwood (Grampn) 227
Morte Point (Devon) 31
Mortimer Forest (H&W/Shrops) 86
Morton Lochs (Fife) 223
Morvich (Highl) 233
Mould's Bog (Kildare) 259
Mound Alderwood (Highl) 237
Mount Caburn (E.Susx) 55
Mount Stewart (Down) 276
Mounts Bay (Corn) 20
Mourne Coastal Path (Down) 274
Mousa (Shetld) 246
Moy Estuary (Mayo) 261
Muckle Moss (Northum) 162
Muckross Wood (Kerry) 251
Mugdock Country Park (Strath) 211
Muggleswick Common (Durham) 153
Muir of Dinnet (Grampn) 228
Muiravonside (Lothian) 217
Muirshiel (Strath) 210
Mull, Island of (Strath) 215
Mull of Galloway (D&G) 202
Mullagh More (Clare) 255
Mullyfamore (Tyrone) 271
Mullygollan (Roscommon) 262
Mumbles (W.Glam) 170
Murlough (Down) 274
Murlough Bay (Antrim) 280
Murrins, The (Tyrone) 272
Murrough, The (Wicklow) 260
Musselburgh Lagoons (Lothian) 217

Mynydd Du (Powys) 184
Mynydd Froesidoes (Powys) 186
Mynydd Mawr/Aberdaron Head (Gwyn) 193

N

Nagshead (Glos) 190
Nant Irfon (Dyfed) 181
Narborough Railway Embankment (Norf) 121
Nash Point (S.Glam) 172
Naze, The (Essex) 111
Needles, The (I of W) 46
Nene Washes (Cambs) 116
Ness Wood (Londonderry) 278
Nethan Gorge (Strath) 210
New Buckenham Common (Norf) 119
New Forest (Hants) 48
New Hill Wood (Somer) 39
Newborough Forest & Warren (Gwyn) 194
Newbourne Springs (Suff) 117
Newbury Pond (E.Susx) 56
Newtown Harbour (I of W) 47
Nigg Bay (Highl) 237
Noir Mont Headland (Jersey, C.I) 44
Norfolk Beaches & Cliffs (Norf) 124
Norsey Wood (Essex) 109
North Antrim Cliff Path (Antrim) 281
North Bull Island (Dublin) 260
North Cliffe Wood (Humbs) 134
North Ford (Benbecula, W.Isles) 240
North Grove Wood (Berks) 67
North Hill (Papa Westray, Orkney) 244
North Hill Nature Trail (Somer) 38
North Meadow (Wilts) 65
North Ronaldsay (Orkney) 244
North Sands (Humbs) 135
North Warren (Suff) 119
Northam Burrows (Devon) 31
Northaw Great Wood (Herts) 112
Northward Hill (Kent) 60
Noss, Isle of (Shetld) 247
Noup Cliffs (Westray, Orkney) 244
Nunhead Cemetery (G.Lon) 72

O

Oakpark (Kilkenny) 253
Oare Meadow (Kent) 60
Oban Bay (Strath) 214
Ogmore River (M.Glam) 172
Ogof Ffynnon Ddu (Powys) 184
Ogston Reservoir (Derby) 106
Old Hall Marshes (Essex) 110
Old Head Wood (Mayo) 261
Old Man of Storr (Skye, Highl) 232
Old Park Wood (Herts) 73
Old River Lea (Essex) 113
Old Sulehay Forest (Northnts) 94
Orcombe Point (Devon) 29
Orkney Islands (Scotland) 242-5
Orwell Estuary (Suff) 117
Ot Moor (Oxon) 77
Otter Estuary (Devon) 29
Oughton Head Common (Herts) 81
Ouse Washes (Cambs) 116
Outwoods, The (Leic) 99
Owlsmoor Bog & Heath (Berks) 68
Oxford Island (Armagh) 273
Oxwich (W.Glam) 170
Oysters Coppice (Wilts) 61

P

Pagham Harbour (W.Susx) 52
Pamber Forest (Hants) 66
Papermill & Knapp Nature Reserve (H & W) 85
Park Hall Country Park (Staffs) 97
Parkhurst Forest (I of W) 47
Parkland Walk (G.Lon) 73
Parkmill (W.Glam) 170
Parsonage Wood (E.Susx) 57
Pass of Ryvoan (Highl) 234
Patmore Heath (Herts) 113
Peatlands Park (Armagh) 273
Peckforton Hills (Ches) 104
Pelyn Woods (Corn) 23
Pembreym Country Park, Burrows & Forest (Dyfed) 175
Pembrokeshire Coastal Path (Dyfed) 178
Penallt Old Church Wood (Gwent) 190
Penarth Flats (S.Glam) 173
Pendaroes Wood (Corn) 21
Penderi Hanging Oakwood/ Creigiau Pen y Graig (Dyfed) 182
Pengelli Forest (Dyfed) 178
Penhale Camp (Corn) 22
Penhow Woodlands (Gwent) 188
Penmon Point (Gwyn) 196
Pennington Flash Country Park (G.Man) 130
Pennington Marsh (Hants) 47
Pensarn (Clwyd) 199
Pensnett Pools (W.Mids) 87
Pentwyn Reservoir (M.Glam) 184
Pepperbox Hill (Wilts) 61
Perran Sands (Corn) 22
Peterhead Bay (Grampn) 229
Peter's Wood (Corn) 24
Peterstone Wentlooge (Gwent) 188
Pett Pools (E.Susx) 56
Pewsey Downs (Wilts) 65
Phillip's Point Cliffs (Corn) 24
Pickering's Pasture (Ches) 104
Pilling Marsh & Shores (Lancs) 137
Pillmore (Cork) 250
Pitsford Reservoir (Northnts) 92
Pleinmont Point (Guernsey, (C.I) 45
Plex Moss (Mers) 128
Plymouth Sound (Devon) 26
Point Lynas (Gwyn) 195
Point of Ayr (Clwyd) 199
Pollardstown Fen (Kildare) 259
Pont Burn Wood (Durham) 153
Pontoon Woods (Mayo) 261
Poole's Cavern (Derby) 107
Porlock Bay & Common (Somer) 38
Port-Eynon (W.Glam) 170
Port Holme Meadow (Cambs) 115
Port Meadow (Oxon) 77
Porthgwarra (Corn) 20
Portland, Isle of (Dorset) 35
Portrush (Antrim) 281
Portsdown Hill (Hants) 50
Portsteward Dunes (Antrim) 281
Possil Marsh (Strath) 211
Potteric Carr (S.Yks) 133
Poulevallan (Clare) 255
Poulnasherry Bay (Clare) 255
Poulsallagh (Clare) 255
Powerstock Common (Dorset) 34
Prawle Point (Devon) 27
Prestatyn Hillside (Clwyd) 199
Priddy Mineries (Somer) 41
Priory Road (Gwent) 189
Prisk Wood (Gwent) 190
Puffin Island (Kerry) 251
Pulfin Fen (Humbs) 135
Pulpit Hill (Bucks) 78-9
Pumlumon (Dyfed/Powys) 183
Purbeck Marine Wildlife Reserve (Dorset) 35
Purwell Ninesprings (Herts) 81
Puttenham Common (Surrey) 71
Pwll-gwyn Wood (Clwyd) 199
Pwyll y Wrach (Powys) 185

Q

Quantock Hills (Somer) 39
Queen Down Warren (Kent) 59
Queen Elizabeth Country Park (Hants) 50
Queen Elizabeth Forest Park (Central) 220
Queens Wood (H & W) 86
Quoile Pondage (Down) 275

R

Raby Castle (Durham) 152
Rack Hill (Wilts) 64
Radipole Lake (Dorset) 35
Rahasane Turlough (Galway) 256
Rahoy Hills (Highl) 230
Raincliffe Woods (N.Yks) 145
Raisby Quarry (Durham) 155
Rame Head (Devon) 26
Ramore Head (Antrim) 281
Ramsden Corner Plantation (Northnts) 89
Ramsey Island (Dyfed) 176-7
Randalstown Forest (Antrim) 279
Ranmore Common (Surrey) 71
Rassal Ashwood (Highl) 236
Rathdrum Woods (Wicklow) 259
Rathlin Island (Antrim) 281
Raven Meols Hills (Mers) 127-8
Raven, The (Wexford) 254
Ravenscar (N.Yks) 146
Ravensthorpe Reservoir (Northnts) 89
Rea's Wood (Antrim) 279
Reculver Marshes (Kent) 60
Red Hill (Lincs) 102
Red Moor (Corn) 23
Red Moss of Balerno (Lothian) 216
Red Rocks (Mers) 126
Red Wharf Bay (Gwyn) 195
Redbog (Kildare) 259
Redcar Rocks (Cleve) 159
Redgrave Fen (Suff) 119
Redwood Bog (Tipperary) 253
Reilly Wood (Fermanagh) 266
Rhinefield (Hants) 49
Rhinog (Gwyn) 192
Rhos Goch Common (Powys) 185
Rhos Llawr Cwrt (Dyfed) 180
Rhos Pil-bach (Dyfed) 180
Rhos Point (Gwyn) 196
Rhossili (W.Glam) 170
Rhum, Isle of (Highl) 231
Ribble Estuary (Mers) 129
Ribble Valley (N.Yks) 144
Richmond Park (G.Lon) 72
Ridge Way Path, The (Wilts) 65
Rigsby Wood (Lincs) 103
Ringwood Gravel Pit (Hants) 48
Risley Moss (Ches) 104-5
Riverside Country Park (Kent) 59
Rivington Reservoirs (G.Man) 130
Roaches, The (Derby/Staffs) 98
Robin Hood's Bay (N.Yks) 146
Rockcliffe Coast (D & G) 203
Rockland Marsh (Norf) 122
Rodborough Common (Glos) 74
Roding Valley Meadows (Essex) 73
Roe Estuary & Valley (Derby) 278
Rogerstown Estuary (Dublin) 260
Roman River Valley (Essex) 110
Roman Road (Cambs/Suff) 114
Ronas Hill (Mainland, Shetld) 247
Ropsley Rise Wood (Lincs) 102
Rosa Shaftoe (Durham) 153
Roseberry Topping (Cleve/N.Yks) 158
Ross Island (Kerry) 251
Ross Lough (Fermanagh) 270
Rossaa Wood (Leitrim) 267
Rossall Point & Promenade (Lancs) 136
Rossbehy (Kerry) 251
Rostellan Lake (Cork) 250
Rostherne Mere (Ches) 105
Rostrevor Forest (Down) 274
Rothiemurchus (Highl) 233-4
Roudsea Mosses & Wood (Cumbr) 148
Roughdown Common (Herts) 112
Roughting Linn (Northum) 166
Roundton Hill (Powys) 186
Roundway Hill Covert (Wilts) 64
Rowley Green Common (G.Lon/ Herts) 112
Royal Victoria Country Park (Hants) 50
Royden Park (Mers) 126
Roydon Common (Norf) 121
Rudry (S.Glam) 173
Rudyard Reservoir (Staffs) 98
Rufford (Notts) 108
Rutland Water (Leic) 100-1
Rye Harbour (E.Susx) 56
Rye House Marsh (Herts) 113
Ryhope Dene (Durham) 154
Ryton Willows (T & W) 161
Ryton Wood (Warw) 89

S

St Abbs Head (Border) 207
St Agnes (I of S) 18
St Alban's Head (Dorset) 36
St Andrews Bay (Fife) 223
St Anne's Dunes & Shore (Lancs) 136
St Bees Head (Cumbr) 150
St Catherine's Hill (Hants) 51
St Catherine's Point (I of W) 46
St Cuthbert's Churchyard (Durham) 153
St David's Head (Dyfed) 177
St Ives Head (Corn) 21
St John's Lake (Devon) 26
St John's Point (Down) 275
St John's Wood (Roscommon) 262
St Kilda (W.Isles) 241
St Leonard's Forest (E.Susx) 56
St Martin's (I of S) 18
St Mary's (I of S) 18
St Mary's Island (T & W) 161
St Peter's Valley (Jersey, C.I) 44
Salcey Forest (Bucks/Northnts) 89
Salcombe Hill (Devon) 29
Sale Water Park (G.Man) 130
Saltburn Wood (Cleve) 158
Saltfleetby-Theddlethorpe Dunes (Lincs) 103
Salthouse & Kelling Heath (Norf) 125
Salthouse Marsh (Norf) 125
Saltmarshe Delph (Humbs) 134
Saltwells Wood (W.Mids) 87
Sand Point (Avon) 43
Sandbach Flashes (Ches) 104
Sandwell Valley (W.Mids) 96
Sandwich Bay (Kent) 59
Sands Club Lake (Mers) 128
Sandscale Haws (Cumbr) 148
Sankey Valley Park (G.Man/Mers) 130
Santon Downham Bird Trail (Suff) 119
Sapey Brook Valley (H & W) 85
Savernake Forest (Wilts) 64
Sawbridge Marsh (Herts) 113
Scadbury Park (G.Lon) 72
Scaling Dam & Reservoir (Cleve) 158
Scolt Head Island (Norf) 123
Scolton Manor (Dyfed) 176
Scout Scar (Cumbr) 148
Scrabo Country Park (Down) 276-7
Scragh Bog (Westmeath) 260
Seaford Head (E.Susx) 54
Seaforth Coastal Nature Reserve (Mers) 126
Seaham Harbour (Durham) 154
Seal Sands (Cleve) 159
Sealife Centre (Strath) 215
Seaton Cliffs (Tays) 226
Seaton Sluice (T & W) 161
Sefton Park (Mers) 126
Selborne Hill (Hants) 51
Selsey Bill (W.Susx) 52
Selsey Common (Glos) 74
Semer Water (N.Yks) 146
Serpentine, The (G.Lon) 72
Seven Sisters Country Park (E.Susx) 54-5
Severn Barrows (Berks) 69
Severn Beach (Avon) 43
Severn Ham (Glos) 76
Shadwell Wood (Essex) 114
Shanes Castle (Antrim) 279
Shannon Estuary: Aughinish/ Asheaton (Limerick) 252
Shapwick Heath (Somer) 39
Sheffield Park (E.Susx) 56
Shepherds Trail (I of W) 46
Sherburn Willows (N.Yks) 142
Sherrardspark Woods (Herts) 112
Sherwood Forest (Notts) 108
Sheskinmore Lough (Donegal) 265
Shewalton Sandpits (Strath) 209
Shibdon Pond (T & W) 160
Shingle Street (Suff) 117
Shining Cliff Wood (Derby) 106
Shipley Country Park (Derby) 106
Shipley Wood (Durham) 152
Shoreham Black (W.Susx) 52-3
Short Wood (Northnts) 93-4
Shotover Country Park (Oxon) 77
Shotton Pools (Clwyd) 198
Shrawley Wood (H & W) 85
Shropshire Union Canal, Montgomery Section (Powys) 186, 187
Shropshire Union Canal, Prees Branch (Shrops) 95
Siblyback Lake (Corn) 23
Siccaridge Wood (Glos) 74
Sidings Lane Nature Trail (Mers) 127
Sidney Wood (Surrey) 70
Silbe Nature Reserve (Guernsey, C.I) 45
Silchester Common (Hants) 66
Skelton Beck (Cleve) 158
Skipwith Common (N.Yks) 134
Skokholm Island (Dyfed) 172-3
Skomer Island (Dyfed) 176
Skye, Island of (Highl) 232
Slaghtfreeden (Tyrone) 272
Slapton Ley (Devon) 27
Slemish (Antrim) 279
Slieve Bloom Mountains (Laois/ Offaly) 258
Slieve Gullion Summit (Armagh) 274
Slieve League (Donegal) 265
Slieveanorra Forest & Moor (Antrim) 280
Slievecarran Wood (Clare) 256
Slimbridge (Glos) 74
Slit Woods (Durham) 153
Snelsmore Common Country Park (Berks) 67
Snettisham (Norf) 123
Snipe Dales Nature Reserve & Country Park (Lincs) 102
Snowdon/Yr Wyddfa (Gwyn) 193
Soham Meadows (Cambs) 116
Solway Coast, North (D & G) 204
Somerford Common (Wilts) 65
Somerset Levels (Somer) 39
Sontley Moor (Clwyd) 197
Sound of Taransay (Harris, W.Isles) 241
South Foreland Cliffs (Kent) 58
South Gare (Cleve) 158-9
South Gower (W.Glam) 170
South Swale (Kent) 60
South Uist Machairs (W.Isles) 240
Southend Flats (Essex) 109
Southern Upland Way (Border) 207
Southerndown (M.Glam) 172
Southport, Botanic Gardens (Mers) 129
Southport Foreshore (Mers) 129
Southport Marine Lake (Mers) 128
Southwick Coast Wildlife Reserve (D & G) 203
Sovell Down (Dorset) 49
Spey Bay (Grampn) 229
Spittles, The (Dorset) 34
Sprotbrough Flash (S.Yks) 133
Spurn Head (Humbs) 134
Stack Rocks (Dyfed) 174
Stackpole (Dyfed) 174
Staffhurst Wood (Surrey) 57
Staines Reservoir (Surrey) 72
Stanford Reservoir (Northnts) 92
Stanmore Common (G.Lon) 73
Stanner Rocks (Powys) 186
Stanpit Marsh (Dorset) 37
Start Point (Devon) 27
Staunton Harold Reservoir (Derby) 106
Stedham Common (W.Susx) 70
Steep Holm Island (Somer) 40
Stevington (Beds) 82
Stewartby Lake (Beds) 81
Stinchcombe Hill (Glos) 74
Stiperstones (Shrops) 94
Stithians Reservoir (Corn) 21
Stockbridge Down (Hants) 50-1
Stockgrove (Beds) 81
Stocks Reservoir (Lancs) 137
Stocksmoor Common (W.Yks) 132
Stockton Earthworks & Wood (Wilts) 61
Stodmarsh (Kent) 60
Stoneycliffe Wood (W.Yks) 132
Stornoway Woods (Lewis, W.Isles) 241
Stour, River (Dorset) 37
Stour Woods (Essex) 117
Stow Cum Quy Fen (Cambs) 115
Strabane Glen (Tyrone) 272
Straidkilly (Antrim) 279
Strangford Lough, north (Down) 277
Strathclyde Country Park (Strath) 210
Strathfarrar (Highl) 235
Strathsuardal (Skye, Highl) 232
Strathy Point (Highl) 239
Strawberry Cottage Wood (Gwent) 185
Straythe, The (Corn) 22
Strensall Common (N.Yks) 143
Strid, The (N.Yks) 142
Strumble Head (Dyfed) 178
Strumpshaw Fen (Norf) 122
Stubhampton Bottom (Dorset) 36
Studland Heath (Dorset) 37
Styal (Ches) 105
Sugar Loaf (Gwent) 185
Sumburgh Head (Mainland, Orkney) 246
Sunbiggin Mires & Tarn (Cumbr) 150
Sunderland Point (Lancs) 137
Sundon Hills (Beds) 80
Surlingham Marsh (Norf) 122
Sutton Bank (N.Yks) 145
Sutton Bingham Reservoir (Somer) 38
Sutton Park (Warw/W.Mids) 88
Swaby Valley (Lincs) 103
Swallow Moss (Staffs) 98
Swansea Bay (W.Glam) 170-1
Swansea Canal (W.Glam) 171
Swift's Hill (Glos) 75
Swithland Reservoir (Leic) 99-100
Swithland Wood (Leic) 99
Sychnant Pass/Bwlch Sychnant (Gwyn) 196
Sydenham Hill Wood (G.Lon) 72
Syderstone Common (Norf) 123
Symonds Yat Rock (Gwent/H & W) 190
Sywell Country Park (Northnts) 93

T

Tacumshin Lake (Wexford) 254
Tailend Moss (Lothian) 216
Talybont Reservoir (Powys) 185
Tal-y-llyn (Gwyn) 191
Tamar Estuary (Devon) 26
Tamar Lakes (Corn) 25
Tan Hill (N.Yks) 146
Tandle Hill Country Park (G.Man) 131
Tantallon Castle (Lothian) 218
Tardree Forest (Antrim) 279
Tatton Park (Ches) 105
Tavy, River (Devon) 27
Taw Estuary (Devon) 31
Taw Marsh (Devon) 27
Tay Shore: Kingoordie and Broughty Ferry (Fife) 223
Taynish (Strath) 213-14
Teal Lough (Londonderry) 272
Tees Mouth (Cleve) 159
Teign Estuary (Devon) 28
Teign Valley Woods (Devon) 28
Tennyson Down (I of W) 46
Tentsmuir Point (Fife) 223
Termon Glen (Tyrone) 272
Termoncarragh Lake (Mayo) 261
Tetney Marshes (Lincs) 103
Teviot, River Walk, Kelso (Border) 206
Thames, River (Berks) 67
Thameside Ecological Park (G.Lon) 72
Thatcham Reed-Beds (Berks) 67
Theale Gravel Pits (Berks) 67
Theddlethorpe-Saltfleetby Dunes (Lincs) 103
Therfield Heath (Herts) 114
Thompson Common (Norf) 121
Thorncombe Wood (Dorset) 36
Thorndon Park, North & South (Essex) 109
Thorpe Marsh (S.Yks) 132
Thrapston Gravel Pit (Northnts) 93
Threave Wildfowl Refuge (D & G) 203
Three Cliffs Bay (W.Glam) 170
Thrislington Plantation (Durham) 155
Thrunton Wood (Northum) 164
Thursaston Common (Mers) 126
Thursley Common (Surrey) 70-1
Tickenham Hill (Avon) 42
Tiddesley Wood (H & W) 85
Tilehill Wood (Warw) 88
Tillington-Doxey Marshes (Staffs) 96
Timahoe Eskers (Laois) 258
Tiptree Heath (Essex) 110
Tiree, Isle of (Strath) 215
Titchfield Haven (Hants) 50
Titchmarsh Gravel Pit (Northnts) 93
Titchwell Marsh (Norf) 123
Tomies Wood (Kerry) 251
Torc Cascade (Kerry) 251
Torrent Walk (Gwyn) 191
Torridge Estuary (Devon) 31
Torridon (Highl) 236
Torry Bay (Lothian) 217
Totternhoe Knolls (Beds) 80
Town Kelloe Bank (Durham) 155
Townsend (Dorset) 36
Toys Hill (E.Susx) 57
Traeth Lafan/Lavan Sands (Gwyn) 196
Traeth Mawr (Powys) 184
Tramore Dunes & Mudflats (Waterford) 252
Trelissick (Corn) 21
Trench Wood (H & W) 85
Trentabank Reservoir (Ches) 105
Tresco (I of S) 18
Tring Reservoirs & Woodlands (Herts) 80
Trosley Country Park (Kent) 59
Trough of Bowland (Lancs) 137
Trumland (Rousay, Orkney) 244
Tullecombe Forest (Hants) 70
Tummel Forest (Tays) 225
Tummel, River Walks (Tays) 226
Tunstall Reservoir (Durham) 153
Tweed, River, Berwick-upon-Tweed (Border/Northum) 206
Tweed, River Walk, Newtown St Boswells (Border) 206
Tweed, River Walk, Peebles (Border) 205

SITE INDEX

Ty Mawr (Clwyd) 197
Ty'n-Coed (M.Glam) 173
Tyndrum (Central) 221
Tyne & Wear Heritage Coast (T&W) 161
Tynron Juniper Wood (D&G) 205
Tywyn Aberffraw/Aberffraw Dunes (Gwyn) 194-5

U

Udale Bay (Highl) 237
Ufton Fields (Warw) 88-9
Umbra, The (Londonderry) 279
Union Canal, Edinburgh-North Falkirk (Lothian) 216
Upper Hamble Country Park (Hants) 50
Upper Wood (G.Lon) 72
Upton Country Park (Dorset) 37
Upton Warren (H&W) 85
Uragh Wood (Kerry) 251

V

Vale Pond (Guernsey, C.I) 45
Vane Farm (Tays) 224
Vazon Bay (Guernsey, C.I) 45
Velvet Bottom (Somer) 41
Ventnor Downs (I of W) 46
Victoria Park, Belfast (Antrim) 277
Virginia Water (Berks) 69
Vyrnwy, Lake (Powys) 187

W

Waggoners Wells (Surrey) 70
Walberswick (Suff) 119
Walbury Hill (Berks) 69
Waldridge Fell (Durham) 154
Wallington Hall (Northum) 163
Walmsley Sanctuary (Corn) 22-3
Walney Island (Cumbr) 149
Wandlebury (Cambs) 114
Wappenbury Wood (Warw) 89
Warburg (Bucks/Oxon) 78
Warden Hill (Beds) 80
Waresley Wood (Cambs) 82
Warkworth Gut (Northum) 165
Warley Place (Essex) 109
Warsash & Hook Nature Reserve (Hants) 50
Warton Crag (Lancs) 138
Washburn Valley (N.Yks) 143
Washington Wildfowl Park (T&W) 154-5
Wat Tyler Country Park (Essex) 109
Wath Ings (S.Yks) 133
Wayland Wood (Norf) 121
Wayoh Reservoir (Lancs) 131
Wealden Edge Hangers (Hants) 51
Weardale (Durham) 153
Weaver Bend (Ches) 104
Weeting Heath (Suff) 119
Welbeck Park (Notts) 108
Walland Marsh (E.Susx) 56

Wellington Country Park (Berks) 66
Wellington Hill (Somer) 30
Welney (Cambs) 116
Wem Moss (Shrops) 95
Wembury (Devon) 26
Wenallt (S.Glam) 173
Wenlock Edge (Shrops) 94
Wepre Park (Clwyd) 198
West Bexington (Dorset) 34
West Highland Way (Central) 220, 221
West Kirby Foreshore & Marine Lake (Mers) 126
West Loch Tarbert (Strath) 212
West Sedgemoor (Somer) 39
West Stow (Suff) 118-19
West Williamston (Dyfed) 174
Westfield Wood (Kent) 59
Westleton Heath (Suff) 120
Weston Moor & Woods (Avon) 42
Wexford Wildfowl Reserve (Wexford) 254
Wharram Quarry (N.Yks) 143
Wheldrake Ings (N.Yks) 134-5
Whippendell Wood (Herts) 112
Whipsnade Downs (Beds) 80
Whitbarrow Scar (Cumbr) 148
White Down (Surrey) 71
White Hill (Hants) 66
White Nothe Undercliff (Dorset) 35
White Sheet Hill (Wilts) 61
Whitegate Marshes (Cork) 250
Whitehorse Hill (Berks) 69

Whitewell (Highl) 234
Whittle Dene Reservoir (Northum) 162
Wicken Fen (Cambs) 115-16
Wicksteed Park (Northnts) 93
Widdybank Fell (Durham) 152
Widemouth Bay (Corn) 24
Widewall Bay (South Ronaldsway, Orkney) 242
Widewater (W.Susx) 52-3
Wigan Flashes (G.Man) 130
Wigtown Bay (D&G) 203
Willoughby-Farlesthorpe Railway Line (Lincs) 103
Willow Garth (W.Yks) 142
Willsbridge Mill (Avon) 43
Wimbleball Lake (Somer) 38
Wimbledon Common (G.Lon) 72
Windmill Hill (H&W) 85
Windsor Great Park (Berks) 69
Windsor Hill (Bucks) 78
Wingate Quarry (Durham) 155
Winkworth Arboretum (Surrey) 71
Winmarleigh Moss (Lancs) 136
Winnall Moors (Hants) 51
Winspit (Dorset) 36
Wintersett Reservoir (W.Yks) 132
Winterton Dunes (Norf) 122
Witherslack Woods (Cumbr) 148
Witley Common (Surrey) 71
Witton-le-Wear (Durham) 152
Wokefield Common (Berks) 66
Wolves Wood (Suff) 117

Wood of Cree (D&G) 203
Woods Mill (W.Susx) 53
Woodspring Bay (Avon) 42
Woodwalton Fen (Cambs) 115
Woolsbarrow (Dorset) 36
Woodspring Bay (Avon) 42
Wormley Wood (Herts) 113
Worsley Trail (I of W) 46
Wotton Hill (Glos) 74
Wren's Nest (W.Mids) 96
Wycoller Country Park (Lancs) 136
Wye Downs (Kent) 58
Wye Gorge (Glos/Gwent) 189-90
Wye, River (H&W) 84
Wye Valley Woodlands (Glos/Gwent) 189
Wylye Down (Wilts) 61
Wyre Forest (H&W/Shrops) 87
Wyre, River Gravel Pits (Lancs) 137

Y

Yarner Wood (Devon) 28
Yateley Common (Hants) 68
Yellands Meadow (N.Yks) 146
Yes Tor (Devon) 27
Yetholm Loch (Border) 206
Ynmys Eidiol (Dyfed) 182-3
Ynys Enlli/Bardsey Island (Gwyn) 193
Ynys Hir (Dyfed) 182-3
Yockletts Bank (Kent) 58
Yr Wyddfa/Snowdon (Gwyn) 193
Ythan Estuary (Grampn) 229

Photographic Credits

All photographs supplied by Natural Selection picture library.
Paul Morrison pages 9, 11, 12, 13, 16, 25, 45, 62, 63, 73, 77, 81, 82, 90, 110, 120, 133, 167, 177, 244, 257, 259, 269, 281. **J. F. Young** pages 3, 67, 85, 86, 116, 125, 140, 141 (bottom), 197, 201, 211, 223, 263, 266, 268, 277. **W. S. Paton** pages 17, 31, 43, 60, 112, 121, 143, 156, 161, 219, 245, 249, 254. **Geoffrey Kinns** pages 10, 33, 83, 91, 157, 165, 187, 200, 207. **Iain Malin** pages 8, 23, 109, 139, 141 (top), 208. **Ken Willmott** pages 53, 79, 169. **R. T. Mills** pages 195, 253, 264. **Alan Goodyear** pages 105, 168. **E. A. Janes** page 179. **Chris Knight** page 123. **David Sewell** page 32. **Geoff Nobes** page 171. **J. V. and G. R. Harrison** page 19. **Alan Blair** page 248. **Henry Goodall** page 183.

Editorial and design

Editorial director
Andrew Duncan
Assistant editors
Gwen Rigby, Linda Hart, Shelley Turner
Proofreading
Nikki Aduba
Editorial assistant
Laura Harper
Index
Rosemary Dawe

Art director
Mel Petersen
Designers
Chris Foley, Beverley Stewart, Lyn Hector